JOHN MARSHALL
1800-1801

MADISON
1801-1809

SMITH
1809-1811

MONROE
1811-1817

LIVINGSTON
1831-1833

MCLANE
1833-1834

FORSYTH
1834-1841

CLAYTON
1849-1850

EVERETT
1852-1853

MARCY
1853-1857

CASS
1857-1860

SECRETARIES
OF
STATE
1784-1869

John Mitchell Justice

AMERICAN DIPLOMACY

ROBERT H. FERRELL
INDIANA UNIVERSITY

AMERICAN

☆ ☆ ☆ ☆

DIPLOMACY

A History

W · W · NORTON & COMPANY · INC · *New York*

FIRST EDITION

Cartography by E. D. Weldon

Library of Congress Catalog Card No. 59-6082

PRINTED IN THE UNITED STATES OF AMERICA
FOR THE PUBLISHERS BY VAIL-BALLOU PRESS

For Lila

Contents

Maps and Illustrations

Preface

This new book is a short text, for either one- or two-semester courses in American diplomacy. It aims to be long enough to give sufficient narrative continuity to courses, concise enough to free the lecturer to develop special themes and topics and allow the student to acquaint himself with some of the excellent monographic and biographical literature dealing with American foreign relations. Even so, it seeks also to offer analysis as well as narrative, in the hope that the author's opinions, freely ventured, will stir up the student and encourage him to think for himself about the purposes and achievements and shortcomings of American policy—encourage him to learn more than the details of foreign relations. Lastly this book emphasizes the diplomacy of the twentieth century. One cannot, of course, understand American foreign policy without considering its historic beginnings at the end of the eighteenth century and its development throughout the nineteenth century, but this prelude to our own crucial twentieth century needs now to have its emphasis reduced. To put twentieth-century events in their historical perspective has required a certain condensation of the traditional narrative of American diplomatic history prior to the 1890's and a subordination or omission of parts of it that have sometimes been discussed at length.

The following individuals have read and criticized chapters of the manuscript, and to them the author records his appreciation and gratitude—for without the help of friends it is impossible for anyone to study or write: Russell Bastert, F. Lee Benns, John W. Davidson, Alexander DeConde, John A. DeNovo, Louis P. Galambos, Norman Graebner, Hajo Holborn, Reginald Horsman, Lawrence Kaplan, William W. Kaufmann, William L. Neumann, Bernard F. Nordmann, William E. Scott, Charles Seymour, Paul Varg, P. J. Vatikiotis, J. Chalmers Vinson, and Richard L. Walker. Several colleagues in the department of history at Indiana University, who meet together regularly to discuss each other's historical writings, have likewise been of great assistance—Maurice G. Baxter, John W. Snyder, Leo F. Solt, James Sutton, Robert E. Quirk, Piotr S. Wandycz.

Maps have been checked for accuracy against standard authorities, including the following: C. O. Paullin (ed.), *Atlas of the Historical Geography of the United States* (Washington, 1932); William R. Shepherd, *Historical Atlas* (7th ed., New York, 1929); C. L. Lord and E. H. Lord, *Historical Atlas of the United States* (New York, 1944); *Geological Survey Bulletin 817* (*Boundaries, Areas, Geographic Centers and Altitudes of the United States and the Several States*); Samuel Flagg Bemis, *A Diplomatic History of the United States* (rev. ed., New York, 1942).

E. D. Weldon of the American Geographical Society designed and drew the maps. Mrs. Grace Parker compiled the index.

AMERICAN DIPLOMACY

CHAPTER

☆ 1 ☆

The American Revolution

Almost two hundred years have passed since the American people took up arms and fought a long, bitter, and at length successful revolution against the mother country for their national independence. With lapse of time and the renewal in many ways and on numerous occasions—most recently in two World Wars—of ties and friendships between the United States and Great Britain, the peoples of the two principal English-speaking nations of the world have gladly forgotten the tensions of the revolutionary era. The mid-twentieth century is much different in thought and action from the eighteenth. The average American today has little knowledge of the War for American Independence. He has read a few romantic accounts of guns flashing at Bunker Hill, of long lines of redcoats wavering and stumbling before entrenched sharpshooting patriots. He has little acquaintance with the causes of the revolution or the manner in which it was fought or, especially, of the way in which the historic revolt in America tied itself diplomatically to the contemporary combinations and collisions of European politics.

1. *America and the Revenge of France*

The key to understanding the successful course of the American revolution, once fighting had broken out between patriots and British troops in 1775, is the fact of French assistance: the revolution would have failed without the alliance of the United States with

3

monarchical France in 1778.

The reason for French assistance to the rebellious colonials in North America had little to do with future American greatness. No individuals in 1775–1783 could have foretold the phenomenal success of republican principles in the New World, the expansion of the United States from sea to sea, America's rise from the obscurity of colonial struggle against Great Britain to a position in the sixth decade of the twentieth century as the most powerful nation in the world. The French nation did not foresee, by momentary vision into the grand processes of history, that in the twentieth century the United States would itself fight to preserve French independence, that America would, a hundred times over, "repay the debt to Lafayette." No such notions moved French statecraft in the eighteenth century. To Europeans of the day the American revolution was little more than an obscure legal conflict between mother country and colonies, which had no importance in itself but presented Britain's principal opponent, France, with opportunity to revenge herself for the defeat suffered at the hands of the British during the recent Seven Years War.

The latter conflict was a notable affair, and in a very real sense it set in motion a train of events that gave Americans their independence. The Seven Years War was fought out mostly in Europe between France and Great Britain, and ended in a Peace of Paris of 1763 whereby Canada passed under British control, Louisiana went from France to Spain, and Spain gave Florida to Great Britain. For its day, this territorial settlement was drastic, and contrary to the custom in European wars of the eighteenth century whereby victor nations were not to take undue advantage of the vanquished. Britain had come under the sway of the elder William Pitt, who had caught the vision of a large British empire, and Pitt had pursued the war beyond its customary bounds. The peace of 1763 was a harsh peace. For the French nation, cherishing the memory of France's greatness under the late king Louis XIV, it was an impossible peace. The French statesmen at once set about getting revenge against Britain, and out of this purpose came, eventually, American independence.

The French foreign minister during and after the Seven Years War, Étienne-François Duc de Choiseul, a wily diplomatic practitioner, devoted servant of the Bourbon monarchy and the interests of France, could not get the Seven Years War out of mind. Obsessed by what he considered the enormous wrong done to France by Britain in 1763, he laced his instructions to French ministers and ambassadors with angry sermons on British wickedness. The Seven Years War had begun, Choiseul asserted, when England "threw at its feet the most sacred rules of equity, the most inviolable maxims of the rights of nations." "All the powers of Europe were alarmed at the scandalous rupture." "Its purpose was to invade France's American colonies, drive France from that continent, and seize all its commerce there." "But even this did not bound its ambitions." "It proposed to seize all of Louisiana, to penetrate by this way to New Mexico, and thus open for itself gradually the road to all the Spanish possessions." Oliver Cromwell had dreams of the sort when that militant Puritan ruled England in the mid-seventeenth century. Indeed, Choiseul believed, the English of his own day would go further. "They would stifle our marine in its birth, rule the sea alone and without a rival." Choiseul told his frivolous sovereign, Louis XV, that England "is, and will ever be, the declared enemy of our power, and of your state. Her avidity in commerce, the haughty tone she takes in the world's affairs, her jealousy of your power, the intrigues which she has made against you, make us foresee that centuries will pass before you can make a durable peace with that country which aims at supremacy in the four quarters of the globe."

Filled with hatred of Britain's ambition, incapable of forgetting the peace of 1763, Choiseul in 1764 sent out to the American colonies the first of several French observers whom he instructed to examine the prospects of dissension between colonists and Great Britain. Hopefully, wishfully, he read the reports of his men in America. From all save one he read what he wanted to read, for the requirements of diplomatic reporting in monarchical France were not unlike those in present-day dictatorships, and perhaps even in democracies: diplomatic correspondents reported what their superiors liked to read, for such was the way to promotion and preferment, whereas the truth, if sour and unattractive, made only for trouble. All the reporters except one sent back word of agitated colonial feelings, of unrest, of colonial desires for independence, of imminent revolt. As for the Baron de Kalb who went out to America in 1767, that honest gentleman reported that while the colonies seethed with unrest and tensions, there was no colonial desire to break the ties with England. In irritation and disappointment Choiseul charged Kalb with superficiality and pronounced the baron's labors useless.

Kalb was right about the popular temper in the colonies. Despite British provocation, colonial sentiment for a complete separation from Britain remained wavering and unsure until July 1776, when the colonists at last abandoned all their ties by a declaration of independence. Prior to that time, from the close of the Seven Years War until the signing of the declaration colonial hopes often burned brightly for reconciliation with Great Britain. When Benjamin Franklin was in London on colonial business in 1767 he wrote to his son that "that intriguing nation [France] would like very well to meddle on occasion, and blow up the coals between Britain and her colonies; but I hope we shall give them no opportunity." While French observers watched for a break between the American colonies and the mother country, while the Stamp Act of 1765 and the Townshend Duty Acts of 1767 and the Boston Massacre of 1770 marked a growing dissension, hope remained in both England and America that the troubles were only family troubles, capable of solution within the accustomed constitutional procedures of the English-speaking family. Americans as well as Englishmen cherished the principles of the common law—their rights to life, liberty, and property. The American colonies had been tied to Great Britain since 1607 and it seemed impossible that the common inheritance could not preserve peace.

Relations between the old country and the new had long been close. Englishmen on occasion had accustomed themselves to speak lightly, condescendingly, even harshly of Americans, but most thinking people in the homeland refused to take such sentiments seriously. That stentorian representative of English conservatism, Dr. Samuel Johnson, had expressed his opinion of Americans as early as the year 1769 when he told a friend that "Sir, they are a race of convicts, and ought to be thankful for anything we allow them short of hanging." The faithful Boswell, hearing of this remark, permitted himself a gentle difference with his master. Johnson's comment, Boswell wrote, lacked "that ability of argument, or that felicity of expression, for which he was, upon other occasions, so eminent. Positive assertion, sarcastical severity, and extravagant ridicule which he himself reprobated as a test of truth, were united in this rhapsody." And surely, the Boswells far outnumbered the Johnsons in eighteenth-century

British appraisals of American character. The High Tories ranted, as they had done for decades and would continue for decades after, but the majority of Englishmen thought better of Americans, were proud of the growing American colonies, and sided with such men as William Pitt the Elder, and Edmund Burke, who saw positive good in the existence of three million thriving colonials across the Atlantic. America, Pitt once exclaimed, was "indeed, the fountain of our wealth, the nerve of our strength, the nursery and basis of our naval power." Britain at the time of the American revolution had herself a population of only about eight million, as opposed to the French population of sixteen million, and many Englishmen agreed with Burke that it was desirable to increase the race in America, if only as a counterbalance to French power.

Unfortunately the British government after 1763 lay in the hands of the enemies of a moderate colonial policy. The young George III, whom contemporaries dubbed the Patriot King, had determined to secure a personal ascendancy over Parliament, and by judicious bribery he did so. Not himself a reactionary, the king in his campaign to increase the power of monarchy in England forced himself into reliance upon the reactionary Tories of his realm, antagonizing the forces of liberty, the forces of moderation. Under the personal direction of the king there began after 1763 the heavy-handed effort of the British government to tax the colonials for the support of government in the New World. This rational purpose was pursued from London with little understanding for colonial feelings. The British wished the Americans to pay. The Americans did not want to pay. The British failed to enlist the sympathy and good will of their colonials, and the government in London blundered its way into the American revolution. If the landlords then in control of Parliament had increased the tax on land even slightly, there would have been no need to tax the colonies. This might have been the procedure at the moment, after which the government could have gingerly approached the colonial legislatures with moderate revenue schemes and, with sufficient tact, could probably have obtained colonial consent. The British government after 1763 chose instead to pursue an appallingly tactless course that drove the colonials to revolt and that inspired the watchful French government to begin a general European war against Great Britain for the purpose of humbling France's traditional foe.

2. *The Beginning of the Revolution*

In the years immediately after the Duc de Choiseul's retirement from the foreign office in 1770 there was a let-up in Britain's colonial troubles in America, which might have ended if the British government had calculated the temper of the colonists in America and shaped colonial legislation accordingly. Statesmanship in London in the half-decade after 1770 could easily have prevented further trouble by the colonists. Instead there came that crowning blunder of British colonial policy, the Tea Act of 1773, a subsidy for shipment of East India tea to the colonies. Colonial merchants, the shelves of their stores groaning under the weight of smuggled Dutch tea, raised an argument about the constitutionality of such legislation, and afterward in quick succession came the Boston tea party, the British "intolerable acts" of 1774 in reprisal, and the opening shots of revolution in the springtime of 1775 at Concord and Lexington.

A worthy successor to Choiseul, Charles Gravier Comte de Vergennes, meanwhile had come into the French foreign office in 1774. He took up the problems of colonial revolt at the place where Choiseul had left them. Vergennes found the foreign-office archives full of letters, diaries, and special reports on the prospects of a revolt against Britain by the English-speaking colonies in the New World. The foreign minister, like his predecessor, held no love for the English. Britain, he believed, was "an enemy at once grasping, ambitious, unjust, and perfidious. The invariable and most cherished purpose in her politics has been, if not the destruction of France at least her overthrow, her humiliation, and her ruin." "It is our duty then to seize every possible opportunity to reduce the power and the greatness of England." Vergennes felt that civil war in the British colonies would not occur for some years, and so at the outset of his duties as foreign minister he leisurely contemplated North American affairs but concerned himself with what seemed to be the more immediate problems of European diplomacy. He found himself happily surprised when the revolution began in 1775. A cautious man, he waited to see how resolute the colonists would be, to see whether the revolt would become extensive and bitter enough to warrant France's open intervention. Whereupon there appeared before him an enterprising Frenchman, Pierre Augustin Caron de Beaumarchais, watchmaker, courtier, author of the *Marriage of Figaro* and the *Barber of Seville*, lover of intrigue and liberty.

Beaumarchais was the spirit of Benvenuto Cellini, reborn in the eighteenth century. He had first come to the attention of high French society when as a young watchmaker he produced a watch so small that it could be worn in a ring on a lady's finger. Knowing exactly what to do with such a gimcrack, he presented a watch ring to Mme. de Pompadour, mistress of Louis XV, and soon had orders for rings from all the courtiers of Versailles. Thereafter he engaged in a number of escapades. Early in 1776, anxious for more excitement and adventure, Beaumarchais offered a special proposition to Vergennes, namely, that France secretly assist the American revolution by sending munitions through a bogus firm, to be headed by himself and to be known as Roderique Hortalez and Company.

The scheme was a clever one, befitting the talents of its author. Beaumarchais would receive a gift of money from the French government, perhaps also from the Spanish government, and employ the funds to purchase arms and other necessary military equipment for dispatch direct to America. All this activity was to be under the guise of private commerce, the simple business venture of Hortalez and Company. Thus if the curious and alert British ambassador at Paris, Lord Stormont, made inquiries and complained that France was intervening in the private affairs of Great Britain, the French government could answer that Beaumarchais's operations were those of a private citizen with no connection with the government.

The idea appealed to Vergennes and the foreign minister lost no time in persuading his colleagues of the French cabinet to approve a secret gift to the Americans, via Beaumarchais, of 1,000,000 livres, about $200,000. This took, one should add, some considerable persuading, for Louis XVI was squeamish about the ethics of the Beaumarchais proposal. Moreover, the king's finance minister, Baron Turgot, predicted that the scheme would bankrupt France, and he was eventually proved right: the indirect aid turned after a while into direct aid; the cost of France's war against Britain by 1783 totaled perhaps 1,200,000,000 livres, emptied the French treasury, and helped bring on the French revolution in 1789. But Vergennes in 1776 could not look that far ahead. He overcame the opposition of Turgot and the king and in May of that year came to an arrangement with Beaumarchais before any American agent had set foot in France, indeed before the American declaration of independence. The king of Spain, Charles III, uncle of Louis XVI, matched this gift, sending Beaumarchais another million livres. Charles's foreign minister reasoned deviously that such a gift, keeping alive the war in the New World, might cause the Americans and British to exhaust each other. In ensuing months there were further French contributions to the company of M. Hortalez, some in the form of outright gifts from French government arsenals. Across the Atlantic, from France to the United States, came a life-giving stream of military articles that the Americans so sadly lacked—powder, guns, clothes, drums, fifes, medicines of every sort, surgical instruments, and even cannon with the Louis XVI monogram. Beaumarchais wrote to the Spanish ambassador in Paris, Count Aranda, that the first shipment by Hortalez and Company in the summer of 1776 consisted of 300 "thousands" of powder for cannon, 30,000 muskets, 3,000 tents, 200 cannon with full train, 27 mortars, 100,000 cannon balls, 13,000 bombs, clothing for 30,000 men.

It is impossible to overemphasize the importance of French support for the American revolution, for without the munitions sent to America in 1776 and 1777 the revolt would have collapsed. There was, to mention only one need of the revolutionary armies, an acute shortage of powder, so much so that on Christmas day, 1775, Washington wrote: "Our want of powder is inconceivable. A daily waste and no supply administers a gloomy prospect." Three weeks later no powder was to be had at all, and if the British could have learned this they might have marched out to Cambridge and destroyed the new colonial army, probably ending the revolution. Arrival of French powder shortly thereafter was of crucial importance to the American cause. According to a computation later made by an American historian, French powder comprised nine-tenths of the American supply during the early years of the revolution.

In addition to furnishing munitions of war, France in the first years of the revolution assisted American commerce upon the seas. That commerce faced grave dangers from British warships, and the French government did its best to prevent captures of American vessels. A French naval squadron was stationed off the Channel ports to discourage too close scrutiny of French roadsteads for American ships. Another squadron went out to the French West India Islands in May

1776, with instructions to protect "insurgent" vessels which, pursued by British warships, might seek asylum under the French flag. The government of Louis XVI allowed American privateers to operate from French harbors, equipping themselves there and bringing back prizes to be sold to the highest bidder. This accommodation was in complete contravention of France's duties as a neutral, for France had not yet declared war on the British. Vergennes time after time winked at the practices of American privateersmen and at assistance given them by French citizens and government officials. When the foreign minister was confronted by affidavits sworn on "the Holy Evangelists of Almighty God" that in the French islands British sailors captured by American privateers were being held in prison and dying by "inch-meal," he resorted to the baldest evasions, promises, and denials. The British ambassador on one occasion asked the French government to restore prizes brought in by American privateers. Vergennes answered, "You cannot expect us to take upon our shoulders the burden of your war; every wise nation places its chief security in its own vigilance." Stormont replied, "The eyes of Argus would not be too much for us." Vergennes, unperturbed, answered with unction, "And if you had those eyes, they would only show you our sincere desire of peace." Stormont ventured that French officers were hurrying to America to enlist in the rebel forces. "Yes," said Vergennes, "the French nation has a turn for adventure."

This was the state of affairs—virtually a recognition by France of American belligerency, though such a judicial distinction was then unknown in international law—when in the late autumn of 1777 a new development in the civil war between the British and their colonies brought French intentions into the open. For a number of months the ships of Beaumarchais had been landing supplies at Portsmouth, New Hampshire, whence the munitions were carried westward to the gathering forces of General Horatio Gates. When in the summer and autumn of 1777 the lumbering troops of General John ("Gentleman Johnny") Burgoyne came down from Canada, they encountered the French muskets and powder of Gates's forces. Burgoyne's surrender on October 17, 1777 was almost a French victory. The battle of Saratoga, most decisive battle of the revolution, persuaded France to support openly, with ships and troops, the new government of the United States.

3. *The French Alliance*

By the time of Saratoga a number of American diplomats had been sent abroad, to use the successes of American arms to gain foreign support for the revolution. The special hope of this "militia diplomacy"—sending American diplomats to the principal courts of Europe, whether or not those courts desired to receive them—was to obtain recognition of the United States by the various nations. Recognition, and perhaps a loan or gift of arms.

At the beginning it had proved difficult to convince the American Congress, the second Continental Congress which in 1775 had turned itself into a national congress, that diplomatic representation abroad was necessary or even advisable. When John Adams first suggested to his congressional colleagues that the United States apply for assistance to Britain's enemies in Europe, he received "grimaces" and "convulsions" from the members, for whose nerves, already shaken by the emotional difficulties of cutting the ties of the British empire, the idea of sending diplomats abroad was too much. There was feeling in Congress that it would be unwise to employ such "foreign papists" as the French in American service. Still, hesitation could not stand in face of the evident need for foreign alliance. The members of Congress quailed at the prospect of war with England without the aid of France, and in 1776 Congress authorized dispatch of three representatives to the French court: Benjamin Franklin; Arthur Lee, previously the agent of Massachusetts in London; and Silas Deane, a wealthy and respected member of Congress from Connecticut. Deane and Lee were already in Paris, where Deane was having a number of dealings with Beaumarchais on behalf of the American government.

Of these three American diplomats—the first accredited diplomats in the history of the United States—the most impressive and able, by far, was Benjamin Franklin. The diplomatic services rendered by Franklin to the revolution were, as events proved, invaluable. When Franklin arrived in Paris in December 1776 he met a welcome such as a king would have enjoyed. He was one of the two best-known men in the world during the latter eighteenth century, the other being Voltaire, but the aging American could not have dreamed that Frenchmen would find his presence so irresistible. He made the most of his opportunities. Frenchmen for some reason believed Franklin, a citizen of Philadelphia, to be a Quaker fresh from Penn's Woods, and the venerable scientist obliged them by dressing to the role. Three weeks after he had settled down, the police reported that "this Quaker wears the full costume of his sect. He has an agreeable physiognomy. Spectacles always on his eyes; but little hair—a fur cap is always on his head." Franklin found his benign features on snuff-box lids and medallions, and his pictures and busts were everywhere. These, so he wrote his daughter in 1779, "have made your father's face as well known as that of the moon . . . It is said by learned etymologists that the name *Doll*, for the images children play with, is derived from the word Idol; from the number of dolls now made of him, he may be truly said, *in that sense* to be *i-doll-ized* in this country." *Le grand Franklin*—deist and freethinker, a Quaker in France—was a striking figure. The simplicity of his dress hid the fact that he was a wealthy man. The humility of his bearing, the modesty of his speech, shielded from French minds his subtle and refined intellect that could take the measure of any person of his generation, even the most mannered courtiers and diplomats of Europe.

Franklin moved in triumph through French society during the year 1777, the year which, as he knew, was a crucial one for American independence. He established cordial relations with Vergennes, and constantly importuned the foreign minister—though his skill in personal relations made his inquiries seem not at all like importuning— for loans to the United States (he had secured 18,000,000 livres by 1782). He also sought French recognition of the independence of the United States, and a treaty of alliance between France and the United States, such a treaty to be followed by military and naval assistance. Vergennes held off, despite the blandishments of the American Poor Richard, until news of Burgoyne's defeat at Saratoga gave assurance that revolt in the New World was meeting with considerable success. A courier bearing word of the American victory arrived early in December 1777. The foreign minister sent his secretary to the American commissioners in Paris, offering congratulation and inviting the Americans to renew their offer of a treaty of alliance. He required a short time to draw the treaty, which he signed with the Americans on February 6, 1778.

There were in fact two treaties which Vergennes made with the Americans. The first, the treaty of alliance, announced the "liberty, sovereignty, and independence absolute and unlimited of the United

States." Here was formal French recognition of American independence. There followed stipulations that in case of war between France and Britain the United States should have a free hand to conquer Canada and the Bermuda Islands, and that France might seize the British West Indies. Each nation guaranteed the territory of the other, a customary amenity in alliances. There was the important proviso, essential to any alliance, that neither nation would conclude a truce or peace with the foe without the other's consent. In a separate treaty of amity and commerce the two nations established in general terms their commercial relations, with a promise by each to adhere to specified principles of neutral rights in the event of future wars. These principles need not detain us at this point, as their importance appeared later when war broke out in Europe after the French revolution of 1789.

"No American should ever forget the alliance of 1778. No Frenchman ever will." This remark by the leading historian of the diplomacy of the American revolution, Samuel Flagg Bemis, well characterizes the most signal American diplomatic achievement of the eighteenth century. Without the alliance there could never have been American independence. Prior to 1778 the shipment of French munitions to the New World ensured survival of the revolutionary armies during their first clashes with the well-supplied British regulars and enabled the Americans to win the battle of Saratoga. After 1778 the open assistance of French ships and troops made possible the final triumph of American arms, the victory at Yorktown in 1781, in which more Frenchmen participated than Americans.

French help, as we have seen, came because of the traditional enmity of Frenchmen and Britishers, and more specifically because of the defeat of France in the Seven Years War. American diplomats were under no illusions as to the reason for French intervention in the American war for independence, and it was with full awareness of the circumstances that they courted French assistance. They knew that they were precipitating—for their own advantage, they hoped—a large-scale war in Europe, another war on the scale of the Seven Years War, or the previous War of the Austrian Succession (1740–1748), or the War of the Spanish Succession (1702–1713). They knew that with the treaty of alliance of February 1778 there would follow open conflict between France and Britain, that France would enlist the support of her traditional Bourbon ally Spain, that other nations of Europe, in particular Prussia and Austria, might use the occasion to settle their own quarrels. There would probably be a general European war, once France had declared herself in favor of the Americans, and American diplomats would have to snatch their country's independence out of this European turmoil. It was risky business for the United States. No nation in Europe cared greatly about the success of republican principles in the New World, and even the French ally might abandon the cause of American independence if circumstances made such a course desirable.

Hostilities in Europe began on June 17, 1778, when French and British naval forces drifted into a skirmish along the Channel coast. Almost at once American diplomatic representatives saw their country drawn into European politics because of the necessity of the alliance with France.

4. *The Wiles of Europe*

Vergennes sought a formal connection between France and Spain, hoping that in the war with Britain he could gain the help of the Spanish fleet, which if grouped with the French fleet would give naval superiority against England. The Spanish backed and filled during most of the year 1778, and only in the following year decided to join the French.

France's negotiation with Spain proved unsuspectedly difficult and time-consuming, for several reasons. For one, the Spanish monarchy —despite its decline in vigor during the eighteenth century—cherished dreams of past importance, and the Spanish felt, not without justice, that the French had been too quick in calling the tune with the Americans. Vergennes had concluded his alliance with the United States too hastily, the Spanish believed; Spain had not been consulted with sufficient deference to her wishes. One cannot altogether blame Vergennes in the matter. He had sought to obtain prior Spanish consent to his alliance with the Americans, and when the Spanish government dallied and procrastinated he had gone ahead and made his treaties. Having done this he found his task of bringing Spain into the war exceedingly difficult.

Two other factors explain why Spain at first sought to remain aloof from the conflict, despite all the alleged friendliness, the fond emotional attachments, of the Bourbon family compact. For one, the

Spanish were worried that an independent nation established close to their colony of Louisiana might prove a military threat. Then too, there was the possibility of persuading the British to cede Gibraltar (which Britain had taken from Spain in 1704). The Spanish dealings over Gibraltar with the British took the peculiar form of a proposal of mediation, with Gibraltar as its price, between Great Britain and the Americans. The mediation would have been the basis of *uti possidetis*, the war map of the moment, which favored the British inasmuch as they were in possession of good-sized portions of the American seaboard. The British, as we now can see, should have signed up with the Spanish, for they would have lost far less than they eventually did. Admittedly the Americans had an alliance with the French, which stipulated that there should be no separate peace by either ally until American independence had been recognized by Great Britain, and so one might argue that whatever arrangements Spain made with the British did not relieve France of the obligations of the alliance of 1778. Still, if the Spanish had pushed through an arrangement over America with the British government it would have been difficult for the French to fight on singlehandedly for American independence. The government of Louis XVI would have had to go back on its word, a not-unheard-of procedure in eighteenth-century European international relations. Spanish dickering with Britain had considerable danger for the future of the American republic, but fortunately the government of Lord North refused to listen to the propositions of the Spanish ambassador in London.

Spain's efforts to secure Gibraltar out of the Franco-American-British struggle were little more than blackmail of Britain during its time of trouble. As the Spanish foreign minister wrote to his ambassador in London in 1778, the British "must know that what we do not get by negotiation we know how to get with a club." The price of Spanish neutrality was "that pile of stones of Gibraltar." The Spanish ambassador in London said all this to Lord Stormont, the erstwhile ambassador in Paris who had become foreign secretary of the Lord North government. Stormont was not averse to the idea of buying Spain out of the war, but there were a number of difficulties in working out the purchase, a series of cessions between France, Spain, and England in the New and Old Worlds. In the course of the proposed roundabout exchange of Haiti, Corsica, Minorca, and Gibraltar all sorts of arrangements were necessary, and while the dickering went

Great Britain. Irrespective of French wishes, the Austrians took advantage of the death of the ruler to annex Bavaria in the winter of 1777–1778, thereby beginning a war with Frederick the Great of Prussia. The problem for France was to stop the dreary campaigns of the Kartoffelnkrieg, the Potato War, so-called because the ill-fed soldiers of Austria and Prussia spent the winter of 1778–1779 digging frozen potatoes. Mediation of the War of the Bavarian Succession was accomplished in 1779 by the French court acting with Russia. Whereupon the Austrian emperor, furious at this intervention in his affairs by a supposed ally, undertook to reciprocate the French favor, and offered to mediate between Britain and France. In this mediation effort Austria was joined by Russia. It happened that the offer from these two powers coincided with a low point in the military fortunes of the French and Americans, and, as we have seen, Vergennes was willing to accept a mediation if necessary, and believed that he saw a way out of the embarrassments of the Franco-American treaty by getting Austria and Russia to propose the *uti possidetis*.

One should mention, among the European projects of these years, the armed neutrality of 1780, announced by the Russian empress Catherine the Great as a defense of the neutral rights of small powers. This scheme would have brought together the neutral navies of Northern Europe, which in concert could have demanded the right to trade with Britain's enemies in all goods except those obviously useful as implements of war. The British had been denying the neutrals this right. In actuality the armed neutrality never got beyond the stage of a project, for no nation went so far as to support by force the proposal of the tsarina. Nevertheless the British government had some difficult moments contemplating what might happen if the neutral navies of the European powers marshaled themselves against the Royal Navy. The result would not have been pleasant, for in the late eighteenth century the Scandinavian nations maintained formidable navies, and if coupled with the Russian navy they might have secured a concert of power sufficient to take control of the seas from Great Britain. Happily for the English the armed neutrality came to nothing. It never emerged from the ideal to the real, proving to be naught, as Catherine herself described it, but an armed nullity.

During these European moves and countermoves—armed neutrality, Austro-Russian mediation, Hussey-Cumberland negotiations, Spanish mediation offer—the Netherlands entered into the war against

Great Britain.

In the first hopeful months of militia diplomacy, Congress had sought recognition of independence of the United States from the Dutch Estates General; but the Dutch, knowing that recognition would invite British reprisals and probably war, refused to take any formal step in that direction. Meanwhile, in the Dutch West Indian island of St. Eustatius, a thriving trade in contraband goods arose between the Dutch and other European nations on the one hand and the Americans on the other. This trade, together with participation of Dutch vessels in the French coastal trade after France entered the war in 1778, led Great Britain to declare war on the Estates General in 1780. The British pretext was as flimsy as it could possibly have been. Britain declared war after capturing at sea a draft of a treaty between Holland and the United States, which bore only signs of unofficial discussion between an American agent and a representative of the burgomasters of Amsterdam. But with the beginning of hostilities Great Britain brought to an end the coastal trading by the Dutch with France, and early in 1781 Admiral Sir George Rodney descended on the island of St. Eustatius and sacked it as completely as any island had been sacked since the freebooting years of Drake and Raleigh on the Spanish Main.

The conquest of St. Eustatius was of more than passing interest in the history of the American revolution. The island, as mentioned, had been providing immense quantities of munitions to the Americans. Rodney himself said, with some exaggeration, that "This rock, of only six miles in length and three in breadth, has done England more harm than all the arms of her most potent enemies, and alone supported the infamous American rebellion." The Dutch free port, popularly known as Statia, had a mile-long street of warehouses for contraband goods. Here a privateer could arm for a cruise, and the smuggler could purchase false papers together with gunpowder in tea chests or rice barrels. Its loss to the patriot cause was serious. Admiral Rodney's triumph, however, was less than he at first believed, for the French recaptured much of his booty, including the admiral's personal haul of over half a million dollars in cash, seized when the French came back to the island before the admiral's agent had moved the loot to safety. Then too, when Rodney sold his other acquisitions at a gigantic auction in the West Indies, many of them went to the American cause for far less than their value, a far lower price than the

Americans had been obtaining such supplies from St. Eustatius under Dutch rule. And there was a crowning disappointment in the St. Eustatius operation: by lingering at the island, engaged in gathering together his booty, Rodney failed to apprehend the fleet of the French admiral the Comte de Grasse, then in the West Indies. Grasse shortly thereafter supported an operation of French and American troops before the Virginian village of Yorktown, and the capture of Cornwallis's entire force of more than seven thousand men on October 19, 1781 marked the concluding battle of the revolutionary war.

It was good news to Benjamin Franklin at Passy, near Paris, when the word came of Yorktown. For Franklin the years had passed slowly after 1778. They were years of advancing age—the philosopher was seventy-five in 1781—and he had absented himself from the family circle in Philadelphia. He attended scientific meetings, pursued his huge correspondence with individuals all over Europe, flirted with Mme. Helvetius. He read avidly the reports from America. At long last came the defeat of Cornwallis and with it the possibility of peace.

5. A Lack of Bienséance

After Yorktown a peace party began to gain adherents in England. With the slowness of the war and lack of important British victories the opponents to the personal rule of George III in Britain took heart, and a strong feeling for peace emerged. The opposition managed to carry a resolution through the House of Commons, early in 1782, declaring enemies of their country all those who should advise or in any way attempt to prosecute an offensive war in America for the purpose of reducing the colonies to obedience by force. Lord North resigned as prime minister in March 1782. George III drew up a message of abdication, and was dissuaded only by the thought that through appointment of Lord Rockingham as North's successor he could work with the ministry not completely under control of his enemies. The Rockingham ministry decided to make peace with America, and Franklin in Paris received visits from a British emissary, an elderly philosopher and one-time slave trader named Richard Oswald. With this change of affairs everything was set for a triumph of American diplomacy under Franklin's guiding genius.

The problem was to get out of the war and, at the same time, maintain good faith with France. Americans had no desire to continue fighting for Spanish aims in Europe, but they were bound indirectly, via the Franco-American alliance, to the Treaty of Aranjuez. It was Franklin who found a way out of the inconveniences of the French alliance and at the same time managed to preserve a substantial amount of American good faith.

The first important move in negotiations to end the war was made by one of Franklin's colleagues, John Jay. Jay had been sent to Spain by Congress in a tactless effort to obtain Spanish recognition. According to the Spanish foreign minister, Floridablanca, Jay's "two chief points were: Spain, recognize our independence; Spain, give us more money." After the futilities of such a mission eventually impressed themselves upon Congress, Jay received a new appointment as commissioner, together with Franklin and John Adams, to negotiate peace with Great Britain. Adams had arrived at Paris after a mission similar to Jay's, to the Dutch in 1780 upon their involvement in war with Britain.

The three American commissioners were unlike in temperament and outlook. Franklin was full of equanimity and hope, trusting to time and the advantages of history. Adams was irascible, pugnacious, eager to force his presence upon the French court, desirous of defending every shred of American rights against France and all other powers on earth. Jay was distrustful, suspecting intrigue by Vergennes to deprive the American nation of its independence. Jay in his suspicions came to believe that Vergennes was dealing behind the backs of the Americans, ready to abandon their cause as soon as the occasion proved convenient. When he heard that Vergennes's private secretary had gone off to London on a special mission he was sure that the French foreign minister was conniving to defraud the Americans, and he entered into confidential negotiations without consent of his fellow commissioners, with the British agent Oswald.

Franklin, on learning of Jay's negotiations, at first had misgivings about them, for such parleys contradicted the spirit if not the letter of the alliance with France, according to which neither France nor the United States was to conclude a peace or truce without the consent of the other. Even so, there was reason to allow continuance of Jay's conversations. Although Franklin put little faith in Jay's fear that Vergennes was negotiating privily with the British, the foreign minister had placed the American peace commissioners in a most awkward position because of a roundabout arrangement he had made with the American Congress through the French minister to the United States, La Luzerne. The latter, by extraordinary diplomatic talents coupled with careful use of money, had acquired influence over the American government. He claimed, in a letter to Vergennes, to have procured the election of Robert R. Livingston as secretary of foreign affairs, and Livingston appears to have been grateful for this assistance and showed appreciation by appointing a French officer as his assistant. The minister to the United States had persuaded Congress to instruct the peace commissioners in Paris to negotiate with the British only under step-by-step consent of the French government. The single *sine qua non* in negotiations was American independence, and on all other matters—boundaries, navigation of the Mississippi, fishing rights off Newfoundland and Nova Scotia—the commissioners found themselves submitted to the advice of the French court.

This was a highly unsatisfactory state of affairs. "Blush, blush, America," an angry member of Congress wrote to John Adams. The devious French prompting of the commissioners at Paris, sent to Franklin, Jay, and Adams as a formal instruction from their government, so tied the hands of the commissioners that if they had followed their instructions they would have been little more than clerks of the French foreign minister. Vergennes believed that he had maneuvered himself into controlling the American commissioners. The commissioners, vigorous personalities in their own right, wished no such control. Franklin felt that the French deserved a modicum of bad faith, and was willing to carry on separate and secret negotiations with the British.

The result was a "preliminary treaty" between Great Britain and the United States signed on November 30, 1782.

Here, in truth, was what in all but name amounted to a separate peace. Once the British and Americans had come to agreement, if only in a preliminary treaty, what more was there to negotiate? In this treaty Great Britain recognized American independence; set the Canadian-American boundary (in part based on imaginary geographic features) as the St. Croix River dividing Maine and Nova Scotia, the St. Lawrence-Atlantic watershed divide, the forty-fifth parallel to the St. Lawrence and then to the Great Lakes and their connecting waterways to the Lake of the Woods and the Mississippi; recognized the American "liberty" to fish in the territorial waters of British North America; stipulated that British forces would evacuate American soil and waters "with all convenient speeds"; validated all debts due creditors of either country by citizens of the other; and provided that Congress "earnestly recommend" to the state legislatures a restoration of Loyalist rights and property. Vergennes was told of the provisions of this treaty on the night before it was signed.

At the time the foreign minister said nothing. Two weeks later he registered formal complaint. Franklin in a classic reply admitted that the American commissioners in concluding virtually a separate peace may have shown a lack of propriety, a lack of *bienséance*, but protested that they meant no disrespect for the king of France. The astute American remarked his hope that "the great work" of peace would not now be ruined "by a single indiscretion of ours," adding: "The English, I just now learn, flatter themselves they have already divided us. I hope this little misunderstanding will therefore be kept a secret, and that they will find themselves totally mistaken." Vergennes, catching at once the hint that the Americans in case of continued French objection might turn to alliance with England, essayed no more criticism of the American preliminary treaty.

If Vergennes had chosen to insist upon the right of the French government to advise the American peace commissioners in all matters save independence, it is doubtful what might have been the final outcome of Franklin's private negotiations with the British. Perhaps Congress, under control of the French minister to the United States, would have reprimanded its commissioners in France and refused ratification of the preliminary treaty. Perhaps Franklin might have been able to gain the support of Congress notwithstanding the opposition of Vergennes.

Certainly the American minister's hope as expressed to Vergennes, that the little misunderstanding between the two allies be kept secret, was at once nullified, through no fault of Franklin. The sage of Passy's private secretary, Dr. Edward Bancroft, who had become secretary to the American peace commission, was a British spy, and regularly sent reports to London of everything that concerned the American negotiations. Bancroft each week dispatched information to the British which he wrote in invisible ink between the lines of love letters addressed to "Mr. Richardson." The love letters he placed in a sealed bottle let down by a string into a hole in a tree on the south side of the Tuileries gardens. He must have sent the British foreign office a bottleful of information about the meeting between Franklin and Vergennes.

But was Franklin in reality going beyond the bounds of propriety in signing the preliminary treaty with Great Britain? In one of his Poor Richard almanacs there was a homely bit of advice, offered by Poor Richard to his readers: "When you come to a low place, stoop." Did Franklin stoop in 1782?

Actually he did not. Franklin's intelligence apparently had penetrated to the center of Vergennes's thinking on the business of peace, weeks before his meeting with the French foreign minister. Franklin had seen that Vergennes was growing weary of the connection with Spain. The war for Gibraltar had come almost to a standstill, with a combined French-Spanish force repulsed before the fortress and some notable English naval victories against the Bourbon allies. Spanish hopes of taking Gibraltar were becoming impossible of achievement, and Franklin in his separate peace with the British seems to have done exactly what Vergennes desired: he offered to the foreign minister an excuse to get out of the Spanish attachment. Vergennes could now say to the Spanish government that because the unfaithful Americans had negotiated separately with the British he was no longer able to keep his country in the war, despite his deepest, most sincere, most heartfelt desires for Spanish recapture of Gibraltar. The American impropriety of November 30, 1782 served French as well as American advantage.

At once the powers set about arranging a formal and final peace with Britain, which was signed at Paris in separate treaties by the United States, France, Spain, and the Netherlands, on September 3, 1783. In this final peace Great Britain relinquished to Spain the Floridas, which the British had taken from Spain in the Treaty of Paris of twenty years before.

In such wise, out of the combinations and collisions of European powers, the United States secured independence. Thirteen British colonies, which in 1763 were protesting in tones of gravity and conviction their attachment to the mother country, twenty years later had fought a successful revolution against Great Britain, invoked a hostile combination of European powers against the homeland, and obtained through wise and discreet diplomacy the independence of a new nation, the United States of America. American fortunes had changed completely within a single generation. At the time this change wrought little impression upon the powers of Europe, who concerned themselves not with distant revolts in a far-off hemisphere but with their own animosities and ambitions. The American revolt had provided an occasion for France's revenge on Britain, and for a new attempt by Spain to take back Gibraltar, and for an effort of Austria to annex Bavaria. Few individuals in Europe worried about the future of the nation across the Atlantic. That nation was a republic and everyone knew that republics were by nature weak governments, prone to division and contention, incapable of expansion and growth. The Americans, so Europeans thought, could have their new form of government, since by their revolution they had served so admirably the purposes of Europe.

The American revolution, seen by Europeans as a convenient incident in the course of their own struggles, seen by Vergennes as a heaven-sent opportunity to humble the hated English, nonetheless was to prove itself of large importance, in two major respects. In the long perspective of history it marked the beginning of a new nation which would become the greatest in the world. It also placed before the peoples of Europe, as apart from their unsympathetic and indifferent governments, the example of a new nation dedicated to republican principles. The spirit of liberty would make startling changes in European life during the nineteenth and twentieth centuries.

ADDITIONAL READING

For events national and international pertaining to the New World the best place to start is the voyages of Columbus, and here the student can find a vastly readable account in Samuel Eliot Morison's *Christopher Columbus, Mariner* (Boston, 1955; available in paperback edition). This is a condensation of a larger work published some years ago that won the Pulitzer prize. Also worth reading are Charles E. Nowell, *The Great Discoveries and the First Colonial Empires* (Ithaca, 1954), J. H. Parry, *Europe and a Wider World: 1415–1715* (London, 1949), and Arthur H. Buffinton, *The Second Hundred Years War: 1689–1815* (New York, 1929).

The best single volume on the American revolution from the diplomatic point of view is Samuel Flagg Bemis, *The Diplomacy of the American Revolution* (New York, 1935; available in paperback), a thorough, well-written book that has become a classic. Its author is justly considered the dean of American diplomatic historians. Supplemental to this work are two earlier books, E. S. Corwin, *French Policy and the American Alliance of 1778* (Princeton, 1916) and Claude H. Van Tyne, *The War of Independence: American Phase* (Boston, 1929). A. B. Darling, *Our Rising Em-*

pire (New Haven, 1940) contains chapters on the revolution. An excellent general treatment in the light of the latest scholarship is Edmund S. Morgan, *The Birth of the Republic: 1763–89* (Chicago, 1956).

The skulduggery of the revolution appears in Helen Augur, *The Secret War of Independence* (New York, 1955), Carl Van Doren, *Secret History of the American Revolution* (New York, 1941), and the still intriguing article by J. Franklin Jameson, "St. Eustatius in the American Revolution," *American Historical Review*, vol. 8, (1902–1903), 683–708. Jameson was one of the pioneers of American historical scholarship.

Biographies dealing with the revolution naturally center on Benjamin Franklin, the most famous American of the eighteenth century, the revolution's best diplomat. Carl Van Doren's *Benjamin Franklin* (New York, 1938) remains the leading work, although it doubtless will be replaced within the next dozen years or so by accounts written from the voluminous Franklin papers being collected at Yale for publication under the editorship of Leonard W. Labaree. Van Doren's book should be read with such books as Gerald Stourzh, *Benjamin Franklin and American Foreign Policy* (Chicago, 1954), Verner W. Crane, *Benjamin Franklin and a Rising People* (Boston, 1954), and William B. Clark, *Ben Franklin's Privateers* (Baton Rouge, La., 1955). Georges Lemaitre, *Beaumarchais* (New York, 1946) provides a light sketch of that light-hearted character. Frank Monaghan, *John Jay* (New York, 1935) offers the distinguished Mr. Jay in all his colors. Aptly titled is Gilbert Chinard's *Honest John Adams* (Boston, 1933).

CHAPTER

☆ 2 ☆

The Early Years of Independence

American diplomacy after the revolution and down to the Monroe Doctrine of 1823 divides conveniently into two periods. The first, from 1783 to 1803, saw the new nation pass through a series of problems mostly domestic in nature, the central fact of the era being establishment of a new government in 1789 on the basis of an ingenious federal constitution. In this first period there were some few difficulties with European nations, in particular the problem of preserving neutrality when the European great powers, France and Britain, commenced a major war in 1793. The era closed when President Thomas Jefferson managed by luck to purchase the vast territory of Louisiana, sold to the United States by Napoleon Bonaparte in 1803 just two weeks before France and Britain embarked upon another major European war.

The second period in American diplomacy, which will be treated in a subsequent chapter, began with protest and argument over neutral rights, went through the War of 1812, and concluded on a note of republican optimism, the Monroe Doctrine. With this grand declaration that the Western Hemisphere was closed to further European interference, the founding era in American diplomacy, encompassing the years from 1775 onward, was brought to a fitting end.

1. *The Diplomacy of the Confederation*

The few years between the Treaty of Paris of 1783 and establishment of the new federal government sometimes have been described as the critical period in American history. This is a dubious appellation for the domestic politics of the United States, and likewise inaccurate for American foreign policy at that time. In domestic politics there was a quiescent time from 1783 to 1789. In foreign affairs the United States in the 1780's was so weak as to count for nothing in its occasional representations at the courts of Europe, and the sole development in American diplomacy during the period which deserves any retelling was the abortive negotiations between John Jay, who was secretary of foreign affairs under the Confederation government during this time, and the Spanish minister to the United States, Diego de Gardoqui.

Don Diego and Jay had some serious conversations in 1785–1786 over navigation of the Mississippi River and over the boundary between the Florida possessions of Spain and the territory of the United States. In regard to the Mississippi, the Spanish wished to cut off American trade down that artery of commerce, and in fact had done so in 1784 when the Spanish governor at New Orleans closed the port to American shipping. As for the boundary between Spanish Florida and the United States, the Spanish wished a boundary a hundred miles north of the line on which Jay desired to fix it—Jay wished the thirty-first parallel and the Spanish desired a line to the north (Florida at that time consisted of East and West portions, the former equivalent to present-day Florida, the latter a strip of territory comprising southern portions of present-day Louisiana, Mississippi, and Alabama; see map, p. 30.) As events turned out, the Florida boundary was left for a later settlement with Spain in a treaty negotiated by John Quincy Adams in 1819. Trade with Spain, together with navigation of the Mississippi, proved the crux of the negotiations of the mid-1780's.

Gardoqui, something of a Spanish dandy, flattered Jay assiduously, thus—so the Spanish minister believed—facilitating the conversations. Whether the fine talk and hospitality did help matters is, one must suspect, doubtful, but Gardoqui did his best. As he reported to Madrid, "The American, Jay, who is generally considered to possess talent and capacity enough to cover in great part a weakness natural

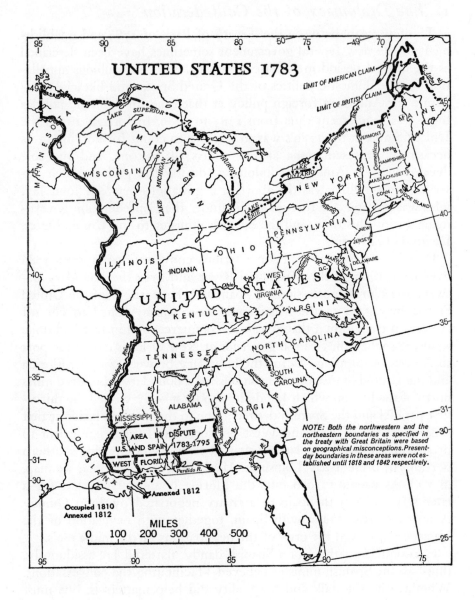

UNITED STATES 1783

LIMIT OF AMERICAN CLAIM

LIMIT OF BRITISH CLAIM

NOTE: Both the northwestern and the northeastern boundaries as specified in the treaty with Great Britain were based on geographical misconceptions. Present-day boundaries in these areas were not established until 1818 and 1842 respectively.

Occupied 1810
Annexed 1812

Annexed 1812

AREA IN DISPUTE
U.S. AND SPAIN 1783-1795

WEST FLORIDA

MILES

0   100   200   300   400   500

to him, appears (by a consistent behavior) to be a very self-centered man, which passion his wife augments, because . . . she likes to be catered to and even more to receive presents. This woman, whom he loves blindly, dominates him and nothing is done without her consent, so that her opinion prevails, though her husband at first may disagree; from which I infer that a little management in dealing with her and a few timely gifts will secure the friendship of both, because I have reason to believe that they proceed resolved to make a fortune."

The minister entertained lavishly at a house in New York, and the Jays often were his guests. He gave special attention to Mrs. Jay, and took her to dances and public festivities. He suggested to his superior in Spain, the foreign minister Count Floridablanca, that the secretary for foreign affairs of the United States be presented with a handsome Spanish stallion. In due time Jay received a horse from Gardoqui, albeit not before the secretary asked for and obtained the consent of Congress for his acceptance of the gift. One might perhaps conclude that the amenities of the Spanish envoy did not hurt relations between Spain and the United States, and it is probably true that Jay was flattered by the attentions of an envoy of a country that during the American revolution had treated him poorly during a mission to Madrid. Still, whether the secretary allowed Spanish entertainment to sway his judgment on matters of state appears doubtful.

It is true that Jay, after a year of talk with Gardoqui, asked Congress to "forbear" American navigation rights on the Mississippi River in return for a favorable commercial treaty with Spain; but Jay at the time believed that this move would be advantageous to his country. Congress debated the proposal at length, and eventually authorized Jay to negotiate a treaty along these lines, but the debate was so bitter that Jay at last realized the impossibility of getting ratification of a treaty with Spain, and his entire negotiation came to naught. According to the Articles of Confederation nine states had to consent to any treaty with a foreign nation. Jay's instructions had obtained in Congress the inadequate margin of seven states in favor and five against.

By the mid-1780's the economic depression of the Confederation period was in full swing, and questions of commerce seemed important in American diplomacy. The trouble was that with the end of the revolution the United States discovered itself outside the British commercial system and without trading rights in such places as the

British West Indies. The Americans were in a position where it was necessary to establish commercial rights by treaty with the various nations of Europe with whom they intended to trade. The British at the end of the revolution sent over dozens of ships loaded with merchandise and flooded the American market. Because of the weak Articles of Confederation, the United States had no practical way of keeping out these goods by tariff. Without ability to place a tariff there was no way in which America could bargain with Britain or the other European commercial powers. The British could sell their goods in the markets of New York, Boston, and Philadelphia without hindrance, and why should they make a treaty granting any privileges of trade to the United States?

The Articles were indeed a difficult form of government for a sovereign nation, and it is fair to say that if the United States had remained under them during the 1790's when European politics took a turn into revolution and war, there might have arisen grave dangers for the new nation of the Western Hemisphere. All kinds of problems presented themselves in the 1790's, not merely treaties of commerce but the matter of American neutrality toward the European wars, and the Articles of Confederation would have given no means of national protection. According to Article 2, "Each state retains its sovereignty, freedom and independence . . ." Article 3 stipulated that the states "severally enter into a firm league of friendship . . ." This weak unity was not enough to present any kind of front to the powers of Europe. Fortunately the new constitution, drawn up in 1787, went into effect in the nick of time, in 1789, the beginning year of the French revolution.

2. *The Early 1790's*

At the outset of this most dramatic revolution in modern world history, the cause of revolutionary France found much sympathy in the United States. Lafayette sent President George Washington the key to the Bastille, and lovers of freedom on both sides of the Atlantic rejoiced. Soon, however, Americans began to divide in their admiration of revolutionary France. Issues between factions in France touched on issues between viewpoints in the United States. The French problem became acute for the United States when France on February 1, 1793 dramatically declared war on Great Britain,

Spain, and the Netherlands.

The problem of American diplomacy was an obvious one: what to do with the Franco-American alliance of 1778, still in effect in 1793. Should Americans rally to the side of France, as the French nation fifteen years before had come to the help of the infant United States? Or had the change of government in France ended the obligations under the treaty of 1778? President Washington's most trusted aide, Secretary of the Treasury Alexander Hamilton, wished to abandon the French alliance, and argued that the alliance was with the monarchy and hence not valid under the republic—this despite the well-known rule of international law which said that changes of regime did not invalidate a nation's treaties.

Thomas Jefferson, first secretary of state of the United States, argued against Hamilton—correctly by international law—that the treaty of alliance with France should not be abandoned, although he was not anxious to see the United States enter the war in Europe. In 1793 he was willing to help the French only with measures short of war. He would have allowed France to outfit privateers in American ports and use the facilities of American territory to raise troops. He would have been willing to assist the French revolutionists by placing his country in what in a later period would have been described as American nonbelligerency.

As events turned out, neither Hamilton nor Jefferson succeeded in influencing President Washington. The French alliance was not abrogated, but the United States at the outset of the war declared a strict neutrality. Jefferson's point of view soon found expression in American politics, however, through the actions of the new French minister to the United States, Edmund Genêt, who reached American soil on April 8, 1793 with a revolutionary mandate to obtain American co-operation as a benevolent neutral in the war.

Genêt was a Frenchman of moderate revolutionary desires, a Girondin, filled with the spirit of liberty, equality, and fraternity, willing to do his best for his country in its time of danger from counterrevolutionary attack in Europe. He landed at Charleston, South Carolina, under instructions to win American aid and negotiate a new treaty of commerce, virtually a new alliance. Even before he had presented his credentials to President Washington he set about commissioning four privateers, and dispatched them to prey upon British vessels along the American coast.

But at this juncture the French minister ran into trouble. Moving northward from Charleston he found himself warmly greeted by fellow republicans of North America and must have come to believe that he would have no difficulty with the government, then located in the city of Philadelphia. Here he was disappointed, for Washington, who had already issued a proclamation of neutrality on April 22, received him on May 18 with cool formality. Secretary Jefferson, acting under Washington's instructions, presented Genêt with a communication to the effect that grants of military commissions on American soil constituted an infringement of American sovereignty. Genêt was told that the privateers commissioned by him would have to leave American waters and could not send their prizes into American ports. Undaunted, the minister authorized the arming of *The Little Sarah*, a prize brought in by a French vessel, renamed her *La Petite Démocrate*, and threatened to send her to sea. Because the vessel was outfitting in the port of Philadelphia, the governor of Pennsylvania sent an emissary to Genêt to persuade the French minister to detain the vessel. Genêt "flew in a great passion" and made it clear that he cared little for "old Washington" and that if necessary "he would appeal from the President to the People." The vessel sailed. Washington with the consent of his cabinet thereupon demanded Genêt's recall.

The minister might have gone home to the guillotine, had the Washington administration carried out its order, for Genêt's successor arrived in the United States in February 1794 with a warrant for Genêt's arrest and deportation to France, now under the control of Robespierre and the Jacobins. The American government congenially allowed the errant minister to remain in the New World. Genêt removed himself, "in retreat and silence," to a farm at Jamaica, Long Island, there to meditate upon "the great revolutions of the world" and to isolate himself "from the detestable intrigues of Courts and the discouraging cabals of nations." The "comet," as Hamilton had described him, disappeared from the political horizon, married the daughter of Governor George Clinton of New York, and lived happily ever after.

Because of the embarrassments of Genêt's mission, the United States decided to make clear its stand toward the European war, and in a neutrality act of June 1794, reinforcing the proclamation of neutrality made by Washington in April 1793, the government set forth its position. The act forbade citizens of the United States to enlist in the service of a foreign power and prohibited the fitting-out of armed vessels in American ports. The revolutionary government of France by this token should have known that it would be futile to invoke the alliance of 1778, but Genêt's successors, Joseph Fauchet and Pierre Adet, boldly continued his efforts to obtain assistance from the United States.

Upon conclusion of the Genêt affair and with the second announcement of neutrality there remained during the Washington administration the negotiation of two important commercial treaties, one with Britain and the other with Spain. These treaties would have been impossible to negotiate under the Articles of Confederation, but they were easily concluded under the constitution. The two treaties were, each in its own way, considerable achievements of American diplomacy. In conclusion of the so-called Jay's Treaty, signed by John Jay with Great Britain on November 19, 1794, the Washington administration braved anti-British sentiment to establish regular commercial relations with the former mother country. There was much criticism of the president and his cabinet for this treaty, under claim that it marked a capitulation to Britain. In truth Jay's Treaty preserved American nationality, for a large part of the revenues of the new government under the constitution came from customs receipts, and if no satisfactory arrangement for commerce had been made by the American government with the British it would have been quite possible for Britain to destroy the government by withholding commerce. To be sure, there were other sources of trade, but Americans preferred British goods. As for Pinckney's Treaty with Spain, signed October 27, 1795, it was less important than Jay's Treaty, for American commerce with Spain was not large, but among other provisions it did give a legal basis to American transshipment of goods at the Spanish port of New Orleans—from Mississippi flatboats to ocean sailing vessels—and in this sense complemented Jay's Treaty with Great Britain.

John Jay, after leaving the post of secretary for foreign affairs, became chief justice of the supreme court, and it was in this capacity that he undertook in 1794 a special mission to Great Britain to conclude the commercial treaty that bears his name. He found himself in London without many advantages in his negotiation, for the British government knew that trade was necessary for the survival of the new federal republic in America. In addition to this difficulty Jay was hindered by the indiscretions of Alexander Hamilton to the British minister in Philadelphia, George Hammond. Hamilton gratuitously told Hammond in the midst of Jay's dealings with the British that the United States would not join the new armed neutrality of 1794, and thus gave away a possible threat—and Jay had few of them—which the chief justice might have used in London. But Hamilton's indiscretion was perhaps not as damaging as it at first seemed, for although Jay was not aware of the fact, the British had a copy of the secret cipher by which he corresponded with the Department of State. Thus, reading at will his messages to and from America, they anticipated his requests and knew always how far they might push him before meeting his final position on each issue.

Jay's Treaty was negotiated in difficult circumstances, and the result for that reason alone was notable. The British pledged themselves to evacuate the frontier posts in territory around the Great Lakes. Britain promised to compensate the United States for spoliations on American shipping made since the outbreak of the European war. A mixed commission—half Britishers, half Americans—was to fix the amount of these damages while two others were to close the gaps in the boundaries stipulated in the Treaty of Paris whereby the line between Maine and Canada and to the west of Lake Superior had remained uncertain. Another mixed commission was to determine a fair compensation for the private debts contracted by citizens of the United States prior to the Treaty of Paris and never paid. Jay's Treaty, incidentally, was something of an innovation in diplomacy in that it established so many mixed commissions to settle outstanding disputes. The United States in this way became a leader in what was to be a favorite nineteenth-century procedure of settlement between nations —arbitration.

John Jay in his treaty with Great Britain failed to obtain recognition of American neutral rights, and this failure deserves a brief explanation. Neutral rights, the right of a neutral to trade under specified rules with belligerents during wartime, were from the outset of the war in Europe in 1793 a large American concern, for the United States in the late eighteenth and early nineteenth centuries was one of the world's leading carriers of ocean commerce, second only to Britain herself in tonnage on the high seas. The Americans were much interested in obtaining recognition of commercial rights from belligerents in any European war, and the more privileges accorded to American commerce the better. The problem was to obtain recognition of neutral rights from Britain, for the queen of the seas would be able to suppress any rights with which she was not in accord, and, on the other hand, if the British approved of wide commercial privileges for American traders then the other nations of the world would probably agree to British trade definitions, and America's arrangements with Britain would by that fact become international law. The history of neutral rights is a complicated matter, but here it is enough to say that the United States early in its history, actually in 1776, set forth three American principles of neutral rights to be established in commercial treaties with foreign nations, and to these three principles there was joined a fourth in 1784. The plan approved by Congress in 1776, the Plan of 1776 as it was called, stipulated first that free ships made free goods—that the cargo of a neutral ship, with the exception of contraband, should not be subject to capture. Second was the principle that contraband should be narrowly defined, excluding foodstuffs and naval stores. Third was the idea that neutral ships had the right to trade between belligerent ports, that is, to take over a belligerent's carrying trade. To these principles the congressional Plan of 1784 added the notion that a blockade to be effective must involve "imminent danger" to vessels seeking to enter a blockaded port. After the United States concluded treaties in the 1780's in which Sweden and Prussia recognized the American interpretation of neutral rights, Jay during the negotiations with Great Britain sought to obtain a similar engagement, but met with prompt and unequivocal refusal. The American envoy was sorry not to have succeeded in this regard, but wrote home realistically that he could not expect the British to sign any agreement that would limit the effectiveness of their war with France. That Britain "at this period, and involved in war," he wrote, "should not admit principles, which would impeach the propriety of her conduct in seizing provisions bound to France, and enemy's property in neutral ships, does not appear to me extraordinary." He had managed to gain one concession: "The articles as they now stand secure compensation for seizures, and leave us at liberty to decide whether they were made in such cases as to be warranted by the *existing* law of nations." This concession was not enough for many of his countrymen, who observing Jay's failure to obtain recognition of American neutral rights were willing to believe that the envoy had purposely given away those rights to Great Britain.

If this accusation were not sufficient to discredit his negotiations, it was Jay's further ill luck that his treaty fell afoul of domestic politics in the United States. By the time that the Senate in 1795 undertook consideration of the treaty American domestic politics were taking a new course: political parties were appearing; lines were forming between the friends of France and those of Great Britain; the Hamiltonian Federalists, as they were coming to be called, stood forth in opposition to the Jeffersonian Republicans, to the complete disgust of President Washington who like most of the founding fathers had not anticipated appearance in the United States of political parties. Jay's Treaty turned out to be one of the issues on which parties took their separate stands. There was a great outcry over the treaty. Jay, a Federalist, was hanged in effigy by some of the more enterprising Republicans, and other indignities were directed at the man who had dared to sign a treaty with Great Britain, the nation that was the enemy of France. Some nameless American reportedly wrote the following sentiments on a fence: "Damn John Jay! Damn every one that won't damn John Jay! Damn every one that won't put lights in his windows and sit up all night damning John Jay!" Whereupon Jay's Treaty passed the Senate, then dominated by Federalists, by a comfortable margin.

In the same year that saw the passage of Jay's Treaty, the American special commissioner in Madrid, Thomas Pinckney, negotiated his commercial treaty with Spain, an agreement more favorable to the United States. Spain, of course, was a weak power, far easier to deal with than Great Britain. In this treaty the Spanish recognized the boundary of the United States as set forth in the Treaty of Paris in 1783 with Great Britain: the Mississippi at the west and the thirty-first parallel at the south. The treaty gave Americans free navigation of the Mississippi and, as already mentioned, the privilege of deposit for their goods at New Orleans, this latter provision to last for three years, after which the place of deposit might be changed if desirable to another point to be designated.

The precise reason for Spain's agreement to Pinckney's Treaty, its willingness to give in on almost all issues outstanding between the two countries, would later be debated by scholars, Arthur P. Whitaker maintaining that Pinckney's Treaty was a frontier treaty forced upon Spain by the threats of American frontiersmen to Spanish New World possessions. Whitaker contends that the movement of lawless American settlers into Spain's possessions in the Floridas and their importunities along the Mississippi River led the government in Madrid to give the Americans a generous commercial treaty. Samuel Flagg Bemis, on the other hand, has contended that Pinckney's Treaty came out of the requirements of European politics, that the Spanish having gone to war against France in 1793 had decided by 1795 that they would change their allegiance and go over to the side of France against their traditional enemy Britain, and that the court in Madrid believed there was a secret article of alliance in Jay's Treaty which led them to make a commercial treaty with Pinckney far more favorable than the minister could otherwise have expected.

Where the truth lies in these contentions is difficult to prove. The two authorities on Pinckney's Treaty, Bemis and Whitaker, have taken their argument so far as to examine sailing schedules between England, Spain and the United States, so as to prove (or disprove) that when Jay's Treaty got to the United States for ratification its terms were soon known (or unknown) to Spanish authorities in Madrid. Bemis in the present writer's judgment has the better of this involved argument. Pinckney's Treaty appears to have been an illustration of one of the basic principles of American diplomacy toward Europe during the founding era, namely that, as Bemis puts it, "Europe's distress was America's advantage." For whatever reason, let us conclude, Pinckney's Treaty of 1795 like its distinguished predecessor of 1794 secured American relations with one of the important powers of Europe during the confusions of a major European war.

There followed in the last year of Washington's administration the president's famous Farewell Address. This announcement to Washington's countrymen was not an address but a presidential manifesto, given out in reality to secure election of the president's chosen successor, John Adams. In the course of this political statement Washington said some truths about American foreign policy which were remembered long after the politics of the occasion had been forgotten. "Europe has a set of primary interests," he said, "which to us have none or a very remote relation. Hence she must be engaged in frequent controversies, the causes of which are essentially foreign to our concerns. Hence, therefore, it must be unwise in us to implicate ourselves by artificial ties in the ordinary vicissitudes of her politics or the ordinary combinations and collisions of her friendships or enmities."

Nowhere in this address, one should add, was the phrase "entangling alliances," which Jefferson first used in his inaugural of 1801. And Washington had not advised against American participation in the extraordinary affairs of Europe—he had counseled only against "ordinary combinations and collisions." This adjectival distinction was overlooked in subsequent references to the Farewell Address by political leaders and publicists, who sought for their own purposes to show that the first president of the United States was an isolationist and against any political contacts between his country and the nations of Europe.

Taken in the way in which Washington meant it, the Farewell Address was a memorable statement of American foreign policy. It set out his own achievement in foreign affairs. His leadership during a large European war had preserved the republic in strength and neutrality, despite the willingness of some Americans in 1793 and thereafter to take sides in a conflict that did not vitally concern them. The first president was a prudent man, and it fell to some of his successors to discover how incautious diplomacy could endanger American national existence.

3. *The XYZ Affair*

In his Farewell Address Washington asked his countrymen to stay clear of ordinary foreign entanglements, although he had not used those words, and his advice was well taken but soon forgotten. Political parties had been forming in his second administration, and by the time he was ready to leave office there was some question as to whether he could control the choice of his successor. The Hamiltonian Federalists were in essence the party of strong central government, and the Jeffersonians favored a more federal, less centralized, national regime. The parties also took stands on issues of foreign relations, the Hamiltonian Federalists being pro-British, the Jeffersonian Republicans pro-French. Both sides injected into the electoral contest of 1796 their views on foreign affairs, and John Adams, whose views internationally might well be denominated pro-American, almost failed of election despite support by Washington. Adams soon afterward ruined his chances for re-election in the year 1800 when he became involved in a serious diplomatic crisis with France known as the XYZ affair. He supported a peaceful solution to it, rather than war, which latter course many of the Federalists desired.

The changing course of the French revolution explains this diplomatic crisis in 1797–1798. The revolution had by this time passed through the reign of terror and turned conservative, for the country had had enough of revolutionary turmoil. After Robespierre the direction of the French government came under a five-man executive known as the Directory, for which the minister of foreign affairs was the wily statesman Talleyrand. The Directory in due time was swept away by the revolutionary general from Corsica, Napoleon Bonaparte, who in 1797 was twenty-eight years old and engaged in a campaign in Italy. The revolution, thus, was in a period of transition at the time of the XYZ affair; the Directory was giving way to Bonaparte. French military prestige was rising in Europe. All in all it was an ill-advised moment for the United States to send a mission to France to adjust outstanding issues.

The American commission, composed of John Marshall, Charles C. Pinckney, and Elbridge Gerry, sailed in the summer of 1797, and when they arrived in Paris they were approached by three intermediaries of Talleyrand, who demanded a bribe for the foreign minister before the mission could hope to do business with the Directory. Talleyrand demanded $250,000 for himself as well as a loan to France, really a gift, of several million dollars. It was an unblushing diplomatic holdup, albeit one not unusual in diplomatic practice in the eighteenth century. Pinckney and Marshall, insulted, refused to consider such a proposition, and on one occasion Pinckney is reported to have said to Talleyrand's contact man, "No, no, not a sixpence!" Gerry was less certain of his position than were his fellow commissioners, both ardent Federalists, and he continued to treat with the foreign minister after the two other men had left Paris in disgust.

The upshot of Talleyrand's effrontery was that President Adams in the spring of 1798 sent a special message to Congress, and as more dispatches arrived from his commissioners he sent these to Congress. He substituted for the names of Talleyrand's agents the letters X, Y, and Z, but otherwise kept Congress fully informed. On June 21, 1798 he made known his final condition: "I will never send another minister to France without assurances that he will be received, respected, and honored, as the representative of a great, free, powerful, and independent nation."

The Federalists in Congress were eager for war, and a series of measures, many of them Hamilton's, were enacted to raise an army and to authorize attacks by privateers and by public vessels upon French ships found preying upon American commerce. The treaties of 1778 and a consular convention in 1788 with France were abrogated unilaterally. Congress voted to authorize a Navy Department and set on foot measures to obtain frigates and other vessels. In the quasi war that followed, the undeclared hostilities against the government of France, there were several notable naval actions, including capture by the French of the American vessel *Retaliation* off Guadeloupe on November 20, 1798, capture of the French *L'Insurgente* by the American frigate *Constellation* on February 9, 1799, and taking of *Le Berceau* by the *Boston* on October 12, 1800.

All this was contrary to Talleyrand's expectation in originally asking the American commissioners for a large bribe. The foreign minister had lived in the United States in 1794–1796 during the Jacobin era in his own country, and he knew the strength of the American republic. He did not wish the Americans harm to an extent that he wanted a war with them. He, along with many other Frenchmen, hoped in fact to build a new colonial empire for France based on the French West Indies, and he was conspiring already for the retrocession of Louisiana from Spain to France. The idea was that Louisiana would be a large granary to feed the Negro labor in Santo Domingo which would in turn raise sugar to export to France, and for this project the French foreign minister needed peace, not war, with the United States. The uproar in the United States over his attempted bribery made him realize that he had gone too far, and when he heard that President Adams had advised Congress that no more missions would go to France unless received with respect, he wrote a private letter to the French chargé d'affaires at The Hague, repeating almost word for word Adams's condition and adding that he, Talleyrand, would most certainly accede to such sentiments. The chargé was empowered to show this missive to the American minister at The Hague, William Vans Murray. Murray sent a message at once to Adams about this new intelligence, and followed his message with the actual letter from Talleyrand to his colleague in the Dutch capital.

The receipt of this instruction from The Hague placed John Adams in a quandary. The country was unified behind his administration in a desire to stand up to the French, and the Federalists had joined ranks with Adams. If he accepted the proffer of renewal of relations which Talleyrand left-handedly had extended to him, he would stir the extremists in the Federalist Party to fury, give a new lease on life to the Jeffersonian Republicans, take a chance that Talleyrand upon the arrival of a new American mission in France would refuse anyway to see them and disavow his letter to the French chargé at The Hague. On the other hand, Adams knew that his country needed peace above all else, for with time the sprawling United States could tie itself more strongly together, the bonds of economics and politics would with years bind the parts of the republic together, and then —and only then—could a statesman safely chance a foreign war. Adams knew that statesmanship required him to send a new mission to France. In later years he expressed the desire to be remembered by the epitaph: "Here lies John Adams, who took upon himself the responsibility of the peace with France in the year 1800." To his everlasting credit he chose the path of statesmanship and announced to a startled country in the autumn of 1798 that he would send a new commission.

Arriving in France in 1799 the second commission (Oliver E. Ellsworth and William R. Davie, together with William Vans Murray) negotiated the Treaty of Mortefontaine, signed September 30, 1800. This convention abrogated the treaty of alliance of 1778, in return for which the United States abandoned claims for spoliations from France in the European war that had begun in 1793. The treaty was also the basis for reopening diplomatic relations between France and the United States.

4. The Louisiana Purchase

The final development in American foreign relations during the first twenty years after the Treaty of Paris in 1783 was the Louisiana Purchase, by which President Jefferson without much diplomatic planning or thought managed, through Europe's distresses, to double the territory of the United States. That the Louisiana Purchase was an unexpected development seems obvious from the American president's embarrassment as to how to accept this new territory into the United States. Jefferson in the latter 1790's had been seeking to limit the power of the federal government, for the government was controlled by the Federalists, his political enemies. To assist him in this good end he had developed a constitutional theory to the effect that the proper construction of the American constitution was a strict construction: the national government, according to Jefferson in this phase of his thinking, had no more power over the people of the United States than the government had expressly received from the constitution; as one of the amendments accepted in 1791 stated, all powers not delegated to the federal government or withheld by it from the states were reserved to the states or to the people. Jefferson did not wish the federal government to have any such wide authority as did Chief Justice John Marshall. In the course of taking this constitutional position, Jefferson put himself into such a tight place that he well could wonder in 1803 whether he had the power as president to purchase so large a territory as Louisiana from a foreign government. Events, of course, and opportunity, outran his constitutional scruples once the possibility of the Louisiana Purchase appeared.

The first step of diplomacy that led to the purchase of the Louisiana territory from France was, properly enough, not a step taken by Jefferson. Talleyrand at the time of the XYZ affair was thinking in terms of a new French empire in America, in which Louisiana would serve as the granary of Santo Domingo. In furtherance of this project the foreign minister negotiated with Spain—which country had received Louisiana from France at the end of the Seven Years War in 1763—a secret treaty of retrocession, the Treaty of San Ildefonso, which was signed on October 1, 1800, one day after the treaty that ended the quasi war between the United States and France, the Treaty of Mortefontaine. The *quid pro quo* obtained by Spain from retroceding Louisiana was a promise by the French government of a kingdom in Italy for a young Spanish princeling.

The initial French move for Louisiana, the Treaty of San Ildefonso, was secret from the United States, but after the French and Spanish signed a second treaty, the Treaty of Madrid of March 21, 1801, confirming the treaty of 1800, President Jefferson learned of what was afoot. The American minister in Great Britain, Rufus King, transmitted definite news of the treaty of retrocession of Louisiana in November 1801. Two problems at once arose for the Americans: first, the threat of an aggressive power to the west of American territory, thwarting American expansion—"our rising empire," as Ben-

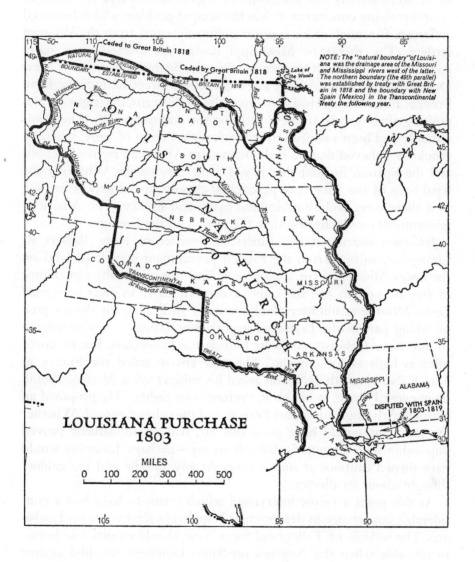

NOTE: The "natural boundary" of Louisiana was the drainage area of the Missouri and Mississippi rivers west of the latter. The northern boundary (the 49th parallel) was established by treaty with Great Britain in 1818 and the boundary with New Spain (Mexico) in the Transcontinental Treaty the following year.

Ceded to Great Britain 1818

Ceded by Great Britain 1818

Lake of the Woods

NATURAL BOUNDARY ESTABLISHED WITH GREAT BRITAIN 1818

POINT OF LOUISIANA

Missouri River

Yellowstone River

MONTANA

NORTH DAKOTA

MINNESOTA

SOUTH DAKOTA

WYOMING

Missouri River

NEBRASKA

IOWA

Platte River

COLORADO

TRANSCONTINENTAL

Arkansas River

KANSAS

MISSOURI

SPANISH

OKLAHOMA

ARKANSAS

TREATY LINE 1819

Red R.

MISSISSIPPI

ALABAMA

Sabine River

LOUISIANA

DISPUTED WITH SPAIN 1803-1819

Perdido River

LOUISIANA PURCHASE
1803

MILES

0   100   200   300   400   500

jamin Franklin once described American territorial ambitions; and second, the problem of navigation of the Mississippi and the demands of Western settlers that the father of waters remain free and open to their increasing commerce. It was this second problem which bothered Jefferson, for much of his support politically came from the Western settlers. The threat to Mississippi navigation loomed even more dangerously when on October 16, 1802 the Spanish governor at New Orleans, apparently without any instruction direct or indirect from French authorities, refused to give the Americans the right of depositing their goods at New Orleans for transshipment. There admittedly had been a confusion in Pinckney's Treaty of 1795, whereby Pinckney believed that he had obtained an American right of deposit and the Spanish insisted that it was a mere privilege. Whatever the legal basis of the American practice of deposit, it did appear in 1802 as if there were collusion between Spain and France. The American government moved to negotiate the issue with the French.

Jefferson instructed the American minister in Paris, Robert R. Livingston, to buy from the French government a tract of land on the lower Mississippi for a port, or failing this, to obtain a guarantee of free navigation and the right of deposit. Early in 1803 he named James Monroe as minister plenipotentiary to France for the purpose of taking part in the Louisiana negotiations. Monroe was instructed to buy New Orleans and West Florida for $2,000,000, but he could offer as high as $10,000,000. The new envoy sailed for France in March. Next month Jefferson asked his cabinet what Monroe should do in event France, as he put it, "refused our rights." He proposed an alliance with England against France, and the cabinet agreed. Whether the president would have gone this far, had an adjustment proved impossible with France, is difficult to say—perhaps Jefferson would have turned cautious at such a time. At any rate he and the cabinet thought about an alliance.

At this point a factor intervened which seems to have had a considerable importance in determining Napoleon's final views on Louisiana. The scheme of Talleyrand for a New World empire had begun to crumble when the Negroes on Santo Domingo revolted against French rule and came under the inspired leadership of the former Negro slave Toussaint l'Ouverture. Toussaint reasoned, naturally enough, that liberty, equality, and fraternity meant just that, and he undertook to secure those precepts in Santo Domingo where the

Jacobins during their short-lived rule had introduced them. The Directorate in a strenuous effort sought to put down this Negro revolt, but the unhealthy climate of Santo Domingo consumed thousands of troops and the revolutionary ardor of the islanders would not be extinguished. Even after Toussaint himself was taken to France the fighting continued. News arrived in France early in January 1803 that General Charles Leclerc, Napoleon's brother-in-law, had died of yellow fever on the pestilential island, that his army was annihilated, and the Negroes were completely out of French control. Napoleon during the autumn of 1802 had gathered a relief expedition in the Dutch Channel port of Helvoet-Sluis. The expedition was ready but unable to sail when it was frozen in by ice during an extraordinarily hard winter. Prior to Leclerc's death Napoleon seems to have been secure in his determination to exterminate the revolt in France's prize West Indian island. When the dismal news arrived in January 1803 he apparently began to waver. What happened to Santo Domingo was of large importance to the United States, for of what use was Louisiana to France without Santo Domingo?

In Europe, Napoleon may have reasoned, war could be made to support war. In Santo Domingo every military move was costly, and could not pay for itself for years and decades thereafter. Napoleon encountered a difficult situation. Perhaps the colonial scheme of Talleyrand had never suited his tastes, and perhaps he had waited only until he could be certain enough of his power in France to back out of the foreign minister's project. Another military failure at Santo Domingo certainly would hurt his personal credit, by disgusting both the French public and the army. He decided to turn his attentions to a more profitable area. The war in Europe had been temporarily adjourned in the Treaty of Amiens of 1802, and he determined to re-open it.

The cunning First Consul (France had changed its government from the Directory to a Roman-like republic known as the Consulate; in 1804 Napoleon became emperor), having made his decision, did not so much as tell his brothers what he was going to do. Talleyrand too was deceived, for as late as mid-February 1803 the foreign minister believed that Louisiana in due course would pass under French control as part of the imperial plan. The first clear evidence of his master's change of mind came in the well-known scene at Madame Bonaparte's drawing room, where Napoleon on March 12 met the British ambassador, Lord Whitworth. "I find, my Lord, your nation wants war again!" said the First Consul. "No, sir," replied Whitworth, "we are very desirous of peace." "I must either have Malta or war!" was the rejoinder. Within a few days the alarm spread through Europe.

Easter Sunday, April 10, 1803 appears to have been the day of decision in regard to Louisiana. Napoleon after attending Mass called together two of his ministers and (according to an account by one of them, François Barbé-Marbois, written a quarter-century later) explained his views about the New World territory. "I think," he began, "of ceding it to the United States. I can scarcely say that I cede it to them, for it is not yet in our possession. If, however, I leave the least time to our enemies, I shall only transmit an empty title to those republicans whose friendship I seek. . . . it appears to me that in the hands of this growing Power it will be more useful to the policy, and even to the commerce, of France than if I should attempt to keep it."

The next day Talleyrand, always the imperturbable negotiator even when making a complete *volte-face*, suddenly said in talk with Livingston about Louisiana: "What will you give for the whole?" The American minister was so startled as to be almost speechless.

Recovering poise, Livingston began the final negotiations for all of Louisiana, and had virtually made the arrangements by the time Monroe arrived on Wednesday. Some days passed in last-minute haggling over the price, Livingston attempting to beat down the French but with no success. He ran some chance of losing everything in this haggle for a few million dollars, but luck was with him. The treaty of cession was dated April 30, 1803 and the price was $11,250,000. The United States by a separate claims convention assumed the debts due from France to American citizens estimated at $3,750,000, making $15,000,000 as the total price for Louisiana. On May 15, little more than two weeks after the Louisiana treaty, Great Britain declared war on France.

Afterward in the United States there was a small to-do over the addition to the nation of so much new territory. The Federalist Party, fearing rightly that to double American territory in the West would mean a large increase of strength in the Jeffersonian Republican Party, stood against the treaty of cession. Federalists spoke openly and violently about Jefferson's assistance to the French cause, of how the president had indulged in the immorality of receiving stolen goods from the greatest cutthroat of modern times. Jefferson had his constitutional doubts about buying Louisiana and found himself in a position where he had to go back on some of his most elaborate constitutional reasoning. He murmured for a while about the need for a constitutional amendment to bring the territory into the union, but settled for ratification of the treaty made by Livingston and Monroe. Perhaps he sensed that his reputation in American history would come to rest, in considerable part, on this addition to the national domain of Louisiana, though he did not have much to do with Napoleon's decision to sell. The Louisiana Purchase of 1803 derived from Europe's distress, which so often in the founding years of American history was America's advantage.

ADDITIONAL READING

The only general account is A. B. Darling, *Our Rising Empire* (New Haven, 1940). On Britain and Canada there is the detailed and scholarly book with the eighteenth-century title by A. L. Burt, *The United States, Great Britain, and British North America from the Revolution to the Establishment of Peace after the War of 1812* (New Haven, 1940). Bradford Perkins has considered *The First Rapprochement: England and the United States, 1795–1805* (Philadelphia, 1955)—the second *rapprochement* being the Anglo-American friendship which began to develop at the end of the nineteenth century. Two books dealing in part with diplomatic affairs are Merrill Jensen, *The New Nation: A History of the United States during the Confederation, 1781–1789* (New York, 1950) and Edward Channing's *A History of the United States: Federalists and Republicans, 1789–1815* (New York, 1917). Channing remains one of the most readable and instructive of historians, and his multivolume history is a monumental tribute to his genius and industry. A recent study, very ably done, is Alexander DeConde, *Entangling Alliance: Politics and Diplomacy under George Washington* (Durham, N.C., 1958). See also Manning J. Dauer, *The Adams Federalists* (Baltimore, 1953); and Stephen G. Kurtz, *The Presidency of John Adams* (Philadelphia, 1957). For a broad view of American life at the beginning of the new century there is no better source than the first six chapters of Henry Adams's *History of the United States during the Administrations of Jefferson and Madison* (9 vols., New York, 1889–1891); these chapters are reprinted in paperback as *The United States in 1800* (Ithaca, 1955). In the multivolume edition Adams's description of the Louisiana Purchase is delightfully done. As one might expect, he allots no extra credit to Thomas Jefferson, who defeated his great-grandfather for the presidency. For the Louisiana Purchase see also E. W. Lyon, *Louisiana in French Diplomacy: 1759–1804* (Norman, Okla., 1934).

Opposing in their interpretation of the forces behind American diplomacy in the 1780's and 1790's are S. F. Bemis's *Jay's Treaty* (New York, 1923) and *Pinckney's Treaty* (Baltimore, 1926) and A. P. Whitaker's *The Spanish-American Frontier: 1783–1795* (Boston, 1927) and *The Mississippi Question: 1795–1803* (New York, 1934).

For the statesmen see Frank Monaghan, *John Jay* (New York, 1935); A. J. Beveridge, *Life of John Marshall* (4 vols., Boston, 1916–1919); Gilbert Chinard, *Honest John Adams* (Boston, 1933); John A. Carroll and Mary Wells Ashworth, *George Washington: First in Peace* (New York, 1957); Irving Brant, *James Madison: Secretary of State, 1800–1809* (Indianapolis, 1953); E. W. Lyon, *The Man Who Sold Louisiana: The Career of François Barbé-Marbois* (Norman, Okla., 1942). A readable one-volume biography of Jefferson is Gilbert Chinard, *Thomas Jefferson* (Boston, 1939). Multivolume biographies are Marie Kimball, *Jefferson* (3 vols., New York, 1943–1950), which will remain unfinished because of the death of the author, and Dumas Malone, *Jefferson and His Time* (2 vols., in process, Boston, 1948–   ). The Library of Congress is presently undertaking a vast publication of all of Jefferson's correspondence. This project, begun during the presidency of Harry S. Truman, has been described by Mr. Truman as his most outstanding presidential accomplishment.

The War of 1812 and the Monroe Doctrine

At the beginning of the first administration of President Thomas Jefferson it truly seemed as if the difficulties of the American republic had resolved themselves, that the new republic on the western side of the Atlantic had survived the troubles of its birth and early years of independence and was now established in the world family of nations. Such was the impression that Jefferson gained in his first year or two of office. He ratified the Convention of 1800, ending the virtual state of war between the United States and France. He watched Britain and France make peace with each other at Amiens in 1802. At home he saw his administration politically secure, for the Federalist Party had suffered in the elections of 1800. All these events combined to make Jefferson believe that he had, to use one of his favorite phrases, completed the circle of his felicities.

Unfortunately he had not, as he discovered when the European war broke out once more in 1803, raising anew the old problems of American neutrality, churning up American domestic politics as the Federalists again sided with Britain and the Republicans with France. The president's troubles thereafter multiplied until the end of his second term, when they devolved upon his successor James Madison —who pursued a dangerous course in foreign policy which led the United States into the European war. There was indeed no easy time in American national life, at home or abroad, from 1803 until the year 1815, the end of the war in Europe. Every tremor of the European balance of power meant, as Jefferson and his successor knew so well, a potential or actual threat to American nationality. The United States had to move with each European change, hoping to avoid upsetting the balance and presenting to one of the major European belligerents, France or Great Britain, an opportunity to end the republican experiment in the New World.

Happily, just before the war in Europe closed in 1815 the American government managed, in the nick of time, to conclude peace with Britain. In subsequent years President Madison's successor James Monroe arranged, through the inspired diplomacy of his Secretary of State John Quincy Adams, a treaty with Spain setting the boundary between American Louisiana and Spanish Texas and California. The final act of this era of American diplomacy, 1803–1823, came when President Monroe proclaimed his famous doctrine, pointing out to the Old World the peculiar interests of the New. The doctrine of 1823 brought to an end the diplomacy of American independence. It completed the work of separation begun in 1775.

1. *America versus the European Belligerents, 1803–1809*

Why was it that, when war broke out in Europe in 1803, the United States could not avoid being slowly drawn into the fighting, eventually entering the war on the side of France and against the mother country? Why did the United States, before having fully ensured its national survival, undertake a war against the greatest power in the world? The War of 1812 could and should have been avoided. It was not a necessary war, and became inevitable only after diplomacy hardened around principle and changed, in fact, from diplomacy to dogmatic argument. There might have been no hostilities if during the decade preceding the outbreak of war the United States had fixed its attention upon what should have been its chief purpose, strengthening the foundations of its nationality, and pursued in foreign affairs a policy of accommodation instead of freedom of the seas.

The Americans, possessing a small navy and a large merchant marine, were seeking to trade in Europe at the height of the Napoleonic wars with any nation that would purchase their cargoes. The British government refused to allow such a free American wartime trade.

The British were determined, first, to prevent assistance to Napoleonic France and, second, to permit as little competition as possible with British merchant shipping. The United States contended that international law sanctioned wartime trade by neutrals, in noncontraband goods, to belligerent ports not blockaded. The British challenged the freedom of the seas. Moreover, they approached the problem of neutral trade from the other end of the American argument, by extending their definition of blockade to include ports merely announced as blockaded: they imposed upon numerous French or French-controlled ports a paper blockade. The exigencies of Great Britain during a war against Napoleon Bonaparte stood in conflict with American principle. The Royal Navy had six hundred ships of war, and the American navy numbered sixteen seaworthy vessels. For Americans, a war with Britain for the purpose of enforcing freedom of the seas was a quixotic undertaking.

The manner in which freedom of the seas led to war in 1812 thus forms a melancholy chapter in American history. Presidents Jefferson and Madison failed to make the most elementary calculations of American military weakness and British power, of the risks involved in war versus those involved in diplomatic accommodation. They chose to stand for a principle that was far from accepted in international practice, especially in the practice of Great Britain. Freedom of the seas set a standard that if followed would have limited the operations of belligerents in wartime, but it lacked acceptance by the British government and this made it an impractical diplomatic principle for the American nation.

There was another principle at stake in the diplomacy that preceded the War of 1812, namely impressment of seamen from American ships by the British navy. This hateful practice figured amply in the diplomatic exchanges between Washington and London in the years before 1812, notably in the period 1803–1807, but it never became as important an issue as freedom of the seas. In regard to impressment the British government always refused to admit any rights by the American government. Lord Harrowby, the younger Pitt's foreign secretary, wrote to the British minister in Washington in 1804 that "the Pretension advanced by Mr. Madison that the American Flag should protect every Individual sailing under it on board of a Merchant Ship is too extravagant to require any serious Refutation." The problem of obtaining sailors for the British navy was a difficult one, admittedly, for when the war resumed in 1803 many sailors were needed and only the most heroic measures obtained them. The attractions of American service were such that British sailors deserted to American vessels in droves. The ship that brought the British minister to the United States in 1803 lost fourteen men by desertion. Nelson reported that 42,000 British sailors had deserted during the war that ended in 1801. The British were incensed by the lenient American naturalization laws, according to which—so said Lord St. Vincent, first lord of the Admiralty—"every Englishman . . . may be made an American for a dollar." Impressment, of course, was no novel policy, and had long been practiced by the British navy. For decades the press gangs had been recruiters for the navy, and statutes implying the right of the crown to make impressments had been in force since the time of Richard II. John Adams acquired fame in 1769 for defending Michael Corbet, who had thrown a harpoon into Lieutenant Panton and killed him in resistance of impressment. But whatever its antecedents, impressment took on new dimensions as an issue between the United States and Britain prior to the War of 1812. Approximately 9,000 bona fide American citizens were impressed from American ships before the War of 1812, the most notable incident in this inhuman business being the encounter of the *Chesapeake* and *Leopard* on June 22, 1807, when the British ship attacked the *Chesapeake* and took off four men as deserters. Jefferson that summer could easily have had war with Great Britain, had he not so ardently desired peace.

Impressment, it seems fair to say, was the chief point at issue between the two English-speaking nations between 1803 and 1807, during which it was the basis of constant American protests to the government in London. At the outset of the European war there was little trouble over what later became the prime bone of contention between London and Washington—neutral rights, freedom of the seas. In the first two years after rupture of the Peace of Amiens there was little restriction of American commerce by the European belligerents. Tonnage expanded at a rate of about seventy thousand tons annually, a large increase if one realizes that the ordinary ocean-going vessel of the early nineteenth century carried a freight of about two hundred and fifty tons. The increased American tonnage was used for trade between belligerent ports in Europe, and especially for taking over the French and Spanish West India trade, normally carried by French and Spanish ships but now interrupted by the war. There was also a lively American competition for the British West India trade during these years. American-produced exports remained at about $42,000,000 annually, in the period 1803–1805. The value of foreign goods transshipped from American ports increased from $13,-000,000 in 1803, to $36,000,000 in 1804, to $53,000,000 in 1805.

All was well for the first two years after renewal of the European war, but then came difficulty. The British government first cut off American carrying trade between the French and Spanish West Indies and Europe by a prize-court decision, the so-called *Essex* case of May 1805. This stopped the American practice of shipping Spanish or French West Indian produce to American ports, paying duty on such cargo, and shipping it out again to Europe as American goods—after a drawback of the duty. The British considered this sort of trading as, to use the title of a contemporary pamphlet by the publicist James Stephen, *War in Disguise; or, the Frauds of Neutral Flags.* Jefferson sent William Pinkney of Maryland to the British capital to assist the American minister, James Monroe, in straightening out these Anglo-American commercial difficulties. To no avail, for shortly after the *Essex* decision the war in Europe took a turn toward more rigorous measures between Britain and France and by both of them toward neutrals. The tempo of the war quickened when Britain at Trafalgar (October 21, 1805) obtained overwhelming mastery of the seas and Napoleon at Austerlitz (December 2, 1805) gained near-complete ascendancy on the Continent. Napoleon on November 21, 1806 announced his famous Berlin Decree, declaring the British Isles in a state of blockade. The emperor forbade commerce and communication with his enemy, and authorized seizure and confiscation of any vessels that violated his instructions. He announced on December 17, 1807 in the Milan Decree that he would regard vessels searched by the British or obeying their maritime regulations as denationalized and liable to seizure and confiscation as British property. Not to be outdone, the British government in a series of orders in council (that is, executive decisions of the British cabinet taken in council with the sovereign) during the year 1807 barred shipping from the coastal trade of France and France's allies, prohibited commerce with Continental ports from which the British flag was excluded, and permitted only those neutral vessels which had first passed through a British port, and there paid customs duties, to call at "non-blockaded" Continental ports.

One should perhaps remark, concerning the French decrees and British orders in council, that the theory behind the opposing measures was simple enough, although it can easily sound complicated. Neither the orders in council nor the Continental System, as Napoleon liked to describe his measures, aimed actually at cutting off supplies from the foe. They were primarily financial measures, by which each side sought to obtain a bloodless victory over the other. Napoleon allowed Continental produce to be sold in England, to drain away British gold. The British in turn brought sugar, coffee, tobacco, and other articles to the Continent and would have sent over anything else, simply for the purpose of making a profit in the business. The British hoped also to force their manufactured goods upon the Continent, and to do so, if possible, with their own ships, and if that were impossible, then with neutral ships.

Within this pattern of belligerent measures and countermeasures the American merchant marine had to operate, and the choice open to American mariners was not attractive, for if they followed the rules of the British they were liable to capture by Napoleon, and if they followed the rules of the emperor they exposed themselves to British seizure. A ship to be fully protected had to have a set of false papers, verified by the oath of the captain. The Philadelphia merchant Stephen Girard took the precaution to have an extra person of French extraction aboard his ships, who could take command in event a French cruiser appeared. The situation was deeply humiliating to a small new nation such as the United States. Jefferson was saying in 1806 (according to the French minister in Washington who sent the following in a dispatch to his chief, Talleyrand) that "we have principles from which we shall never depart. Our people have commerce everywhere, and everywhere our neutrality should be respected. On the other hand, we do not want war, and all this is very embarrassing." Matters gradually reached a point where the president saw only one course of action conducive to American self-respect—a complete and self-imposed embargo upon American shipping to Europe.

In essence this embargo meant an effort to force the British to remove their restrictions on neutral shipping, for the structure of American trade gave the United States a better chance of success with the British than with the French. "I never expected to be under the necessity of wishing success to Buonaparte," Jefferson said in

1807. "But the English being equally tyrannical at sea as he is on land, & that tyranny bearing on us in every point of either honor or interest, I say 'down with England' and as for what Buonaparte is then to do to us, let us trust to the chapter of accidents . . ." The British had been selling one-third of their manufactures to the United States. American foodstuffs were needed in the British West Indies. The American government apparently could exert a considerable economic pressure. Jefferson's program of economic coercion was the same sort of coercion which the American colonies had applied with some success against the British imperial system prior to the revolution, and there seemed little reason why such pressure would not work again. The president signed the Embargo Act on December 22, 1807.

Unfortunately, when it was repealed fifteen months later it had proved a complete failure. It enjoyed no success in forcing the belligerents to give up their commercial restrictions. The reasons for the embargo's becoming a fiasco were numerous, and some of them complicated. Manufacturers of cotton and tobacco in Great Britain were pressed, but simultaneously British shipowners were conveniently relieved of American competition. Moreover, at this time the ports of Spanish and Portuguese America were opened to British commerce. The people of Spain on May 2, 1808 rose up in revolt against their government, then under domination of Napoleon. The British army this same year landed in Portugal. Revolt in Spain and British action in Portugal enabled colonial authorities in the New World to open their ports to British and other foreign merchant ships, reversing the commercial policy of more than three centuries. The British being the chief trading nation on the seas in the year 1808, opening of the Latin American ports redounded to the benefit of British shippers just at the time that trade with the United States had closed.

Moreover, the American Embargo Act was outrageously violated by American citizens and thus much reduced in effectiveness. An amendment to the act passed in 1808 enabled vessels of the United States to sail in ballast for the purpose of bringing home property stored in European warehouses but belonging to American citizens. As Edward Channing has pointed out, eight hundred vessels went out on this errand, and only a small proportion returned home before March 1809 and expiration of the embargo. Whaling ships were permitted to clear under the embargo, and this led to trouble. One citizen of Boston took a ship out after whales, so he said, and carried for the job—perhaps as whale bait—five hundred casks of bacon. He returned from Halifax with one cask of whale oil and several hundred bales of Yorkshire woolens.

To violate the act by trading across the border to Canada was ridiculously easy, and many New Englanders used this opportunity. During the first year of the embargo 150,000 barrels of Yankee flour went to Eastport, Maine, whence they were carted over the border. The price of flour was $5 a barrel in the United States, $12 in Canada, and $25 in Jamaica. At the outset of the illicit trade to Canada it cost just 12½ cents to take a barrel over the line, and it was still easy to make out financially when transport rose in cost to $3. One man made $47 in a night, a large sum for the early nineteenth century. Not until the prohibition era a hundred years later was smuggling so profitable.

As if this sort of trouble were not enough for the harassed Jefferson administration seeking to enforce the embargo, another problem appeared: the embargo raised against the administration a serious political threat in the form of a revived Federalist Party. The Federalists made political capital out of the misfortunes consequent on the embargo. Most of their case was, of course, manufactured, for the embargo did not cause all the harm that the Federalists claimed. In Boston, for example, where to catch the eye of the electorate they established soup houses for starving sailors, it developed that no one was starving and no one needed Federalist soup—a canvass by the *Independent Chronicle* revealed that "the astonishing number of twenty-five daily apply for this excellent refreshment." Such failure did not restrain party warfare over the embargo, and the Federalists turned to circulating the old argument that Jefferson was in league with Napoleon—that the American president, acting as the lackey of the French emperor, had joined the Continental System. The embargo, they said, capped Napoleon's restrictive measures in Europe. The embargo conveniently supplemented the Continental System by denying to the British the use of American neutral carriers to take English manufactures to European ports. Federalists seized upon this apparent Franco-American co-operation, and proclaimed to the people of New England and to anyone else who would listen, not excepting the British minister in Washington, that Jefferson had made a deal with the Tyrant of Europe. There arose the specter of Thomas Jefferson, the American Robespierre. The arch-Federalist Fisher Ames drew a sobering picture of the state of affairs of the American nation. "Our days," he wrote to a friend in early 1808, "are made heavy with the pressure of anxiety, and our nights restless with visions of horror. We listen to the clank of chains, and overhear the whispers of assassins. We mark the barbarous dissonance of mingled rage and triumph in the yell of an infuriated mob; we see the dismal glare of their burnings, and scent the loathsome steam of human victims offered in sacrifice." Ames's colleagues gloomily, and with an eye to the New England electorate, recalled the fate of the city states of Greece, the Roman Republic, the communes of Italy, the Republic of France.

Discounting such rhetoric, was there anything in these Federalist claims of a conspiracy between Jefferson and Napoleon? It is true that Jefferson's Embargo Act came at the precise moment that Napoleon had closed almost every Continental port to British trade. After the capitulation of Russia to France in 1807 the Continental System came quickly to its peak of effectiveness. The American embargo was a sort of keystone to the arch of the emperor's system, for it closed the United States to British goods and prevented American neutral carriers from trying to sneak British goods into the Continent as American goods. Was there some bare possibility that Jefferson, who though a philosopher in speech and appearance was a realist in politics national and international, had timed his measure to suit Napoleon's plans in Europe?

No evidence that the American president was in league with Napoleon has ever developed, despite the most diligent search by Jefferson's political opponents. No one to this day has proved that Jefferson produced the embargo at the imperial command. Despite the cherished revolutionary memories of the alliance of 1778, Napoleonic France was not admired by most Americans of the early nineteenth century. This became evident in 1812 after war was declared against Great Britain, when President Madison never considered making an alliance with Napoleon. Memory of the unfortunately timed Embargo Act nonetheless lingered on in the cynical chancelleries of Europe, where secret understandings were commonplaces of diplomatic intercourse. After the American declaration of war in 1812 the tsar of Russia made an apparently friendly inquiry of the United States minister at St. Petersburg, John Quincy Adams, as to whether President Madison had an understanding with Napoleon. Adams wrote for explicit assurances from Secretary of State Monroe, and gave a negative answer to the tsar's foreign minister, but that wily official, just to be certain, had the American minister's mail opened, and also decoded the cipher dispatches between Adams and the American minister in Paris. He discovered no trace of a plot.

2. The Coming of the War of 1812

Jefferson during his second administration established the pattern for American response to the measures of the European belligerents. In defense of the principle of freedom of the seas and against the competing restrictive systems of Britain and France the president elaborated an American system of economic coercion. The complete embargo as a feature of this system did not work as expected. Jefferson's political protégé and successor in the presidency, Madison, nonetheless determined to defend freedom of the seas in the same fashion as his mentor, through economic coercion, but changing from an embargo to other devices.

After the embargo, a number of American efforts toward economic coercion of Britain and France led finally to the War of 1812. The embargo gave way to a Nonintercourse Act on March 1, 1809, opening trade with all the world except Britain and France. This act, it was soon seen, was ineffective for extracting concessions from the belligerents. Congress fussed and fumed and debated in what Madison described as an "unhinged state," and passed on May 1, 1810 a truly important piece of legislation known as Macon's Bill Number 2, an attempt to bargain between the belligerents in Europe, playing off one against the other. It opened the commerce of the United States with all the world, including Britain and France. If one of the belligerents repealed its commercial measures insofar as they affected the United States, the American government would apprise the other belligerent of the repeal and institute nonintercourse against that belligerent, should it not also repeal its restrictions. The result of Macon's Bill Number 2 was that Napoleon on August 5, 1810 gave superficial acceptance of the American proposal and Madison a few months later instituted nonintercourse against Great Britain. The British refused to abandon their orders of council, and argued with the Americans that the French had not really abandoned the Berlin and Milan decrees. They pointed out that in dealing with Napoleonic France one had to have more assurance than words. As late as June 14, 1812 the British minister in Washington in his last communication to the American government stated that "If you can at any time produce a full and unconditional repeal of the French decrees . . . we shall be ready to meet you with a revocation of the orders in council." Madison remained adamant, choosing even at the risk of war to use Napoleon's promises to force concessions from the British. Congress in 1812 voted for war against Great Britain, in defense of freedom of the seas.

The cause of the War of 1812—freedom of the seas—seems clear enough, despite an argument among historians which for years has swirled around American entry into war in 1812. At the time of the outbreak of the war, and throughout the nineteenth century, it was generally assumed that defense of neutral rights had brought the United States into the War of 1812. This still seems a convincing view, although for some years now it has been argued that other causes took the country to war: Western desire for Canada, Southern desire for the Floridas, Western land hunger, frontier anger against British support of the Indians from Canada and Spain's inability to prevent Indian raids out of the Floridas, an agricultural depression in the West and South which stirred frontiersmen into ascribing their woes to Britain's restrictive maritime measures. Woodrow Wilson, a well-known scholar at the turn of the twentieth century, announced in 1902 that the causes of the War of 1812 were "singularly uncertain," and this argument as to what brought the war has gone on for more than fifty years.

A seeming paradox has encouraged some of the debate. In the voting in Congress for war in 1812, representatives from New England opposed American belligerency against Great Britain, while congressmen from the agricultural portions of the country, the West and South, voted in favor of war. This has led scholars to question the traditional view that the issue of freedom of the seas caused the war, for the West and South possessed almost no ocean shipping. In a pioneer work, *Expansionists of 1812*, Julius W. Pratt has concluded that because of opposition to war by New England the War of 1812 was in large part a Western and Southern war for Canada and the Floridas. Pratt's book on the origins of the War of 1812 was a masterly survey of its subject, in many ways representing American historical scholarship at its best, and it has inspired a generation of students. Even so, there does seem to be another explanation possible for the sectional vote on the war. Westerners and Southerners had cotton, grain, and other products to sell in Europe and they became aroused over Britain's restrictive maritime measures, against which by 1812 they were willing to go to war. The New England shippers, on the other hand, were able as late as 1812 to make considerable profits in trade, despite British restrictions, and opposed war.

Indeed, Western and Southern anger over Britain's maritime measures seems to have given rise to the talk in Congress in the years before 1812 about the possibility of conquering Canada and the Floridas. A recent student, Reginald Horsman, has shown in a brilliant unpublished study that Americans were interested in Canada chiefly because, given the weakness of the American navy, Canada was the only area in which they might effectively attack Great Britain. Canada, Horsman contends (and part of his argument is a repetition of the thesis offered some years ago by A. L. Burt), was the means to an end, and the end was the freedom of the seas. As for the Floridas, owned by Britain's ally Spain, they were of some minor value as a further means of retaliation against the British, but their susceptibility to capture was of slight importance in bringing on the War of 1812. They figured in congressional debates, but they were being acquired piecemeal in the years after 1803. President Madison took part of West Florida in 1810 and the remaining part in 1812; after negotiation with the Spanish, East Florida (present-day Florida) was acquired in 1819. There was never much question but that the Floridas might be taken in entirety by means well short of war.

The thesis incautiously advanced by Louis M. Hacker, that land hunger was the reason for Western interest in attacking Great Britain, has had a wide circulation but little acceptance. Perhaps it is incapable of proof one way or the other. Although Western frontiersmen were always hungry for land, there was by 1812 much good land yet available in the Old Northwest—Indiana by 1812 had only a scattering of population, Michigan was virtually unoccupied outside of Detroit, Illinois was largely wilderness. It is difficult to show why 1812 was the year for this sort of war.

The Indian menace, much talked about prior to 1812, in recent years argued by some historians as a leading cause of the war, seems to have been a strictly secondary reason for war against Great Britain, although Governor William Henry Harrison of Indiana became so certain of the Indians' hostility that he provoked them into the famed battle of Tippecanoe on November 7, 1811. This battle, fought against the confederacy of Tecumseh and his brother the Prophet, resulted in nearly two hundred American casualties. Frontiersmen were persuaded that the British in Canada had been stirring up the Indians from the frontier trading post of Amherstburg, and they were determined to strike before the Indians became too strong, too well supplied with British powder and guns. Actually, while there is no question of the British supplying the Indians and even inciting them, the policy of the royal governors in Canada and their agents along the border was defensive—the government in London was concerned for the safety of Canada in event of hostilities with the United States, and Canadian authorities took precautionary measures. These measures were susceptible to misinterpretation by both the Americans and the Indians, for it was not easy to hand out weapons to the Indians and tell them at the same time that they were not to fight the Americans who all the while were encroaching on Indian lands. Still, British Indian policy in the crucial years before 1812 was defensive in intent. This fact appears to have been fairly well understood by congressional representatives of the American West and South, who in debate seldom failed to put Britain's maritime pretensions far ahead of their concern over British Indian policy.

The West and South were suffering from an agricultural depression by 1812 and here, as George Rogers Taylor has clearly shown, was an important if subsidiary reason for American entrance into the War of 1812. Although the economic distresses of the frontier region lay probably in lack of transportation, communication, and marketing and financial organization, it does seem possible that Britain's restrictive maritime measures added to Western troubles. The frontiersmen felt that they did. They were ready to believe that the 1807 orders in council lay at the root of the agricultural depression.

But the prime reason for American entrance into the war against Great Britain in 1812 seems to have been the principle of the freedom of the seas, for without the rankling British commercial measures the United States would have stayed out of the war. In 1812 the war hawks, as John Randolph called them, were vastly exercised over freedom of the seas, and they equated it with American national honor. Their patriotism was roused by the rigid attitude of Great

Britain on neutral rights. Hurt pride and roaring patriotism were marshaled behind freedom of the seas when the war-hawk Congress assembled in November 1811. The cry for war became irresistible. Such young men as Henry Clay and John C. Calhoun, from the West and South respectively, agitated with enormous effect for war. They were the new generation which had not known, but only heard of, the American revolution. They were brought up on a diet of British iniquity, they had heard from childhood about British outrages, they had observed in their early adult years the countless tragic instances when British boarding parties had seized American citizens, often from vessels just outside American ports, and sent them to forced service and frequently to death. Confronted with this issue of impressment, raised on tales of British iniquity, far less cautious than their aging revolutionary fathers, they exploded in indignation when Britain denied to the United States the freedom of the seas. The indignity was too much. The indignant leaders wanted war and got it. In vain did some individuals tell them the nation was unprepared and altogether no match for Great Britain. "What!" Randolph had cried several years earlier during a congressional debate over war, "shall this great mammoth of the American forest leave his native element and plunge into the water in a mad contest with the shark?" To no avail. Americans did not need to fight the British navy—they could take Canada.

Curiously, if the war hawks had held off a little longer they could have obtained the freedom of the seas without a fight, for the British government by the spring of 1812 was willing to make large concessions. What had happened was that the manufacturing regions of England, like the American West and South, were in the throes of a depression. The depression apparently had been touched off by overspeculation in Latin American markets in 1808 and thereafter, although in its origins it went back to problems growing out of the industrial revolution and the war with France. Because of it the manufacturers were eager to regain trade with the United States and hoped that they could do so if the 1807 orders in council were repealed. The British position by 1812 defies easy explanation, but its broad outlines can be stated. As Horsman has established in his researches, a combination of British shipping interests and West India planters had urged the restrictive measures against American commerce which began in 1805 with the *Essex* decision. The shipping interests desired to cut off the lucrative American carrying trade with the Continent. The West India planters desired to prevent the Americans from carrying the produce of French and (until 1808) Spanish West India colonies to Europe, which there entered into competition with their own produce. The West India planters for a time hung back from joining the home shipping interests to cut off American trade, for they needed American foodstuffs to maintain their own specialized economies in the islands. But gradually it became apparent that the Americans were doing more damage in carrying French produce to Europe than they were assisting the British West Indies by bringing foodstuffs from the United States. The West India interests thereupon joined with shipping interests in England to demand restrictions on the Americans. Many Britishers meanwhile had been angered by the American demand for freedom of trade at a time when the mother country faced the most dire perils, and this feeling—coupled with hostility that went back to the American revolution and added to the demands of the West India planters and the shipping interests—brought the restrictive maritime policies.

This restriction was not to the advantage of Britain's manufacturing regions, in view of their large trade with the United States, and they objected from the outset. When Jefferson placed an embargo on American shipping in 1807 and closed American ports to foreign vessels, the British manufacturing interests took temporary relief by trading in the new Latin American markets. As time passed, those markets proved not as lucrative as they first appeared. The Americans during these years failed to reopen trade with Britain, replaced the embargo with a Nonintercourse Act in 1809, allowed only a temporary commerce—for a few months in 1810—through Macon's Bill Number 2, and again closed commerce early in 1811. It became obvious that the American market was important and worth maintaining even at the expense of British concessions, and matters finally reached a point by early 1812 where the manufacturing interests in Britain, suffering intensely from the business depression, demanded withdrawal of the 1807 orders in council and obtained enough popular support to move the Tory ministry to action. The manufacturers reasoned that this would conciliate the United States, persuade the Americans to lift their nonintercourse with Britain, and give the Americans sufficient money from the Continental trade to buy British products.

The irony of the situation is that by this time the effect of the orders in council had been virtually nullified—first via a system of licenses which had started in earnest in 1807 and which, although it reached its peak in 1810 (18,000 licenses were granted that year), had opened all sorts of possibilities for trade between Britain and the Continent; and secondly by an act of the tsar of Russia who, tiring of the Continental System, in 1810 opened the Baltic ports to trade. There were many opportunities for enterprising American ship captains in the three years after repeal of the Embargo Act. Still the Americans persisted—that is, the Americans in the West and South persisted—in demanding withdrawal of the orders in council. The United States government under the Jeffersonian-Madisonian Republicans had so unwaveringly stated its diplomatic position, had nailed its principle of freedom of the seas so firmly to its diplomatic masthead, that by 1812 nothing less than a repeal of the orders would do. The British had to take this gesture to obtain withdrawal of the American trade embargo against Great Britain. The British government on June 16, 1812 announced suspension of its rules affecting American commerce. Lacking an Atlantic cable, the United States knew nothing of this long-sought-for move, and two days later on June 18, 1812 President Madison signed the declaration of war.

3. *The Peace of Ghent*

In America the Federalist Party, concentrated in New England, bitterly opposed the war and talked of secession. The canard that the Republicans were supporting Napoleon again appeared, gravely embarrassing the Madison administration, which detested Napoleonic France only less than it hated Great Britain. There had been consideration of double war in 1812, with both Britain and France. This made no difference to New Englanders who saw their commerce choked and the mother country "stabbed in the back" at a moment of peril.

It was indeed a tremendously exciting and crucial moment in European and world history when the United States in 1812 rushed into the war against Britain. Napoleon on June 22 embarked on what he hoped would be the conquest of Russia, after which he would pass on to India by way of Persia. He planned to use the Russian army as an auxiliary force, after its defeat, and who can tell what might have happened to this dream of conquest if his troops had not been destroyed by the Russian winter? The United States entered the war at its most dramatic time, and during the summer and autumn of 1812 the same fears for the survival of Russia circulated throughout Europe as appeared again in 1941 when a new Napoleon sought to reach Moscow. Instead there came France's defeat. On the last day of 1812 John Quincy Adams at St. Petersburg set down in a letter to his mother the disaster that had befallen the Napoleonic armies. "Of the immense host with which six months since he invaded Russia," he wrote, "nine-tenths at least are prisoners or food for worms. They have been surrendering by ten thousands at a time, and at this moment there are at least one hundred and fifty thousand of them in the power of the Emperor Alexander. From Moscow to Prussia, eight hundred miles of road have been strewed with his artillery, baggage wagons, ammunition chests, dead and dying men, whom he has been forced to abandon to their fate . . . In all human probability the career of Napoleon's conquests is at an end. France can no longer give the law to the continent. . . . A new era is dawning upon Europe."

This was the drama of the times, beside which the grievances of the American nation and its entrance and eventually its exit from the European war were small matters. Adams had not exaggerated the reports of French losses, for of the 600,000 men whom Napoleon took into Russia—the largest armed force ever assembled under one command up to that time—only 30,000 managed to escape back across the Niemen River in December 1812. Napoleon returned to Paris without a personal guard. France's entire position in Europe by the end of 1812 was on the verge of collapse.

Britishers quite naturally were infuriated over the American declaration of war in, of all moments, June of 1812, and it was fortunate for the United States that the British then and for some time thereafter were occupied by the fighting in Europe. The only serious danger to American fortunes came in the spring of 1814, after the first defeat of Napoleon (and before he returned from temporary exile on Elba), when large British forces became available for campaigns in the New World. At this particular moment peace negotiations had not yet begun between the British and Americans. The tsar of Russia had offered his services as a mediator as early as the summer of 1812, and by 1814 his offer had brought arrangements for a meeting of peace commissioners at the Flemish city of Ghent, but the British procrastinated when in the spring of 1814 the Allies marched into Paris and Napoleon abdicated. The British public wanted "to give Jonathan a good drubbing." The peace commissioners, already nominated, were instructed to proceed to Ghent in a leisurely fashion, and to string out negotiations until the Duke of Wellington's veterans, en route from Bordeaux to North America, could win some victories.

Wellington's soldiers, fortunately not under command of the Iron Duke, were split into two expeditions, one to come down from the St. Lawrence estuary to conquer the Champlain and Hudson valleys, a second to attack the Atlantic seaboard and then move upon New Orleans and the Mississippi valley. Though the British troops in 1814 should have had a field day marching up and down the United States, luck favored the Americans. General Sir George Prevost with 11,000 men met defeat on September 11, 1814 at Lake Champlain and Plattsburg. The second British expedition burned Washington but was repulsed at Baltimore and on January 8, 1815, two weeks after peace had been concluded in Europe, was disastrously routed at New Orleans. Months before this, however—with the prospect of quick military victory in America fading during the summer and autumn of 1814 and with the simultaneous worsening of affairs in Europe, where Napoleon was plotting his return from Elba to Paris—the British, prompted by advice from the Duke of Wellington, had decided to make peace with the United States on a basis of no annexations, the *status quo ante bellum.*

When the British commissioners at Ghent started their parleys with the American negotiators, they asked for a peace with several conditions, including an Indian barrier state encompassing the area of the present states of Michigan, Wisconsin, Illinois, Indiana, and Ohio. This the American delegation refused. Next came a demand for peace on the principle of *uti possidetis,* the military situation of the moment, meaning that the British would have kept part of Maine along with other portions of American territory. The Americans held out for the *status quo ante bellum.* Their persistence, combined with British concern over the deteriorating military situation in Europe, lack of military success in the New World, and the fragile state of the British exchequer, brought about what may be described as an American diplomatic victory. France was seething with unrest (Napoleon returned from Elba on March 1, 1815, to meet final defeat at Waterloo, June 18). Moreover, the British negotiators at the Congress of Vienna were encountering difficulties in drawing a European treaty, and they believed it was best to end the war in America. As the prime minister, Lord Liverpool, wrote to his foreign secretary Lord Castlereagh, November 18, 1814; "I think we have been determined, if all other points can be satisfactorily settled, not to continue the war for the purposes of obtaining or securing any acquisition of territory. We have been led to this determination by the consideration of the unsatisfactory state of the negotiations at Vienna, and by that of the alarming situation of the interior of France. We have also been obliged to pay serious attention to the state of our finances . . . under such circumstances, it has appeared to us desirable to bring the American war if possible to a conclusion."

The American peace commissioners—John Quincy Adams, Henry Clay, James A. Bayard, Jonathan Russell, Albert Gallatin—eagerly accepted when offered the *status quo ante bellum*. They signed the peace on Christmas Eve, 1814. John Quincy Adams, speaking for the delegation, remarked that "I hope it will be the last treaty of peace between Great Britain and the United States."

Henry Clay is reported later to have described the Treaty of Ghent as "a damned bad treaty," but the former war hawk signed it. He was relieved to be through the war, as was the Senate of the United States, which approved the treaty unanimously.

The Peace of Ghent left a number of issues undecided. There was no mention of impressment, although the question had become academic with the end of the war in sight and Great Britain never afterward resorted to the practice. There was no mention of freedom of the seas, in defense of which the United States had gone to war—but the issue of neutral rights could be safely left for time to heal, and when the United States later became involved in the Civil War and in two world wars it proved convenient to forget neutral rights. At Ghent there had arisen several other issues: the northeast and northwest boundaries; control of armaments on the Great Lakes; fishing privileges off Newfoundland and Nova Scotia; British free navigation of the Mississippi. The latter point, prior to the heyday of river steamboats, did not seem too important to the British. They had no way to get down to the Mississippi from Canada without traversing American territory, and to obtain a right to go up the Mississippi was at the moment a useless acquisition. The fishing privileges remained in an uncertain state until 1910, when they were amicably arbitrated.

As for armaments on the Great Lakes, this problem received settlement in the Rush-Bagot Agreement of April 28–29, 1817, which, although it allowed a limited number of gunboats to both Canada and the United States on Lake Champlain and the Great Lakes, foreshadowed the total disarmament that was achieved shortly after the Civil War. The question of the boundaries, northeast and northwest, was left to mixed commissions under the terms of Ghent, but not finally settled until the 1840's (see below, chapter 7).

What can one conclude about the diplomacy of freedom of the seas that led to the War of 1812 and the Treaty of Ghent of 1814? Some writers have stressed that this controversy over neutral rights, together with the war that followed, brought Great Britain to the realization that at last the United States must be treated with dignity and respect. Doubtless an improved British acceptance of America and Americans did result from the War of 1812. Still, the British respect that America gained was an unintentional dividend. The war was not fought for general respect but for preservation of the principle of neutral rights, and in this sense it failed, as did also the diplomacy which ended in hostilities.

Surely American diplomacy toward the European belligerents, Britain and France, was not carefully and thoughtfully based on any realistic conception of the American national interest. It was not wise to risk the existence of the American nation for the abstract principle of freedom of the seas. If the European war had gone another way, if Napoleon had been victorious over Russia, or Russia had not challenged Napoleon, Britain might have fallen in 1812–1814. If Britain had failed, what would have been the judgment of history on the War of 1812 and its diplomatic preliminaries?

This is an interesting line of speculation. If Britain had lost, Napoleon could have reformed the British government, and established himself and his brothers in Buckingham Palace. During his lifetime he might have controlled Europe and Asia from London to Peking. He could have sent a few frigates and divisions to the New World and taken care of the bumptious American democracy, an outpost of liberty threatening his autocratic imperial power.

Such visions seem not to have occurred to Thomas Jefferson and James Madison, either on the hilltop at Monticello or at the Executive Mansion in the District of Columbia. They never thought out their position on freedom of the seas, and luckily everything turned out all right.

4. *The End of an Era*

With the close of the War of 1812 and the final victory of the coalition in Europe against Napoleon, the time arrived when the entire Western world could settle down and relax in the quietness of peace. For Europe there had been almost constant war since 1789, the beginning of the French revolution. For the United States there had been an even longer time of troubles. Americans, before being subjected to the rigors of the opposing belligerent systems of Europe during the wars of the French revolution and Napoleon, had gone through their own revolution and the uncertain period of federal government under the Articles of Confederation. It was time for a rest. The diplomacy of the United States after the Treaty of Ghent was a relaxed sort of diplomacy, with far less than the usual perils and crises, and there occurred in subsequent years only three major developments, one of which was more military than diplomatic—the liquidation of the Barbary pirate troubles, the Transcontinental Treaty of 1819, and the Monroe Doctrine of 1823. All three marked the growing national consciousness of the American people. The Barbary pirates had been making trouble for a long time, and after the War of 1812 the United States sent a large squadron into the Mediterranean and overawed them. There was a feeling, in the case of the Transcontinental Treaty, that the boundaries of the republic should be precisely laid down against any possible foreign challenge as Americans moved westward into the new lands of the Louisiana Purchase. In the case of the Monroe Doctrine, Americans believed that it was well to draw a line between the New World and the Old, to let the powers of Europe know clearly and finally that their political systems were no longer welcome in the Western Hemisphere.

Difficulties with the piratical potentates of North Africa, the rulers of Morocco, Algiers, Tunis, and Tripoli, were a heritage of the treaty of peace with Great Britain in 1783: having detached itself from British protection during the revolution, the United States after 1783 had to make its own arrangements with the Barbary pirates without advantage of the British fleet. In the case of Morocco this was not too difficult, and assisted by the good offices of Spain the American government managed during the mid-1780's (when the Spanish were hopefully negotiating the Jay-Gardoqui Treaty) to obtain a Moroccan treaty without payment of tribute. The treaty was concluded in 1787. There followed, a few years later, treaties with the other Barbary powers: Algiers, 1795; Tripoli, 1796; Tunis, 1797. These later treaties unfortunately had to be paid for dearly. The treaty with Algeria cost $642,000 in ransom money, presents, commissions and other charges, and the United States agreed to pay an annual tribute in naval stores to the value of $21,600. The treaties were likely to be violated by the pirates at the first favorable opportunity.

Nothing effective was done about the Barbary pirates until after the War of 1812. Beginning in 1801 and until 1807, the United States maintained frigates in the Mediterranean; there were some small naval actions, and even an overland expedition to depose the pasha of Tripoli, led by the consul in Tunis, William Eaton. The measures taken were halfhearted and ill-starred, as witness the capture by the pirates of the frigate *Philadelphia*, which had become stuck on a shoal with her crew of over three hundred men, an episode relieved only by the heroic action of Lieutenant Stephen Decatur, who with a small boatload of assistants worked his way into Tripoli harbor and fired the captured ship as it lay at anchor. In 1807, with British and French maritime measures tightening around American trade in the Atlantic, the Mediterranean naval vessels were withdrawn. They finally reappeared in 1815 and extracted from the dey of Algiers a treaty that forced him to pay $10,000 reparations. This American action was followed by a decisive Anglo-Dutch sortie against Algiers in 1816.

As for the Transcontinental Treaty of 1819, the second American action of the years after the War of 1812, it—so Samuel Flagg Bemis has written—was the greatest diplomatic victory won by a single individual in the history of the United States. Had it not been for the tenacity, the diplomatic shrewdness, of John Quincy Adams, secretary of state under President Monroe, this treaty which set the bounds between Spanish and American possessions would have been signed in a far less advantageous form than it was. Adams kept pressing the Spanish minister in Washington, Don Luis de Onís, to move the boundary westward, and when the Massachusetts statesman was finished, Don Luis had given up almost everything that he could.

The manner in which the American secretary of state maneuvered his Spanish adversary was a classic example of diplomatic skill. Adams began by taking the position previously assumed by President Jefferson and successive presidents, namely that West Florida—the portion of territory below the thirty-first parallel that today comprises parts of the states of Louisiana, Mississippi, and Alabama—had been ceded to the United States in the Louisiana Purchase. This was a dubious claim but Adams adhered to it. From this position he argued that East Florida—present-day Florida—should pass to the United States because Spain before and during the War of 1812 had not controlled the Indians in that area, as she should have done according to Pinckney's Treaty of 1795. There were also, so Adams argued, spoliations of American commerce during the Napoleonic wars, for which the Spanish had never paid, and these American claims could be adjusted by cession of East Florida together with a favorable boundary to divide Spanish Texas and California from the lands of the Louisiana Purchase. This was Adams's contention, and he barbed it by intimations from time to time that it might be necessary for the United States to possess itself of East Florida by force, in the event the Spanish did not voluntarily relinquish it. Indians and escaped Negro slaves were raiding from Florida into the United States, and these raids, Adams said, had to be stopped. When the Monroe administration sent General Andrew Jackson on a punitive expedition into East Florida in 1818 with a force of 3,000 men there was consternation in Madrid, for the Spanish knew that the territory could not remain much longer in their hands. Jackson, contrary to his orders, occupied the city of Pensacola, and this act of frontier enthusiasm threw the Spaniards into the depths of despair.

The Spanish government through Onís in Washington tried as best it could to avoid the inevitable, but Onís could do nothing against so redoubtable a diplomatic opponent as John Quincy Adams. Adams took advantage of the Florida negotiations to arrange a steplike boundary between Spanish western possessions and the American territory comprising the Louisiana Purchase. He also conceived the idea of extinguishing Spanish claims along the Pacific Coast above the forty-second parallel. Gradually he pressed Onís into agreement.

Typical was his stand over Article 2 of the proposed treaty, which stipulated that the king of Spain ceded to the United States "all the territories which belong to him, situated to the Eastward of the Mississippi, known by the name of East and West Florida." A comma placed in Article 2 between the word "territories" and the word "which" would have made clear the king of Spain's possession of West Florida. The secretary refused to admit that West Florida belonged to Spain. Adams would not give poor Onís a comma.

At the final stage of the negotiations he was debating with Onís the river boundaries—part of the steplike boundary of the Transcontinental Treaty was along the courses of western rivers—and although it was customary in diplomacy to take the mid-channel of rivers for boundaries Adams demanded the farthest edge. Monroe by this time was nervous, eager to close the negotiation for mid-channel of the boundary rivers. During a reception at the White House the president said to Onís: "I will do anything you want. I have had a personal esteem for you ever since the first day I dealt with you. Have a glass of wine with me." When the choleric Adams heard of this presidential indiscretion, he let Onís know that he, Adams, was negotiating the treaty. The secretary of state stood fast and obtained the farthest edge of the boundary rivers.

Adams and Onís signed the Transcontinental Treaty on Washington's Birthday 1819. After some delay in ratification the treaty went into effect in 1821. Mainly the work of John Quincy Adams, it was a personal triumph. Adams had every right to be proud of his handiwork, although it eventually became apparent that he might have obtained Texas from Onís if he had held out a little longer. Lacking a secret service he was unable to divine this opportunity.

Two years after ratification of the Transcontinental Treaty came the final event of the era, later so celebrated in American and world history: President Monroe announced the Monroe Doctrine in his annual message to Congress in December 1823.

The doctrine of 1823 was eventually transformed into perhaps the most honored principle of American foreign policy, but strangely enough it was not considered of large importance at the time. It was not taken seriously outside the United States, and to Monroe himself it was little more than a temporary expedient required by the diplomatic situation of the moment. Little further was heard from it until President James K. Polk's first annual message to Congress in 1845. Polk, interested in the fate of Oregon and California, concerned over possible machinations for these territories by Great Britain, announced that Monroe's principles applied "with greatly increased force" to the establishment of any new colony in North America. The doctrine of 1823 did not receive its name of Monroe Doctrine until 1852. Not until 1895 did an American president, Grover Cleveland, invoke it in the form originally announced by Monroe, and only in the twentieth century did it obtain recognition from the nations of the world.

There was not, one might add, much that was original in Monroe's famous message to Congress. Throughout the latter eighteenth century there had been a feeling in America that the New World possessed institutions and a culture different from the Old, and Thomas Paine in his *Common Sense* easily had obtained agreement when he wrote that "It is the true interest of America to steer clear of European contentions, which she never can do, while, by her dependence on Britain, she is made the make-weight in the scale of British politics." John Adams along with other revolutionary patriots urged the same course, and later wrote that "we should separate ourselves, as far as possible and as long as possible, from all European politics and wars." The principle of nonentanglement broke down in 1778 because of the need for help against Great Britain, but the uneasiness of association with France became manifest in the peace negotiations of 1782. At one point in the negotiations in Paris there occurred the conversation between Franklin and the British emissary Oswald, in which the latter said that "You are afraid of being made the tools of the powers of Europe." Replied Franklin: "Indeed I am. It is obvious that all the powers of Europe will be continually maneuvering with us, to work us into their real or imaginary balances of power. They will all wish to make of us a makeweight candle, while they are weighing out their pounds." Instances of this feeling that America should stay clear of European politics occurred time and again in the early diplomacy of the United States, one being Washington's neutrality proclamation of 1793. In the Farewell Address of 1796 there was the sensible inquiry, "Why, by interweaving our destiny with that of any part of Europe, entangle our peace and prosperity in the toils of European ambition, rivalship, interest, humor or caprice?" President Jefferson in his inaugural address of 1801 struck the familiar note: "peace, commerce and honest friendship with all nations, entangling alliances with none." Events in Europe in 1823 called forth a restatement of this tradition of American detachment.

The course of European politics after Waterloo resulted in the Monroe Doctrine. The powers of the Continent had managed by the most profound exertions to defeat Napoleon, and the narrrowness of their victory had impressed upon all of them the importance of maintaining their wartime coalition during the first uneasy years of peace. At the outset there was little difficulty among the allies. As the years

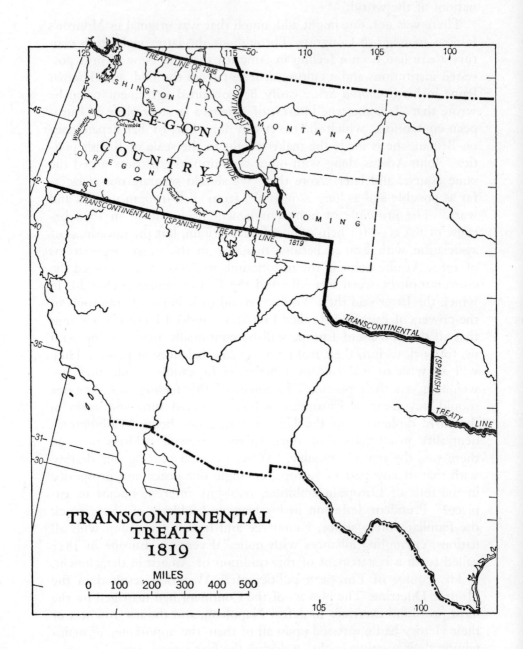

TRANSCONTINENTAL
TREATY
1819

MILES

0   100   200   300   400   500

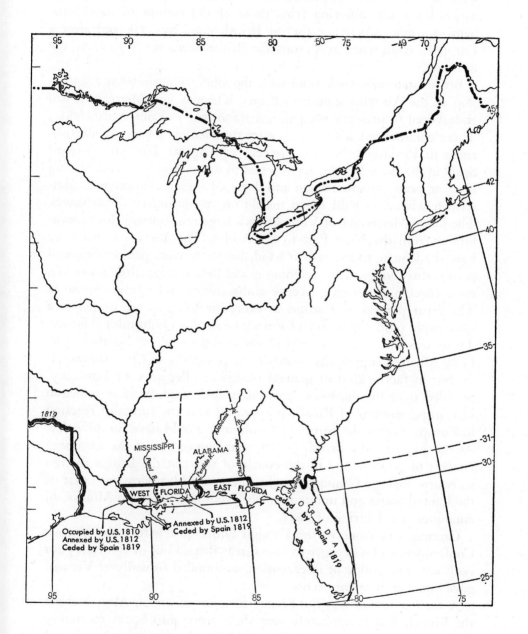

MISSISSIPPI

ALABAMA

Alabama R.

Pearl R.

Perdido R.

Chattahoochee R.

WEST FLORIDA

EAST FLORIDA

F L O R I D A ceded by Spain 1819

St. Johns R.

1819

Occupied by U.S.1810
Annexed by U.S.1812
Ceded by Spain 1819

Annexed by U.S.1812
Ceded by Spain 1819

went by differences appeared. Great Britain, especially, found its national interests differing from those of the nations of the Continent—no new experience for the British—and by 1822 and after a European conference at Verona the British were ready to leave the coalition.

British statesmen took issue with the allies, who under the leadership of the Austrian statesman Prince Klemens von Metternich had endeavored to preserve the political *status quo* in Europe after 1815. There commenced, a few years after the victory, a series of disturbances in Piedmont, Naples, Greece, and Spain. The provinces of Spain in the New World, accustomed to virtual independence during the war years, revolted again and declared their independence. Metternich wished to hold down the lid on revolutionary disturbances. The job of Metternich at Verona was a large one, putting down revolutions from the Near East to the Andes. The Verona Conference looked adequate to the task at hand, for there were present two emperors, three kings, three reigning grand dukes, a cardinal, a viceroy, three foreign secretaries, twenty ambassadors, and twelve ministers. The great powers of Europe, as everyone knew, were united in a Quadruple (and after entry of France in 1818, a Quintuple) Alliance. There was also a rather amorphous engagement among them, the Holy Alliance, supposedly based on the principles of Christian morality but in fact a kind of general pledge of allegiance to autocracy, presided over by the most reactionary and unpredictable monarch of Europe, the tsar of Russia. It appeared as if the forces of reaction in Europe, facing the forces of revolution, would have no difficulty. At this juncture the British government moved out of the European concert of powers, and in the course of this exit the British foreign secretary, George Canning, sought to concert his policy with that of the United States and unintentionally prompted President Monroe to announce the doctrine of 1823.

Canning had come to the Foreign Office just before the Verona Conference, and was eager to take Great Britain out of the European coalition. The policy of intervention, announced formally at Verona, gave him a convenient excuse.

A further reason was the French invasion of Spain. After Verona the French had precipitately sent their army into Spain to restore that country to its monarch, Ferdinand VII, who was being humiliated by a revolutionary Constitutionalist government. The French prime minister, Comte Jean de Villèle, later said that he sent French troops to Spain to avoid invasion of Spain by Russian troops, for the tsar at that time had a million men under arms and was anxious to use them to put down revolution in Europe. Villèle's foreign minister, Vicomte François de Chateaubriand, believed that the reason for sending French troops to Spain was simply to suppress the revolution—but Chateaubriand, one suspects, was being emotional. Villèle was in charge of the French government and knew what he was about. At any rate, after this expedition there was desultory talk in French cabinet meetings about sending French princelings to the New World in the wake of French troops, to take over the governments of the revolting Spanish colonies. This talk had little chance of turning into action. Villèle never envisioned more than detachments of French troops, and there was no possibility of an expedition. All French measures were dependent upon Ferdinand VII assuming a reasonable attitude, but Ferdinand was the most unreasonable man in Europe— since he would never have been satisfied with anything less than absolute restoration of Spanish America to his personal rule; hence the French could hardly have seen their way clear to send an expedition to the New World. If by some miracle Ferdinand VII had changed his mind and the French sent an expedition, the British navy would have destroyed it en route, for Canning instructed the British ambassador in Paris on March 31, 1823 that he would not allow France to restore the Spanish colonies to Ferdinand VII. He apparently feared that British commerce with the Spanish colonies might pass back, under a restoration, to Spain.

Too, Canning wished to mitigate the effects of any aggrandizement of French power on the Continent. As he later boasted, "I resolved that if France had Spain, it should not be Spain 'with the Indies.' I called the New World into existence to redress the balance of the Old." When he sought American help in 1823 for his antirestoration policy he also seems to have desired to please the United States, which was Great Britain's largest commercial customer, at this time taking one-sixth of Britain's foreign trade.

Canning moved to restrain the French, and the unanticipated result was the Monroe Doctrine. He approached the American minister in London, Richard Rush, on August 16, 1823, and on August 20 sent "unofficial and confidential" terms on which the United States and Britain could concert their policy toward any possible French intervention in the New World. Rush, without instructions, deferred agreement, but said that if Canning would recognize the independence of the revolted Spanish colonies he, Rush, would make an agreement with the foreign secretary even without instructions. Canning demurred, vaguely mentioning a future recognition of the nations of Latin America. The French expedition in Spain took the last Constitutionalist stronghold, Cadiz, on October 10, 1823. Anticipating its capture, Canning held a series of conversations early in October 1823 with the French ambassador, Prince Jules de Polignac, in which the two men agreed that France could not reconquer the Spanish colonies and return them to Spain. Canning had already warned the French against such a move in March 1823. The American minister, Rush, did not learn from Canning of the so-called Polignac Memorandum—an account of the British position, given to Polignac on October 9—until November 24, and Canning did not communicate its essence to Rush until December 13. Meanwhile, and unaware of the British pressure on France, President Monroe made his own announcement.

Monroe did not understand the situation in Europe and believed that there was some danger of intervention by France in the New World. He had before him the examples of Spain, Naples, and Piedmont, where the Continental allies had snuffed out revolutions. He knew that there was talk of an invasion of Latin America. His secretary of state, Adams, sensed the true arrangement of forces in Europe, that there was never serious danger of a French expedition, that Canning had frustrated even the remote possibility of such an expedition, and it was Adams who urged Monroe and the cabinet to seize the occasion and make a unilateral statement of American principles. Upon Monroe's suggestion the statement was placed in the annual message to Congress in December 1823. Adams persuaded the president to cut out any acknowledgment in the message of the independence of Greece, which Monroe wished to put in, and Adams also excised some presidential strictures on the French invasion of Spain. The resultant doctrine contained the following three essential points: noncolonization, "hands off" the New World, American abstention from the quarrels of Europe.

Noncolonization came from Adams's experience with Russian designs along the Pacific Coast. The tsar in a mood of impetuosity had announced in a ukase of 1821 that Russia possessed sovereignty to Pacific Coast territory and waters from Alaska south to the fifty-first parallel. This was an extension southward of the tsar's dominions, and Secretary Adams in a plucky note to the Russian minister in Washington in the summer of 1823 announced the principle of noncolonization. As repeated in the Monroe Doctrine, this principle stated that "the American continents, by the free and independent condition which they have assumed and maintain, are henceforth not to be considered as subjects for future colonization by any European powers."

The second idea of the Doctrine, hands off the New World, appeared in Monroe's message of 1823 as follows: "We owe it, therefore, to candor and to the amicable relations existing between the United States and those powers [of Europe] to declare that we should consider any attempt on their part to extend their system to any portion of this hemisphere as dangerous to our peace and safety."

In regard to abstention the president remarked that "In the wars of the European powers in matters relating to themselves we have never taken any part, nor does it comport with our policy so to do."

Such was the doctrine announced by President Monroe. The president, as mentioned, did not consider it a large and special pronouncement but a prudent diplomatic move called forth by the state of European politics in the year 1823. As he well knew, the British government would take care of its enforcement. As for the European reaction to the doctrine, it was, quite naturally, one of surprise and disgust. The United States, the powers believed, was taking credit for a British policy, and was doing so in an officious way. The powers found Monroe's principles monstrous, haughty, blustering, and arrogant. The Russian minister in Washington was told by his government that "the document in question . . . merits only the most profound contempt." The doctrine thereupon passed into history and slumbered until the turn of the twentieth century when the United States brought it out and dusted it off and the European powers came to realize that the principles of Colonel Monroe were worthy of respect.

A word remains about the recognition of the Latin American governments, proposed by Rush to Canning in the autumn of 1823. The United States in 1822 had taken the first step toward recognizing the revolting Spanish colonies when Monroe on March 22 proposed to Congress recognition of the independence of Buenos Aires (the United Provinces of the Rio de la Plata), Colombia, Chile, Peru, and Mexico. Congress answered by appropriating $100,000 to maintain the expenses of "such missions to the independent nations on the American continent as the President might deem proper." Monroe signed an act to this effect on May 4, 1822. In Britain there was enormous opposition to such a course, which explains Canning's reluctance to meet Rush on the issue in 1823. The reactionary Tories of Lord Liverpool's government, while willing to allow Canning to detach Britain from the Continental allies, were unwilling to assist by recognition the revolutionary governments in the New World. As events turned out, Britain had to recognize the Latin American governments if she desired to continue her trade in that region of the world. The British recognized Colombia, Mexico, and the United Provinces on December 31, 1824. It thereupon became the unpleasant duty of the Tory peer Lord Eldon as Lord Chancellor to read to Parliament on February 7, 1825 the King's Speech affirming the government's decision to recognize. Eldon did so with a very bad grace; the king himself, George IV, declined to have anything to do with the speech. His Majesty said that he was suffering from a bad attack of gout and that, in any case, he had mislaid his false teeth.

In this manner there ended an era in American diplomacy, which began with a challenge to American maritime principles improvidently accepted by President Madison, and finished with Britain's recognition of the New World.

ADDITIONAL READING

The literature of American diplomacy during the years 1803–1823 concentrates either on the War of 1812 or questions affecting Spain and Latin America. For the War of 1812, its origin, outbreak, and end, the classic account is Henry Adams, *History of the United States during the Administrations of Jefferson and Madison*. See also A. L. Burt, *The United States, Great Britain, and British North America from the Revolution to the Establishment of Peace after the War of 1812* (New Haven, 1940). The maritime technicalities are set out in Alfred Thayer Mahan's *Sea Power in Its Relations to the War of 1812* (2 vols., Boston, 1905); F. E. Melvin, *Napoleon's Navigation System* (New York, 1919); E. F. Heckscher, *The Continental System* (Oxford, 1922); and Robert G. Albion and Jennie B. Pope, *Sea Lanes in Wartime: The American Experience, 1775–1942* (New York, 1942). The last is a thoroughgoing analysis, full of sharp reasoning. The Melvin and Heckscher volumes, appearing after the first World War and inspired by the maritime troubles of that war, differ in quality; the Melvin volume is a more careful study than that by Heckscher. The latter writer was an expert on mercantilism in an earlier era. The account by Mahan is graced by that sailor-scholar's literary style and well-known theory that sea power constitutes the essence of national greatness. Special studies of merit are those by Bradford Perkins, *The First Rapprochement: England and the United States, 1795–1805* (Philadelphia, 1955); Lawrence S. Kaplan, "Jefferson, the Napoleonic Wars, and the Balance of Power," *William and Mary Quarterly*, vol. 14 (1957), 196–217; and Louis M. Sears, *Jefferson and the Embargo* (Durham, N.C., 1927).

The two best introductions to historical writing on the War of 1812 are Warren H. Goodman, "The Origins of the War of 1812: A Survey of Changing Interpretations," *Mississippi Valley Historical Review*, vol. 28 (1941–1942), 171–186; and Reginald Horsman, "The Causes of the War of 1812," a doctoral thesis at Indiana University, 1958. Goodman's article, cited for nearly twenty years for its commentary on the clash of interpretation, is a careful work although it sidesteps in some of its conclusions. The Horsman thesis has the advantage of later research and an outright appraisal of the historical argument. The major interpretations of the War of 1812, other than the traditional view that violation of neutral rights brought the war, are J. W. Pratt, *Expansionists of 1812* (New York, 1925); Louis M. Hacker, "Western Land Hunger and the War of 1812," *Mississippi Valley Historical Review*, vol. 10 (1923–1924), 365–395; and George Rogers Taylor, "Agrarian Discontent in the Mississippi Valley preceding the War of 1812," *Journal of Political Economy*, vol. 39 (1931), 471–505. Abbot Smith, "Mr. Madison's War," *Political Science Quarterly*, vol. 57 (1942), 229–246, a beautifully written piece, contends that Madison tried to gather the interests together that wanted war, in the manner of the *Federalist* No. 10 where he had argued that the statesman's job was to deal with forces at hand. And so instead of pursuing his own policy in an active way, getting support for it by stirring up public opinion, he waited through two years of national indecision until he had support of the war hawks in 1811, whereupon he came out for war.

For post-1815 diplomacy until 1823 and the Monroe Doctrine, the best introduction is George Dangerfield, *The Era of Good Feelings* (New York, 1952), a masterful account written with grace and understanding. Turning to the Middle East, one might point out three studies dealing with early American relations toward the area: C. O. Paullin, *Diplomatic Negotiations of American Naval Officers: 1778–1883* (Baltimore, 1912); R. W. Irwin, *The Diplomatic Relations of the United States with the Barbary Powers: 1776–1816* (Chapel Hill, N.C., 1931); and L. B. Wright and J. H. Macleod, *The First Americans in North Africa: William Eaton's Struggle for a Vigorous Policy against the Barbary Pirates, 1799–1805* (Princeton, 1945). The Adams-Onís Treaty appears in P. C. Brooks, *Diplomacy and the Borderlands* (Berkeley, 1939). For American diplomacy affecting Latin America the best general work is Samuel Flagg Bemis, *The Latin American Policy of the United States* (New York, 1943). The independence of Latin America has several historians: C. C. Griffin, *The United States and the Disruption of the Spanish Empire: 1810–1822* (New York, 1937); Arthur P. Whitaker, *The United States and the Independence of Latin America: 1800–1830* (Baltimore, 1941); J. F. Rippy, *Rivalry of the United States and Great Britain over Latin-America: 1808–1830* (Baltimore, 1929); William W. Kaufmann, *British Policy and the Independence of Latin America: 1804–28* (New Haven, 1951). The historian of the Monroe Doctrine is Dexter Perkins, who in addition to a general work, *A History of the Monroe Doctrine* (2d ed., Boston, 1955), has written three sequent volumes for the years 1823–1826 (Cambridge, Mass., 1927), 1826–1867 (Baltimore, 1933), and 1867–1907 (Baltimore, 1937).

Biographies include the indispensable *John Quincy Adams and the Foundations of American Foreign Policy* (New York, 1949) by Samuel Flagg Bemis, a Pulitzer prize volume; J. H. Powell, *Richard Rush, Republican Diplomat: 1780–1859* (Philadelphia, 1942); Marquis James, *Andrew Jackson: The Border Captain* (Indianapolis, 1933); Bernard Mayo, *Henry Clay: Spokesman of the New West* (Boston, 1937); Glyndon G. Van Deusen, *The Life of Henry Clay* (Boston, 1937); and Irving Brant's *James Madison: Secretary of State, 1800–1809* (Indianapolis, 1953) and *The President, 1809–1812* (Indianapolis, 1956). For Jefferson, see the titles listed as additional reading at the end of chapter 2.

CHAPTER
☆ 4 ☆

Manifest Destiny

In the history of American diplomacy few ideas have been more important than "manifest destiny"—the belief of the people of the United States that the North American continent, despite prior claims by France, Spain, Russia, Great Britain, and Mexico, was destined to become American territory. This mystic conviction translated itself into reality in the years from the beginning of the nineteenth century to the end of the Civil War. It was the presiding force behind the Mexican War of 1846–1848, the subject of the present chapter. French claims to North America vanished with the Louisiana Purchase of 1803. Spanish claims received settlement in the Adams-Onís Transcontinental Treaty of 1819, after which Spain's lands contiguous to the United States passed under control of the new government of Mexico. Russia's claims to Pacific territory withdrew northward to Alaska in a Russian-American agreement of 1824. British claims to Oregon territory disappeared in a treaty signed in 1846. And by 1848 Mexico's claims to Texas, New Mexico, and California were no more. "Away, away with all those cobweb tissues of rights of discovery, exploration, settlement, continuity, etc.," cried the New York editor, John L. O'Sullivan, who in the year 1845 coined the phrase "manifest destiny." It was, O'Sullivan claimed, "the right of our manifest destiny to overspread and to possess the whole of the continent which Providence has given us for the development of the great experiment in liberty and federative self-government entrusted to us."

Some exponents of manifest destiny believed that the United States should not confine its territorial ambitions to the continent of North America. According to one writer "Its floor shall be as a hemisphere, its roof the firmament of the star-studded heavens, and its congregation an Union of many Republics, comprising hundreds of happy millions . . . governed by God's natural and moral law of equality." Such hopes, of course, were never to be realized, and manifest destiny in its more practical vision limited itself to North America.

Two questions might arise at this point, the first of which can be stated as follows: Was manifest destiny nothing but imperialism, an American brand of a well-known nineteenth-century European practice? The nineteenth century was the age of imperialism in Europe, and although European nations undertook their vast colonial conquests in the latter part of the century, whereas the United States pursued its manifest destiny and continental ambition in earlier years, still it might well seem that there was little difference between imperialism and manifest destiny.

In actual fact there was a considerable difference. Manifest destiny was not imperialism if the latter term is properly defined as "rule over alien peoples." There were few Indians in the American West, hardly any at all if compared to the millions of inhabitants of Africa and the hundreds of millions of Asians. It is true that American policy toward the Indians frequently adhered to the frontier maxim that the only good Indians were dead Indians, and it is true that new diseases brought by the settlers decimated the Indians. But in view of the few Indians in the United States one must say that only in an extremely legalistic sense was the American nation imperialist during the early nineteenth century.

A second question in connection with manifest destiny concerns specifically the Mexican War: Was not this war, one of the most important chapters in American territorial expansion, a war of aggression—did not Americans pick a quarrel in 1846 with a weak and divided Mexico for the purpose of despoiling the Mexicans of New Mexico and California, and could not one therefore say that manifest destiny, at least as avowed in 1846–1848, was only an excuse for a war of conquest?

The reader, having noticed the opening page of this chapter, can see that the author does not believe manifest destiny was thus an excuse, but this argument, often made, deserves investigation. Many

Americans have felt embarrassment because their country went to war against a feeble sister republic of the New World and took from her a large expanse of territory. Present-day psychologists would perhaps diagnose this feeling as a guilt complex, the persistent belief of many good-hearted and well-intentioned citizens of the United States that their country in the mid-nineteenth century had not lived up to minimum standards of behavior. This lingering guilt complex, a hundred years after the event, becomes the more intense when one realizes that the nation in the twentieth century could not possibly give back to Mexico the territories won in 1846–1848. It might therefore be advantageous to look back to the details of Mexican-American relations in the early nineteenth century, to see whether the Mexican War was in fact a war of aggression, a war of conquest pure and simple, the sort of war which the government and people of the United States would condemn in the twentieth century, against which Americans have fought two world wars and accepted the possibility of a third, a war in which the idea of manifest destiny was only a sort of rationalizing veneer.

1. *Mexico and the Texas Revolution*

At the turn of the nineteenth century the lands of Mexico belonged to Spain, and it was only after some years of uncertainty during the Napoleonic wars, after reconquest of Mexico by Spain at the end of the wars, that Mexico in 1821 became an independent nation. Twenty-five years of independence followed before the government in Mexico City had to face war with the United States.

The tasks of the Mexican government in its early years were, by any standard, large. The lands of Mexico began in Central America, at the border of Guatemala. Mexican territory reached eastward through Yucatan, northward through the isthmus of Tehuantepec to spread like a gigantic fan across twelve hundred miles of virgin territory from the Sabine River in the east to California in the west. Over these distances the government in Mexico City had to exert its authority, distances that in the early nineteenth century rendered them much more remote from the Mexican capital than mid-twentieth century Fairbanks or Honolulu from Washington, D.C. The task of administering the territory of Mexico from the capital in Mexico City was therefore almost impossible. The northern Mexican provinces of Texas, New Mexico, and California were distinctly separated by geography from the populous region about Mexico City, and were oriented economically to the United States. From the Nueces River to the Rio Grande was a desert tract. South of the Rio Grande for hundreds of miles there was almost no cultivation. Westward for hundreds of miles stretched sheer wilderness and desert.

Was there any chance that with time Mexico might have peopled its northern empire? Not unless time were reckoned in terms of several decades, perhaps a century or more, and even this might not have sufficed. Some six million Indians and half-castes lived in Mexico —no one knows, of course, just what the population really was—and controlling this ignorant and poverty-stricken mass were only some 60,000 Spanish-speaking and Spanish-descended persons who were the government officials and landholders and priests and army officers. Nearly all of the 60,000 Spanish lived in the area now embraced within the republic of Mexico. They had little desire to migrate to the northern provinces, Texas and New Mexico and California. They remained in their comfortable towns and ranches, and only a trickle of people from Mexico proper entered the upper territories. This trickle could do little when the Yankee flood began coming across the Sabine shortly after signature of the Transcontinental Treaty in 1819.

One cannot stress sufficiently the point that Texas and the other northern territories of Mexico were virtually empty lands, lacking Mexican settlers, and because of distance lacking almost any control from Mexico City.

Mexican establishments in California, like those in Texas, were pitiful in their poverty and unimportance. If in Texas there were only about three thousand Mexicans of Spanish origin in the 1830's, there were little more than four thousand in California, a mere handful consisting chiefly of priests and monks about the missions, soldiers employed to keep the Indians submissive, and a few large landowners and cattle raisers. In California the area of Mexican control never extended north of San Francisco, nor inland beyond the coastal area. The first Mexican settlers had come at about the time of the American revolution, and few settlers followed them. Certainly there could be no comparison between the Mexican attempt to settle California and the effort by Englishmen a hundred and fifty years earlier to settle the province of New England, for in the Great Migration of

1630–1642 some 16,000 Englishmen from the Old World came there, to say nothing of simultaneous English migrations to other parts of America.

Aside from the difficulty of holding the northern territories there was the more serious problem of the debility and incompetence of the Mexican government. The revolution against Spain had broken out in 1810, and the Mexicans triumphed conclusively over the forces of their mother country in 1821. In the next year a military adventurer, Agustín de Iturbide, made himself emperor of Mexico with the title of Augustus I. After a short time he fell from power, went abroad, returned, and was shot. The Mexicans in 1824 established a federal constitution on the United States model, and this constitution managed to stay in effect for five years, after which another military leader, Bustamante, subverted it and took office for three years. He was displaced by Antonio López de Santa Anna, the prince of Mexican adventurers, who was in and out of power several times in the next two decades. There was no peace in Mexico before 1877 when General Porfirio Díaz took the reins of government and held them with absolute authority until 1911, after which came a new time of trouble for government in Mexico.

It was nominally the effort of Santa Anna in 1835 to centralize the Mexican government that led to a revolt in Texas in 1835–1836, but behind the constitutional issue lay the weakness of Mexican control in Texas, the thinness of Mexican settlement, and—above all—the fact that in the fifteen years preceding the Texas revolution some thirty thousand Americans had moved into the Mexican province.

Land hunger had drawn American settlers to Texas during the years after the first group arrived in 1821 under the guidance of the *empresario* Stephen F. Austin. Austin had contracted with the Mexican government for many thousands of acres of land in return for bringing in families of settlers. The families paid about ten cents an acre for their land, with liberal arrangements of credit, at a time when inferior land was selling in the United States for $1.25 cash. The United States government, following a financial panic in 1819, had tightened its land policy, and the Bank of the United States, then the principal bank of credit in the country, had drastically reduced its loans and raised its rates of interest, so that settlers seeking cheap lands were driven by force of circumstance to accept the propositions of such men as Stephen Austin. Few of these early American settlers in Texas stopped to inquire as to the type of government they would encounter in their new country. Even the demand of Mexican authorities that they become converts to Catholicism did not disturb their consciences, and they accepted the forms of Catholicism as easily as they accepted other Mexican laws exercised through the Texas organs of the Mexican government—always provided that government, law, and religion did not interfere with their whole-hearted search for cheap land.

Naturally the carefree attitude and abandon with which settlers moved into Texas changed when, after a few years, prosperity permitted leisure for thought and consideration. What in early days had proved acceptable began to irk. Especially the effects of frontier religious revivals must be considered, for as Methodist and Baptist preachers took up superintendence over the souls of American frontiersmen, there came advice from the new ministers that it was blasphemous for the settlers to participate in any way in the forms of the Catholic Church. By the latter 1820's, when signs of civilization were appearing at every hand and settlers were becoming annoyed by increased numbers of Mexican government officials, a new spirit of discontent swept the scattered communities of Texas. Settlers remembered their old allegiance to the United States. When General Andrew Jackson took office as president of the United States in 1829, a wave of enthusiasm and hope rose in the American West. No frontier settlement, even in Mexican Texas, could forget that the "Ginral" was a man of the people. Meanwhile life kept improving. "Within four miles of me," wrote one Texan settler in the mid-1830's, "there are more than one thousand inhabitants, chiefly new emigrants, and within the same distance we have four small stores, two blacksmith shops and two schools. We have a dancing frolick every week and preaching allmost [sic] every Sunday."

In a bare decade and a half more settlers came to Texas than in centuries of Spanish administration. This was the inescapable statistic of the Texas situation by the time of the Texas revolution. By the early 1830's the American settlers outnumbered the Spanish-Mexican population by ten to one. Mexican administrators in Mexico City and in Texas took alarm. The Americans had been fairly happy under the short-lived constitution of 1824, the easy requirements of which were laxly enforced. The processes of Mexican government had not touched them to any important extent. But when the government of Santa Anna sought in 1835 to tighten the administration in Texas, trouble began, which might have been foreseen from the moment the first American immigrants entered Texas in 1821. It was not foreseen, and by 1835 time had run out on Mexican claims to Texas. There followed during the winter and early spring of 1835–1836 the chief events of the Texas revolution.

Some settlers in Texas had risen in November 1835 and in an unorganized but effective fashion had expelled the few Mexican soldiers and administrators then present on Texan soil. To quell this rebellion, Santa Anna led a large army of 3,000 men into Texas and began his assault with the famous attack on the Alamo. There the rapacious Mexican leader isolated 188 Americans under Colonel William B. Travis and raised from the cathedral the black flag of No Quarter. For seven or eight days the Texans held out, issuing a defiant call for help to "all Americans in the world." But no help arrived, and the Mexican troops closed in on the defenders and slaughtered them to the last man. The Alamo, to indulge in an understatement, incited Texans to fury. "Thermopylae had her messenger of defeat—the Alamo had none," roared General Edward Burleson when he heard the news of the tragedy. Foolishly Santa Anna followed up this slaughter by an even larger carnival at Goliad, where he shot down more than 300 American prisoners in cold blood. News of these massacres spread terror among thousands of the Texas settlers, and as Santa Anna advanced there began a wild flight to the border of the United States, the Sabine River. A long, suffering procession of refugees, women and children and Negro slaves, struggled to reach American territory. The exodus took place in cold weather, with incessant rain. Fortunately Santa Anna shortly thereafter met his downfall when General Sam Houston caught him encamped in a trap. Houston had only to attack. This the Texan leader vigorously did, to the embarrassment of the Head of the Mexican State, who at the crucial moment was taking a siesta. With the Battle of San Jacinto on April 21, 1836, the capture of Santa Anna and dispersal of his army, Texas became independent.

One should perhaps point out, in discussing the Texas revolution, that it was in the main a revolt fought by volunteers from the United States. Of the approximately 700 men killed in action or massacred as prisoners by the Mexicans in the spring of 1836, less than a fifth had lived in Texas at the beginning of hostilities in the autumn of

1835. Companies of Americans descended the Mississippi as soon as news of the revolt arrived in the United States, and these forces, thinly disguised as emigrants, fought the revolution. Volunteers came from all over the United States, traveling even from Maine. The emigrants from Maine vowed solemnly that they would "fite or dye" for Texan liberty. American neutrality laws, of course, should have prevented this interference in the Texas revolution, for according to international law it is not permissible for citizens of a country to organize military companies on their own soil and travel as a unit to another country engaged in war. Two years after the Texas revolution, in 1838, when the Canadians had a large-scale revolt against British rule and when organized military units from the United States sought to interfere in the hostilities between the British government and its colonials, the United States hastily passed a stringent neutrality statute, which showed that American neutrality during the Texas revolt had been something less than proper.

As for the meaning of Texan independence for the continental expansion of the United States, the precise manner in which the events of 1835–1836 fitted into the course of manifest destiny, this was not immediately apparent in 1836. The Texans after their revolution made a desultory effort to be independent, and obtained recognition by several foreign states, including the United States, Great Britain, and France, and some nine years elapsed before March 1, 1845, when the American Congress by joint resolution annexed Texas to the United States.

To the Texans of today—many of whom, like the inhabitants of present-day California, have spent most of their lives in other localities but have acquired a pride in their adopted state—the period of independence bespeaks the demonstration of Texan prowess before the entire world, after which the people of Texas joined the union. Actually the Texan republic was a feeble affair, which ran up a huge debt and almost from fear of bankruptcy joined the American union. The republic lived anything but a serene existence. In the days when the Mexicans were carrying everything before them in the spring of 1836, the head of the Yanqui rebels in Texas—the newly installed rebel governor—and his council were at loggerheads, trading recriminations rather than seeking ways of halting the foe. The governor at one point sent a message denouncing his council as Judases, scoundrels, wolves, and parricides. The council responded by brand-

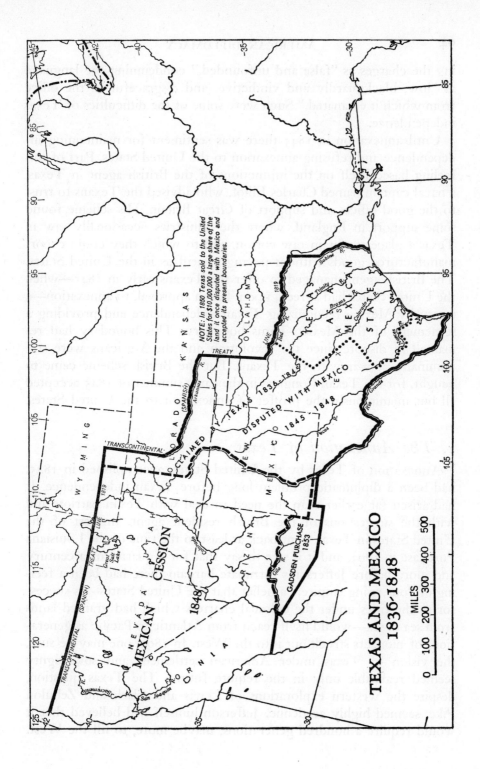

TEXAS AND MEXICO
1836-1848

NOTE: In 1850 Texas sold to the United States for $10,000,000 a large share of the land it once disputed with Mexico and accepted its present boundaries.

MILES
0   100   200   300   400   500

ing the charges as "false and unfounded," condemning the language as "low, blackguardly and vindictive, and disgraceful to the office from which it emanated." Such were some of the difficulties of Texas independence.

Until annexation in 1845 there was sentiment for maintaining independence and refusing annexation to the United States. Part of this feeling based itself on the injunctions of the British agent in Texas, a naval captain named Charles Elliot, who advised the Texans to trust to the good offices and support of Great Britain. His scheme found some support in England, where the ministries occasionally saw in Texas a place to obtain raw cotton, and to which they could export manufactured goods without paying a tariff as in the United States. The British agent managed to offer the Texans early in 1845—when the United States had agreed, upon Texan approval, to annexation—a treaty by Mexico recognizing Texan independence and providing a settlement of the Mexico-Texas boundary. This boundary had remained in dispute since the revolution and the Mexicans were still nominally at war with the Texans. But the British scheme came to naught, for the Texan Congress in the early summer of 1845 accepted all but unanimously the proffer of annexation to the United States.

2. The Annexation of Texas

Annexation of Texas by the United States, accomplished in 1845, had been a diplomatic problem long before Texan independence. It had arisen far earlier than the need to deal with Texan patriots and with the suggestions of the British resident agent. Interest of the United States in Texas went back at least to the time of the Louisiana Purchase in 1803, and it is safe to say that for a quarter of a century and more before Jefferson's fortunate bargain there had been a feeling of "our rising empire," a belief that the United States—as successor to the titles under the colonial charters which had granted lands from sea to sea—would itself reach from Atlantic to Pacific as generations of pioneers struck out into the West. In 1803, one may be sure, the vision of Texas under American settlement and sovereignty seemed realizable only in the remote future. The Texas question, despite the western explorations of Lewis and Clark and Zebulon Pike, seemed highly academic. Jefferson himself had believed that it would require a hundred generations, maybe more, to fill the West.

American ambitions, it is fair to say, changed with startling rapidity in the years after the War of 1812. John Quincy Adams in 1819 reluctantly agreed with Don Luis de Onís that the Sabine River would form part of the western boundary of the Louisiana territory. At the moment, Monroe's entire cabinet and General Andrew Jackson agreed that the Sabine was the best boundary that the United States could get. The Sabine boundary turned out to be a mistake, for within months after signature of the Adams-Onís Transcontinental Treaty opinions began to change. Jackson in patriotic old age asserted that he never agreed to the Sabine. Other patriots found themselves declaiming that the Sabine boundary was a fraud. John Quincy Adams had to defend his choice of the Sabine for the rest of his long life.

During his presidential administration Adams had sought to buy Texas from Mexico, but to no avail, perhaps because the New Englander was only willing to offer the paltry price of a million dollars. His secretary of state, Henry Clay, used every possible argument to make the proud and newly independent Mexicans sell their northern province, even pointing out that if Texas were ceded to the United States the capital of Mexico would be situated nearer the center of the country. Nothing came of such negotiation.

Andrew Jackson turned to a sharper diplomacy, and his minister to Mexico City, Colonel Anthony Butler, made persistent efforts to acquire Texas and did not shy from proposals to his chief that the United States bribe Mexican political leaders. This idea was not completely foolish. It was not uncommon for many Mexican political leaders of the early nineteenth century to accept bribes in one form or another, and Butler was only being realistic when he wrote to Jackson in 1831 that "As the influence of money is as well understood and as readily conceded by these people as any under Heaven, I have no doubt of its doing its office." The general scrawled on the back of one such letter, "A. Butler. What a Scamp." The scamp remained in Mexico City from 1829 to 1836, and we may be sure that Butler kept busy during that time, hatching one plot after another. The historian of Texas annexation and of the Mexican War, Justin H. Smith, later wrote of Butler that he "was a national disgrace . . . personally a bully and a swashbuckler, ignorant at first of the Spanish language and even the forms of diplomacy, shamefully careless about legation affairs, wholly unprincipled as to methods, and by the open

testimony of two American consuls openly scandalous in conduct."
Be that as it may, Butler busied himself after what many Americans
considered the grandly national business of getting Texas from the
Mexicans.

The Texan revolution of 1835–1836 made no change in American
policy. Andrew Jackson, consummate politician that he was, refused
during his second administration to sponsor admission of Texas to the
union. Desiring annexation, he refrained from making political capital
of it, for fear that the Texas question if propelled into politics would
reopen the slavery question, uneasily adjourned by the Compromise
of 1820. Northern congressional leaders were certain that Texas upon
admission to the union would be a slave state, and this would raise
the inconvenient issue of balance of slave versus free states in the
Senate, which then was exactly even, thirteen slave and thirteen free.
Especially they thought of what might happen if Texas upon annexation should split itself into five or ten slave states, for this would ruin
any hope of maintaining the sectional balance. Jackson was aware of
Northern feeling on this matter. The most obtuse statesman—which
Jackson assuredly was not—could hardly remain ignorant of the rising feeling between North and South. Jackson moved gingerly and
with complete impartiality of action, if not of feeling, when the
Texans in 1836 declared their independence. At one point Sam
Houston asked the general if Texas, desperately in need of money,
might have a share in distribution of surplus revenue from the treasury. Jackson commented on this request: "The writer did not reflect
that we have a treaty with Mexico, and our national faith is pledged
to support it. The Texans before they took the step to declare
themselves Independent which has aroused all Mexico against them
ought to have pondered well—it was a rash and premature act, our
neutrality must be faithfully maintained." Giving as excuse for his
inaction the existence of a treaty between his country and Mexico,
and the proprieties of international intercourse, Jackson had in mind
the delicate political situation in the United States.

With the refusal of the Jackson administration to annex Texas
after San Jacinto, relations between the two sovereign English-speaking states of North America settled down to a brief and quiet interlude. Jackson recognized Texan independence eleven months after
San Jacinto, four months longer than the American government had
waited to recognize Mexico after its successful revolution against

Spain in 1821. The Mexicans nonetheless protested American recognition of Texas, and refused themselves to recognize Texan independence, a policy in which they persisted to the bitter end. Events continued in this course—Texan independence, American recognition, Mexican nonrecognition—until President John Tyler in 1844 sponsored in the Senate a treaty of annexation, and failing in that effort resorted early in 1845 to a joint resolution of annexation.

There is no point in detailing the fortunes and misfortunes of the Tyler treaty of 1844 which failed in the Senate. The treaty failed not because of antislavery or proslavery agitation but because the Senate split along partisan lines, with Southern Whigs voting against the treaty. There followed the presidential election of 1844, an election which many students later would describe as one of the three American elections turning on a question of foreign affairs—the other two being 1796 and 1920. The election of 1844 was a confused contest, as are most contests for the American presidency, and the winning candidate James K. Polk appears to have won not so much because he came out for annexation of Texas as because the national balance between Whigs and Democrats was just about even anyway and luck favored Polk in the electoral college. Whatever the confusion involved in electing Polk, who incidentally was the first "dark horse" candidate for the presidency, the new president after election chose to interpret his mandate as requiring annexation of Texas, and his eager predecessor Tyler, still in office, arranged for and signed the joint resolution on March 1, 1845.

Southern statesmen in the mid-nineteenth century, speaking for annexation of Texas, adduced some ingenious proslavery claims. Henry Wise of Virginia asserted, perhaps with tongue in cheek, that annexation would benefit Northern abolitionists: so long as Texas remained a foreign country the abolitionists could do nothing about freeing the slaves there, but when it became part of the union they could work on slavery there to their hearts' content. Secretary of State John C. Calhoun, in 1844 during the debate over ratification of the Tyler annexation treaty, took advantage of a diplomatic note received from the British minister in Washington, Richard Pakenham, to write a reply giving in large detail the proslavery reasons for annexation of Texas. The argument was, in sum, a statement that slavery benefitted both the master and the slave, that it was an institution of piety and love rather than force and brutality, that its defense was the duty of the government of the United States. That government, Calhoun argued, intended to annex Texas to prevent antislaveryites in England from undertaking, via British diplomacy, to free the slaves in Texas.

Just why Calhoun wrote this saucy diplomatic note in 1844 is not quite clear. His most recent biographer has asserted that he did not mean to raise a row in England or in the American North, but was only stating reasons for annexation as he understood them. He may have hoped to end the abolition propaganda, then beginning to pour in large quantities from the printing presses of the North. He may have hoped to rally antiabolition opinion to his side. He may have hoped to hasten the impending split of the nation into North and South, and to precipitate then and there, in 1844, a war for Southern independence.

Antislavery men, opposing the slavery advocates, counseled that admission of Texas to the union as a slave state would be contrary to the constitution, and that the free states of the North had the right to nullify—that is, to deny the legality of—any federal statute passed to this effect. There was even some feeling that admission of Texas was sufficient reason for the North to dissolve the union. John Quincy Adams, old in years but young in heart, told the young men of Boston that "Your trial is approaching. The spirit of freedom and the spirit of slavery are drawing together for the deadly conflict of arms. The annexation of Texas to this union is the blast of the trumpet for a foreign, civil, servile, and Indian war, of which the government of your country, fallen into faithless hands, have already twice given the signal—first by a shameless treaty, rejected by a virtuous senate; and again by the glove of defiance, hurled by the apostle of nullification, at the avowed policy of the British empire peacefully to promote the extinction of slavery throughout the world. Young men of Boston: burnish your armor, prepare for the conflict, and I say to you, in the language of Calgacus to the ancient Britons, think of your forefathers! Think of your posterity!"

To no avail were the antislavery arguments against annexation. The feeling of manifest destiny was too strong and too popular in 1845, antislavery sentiment not yet strong enough. Tyler's joint resolution passed Congress with a whoop. "You might as well attempt to turn the current of the Mississippi," Old Hickory declared in a letter given to the press at the crucial political moment, "as to turn the democracy from the annexation of Texas to the United States . . . obtain it the U. States must—peaceably if we can, but forcibly if we must."

All but forgotten in the uproar were the pretensions of the Mexican government. Texas, Mexican diplomats had been claiming, was still part of Mexico, and annexation by the United States would be tantamount to a declaration of war. Upon passage of the joint resolution of March 1, 1845, the Mexican minister in Washington asked for and received his passports.

3. *The Mexican War*

A year elapsed after the annexation of Texas before the war with Mexico began. There followed after Tyler's resolution of March 1845 a period of maneuvering and uncertainty during which President Polk waited to see what the Mexicans would do. The president was not averse to war. Still, he did not wish war if he could get its fruits without any fighting. He therefore sent a representative to Mexico City, John Slidell, in the hope of obtaining Mexican recognition of a Texas boundary at the Rio Grande, in exchange for which the United States would assume payment of claims of its nationals against the Mexican government. (Because Mexico had been in turmoil for thirty years and more, many Americans had found their properties confiscated and sometimes their lives endangered by the various revolutionary troubles; these claims had been settled by a mixed claims commission for approximately two million dollars, but the Mexicans had refused to pay the claims.) This was Slidell's minimum proposal: recognition of the Rio Grande boundary in return for American assumption of the claims payments. In addition the emissary was empowered to purchase New Mexico and California for $25,000,000. Polk would have gone as high as $40,000,000. He especially desired California with its fine harbor of San Francisco.

The president's representative, Slidell, unfortunately for Mexico, met with rebuff. Before Slidell's journey to Mexico City Polk had received a statement in writing from the Mexican foreign minister to the effect that an American commissioner would find a friendly reception. The Mexican government upon Slidell's arrival refused to treat with him, on the technicality that his credentials were those of a minister plenipotentiary rather than a special *ad hoc* representative.

What happened was that the Mexican government of the moment, led by General Mariano Paredes, was in imminent peril of being thrown from office, and could not face the hostility of popular opinion in the capital city, should it undertake to negotiate with the Americans. The Mexican people—when one spoke of a "people" of Mexico in the nineteenth century he meant little more than the literate inhabitants of the capital—were determined that annexation of Texas would be tantamount to war.

Whatever sort of government was in control, it was a fatuous act in 1846 to turn down an overture from the government of the United States. Mexico was in the position of refusing to sell territories that she could not keep anyway. Napoleon in 1803, seeing that he could not hold Louisiana, had sold it. There were no Napoleons in Mexico in 1846 but only factional politicians who found momentary power too sweet to relinquish, be the responsibilities of their decisions ever so serious for the future of their country.

And so John Slidell went away, and President Polk, tired of the irresolution of his adversary, disposed American troops under Brigadier General Zachary ("Old Zach") Taylor in the disputed border area of Texas between the Nueces River and the Rio Grande. The local Mexican commander on April 25, 1846 surprised a company of American soldiers, killing or wounding sixteen and capturing the remainder, and the war was on. This even before news had reached the Mexican commander that the government in Mexico City had declared a "defensive war" against the United States. In Washington, Polk was preparing a war message to Congress when the welcome news arrived of the Mexican attack. War, Polk then could assert, had been forced upon the United States by act of Mexico. Congress declared on May 13, 1846 that "by the act of the Republic of Mexico, a state of war exists between that Government and the United States."

That this war with Mexico in the mid-nineteenth century was not a popular conflict soon became obvious to everyone. The war with Mexico of 1846–1848 never evoked the popularity that surrounded the first or second World Wars or the war with Spain in 1898. Not merely was there grumbling and disgruntledness in New England, but outright speeches against the war by such Western opponents as Congressman Abraham Lincoln of Illinois. The issue on which opposition arose was, of course, the extension of slavery. Northern opposition to the war found expression everywhere from pulpits, rostrums, and "stump" platforms. No sooner had the war begun than it received a name indicating its alleged origin—President Polk's War. It was the dishonored successor of President Madison's War, un-honored predecessor to Mr. Lincoln's War, forerunner of the wars of Mr. McKinley, Mr. Wilson, Mr. Roosevelt, and Mr. Truman. The Mexican War, according to the critics of James K. Polk, was an "unhappy war, in which, by his own deliberate, unauthorized and criminal act, he has involved the country." On the floor of the House of Representatives the cantankerous abolitionist Joshua R. Giddings declared the conflict "a war against an unoffending people without adequate or just cause, for the purpose of conquest; with the design of extending slavery; in violation of the Constitution, against the dictates of justice, humanity, the sentiments of the age in which we live, and the precepts of the religion which we profess. I will lend it no aid," Giddings said during debate over an appropriation bill, "no support whatever. I will not bathe my hands in the blood of the people of Mexico, nor will I participate in the guilt of those murders which have been and will hereafter be committed by our army there. For these reasons I shall vote against the bill under consideration and all others calculated to support the war."

President Polk in taking the country to war against Mexico did not, incidentally, act from proslavery motives. Polk was dismayed at the debates over the slavery issue, and became embittered after the war began by the reintroduction into Congress in January 1847 of the Wilmot Proviso to prevent the expansion of slavery into new territory. Slavery as an institution, the president always maintained, had no connection with the war or the peace. "Its introduction in connection with the Mexican War," he recorded in his diary, "is not only mischievous but wicked." Although a citizen of Tennessee and a slaveholder, like his predecessor Andrew Jackson, he had in mind first and foremost the territory and Pacific ports of California, and only after this goal was achieved would he concern himself over the slavery question. Economic interests, but of a territorial sort, moved Polk in his actions, peaceful and otherwise, toward Mexico.

The actual fighting of the Mexican War is not of immediate con-cern to the student of American diplomatic history, but is of some interest. After Mexico's attack on General Taylor's forces along the Rio Grande there followed some of the finest campaigning in Amer-ican military annals. Taylor led his troops into Mexico from their positions at the border, and on February 23, 1847 won the battle of Buena Vista. Meanwhile, after a period of indecision in Washington, General Winfield Scott received permission to land a force at Veracruz, which he did on March 9, 1847 and marched overland to Mexico City itself. Scott advanced in record time and reached the capital in September 1847. There is no better story of the valor of American arms than the expedition of Scott's troops to the Halls of Montezuma, much of it across difficult and ruggedly mountainous terrain, ending with the storming of the causeways and gates of the imperial city of the Aztecs. Winning a brilliant victory, with fewer than 6,000 troops, Scott consented to a peace arranged by an accompanying representative of the State Department, its erstwhile chief clerk Nicholas P. Trist.

The Treaty of Guadalupe Hidalgo was concluded on February 2, 1848, and had a most interesting background. It was signed by Trist after his commission had expired. President Polk through Secretary of State James Buchanan had annulled Trist's commission, fearing that to have a negotiator accompanying Scott's army would seem to the Mexicans like a sign of American weakness. But Trist at this point began to fear that without an immediate peace there might develop a sentiment in the United States for taking all of Mexico. The Mexican government had been reconstituted through the efforts of General Scott, whose troops were billeted comfortably in the Mexican capital. The abject defeat of the Mexicans was so obvious that, as Trist knew, it might well encourage the more ambitious apostles of manifest destiny to stretch the American eagle's wings all the way to Guatemala. Even as Trist was deliberating his course of action, Senator Hannegan of Indiana introduced a resolution in the Senate, "That it may become necessary and proper, as it is within the constitutional capacity of this government, for the United States to hold Mexico as a territorial appendage." Two months later Senator Dickinson at a Jackson Day dinner offered the toast, "A More Perfect Union embracing the entire North American Continent." It was a serious situation. Trist from his point of view made the most of it. With Scott's consent, for the general was agreeable to finishing off the war, Trist negotiated his treaty at the little village of Guadalupe Hidalgo just outside Mexico City and sent the treaty off to Washington to see what Polk would do with it.

Polk was furious. The president, an able, conscientious, sincere man, was intensely suspicious of political plots during his administration—and he saw a plot in Trist's treaty.

Polk, it seems altogether fair to say, had begun the Mexican War not out of partisan but for national reasons. The president believed that his country's future demanded a border of Texas at the Rio Grande, and in addition he wanted to acquire New Mexico and especially California. This was a broadly national purpose, but as Whig opposition to the war became more vehement Polk found that matters of politics plagued his every move, that he had to be circumspect in his every act to fend off the Whigs and keep the war going to a victorious conclusion. He managed to do this, but only with difficulty, and one of his worst problems in the conduct of the war was that the two leading military commanders, Generals Taylor and Scott, were both Whigs and likely to profit personally from the war by being nominated on the Whig ticket for the presidency. Taylor, old "Rough and Ready," quickly became a popular figure, and as Taylor's political prospects rose Polk's opinion of his generalship went lower and lower. The president decided that Taylor was lacking in initiative, and complained that he "simply obeys orders and gives no information to aid the administration in directing his movement." Still, there was no question but that Taylor was an effective field commander, and after the general's triumphs Polk finally had to admit that "After the late battles, which were well fought, the public opinion seems to point to him as entitled to the command." As for Scott, the political prospects were just as disquieting. The president wanted Scott out of Washington, where his presence was embarrassing to the secretary of war, but it was equally annoying to have to send Scott to command the Veracruz expedition, for there was no telling what laurels this duty might bring. Polk had to circumscribe, if possible, the reputations of Taylor and Scott and conclude somehow an acceptable peace with Mexico. It was a difficult program.

The president believed that he had chosen the right man for the job of peacemaking when he picked out Nicholas P. Trist. Trist's background was irreproachable. The chief clerk of the State Department was a longtime Democrat, and had served for a while as General Jackson's private secretary. There could be, so Polk must have thought, no political difficulty in sending Trist to Mexico. Moreover, the chief clerk was not a person of stature in the Democratic Party, and hence there could be no chance of offending any faction of the party by appointing Trist. Too, by commissioning Trist as an executive agent the president left the way open for a regular diplomatic mission under Secretary Buchanan, should such later seem feasible. And if Trist were a success the credit for the enterprise would fall to his superiors, and if he were a failure he might conveniently be disowned. It seemed a perfect situation.

As luck would have it, Trist proved in no sense as useful as Polk imagined. The chief clerk had a mind of his own, as evidenced in his singular decision to sign a treaty with the Mexicans after his commission had expired. And to add to this difficulty of Trist was the fact that Polk's envoy became, before signature of the Treaty of Guadalupe Hidalgo, a fast friend and confidant of General Scott. At first Trist and Scott had been bitter enemies. Both men were adepts as letter writers, and there followed a vindictive correspondence in which each sought to insult, in the grossest manner, the other. Observing this verbal battle with some amusement, one of Polk's supporters in Washington remarked that Scott and Trist would produce "a most voluminous, if not a luminous correspondence." Trist complained bitterly to the State Department about Scott. Scott could not stand the thought of Trist, and declared that the latter, armed with "an ambulatory guillotine," would be "the personification of Danton, Marat, and St. Just, all in one." Then the two men came together in friendship. Scott soon was reporting to Secretary of War William L. Marcy that he regarded Trist as "able, discreet, courteous, and amiable." The general added that "So far as I am concerned, I am perfectly willing that all I have heretofore written to the Department about Mr. Trist, should be suppressed." Similarly Trist praised Scott to the Department of State. To his wife he wrote that Scott was "the soul of honour and probity, and full of the most sterling qualities of heart and head: affectionate, generous, forgiving, and a *lover of justice.*" When Trist of a sudden became ill, Scott put him in the charge of their mutual friend, General Persifer F. Smith, sent him some guava marmalade from his personal stores, and to top it all made Trist his guest at headquarters.

It was not unnatural that the Polk administration, surveying these developments, saw political complications in this Trist-Scott *rapprochement*, and Polk became obsessed by what he considered Trist's perfidy, disowning his peace commissioner and even refusing to pay him, making it necessary for Trist to petition the government to obtain recompense, twenty-two years later, for his personal expenses in Mexico. Polk felt that "Mr. Trist, from all I can learn, has lent himself to Gen'l Scott and is his mere tool, and seems to be employed in ministering to his malignant passions." The president in his diary for January 15, 1848 recorded having received "a very long despatch from Mr. Trist. It was dated on the 6th of Decr. last, and is the most extraordinary document I have ever heard from a Diplomatic Representative. . . . His despatch is arrogant, impudent, and very insulting to his Government, and even personally offensive to the President. He admits he is acting without authority and in violation of the positive order recalling him. It is manifest to me that he has become the tool of Gen'l Scott and his menial instrument, and that the paper was written at Scott's instance and dictation. I have never in my life felt so indignant, and the whole Cabinet expressed themselves as I felt. I told Mr. Buchanan that the paper was so insulting and contemptably [sic] base, that it require[d] no lengthy answer, but that it did require a short, but stern and decided rebuke, and directed him to prepare such a reply. . . . If there was any legal provision for his punishment he ought to be severely handled. He has acted worse than any man in the public employ whom I have ever known. His despatch proves that he is destitute of honour or principle, and that he has proved himself to be a very base man. I was deceived in him. I had but little personal knowledge of him, but could not have believed [it] possible that any man would have acted so basely . . ."

Even so, the president had little choice but to submit Trist's treaty. As he wrote in his diary for February 21, 1848, "I looked, too, to the consequences of its [the treaty's] rejection. A majority of one branch of Congress is opposed to my administration; they have falsely charged that the war was brought on and is continued by me with a view to the conquest of Mexico; and if I were now to reject a Treaty made upon my own terms, as authorized in April last, with the unanimous approbation of the Cabinet, the probability is that Congress would not grant either men or money to prosecute the war. Should this be the result, the army now in Mexico would be constantly wasting and diminishing in numbers, and I might at last be compelled to withdraw them, and thus loose [sic] the two Provinces of New Mexico & Upper California, which were ceded to the U.S. by this Treaty. Should the opponents of my administration succeed in carrying the next Presidential election, the great probability is that the country would loose [sic] all the advantages secured by this Treaty. I adverted to the immense value of Upper California; and concluded by saying that if I were now to reject my own terms, as offered in April last, I did not see how it was possible for my administration to be sustained."

Trist's treaty, despite the improprieties of its conclusion, was not unwelcome, for Polk's agent had secured New Mexico and California plus Mexican acceptance of the Texan boundary at the Rio Grande, and the United States was to pay $15,000,000 and assume the adjusted claims of its citizens against the Mexican government. These terms, Polk realized, were virtually the maximum that Slidell had been empowered to negotiate in the abortive mission of 1846, and despite his intense disgust with Trist for acting without commission the president sent the treaty to the Senate, which gave its advice and consent on March 10, 1848. After ratification by Mexico, Polk proclaimed the treaty in effect on the anniversary of American independence, July 4, 1848. By this stroke of war, following upon the stroke of diplomacy which had gained Texas in 1845, the United States had added altogether (including Texas) 1,200,000 square miles to its domain, an increase of more than sixty-six per cent.

What could one say about manifest destiny, as it had found fulfillment in the events of 1845–1848? The peaceful process by which the United States of America had been expanding across the enormously valuable North American continent had been punctuated by a short and sharp and altogether victorious war. At the time, people were asking whether political leaders from the Southern portion of the United States had not forced the war with Mexico for the enlargement of their slave domains, for the miserable purpose of obtaining "more pens to cram slaves in." This fear, so far as concerned the reasoning of President Polk himself and probably many of his supporters, was unfounded. Even so, in the twentieth century when war led to the near-destruction of Western civilization, many people were again going to ask if the Mexican War were not an unjust war of aggression. Was, then, the Mexican War a conflict that for this latter reason should have been avoided? Should not the United States in 1846–1848 have trusted to its diplomacy and restrained its pursuit of manifest destiny, if that were possible?

The answer to this question is not easy. No American today would like to give up the territories secured from Mexico. Those expanses so varied in their riches gave us first gold, then oil, now uranium, and have increased enormously the power of the United States. If one may be permitted the luxury of reading the present into the past— assuredly a most unhistorical operation—he can easily see that at a time in the mid-twentieth century when the power of the United States and the Union of Soviet Socialist Republics is so neatly balanced, any large subtraction from American power might have changed the course of history. This is no fanciful notion, pleasantly speculated upon in these pages, but an idea that bears some consider- able possibilities for thought. What might have happened if the United States during the second World War had not had enough economic and military strength to throw the victory to the Allies? Or for that matter, what might have happened in the gray spring of 1918 when the German offensive came within an ace of success, if the morale of Allied troops had not been bucked up by the prospect, soon to be realized, of two million American soldiers in France? If the nation had stopped at the Sabine River, if such statesmen as John Tyler and James K. Polk had taken Mexican complaints and protests as insuperable obstacles to realization of manifest destiny, the Amer- ican people might today find their personal and public circumstances altogether unenviable.

If Texas had been allowed to go her own way in 1845, if the Amer- ican government had continued timid and unresponsive to Texan requests for annexation there might have developed another large North American republic between the United States and Mexico. If the manifest destiny of the American people had received this blow there might have followed an independent California on the Pacific Coast, perhaps an independent Oregon. The North American con- tinent, already split south of the Rio Grande into half a dozen or more weak governments, would have gone the way of South Amer- ica.

But the above comments are admittedly retrospective. The question remains as to whether the Mexican War was a just conflict—whether Americans should in good conscience have avoided the war by which their country took New Mexico and California from a weak Latin government, whether manifest destiny offered only an excuse for a land-hungry nation.

Americans may as well admit that in 1846–1848 they fought a war of aggression against Mexico. Such a confession is discomforting to make in the aggression-ridden twentieth century, but the facts of the case substantiate it. President Polk touched off the war when he ordered General Taylor to the line of the Rio Grande. He hoped to provoke the Mexicans and managed to do it. The war was an act of aggression by the United States for the purpose of conquering territory from a helpless neighbor. Mexico had little chance of defending herself. Although the American people were divided in their support of the war, the outcome was hardly ever in doubt, and the United States triumphed so completely that if there had been more unanimity at home the American flag might well have waved permanently over all of Mexico. Americans, surveying the Mexican War, can argue that their country brought order and prosperity to the regions it conquered, and especially that for the preservation of democracy in the twentieth century this nineteenth-century war was a fortunate affair. Such argument does not alter the fact that the method employed in 1846–1848 to extend American sovereignty westward to the Pacific was aggression and that the war against Mexico was not a just war.

This statement of fact, however, does not dispose of the justification for the war, manifest destiny, the mystic notion that the North American continent was destined to belong to the people of the United States. As one examines the course of Mexican-American relations in the early nineteenth century it does seem that, apart from the rightness or wrongness of the Mexican War, there was an undeniable logic in United States possession of Texas, New Mexico, and California. One has therefore the uneasy feeling that the result of the war was good but the means were bad, and that perhaps if the American people in 1846–1848 had been possessed of more wisdom they would have found another method, besides war—presumably a correct diplomatic method—by which to realize their good end, their manifest destiny.

ADDITIONAL READING

Edward Channing's *History of the United States*, despite the years that have elapsed since its writing, remains one of the best introductions to American history prior to the end of the Civil War, and his fifth volume, *The Period of Transition: 1815–1848* (New York, 1921) offers shrewd insight to the manifest-destiny viewpoint of that era. A colorful if controversial account of the times is Arthur M. Schlesinger, Jr., *The Age of Jackson* (Boston, 1945; abridged edition available in paperback). The author of this latter work is one of the most talented historical writers in the United States whose views are always interesting even if inspired by a large-D Democratic enthusiasm. A glancing and general account is Nathaniel W. Stephenson, *Texas and the Mexican War* (New Haven, 1921), one of the *Chronicles of America* series of 50-odd volumes allegedly written for the tired business man, the student, and the professor who needs a quick prelecture briefing. Two older but useful works are Jesse S. Reeves, *American Diplomacy under Tyler and Polk* (Baltimore, 1907) and G. L. Rives, *The United States and Mexico: 1821–1848* (2 vols., New York, 1913). Albert K. Weinberg, *Manifest Destiny* (Baltimore, 1935) shows the logical inadequacies of its subject, without recognizing its virtues.

The Texas revolt and annexation appears in several books: William C. Binkley, *The Texas Revolution* (Baton Rouge, La., 1952), a series of four lectures; E. C. Barker, *Mexico and Texas: 1821–1835* (Dallas, 1928); Joseph W. Schmitz, *Texan Statecraft: 1836–1845* (San Antonio, 1941); and Stanley Siegel, *A Political History of the Texas Republic: 1836–1845* (Austin, 1956). Justin H. Smith's *The Annexation of Texas* (New York, 1911) is a thorough monograph.

For the Mexican War see Justin H. Smith, *The War with Mexico* (2 vols., New York, 1919); and Alfred Hoyt Bill, *Rehearsal for Conflict* (New York, 1947). The latter author believes that the Mexican War was a proving ground for the American army and gave to a number of American officers the experience necessary to wage the Civil War.

A new interpretation, that it was not so much manifest destiny as desire for Juan de Fuca Strait, San Francisco, and San Diego that took Americans to California and Oregon, appears in Norman A. Graebner, *Empire on the Pacific: A Study in American Continental Expansion* (New York, 1955), a lively book written from manuscript materials. Graebner believes that the large movements of American diplomacy must be understood in terms of concrete objectives rather than philosophical notions. Perhaps, however, both might operate at the same time.

Biographies include E. C. Barker, *The Life of Stephen F. Austin* (Nashville, 1925); Allan Nevins, *Frémont* (2 vols., New York, 1928); Marquis James, *The Raven: A Biography of Sam Houston* (Indianapolis, 1929); W. H. Callcott, *Santa Anna* (Norman, Okla., 1936); Marquis James, *Andrew Jackson: Portrait of a President* (Indianapolis, 1937); Oliver P. Chitwood, *John Tyler: Champion of the Old South* (New York, 1939); Herbert P. Gambrell, *Anson Jones* (Garden City, N.Y., 1948); Charles H. Wiltse, *John C. Calhoun, Sectionalist: 1840–1850* (Indianapolis, 1951); Llerena Friend, *Sam Houston: The Great Designer* (Austin, 1954). For Polk see Eugene I. McCormac, *James K. Polk* (Berkeley, 1922). Worth careful examination is Milo M. Quaife, ed.,

The Diary of James K. Polk: During His Presidency, 1845 to 1849 (4 vols., Chicago, 1910), which has been boiled down in Allan Nevins, ed., *Polk, The Diary of a President: 1845–1849* (New York, 1929). The excellent multivolume biography of Polk by Charles G. Sellers has not yet reached the presidential period; the first volume is entitled *James K. Polk: Jacksonian, 1795–1843* (Princeton, 1957).

Samuel Flagg Bemis's second volume on the indefatigable "JQA," *John Quincy Adams and the Union* (New York, 1956), contains within a biographical framework the latest scholarship on Texas and the Mexican War. It would be a worthwhile project for another American scholar to do what Bemis has done but on a larger scale, bringing together the miscellaneous—and in the case of some of it, dull and tedious—literature of manifest destiny in a medium-sized and well-written book.

CHAPTER
☆ 5 ☆

The Era of the Civil War

For a number of years after the Mexican War, Americans continued to think in terms of manifest destiny, of boundaries and expansion, and in the 1850's the sense of manifest destiny took new form in the idea that there was something youthful about the American nation, that "young America" stood erect in the strength of early manhood, shoulder to shoulder with such new nations of Europe as young Hungary, young Italy, and young Ireland, facing the worn-out older nations of Great Britain, France, and Spain. When the Habsburgs suppressed the Hungarian revolution in 1849, young America in the pride of manifest destiny sent a thunderous warning to the Austrian government. A few years later it apprised Spain in no uncertain terms of the need for American annexation of Cuba. In the 1850's there was filibustering in Cuba and Nicaragua. There was speechmaking in Congress about Mexican annexation. Where the American eagle would range was limited only by the youthful American imagination.

It may appear odd that no sooner had such sentiments of young America filled the halls of Congress than there arose the oratory of secession, seemingly the negation of manifest destiny. Actually, the new government of the Confederate States of America considered its independence required for the fulfillment of manifest destiny. And not a few Southerners in 1861 envisioned their own special continuance of manifest destiny through taking lands in Mexico and Central America and the Caribbean, territories that the United States had

111

neglected to take during the 1850's. As for the men of the Union, they too acted in accord with manifest destiny, believing it the will of God that there should be one great republic, instead of two, on the continent of North America. The Civil War was fought by both sides under the compulsions of this mystic spirit of American destiny, variously interpreted.

After the end of the war came expulsion of the French from Mexico, where they had ensconced themselves behind a phantom emperor named Maximilian. The diplomatic actions of Secretary of State William H. Seward toward France were taken under the Monroe Doctrine, and the doctrine of 1823 was assuredly a statement of manifest destiny. In the same year, 1867, Seward bought Alaska from the Russians, again a sign of this spirit of the times.

It is not too much to say, therefore, that the years before, during, and after the Civil War, the two decades that followed the Treaty of Guadalupe Hidalgo, like the years that preceded it, were filled with the notion of manifest destiny. In the period from 1848 to 1867 the diplomacy of the United States was not, as historians have sometimes drawn it, a series of unconnected episodes tenuously ordered by the rise and fall of presidential administrations. It showed clear evidences of the same motive force that had demonstrated itself in previous decades of American diplomatic history.

1. *Young America*

Young America was the form taken by manifest destiny after the Mexican War. By chance, the European revolutions of 1848 occurred in the same year that the United States concluded the Treaty of Guadalupe Hidalgo, and this coincidence gave support to the idea of young America, to the belief that America was young and that the powers of Europe were old. Edwin de Leon, in an 1845 address at South Carolina College, had observed, perhaps for the first time, that as there was a young Germany, a young Italy, and a young Ireland, so there might well be a young America. For "nations, like men, have their seasons of infancy, manly vigor, and decrepitude." The young giant of the West, America, stood at the full flush of "exulting manhood." The worn-out powers of the Old World could not hope to restrain or impede the giant's progress. Senator Lewis Cass of Michigan hence could remark in 1852 that American power should make itself felt in Europe. The nation, Cass urged, must not remain a "political cipher." The world must know that there are "twenty-five millions of people looking across the ocean at Europe, strong in power, acquainted with their rights, and determined to enforce them."

Americans, filled with such feelings of national importance, could not have been expected to look with indifference upon the suppression of youthful nations in Europe. Thus when the emperor of Austria, with the help of his fellow monarch the tsar of Russia, suppressed young Hungary in 1849 there was an almost national urge in the United States to do something. Daniel Webster, then secretary of state, found occasion in 1850 to insult Austria through the Austrian chargé in the United States, an unfortunate man named Huelsemann. The Huelsemann Note, as it thereafter was known, informed the Austrians that the events in Hungary "appeared to have their origin in those great ideas of responsible and popular governments on which the American constitutions themselves are founded. . . . The power of this republic, at the present moment, is spread over a region, one of the richest and most fertile on the globe, and of an extent in comparison with which the possessions of the House of Habsburg are but as a patch on the earth's surface." As to possible retaliation, "the government and people of the United States are quite willing to take their chances and abide their destiny." This, of course, was a preposterous note from a fresh young republic such as the United States to one of the most ancient monarchies of Europe. It was all the more extraordinary because the Hungarian revolution was, in a very real sense, none of the United States's business. The Imperial Austrian Government must have been incensed at Webster's brash and gratuitous lecture.

The most impressive demonstration of American solidarity with the cause of the defeated Hungarians came when the Hungarian leader Lajos Kossuth visited the United States in 1851–1852. The entire country feted this European revolutionary. Memorable were the demonstrations of affection in the American West. The Middle West —the West, as it was then—received Kossuth with open arms. His progress through Ohio in 1852, between Columbus and Cincinnati, marked the largest popular demonstration ever seen in that region. Perhaps 100,000 people lined the railroad tracks, and when Kossuth arrived in Cincinnati the shouts that went up from the mighty throng may have reached the throne of Francis Joseph himself. The exiled Hungarian leader, engaged in collecting donations, told the Ohio legislature in a special session that he and the state of Ohio were the same age, that Ohio had been admitted into the union in 1803, the year of his birth. Thus, he said, his heart had always throbbed with excitement at the name "Ohio." "It was like as if something of supreme importance lay hidden in that name for me to which my future was bounded by the very year of my nativity. This day my anticipations are realized."

Kossuth gradually discovered that American sympathies did not extend to the point of large cash donations, nor farther than verbal diplomatic support, and he returned crestfallen to Europe. Still, he had found a warm welcome in the United States. The defeated European revolutionaries of 1848 found that the United States was friendly and sympathetic to their national aspirations. In England in 1854 the American minister, James Buchanan, played host at the legation one night to a gala dinner party of a dozen or so expatriate revolutionaries, including Kossuth, Herzen, and Mazzini. To an American friend Buchanan afterward asked, "Weren't you afraid they would blow you up?" The friend was not afraid. It seemed natural that youthful America should sponsor the revolutionaries of other young nations.

So much for young America versus old Europe in the decade of the 1850's. How did this boisterous era in American history affect the Western Hemisphere? The idea of young America brought a burst of diplomatic activity in Central America and the Caribbean. Interest of the United States in Central America had appeared before the mid-nineteenth century, but with the annexation of California, the gold rush of 1849, and the popularity of the idea of manifest destiny, Central America and the Caribbean became highly important in the diplomacy of the United States.

The first move, the Clayton-Bulwer Treaty, concerned the isthmus of Panama. The then secretary of state of the United States, John M. Clayton, concluded it on April 19, 1850 with the British minister in Washington, Henry Lytton Bulwer—brother of the author of *The Last Days of Pompeii*. The treaty stipulated that neither Britain nor the United States would ever "obtain or maintain for itself any exclusive control" over a canal across the isthmus, and that "neither will ever erect or maintain any fortifications commanding the same, or in the vicinity thereof, or occupy, or fortify, or colonize, or assume, or exercise any dominion over Nicaragua, Costa Rica, the Mosquito Coast [the coast of present-day Nicaragua and Honduras], or any part of Central America." In an accompanying statement the British plenipotentiary announced that Her Majesty, Queen Victoria, "does not understand the engagements . . . to apply to Her Majesty's settlement at Honduras or to its Dependencies." This was to reserve British rights to an area which at about this time had become a crown colony. The Clayton-Bulwer Treaty had no immediate effect upon American history, and did not become important until fifty years later. It is worth mention at this point because it reflected the new continental interests of the United States and because it gave the appearance, no matter how insecure legally, of a national interest in the area of the Caribbean and Central America.

The American government meanwhile was making a strenuous diplomatic effort to purchase Cuba. American government leaders had long shown interest in Cuba, and the Cuban historian Herminio Portell-Vilá has compiled a list showing that every president from Jefferson to McKinley, excepting only Lincoln, who was too busy with the Civil War, coveted the Pearl of the Antilles. Jefferson had shown interest in Cuba, and John Quincy Adams, that soul of rectitude, had remarked in a memorable instruction to the United States minister in Spain that "the annexation of Cuba to our federal republic will be indispensable to the continuance and integrity of the Union itself." Polk in 1848 tried to open negotiations for purchase of Cuba, and instructed the American minister to Spain to offer as much as $100,000,000. This was a considerable price, for Polk in 1845 had been willing to give Mexico only between $25,000,000 and $40,-000,000 for the boundary of the Rio Grande, together with New Mexico and California.

In 1854, during the administration of President Franklin Pierce, Secretary of State Marcy directed the American minister in Madrid, Pierre Soulé, to try to get Cuba for $130,000,000. This diplomatic effort is worth examination in some detail. The secretary had informed Soulé that if the American overture met refusal, Soulé should bend his efforts to make Cuba independent. By this he meant that the minister should use good offices and the arts of gentle persuasion to make the Spanish see that Cuba should be independent. The secretary forgot what sort of minister he was addressing in Madrid. Pierre

Soulé was a typical American shirt-sleeves diplomat of the sort that so often obtained foreign posts of importance in the nineteenth century. A politician who had antagonized some of his fellow politicos in his native Louisiana, he was packed off to Spain in the hope that there he would be safely out of the way. Soulé at once embroiled himself with the Spanish. First he fought a duel with the French ambassador at Madrid. Next he presented the Madrid government an unauthorized ultimatum in the affair of the *Black Warrior*, an American ship that the Spanish authorities had detained in Cuba. Soulé gave the Spanish foreign office forty-eight hours to make amends for the seizure, without which he would demand his passports and leave. The Spaniards took him at his word and he left. Not content with this melodrama, he repaired to Belgium—he could not stay in France—and there on October 18, 1854 with his colleagues from London and Paris, James Buchanan and John Y. Mason, drew up a report on the Cuban question which became known, although it was signed in Aix-la-Chapelle, as the Ostend Manifesto.

Sent to Marcy as a private document, the Manifesto's contents leaked out, and Congress in March 1855 published the dispatch. The administration had to repudiate the pronouncement of its three principal European diplomats, although it added luster to Buchanan's personal reputation and helped him win election to the presidency in 1856. The American diplomats had bluntly said in their Ostend Manifesto that "self-preservation is the first law of nature, with states as well as with individuals." This was no original idea. From there, however, they proceeded to a question: "does Cuba, in the possession of Spain, seriously endanger our internal peace and the existence of our cherished Union?" Should this question be "answered in the affirmative," said Messrs. Buchanan, Soulé, and Mason, "then, by every law, human and divine, we shall be justified in wresting it from Spain . . . upon the very same principle that would justify an individual in tearing down the burning house of his neighbor if there were no other means of preventing the flames from destroying his own home." The flames—and here was the rather shocking reasoning behind the Manifesto—were the possibility that the revolt going on in Cuba would come under the control of Cuban Negroes, that Cuba would be "Africanized and become a second St. Domingo, with all its attendant horrors to the white race, and suffer the flames to extend to our own neighboring shores, seriously to endanger or actually to consume the fair fabric of our Union." The diplomats in Europe, whether through conviction or a sense of political expediency or both, were appealing to the proslavery American South, which had just taken alarm over the Kansas-Nebraska Act of 1854 and was beginning to pursue tactics that were to lead to the Civil War. As had happened before, and would again, American diplomacy had become the plaything of domestic politics.

The Ostend Manifesto was, to be sure, a sensational expression of manifest destiny, but other such evidences of America's bumptiousness and territorial cupidity were not lacking in the mid-nineteenth-century. There were notably the filibustering exploits—the freebooting adventures, organized from the United States, against governments with which the American government was at peace—of Narciso López in Cuba and William Walker in Nicaragua and the filibustering plans (they never reached the stage of exploits) of George W. L. Bickley for Mexico. The decade of the 1850's, especially the early 1850's, was the heyday of filibustering in the Caribbean and Central America, and such exploits were intrinsic to the idea of young America. Contrary to belief then and later, this mid-century filibustering was not in its beginnings the scheming of slavery supporters in the southern United States, though it became more so by the end of the decade. The two principal freebooters of the era, Narciso López in Cuba and William Walker in Nicaragua, were moved by desire for adventure and personal power rather than by missionary zeal to propagate slavery. George W. L. Bickley was interested as much in adventure and the promotion of a secret fraternal order as in the spread of slavery. In the American North it was usually believed that filibustering was part of a Southern slave plot, that the expansion of slavery, having failed with Trist's treaty in 1848, was being secretly furthered through encouragement of expeditions into the weakly governed states of Central America and the Caribbean. The fact that many of the men who gathered around López and Walker were Southerners was largely the result of geography, for it was convenient to recruit men from the nearby American South. The filibustering of the 1850's was a personal matter, and such support as it received in the United States came from feelings of manifest destiny rather than desire to expand the institution of Negro slavery.

Narciso López, a native of Venezuela, counting on support from American citizens, attempted three expeditions to Cuba (1849, 1850,

1851) to free Cuba from Spanish rule. If successful, he presumably would have arranged the subsequent annexation of Cuba by the United States. López acted with the support of Southern slaveholders, and the institution of slavery beyond question would have continued had he been able to expel the Spanish. Still, as was mentioned, it was love of adventure rather than proslavery notions that moved him in his attempts to revolutionize Cuba. On the first attempt in 1849 he failed to get away from New York, where federal authorities detained him. The following year he did make it to Cuba but found the natives uninterested in liberation, and he barely got back to Key West ahead of a pursuing Spanish warship. The 1851 effort was disastrous, for the Spanish caught López and his men, executed the Venezuelan general and fifty of his followers, and gave the others long penal terms. In retaliation a mob sacked the Spanish consulate in New Orleans, and in further retaliation a mob in Madrid attempted to sack the American legation. Eventually the affair died down with President Millard Fillmore's secretary of state, Webster, acknowledging his country's error in permitting the filibustering expeditions. The Spanish pardoned the American survivors of the third López foray, and Congress voted $25,000 compensation to Spain for damage done the Spanish consulate by the New Orleans mob. Parenthetically one might note that during this episode of filibustering by López the five-barred flag with a single star which two generations later became the flag of the Republic of Cuba first appeared, hanging in New York City from a staff above the offices of the New York *Sun*.

William Walker was a more interesting character than López, and in his activities he was for a while more successful. Short, slight of build, and shy, he had gone to California to work on a newspaper, only to desert that prosaic calling for adventure in Nicaragua in the late 1850's. His efforts there would have come to naught had it not been for the existence of the Accessory Transit Company, an American-owned organization whose business it was to convey across Nicaragua travelers to and from California. The Transit Company had facilitated the travel of tens of thousands of Americans. Passengers from New York and New Orleans landed at Greytown, proceeded in boats of light draft up the San Juan River to Lake Nicaragua, crossed the lake in steamers to a point on the west shore called Virgin Bay, and from there were conveyed in carriages over a macadamized road to San Juan del Sur and the steamer for San

Francisco. It was like a picnic excursion, and a far cry from the disease-ridden and longer route across the Isthmus of Panama.

As the income from this route became lucrative in the 1850's, the Transit Company sought to protect itself from the volcanic animosities of Nicaraguan politics and employed Walker to keep the tiny republic in order. This was no difficult job, and Walker inaugurated himself president of Nicaragua. A faction of the Transit Company conspired with El Presidente Walker to cancel the company's charter and issue a new charter to themselves. Commodore Cornelius Vanderbilt, part owner of the company, found himself tricked and outwitted by Walker and the conniving faction. He therefore sent his own agent to the scene, who started a liberation movement of the Nicaraguans via neighboring Costa Rica. After a sanguinary campaign, directed by opposing groups of American capitalists, Walker was deposed, although in the general confusion of this so-called revolution of 1857 Nicaragua really lost out, for American interest in isthmian transit thereafter focused on Panama rather than Nicaragua and the latter country was obliged to turn to the cultivation of cotton, coffee, and bananas. Walker made two attempts to regain power in Nicaragua. On the first occasion in November 1857 he failed. On the second, in 1860, a British captain arrested him on the coast of Honduras and handed him over to unfriendly Nicaraguans, who shot him.

Last of the American filibusters was General George W. L. Bickley, President General of the American Legion, KGC. The "KGC" stood for Knights of the Golden Circle. A doctor of medicine in Cincinnati, Bickley in the late 1850's conceived the idea of a grand secret lodge that would advance American manifest destiny into the regions south of the Texas border. He organized his lodges throughout the South, and began to prepare for possible military expeditions to Mexico. The president general was a suitable man for the task, being "a tall, fine looking, middle-aged gentleman, having an uncommonly fine expression of countenance, and a high intellectual forehead." He was disturbed by that "crookedest of all boundary lines, the Rio Grande," and decided that he could do something about it. His purposes he smoothed over with a frosting of morality, although it was common knowledge that Mexico was his goal. No matter that, as a Richmond newspaper remarked in 1860, it was difficult to elevate the morals of our neighbors by stealing their country. Bickley's imagination foresaw "energetic Anglo-Saxons" settled in Mexico, who would proceed with the "Texasizing" of that country, that is, annexing it to the United States as slave territory. To proslavery Americans of the late 1850's Bickley held out the prospect of dividing Mexico into twenty-five slave states. Fifty new slavery senators in Washington! The prospect was as impossible as it was alluring, for slavery could not easily flourish in the arid reaches of Mexico, a country devoid of both cotton lands and adequate facilities for transportation. Eventually "that arrant knave and unmitigated humbug, 'General' Bickley" met with failure, for his movement suddenly found itself overshadowed in 1860–1861 by the North-South slavery controversy which led to the Civil War. Perhaps, if this larger issue had not intervened, General Bickley would have become as famous as General Sam Houston twenty-five years before.

Thus passed a decade of expansive projects, and the Civil War came upon the expansionists before they knew what had happened.

2. *The Civil War—Relations with Great Britain*

The diplomacy of the United States—the diplomacy of the Union, as the federal government soon was called—was in a perilous state at the beginning of the Civil War. The North had few friends among the European governments in 1861. Most of the governments of Europe, disliking republican institutions, were glad when in 1861 the American republic divided into two warring parts. Europeans had watched the Americans move with the current of manifest destiny during the 1840's and 1850's, and at the outset of this expansive period the swift advance of the American government across the continent led to some considerable worry, for the United States might in time become the rival of Europe. But during the 1850's the accretions in pursuit of manifest destiny were small: only the purchase of a rectangular strip of desert territory about 45,000 square miles in extent in the Mesilla Valley south of the Gila River, the Gadsden Purchase of December 30, 1853, to facilitate a transcontinental railroad across the Southern states to the Pacific. The filibustering in Nicaragua and Cuba, the talk of Mexico, all came to nothing. European nations were not impressed. And then came the beginning of the Civil War, opening in earnest with the first battle of Bull Run fought outside Washington in July 1861—a chaotic rout so obvious that it could not be hidden, a debacle in which 30,000 raw Union soldiers ran for miles to get away from the avenging Confederates and abandoned most of their equipment en route. In midsummer 1861 Union diplomacy stood at its lowest point.

It might well have seemed at the beginning of the Civil War that there was no hope for the Union, and there would have been none if two of the most talented individuals in American history had not headed the government of the United States. American diplomacy during the war engaged the talents of two illustrious men, President Abraham Lincoln and his secretary of state, William H. Seward. As Henry Adams remembered him, Seward was a "slouching, slender figure" with "a head like a wise macaw; a beaked nose; shaggy eyebrows; unorderly hair and clothes; hoarse voice; offhand manner; free talk, and perpetual cigar." The secretary of state was not, one should add, the wisest of men: witness his April Fool's Day proposition of 1861 to Lincoln, urging the president to give him the reins of office so that he could then save the Union by starting a foreign war with France or Spain! At such points as this in the conduct of America's Civil War diplomacy, Lincoln intervened and kept affairs in balance. The president on more than one occasion had to cut off the projects and limit the activities of his secretary of state. Lincoln's contribution to American diplomacy during the Civil War was a wonderful touch of wisdom, the sure touch of the born leader of men, which enabled the brilliant but effervescent Seward to conduct diplomacy with such deftness that, as a result, Seward would go down in history as one of the greatest of American secretaries of state. Somehow Lincoln was able to reach out at the crucial moments and restrain Seward, all the while carrying on the task of organizing and prosecuting a war against six million rebellious Americans.

Britain was the chief object of this Seward-Lincoln diplomacy— the crucial diplomatic need of the Union during the Civil War was the neutrality of Great Britain. The British government at the beginning of the war was delighted that the Americans were in trouble. Upperclass Britishers had always disliked the American experiment in democracy, and predicted year after year that it would degenerate into anarchy and chaos, as democracies had done before. All the doctrines of political economy and public philosophy taught that republics could exist only in a limited territory, and that the larger a republic's expanse the weaker became its hold over its citizens. The Mexican War offered the spectacle of the American glutton eating itself to death. The denouement of 1861 proved the wisdom of history. A distinguished English historian, Edward A. Freeman, published in 1863 the first volume of a work entitled *History of Federal Government, from the Foundation of the Achaian League to the Disruption of the United States.* That Freeman would never conclude his second volume was not apparent at the time the initial tome appeared.

The danger of an unfriendly British action against the Union was for a while the chief foreign concern of the Lincoln administration. The British government, most powerful in all the world, could have broken the North's blockade of Southern ports in 1861 and so reinforced the South that a Northern victory would have been impossible. In South America in 1828 Britain had sponsored the dissolution of Brazil into Brazil and Uruguay under a policy of *divide et impera.* Why not do the same with the United States? The British prime minister in 1861, Lord Palmerston, according to the later recollection of William E. Gladstone "desired the severance as a diminution of a dangerous power," but—Gladstone added—Palmerston in 1861 was uncertain of the outcome in America and "prudently held his tongue." Still, to the wondering Union diplomats in the first year of the Civil War the position of Great Britain was a huge question mark. When the new American minister to London, Charles Francis Adams, set foot on British shores in May 1861, it was to learn that the London government had just recognized the belligerency of the South. Adams's young son Henry thought his father's mission hopeless. He saw no friendship for the North in Great Britain, and believed that the Adamses, venturing to London, were like "a family of early Christian martyrs about to be flung into an arena of lions, under the glad eyes of Tiberius Palmerston."

Whatever the odds against the Union cause in 1861, one thing was certain: the wisdom of the appointment to London of Charles Francis Adams. This was a stroke of genius on Seward's part. There could have been no better choice for the difficult work in London than Charles Francis Adams. Son of John Quincy Adams, grandson of John Adams, third Adams to hold appointment by his country to the Court of St. James, C. F. Adams had been brought up in an English public school and thoroughly understood the proprieties of English society. Unlike the Confederate commissioner to England, James M. Mason (not to be confused with the John Y. Mason of Ostend Manifesto fame), who while listening to the House of Commons debates would spit tobacco juice over the carpet in front of him, Adams knew perfectly how to behave. When he faced the British foreign secretary of the day, Earl Russell, it was as one noble lord speaking to another. Russell resembled no one so much as Adams's own father, John Quincy Adams. Adams and Russell were both small, funereal men, and their meetings and epistolary exchanges were conducted with such icy propriety that there soon emerged something close to mutual understanding if not appreciation.

But there was more to the diplomatic situation in England than mere personal relations, and more than upper-class dislike of the Union. The economic ties of England to the Confederacy were the principal hope of Confederate leaders and diplomats. They felt certain that England's need for Southern cotton would drive Britishers to support the South, even to the extent of opening the blockade. Cotton was king, so Southerners believed, and their diplomacy in Great Britain need only be a kind of cotton diplomacy. *King Cotton Diplomacy*—so the twentieth-century historian Frank L. Owsley would entitle his history of Southern diplomacy during the Civil War. One-fifth of the population of England in 1861 lived, directly or indirectly, from the production of cotton products. The overwhelming bulk of British supplies of cotton came from the American South. Beginning with the year 1850 there had been a tremendous increase of cotton production in the Southern states. In the years 1849–1851 something over a million bales of American cotton had been exported annually to Great Britain. By the years 1858–1860 nearly two million bales went to Britain each year. This quantity was only four hundred thousand bales short of all British cotton imports in the same years. King Cotton Diplomacy, so it appeared in 1861, would almost without effort prove successful in ensuring Southern independence, especially when the British ruling classes were already prejudiced in favor of the aristocratic South.

It was perhaps the crowning misfortune of the South during the Civil War that cotton proved, by a quirk of fate, a poor diplomat. One may even venture the observation that the failure of King Cotton Diplomacy rang the knell of Southern hopes more certainly than did the South's defeat on the field of battle. The South had some chance of independence if it could gain support abroad. It had little chance, in view of the superior economic resources of the Northern states, if diplomatic support were for some reason denied. What happened, curiously, was that the opening of the Civil War found the Southern cotton crop of 1860 almost entirely exported. Moreover, a surplus both of raw cotton and of manufactured cotton goods had accumulated in Britain; the mill operators in Lancaster were delighted to find an excuse to close down their mills and wait for a rise in price of their warehoused cotton and cloth. The operators had already been closing mills prior to the beginning of the war in America, and the guns at Sumter gave them a golden opportunity for profit. If the Southern leaders in Richmond, planning a triumph over the North with what they supposed was the irresistible logic of King Cotton Diplomacy, had realized the weakness of cotton as a diplomatic bargaining device in England, they might have been dissuaded from seeking Southern independence. The cotton famine in England which they planned for 1861 or, at the latest, 1862, came in the winter of 1862–1863, and before Southern diplomacy had been able to exploit the famine the North won the battles of Vicksburg and Gettysburg and the fate of the South was sealed.

One should mention the Northern belief during the war that by wheat, rather than arms, Northern diplomacy had triumphed—that Northern exports of wheat to England during the years 1860–1863, years of poor European crops, had tied Britain to the Northern cause as effectively as Southerners had dreamed would be the case with cotton. According to a contemporary jingle,

> Old King Cotton is dead and buried,
> Brave young Corn is King.

Exports of wheat to Britain increased greatly in 1861–1863, and by the latter year the embarrassments both of Northern diplomacy and Britain's need for Northern grain nicely disappeared together. Whether the need of Britain for grain was so great as to attach that nation to the Northern cause must be a matter of doubt. Doubtless it helped relations between the two countries. Perhaps Britishers thought that they were more dependent on Northern grain than they actually were, and in such case the thought would have been equivalent, in diplomatic effect, to actuality. The grain crisis of 1860–1863 was general in Europe, and the usual sources of British supply during lean harvests, the Baltic and Balkan countries, were exporting their surpluses to Western Europe, leaving Britain no recourse but to turn to America. Grain imports may have had some diplomatic effect.

But to turn now to the specific diplomatic events of the war. In the early years of the Civil War there came two crises, the *Trent* affair and the dispute over the Laird rams.

3. *The Trent Affair and the Case of the Laird Rams*

The affair of the steamer *Trent* was the more serious. The British government had recognized Southern belligerency in May 1861, a move that followed naturally from Lincoln's proclamation of a blockade of Southern ports, and the danger was that (1) recognition of belligerency might change into (2) recognition of Southern independence and (3) destruction of the blockade. The *Trent* affair raised British tempers near to a point of explosion in the winter of 1861–1862 and threatened to force the London government to take the second and third steps mentioned above. Henry Adams in London telegraphed his father frantically—Charles Francis Adams was visiting in the country—when the legation learned that Captain Charles Wilkes of the United States navy on November 8, 1861 had forcibly removed two Confederate commissioners from the British mail steamer *Trent*, then passing through the Caribbean, and taken the commissioners to Boston where federal authorities had imprisoned them. Kidnaping of nationals from the vessels of a neutral had been a favorite practice of Great Britain for decades, and had been a factor in bringing on the War of 1812. But by 1861–1862 the views of the British had changed as a result of the nearly fifty years of relative peace after the Napoleonic wars. Humanitarian sympathies enlisted during the Crimean War of 1854–1856 had brought the Declaration of Paris of 1856, wherein Britain accepted a number of small-navy principles of naval warfare and neutrality. By the time of Captain Wilkes's action with the *Trent* the British government had turned turtle its ideas about impressment, and was willing to challenge anything resembling impressment.

Captain Wilkes, it is true, had not taken off the two Confederate commissioners as an act of impressment. After consulting hastily some law books in his cabin he had reasoned to himself that the two Confederates, Mason and Slidell—the latter the same man who had gone to Mexico for President Polk in 1846—were embodied dispatches from a belligerent power, or else rebellious citizens of the United States, and in either case removable from the *Trent*. Wilkes should have taken the steamer into port, for it was carrying Southern diplomatic dispatches to Europe, but such a course although technically correct would have wrought even stronger feeling in Britain than occurred when Wilkes removed only the Southern commissioners.

The impressment of Mason and Slidell, or the seizure of these two rebellious citizens, or embodied dispatches, was in its details a comic-opera affair, and anyone who recalls the manner in which this Caribbean contretemps occurred must wonder what had happened to the American and British senses of humor. People in 1861 should have laughed at the *Trent* affair rather than become angry. Captain Wilkes had insisted, prior to the capture, in firing two shots across the bow of the British steamer, and this began the comic tragedy. He then sent on board the *Trent* his representative, Lieutenant D. M. Fairfax, who asked for Mason and Slidell. A British naval commander, at the moment a passenger on the ship, thereupon appeared in full uniform and made a long speech to the effect that "In this ship I am the representative of her majesty's government, and I call upon the officers of the ship and passengers generally to mark my words, when, in the name of the British government, and in distinct language, I denounce this as an illegal act . . ." Fairfax ignored the speech and asked once more for the two Southern envoys. Mrs. Slidell expressed surprise that Captain Wilkes would wish to take off the two eminent passengers, thus arousing England. Mr. Mason suggested to Mrs. Slidell that she keep quiet. The two Southern diplomats refused to go peaceably, and a boatload of marines was summoned from the American ship, the *San Jacinto*. Messrs. Mason and Slidell repaired to their respective cabins and arranged their luggage but still insisted that force would be necessary to move them. Lieutenant Fairfax said to his men, "Gentlemen, lay your hands upon Mr. Mason." They did so, seizing him by the shoulders and the coat-collar. The problem then became Mr. Slidell, who insisted that considerable force would be necessary to remove him. He attempted to jump out of a window, perhaps to escape, but two officers seized him and conveyed him to the boat with Mason. Meanwhile had occurred an incident with Miss Slidell, the Confederate diplomat's fair young daughter, aged perhaps seventeen. Some accounts have it that she screamed and slapped Lieutenant Fairfax in the face, but apparently nothing more happened than that, as she was confronting Fairfax, the ship rolled slightly and she involuntarily touched the lieutenant's shoulder. The entire party soon was transferred to the *San Jacinto*, and taken north to Fort Warren in Boston harbor. During the voyage the prisoners were treated to every courtesy. Captain Wilkes gave up his cabin to his guests and they dined at his table.

But upon Wilkes's arrival in the United States the trouble began. The captain was treated to an enthusiastic public demonstration by his fellow countrymen. The tumultuous nature of his welcome, the laurels which came his way for his exploit, were so numerous and sincere and heartfelt that the Lincoln administration in Washington was faced with a grave situation, in terms of coming to agreement with Great Britain over the capture. The American public, having heard for months about Northern military defeats, became almost hysterical at the capture of Mason and Slidell, and in the height of this enthusiasm it was extremely difficult for Seward and Lincoln to back down in any diplomatic dealings with England over the matter. Congress voted Wilkes a gold medal, Secretary of the Navy Gideon Welles commended and promoted him, Governor Andrews of Massachusetts at a banquet tendered Wilkes in Boston on November 26 called Wilkes's action "one of the most illustrious services that had made the war memorable," and added "that there might be nothing left [in the episode] to crown the exultation of the American heart, Commodore Wilkes fired his shot across the bows of the ship that bore the British lion at its head." The *New York Times* was certain that Great Britain "will applaud the gallant act of Lieut. Wilkes, so full of spirit and good sense, and such an exact imitation of the policy she has always stoutly defended and invariable pursued . . . as for Commodore Wilkes and his command, let the handsome thing be done, consecrate another *Fourth* of July to him. Load him down with services of plate and swords of the cunningest and costliest art. Let us encourage the happy inspiration that achieved such a victory." Fortunately the Atlantic cable which Cyrus Field had laid in 1858 had gone dead soon thereafter, and by 1861 there was no instantaneous communication with England. Had there been, a war might have followed between the two English-speaking nations, Britain and America—for the British, once they heard the news late in November 1861 of Wilkes's "victory," were as incensed as Americans were pleased. An American long resident in London wrote to Seward on November 29, 1861 that "There never was within memory such a burst of feeling as has been created by the news of the boarding of [the *Trent*]. The people are frantic with rage, and were the country polled, I fear 999 men out of a thousand would declare for immediate war. Lord Palmerston cannot resist the impulse if he would."

The first impulse of the British government was to prepare for war, and on November 30 orders went out to hold the British fleet in readiness, to begin preparations for sending troops to Canada, and initiate munitions and supply activities. But the more the British government considered the matter the less certain it became that war was the proper course. For one thing there was the embarrassment of Canada. The British minister in Washington, Lord Lyons, wrote to Russell on December 3, 1861 that "Mr. Galt, Canadian Minister, is here. He has frightened me by his account of the defencelessness of the Province at this moment." Russell himself perused Alison's book on the War of 1812 and came to a startling conclusion: he wrote to Palmerston on December 11 that although the American army for invasion of Canada in 1812 had numbered but 2,500 men, "We may now expect 40 or 50,000." A few days later he informed the prime minister that "Lyons gives a sad account of Canada."

Another factor in effecting a peaceful solution of the dispute was the pacific feeling of Queen Victoria's consort, Prince Albert, who as the queen's private secretary and confidential adviser softened a note that Russell had been ready to send to Washington. The foreign secretary apparently had been ready to send an ultimatum, but Prince Albert toned down the note so that it only empowered the British minister in Washington, Lyons, to make an inquiry and ask for reparation. In the *Trent* affair the prince regent engaged in the last official act of his career. When he was reading the papers of the case he was already without appetite, "very wretched," could eat no breakfast, and soon died, on December 14, 1861. His death plunged the nation into mourning, and the enforced period of devotion was not without its soothing effect on Anglo-American relations. The misfortune of the royal house became the fortune of the American government. Queen Victoria ever afterward harbored friendly feelings for the United States, for had not the beloved prince recommended moderation toward the Americans as his last official act in this world?

After public opinion had had its day and the incident of the *Trent* began to lose its immediacy, the diplomats on both sides of the Atlantic set to work and settled the affair amicably. The Lincoln cabinet met on Christmas day 1861 and was unable to arrive at a solution, but a further meeting the next day made possible the release of the Confederate commissioners, who went harmlessly off to Europe. The crisis was over, and the astonished son of Minister Adams found that "the *Trent* Affair passed like a snowstorm, leaving the Legation, to its surprise, still in place."

As a kind of aftermath to the case of the *Trent*, 11,000 British troops were sent to Canada after the *Trent* affair had blown over. Their arrival served to accentuate rather than relieve the hostage-like geographical position of Canada next to the United States. Arrival of the troops gave Seward a chance to play on the English what Lord Lyons described disgustedly as a trick. A private company in Montreal asked the secretary of state's permission to land some officers' baggage at Portland and transport it across Maine—the St. Lawrence River was then full of ice—and this gave Seward his chance to offer to the British all facilities for landing and transporting to Canada or elsewhere their troops, stores, and munitions of war.

It thus appeared that the Americans had the last word in the famous *Trent* affair.

As for the second crisis in British-American relations—the crisis of the Laird rams—this controversy arose in September 1863 over construction by the British shipbuilding firm of William Laird and Sons of some new-style ironclad rams for the Confederate government. The destination of these vessels was thinly disguised by consigning them to the private Paris firm of Bravay and Company. The rams were being built for M. Bravay, who supposedly had bought them for His Serene Highness the Pasha of Egypt. To deceive the unwary the vessels received fine-sounding Eastern names, *El Tousson* and *El Monassir*. Still, what M. Bravay would do with two such vessels was cynically plain: he would sell them to the Confederacy. The task of Minister Adams in London was to stop the sailing of these vessels. Adams had been unable to halt the *Alabama* in 1862 and several other Confederate vessels had gotten to sea despite the vigilance of American consuls in British shipbuilding ports. He determined to stop the rams, for if they escaped they might break the Northern blockade.

What were these so-called naval rams that dominated Anglo-American diplomacy in the year 1863? The construction of these vessels was interesting, for their design signalized the revolution in naval warfare which had begun some few years before the Civil War and already had made obsolete all the wooden navies of the world. Of this revolution, more in another chapter. The Laird rams were revolutionary enough in design to have destroyed the Union blockade of the South, had they gotten to sea and arrived off the American coast. By present-day standards they were tiny ships, perhaps the size of a destroyer, about 1,500 tons displacement, but they were armored with four and a half inches of iron plate and each was equipped with a formidable wrought-iron "piercer" at the prow, about seven feet in length. This piercer gave to the ships the name of rams, and the idea was that the piercer, three feet under the surface of the water, could be rammed into the wooden blockade ships of the Northern navy and sink them. The Laird vessels, being ironclad, would be impervious to shot and shell while they made the run into a Northern sailing vessel. The idea was ingenious and had some short-term value, though the continuing revolution in ship design soon made the rams obsolete. After the Civil War, Charles Francis Adams in 1867 watched the great naval review at Portsmouth, where one of the two Laird rams (by this time they had been bought by the British navy) was pointed out to him. He afterward wrote that "as I looked on the little mean thing, I could not help a doubt whether she was really worthy of all the anxiety she had cost us."

Still, at the time, in 1863, Adams and other individuals believed that their escape from England might well decide the course of the war. The chief Confederate naval agent in England, James D. Bulloch, wrote on July 9, 1863 to the South's secretary of the navy, Stephen R. Mallory, that "our vessels might sail southward, sweep the blockading fleet from the sea front of every harbor . . . , and cruising up and down the coast could prevent anything like permanent, systematic interruption of our foreign trade in the future." And if the rams had opened the South's trade, if cotton again had entered English ports in large quantity, the South would have gained much-needed foreign exchange with which to buy military supplies in Europe. Then, equipped from abroad, the Confederate armies in Virginia and elsewhere could take the offensive in earnest, whip the Northerners, and, perhaps, end the Civil War.

What to do about the Laird rams was Minister Adams's most pressing diplomatic problem in 1863. The British government through

Earl Russell had announced to the American government in April of that year that it would allow no more vessels to be constructed in British ports for sale to the Confederates. Adams was uncertain how far British intentions would be accompanied by actions, for the famous *Alabama* had escaped when the queen's advocate through an understandable but unfortunate coincidence had gone insane at the time that the *Alabama* papers were on his desk. There eventually followed an altogether unnecessary crisis. On September 3, 1863 Earl Russell wrote to Palmerston that he was seizing the rams as a matter of public policy, if not of law. On September 4 he wrote to Minister Adams that the question was under "serious and anxious consideration." The latter, having not yet received Russell's note (it arrived in the afternoon of September 5), on the morning of September 5 sent off a note to Russell containing the blunt phrase, "It would be superfluous in me to point out to your lordship that this [the escape of the rams] is war." On September 8 a note from Russell reached Adams that the government had detained the rams, which then were bought by the Royal Navy.

Russell's diplomacy during the rams affair, as we now see, was something less than skillful. If there were any blame for the diplomatic crisis of September 1863 it was his. The foreign secretary should have realized early in the Laird rams affair that the Foreign Enlistment Act of 1819 under which the British government sought to maintain its neutrality during the American Civil War was utterly inadequate for the situation of 1861–1865. It had a loophole which permitted vessels to be constructed so long as they were not armed. It made no provision for seizing vessels on suspicion of unneutral destination. Having realized these inadequacies of the act, Russell might have persuaded his chief Lord Palmerston to obtain from Parliament an adequate neutrality act, or else announced clearly and unequivocally and often to the worried American minister that as a matter of policy the government would not allow the Laird rams to put to sea and obtain armament in some remote West India island as had other Confederate raiders constructed in England. Having allowed the *Alabama* to put to sea—which resulted later in a most expensive arbitration with the American government—Russell's diplomacy, fumbling the Laird case, was less than successful. Worse yet, so Henry Adams concluded, the foreign secretary "had put himself in the position of appearing to yield only to a threat of war."

But the crisis passed, as had the *Trent* affair before it, and this was all that really mattered. The South had no opportunity to gain recognition from the British government. The blockade of Southern ports tightened each year that the war continued, without the slightest effort by Great Britain to intervene. The shadow of defeat fell over the Confederacy as the South failed to defend its manifest destiny at home and abroad.

One other factor—namely, Negro slavery—made difficult the work of Southern supporters in England. The British people in the early nineteenth century had led a world campaign to abolish slavery, their diplomats had sought to commit all the powers of Europe against slavery and the slave trade, and it was extremely difficult for the South to make its way diplomatically in Great Britain when Southern views on slavery were so well known. It was not possible to disguise the South's position on Negro slavery. Vice President Alexander Stephens of the Confederacy had said in 1861 that "Our new government is founded . . . its foundations are laid, its cornerstone rests, upon the great truth that the negro is not equal to the white man." When Lincoln announced after the battle of Antietam in 1862 his preliminary emancipation proclamation, his Southern opposite, Jefferson Davis, with incredible ineptitude seized the occasion to declare that on Washington's birthday, February 22, 1863 all free Negroes resident in the South would be enslaved, "they and their issue forever." The maladroit Davis continued: "The day is not distant when the old Union will be restored with slavery nationally declared to be the proper condition of all of African descent." Many of the great Victorians, it is true—Acton, Bulwer-Lytton, Charles Dickens, Matthew Arnold, Herbert Spencer, Charles Darwin—had ranged themselves on the side of the South at the beginning of the war. They liked the aristocratic traditions of the American South, and saw in them a reflection of their own upper-class English way of living. Still, it was difficult to keep them in support of slavery. The North during the Civil War had the advantage of a moral cause. Alfred Lord Tennyson, certainly one of the leaders of mid-Victorian society, admitted his sympathy for Southern culture and traditions but found that the "Battle Hymn of the Republic" haunted him. He discovered himself unwittingly humming the republican melody, and he wondered why the South had failed to produce such a glorious call to arms.

As for the middle classes and the workingmen of England, it proved impossible for the South to convert them to its cause, for they saw in the Union's fight for life nothing less than the cause of liberty itself. With the emancipation proclamation in effect after January 1, 1863, and supported by the blunders of his opponent in Richmond, Lincoln found that his diplomacy toward antislavery England was growing markedly easier. Escaped slaves, such as the former coachman of Jefferson Davis, were introduced at emancipation meetings. George Francis Train, a private American citizen living in Britain, did valiant work for the cause—resorting to such tricks as advertising a debate and "for want of speakers on the Southern side" appointing himself to defend the Confederacy. He would begin the South's defense by stating, "We in Secessia have based our Constitution and reared our Temple of Despotism on one acknowledged cornerstone—NEGRO SLAVERY." John Bright and Richard Cobden, the two prominent English reformers, sided with the North. The only real cause of the Civil War, Bright contended at emancipation gatherings, was slavery, slavery, slavery.

Thus went American diplomacy toward Great Britain during the Civil War. By the year 1865 and the end of the great war in the Western Hemisphere, American diplomacy had proved in every way successful. The government of the United States, having triumphed over an unprecedentedly large revolt by almost an entire section of the nation, found its prestige more than restored in Europe. When the Union survived with its territory undiminished there was extreme embarrassment among many British men of prominence. William E. Gladstone in 1862 had proclaimed—and not without thought, for he was sending up a trial balloon for Earl Russell who at the moment wished to recognize the Confederacy—that "Jefferson Davis and other leaders of the South have made an army; they are making, it appears, a navy; and they have made what is more than either,—they have made a nation. . . . We may anticipate with certainty the success of the Southern States so far as regards their separation from the North." This was the same Gladstone who later said that the American constitution was "the most remarkable work . . . to have been produced by the human intellect, at a single stroke, in its application to political affairs." In 1896, when the American nation had become a world power potentially far greater than England, Gladstone confessed his sin of 1862, "that incapacity which my mind so long retained, and perhaps still exhibits, an incapacity of viewing subjects all round."

Englishmen in such manner recanted their support of the South. By the spring of 1865 the international prestige of the government of the United States had been restored. Because of its championing of the antislavery cause, the Lincoln administration by the end of the war achieved popularity in England. When news of the president's assassination reached England in the spring of 1865 there was a near panic. One newspaper reported that not since Henry IV of France had been slain by Ravaillac had "the whole of Europe rung with excitement of so intense a character." The House of Commons adjourned. The House of Lords adjourned, an act which some said was unprecedented. Queen Victoria wrote a personal letter to Mrs. Lincoln comparing the president's untimely demise to that of her own lamented husband. The magazine of British humor, *Punch*, made one of the most famous apologies in British literary annals. *Punch*, like the *Times* of London, had filled hundreds of columns with sneeringly sarcastic comments about the Lincoln government and many of its sallies had been at the expense of the dead president himself. *Punch* apologized in the well-known lines,

> Between the mourners at his head and feet,
>   Say, scurril-jester, is there room for you?
>
> Yes, he had lived to shame me for my sneer,
>   To lame my pencil, and confute my pen—
> To make me own this hind of princes peer,
>   This rail-splitter a true-born king of men.

4. *Relations with France, Mexico, and Russia*

Anglo-American relations were admittedly of prime importance in the diplomacy of the Civil War, but they were not the only diplomatic relations of the time, nor always the most important, for Lincoln and Seward planned carefully their diplomacy in respect to several other nations: France, Mexico, and Russia. To Britain had gone the best of the American diplomats abroad in the 1860's, Charles Francis Adams. To Mexico in 1861 had gone a friend of Mexico and a former senator from Ohio, Thomas Corwin. To France went a deserving and capable political leader, William L. Dayton. Dayton's consul general was John Bigelow, second only to Adams in ability.

The Union men in France had two difficult individuals to watch. One was the emperor of the French, Napoleon III, who while ever willing to fish in the troubled American waters, took care to keep his feet dry. The other individual, more devious than Napoleon III, was the Confederate commissioner John Slidell, whose principal activity was to arrange a Confederate loan based on cotton futures, a promise of future delivery of cotton as basis for the loan. The project failed when news of Vicksburg and Gettysburg sent the price of Confederate bonds tumbling, and when Seward's financial trouble-shooter in Europe, Robert L. Walker, went to France for the express purpose of ruining Slidell's bond scheme. At crucial moments Walker offered to buy large blocks of Confederate bonds at extremely low prices, or else threw blocks of bonds on the market. The Confederate bond house, under control of a friend of Slidell, a banker named Emil Erlanger, found itself spending its funds buying out Walker to prevent a market collapse. When Walker left France, the Confederate banker, no longer able to bull the market, was helplessly watching the bonds fall to zero.

As for Lincoln's minister to Mexico, Tom Corwin, he was every bit as agile and discreet as the president's other leading diplomatic representatives, and American diplomacy maintained itself handsomely in Mexico. Corwin had been adamantly against the Mexican War, and after the Treaty of Guadalupe Hidalgo had written sarcastically to a friend that the treaty gave to the United States a third of Mexico immediately "with the implied understanding that the ballance [sic] is to be swallowed when our anglo-saxon gastric juices shall clamor for another Cannibal breakfast." By the time of the Civil War he could ably represent his country in the sovereign state of Mexico. He got along famously with the Mexicans after he persuaded Mexican espionage agents to open the mail of his Confederate rival, Colonel John Pickett. The Mexicans discovered to Corwin's delight that Pickett had been calling them "a race of degenerate monkeys . . . robbers, assassins, blackguards and lepers," and had been urging the South to conquer Mexico. Minister Corwin had no difficulty ingratiating himself with the government of Mexico, then headed by the full-blooded Indian Benito Juárez.

As for Russia, Lincoln's choice as minister in the early period of the Civil War was the colorful Cassius Marcellus Clay of Kentucky, before the president translated to that remote land his discredited secretary of war, the Pennsylvania spoilsman Simon Cameron. Clay had been one of the "fightingest" men in a fighting state. His political rivals once imported into Kentucky for the special purpose of ending Clay's career a man from New Orleans named Sam M. Brown, "hero of forty fights and never lost a battle." The fight began when Clay heckled Brown at a political meeting. Brown knocked Clay down with a club. Clay rose with bowie knife in hand. Brown shot Clay with a pistol at point-blank range. The shot struck the scabbard of Clay's knife which hung around his neck. Clay then worked Brown over with the bowie knife, cutting off an ear, skewering out an eye, and threw the hero of New Orleans over a wall into a pond of water. In Russia, naturally, Clay made a considerable impression. He carried a bowie knife on all occasions. For formal dress he wore an eighteen-inch blade with a pearl handle and an eagle on the haft. For street wear he preferred bone-handled knives. He was the despair of Russian gentlemen seeking duels. Never the challenger, Clay always had a choice of weapons, and out of a wide variety of lethal instruments, including all manner of guns, daggers, and pistols, the American minister unfailingly chose the bowie knife.

Russian-American relations, as opposed to relations with Britain and France, remained friendly through the Civil War. In September and October 1863, when it seemed that England and France were about to declare war on Russia because of Russia's suppression of a revolt in Russian Poland, the tsarist Baltic and Asiatic fleets arrived in New York and San Francisco. The Russian admiralty hoped that in event of war their ships in American waters might be able to venture forth and attack Anglo-French commerce. Unwilling to recognize the purpose of this maneuver, Americans saw only support for their Civil War. The Russians were wined and dined, and everyone recalled that both nations had enjoyed a long era of friendship, that both were fighting rebellions, that Lincoln had freed the slaves in 1863 and the tsar had liberated the serfs in 1861.

After the war and in memory of such friendly relations there came in 1867 the sale of Alaska to the United States. The tsar had observed the workings of manifest destiny in the American subcontinent. He had seen the speed with which Americans during the gold rush had populated California, he knew that there was gold in Alaska, and he knew that Alaska was militarily indefensible in the event of any future war between Russia and one of the great powers of Europe. The best course was to make a virtue of necessity, and he decided to remind the Americans that in his deep friendship for them and their cause of union and manifest destiny he was willing to sell Alaska. Among Americans in the year 1867 there was, unhappily, almost no sentiment for annexing Alaska. Interest in manifest destiny had not yet extended to it. As would happen thirty years or so later in annexing the Philippine Islands, citizens of the United States did not know whether Alaska was a city, an animal, or a new kind of drink. Secretary Seward, who knew the riches of that remote northern peninsula of North America, jumped at the chance to buy it, and opened the State Department in the middle of the night to sign a treaty with the Russian minister Baron Edouard de Stoeckl, at 4:00 A.M. on March 30, 1867. To get his measure through the Senate, Seward enlisted Senator Charles Sumner. The treaty passed. But the House of Representatives balked, and it appeared that there would be no appropriation of the paltry $7,500,000 which Seward had agreed to as the purchase price. Stoeckl calculated that since he had received $2,500,000 more than the tsar's government expected, there was money left for bribery. The minister took American post-Civil War politics as he found them, and after distribution of funds among needy congressmen the Alaska appropriation bill passed the House. The disgusted Stoeckl— who need not have been so disgusted; bribery was common enough in tsarist Russia—asked his government for relief from his post in the United States so that he might go some place where he could "breathe for a while a purer atmosphere than that of Washington."

Seward got nowhere, however, with a largely private and entirely unsuccessful effort to purchase the Danish West Indies, or with his wish, in later years supported by President Ulysses S. Grant, to annex the willing Dominican Republic.

An American naval officer in August 1867 occupied the Midway Islands, a thousand miles west of Hawaii; at the moment they did not seem important, but seventy-five years later, during the second World War, they proved a convenient base against Japan.

The last piece of important diplomacy during the 1860's was expulsion of the French from Mexico. The American government had accredited Thomas Corwin to the Juárez government of Mexico, the legitimate government, in 1861, and Corwin had put into disrepute the conduct of his Confederate opposite, Pickett. When in October 1861 the British, French, and Spanish governments decided to invade Mexico to obtain redress for overdue debts, there was nothing that Corwin could do other than express American sympathy for the Mexicans and await the outcome of the American Civil War. He could rest assured that there would be a day of reckoning over the Allied expedition to Mexico, an expedition so obviously contrary to the principles of the Monroe Doctrine. During the war, Secretary Seward was careful not to press too hard upon the sensibilities of France (the expedition to Mexico in May 1862 became entirely a French enterprise). Seward did nothing more than register the position of his government and reserve its rights for the future. When the French took Mexico City on June 7, 1863, Seward—who had wanted to fight the world in 1861—wrote Bigelow in Paris that the United States "are too intent on putting down our own insurrection . . . to seek for occasions to dispute with any foreign power." The Austrian archduke Maximilian, younger brother of the Habsburg emperor Francis Joseph, was proclaimed emperor and landed at Veracruz with his consort Carlotta (the Belgian princess Charlotte) on May 28, 1864. Again Seward refrained from action. But when the war was over the secretary began to put diplomatic pressure on Napoleon III, who by that time was none too anxious to continue what had become an enormously expensive venture. The emperor made a show of resistance, then announced that he would withdraw the French troops completely.

Napoleon's puppet emperor should at that moment have retired quietly to Europe, leaving Mexico for the Mexicans, but Maximilian possessed too much pride for this maneuver. He declared that he would stand by his own country, meaning Mexico, that he had become a Mexican and could not return to Europe. For this statesmanship Maximilian's subjects captured and executed him in 1867. To no avail had the Spanish ambassador pleaded personally with Secretary Seward for assistance in saving the young monarch's life. Seward had replied (crunching a radish), "His life is quite as safe as yours and mine." To no avail had Maximilian's wife, the beautiful Empress Carlotta, taken her husband's case to Napoleon III who would do nothing, and to the pope, who could do nothing. Her reason departed and she lived on in almost complete insanity, a pathetic relic of Napoleon III's expedition to found a monarchy in the New World.

When she died in 1927 in the era of Calvin Coolidge, the Habsburgs and Napoleons had long since retired from the stage of public affairs.

Such was the diplomacy of the United States in the twenty years after the Mexican War. The stirrings of the 1850's, the strivings in the Civil War of the early 1860's, the purchase of Alaska and the retreat of France from Mexico in 1867: these developments found their motive, in one way or other, in the belief of Americans in manifest destiny, that the most valuable portions of the North American continent were destined to fall under the sovereignty of the government of the United States. What at first might appear as a series of unrelated episodes becomes intelligible when one considers the factor of manifest destiny. In the perspective of the twentieth century this idea may seem a peculiarly nineteenth-century proposition, a confusion of national ambitions with historical inevitability and divine guidance. Still, if one surveys the territorial expanse of the American nation as it stood in the year 1867, there does seem to have been something mystical, something defiant of ordinary logic, in this growth of an infant nation to proportions of world power during little more than eighty years of independence.

ADDITIONAL READING

For the spirit of the 1850's the best introduction is Merle E. Curti, "Young America," *American Historical Review*, vol. 32 (1926–1927), 34–55. The Kossuth craze appears in J. W. Oliver, "Louis Kossuth's Appeal to the Middle West—1852," *Mississippi Valley Historical Review*, vol. 14 (1927–1928), 481–495. See also M. E. Curti, "Austria and the United States, 1848–1852," *Smith College Studies in History*, XI (1926), no. 3; A. J. May, *Contemporary American Opinion of the Mid-Century Revolutions in Central Europe* (Philadelphia, 1927); A. A. Ettinger, *The Mission to Spain of Pierre Soulé* (New Haven, 1932); and Andor Klay, *Daring Diplomacy* (Minneapolis, 1957).

The filibusters in Latin America have inspired a few books and articles: R. G. Caldwell, *The López Expeditions to Cuba: 1848–1851* (Princeton, 1915); W. O. Scroggs, *Filibusters and Financiers* (New York, 1916), dealing with William Walker; Ollinger Crenshaw, "The Knights of the Golden Circle: The Career of George Bickley," *American Historical Review*, vol. 47 (1941–1942), 23–50; and Roy F. Nichols, *Advance Agents of American Destiny* (Philadelphia, 1956). Also consult Dexter Perkins, *The Monroe Doctrine: 1826–1867* (Baltimore,

1933).

The best one-volume general treatment of the diplomacy of the Civil War is Jay Monaghan's *Diplomat in Carpet Slippers: Abraham Lincoln Deals with Foreign Affairs* (Indianapolis, 1945). This book is beautifully written and filled with colorful detail. See also the scattered chapters in Edward Channing, *A History of the United States*, vol. 6, *The War for Southern Independence: 1849–1865* (New York, 1925); and J. G. Randall, *Lincoln the President* (4 vols., New York, 1945–1955), the last volume written in large part by Richard N. Current. A masterful analysis is E. D. Adams, *Great Britain and the American Civil War* (2 vols., London, 1925), composed after meticulous and skeptical examination of available material, manuscript and printed. A view of Southern diplomacy during the war is Frank L. Owsley, *King Cotton Diplomacy* (Chicago, 1931).

The *Trent* affair, surprisingly neglected by historians, appears only in two old and inadequate accounts, Thomas Harris's *The Trent Affair* (Indianapolis, 1896); and Charles Francis Adams, "The *Trent* Affair," *American Historical Review*, vol. 17 (1911–1912), 540–562. For British neutrality during the war there is the reflective article by James P. Baxter, 3d, "The British Government and Neutral Rights, 1861–1865," *American Historical Review*, vol. 34 (1928–1929), 9–29. See also M. P. Claussen, "Peace Factors in Anglo-American Relations, 1861–1863," *Mississippi Valley Historical Review*, vol. 26 (1939–1940), 511–522; and D. Jordan and E. J. Pratt, *Europe and the American Civil War* (Boston, 1931).

Biography, autobiography, and diary appear in such volumes as Brainerd Dyer, *Zachary Taylor* (Baton Rouge, 1946); Holman Hamilton, *Zachary Taylor* (Indianapolis, 1951); Roy L. Nichols, *Franklin Pierce* (Philadelphia, 1931); Dexter Perkins, "William H. Seward as Secretary of State," in Glyndon G. Van Deusen and Richard C. Wade, eds., *Foreign Policy and the American Spirit: Essays by Dexter Perkins* (Ithaca, 1957); Margaret Clapp, *Forgotten First Citizen: John Bigelow* (Boston, 1947); S. A. Wallace and F. E. Gillespie, eds., *The Journal of Benjamin Moran: 1857–1865* (2 vols., Chicago, 1949), by the secretary of the American legation in London; Henry Adams, *The Education of Henry Adams* (Boston, 1918), a classic memoir by the son of the American minister, dealing not merely with the Civil War but politics, society, and life in the latter nineteenth century.

The best source for the Maximilian affair is E. C. Corti, *Maximilian and Charlotte of Mexico* (2 vols., New York, 1928).

On relations with Russia there are several articles by Frank A. Golder, who prior to the Bolshevik revolution was able to exploit the Russian archives: "Russian-American Relations during the Crimean War," *American Historical Review*, vol. 31 (1925–1926), 462–476; "The American Civil War through the Eyes of a Russian Diplomat," *AHR*, vol. 26 (1920–1921), 454–463, an analysis of the dispatches of Baron de Stoeckl;

"The Russian Fleet and the Civil War," *AHR*, vol. 20 (1914–1915), 801–812; "The Purchase of Alaska," *AHR*, vol. 25 (1919–1920), 411–425. More general treatments appear in Foster Rhea Dulles, *The Road to Teheran* (Princeton, 1944); and Thomas A. Bailey, *America Faces Russia* (Ithaca, 1950).

CHAPTER

☆ **6** ☆

Boundaries and Arbitrations

Somewhere, at some point, in recounting the history of American diplomacy it is necessary to turn aside from chronological narrative and relate how the United States and Great Britain, during the nineteenth and at the beginning of the twentieth century, accommodated each other in four large controversies: the Northeast boundary; the Northwest boundary; the *Alabama* claims arbitration; and the Alaska boundary. These controversies in their full details are assuredly most uninteresting, and it is not the purpose of the present chapter to deal with every small geographical argument, every rhetorical flourish before an arbitral tribunal. Rather, it is to set down these controversies with Great Britain in detail sufficient to make them understandable in their larger political meaning, namely, that after the War of 1812 it was in every case possible for the United States to adjust its disputes with Great Britain, through treaty or through arbitral award, by measures short of war.

1. *The Northeast Boundary Dispute*

The first adjustment came with the Webster-Ashburton Treaty of 1842, concluded at Washington between the American secretary of state, Daniel Webster, and the British plenipotentiary, Lord Ashburton. This treaty ended an argument over the Northeast boundary between the United States and Canada which had continued since the Treaty of Paris of 1783.

In its origins the Northeast boundary controversy was easily understandable. To determine the boundary between Maine and Canada
was one of the lesser problems of Benjamin Franklin and his fellow
peace commissioners at the end of the revolution. When Franklin,
Jay, and Adams were negotiating with Richard Oswald in 1782 they
did not, of course, act from carelessness, even in small matters. They
did their best to avoid controversial articles in the treaty of peace.
The maps of the day unfortunately were inaccurate, and the map used
in 1782, a 1775 edition of Mitchell's Map of North America, was
rather imaginative in its descriptions of the terrain along the Northeast boundary of the former British colonies. In the preliminary
articles of peace signed in 1782 the Americans using Mitchell's Map
agreed unwittingly to a boundary that did not exist. The boundary
was to begin on the Atlantic coast with the St. Croix River. There
was no St. Croix River. Moreover, the negotiators of 1782 failed to
append to their accord a copy of Mitchell's Map, nor did they even
mention that they had used Mitchell's Map. The result of this confusion was to place in dispute an area over one hundred miles in
length. The north-south gap between British and American claims
spread out over 7,697,280 acres.

There followed efforts by mixed commissions, one created by Jay's
Treaty and another twenty years later by the Treaty of Ghent, to
patch up this boundary. The commission created by Jay's Treaty
decided in 1798 that a river then called the Schoodiac was in truth the
St. Croix, but beyond running the boundary up that river to its source
the commission failed, and the remainder of the Northeast boundary,
up around the hump of present-day Maine and New Hampshire and
almost straight westward across the top of Vermont and New York
to the St. Lawrence River, remained in dispute. With the clause appointing a second mixed commission in the Treaty of Ghent there
was another anticipating what might happen should the new commission disagree: in such case the two nations would refer their differences to a friendly sovereign or state, and would consider his decision
as "final and conclusive on all the matters so referred." The second
commission disagreed, and after some considerable further negotiation
during the 1820's the dispute was given to the king of the Netherlands.

That monarch apparently put aside all the voluminous evidence
offered by the opposing parties, British and Americans, and split the

difference between the two nations, running a line roughly through the middle of the disputed area. The British government was willing to accept this award, though it admitted that the Dutch king had erred technically, for his duty as an abitrator was to decide between the opposing claims and not to set out a compromise boundary. The American government under President Andrew Jackson—the year was 1831—was not unwilling to accept the royal error, to take the king's award, but Jackson was unwilling to accept responsibility for giving away what, to the citizens of Maine, was the territory of their state, and so he asked the advice of the Senate, which voted against the proposed compromise boundary. There matters rested through most of the decade of the 1830's.

In the later thirties some new factors entered, which urged a settlement of the Northeast boundary. Of first importance was the large-scale insurrection by the Canadians against British rule which broke out in 1837 and received encouragement and supplies from the American side of the border. A band of pro-British Canadians crossed the river above Niagara Falls on December 29, 1837, seized the American ship *Caroline* (a notorious munitions-runner) as she was tied up on the American side of the river, cut her loose and sent her over the falls. This incident raised tempers mightily in America. When a Canadian named Alexander McLeod boasted in 1840 that he had taken part in the *Caroline* fracas and had killed an American during the affair, there was an enormous hullabaloo. McLeod was tried in New York State and acquitted. But the McLeod affair, following the *Caroline* affair, both so exasperating to American public opinion, stirred British fears for retention of Canada in case of a war with the United States. From these fears came a British conviction that when the Northeastern boundary should be settled there should be enough territory ceded to the Crown so that during winters when the St. Lawrence was frozen it would be possible to run military supplies overland from Halifax and Saint John to Quebec and Montreal. In summer the land passage was a painful route, impassable to all save single travelers, but in winter, ice and snow supported sledges and permitted movement of larger groups and of bulk goods and artillery.

Then during the 1830's there was realization by the citizens of Maine that the Aroostook Valley, part of the disputed area, was worth a diplomatic fight with Great Britain. The valley was a pocket of unusually rich limestone soils in the northern hump of Maine, isolated from the rest of the state by a stretch of wilderness even in the twentieth century unpeopled. It lay undiscovered until the 1830's. Citizens of Maine had supposed that it was simply another forested area, with unyielding acid soil, a wilderness of conifers and ponded streams. Partly through exploration for proposed railroads, partly as a result of an expanding frontier movement, the "Roostook" Valley now took on importance. As one of the surveyors wrote upon return from this attractive area, "Are you a young man just starting in life, but with no capital save a strong arm—good courage, and a *narrow axe?* Go to the Aroostook; attend assiduously and carefully to your business; select a lot suitable for your purpose, and with the common blessings of providence, you will, in a very few years, find yourself an independent freeholder, with a farm of your own subduing, and with a capital of your own creating." To the able-bodied young men in the stony hill country of central and southern Maine, this was good news. When the British province of New Brunswick began granting land titles and claiming jurisdiction within this land that the residents of Maine deemed their own territory, there began in 1838 a small border strife known as the Roostook War. A fragile peace was arranged in March 1839 by intercession of the American general, Winfield Scott, but who knew when another Roostook War would erupt, perhaps bringing full-scale hostilities between the British and American peoples? This trouble incident to the discovery of the Aroostook Valley—like the trouble incident to the Canadian rebellion of 1837–1838—pointed up the need for a settlement of the Northeast boundary controversy.

Such was the situation when Lord Ashburton came to Washington as a special British plenipotentiary in 1841, to reopen negotiations on the Northeast boundary with President John Tyler's secretary of state, Webster. The Americans desired the Aroostook Valley. The British wished a military road. The boundary by this time had been in dispute for sixty years.

The adjustment arrived at between Ashburton and Webster came quickly and easily. The treaty of 1842 was in reality Webster's treaty, for the secretary of state pushed his negotiation to a conclusion as rapidly as he could, even at the expense of American rights in the disputed area. Webster seems to have coveted an appointment as American minister to Great Britain, and believed that if he accommodated the British in 1842 he might facilitate his welcome in the

British capital. He needed, however, some sort of argument to present to the people of Maine and the people of Massachusetts (which state had retained half ownership in Maine's public lands after Maine detached itself from Massachusetts in 1820 and became a state) and also to the Senate of the United States, which had to advise and consent to any treaty that Webster obtained. If, say, he could obtain a map or two seeming to prove the rightness of the British claim in Maine, he could show this evidence to his countrymen and sign with Ashburton.

For his sly purpose—persuading Maine, Massachusetts, and the Senate—Webster enrolled an acquaintance and professor at Harvard College, Jared Sparks, who was a biographer of Washington, author and editor of many volumes, later president of Harvard; Sparks volunteered his services to Webster in a letter of February 1842, in which he related how during a residence in France he had studied the French archives and found a small map on which, so he guessed, Franklin in 1782 had marked "with a strong red line" the boundary between Maine and Canada. Sparks had taken notes on this map and its line, and in his letter to Webster he enclosed a nineteenth-century map of Maine on which he marked what he remembered seeing in the French archives. His marking coincided with the British claim in Maine. His map, needless to add, was exceedingly welcome to Webster, for the secretary could use it to argue for any concessions made to the British. Webster already had in his possession a map that he had picked up from a second-hand dealer, a Mitchell Map formerly belonging to Baron von Steuben, on which someone (Franklin, so Webster assumed) had also marked a boundary coinciding with the British claim in Maine.

Webster on August 9, 1842 concluded a treaty with Ashburton, and apparently received about $14,500 from the British plenipotentiary to pay Jared Sparks to go up to Augusta, the capital of Maine, and show the two maps to the people there as an argument that it was best to give in to the British.

At the time of passage of the Webster-Ashburton Treaty through the Senate, it was thought that Webster had followed the path of statesmanship in concluding a treaty that accepted roughly the line proposed by the king of the Netherlands in 1831. Webster in fact had accepted a line giving up more territory than the United States would have lost under the award of 1831, but compromise seemed proper in view of Webster's cartographical discoveries. When the secretary

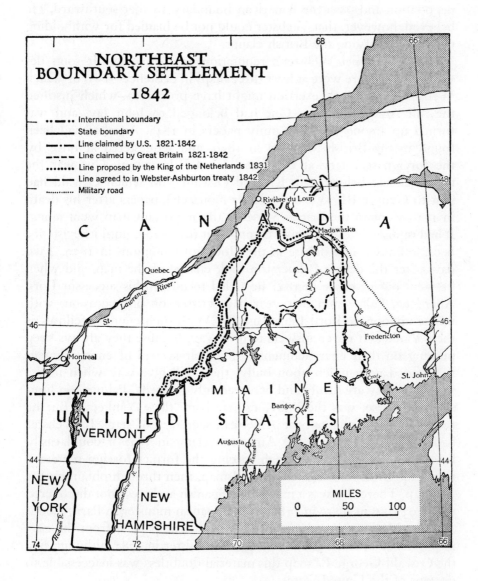

NORTHEAST BOUNDARY SETTLEMENT 1842

- ..—..— International boundary
- ——— State boundary
- —·—·— Line claimed by U.S. 1821-1842
- — — — Line claimed by Great Britain 1821-1842
- •••••••• Line proposed by the King of the Netherlands 1831
- •••••••• Line agreed to in Webster-Ashburton treaty 1842
- ·········· Military road

CANADA

Rivière du Loup

Madawaska

Quebec

Lawrence River

St.

Montreal

Aroostook R.

John R.

Fredericton

St. Croix R.

St. John

MAINE

Penobscot R.

Bangor

UNITED STATES

VERMONT

Augusta

Kennebec R.

NEW YORK

NEW HAMPSHIRE

Connecticut R.

Hudson R.

MILES
0   50   100

told Ashburton about the two maps, just prior to signature of the treaty, the Britisher felt that it was a shame he could not reopen the negotiation and push the American boundary further southward. He believed, however, that Webster could not be blamed for withholding the maps justifying the British claims.

Alas for Daniel Webster's reputation as a diplomat. It soon developed that there were at least three maps in existence—two of which Webster with a little exertion might have procured—which justified the full American claim. One had belonged to John Jay, and was turned up among the Jay family papers in 1843. Another had been found in the British Museum in 1839, and sequestered at once by the foreign secretary at that time, Lord Palmerston. This was the map that had belonged to Richard Oswald, and which Oswald had sent to George III. When the latter monarch's papers after his death in 1820 went to the British Museum the important map went along. It had reposed in the Museum throughout the 1830's, until its existence became known in a debate in the House of Commons in 1839. Two days after the debate Palmerston took charge of the map, and when he went out of office in 1841 he failed to inform his successor Lord Aberdeen. Palmerston that year had written on one occasion, with undue unction, to Lord John Russell: "With such cunning fellows as these Yankees it never answers to give way, because they always keep pushing on their encroachments . . . their system of encroachment is founded very much upon bully, they will give way when in the wrong, if they are firmly and perseveringly pressed." Palmerston himself, of course, was the bully, rather than "these Yankees." But he received assistance from the American secretary of state. If Webster had wished to establish the American claim in 1842 it could easily have been done, if not through forcing the former foreign secretary to relinquish the Oswald-George III map, then through obtaining the Jay map. There also was a map in the Spanish archives (not discovered until 1933), sent there in 1782 by the Spanish minister in Paris, Count Aranda. More evidence was in the Lansdowne papers, from the correspondence of Lord Shelburne, prime minister in 1782, although like the Oswald-George III map this material doubtless was inaccessible to citizens of the United States.

Daniel Webster thus took part in what personally was a discreditable episode, by which Great Britain gained 3,207,680 acres of American soil. The fact remained that he had settled a long controversy with the British government. This in the nineteenth century was a worthwhile achievement, and it marked the first of four major accommodations between the governments in London and Washington.

2. *The Northwest Boundary Dispute*

The second of these diplomatic accommodations, settlement of the Northwest boundary dispute, came four years after the Webster-Ashburton Treaty, when in 1846 President Polk sent to the Senate a British-proposed treaty that ended a quarter-century of argument.

At stake in the Oregon dispute was a large wilderness, an area many times that involved in the Maine controversy: all the land between the parallels 42° and 54° 40', bounded on the west by the Pacific and the east by the Continental Divide. This territory had been in dispute for many years, first between Great Britain and Spain, then between Britain, Russia, and the United States, finally between the two English-speaking nations. Spain and Britain had quarreled in 1789–1790 over an attempt by a British fur-trading expedition to establish a base at Nootka Sound on Vancouver Island, and when the younger Pitt pushed British claims to the point of an ultimatum the Spanish gave in, granting the right of British subjects to trade and settle on the north-west coast of North America north of the area occupied by Spain. Years later, in 1818, the United States signed a treaty with Great Britain stipulating a boundary between American and Canadian soil that ran from Lake Superior to the Lake of the Woods and then along the forty-ninth parallel to the eastern slope of the Rocky Mountains. The decision in 1818 in regard to the western side of the Rockies, the Pacific Coast area, was that it should be "free and open" to settlement by nationals of either of the two states. The United States in 1819 concluded the Transcontinental Treaty with Spain, extinguishing Spanish rights above the northern boundary of Spanish California, the forty-second parallel. The United States in 1824 and Great Britain in 1825 had concluded an arrangement with Russia whereby the southern limit of Russian territory along the Pacific Coast was set at 54° 40'—the negotiators had suggested the fifty-fifth parallel, but the Russians wished to extend their boundary south to keep Prince of Wales Island entirely within Russian jurisdiction rather than have the line run across it. In such manner did the Oregon question become after the mid-1820's an Anglo-American problem: to the south, on the forty-second parallel lay the northern boundary of California; to the north, at 54° 40′ lay the base of Russia's Alaskan panhandle; between these extremes lay the free and open area, to be decided between the British and Americans.

The area in dispute narrowed further, through a natural process, to the land north and west of the Columbia River and south of the forty-ninth parallel. South of the Columbia lay the Willamette Valley, one of the finest pieces of rolling plain and lightly wooded farmland ever to be found in the United States. Settlers moved into that area in the 1830's, and the American settlements were so well rooted by the early 1840's that when the Oregon question came up for solution there was no doubt about American possession of the Willamette. What the Americans wished, however, was to obtain a good port on the Pacific Coast, and since the Mexican War was not at this time in prospect, with its award to the United States of San Francisco and San Diego, it appeared as if the only way in which Americans might obtain a port would be to lay claim to some of the lands around Puget Sound and Juan de Fuca Strait, which meant persuading the British to extend to the Pacific the line of the Treaty of 1818—that is, the forty-ninth parallel. The American government offered to settle the boundary at the forty-ninth parallel in 1818, 1824, 1826, and 1843.

The British unfortunately would not go along with such a proposal. Great Britain during the quarter-century course of the Oregon dispute always intimated willingness to divide the Oregon country at the line of the Columbia River, running the boundary up the Columbia until the river crossed the forty-ninth parallel. It offered such a boundary in 1824, 1826, and 1844. It further offered in 1826 and 1844 to yield to the United States a fragment of the Olympic peninsula fronting both on the Pacific and Juan de Fuca Strait, on which the Americans might construct a port. But this was as far as the British would go, for the London government insisted upon retaining control of the Columbia.

The reason for this stand was the Hudson's Bay Company, which under the energetic leadership of its chief factor, Dr. John McLoughlin, had gained a pre-eminent position in the Oregon country north of the Columbia. The British government in 1821 had granted the company a monopoly of trade in the Pacific regions. Although the American post at Astoria, captured during the War of 1812, afterward had passed back under the stars and stripes, it came under

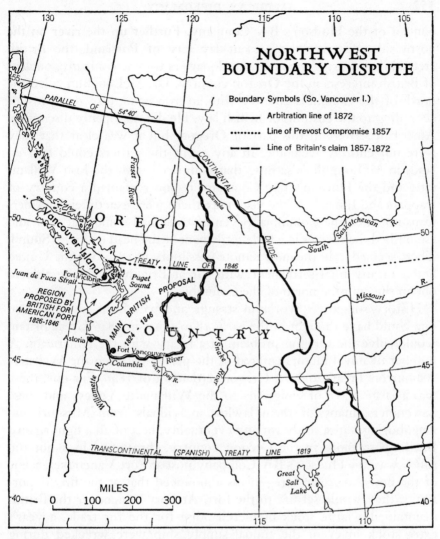

NORTHWEST BOUNDARY DISPUTE

Boundary Symbols (So. Vancouver I.)

———— Arbitration line of 1872

·········· Line of Prevost Compromise 1857

— — — Line of Britain's claim 1857-1872

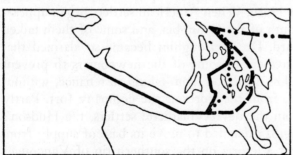

control of the Hudson's Bay Company. Further up the river on the north side, opposite the present-day city of Portland, the British erected their Fort Vancouver, headquarters for the company, nucleus of British interests in the Oregon country. Dr. McLoughlin ruled the north-of-the-Columbia country with an iron hand, dispensing justice according to the customs of British law. He did not openly discourage American settlers in this part of Oregon, but it was clear that they were not entirely welcome. In any event the settlers could find no lands in McLoughlin's satrapy that compared with the lush Willamette, and the Hudson's Bay Company region remained a country of trappers and Indians. In the year 1845 there were exactly eight Americans north of the Columbia. Seven of these had come that year and established themselves in a little settlement at the head of Puget Sound. There seemed only the most remote possibility in 1845 that the United States in any final settlement with Great Britain would be able to obtain the country north of the Columbia.

History sometimes works in strange and wondrous ways, and no one could have thought in the early 1840's that in 1846 Great Britain would solve the Oregon problem in a treaty with the Americans. A number of novel factors entered in the period between the Webster-Ashburton Treaty and the Oregon settlement of 1846. For one, there was a large wave of emigrants to the Willamette Valley, and these newcomers, many of them lawless individuals from Missouri and neighboring states, ready for any eventuality, best of all a fight against British possessions in the Oregon country, threatened in a not too subtle way the Hudson's Bay Company post at Fort Vancouver. Some of the new American Oregonians announced that at the first opportunity they would set fire to the fort. At Fort Vancouver the British maintained a large stock of merchandise for the fur trade, a year's extra stock in event the annual supply ship were wrecked during the course around Cape Horn. When American settlers began appearing in large numbers south of the Columbia, and some of them talked about moving northward, Dr. McLoughlin became so alarmed that in 1843 and 1844 he gave aid to some of the newcomers to prevent the latter in their penniless condition from taking sustenance, without payment or permission, from the stores at the company fort. Partly because of pressure from the new Willamette settlers, the Hudson's Bay Company in 1844–1845 decided to move its base of supply from Fort Vancouver to Fort Victoria on the southern tip of Vancouver

Island. The area south of the forty-ninth parallel also had been trapped out in the past few years, and no longer could support a large trading post. For a decade there had been talk about moving northward. By chance the move occurred at the moment when the Oregon question entered into a period of crisis and then settlement.

But the peculiar turns of British politics in the period 1842–1846, far more than the change of base of the Hudson's Bay Company or the wave of emigration to Oregon, provide the key to understanding the settlement of the Oregon question. In 1841 the Tory government of Sir Robert Peel had come into office in Britain, with the capable and peaceful Lord Aberdeen as foreign secretary. Palmerston had left the Foreign Office, to the relief of all the chancelleries of Europe. One of the first fruits of this change had been the decision of the new government to send Ashburton to America to arrange a settlement of outstanding issues with the Americans. All went well until Ashburton's treaty arrived in England, whereupon—although the vast generality of Britishers favored the treaty, and had good reason to favor it—Palmerston launched a loud campaign against what for purely partisan reasons he described as the Ashburton Capitulation. This had the unfortunate effect of making the Peel government, never too robust in its parliamentary support, hesitant to conclude another boundary treaty with the Americans that could by any stretch of anyone's imagination be described as favoring the United States. In a sense the problem of British political leaders at this point, the solution of which determined the solution of the Oregon question, was Lord Palmerston. Before taking steps in foreign policy they had to block the opposition of the terrible Palmerston, who had gained access to the *Morning Chronicle* and was making trouble for Aberdeen at the Foreign Office. What happened, finally, was that Palmerston found himself not merely opposed by but subject to the instruction of some of his most highly placed fellow members of the Whig Party. After a series of maneuvers including a temporary collapse of the Peel cabinet there arose agreement between Tories and Whigs over another arrangement with the United States. Aberdeen at once —the year was now 1846—sent off a proposal to Washington to extend the Canadian-American boundary along the forty-ninth parallel to the Pacific. Polk cautiously asked the Senate for advice, and the response was favorable. The president signed the treaty on June 15, 1846. The Senate gave its formal advice and consent on June 18. The

Oregon question came to an end.

It was a large victory for the United States, for the Americans had little settlement and no commerce north of the Columbia and the Treaty of 1846 balanced off the diplomatic defeat of 1842 when Daniel Webster negotiated against his own country.

A word remains about the famous outcry of Fifty-Four Forty or Fight, the alliterative slogan for defying Great Britain and taking all of Oregon, raised in early 1845 by Northern Democrats in Congress and among settlers moving out to the Oregon territory. Extending American territory up to the Russian panhandle seemed, for a moment, a patriotic thing to do, when the moment coincided in American-Mexican relations with outbreak of war for manifest destiny. It appeared to be only the course of nature that the United States should cut the British off entirely from the Pacific Coast. When the issue of Texas annexation came to a vote in March 1845, there was talk of taking all of Oregon. Northern Whigs, however, were incensed—certain that, like Texas, there was another plot afoot in the Pacific Northwest. A Vermont editor declared that Oregon had been "wrapped around" Texas, "just as the nurse disguises a nauseous dose in honey to cheat the palate of a rebellious patient." It developed that opposition to annexation of Oregon was much stronger than opposition to the annexation of Texas. Southern Democrats in the Senate, such as Calhoun of South Carolina, were satisfied with annexation of Texas and willing to compromise with Britain on Oregon. President Tyler had resorted to a joint resolution of Congress to annex Texas, and it seemed advisable for Polk to compromise on Oregon. Polk, the expansionist president who welcomed war with Mexico, made a treaty of peaceful settlement on Oregon with Great Britain, the ancient foe.

Some of the more ardent Democrats in Congress were incensed at Polk for his betrayal, as they described it, of Oregon. Senator Edward A. Hannegan of Indiana declared that "so long as one human eye remains to linger on the page of history, the story of his abasement will be read, sending him and his name together to an infamy so profound, a damnation so deep, that the hand of resurrection will never be able to drag him forth." The Washington correspondent of the New York *Tribune* asked in truth what had happened to the alliterative slogan about Fifty-Four Forty or Fight, sometimes known as the four P's, Phifty-Phour Phorty or Phight. As if in reply, a Southern newspaper asserted that Phifty-Phour Phorty or Phight had now "phortunately phallen to phinal phlat phooted phixing at 'Phorty nine' without the 'Phight' against a phoreign phoe." Polk, despite the Hannegans, had given in to Great Britain, at least so far as attempting to get such an impossible boundary on the Pacific Coast as 54° 40'. It was one thing to press territorial claims against a nation such as Mexico, and quite another to stand up to the most powerful nation in the world, as Britain was during the nineteenth century.

3. *Hamilton Fish and the Alabama Claims*

The third of the major accommodations with Great Britain—the only one treated in this chapter which did not concern boundaries—was the *Alabama* claims controversy, settled after the Civil War in the Treaty of Washington of 1871 and the subsequent Geneva arbitration of 1872. According to the dean of American international lawyers, John Bassett Moore, the Treaty of Washington was "the greatest treaty of actual and immediate arbitration" the world has ever seen. This treaty, Moore wrote, occupies a place in the annals of American diplomatic history second only to the Treaty of Paris of 1783. The treaty, one should add, was in many ways the personal triumph of President Grant's secretary of state, Hamilton Fish, and for its happy conclusion students of American diplomacy have generally placed Secretary Fish in the ranks of the truly great secretaries of state, alongside John Quincy Adams and William H. Seward.

It would be incorrect to contend that the Treaty of Washington in its negotiation or outcome elicited great attention at the time, from Americans or Europeans. In the United States people were much more interested in Tammany scandals, amnesty for some of the former Southern leaders, an Indian warrior named Red Cloud who had threatened disaster in areas of the American West, Mrs. Lincoln's request for a pension, and assorted murder trials. In Great Britain there was concern over troubles in Ireland, reform of the English school system, the death of Charles Dickens, reorganization of the British army. The Treaty of Washington was concluded in the summer of 1871 in an atmosphere of quiet indifference, which suited exactly the pacific purposes of the British and American commissioners meeting in the American capital. They might have faced an impossible task, had public opinion in the two countries been aroused and every turn of the negotiation seized upon by newspapers as a subject for emotional outburst.

Both sides in 1871 were eager to come to a conclusion over the vexatious issues separating the two countries—*Alabama* claims, fisheries, joint use of Canadian waterways such as the St. Lawrence. During a crisis with Russia in 1870 the British found themselves without allies in Europe, and were anxious to strengthen ties with the United States. In the midst of the Franco-Prussian War of 1870–1871 the Russian government had denounced the decision arrived at during the Crimean War of 1854–1856, namely that Russia should not maintain a fleet in the Black Sea, and when the Russian foreign minister unilaterally repudiated this engagement the British found themselves facing Russia alone: the Austrian government was weak, the German government was friendly to the Russians, the French government was being overthrown in war by the Germans. During the war scare that accompanied the Russian denunciation there was fear that in event of hostilities there might be a repetition, to Britain's disadvantage, of what had happened during the American Civil War. The Americans might permit the Russians to build a large number of *Alabamas*, to venture forth to prey on British commerce all over the world. It was understandable why in 1871 the British were eager to come to an agreement with the United States.

The Americans had their own reasons for pressing a settlement of issues with Great Britain. In the years after the Civil War there was tremendous development of the American economy, evident in construction of railways across the American West, and railways and other enterprises required capital from abroad, in particular from the center of world finance, Great Britain. So long as relations between the two countries were strained, every small crisis between London and Washington had a marked effect on the value of American bonds and the availability of British capital. It was, therefore, much to American interest to ensure peace with the British. Moreover, it was peculiarly advantageous for the Grant administration to set on foot a grand treaty and arbitration, for in domestic politics there had been a succession of troubles which was leading to a split in the Republican Party in the election of 1872. The Liberal Republicans, as they called themselves, were crying for reform. Grant was unwilling to give it to them, but he was willing to seek a diplomatic triumph that would serve his administration in 1872.

The diplomatic antecedents of the Treaty of Washington reached back before the Grant administration to the time of Secretary of State Seward, for it was he who at the end of the war undertook to clear away the diplomatic issues that had been postponed until the victory. Seward had announced that Great Britain must pay for the depredations of Confederate cruisers built in British ports, and he had raised early in the postwar years the claim that indirect as well as direct damages must be paid. By this he meant that the Confederate cruisers had made so much difficulty that they had postponed Union victory. Britain should pay for the cost of additional war imposed by the cruisers. This claim was taken up by Senator Charles Sumner of Massachusetts. Sumner, who was one of the most vindictive men in American history, demanded that Britain in return for the indirect claims undertake a "hemispheric withdrawal"—from Canada, Jamaica, Bermuda, the Bahamas, Trinidad and other West Indies islands, and British Honduras, British Guiana, the Falklands, and South Georgia. Canada, in Sumner's opinion, might gravitate to the United States, and perhaps the other formerly British territories would follow. Seward in his last months in office negotiated through the American minister in Great Britain, Reverdy Johnson, and the British foreign secretary Lord Clarendon, the Johnson-Clarendon Convention, signed January 14, 1869, providing for general adjudication of American claims against Great Britain, with no specific mention of the *Alabama* claims. The Senate, led by Sumner, rejected this convention on April 13, 1869, by a vote of 54 to 1. The Grant administration under direction of Secretary Fish reopened negotiations.

On New Year's Day, 1871, Sir John Rose, a private British gentleman who was in the complete confidence of the Foreign Office, was on the high seas en route from London to the United States to converse with Secretary Fish. Upon arrival the two men in their first conversation talked for six hours, and at once set on foot a new negotiation. A British commission came to Washington that spring. It met in numerous sessions with an American commission, and these discussions were accompanied by conferences between Fish and the leader of the British commission, Earl de Grey. A spring fox-hunt was arranged in Virginia. De Grey took a house for the commission in Washington, and champagne flowed freely. Reporters had a busy time following the festivities of the occasion. Secretary Fish gave many return dinners, and it was at one of these that a reporter bribed a waiter to conceal him under the table, where he took notes on the conversation. Finally, at the signing of the Treaty of Washington on May 8, 1871, the American and British negotiators took leave of each other, concluding their labors with a repast of strawberries and ice cream.

The negotiations although tortuous had not been difficult. The fisheries question, allowing Americans inshore fishing privileges in British North America, outlasted all the others. Seventeen sessions of the commission were devoted to Canadian questions, chiefly the fisheries, also including American navigation of the St. Lawrence, Canadian navigation of Lake Michigan, Canadian use of certain Alaskan rivers, and reciprocal use of local canals connecting with the Great Lakes-St. Lawrence system along the international boundary. Ten additional sessions went to the claims against England. Four sought to draw the proper boundary in San Juan de Fuca Strait, an issue left unsolved from the Oregon Treaty of 1846. The San Juan channel dispute was submitted for arbitration by the German emperor, who in an award of 1872 gave San Juan Island to the United States. Citizens of the United States were allowed by the Treaty of Washington to use the St. Lawrence. Canadians were granted navigation rights on rivers flowing out of British territory to the sea through Alaska. The Canadians received a temporary, later (in a treaty of 1909) permanent, navigation of Lake Michigan. Reciprocal use of the local canals connecting with the Great Lakes-St. Lawrence system was to be arranged, and was so arranged, with local authorities, state and Dominion.

As for the far more troublesome fisheries question, this was decided for a minimum of ten years, during which citizens of the United States were admitted to Canadian inshore fishing privileges. A commission was appointed to meet in Halifax and determine a cash equivalent for this Canadian concession (when it met it awarded to Canada the sum of $5,500,000). The United States also was to admit without duty Canadian fish and fish oil and to open coastal fisheries of the United States north of the thirty-ninth parallel. The fisheries articles of the Treaty of Washington expired in 1885, and the fisheries dispute thus reopened continued until it was arbitrated in 1910. At the time, in 1871 at Washington, it was considered virtually solved. The Canadian prime minister, Sir John Macdonald, one of the British commissioners, felt badly about the fisheries, and his final surrender was humorously set down in Secretary Fish's diary: "When Sir John

Macdonald was about to sign, while having the pen in his hand, he said to me (in a half-whisper), 'Well, here go the fisheries.' To my reply, 'You get a good equivalent for them,' he said, 'No, we give them away—here goes the signature.'; and thereupon signed his name, and rising from the table, said, 'They are gone.' "

In regard to the *Alabama* claims, so-called for the destruction caused by the most famous of the Confederate cruisers but including claims growing out of depredations by all cruisers built in England, the treaty established an arbitral tribunal of five men, to be named by President Grant, Queen Victoria, the king of Italy, the president of the Swiss Confederation, and the emperor of Brazil. The tribunal was to meet in Geneva at the earliest possible date. It was to act on the American claims in accord with three famous principles laid down in the Treaty of Washington, which are worthy of special notice because they since have passed into international law. First, a neutral government was bound to use "due diligence" to prevent the outfitting or arming of any vessel which it had "reasonable ground" to believe was intended to make war against another nation, and to prevent departure of any such vessel. Second, a neutral government should prevent a belligerent from making use of its ports or waters as a base of naval operations, or for procuring military supplies, arms, or re-cruits. Third, it must exercise due diligence in its ports and waters and over all persons within its jurisdiction to prevent violation of these obligations. At the demand of the American commissioners the Treaty of Washington contained an express British statement of regret "for the escape, under whatever circumstances, of the *Alabama* and other vessels from British ports, and for the depredations committed by those vessels."

The treaty was a triumph for Hamilton Fish, its negotiator. By writing into the treaty the principles of the arbitration, Fish bound the arbitrators to accept in advance a large part of the American case, and only the amount of damages remained in question.

To the treaty the Senate at once gave approval, on May 24, 1871, which was Queen Victoria's birthday. Ratifications were formally exchanged in London on Bunker Hill day, June 17. President Grant proclaimed the treaty in full effect on July 4. There remained only the arbitration itself.

To Geneva the United States sent Charles Francis Adams as one of the five arbitrators. To present the American case Fish and Grant chose William M. Evarts, leader of the American bar, together with Caleb Cushing, the negotiator of the Cushing Treaty with China in 1844 and one of New England's most eminent citizens, and Morrison R. Waite, soon to be chief justice of the United States.

At Geneva the arbitrators—American, British, Brazilian, Swiss, and Italian—heard presentations of the American claims, a presentation almost wrecked by the ill-advised revival of the indirect claims. The British during the Washington negotiations had thought the indirect claims had been put to rest. Secretary Fish and his principal assistant in preparation of the American case at Geneva, J. C. Bancroft Davis, resurrected the claims without advising the British of their peculiar purpose for so doing: they advanced the indirect claims at Geneva only to satisfy American public opinion, and not for the serious attention of the Geneva tribunal. The British government was incensed by the American demands for an award equivalent to the cost of the Civil War after the battle of Gettysburg. Lord Granville, the foreign secretary, estimated these claims with seven per cent interest at $4,500,000,000, "an incredible demand." Prussia's recent exaction of a billion-dollar indemnity from France had made a painful impression upon all Europe, and here were the Americans at Geneva demanding several times that much. The British prime minister, William E. Gladstone, almost lost his temper, for Gladstone estimated that the "war prolongation claim" might come to $8,000,000,000. In a letter to Queen Victoria he compared the American indirect claims to Russia's abrogation of the Black Sea clauses: "Even bearing in mind the proceeding of Prince Gortschakoff in the autumn of 1870, Mr. Gladstone is constrained to say that the conduct of the American Government in this affair is the most disreputable he has ever known in his recollection of diplomacy." Confronted with this sort of accusation, Secretary Fish ruffled momentarily, and foresaw the end of his cherished arrangement of issues with Great Britain, but he recovered his poise, issued suitable disclaimers on the indirect claims, allowed an arrangement at Geneva whereby the arbitrators unanimously threw out these American pretensions, and the arbitration moved forward to its happy conclusion, an award of $15,500,000 to the American government. Fish realized in regard to the indirect claims that it would be poor business for the United States to establish a precedent for them in international law. As he wrote privately to a friend, "I may say to *you*, that I never believed that the Tribunal would award a cent for the 'indirect claims'; it is not the interest of the United States, who are habitually neutrals, to have it decided that a neutral is liable for the indirect injuries consequent upon an act of negligence. We have too large an extent of coast and too small a police, and too much of the spirit of bold speculation and adventure, to make the doctrine a safe one for our future."

The Geneva tribunal labored from the end of June 1872 to mid-September, in the small Salle des Conférences in the Hôtel de Ville —now known as the Salle de l'Alabama. The neutral arbitrators, Swiss, Brazilian, and Italian, were the deciding factors in the arbitration, and the Americans at Geneva left nothing undone which would sway the neutrals toward the American side. Bancroft Davis, present during the deliberations, flattered the neutral arbitrators to a point where they were altogether willing to decide in favor of the United States. He took the additional precaution to bribe the French newspaper press, read by the neutral arbitrators. In this regard he did a thorough job, for as he wrote to Fish, his list included "all the important political papers except the *Debats* and the *France*, and the *Journal de Paris*. The first two are bought by England; the latter I don't know about." One must suspect that in other ways the arbitration was not altogether judicial, for the Brazilian arbitrator at one point seems to have decided against the British on the basis of ability to pay; he told the British counsel that "You are rich—very rich." By such assumptions, together with the American precautionary measures, together with the preliminary surrender of the British position contained in the stipulations of the Treaty of Washington, the United States obtained its diplomatic victory at Geneva.

The financial settlement, as mentioned above, was $15,500,000 to the United States. Simultaneously, the private claims of British citizens against the United States were established at $1,929,819 and an award of this amount was made to Britain. American private claims against Britain were dismissed. If one considers, then, the award in Halifax of $5,500,000 to Canada for inshore fishing privileges, the net American financial gain from the Washington Treaty of 1871 was $7,429,-819, a tidy sum—not to mention the precedent established in favor of American principles of neutrality.

Perhaps, one should say in conclusion, John Bassett Moore over-estimated the importance of the Treaty of Washington and the Geneva arbitration when he described it as the largest triumph of American diplomacy after the Treaty of Paris ending the American revolution. This praise seems a little overdone, for the Treaty of Washington was not itself difficult to conclude, and the arbitration at Geneva after trouble with the indirect claims proceeded easily to its foreordained end. Even so, the Geneva award marked the greatest arbitration in American diplomatic history, perhaps in world history. The achievement of Hamilton Fish in 1871–1872 in arranging all the issues outstanding between the United States and Great Britain must go down as a large act of statesmanship, comparable to John Quincy Adams's negotiation of the Transcontinental Treaty with Spain of more than fifty years before.

4. *TR and Alaska*

The last major boundary dispute that the United States has had with Great Britain concerned the extent of the Alaska panhandle territory, and it was happily settled in 1903. This dispute was of considerably less importance than the controversies that preceded it, but once again showed how Great Britain and the United States were able to dispose of difficulties without war. It also showed, once more, how highly political—in the domestic sense—these disputes with Britain were. If anyone should suppose that whenever the United States had trouble with the erstwhile mother country it was necessary only for diplomats to fix the extent of the difficulty and arrive at an equitable solution, without attention to the exigencies of American politics, he need only trace the negotiations over the Alaskan boundary from 1898 to 1903 to see how politics in the United States simply could not stop at the water's edge.

The origin of the panhandle argument with Britain lay in the uncertainties of the Anglo-Russian treaty of 1825, wherein the two nations had sought to establish the boundary between Russian Alaska and British Canada. According to this treaty the line started at the southern end of the panhandle, at 54° 40'—but the next point chosen turned out after subsequent surveys to be nonexistent. The treaty then confounded this confusion by taking the boundary northward from crest to crest along a mythical mountain range. A third confusion appeared in the section of the treaty that stated that where a line from crest to crest would be more than ten marine leagues (a marine league equals 3.45 miles) from the ocean the boundary should run parallel to indentations of the coastline and not more than ten leagues from it. Because the Alaskan coast was split by numerous islands, large and small, and by long narrow bays (or canals, as they are called), such a line was geometrically impossible. The only saving feature of the Anglo-Russian treaty of 1825 was its intent, which was reasonably clear: Russia was seeking, and to this the British had agreed, to retain control of the coast down to 54° 40′.

No one cared about the panhandle lands until gold was discovered in the Canadian Klondike in August 1896, whereupon it was suddenly realized that the easiest access to the gold fields was across the panhandle. The Canadians in June 1898 laid claim to a boundary which would have given them the narrow bays and hence a free passage to the Klondike fields. Their claim to one of the largest bays, the Lynn canal, threatened to bisect southeastern Alaska. On the Lynn canal were the three important settlements of Pyramid Harbor, Dyea, and Skagway, each harbor leading to a pass over the mountains to the gold fields. The Canadians offered to negotiate, providing the United States would agree in advance to give them Pyramid Harbor. The Canadian claim was a barefaced fraud, a diplomatic holdup. Secretary of State John Hay wrote on June 15, 1899 to the American ambassador in London, Joseph H. Choate, that "It is as if a kidnapper, stealing one of your children, should say that his conduct was more than fair, it was even generous, because he left you two."

From the outset the American government refused to give in to this chicanery, and Secretary Hay in 1899 proposed a commission of six men, three Americans and three chosen by Great Britain, decision to be by majority vote—which meant that the Americans could not lose and, if one Britisher budged, would win. Nothing came of this proposition in 1899. The Canadians would not consent to it. The British were occupied by trouble with the Boers in South Africa (the Boer War began in October 1899 and lasted to June 1902). Hay had other irons in the fire, such as announcement of the open-door policy for the Far East. In Central America he was attempting to amend the Clayton-Bulwer Treaty so as to enable the United States to begin construction of an Isthmian canal. He half expected the British government to attempt to trade concessions in the Isthmus for concessions in Alaska, but the government of Lord Salisbury fortunately played fair with the Americans, perhaps because of the Boer War. Salisbury apparently realized also that the Canadian claims in the panhandle

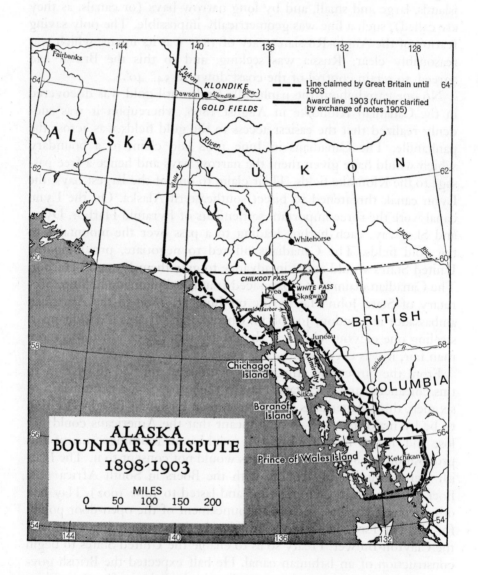

were outrageous.

The issue lapsed until the year 1902 when the Canadian government through Prime Minister Sir Wilfrid Laurier intimated to Ambassador Choate in London that the Hay formula of 1899 would be the best way out of the situation. Laurier had publicly advocated the Canadian position and could not back down before his countrymen, but he wanted to get out of his pledge and wished to do it through the Hay proposal of a six-man commission. Hay in a letter of July 14, 1902, proposed this course to his chief in the White House, President Theodore Roosevelt. The commission would not be an arbitral tribunal, he assured "TR." "I do not think they [the Canadians] have a leg to stand on, and I think any impartial court of jurists would so decide. At the same time I recognize the danger of submitting such a matter to an ordinary arbitration, the besetting sin of which is to split the difference. My suggestion was a submission of the question of the interpretation of the treaty of 1825 to a tribunal of six, three on a side, a majority to decide. In this case it is impossible that we should lose, and not at all impossible that a majority should give a verdict in our favor." This seemed, certainly, a safe course.

Roosevelt at this point, however, began to get difficult, and Hay's biographer, Tyler Dennett, has concluded that the president was trying to drum up a campaign issue for 1904. TR did allow Secretary Hay on January 23, 1903 to sign a treaty with the British ambassador in Washington, Sir Michael Herbert, giving the controversy to a six-man commission. But then he began to make difficulties, small and large. Five days after the treaty went to the Senate for advice and consent the president withdrew it for a significant "correction." He had discovered that the commission of six was referred to in the body of the treaty as a "tribunal" but in the preamble was described as an "arbitral tribunal." The adjective had to come out. Hay's assistant, Alvey A. Adee, reported to the secretary on January 31, 1903 that the first sheet of the treaty had to be "re-engrossed, with the necessary changes. It will be ready on Monday, when the seals can be broken, the treaty untied, the new sheet substituted, and the blame thing re-tied ready for re-apposition of the seals, which can be done without re-signing." The British accepted the treaty with the excised adjective.

There followed two typical Roosevelt maneuvers. First the president appointed, under the terms of the treaty of 1903, the American members of the commission. The treaty stipulated "impartial jurists of repute who shall consider judicially the question submitted to them," and TR chose ex-Senator George Turner of Washington, Senator Henry Cabot Lodge, and Secretary of War Elihu Root. Root was a member of the administration, presumably no impartial individual. Lodge was the president's bosom friend. Turner represented a state which was highly interested in the fate of the panhandle. The Canadian prime minister, Laurier, at this precise moment engaged in getting the treaty through the Canadian parliament, protested bitterly to Hay. The secretary of state was appalled at Lodge's appointment, though he could not intimate this to Sir Wilfrid. He wrote to his good friend Henry White, first secretary of the American embassy in London, how the Massachusetts senator "as if the devil were inspiring him . . . took occasion last week to make a speech in Boston, one half of it filled with abuse of the Canadians, and the other half with attacks on the State Department. He is a clever man and a man of a great deal of force in the Senate, but the infirmity of his mind and character is that he never sees but one subject at a time . . . Of course, you know his very intimate relations with the President . . ."

Not content with this sabotage of Hay's negotiation, Roosevelt then sent his views on the Alaska boundary to Henry White and to Justice Oliver Wendell Holmes of the Supreme Court, visiting in England, and suggested that White and Holmes speak to the British prime minister, Arthur Balfour, and to Joseph Chamberlain, the colonial secretary: the president contended, via his two intermediaries, that if the commission did not decide the way it should, then he, Roosevelt, would run the boundary line and the Canadians and British could make the most of it. Hay gently protested to Roosevelt on September 25, 1903 that "Of course the matter is now *sub judice*. You can say nothing about it . . ."

Finally on October 20, 1903 the commission, meeting in London, voted in favor of the American claim. The two Canadian members championed their side to the end, but to no avail, for the British member, the lord chief justice, Lord Alverstone, voted with the United States. Hay was elated. As he informed his wife in a letter of October 24, the president "loaded me with compliments today in the Cabinet meeting. 'Nobody living could have done the work as I did,' etc. etc. 'It was the biggest success of my life.' Etc." The completeness of the victory, the secretary concluded, was "something amazing. We have got everything we claimed . . ." "I think myself," he wrote, "that Lord Alverstone is the hero of the hour. No American statesman would have dared to give a decision on his honor and conscience against the claim of his own country."

Whether Alverstone gave his decision on the basis of the evidence, or because of the president's carefully communicated views, is difficult to say. He doubtless learned of TR's threat to run the boundary in case the commission did not do its duty. He may have concluded that the advices of law and politics in this case nicely coincided. In a public speech after the decision Alverstone said that "If when any kind of arbitration is set up they don't want a decision based on the law and the evidence, they must not put a British judge on the commission." Perhaps this was the sole basis of the lord chief justice's stand. One should probably be content with this explanation, publicly offered, and with it draw the veil over the Alaska boundary decision of 1903.

Such was the record of accommodation with Great Britain during the nineteenth and early twentieth centuries—the Alaska boundary settlement, the *Alabama* claims arbitration, the Oregon Treaty, the Webster-Ashburton Treaty. American diplomacy had resolved with Great Britain four disputes which otherwise might have passed into war. The record was a good one, considering the way in which such other nations of the time as France, Germany, Italy, Japan, Russia, even Great Britain had resorted to war to settle similar differences. The United States, perhaps because it was by geography detached from the emotions and interests of Europe and Asia, had managed to bring large diplomatic problems to solution by peaceful means.

ADDITIONAL READING

The most recent account of the Northeast boundary dispute is in Samuel Flagg Bemis's *John Quincy Adams and the Foundations of American Foreign Policy* (New York, 1949); settlement of the boundary began at Paris in 1782, and the son of John Adams considered the boundary problem at Ghent in 1814. See also C. M. Fuess, *Daniel Webster* (2 vols., Boston, 1930); A. B. Corey, *The Crisis of 1830–1842 in Canadian-American Relations* (New Haven, 1941); Thomas E. LeDuc, "The Maine Frontier and the Northeastern Boundary Controversy," *American Historical Review*, vol. 53 (1947–1948), 30–41; Richard N. Current, "Webster's Propaganda and the Ashburton Treaty," *Mississippi Valley Historical Review*, vol. 34 (1947–1948), 187–200; and W. D. Jones, "Lord Ashburton and the Maine Boundary Negotiations," *MVHR*, vol. 40 (1953–1954), 477–490.

The historian of the Northwest boundary dispute, Frederick Merk, has published a half dozen articles in the *Mississippi Valley Historical Review* and the *American Historical Review*, and has concentrated on the dispute's earlier history in *Albert Gallatin and the Oregon Problem* (Cambridge, 1950). See the recent biography of Gallatin by Raymond Walters, Jr., *Albert Gallatin* (New York, 1957). John S. Galbraith, *The Hudson's Bay Company as an Imperial Factor* (Berkeley, 1957) has a section on Oregon. Consult also the standard biographies and monographs on Tyler, Polk, and manifest destiny, listed at the end of chapter 4. A clever article showing that the slogan "fifty-four forty or fight" became current in 1845 and that Oregon had minor importance in the election of 1844 is Edwin A. Miles, " 'Fifty-four Forty or Fight'—an American Political Legend," *Mississippi Valley Historical Review*, vol. 44 (1957–1958), 291–309.

For the *Alabama* claims the best account by far is in Allan Nevins, *Hamilton Fish: The Inner History of the Grant Administration* (New York, 1936), a splendid diplomatic biography. See also W. B. Hesseltine, *Ulysses S. Grant: Politician* (New York, 1935).

On the Alaska boundary arbitration see Charles S. Campbell, Jr., *Anglo-American Understanding: 1898–1903* (Baltimore, 1957), together with Tyler Dennett, *John Hay: From Poetry to Politics* (New York, 1933). The Campbell and Dennett books are both fine pieces of historical scholarship. Dennett's *John Hay* has many merits in addition to its pages on the Alaska boundary, for it is one of the most ably written volumes in the literature of American history. Thomas A. Bailey's "Theodore Roosevelt and the Alaska Boundary Settlement," *Canadian Historical Review*, vol. 18 (1937), 123–130 cuts to proper size TR's role in the success of the negotiation and corrects the pages in Henry F. Pringle, *Theodore Roosevelt* (New York, 1931; available in paperback). Biographies of statesmen involved in the Alaska arbitration are Allan Nevins, *Henry White* (New York, 1930); P. C. Jessup, *Elihu Root* (2 vols., New York, 1938); and John A. Garraty, *Henry Cabot Lodge* (New York, 1953).

The New Manifest Destiny

A new feeling of manifest destiny appeared in the United States at the end of the nineteenth century, and it opened an exciting epoch in the history of American foreign relations. This notion differed drastically from its mid-century predecessor, the belief that the United States was destined to extend territorially across the North American continent; according to the newly manifest destiny, America should take its jurisdiction overseas to noncontinental possessions in the Caribbean, Pacific, and Far East. With the purchase of Alaska and expulsion of the French from Mexico in the year 1867, the old spirit of manifest destiny had run out. The old interest in territorial expansion had spent itself by the end of the Civil War, and for thirty years afterward there were few moves of importance in American diplomacy. From the inauguration of President Grant in 1869 to the end of the second administration of Grover Cleveland in 1897, Americans were busy with many other things—this was the period of the emergence of modern America, of change from an agricultural to industrial economy, from rural life to city life. It marked the settlement of the West, the closing of the frontier. Issues of foreign affairs fell from sight. They were occasionally raised by officials in Washington, but only for purposes which smacked of domestic politics. "I have sometimes been inclined to think," Senator George F. Hoar once remarked during this quiescent era, "that when you saw uncommon activity in our grave, reverend, and somewhat sleepy Committee on

Foreign Relations . . . it was circumstantial evidence, not that there was any great trouble as to our foreign relations, but that a Presidential election was at hand." Even so, by the mid-1880's and early 1890's a change began to appear in popular and official sentiment. The period of economic growth was slacking off, the dire memories of 1861–1865 were disappearing, the sectional wounds were closing. There arose talk of overseas possessions, of a novel kind of manifest destiny. The Republican Party in 1892 pledged its belief in "the achievement of the manifest destiny of the republic in its broadest sense." The action to achieve this destiny, so solemnly avowed, in the late 1890's commenced a new chapter in the diplomacy of the United States.

The new manifest destiny differed in several ways from its predecessor. For one thing, it was virtually a carbon copy of the contemporary imperialism of European powers in Africa and Asia. There was, undeniably, an American imperialism at the end of the nineteenth century. The latter years of the nineteenth century were the heyday of European imperialism—Cecil Rhodes was consolidating large territories in Africa, Germany was sending colonists to the Cameroons and other places in Africa, and France in Africa and Asia was bringing millions of strange peoples under its rule. The territories that came to the United States as a result of the new manifest destiny brought several millions of alien peoples under American rule. Some of these peoples eventually became American citizens, but many never did.

Then too, in its peculiar philosophical roots the new manifest destiny stood apart from the old. The views of American destiny current at the time of the Mexican War derived from no philosophy in particular, but had come out of American experience, out of the long-dreamed-about destiny of the settlers of the New World, out of the ambitions of revolutionary patriots who thought that their republican experiment might well be destined to rule a continent. The new manifest destiny, on the other hand, could trace its origin to a distinct body of philosophical ideas, to the views of the so-called Darwinists. Darwinism was highly popular in America in the later nineteenth century. The United States, according to Darwinist beliefs, was a strong nation bound to extend its power over weaker nations, a national instance of what the biologists had found in the plant and animal kingdoms, natural selection, survival of the fittest.

But perhaps most noteworthy about this viewpoint was the essential intolerance of its advocates, their notion of American superiority argued from the biology of Darwin, which made the period of the new manifest destiny a saddening episode in American history. Ever since the foundation of the republic, and for a century and a half before that, the feeling had existed in America that in the New World all men were equal in rights if not in ability. There was thought to be in the Western Hemisphere a view of humanity different from that which prevailed in Europe and Asia. Americans, so it was believed, had banded together to fight intolerance and superiority, so that everyone who wished could pursue his future in his own way. The apotheosis of this belief came during the Jacksonian era in the United States. Democracy thereafter seemed to rule supreme. To be sure, Jackson's view of humanity carried within itself, in the institution of Negro slavery, the seeds of its own destruction, but the slavery incubus was destroyed in the Civil War. After 1865 Europeans and Asians alike began to become accustomed, as Americans long had been, to describing the United States as a model for governments everywhere. Then, at this very moment, the United States succumbed to the idea of American superiority, interpreted in Darwinian terms of natural selection. With this false view of themselves, preening themselves on their destiny, Americans in the last years of the nineteenth century began to look for overseas territory to conquer.

There were some similarities between the new manifest destiny and the old, especially the idea of expansion southward and northward, to Central and South America and to Canada. Under the mid-century expansionist enthusiasm there had been serious projects for Central America and the Caribbean and, as we shall see later, an effort to extend American influence as far into the Pacific as Japan. The drive, the zeal and missionary spirit, the feeling of necessity and inevitability, was present at the end of the nineteenth century as before. In this latter era John Hay found in the impulse to expand an indication of an irresistible cosmic tendency: "No man, no party, can fight with any chance of final success against a cosmic tendency; no cleverness, no popularity avails against the spirit of the age." There was little difference between this outlook of inevitability and the dogmatic assurance about the American future that marked the mid-century. Still, there were drastic differences between the old and new versions of manifest destiny which in sum were far more important than any similarities.

1. *The Philosophy of the New Manifest Destiny*

The intellectual justification for the new manifest destiny began in the year 1859, just before the American Civil War, when Charles Darwin published his *On the Origin of Species,* which referred in its subtitle to *The Preservation of Favored Races in the Struggle for Life.* Its vocabulary included "natural selection," "survival of the fittest," and "struggle for existence." Whatever the gap between Darwinian theories and their application by eager publicists who never read the scientist's words except at fourth- or fifth-hand, politics and diplomacy thenceforth had to live with the notion that life was a struggle in which the fittest survived. From this notion was derived a corollary, that success is an indication of fitness—that survival is, of necessity, fitness—and the secondary corollary that a nation which achieved the ordinary measurements of a great power (large military establishment, economic strength, population) was by this fact a fit nation, a chosen nation, qualified to instruct other and less successful nations in the facts of life. This, to be sure, was an erroneous doctrine. Survival, as anyone who observes the results of war can attest, does not always mean survival of the fittest: the fittest young men are those who go to war and are killed or wounded fighting the fittest young men of the other side. The political Darwinists also forgot or overlooked the phenomenon of mutual aid, to which man owes much of his survival and achievement: by helping each other the members of the human race have risen to wealth and to such security as they have. And there was ignorance on the part of the survival-of-the-fittest enthusiasts that the cause of progress was not the struggle of man against man but the struggle of man against his environment. In the heat of the Darwinian dialectic these subtleties were lost from view. In the United States of the late nineteenth century, even those who rejected biological evolution often accepted without demur the necessity of the struggle of man against man, nation against nation; many cheerfully confused the Christian religion with such beliefs and concluded that the American people, a successful people (and therefore a fit people), were a chosen people, God's anointed. Senator Albert J. Beveridge of Indiana announced in 1899 in a celebrated speech that "God has not been preparing the English-speaking and Teutonic peoples for a thousand years for nothing but vain and idle self-admiration. No! He has made us the master organizers of the world to establish system where chaos reigns. . . . He has made us adepts in government that we may administer government among savages and senile peoples."

There thus seemed no reason to doubt the destiny of the United States. Americans basked in their own excellence. Even Darwin seems to have fallen under the spell of American success, and in his 1871 work *The Descent of Man*, wrote that "There is apparently much truth in the belief that the wonderful progress of the United States, as well as the character of the people, are the results of natural selection; the more energetic, restless, and courageous men from all parts of Europe having emigrated during the last ten or twelve generations to that great country . . ."

From this feeling of American superiority came many vices, which cannot be recited here. One can only guess at how boorish and rude some Americans must have appeared to their contemporaries in other countries at the turn of the century. From available testimony it would seem that they possessed an obnoxious sense of mission, a misplaced zeal that to less successful peoples, peoples perhaps slated for imperial tutelage, made them appear patronizing, greedy, and vain. The traditional American idea that the United States had a mission in the world, a mission to spread to the corners of the earth the values of democracy, began to change into something markedly different: before the Civil War the usual statement of the doctrine of mission had been that the United States should be a witness, in confident but quiet modesty, for democratic principles; after the war the doctrine of mission changed from witnessing to proselytizing. The idea was that if backward peoples did not desire to learn about democratic principles, those principles would be thrust upon them.

The new manifest destiny—taking for its philosophy the Darwinian beliefs, giving a novel and unfortunate interpretation to the American idea of the mission of democracy—also encumbered itself with racism, with the idea of Anglo-Saxon or Aryan superiority. Like the American doctrine of mission, racism in the United States antedated Darwinism, for many Americans had long been convinced of the inferiority of the Indian and the Negro. Racist arguments had been heard at the time of the Mexican War. But racism became a respectable intellectual position after the Civil War when Americans learned the tenets of Darwinism. American scholars in the 1880's and

1890's, many of them fresh from German university seminars where they had imbibed German nationalism as taught by Heinrich von Treitschke and Leopold von Ranke, put forward ideas of racial superiority. When the first important American graduate school was established in Baltimore at Johns Hopkins University, Herbert Baxter Adams, the instructor of a group of brilliant graduate students which included the youthful Woodrow Wilson, advanced the thesis that all that was worthwhile in American and English government could be traced back in "germ" form to the tribal inhabitants of the Teutonic forests. The young Henry Adams, trained as a historian in this period, later wrote that "I flung myself obediently into the arms of the Anglo-Saxons in history." Such outstanding teachers as John W. Burgess of Columbia taught the primacy of the Anglo-Saxon race, the struggle for existence, the survival of the fittest. "Indifference on the part of Teutonic states to the political civilization of the rest of the world," Burgess announced, "is . . . not only mistaken policy, but disregard of duty." John Fiske, a Harvard-trained historian and philosopher, as early as 1880 gave a series of lectures in England to the effect that the dispersion over the world of the magnificent Aryan political system would eliminate war, and was the next step in world history.

That greatest exponent of the new manifest American destiny, Theodore Roosevelt, the individual who more than any other was the leader of American territorial expansion at the turn of the century, had studied under Burgess at the Columbia University Law School. Whatever his inspiration he certainly mirrored the prejudices of his age. "I preach to you . . . my countrymen," he was saying in 1899, "that our country calls not for the life of ease but for the life of strenuous endeavor." Here was an activist manifestation of the idea of survival of the fittest. The typically Rooseveltian preachments against race suicide were the normal notions of a Darwinian enthusiast. Roosevelt believed that every American family should have at least four children, and at Sagamore Hill he raised five. One could not expect an individual like him to have patience with such persons as Henry James who, wearied of the grosser tendencies of American life, sought refuge from the struggle for existence by emigrating to England. Love of country was essential to the struggle for existence, Roosevelt always believed. Without it a nation sank into degeneracy and weakness, exposing itself to conquest by some virile enemy.

Eventually TR thanked heaven that Henry James was "now an avowedly British novelist," for he was a "man in whom intense love of country is wanting . . . a very despicable creature, no matter how well equipped with all the minor virtues and graces, literary, artistic, and moral."

Many of the religious leaders of America were as enthusiastic about social Darwinism and its international corollary, the White Man's Burden, as were the political leaders and college teachers. A notable example was the Reverend Josiah Strong, who in 1885 published a small volume entitled *Our Country: Its Possible Future and Its Present Crisis*. This book sold 170,000 copies and was translated into many foreign languages. Something of an individualist and a believer in the social gospel Strong was nevertheless against immigrants, Catholics, Mormons, saloons, tobacco, large cities, socialists, and concentrated wealth. In his writings he managed to combine these prejudices of rural Protestant America with a strong feeling of manifest destiny. *Our Country* was a diatribe for Anglo-Saxon and American supremacy in the world. The Anglo-Saxon people, he wrote, "is multiplying more rapidly than any other European race. It already owns one-third of the earth, and will get more as it grows. By 1980 the world Anglo-Saxon race should number at least 713,000,000. Since North America is much bigger than the little English isle, it will be the seat of Anglo-Saxondom." Was there room for doubt, he asked, that this wonderful Anglo-Saxon race, "unless devitalized by alcohol and tobacco, is destined to dispossess many weaker races, assimilate others, and mold the remainder, until, in a very true and important sense, it has Anglo-Saxonized mankind?" Strong saw that the future expansion of America was not merely destiny already in part made manifest but the desire of Almighty Providence, whose commandment was "Prepare ye the way of the Lord!" His was a powerful and typical voice in an era when in American colleges thousands of student volunteers for missionary service abroad were striving to realize the vision of the YMCA leader John R. Mott, "the evangelization of the world in this generation."

There were some Americans, many in aggregate, unfortunately few in influence, who opposed Darwinism and the new idea of manifest destiny, but their efforts were unsuccessful. And many of the Darwinists themselves, when faced with the results of their teaching, drew back and became anti-imperialists, opposing the war with Spain in

1898. John W. Burgess of Columbia, stout defender of Darwinism, took himself into the anti-imperialist camp in 1898, arguing that it would be "disastrous to American political civilization" to extend American authority over subject peoples. David Starr Jordan, president of Stanford University, a biologist and Darwinist, opposed imperialism as the wrong means to the right end. Jordan believed that the white race was superior to other races; he contended that the inequality of progress which could be seen among the many races of the world argued biological inequality; but he thought that to use force to advance American manifest destiny—as the United States did at the turn of the century—was degrading and would pull the race down toward the level of the conquered, inferior races.

There were many Americans who held variants of these views, and it would be inaccurate to argue that the new manifest destiny, with its intellectual justification of Darwinism, found acceptance everywhere. But it was difficult to stand against the supporters of the new manifest destiny, given the popularity of the Darwinian ideas. Some anti-imperialists tried to use the arguments of Darwinism to combat the new American foreign policy. Members of the Democratic Party (expansionism was strongest in the Republican Party) could not challenge openly the idea on which imperialism rested, Anglo-Saxon racial superiority, because this would be an uneasy topic to discuss in the American South. Southern Democrats, if anti-imperialist, chose to contend that annexation of overseas territories would dilute American nationality by adding inferior island breeds.

It is a curious fact that Darwinism, the philosophy of the new manifest destiny, met its demise during the first World War, when the Germans advanced the idea of Teutonic superiority in support of their hegemony of Europe. It was ironical that American entrance into the first World War occurred just at the time when it proved necessary to discredit Darwinism, for the Darwinian ideas had extolled the virtues of such a military conflict as the United States entered in 1917.

2. *The New American Navy*

It was under the impulse of the new sense of manifest destiny that there came a most important development for American diplomacy in the 1880's and 1890's: the rejuvenation of the American navy.

Appearance of the new navy at the end of the nineteenth century had a notable effect on American diplomacy, for there is always a correlation between national military power and diplomacy. It increased American stature abroad, making easier the tasks of the republic's diplomats, and it also had special importance for American history because of the way in which it increased the belligerence of public opinion. Americans were proud of their navy and it was no small factor in the outbreak of the war with Spain in 1898.

The navy at the end of the Civil War had been a powerful military arm, so formidable that it may have been the strongest fleet in the world. The military power of the American republic in 1865, both navy and army, was at its peak, and had the United States then desired to set forth on a career of conquest—Canada, Mexico, Central America, the Caribbean—no European nation could have prevented it. There were too many domestic tasks to occupy American energies, and people turned to exploiting the West, building a gigantic industrial power, constructing large cities. The Civil War army disbanded, and in about two years had shrunk from its one-time peak of nearly a million to fewer than sixty thousand men. The American navy likewise lost the edge of its fighting strength. The auctioneer and the axe reduced the Civil War fleet within nine months of Appomattox from 971 ships to 29.

In design these remaining ships were quickly outmoded by construction of new and far more formidable vessels by the navies of foreign powers. There had been a time in history, not far removed from 1865, when after a great war it was wise policy to do nothing with one's ships except lay up some of the vessels and keep the better ones seaworthy. Ship design changed slowly prior to the mid-nineteenth century. Nelson's flagship *Victory* had been laid down in 1759, and was as powerful in 1805 as at the time of her launching nearly half a century before. The year 1865, unfortunately, came at a far different moment in the annals of naval design, for there was in process a revolution in ship construction—the epochal transition from sail to steam and from wood to steel, the latter change inspired by new types of naval ordnance. The revolution had begun when Robert Fulton demonstrated the practicality of steam locomotion. Some years thereafter came the introduction of armor plate and iron hulls, forced by the Paixhans shell gun. A French artillery officer, Henri Joseph Paixhans, in a treatise published in 1822 had recommended that the

French navy be armed with shell guns rather than the old solid-shot cannon, and his proposal was taken up by the French and other navies. An especially acute problem, after invention of new types of naval ordnance, was the vulnerable paddle wheels of the first steam-driven warships; the answer was the screw propeller, in the introduction of which the American navy of the 1840's became the envy of the world with its ship *Princeton*, the first propeller-driven man of war. One thing thus led to another. Construction of ironclad, propeller-driven, modern-gunned warships was well advanced everywhere by the time of their use during the American Civil War.

In such a period of revolutionary ship design no navy could afford to ignore the constantly lengthening list of inventions, yet this was the policy of the American navy after 1865. The navy stood still in the midst of the striking changes in propulsion, armor, and guns. American naval officers on countless occasions were embarrassed when foreign officers, boarding an American warship and observing the collection of marine antiquities and curios which made up the ship's armament and gear, acted as if they were visiting a museum and spoke sadly about the past. While other navies went from new vessel to new vessel there was even a retrograde movement in the American fleet, from steam to canvas. Some American sailing vessels during the Civil War had been equipped with auxiliary steam engines, but policy in the Navy Department afterward became so archaic that according to the navy regulations of 1870 no steam was to be used except when absolutely necessary. As a naval officer of that unhappy period reminisced many years later, "To burn coal was so grievous an offense in the eyes of the authorities that for years the coal-burning captain was obliged to enter in the logbook in *red ink* his reasons for getting up steam and starting the engines." After the Civil War the navy went doggedly downhill under the direction of such unimaginative officers as Admiral David D. Porter, who seems to have thought that steam was an invention of the devil. The reactionary line officers were determined to put the engineer officers in their places, and managed to do so, virtually eliminating them. The technicians could not, so the old salts maintained, take over the navy. When the line officers thought of any advanced type of ship at all, it was the Civil War monitor, and beyond this their horizons of design did not extend. As late as 1887 Admiral Porter was urging the repair of the aged and rotting single-turreted monitors of the war of 1861–1865, and recommended construction of as many new monitors as cruisers, contending that vessels of the monitor type, properly equipped and handled, "would be a match for the heaviest European ironclad that could reach our shores." The officers of the line, unfortunately, were subject to no instruction from the civil secretaries of the navy, who might have interrupted the peace of the Navy Department in Washington and made some changes for the good of the service. This the succession of political secretaries did not do, either from indifference or gross incompetence or ignorance, perhaps the latter more than anything else. It was alleged of Rutherford B. Hayes's secretary of the navy, Richard W. Thompson of Indiana, that he was so densely ignorant of naval affairs as to express surprise upon learning that ships were hollow.

There was some realization of the antiquity of the post-Civil War fleet when during a minor crisis with Spain over capture of a filibuster ship off Cuba the navy engaged in fleet maneuvers in the Gulf early in 1874. The appearance there of the American navy—the "heterogeneous collection of naval trash," of "antiquated and rotting ships" —shook the morale of the entire service. But the turning point in the navy came with the short-lived administration of President Garfield in 1881, when it was suddenly realized in connection with a minor Latin American war that the Republic of Chile had a better navy than the United States. The assertion was made, with some justification, that a single ship of the Chilean navy could have destroyed the entire United States fleet. Apropos this petty Latin American conflict it was rumored that "when Admiral Balch undertook to make some kindly suggestions . . . the Chileans simply told the American admiral, and the American government through him, that if he did not mind his own business, they would send him and his fleet to the bottom of the ocean."

This sort of provocation, if it never happened, was a possibility, and American pride simply could not stand the thought of a Chilean ship sinking an entire fleet and its admiral with it. There also was fear of blockade of American ports, in event of some unforeseen war, and in such a case millions of dollars would have been lost if the blockade would have lasted as long as a week. It seemed good business to pay a little money in advance and have a navy. There was fear, too, of a large indemnity that might be enforced by a victorious enemy nation, such as France after 1871 had to pay to Germany. Worries such as these were churned by the British bombardment of Alexandria in 1882, when the 80-ton British naval guns pounded to pieces the Egyptian fortifications. About this time the U.S.S. *Tallapoosa*, a warship in the American fleet, was run down by a coal barge. It seemed as if something had to be done about the condition of the United States navy. The combination of events and fears and humiliation led in 1883 during the administration of President Chester A. Arthur to an act of Congress providing for three small "protected" cruisers and a dispatch boat, the first step toward a new American navy.

The Act of 1883 was a beginning, and more new construction swiftly followed. The vessels appropriated in 1883, completed in 1885 and 1887 and known as the White Squadron, much admired by the American public, proved rather unsatisfactory. In addition to their engines all of them carried full sail rigs. They had no side armor (in the terminology of the day they were not armored; their deck armor categorized them merely as protected), and they were vulnerable to any armored ship able to catch up with them. In speed they were soon outdistanced by foreign naval construction. And it was belatedly realized that commerce destroyers, in the old American naval tradition, were no longer feasible for the United States in an age when steam vessels required numerous coaling stations to operate outside of coastal waters. During the first Cleveland administration of 1885–1889 the White Fleet gave way, on the designing boards and in appropriation for construction, to new vessels aggregating nearly 100,-000 tons. The ships authorized under Cleveland included the famous *Maine*, which later came to so catastrophic an end. The *Maine* was a typical battleship of its day, displacing less than 7,000 tons, with maximum speed of less than 18 knots, carrying four ten-inch guns. Still, the very year it was launched, 1890, marked its assignment to a second rank in the new American navy, for in the Naval Act of 1890 Congress made appropriation for first-class—that is, high seas—battleships. This program resulted in some famous vessels including the battleships *Indiana, Massachusetts,* and *Oregon.* The *Oregon* class displaced about 10,000 tons, had a speed of 15.5 to 17 knots, was armed with four 13-inch and eight 8-inch pieces, and cost between $5,500,-000 and $6,500,000. The *Oregon* herself, incidentally, became one of the best known ships ever to serve in the American navy and had a long and gallant career of over sixty years—the ship rounded the Horn in 1898 from Pacific to Atlantic to help blockade the Spanish fleet at Santiago, served in the first and second World Wars, and finally was sold to a Japanese firm and broken up for junk in the year 1957.

With the battleship appropriation of 1890 the United States at last gave up its ideas of a navy of commerce raiders. It set out to construct a battle fleet capable of opposing the greatest ships of the world. This was at first not realized by the public, and until the end of the decade —the naval act of 1900 was the first exception to this rule—it proved wise policy to designate the new battleships as "seagoing coast-line battleships."

The navy was building and the appropriation of 1890 was passing through Congress when there appeared a book by Captain Alfred Thayer Mahan, *The Influence of Sea Power upon History*, which in its effect upon history was as important as that other fateful nineteenth-century opus, *On the Origin of Species*. Mahan's book had been finished in 1886, and the author had been giving its contents in the form of lectures at the Naval War College at Newport, but its publication in 1890 was a landmark in the literature of the new manifest destiny. It deeply influenced all the great powers of the world, including Germany and Japan. These latter two nations, together with the United States, were newcomers on the world scene, but they too aspired to national greatness, including if necessary a large navy. Captain Mahan informed them that naval power was the key to national greatness. Mahan taught that nations may rise or decline but never stand still, that expansion was essential, that to support expansion a government must have access to accumulated wealth, that a large and flourishing foreign commerce was the best means of accumulating wealth, that a navy was necessary to secure and ensure foreign commerce, and that a navy required colonies for coaling stations. Mahan had generalized his theories from the rise of England and the British navy, and *The Influence of Sea Power upon History* dealt with the history of English sea power from 1660 to 1783. There is no question that Mahan failed to realize the uniqueness of Britain's historical position athwart the chief western entrances to the Continent of Europe, possessing as well such strategic places as Gibraltar, Malta, and (after 1882) Alexandria, not to mention the Cape of Good Hope and Singapore. He failed to ask whether Britain's success could be attained by a nation not a strategically well-situated island. He underestimated the force of non-naval factors in Britain's

rise to world power, such as the appearance of the industrial revolution in England a century before it spread to the other countries of
the world. His teachings largely ignored the circumstances of the late
nineteenth century, when a great power required many more ac-
couterments than a large and powerful navy. He did manage to stress
the advantages, actual and alleged, of sea power at a time when naval
construction appeared otherwise desirable to great nations of the
world. It was peculiarly appropriate that Mahan should have been an
American, for his writings illuminated the new interest and position
of the United States in world affairs.

What was the outcome of this navalism of Mahan? "It was not that
what he said was profound," Walter Millis has written, "but that he
had the luck to say it at a moment in history when countless prosperous and influential persons were looking for precisely this justification for courses which they wished for their own reasons to pursue.
Mahan taught that sea power, in and of itself, was a good in peace or
war; and in so doing he tossed an apple of discord into the affairs of
nations for which there was to be no lack of ambitious contenders."
In the two world wars of the first half of the twentieth century the
American navy fortunately would find itself allied with the navy of
Great Britain, but the Germans and Japanese, following only too well
the dogmas of Mahan, gave serious international trouble. German determination to best the British navy was one of the several leading
causes of the first World War. Admiral Alfred von Tirpitz cited
Mahan to the effect that a great power needed a large navy, and over-
looked the fact that a navy for Germany was a luxury whereas for
the inhabitants of the British Isles it was a necessity. Likewise the
Japanese navy in due time challenged the apostles of Mahan in the
American navy.

Navalism, one should nonetheless emphasize, was not an invention
of Mahan—he was only its leading prophet. It grew out of the fateful
philosophy of the time, Darwinism, the feeling that life was a race
and that the rewards fell to the fittest. In America it was one of the
major works in support of the new manifest destiny.

3. *Samoa, Chile, Hawaii, and Venezuela—the Beginnings of an American Imperialism*

Americans by 1890 began looking outside the continental United
States for coaling stations and colonies. Mahan had said that these were

necessities for a great nation. The proponents of the new manifest destiny moved out of the realm of theory and into that of action during the successive administrations of Presidents Benjamin Harrison (1889–1893), Cleveland, and McKinley, first pressing their program in diplomatic crises over Samoa, Chile, Hawaii, and Venezuela, ultimately in 1898 in the Spanish-American War.

The Samoan affair, as American difficulties over the Samoan Islands came to be known, took its origin in a treaty negotiated by an American naval officer with Samoan native chieftains in 1872. The treaty failed of ratification in the Senate, but President Grant dispatched in 1873 a special agent, Colonel A. B. Steinberger, who set himself up as premier of the islands. The American government arranged in 1878 for rights to a naval station at Pago Pago. After a confused interlude during which the United States contended for the islands with Britain and Germany, a conference in Berlin in 1889 provided for a three-power protectorate. When this proved unsatisfactory, the islands were partitioned by a treaty among the three powers signed in Berlin on December 2, 1899.

The reasons for the partition were complicated, but boiled down to the fact that the two newcomers to world power, Germany and the United States, wished sole ownership of territory in the Samoas. Britain apparently was indifferent to the islands, and at the moment was thinking of the Boer War which began in South Africa on October 12, 1899—although pressure from New Zealand, where the Samoan question seemed more important, may have moved the British also in the direction of a partition. By the treaty of 1899 Germany received the two largest islands and the United States obtained several islands, including Tutuila with its harbor of Pago Pago. Britain received from Germany a compensation in the form of the Tonga Islands, located just south of the Samoas, together with part of the Solomon Islands and some adjustments in West Africa. All this complication over the Samoas serves to indicate the nature of international dealing in the age of imperialism. The German gains from this bargaining disappeared in 1914 at the beginning of the first World War when New Zealand forces occupied the German Samoas.

During the 1890's also there came a crisis over the government and territory of Hawaii, which derived from a complexity of problems and issues but occurred at the beginning of America's new era of manifest destiny and led, eventually, to American annexation of the Hawaiian Islands. American interest in Hawaii had appeared early in the nineteenth century, after a group of missionaries journeyed to Oahu and undertook to convert the natives to Christianity. The sons and grandsons of this missionary group gained economic control of the islands, and their development of sugar plantations linked the Hawaiian economy closely to that of the United States, so closely in fact that by the early 1890's a change in the American tariff threatened serious economic difficulties. The McKinley Tariff Act of 1890 authorized a bounty of two cents a pound for home-grown American sugar. The two-cent domestic bounty broke Hawaiian sugar prices, which fell from $100 to $60 a ton, with an estimated loss to Hawaiian producers of $12,000,000. To some Americans in the island it appeared desirable to place the islands under American rule for this would permit Hawaiian sugar to receive the two-cent bounty.

But there were other forces at work which explain the course of events in Hawaii over the next several years. It is true that many of the sugar barons on the islands opposed annexation to the United States, though annexation was to their advantage in relief from the tariff. They reasoned that if their plantations came under the American flag there would be no more contract labor from the Orient, especially from Japan, because American law would forbid this practice that amounted at times to virtual slavery. Still, in opposition to this view was the belief of the middle class of whites in the islands that they were in danger of being outvoted in island elections by the Hawaiians of native descent. In the early 1890's the island whites were not yet overly worried about an inundation of Japanese contract laborers, for these latter were not at the moment so numerous or influential as to dispute control of the government with the whites. The native Hawaiians were in a position to do this, and hence the desire for annexation.

In the midst of these feelings there came a crisis in the government of the islands when the native dynasty in 1891 brought to the Hawaiian throne Queen Liliuokalani, an exponent of a firm pro-native policy. The queen had not been in favor of the American naval base at Pearl Harbor, provided for in a Hawaiian-American treaty of 1884, ratified in 1887. Moreover, upon ascending the throne she began to oppose all constitutional limits to her power, threatening to exert her royal prerogatives against the white, American-dominated legislature. The Hawaiian whites, already suffering from fears and worries because of the sugar depression, concerned over the future of their property under rule of this ambitious queen, overthrew her government on January 17, 1893.

The revolution received the enthusiastic support of the American minister to the islands, John L. Stevens, who ordered American marines to land from the cruiser *Boston*. Stevens allowed the revolutionists to raise the American flag over the Honolulu government buildings on February 1, 1893, proclaimed Hawaii a United States protectorate, and with assistance of the revolutionary leader Sanford B. Dole drew up a treaty of annexation. He informed his superiors in Washington that "the Hawaiian pear is now fully ripe, and this is the golden hour for the United States to pluck it."

The minister was mistaken, as the year was 1893, the year when the anti-imperialist Grover Cleveland became president of the United States for a second term (not consecutive; the first was in 1885–1889). The Hawaiian treaty arrived in Washington shortly before Cleveland's inauguration, and President Harrison submitted it to the Senate, but Cleveland five days after taking the oath of office withdrew it for "the purpose of re-examination." He sent out a special commissioner to Hawaii, ex-Congressman James H. Blount, to investigate the revolution together with the conduct of Minister Stevens. Blount appraised the situation in the islands for what it was, and Cleveland refused to resubmit the treaty. The revolutionary government led by Dole had no choice—allowing Liliuokalani back on the throne was no recourse, for she was threatening to behead the revolutionists—but to continue its regime under the guise of an Hawaiian Republic. Appropriately, the new republic was proclaimed on July 4, 1894, and it maintained a tranquil existence until 1898 when the United States annexed it during the Spanish-American War.

What can one conclude about the history of these events in Hawaii, from the dethronement of Liliuokalani to Cleveland's refusal of annexation? They have often been decried as a sorry and shabby episode in American diplomacy, an affair in which a majority of the Hawaiian people was thwarted by a planter clique of white Hawaiians and the American minister. Perhaps this description applies, but one must realize that the Hawaiian situation was complicated. The planters and middle-class whites represented the only substantial economic group in the islands, and their plans for developing Hawaii could not continue under the rule of a backward dynasty. Nor could they easily heed the desires of the Hawaiian people or the contract workers.

Moreover, it was strategically advantageous for the United States to do as it later did, annex the Hawaiian Islands. The Hawaiian archi- pelago offered a well-situated base from which to control the Pacific approaches to the American west coast. If America had not annexed Hawaii in 1898 some other great power, perhaps Germany or Japan, would have done so. The action of Minister Stevens in 1893 must be considered in the light of these circumstances, and in retrospect the effort to obtain annexation does not appear unreasonable.

In the Pacific in the 1880's and 1890's there thus were these minor crises over Hawaii and Samoa. In Latin America there likewise were troubles—albeit not over possible annexation—with Chile and Vene- zuela. The difficulty with Chile can be dismissed rather briefly, and it is of interest to the student of American diplomacy because it il- lustrates the growing sensitivity of American public opinion to all international difficulties, and also because it shows a considerable change both in the American navy and in naval attitudes since the fabled occasion in 1881 when the Chileans threatened to send Admiral Balch and his fleet to the bottom of the ocean. The new trouble came after the United States in 1891 had sought to prevent shipment of arms to some Chilean revolutionists. The revolutionists, as American luck frequently has it in Latin America, took over the government, and they were understandably unfriendly toward the nation which had denied them arms. When an American cruiser, the *Baltimore*, sent some of its crew ashore on leave at Valparaiso, a mob attacked the unarmed American sailors on October 16, 1891, killing two and in- juring sixteen. Some sailors were thrown into the local jail. President Harrison was incensed at this affair, and when his pacific-minded secretary of state, James G. Blaine, sought to defend the Chileans in a cabinet meeting the president leaned forward and with an emphatic gesture declared: "Mr. Secretary, that insult was to the uniform of the United States sailors." Harrison sent a special message to Congress on January 25, 1892, virtually asking for war. The country was enormously stirred by the Chilean insult. The commander of a naval vessel which replaced the *Baltimore* in Chilean waters, Robley D. Evans, found himself known to the American public as Fighting Bob.

Commander Evans had not been involved in the original trouble at Valparaiso; but when his ship, the *Yorktown*, arrived in harbor there appeared the makings of a further fracas which Fighting Bob duly solved. The Chileans in torpedo boats made a number of close passes at the *Yorktown*, on one occasion missing her by less than six feet. Evans "gave orders, if one of them even scratched the paint on the *Yorktown*, to blow the boat out of the water and kill every man in her, so that there could be no question of an accidental collision. I then saw the officer in charge of the drills, and told him that he certainly had great confidence in the steering gear of his torpedo boats; that if anything should jam so that one of them struck me I would blow her bottom out. He replied that the water in the harbor belonged to his Government, and that he proposed to use it for the purpose of drilling his boats. I answered that I was fully aware of the ownership he had stated, but that the *Yorktown* and the paint on her belonged to the United States . . ." Happily, tempers cooled at Valparaiso, and the Chilean government apologized for the attack on the crew of the *Baltimore* and paid an indemnity of $75,000.

A few years later, in 1895, came the much more serious Venezuelan incident, arising out of a controversy between Venezuela and Great Britain over the boundary line of British Guiana. The dispute between the two nations went back to 1814 when the British had taken their part of Guiana from the Dutch. A British engineer, Sir Robert Schomburgk, made a survey of the boundary in 1840 and proposed a line which Venezuela rejected. Whereupon the dispute lapsed because of its essential unimportance until in the 1880's gold was discovered in the contested region. The British in 1887 refused the good offices of the United States in settling the dispute; Cleveland in his annual message of 1894 offered to renew his attempt of 1887 to bring about an arbitration; Britain refused to arbitrate.

Here, assuredly, the British government under Lord Salisbury made a grievous miscalculation, for the new confidence in manifest destiny was waxing strong in America in the early 1890's. On every hand the imperialists were making themselves known. Theodore Roosevelt could describe the anti-imperialists in 1895 as "solemn prattlers" who "strive after an ideal in which they shall happily unite the imagination of a green grocer with the heart of a Bengalese baboo. They are utterly incapable of feeling one thrill of generous emotion, or the slightest throb of that pulse which gives to the world statesmen, patriots, warriors, and poets, and which makes a nation other than a cumberer of the world's surface." When the British navy in April 1895 occupied the port of Corinto in Nicaragua, in an effort to obtain reparation for the expulsion of several British subjects from that little

Central American republic, popular protests in the United States rose to a deafening roar. The Cleveland administration argued cautiously in regard to Nicaragua that the British occupation, avowedly temporary, did not constitute violation of the Monroe Doctrine. Critics at once pointed out the temporary nature of the British occupation of Egypt in 1882. Then the British admiral at Corinto seems to have described the Monroe Doctrine, with a horrendous lack of diplomacy, as an obsolete doctrine and a myth. The patriots raged. Someone discovered—*horribile dictu*—that at a banquet in England the American ambassador, Thomas F. Bayard (who, incidentally, in 1893 was the first American diplomat appointed to ambassadorial rank), had proposed a toast to Queen Victoria. Bayard according to the New York *Tribune* lacked "the superb and indispensable quality of making himself disagreeable at the proper time." He was, in a word, an Anglophile. The Cleveland administration, listening to such criticism from the Republican opposition, hearing it from many Democrats, yielded to popular clamor when after the Nicaraguan affair there came Britain's refusal to arbitrate the Venezuelan boundary. The Cleveland administration took a stand on Venezuela. The first hint of trouble came when a friend of the president made a speech in Detroit to the toast, "Our Veterans: Can They Hear the Bugle Call?"

Cleveland on July 20, 1895 permitted a most remarkable diplomatic note to be sent to Great Britain (Ambassador Bayard did not find an occasion to deliver it until August 7), which testily set forth the American view of the Venezuelan boundary. This was the Olney Corollary to the Monroe Doctrine—that intervention by the United States was permissible and even desirable to force a settlement of any dispute involving the Monroe Doctrine. Cleveland's secretary of state, Richard Olney, announced that "Today the United States is practically sovereign on this continent, and its fiat is law upon the subjects to which it confines its interposition. Why? . . . It is because, in addition to all other grounds, its infinite resources combined with its isolated position render it master of the situation and practically invulnerable as against any or all other powers." One of the most bumptious diplomatic documents ever written by an American diplomat, this note was comparable to the Ostend Manifesto of 1854 and the Huelsemann Note of 1850. Cleveland described it in private as a 20-inch gun. The British government could only have been outraged. Lord Salisbury impolitely waited four months to answer, and asserted in a reply of November 1895 that the Monroe Doctrine was inapplicable to the boundary dispute. He again rejected the American offer of arbitration. Cleveland laid the diplomatic correspondence before Congress, with a blunt affirmation of the applicability of the Monroe Doctrine.

Fortunately for the history of Anglo-American friendship and understanding there was no war over a Venezuelan boundary, for Britain simultaneously was encountering the troubles in South Africa that led to the Boer War. The German emperor William II at this time sent an indiscreet congratulatory telegram to the president of the Boer Republic indicating support for the Dutch-descended Boers in their controversy with Britain. Alarmed, Salisbury backed down over Venezuela. He needed the friendship of the United States, and to him the Venezuelan affair was a minor fracas anyway. Britain agreed to arbitrate the boundary line and the award in 1899 was in accord with the original British claims.

Because of his unbending attitude toward the Venezuelan boundary dispute Cleveland momentarily found himself a popular figure among his fellow Americans. There was applause over the way in which he had dealt with Great Britain. People felt that he at last had taken a strong stand for his country. The imperialists, of course, had failed to convert Cleveland—no special plaudits could have moved that massive conscience. Grover Cleveland was a stubborn man, who would act on a matter when he was convinced of the rightness of his position. In the Venezuelan affair he seems to have believed the dignity of the United States was involved. In regard to Hawaii he saw no reason for annexation, and generally was most unsympathetic toward American overseas expansion. He was by conviction an anti-imperialist, reflecting perhaps the views of the cautious New York business community with which he had been associated in the interim between his two terms of office. A conservative man in ideas and actions, by the end of his second administration in March 1897 he found himself almost completely out of touch with American public opinion. It was primarily because of Cleveland's conservative views on national finance that the Democratic Party deserted his leadership in 1896 in favor of William Jennings Bryan, and the election of 1896 was fought over domestic issues rather than questions of foreign policy. Yet Cleveland had become old-fashioned not merely because of his ideas of domestic economics but because he was an anti-imperialist, an unbeliever in overseas expansion. When he retired to Princeton to live out the remaining few years of his life, his departure from the seat of national government in Washington signified—though this was not at first realized in the flush of McKinley's triumph over "Bryanism"—the passing of the post-Civil War era of inaction in American foreign policy.

ADDITIONAL READING

The best introductions to the new manifest destiny appear in chapters in Ralph H. Gabriel, *The Course of American Democratic Thought* (New York, 1940); Richard Hofstadter, *Social Darwinism in American Thought: 1860–1915* (Philadelphia, 1944; available in paperback); and especially in the first chapter of Julius W. Pratt's *Expansionists of 1898* (Baltimore, 1936). Examples of the literature of the time are Josiah Strong, *Our Country* (New York, 1885) and John W. Burgess, *Political Science and Comparative Constitutional Law* (2 vols., Boston, 1890). A challenge to the new ideas of manifest destiny is Ralph Barton Perry, *The Present Conflict of Ideals* (New York, 1918), a volume inspired by the first World War and Germany's bid for leadership. Also see Edward McNall Burns, *The American Idea of Mission: Concepts of National Purpose and Destiny* (New Brunswick, 1957).

For the new navy see first of all the general account in Harold and Margaret Sprout, *The Rise of American Naval Power: 1776–1918* (Princeton, 1939). Historical and technical background can be found in J. P. Baxter, *The Introduction of the Ironclad Warship* (Cambridge, Mass., 1933). See also William E. Livezey, *Mahan on Sea Power* (Norman, Okla., 1947). A thoughtful view of Mahan is Julius W. Pratt, "Alfred Thayer Mahan," in William T. Hutchinson, ed., *The Marcus W. Jernegan Essays in American Historiography* (Chicago, 1937). Consult Mahan's *The Influence of Sea Power upon History: 1660–1783* (Boston, 1890; available in paperback), and also his magazine articles in the 1890's and after which were collected and published every two or three years under various titles. W. D. Puleston, *Mahan* (New Haven, 1939) is the best biography. See also such accounts as Robley D. Evans, *A Sailor's Log* (New York, 1901) and Edwin A. Falk, *Fighting Bob Evans* (New York, 1931).

As for the events of American diplomacy in this era, there is Albert T. Volwiler, "Harrison, Blaine, and American Foreign Policy, 1889–1893," *American Philosophical Society Proceedings*, vol. 79 (1938), 637–648; Charles C. Tansill, *The Foreign Policy of Thomas F. Bayard: 1885–1897* (New York, 1940); Allan Nevins, *Grover Cleveland: A Study in Courage* (New York, 1932); Nelson M. Blake, "Background of Cleveland's Venezuelan Policy," *American Historical Review*, vol. 47 (1941–1942), 259–

277, a careful and interesting article; Dexter Perkins, *The Monroe Doctrine: 1867–1907* (Baltimore, 1937); Alice Felt Tyler, *The Foreign Policy of James G. Blaine* (Minneapolis, 1927); Robert Louis Stevenson, *A Footnote to History* (New York, 1895), by an eyewitness to the Samoan affair; Richard D. Weigle, "Sugar and the Hawaiian Revolution," *Pacific Historical Review*, vol. 16 (1947), 41–58; Foster Rhea Dulles, *The Imperial Years* (New York, 1956), dealing in part with this period.

CHAPTER
☆ 8 ☆

The War with Spain

In a military sense the Spanish-American War was one of the least impressive conflicts of the nineteenth century. The war boiled up suddenly in the springtime of 1898. It was an exhilarating experience, sensational, not dangerous. The outcome was never in doubt. The antagonist, Spain, had a population of eighteen million compared with the seventy-five million people in the United States. Captain Alfred Thayer Mahan, in Europe when the war started, was asked how long it would last, and he answered, "About three months." By the end of the summer the fighting was over, won by the small but new and efficient American navy against the antiquated seagoing contraptions that passed for the navy of Spain. In the peace that followed the Spanish relinquished the remnants of a once grand empire: Cuba, Puerto Rico, Guam, the Philippine Islands. The war had no visible effect upon the large questions of international politics, especially the European balance of power which at the moment was gaining the attention of the world's statesmen. The Spanish-American War was a ripple on the surface of world affairs, and by the time the peace conference assembled in Paris in October 1898 relations between the United States and Spain were again almost cordial. Perhaps the Spanish realized, although they could not admit it, that if the United States had not taken their colonies, some other power would have.

There was, however, a deeper than military meaning behind this summer turmoil of 1898, which makes the war of interest to the student of diplomatic history. The war suddenly brought into focus the ideas which had been generating in the minds of Americans in the 1880's and 1890's—ideas which, once the weariness and near-exhaustion of the Civil War disappeared, had fired the imagination of the American people. Several years before the war of 1898 the American nation had begun to look outward and exert its influence abroad. This new attitude was not merely a matter of interest in Latin America, interest in a revival of the Monroe Doctrine, for there was interest also in Samoa, an island group far beyond the bounds of the Western Hemisphere as imagined by Colonel Monroe in 1823. Americans perhaps had blundered into Samoa, and failed to realize the difficulties of holding territory deep in the South Seas. Samoa nonetheless indicated that the United States was a world power, and when during the war with Spain an opportunity was presented to take more territory outside the Western Hemisphere, it was hardly to be expected that the United States would hesitate. The meaning of the Spanish-American War lay in its appeal to the emotions of the new manifest destiny. The war focused these emotions and attached them to new and widely dispersed territories.

1. Cuba

Cuba was the precipitating cause of the war. The Ever-Faithful Isle, as it was known because of its loyalty to Spain during the Latin-American revolutionary period, had in the mid-nineteenth century begun to acquire feelings of nationalism. Cuban nationalism produced open warfare for a decade beginning in 1868, a long and savage guerilla conflict between Spanish military forces and the revolutionaries which was confined chiefly to the wild and unsettled eastern end of the island and did not afflict the rich and populous western half which includes Havana. The war of 1868–1878 was led by the revolutionary general Máximo Gómez, a Santo Domingan who seems to have acted under the revolutionary ardor which possessed so many Latin Americans during the period of liberation, for while the era of Bolívar and San Martín had long since passed, in Gómez there still burned the revolutionary fire. It is possible that during the insurrection of 1868–1878 most Cubans did not desire liberation. Perhaps Gómez did not secure enough assistance from Cuban expatriates in the United States. The American government and people in the years after their own Civil War were too weary of warfare and too busy with their own concerns to assist the Cuban revolutionists. The revolt spent itself and on February 10, 1878 there was signed the Pact of Zanjón, by which the insurgent Cubans received amnesty and the island was granted the same system of government enjoyed by Puerto Rico. It developed later that in the weariness and confusion which attended the end of the war neither side knew, when the pact was signed, the nature of the government enjoyed by Puerto Rico.

Had the United States desired to intervene in Cuba during this insurrection there had been at least one opportunity, the famous *Virginius* episode of 1873, when Spanish authorities seized the ship *Virginius* and took it into Havana. Captured on the high seas far beyond Cuban territorial waters, the ship, although flying the American flag, was obviously on a filibustering expedition. The crew and passengers, despite their American-sounding names, were of a strongly Cuban countenance. They were all able-bodied males, and had no legitimate business which they could claim to be pursuing so close to the insurrectionary island of Cuba. After a short trial the Spanish decided to shoot these men as pirates, and fifty-three were killed before a British captain sailed in with a warship and stopped the executions. The *Virginius* affair would have offered an excuse for American action, had the United States in 1873 wished to start a quarrel with Spain. Instead the State Department under Hamilton Fish bided its time, inquired into the circumstances of the case, and ascertained that the ship was falsely flying the American flag. The secretary of state obtained a Spanish apology and indemnity for the dubiously American citizens killed. If the United States had been spoiling for a fight, here was an incident which could easily have been used. Spain at the time was undergoing a civil war, and there could have been no Spanish defense of Cuba against American invasion. But there was no American willingness to invade and take Cuba. Perhaps the coincidence of the *Virginius* incident with a domestic economic crisis, the panic of 1873, had some part in the general American desire to avoid war.

The revolution of 1868–1878 came to an end with the Pact of Zanjón, and there followed a period until 1895—when a new revolt broke out—during which there was peace and something approaching prosperity in Cuba. One of the most important causes of American concern over the island, the continuing existence there of the institution of human slavery, was eliminated when Spain abolished slavery in her colony in 1886 after a gradual emancipation. Meanwhile the sugar plantations expanded, and began to flourish under the beneficent terms of the McKinley Tariff of 1890 which provided for reciprocity agreements. Spain and the United States arranged in 1891, in return for Spanish concessions, for free entrance of Cuban sugar into the United States. Unfortunately, a new American tariff act of 1894 ended the reciprocity. This act followed the business panic of 1893, and the general business stagnation of the mid-1890's together with the new and unfavorable American tariff almost ruined the Cuban economy. The island again was ready for revolt.

At the beginning of the second Cuban revolution in 1895 few individuals in the United States were willing to go to war to liberate Cuba from Spain. American economic interests, about $50,000,000 in Cuban property and $100,000,000 annually in trade, were not large enough to generate enthusiasm for the revolution. There also occurred in 1895 the far more interesting Venezuelan crisis, precipitated by President Cleveland and Secretary Olney against a first-class world power, Great Britain. Then came the election of 1896, when the United States for one of the few times in its history seemed to be dividing politically along economic lines, the poor against the rich. Once that vision had dissolved, the nation concentrated its energies on bettering business conditions which had stagnated after the panic of 1893. Only after the presidential election did the business cycle at last begin to move upward, after four long and grinding years of depression, and in the United States there was little eagerness to risk this gain in the uncertainties of a foreign war.

The Cubans by this time had turned their revolution against Spain into a ferocious contest, and to Americans it seemed evident that the rebels because of their wanton acts deserved no sympathy, though they constantly sought it. They were pursuing a scorched-earth policy, burning crops and destroying food in the hope either of forcing the Spanish government to grant independence or forcing the United States to intervene for independence. These tactics infuriated President Cleveland, who privately referred to the revolutionaries as "rascally Cubans." From his successor after March 1897, President William McKinley, there was more sympathy, but McKinley was determined not to be involved: the Republican administration was a business administration, devoted to the welfare of the American industrialist, and businessmen in 1897 and early 1898 shunned war. The Cuban tactics of destruction had no effect on the policy of the United

States, and little effect upon the Spanish government, which in 1896 had sent over a new captain-general, Valeriano Weyler.

General Weyler undertook a rigorous policy of forcing the population in the disaffected Cuban provinces into concentration camps, separating the people from the revolutionaries, and thereby identifying the latter. His arrival in Cuba marked a turning point in American sentiment toward the Cuban revolution. Before Weyler adopted his policy of herding the Cubans to concentration camps, the government of the United States had stood against intervention. American hesitation over Cuba stemmed, as was mentioned, from dislike of the destructive acts of the rascally Cuban revolutionaries. It came also, one should add, from the problem of disposing of the island once Americans should intervene and expel the Spanish. The Cubans, most informed Americans believed, could not govern themselves. Nor could the island be annexed and brought into the American union. Annexation would have precipitated grave difficulties because of the mixed racial composition of the Cuban population. Moreover, many Cubans were illiterate. Regarding annexation, William Graham Sumner of Yale had spoken much to the point: "The prospect," Sumner said, "of adding to the present Senate a number of Cuban Senators, either native or carpetbag, is one whose terrors it is not necessary to unfold." But Americans could not overlook the miseries of General Weyler's camps. Weyler appears to have been a man of decent intentions who was a victim of the inefficiency of Spanish colonial administration. It was easy to bring the people into the camps, but the subsequent duty of feeding them and watching over sanitation was too much for Spanish bureaucracy. Cuba by late 1897 was in a tragic plight. Perhaps as many as 200,000 Cubans died in the camps. And errors of Spanish administration had been compounded by the actions of the Cuban revolutionaries, who in hope of increasing the general misery on the island took measures to prevent the feeding of the *reconcentrados*.

Americans were shocked by what was going on so close to their shores and there began to be talk of intervention. This was at once encouraged by the famous newspaper circulation war in New York City between the New York *Journal*, owned by William Randolph Hearst, and the *World*, owned by Joseph Pulitzer. These two newspapers took advantage of every little change in American-Spanish relations to increase their circulation. They stopped at nothing to blow up the trouble in Cuba into a crisis of major proportions. As E. L.

Godkin, a more staid and gentlemanly contemporary of Hearst and Pulitzer, said at the time, and without much exaggeration, "Nothing so disgraceful as the behavior of these two newspapers . . . has ever been known in the history of journalism."

One may ascribe the outbreak of the Spanish-American War to several circumstances: the trouble in Cuba following 1895; the yellow journalism of Hearst, Pulitzer, and similar editors; the famous episode of the Dupuy de Lôme letter (February 9, 1898); and the sinking of the battleship *Maine* in Havana harbor on February 15, 1898.

This letter was written to a friend in Cuba by the Spanish minister in the United States, Dupuy de Lôme. The circumstances surrounding its composition were altogether understandable. All diplomats are by the nature of their work repressed individuals—they know and feel so much more than they dare say officially that there is a temptation to confide intimate thoughts to friends. The Spanish minister by the autumn of 1897 was receiving increasing advices about Cuba from American government officials, and he may be excused for finding some of them impertinent. The result was an undiplomatic private letter. Señor Dupuy de Lôme did not like the tone of President McKinley's state-of-the-union address in December 1897, and wrote to his friend in Cuba that "Besides the ingrained and inevitable coarseness with which it repeated all that the press and public opinion in Spain have said about Weyler, it once more shows what McKinley is, weak and a bidder for the admiration of the crowd, besides being a common politician who tries to leave a door open behind himself while keeping on good terms with the jingoes of his party." One can only imagine Dupuy de Lôme's embarrassment when he learned that this letter had been stolen from the desk of his correspondent and was in the hands of Hearst and the New York *Journal*. He hastily resigned his post.

The minister had said of McKinley what many Americans believed and published daily in their own newspapers, but a foreign diplomat must be discreet. McKinley had in truth seemed to many of his countrymen pre-eminently a politician, the more so when compared to the courageous Grover Cleveland. As McKinley talked in meaningless generalities while desire for intervention in Cuba mounted, Theodore Roosevelt found him as "spineless as a chocolate eclair." A current joke went, "Why is McKinley's mind like a bed?" (Answer: "Because it has to be made up for him every time he wants to use it.") But the truth or falsity of Dupuy de Lôme's opinions was no issue in 1898, and the Spanish minister inflamed the American people against Spain when he repeated the popular wisdom.

Almost immediately following this *faux pas* occurred the *Maine* disaster. The battleship was in Havana harbor on the not very convincing pretext of a courtesy visit. Probably the reason for the *Maine*'s visit was that the McKinley administration feared not to have a ship in Havana should trouble break out and American citizens ask for protection. It was risky to send a ship to Havana during the revolutionary chaos, but McKinley was almost forced to protect his countrymen when Americans by the latter 1890's were becoming so sensitive to their rights and position in the world. He did not reckon how desperate the Cuban situation was. The Cuban revolutionaries—perhaps—made their supreme effort to secure American intervention.

The *Maine* on the evening of February 15, 1898 sank at her moorings after a terrific explosion, the detonation of her magazines. Of 350 officers and men aboard, 252 were dead or missing and 14 died afterward. A naval court of inquiry in 1898 found in favor of an external explosion touching off the magazines. When the vessel was raised in 1911 an inward buckling of her plates was evident, and a second court of inquiry then reported, as had the first court, that "the injuries to the bottom of the *Maine* . . . were caused by the explosion of a low form of explosive exterior to the ship." The hulk was towed out to sea in 1912 and sunk in 600 fathoms of water. No one to this day has discovered who or what in 1898 blew up the *Maine*. One can say only that the vessel's destruction greatly benefited the Cuban revolutionaries, already distinguished by the abandon with which they conducted their guerilla actions against the Spanish. The sinking of the *Maine*, as few other events could have done, precipitated the United States into the revolutionary struggle against Spain.

The American people and Washington officials were at first incredulous, and then deeply angered. Years afterward the watchman in the White House remembered McKinley pacing the floor in the first shock of the news, murmuring "The *Maine* blown up! The *Maine* blown up!" Hearst's New York *Journal* emblazoned for its readers, THE WARSHIP MAINE WAS SPLIT IN TWO BY AN ENEMY'S SECRET INFERNAL MACHINE. "Remember the *Maine*," became a national watchword:

Ye who made war that your ships
   Should lay to at the beck of no nation,
Make war now on murder, that slips
   The leash of her hounds of damnation;
Ye who remembered the Alamo,
Remember the *Maine!*

In a Broadway bar a man raised his glass and said solemnly, "Gentle-men, remember the *Maine!*" Through the streets of American cities went the cry, "Remember the *Maine!* To hell with Spain!"

After this disaster at Havana it is doubtful if McKinley or anyone could have checked the course of events. The argument frequently advanced, that McKinley could have defied the war hawks of 1898 in Congress, does not seem plausible, for Congress in such a case would likely have voted a declaration of war and overridden him. If the Spanish government had granted Cuba immediate independence, this alone might have prevented hostilities with the United States. Such an action was impossible for a sovereign nation, especially after the belligerent tone of American public statements about the sinking of the *Maine.* The Spanish did almost everything except grant immediate independence, but to no avail. The American minister to Spain was instructed on March 27 to notify the Madrid government that the United States had no territorial ambitions in Cuba but that there should be a Cuban armistice until October 1, as well as revocation of the concentration-camp policy. The Spanish agreed to the second demand on April 5, and granted the armistice on April 9. President McKinley had this information on April 10. The president hesitated, for the Spanish had met the American terms. The armistice declaration contained a qualifying phrase (the captain-general in Cuba was ordered by Madrid "to grant a suspension of hostilities for such time as he might think prudent to prepare and facilitate peace negotia-tions") and this might be construed as an attempt to stall matters until the Spanish military forces could consolidate their positions and pre-pare to reopen the war. Such was the construction put upon the Spanish offer by Henry Cabot Lodge, who described it casually in his diary as a "humbug armistice."

Yet Spain by this time was in no position to procrastinate with the United States, and the unfortunate wording of the instruction to the captain-general was probably inadvertent. McKinley may have realized this. He may also have realized that he could not control Congress. At this time, while talking about the Cuban crisis to a friend, the president broke down and cried, so his friend later wrote, like a boy of thirteen. The president said he hadn't slept more than three hours a night, he thought, during the past two weeks. This was the period when the belligerent Theodore Roosevelt, coming away from a visit to the White House, angrily asked: "Do you know what that white-livered cur up there has done? He has prepared *two* messages, one for war and one for peace, and doesn't know which one to send in!" McKinley resolved his doubts on April 11 by submitting the matter to Congress.

There could be no question of the outcome. The congressional joint resolution of April 20 demanded the independence of Cuba, withdrawal of Spanish forces, empowered the president to force Spain's withdrawal, and disclaimed any intention by the United States of exercising "sovereignty, jurisdiction or control" over Cuba. This latter clause, the Teller Amendment, passed Congress without a dissenting vote. McKinley signed the war resolution on April 20, dispatched an ultimatum to Spain, and received in return a Spanish declaration of war.

2. *The Course of the War*

During the Spanish-American War there was scarcely a military campaign worthy of the name. The war began in late April, and ended with an armistice on August 12. During this time Commodore George B. Dewey blew up ten old Spanish ships in Manila Bay (May 1) and a minuscule Spanish squadron was sunk near the harbor of Santiago de Cuba (July 3). American land forces under General William R. Shafter accepted the surrender of Santiago after skirmishes and some sharp fighting, and in the Far East General Wesley Merritt on August 14, unaware of the armistice signed in Washington two days earlier, took Manila after a token resistance by the Spanish forces to keep out the insurgent Filipinos. With this, and including the virtually unopposed campaign by General Nelson A. Miles in Puerto Rico, the war came to an abrupt end. The result had never been in doubt. The military operations on some occasions became so ludicrous that Mr. Dooley, the mythical Chicago Irishman created by

Finley Peter Dunne, could remark, apropos General Miles's Puerto Rican expedition, that it was "Gin'ral Miles' gran' picnic an' moonlight excursion . . . 'Tis no comfort in bein' a cow'rd," he added, "whin ye think iv them br-rave la-ads facin' death be suffication in bokays an' dyin' iv waltzin' with th' pretty girls iv Porther Ricky."

Annexation of the Hawaiian Islands came at last during the Spanish-American War. Acquisition of these islands had been urged in the United States for several reasons. There was a moral argument: the islands had been begging for annexation, and had placed themselves in danger, for Spain might attack them. There was another argument to the effect that Hawaii should be annexed as a war measure—the islands were necessary for prosecution of the war. This contention broke down on at least two counts, namely that the war was practically over after sinking of the Spanish squadron at Santiago on July 3 (Hawaii was annexed on July 7), and that Hawaii was a less advantageous stopping place for ships en route to the Far East to support Dewey in the Philippines than was another harbor which the United States already owned, Kiska in the Aleutian Islands. Kiska was a far more commodious harbor than Honolulu, and the Kiska route was several hundred miles shorter than that via Hawaii. Moreover, Kiska was closer to being a halfway point to the Philippines than was Honolulu. A number of ships in the American navy could not carry sufficient coal for the Honolulu-to-Manila run. The northern route also was more healthful for transporting soldiers. But there was real point in a third contention for annexing Hawaii—that the Hawaiians should be annexed to facilitate the future defense of the United States. The defense argument, unlike the war-measure argument and the moral argument, was sound in 1898, before the era of air power made American possession of the Hawaiian chain even more important. The war lent urgency to the defense argument, and the McKinley administration, to play safe with a still doubtful Congress, submitted the proposal for annexation of Hawaii in the form of a joint resolution requiring only a majority vote.

Grover Cleveland, retired in Princeton, remained adamant to the end, and inquired of his friend Olney, "Did you ever see such a preposterous thing as this Hawaiian business?" Cleveland in January 1898 had said that annexation of islands in the Pacific was "a perversion of our national mission. The mission of our nation is to build up and make a greater country out of what we have, instead of annexing islands." His anti-imperialism certainly suggested one way of resolving doubts over annexation. Perhaps, however, there could have been a middle position between that of Cleveland—taking no islands at all —and the decision of the McKinley administration to annex both the Hawaiian Islands and the Philippine Islands. Perhaps Hawaii would have been enough new territory.

The most fateful territorial acquisition of the Spanish-American War was the taking of the Philippines, after Dewey had sunk the Spanish squadron. Annexation of the Philippines was of large importance to the future of American diplomacy. It projected the United States far into the Western Pacific, and so close to Japan and China— two future trouble spots of the world—that American interests, once established in the Philippines, were almost bound to become involved and probably hurt in Far Eastern rivalries quite as remote from the American national interest as had been the European rivalries against which President Washington once had counseled. The British admiral P. H. Colomb, writing in the *North American Review* for October 1898, showed with remarkable prescience what might happen to the United States because of annexation of the Philippines. Taking the islands, the admiral stated, meant that America was "for the first time giving hostages to fortune, and taking a place in the world that will entail on her sacrifices and difficulties of which she has not yet dreamed. . . . with outlying territories, especially islands, a comparatively weak power has facilities for wounding her without being wounded in return." This move into the Far East has seemed in retrospect very unwise. Perhaps, on the other hand, it was only the working out of American destiny, and could not have been humanly avoided. The victor of Manila Bay, surveying his triumph over the Spanish fleet, declared that "If I were a religious man, and I hope I am, I should say that the hand of God was in it." Of this, more later; here is the place and time to recount the administrative intrigue by which the United States became prepared in 1898 to take the Philippines, once war had started over Cuba.

The intrigue was such a natural expression of Theodore Roosevelt's exuberance that perhaps there was no intrigue at all. Roosevelt was assistant secretary of the navy, having been placed in that post (according to "Boss" Platt of New York, who put him there) because "Theodore" could "probably do less harm to the [Republican Party] organization as Assistant Secretary of the Navy than in any other office that can be named." Roosevelt bent his energies to developing the fighting readiness of the new American navy, the readiness of the new battleships and cruisers which in the last decade or so had been coming off the ways of American shipyards. In the spring of 1898 it was obvious to him that a war with Spain was imminent, and he took it upon himself to prepare the American Asiatic squadron. By some string-pulling he arranged the appointment of his friend, Commodore Dewey, to command it. Roosevelt told Dewey, who was a far better sailor than politician, that political influence was being exerted by other candidates for the squadron and that Dewey should seek out a senator. Dewey obtained the assistance of Senator Proctor of Vermont. After he received the appointment he discovered that no influence had been exerted by the other candidates. Roosevelt's left-handed manner of securing Dewey's appointment so annoyed Roosevelt's superior, Secretary of the Navy John D. Long, that Long refused Dewey the temporary rank of rear admiral which went with the Asian command, and Dewey was a commodore at the time of Manila Bay.

Nor was this the only Rooseveltian maneuver, for there was the famous occasion on February 25, 1898 when Secretary Long went home for an afternoon rest and left Roosevelt as acting secretary of the navy. TR broke loose in the department that afternoon, moved ships around as if they were yachts, and among other things ordered Dewey, at last in the Far East at Hong Kong, to coal his ships and prepare for offensive operations in the Philippines in the event of war. Dewey was not to allow the Spanish squadron to leave the islands, for fear it might somehow find its way to the American West Coast and ravage Seattle and San Francisco.

It is difficult to take seriously the fear that the Spanish ships in Manila could endanger the American Pacific coast. One might have thought, too, that when Secretary Long returned from his afternoon rest he could have countermanded his assistant secretary's orders and perhaps demanded Roosevelt's resignation. Nothing happened; Roosevelt stayed at the department, and when war came, Dewey was ready. After the Spanish squadron had been destroyed the commodore requested army troops to the number of 5,000 to invest Manila. The War Department sent 11,000 and Manila was taken.

The investment of Manila went off without a hitch, except for some friction that developed between Dewey and the commander of a

German naval squadron then in Manila harbor. This friction was later interpreted as endangering peace between the United States and Germany. The Germans had originally blundered by sending to Manila a vice-admiral in charge of a squadron slightly stronger than Dewey's, and during the summer there had been trouble over the blockade regulations which, Dewey claimed, the Germans violated. Dewey at Manila told Admiral Otto von Diederichs's flag lieutenant that if Germany wished war she could have it. He also told some newspapermen that he had a plan to engage, if necessary, the German fleet. When Dewey on August 13 was preparing to bombard Manila in support of General Merritt's troops, the squadrons of France, Germany, and England, then in harbor, eagerly jockeyed for position to observe the firing. In the course of the position-taking, the Germans managed to get to the left of Dewey's ships, the French were behind the Germans, and the British in an ungentlemanly maneuver sailed into position immediately in front of the Germans. The German admiral had to move his flagship from its moorings to get a better view of the hostilities. Later the story arose that the German squadron had threatened Dewey's operations, and that the British moved in between the Germans and Dewey to protect the American commodore. But there was never any danger of war with Germany. Dewey later asked Frederick Palmer, who ghosted his *Autobiography*, to omit these *contretemps* from the record.

The Spanish-American War had no serious repercussions upon the European balance of power, for none of the European powers other than Spain became involved in it. Likewise, so far as concerned the two combatants, the war did not permanently impair their good relations—at the peace conference there appeared little enmity between American and Spanish negotiators. The summer of hostilities in 1898 did mark a notable consolidation of American nationalism. The war gave to the entire American people a vague feeling of danger, of risky adventure, and all but remnants of those political passions between North and South which had grown out of the Civil War and reconstruction disappeared in the comradeship of a national war. The events of the Civil War era had by this time slipped far into history. "The youngest boy who could have carried arms at Gettysburg," Paul H. Buck has written, "was a man of fifty when the century closed . . . By far the greater portion of the generation which had listened with awe while the guns boomed in Virginia and the ships

of war steamed on the Mississippi slept in silent graves in which the
issues for which they had contended were buried with them. The old
had given way to the new." McKinley during a speech at Atlanta in
1898 affirmed the care of Confederate graves to be a national duty.
When the president appointed four temporary major generals, he
diplomatically chose two ex-Confederate generals, Joseph ("Fighting
Joe") Wheeler and Fitzhugh Lee. Fitzhugh Lee, nephew of Robert E.
Lee, already had come to public attention in performing his duties as
consul general at Havana at the time the *Maine* was sunk. Fighting
Joe Wheeler went to Cuba and took part in the surrender of the
island. During the campaign before Santiago there occurred the rather
humorous incident when General Wheeler at one point in a battle
cried, "We've got the Yankees on the run!" The nation, both North
and South, fought together in the Spanish-American War, and this to
all American patriots was a heartwarming scene.

There were many touching evidences of this new national unity,
but perhaps no event was more poignant than the demonstration that
occurred when on May 20, 1898 the Sixth Massachusetts Regiment
marched through Baltimore on its way to camp. In 1861 the regiment
had been stoned by hostile mobs as it marched to defend Washington.
The Massachusetts men in their uniforms of blue with the gallant new
leggings, broad-brimmed campaign hats slouched over their faces,
pennants flying, marched through the streets in 1898 with the regi-
mental band playing "Dixie." Senator Lodge, having journeyed up
from the capital to see the parade, wept unashamedly. "It was 'roses,
roses all the way'," he afterward remembered, "—flags, cheers, excited crowds. Tears were in my eyes. I never felt so moved in my
life. The war of 1861 was over at last and the great country for which
so many men died was one again."

3. *The Paris Peace Conference of 1898*

The Spanish ambassador at Paris on July 19, 1898 requested the
French foreign minister, Théophile Delcassé, to mediate between
Spain and the United States. This the foreign minister did through
his ambassador in Washington, Jules Cambon, and Cambon on August
12 signed an armistice on behalf of the Spanish. According to its terms
a peace conference was to assemble in Paris not later than October 1.
President McKinley appointed five peace commissioners: the chair-

man of the Senate committee on foreign relations, Senator Cushman K. Davis; the next ranking Republican member, Senator William P. Frye; the leading minority member of the foreign relations committee, Senator George Gray; Secretary of State William R. Day (who on September 30 yielded his secretaryship to John Hay); and Whitelaw Reid, publisher of the New York *Tribune*. Curiously there was some question over the propriety of McKinley's appointments, because the three senators, so the contemporary argument ran, would have to vote on their own handiwork after returning from Paris. The politically astute McKinley ignored such pleas and set a precedent which Woodrow Wilson twenty years later might well have followed at the peace conference of 1919.

Upon arrival in Paris the commission was treated to an elaborate luncheon of twenty-six covers given by Delcassé at the Quai d'Orsay Palace, September 29, 1898: oysters, lake trout, beef, cutlets Sévigné d'ivoire, duck, partridges, ham, salads, artichokes au champagne, ices (Russian style), fruits, French wines. During the deliberations which followed—the conference lasted two months and two days—the peace commissioners meeting in a large room of the French foreign office had constant access to an anteroom containing a well-stocked larder. In view of the paucity of diplomatic business before the conference, this may explain why its sessions took so long. There were only two unsettled questions, namely the Cuban debt (should the United States assume it?), and the Philippines (should the islands be annexed?). The American commissioners refused to assume the $400,000,000 Cuban debt. As for the Philippines, there was little to discuss because the question would have to be settled in Washington.

Until Dewey encountered the Spanish squadron the Philippines meant little to the American people. McKinley himself said afterward, "When we received the cable from Admiral Dewey telling of the taking of the Philippines I looked up their location on the globe. I could not have told where those darned islands were within 2,000 miles!" As debate grew in volume over disposition of the Philippines Mr. Dooley remarked to his good friend Mr. Hennessy that " 'tis not more thin two months since ye larned whether they were islands or canned goods. . . . Suppose ye was standin' at th' corner iv State Sthreet an' Archey R-road, wud ye know what car to take to get to th' Ph'lippeens? If yer son Packy was to ask ye where th' Ph'lippeens is, cud ye give him anny good idea whether they was in Rooshia or jus' west iv th' thracks?" But the governing fact of the Philippine question was that the United States had taken possession of Manila. Hennessy had begun the above colloquy by remarking that "I know what I'd do if I was Mack. I'd hist a flag over th' Ph'lippeens, an' I'd take in th' whole lot iv thim." After protests from Dooley he still was saying "Hang on to thim. What we've got we must hold." Hennessy captured the essence of the Philippine argument, for possession was nine-tenths of the decision.

Taking the islands was all the easier for the McKinley administration when American businessmen began to see in the Philippines a stepping-stone—vestibule, anteroom, or general entrance—to the China trade. Markets in China, as we shall see in the next chapter, had long intrigued American businessmen. The new sense of manifest destiny had stemmed in part from the feeling of the American business community that the domestic market of the United States was saturated, and that expansion of foreign trade was the only hope of further developing the American economy. Businessmen, down to the beginning of hostilities with Spain, had opposed war, believing that a war could only harm the economy. A war's effects, business leaders maintained, would perhaps include derangement of the currency and a revival of the free-silver agitation. They suspected that most of the jingoes were free-silverites. "Free Silver and Free Cuba," so Senator Lodge believed, would be the Democratic Party's campaign slogan in the election of 1900. With the taking of Manila, business fears began to evaporate. Business pressures to keep the Philippines in anticipation of the China trade converged upon Washington at the same time that retention of the islands was attracting popular support throughout the country. The railway magnate, James J. Hill, declared that whoever controlled the trade of the orient held the world's purse strings. The Philippines, according to another business figure, were the key to the orient. Senator Lodge argued that Manila was the great prize and "the thing which will give us the eastern trade."

The China trade was, one should add parenthetically, a mirage. It has never amounted to anything. In 1898 the mirage was more important than reality, especially after the nation had just emerged from the difficult economic era of the mid-1890's.

There was no chance of the United States taking part of the Philippine Islands—say Luzon with Manila. It was a case of all the islands or none. General Merritt went to Paris from Manila to give his views to the peace commissioners, and while he at first indicated that Luzon might be held alone, under further questioning he admitted that Manila was prosperous only because it was the capital of the archipelago. Militarily, too, there could be little advantage, and positive disadvantage, in allowing the other islands to pass under control of some power other than the United States.

If the United States refused to take the islands they would probably have passed to one of the European powers, perhaps Germany (Japan and England were also interested). Germany after much hesitation had begun a few years before 1898 to acquire an overseas empire. An empire seemed to be a hallmark of a great power—the collection of Asiatic territory, as Walter Millis has pointed out, was the fashionable thing at the moment among all the very best diplomacies—and Germany, a newcomer in the family of powers, wished above all to be fashionable and to "belong" by doing the proper things. The Germans in 1898 were looking for stray bits of territory which might be added to their empire, and would almost certainly have taken the Philippines if the United States had not. Germany made an agreement with Spain, after Spain's armistice with the United States and before the assembling of the Paris Peace Conference, in which it was stipulated that Spain would resist any demands of the Americans for the Caroline Islands, if such demands were made, and that after the peace settlement these islands would be sold to Germany.

President McKinley is reported by many people who saw him at the time to have been much worried about the fate of the Philippines. What, he asked casual visitors to the White House, could he do with the islands? At one juncture he said that "If old Dewey had just sailed away when he smashed that Spanish fleet, what a lot of trouble he would have saved us." Old Dewey had not sailed away, and popular opinion in the United States had risen to such heights of adulation over the hero of Manila Bay (Dewey had still to disappoint his admirers by displaying his political vanity) that the commodore could not have departed from the scene of his triumph even if the national interest dictated it.

A religious factor, albeit one based on something of a misunderstanding, exerted a considerable influence in the American decision to take the Philippines. American Protestants looked to the islands as an area to be Christianized. President McKinley, a devout Methodist who instituted hymn singing in the White House each

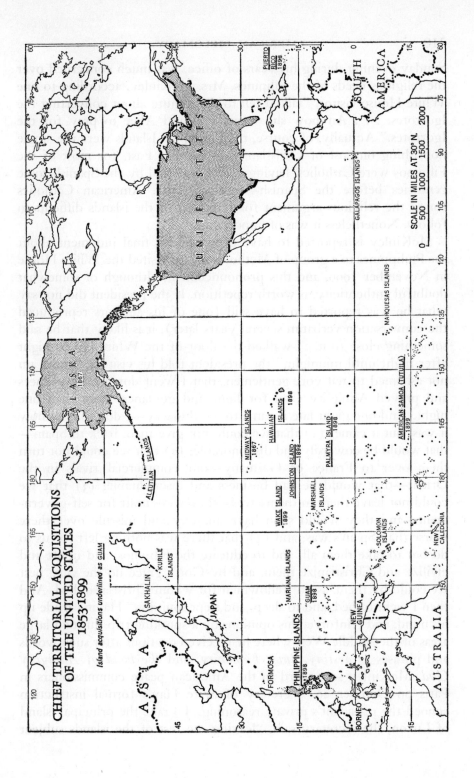

CHIEF TERRITORIAL ACQUISITIONS
OF THE UNITED STATES
1853-1899

Island acquisitions underlined as GUAM

SCALE IN MILES AT 30° N.
0   500   1000 1500 2000

UNITED STATES

ALASKA
1867

ASIA

SAKHALIN

KURILE
ISLANDS

JAPAN

FORMOSA

PHILIPPINE ISLANDS
1898

BORNEO

NEW
GUINEA

AUSTRALIA

ALEUTIAN ISLANDS

MIDWAY ISLANDS
1867

WAKE ISLAND
1899

JOHNSTON ISLAND
1898

HAWAIIAN
ISLANDS
1898

MARIANA ISLANDS

GUAM
1898

MARSHALL
ISLANDS

PALMYRA ISLAND
1898

SOLOMON
ISLANDS

NEW
CALEDONIA

AMERICAN SAMOA (TUTUILA)
1899

MARQUESAS ISLANDS

GALAPAGOS ISLANDS

PUERTO
RICO
1898

SOUTH
AMERICA

Sunday evening during his years of office, was much concerned over the religious needs of the Filipinos. Mrs. McKinley, according to one White House visitor, "talked ten to the minute about converting the Igorrotes. . . . Anyhow she wants you and Alice to pray for the Igorrotes." Actually, of course, the Philippine Islands were the single flourishing outpost of Christianity in the Far East, for most of the Filipinos were Catholics, having been converted by the Spanish some centuries before the Spanish-American War. American Catholics found the religious argument for retention of the islands difficult to follow. Nonetheless it was of importance.

McKinley is reported to have expressed his final judgment about the Philippines to a group of Methodists who visited the White House in November 1900, and this pronouncement, although of somewhat doubtful authenticity, is worth repetition. If the president did not say what he was reported to have said (one of his auditors reproduced the conversation verbatim several years later), it is likely that he said something close to it. "I walked the floor of the White House night after night until midnight," the president told his visitors, "and I am not ashamed to tell you, gentlemen, that I went down on my knees and prayed Almighty God for light and guidance more than one night. And one night late it came to me this way—I don't know how it was, but it came: (1) that we could not give them back to Spain— that would be cowardly and dishonorable; (2) that we could not turn them over to France or Germany—our commercial rivals in the Orient—that would be bad business and discreditable; (3) that we could not leave them to themselves—they were unfit for self-government—and they would soon have anarchy and misrule over there worse than Spain's was; and (4) that there was nothing left for us to do but to take them all, and to educate the Filipinos, and uplift and civilize and Christianize them, and by God's grace do the very best we could by them, as our fellowmen for whom Christ also died. And then I went to bed, and to sleep, and slept soundly." Having made up his mind, and reinforced his opinions by a speaking trip through large areas of the Middle West where he received ovations after such words and phrases as *destiny*, *duty*, *humanity*, and *the hand of Almighty God*, McKinley sent word to the American peace commissioners in Paris on October 26. Secretary of State Hay's formal instruction echoed the president's private reasoning. To take the principal island of Luzon, the secretary said, "leaving the rest of the islands subject to Spanish rule, or to be the subject of future contention, can not be justified on political, commercial, or humanitarian grounds. The cession must be of the whole archipelago or none. The latter is wholly inadmissible and the former must therefore be required." The Spanish commissioners had no recourse except, after a month and more of stalling, to acquiesce.

The terms of the Treaty of Paris, signed on December 10, 1898, were cession of the Philippine Islands, Puerto Rico, and Guam. The latter island, 3,300 miles west of Honolulu, was well situated as a naval station en route to the Philippine Islands, and the decision to retain the Philippines led logically to inclusion of Guam in the peace settlement of 1898. The United States paid $20,000,000 for the Philippines. Spain surrendered all claim to Cuba and agreed to assume the Cuban debt.

There was a small crisis in getting the treaty through the Senate, for until the end of debate the issue lay in doubt and the vote on February 6, 1899 was close, 57 to 27, one vote above the necessary two-thirds majority. William Jennings Bryan, who had felt some of the martial spirit during the war and volunteered as a colonel of cavalry, greatly assisted the McKinley administration in urging the treaty upon some of the reluctant Democratic senators. It was said that the non-Republican senators (Democrats, Populists, and some independents) who voted for the treaty were partly converted by the counsel of Bryan, personally given during a hurried trip to Washington. In the end, some further arguments seem to have been offered to one or two wavering senators. The Democratic Senator Gray, who as a peace commissioner had strongly opposed taking the Philippines, voted for the treaty in the Senate, and shortly thereafter received a federal judgeship from the Republican McKinley. One should add that the McKinley administration could have waited if necessary until March 4, 1899 and the admission of a sufficient number of recently elected Republican senators to approve the treaty.

But the importance of the Spanish-American War in the history of American diplomacy does not lie in the closeness of the vote on the treaty, for that could have been favorably changed a month later, or in the relation of the war to the diplomacies of the European powers who by 1898 were pursuing the rivalries which led to the World War in 1914—the powers did not believe their vital interests challenged by the war, and Germany, while wistful about the disposition of the Philippines, was content with receiving the Caroline and Palau Islands and the Mariana Islands with the exception of Guam. Nor did the new status of Cuba, an American protectorate, affect greatly the course of American history. The importance of the Spanish-American War for the diplomatic history of the United States lies in its appeal to the new sentiment of manifest destiny, its lending of substance and a feeling of achievement to what hitherto had been largely dreams and hopes. America in 1898 "emerged" as a world power, to use the verb of the day. The experience was thrilling to the national psyche. At the moment few individuals foresaw how acquisition of the Philippine Islands had committed the United States in the far Pacific, and that in subsequent years with the rise of Japan to world power there would come difficulties that eventually, forty-three years after 1898, would lead the country into a first-class Asian war.

ADDITIONAL READING

A readable and reliable account of the Spanish-American War, written with a view to the humor and occasional ridiculousness of the conflict, is Walter Millis, *The Martial Spirit: A Study of Our War with Spain* (Boston, 1931). A fascinating volume of pictures and text is Frank Freidel, *The Splendid Little War* (Boston, 1958). A little frothy and impressionistic, Gregory Mason's *Remember the Maine* (New York, 1939) is nonetheless worth attention. Julius W. Pratt's *Expansionists of 1898* deals with Hawaii and the Philippines. See also F. R. Dulles, *The Imperial Years* (New York, 1956) and W. H. Callcott, *The Caribbean Policy of the United States: 1890–1920* (Baltimore, 1942). Two monographs are Joseph E. Wisan, *The Cuban Crisis as Reflected in the New York Press: 1895–1898* (New York, 1934) and John Edward Weems, *The Fate of the Maine* (New York, 1958). Articles by Thomas A. Bailey treat aspects of the war, "Dewey and the Germans at Manila Bay," *American Historical Review*, vol. 45 (1939–1940), 59–81; and "The United States and Hawaii during the Spanish-American War," *AHR*, vol. 36 (1930–1931), 552–560.

For the statesmen of the period see Howard K. Beale's excellent *Theodore Roosevelt and the Rise of America to World Power* (Baltimore, 1956), together with the somewhat dated but eminently readable Henry F. Pringle, *Theodore Roosevelt* (New York, 1931; available in paperback). TR's reminiscences in his *Autobiography* (New York, 1913) are always interesting if at times inaccurate. Other biographies are Tyler Dennett,

John Hay: From Poetry to Politics (New York, 1933), a brilliant book about that *fin de siècle* statesman; H. H. Kohlsaat, *From McKinley to Harding: Personal Recollections of Our Presidents* (New York, 1923), a mine of quotation on McKinley; William Carl Spielman, *William Mc-Kinley: Stalwart Republican* (New York, 1954), an able account; Rich-ard W. Leopold, *Elihu Root and the Conservative Tradition* (Boston, 1954), an extremely able account by a close student of American diplo-macy; Claude G. Bowers, *Beveridge and the Progressive Era* (New York, 1932), best for that Indiana statesman and "jingo"; Merle E. Curti, "Bryan and World Peace," *Smith College Studies in History*, vol. 16, nos. 3–4, lucid analysis, done with sympathy and understanding.

The territorial results of the war appear in parts of J. W. Pratt's *Amer-ica's Colonial Experiment* (New York, 1950). Consult also Earl S. Pome-roy's attractive volume, *Pacific Outpost: American Strategy in Guam and Micronesia* (Stanford, 1951), and Charles S. Campbell, Jr., *Anglo-American Understanding* (Baltimore, 1956).

Paul H. Buck, *The Road to Reunion: 1865–1900* (Boston, 1937) shows a signal result of the war, the consolidation of American nationalism.

CHAPTER

☆ 9 ☆

The Far East, 1784-1921

American diplomacy with the orient has acquired large importance in the twentieth century, especially since the beginning of the second World War, and it is hard to realize that throughout the nineteenth century Far Eastern affairs were of less concern to the United States than relations with Latin America. In the first decades of American diplomacy the interests of the United States in the Far East were chiefly the opening of markets to traders, Christianization of the heathen orientals, and introduction of Western ideas and industrial techniques. The problem of aggression in the Far East, by Japan or China, had no immediacy in the nineteenth century.

Trading, Christianizing, civilizing—these were the purposes of Americans during most of the years between the first contact of Yankee traders with the orient in 1784 and the end in 1921 of the period under consideration in this present chapter. Trading inaugurated the relations of the United States with the Far East, and was the strongest single interest of American diplomacy until the year 1900 and even later. Christianization of the orient began early in the nineteenth century and grew large in fervor in the 1890's when Protestant Americans undertook "the evangelization of the world in this generation." Westernization, the third concern of Americans, always characterized contacts between the United States and the East. At first westernization was thought of in terms of bringing republican government to Asia, rather than technical knowledge, but by the late nineteenth century there was also interest in introducing American

214

mechanical achievements.

The extent to which Americans were able to carry out these initial purposes in the orient is difficult to estimate. By 1921, the year when the Washington Naval Conference met, the United States was turning to more strictly political aims in the Far East. The desire to trade, Christianize, and civilize was still present, but fear of the power of modern Japan was bringing to the fore the idea of American security vis-à-vis that new Asiatic nation. Perhaps the opening of the orient to Western influences had been a mistake. Perhaps it only produced aggressive, ambitious nations such as the pre-1945 Japan and post-1945 communist China. It is at least arguable, to use a theory recently advanced by Arnold Toynbee, that the orient modernized itself too quickly, without acquiring the philosophical foundations of Western civilization, in particular Christianity. In the closely related modern world, power without knowledge is dangerous; and it is possible to contend that when the Western nations opened the orient in the nineteenth century they were creating a new Balkans, an area of half-baked nationalism which would give trouble to later generations.

Still, the orient could not have remained isolated in the nineteenth century. It was to be expected that the nations of the West, including the United States, would open this part of the world to Western civilization. The course of history could hardly have been otherwise. The Far Eastern problem of the twentieth century, the problem of Far Eastern power, could scarcely have failed to appear.

1. *American Far Eastern Relations in the Nineteenth Century*

American commerce with the orient began in 1784 when the *Empress of China* sailed out to Canton with a cargo of furs, raw cotton, lead, and thirty tons of a curious and utterly useless New England root which the Chinese called ginseng, and which they hoped would restore virility. This cargo the Americans exchanged for tea, cotton goods, silks, and chinaware. The profits were about thirty per cent. In the following years there were many more American trading voyages to Canton, and prior to the War of 1812 these voyages were highly profitable. Sometimes the owner of a vessel recovered the total cost of his investment in a single venture. Occasionally owners did better than that, for during a voyage in 1797–1798 the 93-ton vessel

Betsy on an investment of $7,867 earned $120,000. It was, incidentally, in search of goods that would interest the Chinese that Yankee
merchants developed a fur trade in the Pacific Northwest. In the
course of pursuing the trade in furs the ship *Columbia* gave its name
to the largest river of the Northwest, and John Jacob Astor founded
his trading post at Astoria. Sea-otter skins also proved valuable in the
Canton market, and American traders ranged through the South Atlantic and the Pacific, collecting skins in the Falkland Islands, South
Georgia, and the Aucklands. In the Falkland Islands one ship obtained
some 80,000 skins worth three dollars apiece at Canton, and the cargo
of Chinese tea with which this ship returned to America netted
$280,000. In their search for products appealing to the Chinese taste,
Yankee traders collected many items other than skins and furs, such
as sandalwood, tortoise shell, mother of pearl, snails, and—of course
—birds' nests.

Then there was the opium trade, and it was through this that Westerners, including the Americans, made their first large gain in the
markets of China. During the years prior to the Opium War of 1839–
1842 all foreigners traded through the single port of Canton under
the close supervision of designated Chinese intermediaries, the so-
called hong merchants. Conditions of life and trade in Canton were
bearable, but British merchants in the Far East were eager to obtain
more privileges of trade and residence. The Opium War was their
pretext. The trade in opium, one should explain, was only in small
measure an American affair, and when the Chinese in 1839 sought to
end the supplying of opium by Westerners the Americans in China
were not greatly alarmed. As one congressman put it, if the Chinese
ceased to smoke opium they might take up tobacco chewing. But
when the English forces obtained a Chinese treaty opening four new
ports in addition to Canton, the Americans grasped the chance to profit
from Britain's use of military force. The result was the Treaty of
Wanghia, signed at a town near Macao on July 3, 1844 by the special
American plenipotentiary, Caleb Cushing.

In this treaty, sometimes called the Cushing Treaty, the United
States received rights of trade in the four new treaty ports which
China had opened to the British. The treaty also set down clearly,
for the first time in any Western convention with China, detailed
guarantees of extraterritoriality—special privileges on foreign soil—
including the right to hire land, to build hospitals and churches and

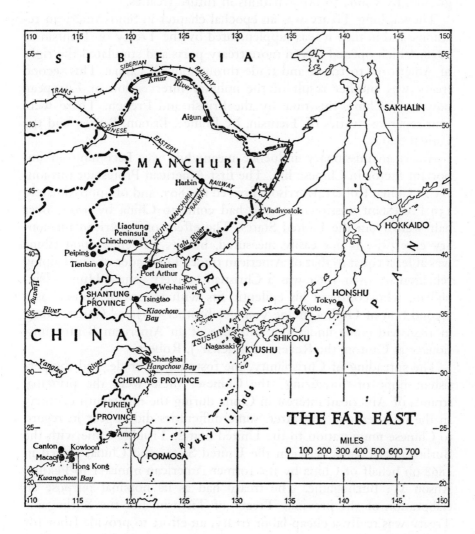

THE FAR EAST

MILES
0 100 200 300 400 500 600 700

cemeteries, and to engage Chinese teachers, interpreters, and servants. There was a "most favored nation" clause to the treaty, according to which the United States would receive automatically any concessions granted by China to other nations in future treaties.

The Cushing Treaty was an epochal chapter in Sino-American relations, and in time it was supplemented by the Treaty of Tientsin of 1858, which opened eleven more treaty ports and stipulated the right of Americans to travel and trade throughout all China. This second treaty was another result of the military intervention of European powers in China, this time by the British and French. There were four separate treaties of Tientsin, by France, Britain, Russia, and the United States.

American missionary influence meanwhile was becoming an important factor in Chinese life. The first American Protestant missionary in China, Robert Morrison, arrived in 1807, and of approximately 150 Protestant missionaries who had come to China by 1851, over half were from the United States. The effect of American missionary enterprise is not easily measured, but its influence upon China was at least equal to that of American trade. The leader of the Taiping rebellion of 1850–1864 was a Christian convert named Hung Hsiu-ch'üan, who confused his epileptic fits with visions of himself as a second Son of God, a divine younger brother of Jesus Christ. Hung in 1846 had come under the influence of an American Baptist missionary at Canton, the Reverend Issachar J. Roberts.

The spreading of Christianity, the fostering of trade, and the persistent hope of "civilizing" the Chinese: these were the principal strands of American interest in China during the nineteenth century. In the mid-century and after, some difficulties did appear in regard to Chinese immigration to the United States. Trouble came with the Burlingame Treaty between the United States and China, signed in 1868 on behalf of China by the former American minister to Peking, Anson W. Burlingame. The treaty had as its nominal purpose an elaboration of the previous Treaty of Tientsin, but the Burlingame Treaty was really a cheap-labor treaty, an effort to provide labor for the building of the transcontinental railroad across the American West. It was estimated that nine-tenths of the construction workers of the Central Pacific were Chinese. Without this source of cheap labor the line would never have been finished in time to receive the promised federal subsidies. As events turned out, the need for cheap labor came to an end just one year after the treaty was signed, for the railroad was completed in 1869. Thereafter the Chinese who had come to America to labor on the road, and whose predecessors had worked in the California gold mines, found themselves forced to turn to occupations competing directly with the labor of native Americans, and the slogan of the American West became "the Chinese must go." Congress in the Chinese Exclusion Act of 1882 forbade further immigration of Chinese laborers, and also stipulated that "hereafter no state court or court of the United States shall admit Chinese to citizenship." Subsequently renewed, the act lasted until 1943 when, under pressure of the enthusiasm for wartime collaboration with Nationalist China, the Chinese were granted an annual quota of 105 immigrants. This applied to all Chinese, rather than just those coming directly from China. This Act of 1943 at last ended a touchy problem of Sino-American relations; for years American missionaries in China had been hearing a great deal about the fact that Christian converts could go to the white man's heaven but not to the white man's country.

In the nineteenth-century history of American relations with the Far East there remains the saga of Commodore Perry and the opening of Japan, a product of the manifest destiny of the 1840's and early 1850's.

Who, first of all, was this Matthew C. Perry, the diplomat and sailor whose dignified and sensible bearing during his expedition to Japan was one of the reasons for the success of his mission? Perry, it should be explained, was one of the outstanding officers in the American navy of his day. He was the younger brother of Oliver Hazard Perry, of Lake Erie fame, and had served in the War of 1812. Ever a forward-looking officer, the younger Perry had helped select the original location for the American Negro settlement in Liberia. He had first demonstrated the efficiency of the naval ram. He commanded one of the navy's first steam vessels, the *Fulton*—an awkward floating battery equipped with paddle wheels and four huge stacks which made a record run down Long Island Sound of twenty-eight miles in an hour and fifty-seven minutes. He was largely responsible for building the steam-propelled frigates *Mississippi* and *Missouri*, notable vessels in the slow progress of the American navy from sail to steam.

Why did manifest destiny result in Perry's opening Japan to Western trade and civilization in the early 1850's? There had been a large growth of the Shanghai trade after the Chinese opened that port to the United States in the Treaty of Wanghia, and this trade made convenient a port of call in Japan. The increase of steam navigation produced the need for a coaling station in the vicinity of the Japanese Islands. The development of whale fisheries in the north Pacific had resulted in a number of wrecks of American vessels off Japanese shores. The sudden acquisition of California in the Mexican War had made Americans far more sensitive to Eastern matters. Upon Perry's departure for the orient his instructions stressed the extent to which the Far East had been brought closer to the United States by "the acquisition and rapid settlement by this country of a vast territory on the Pacific" and "the discovery of gold in that region."

The inspiration of Perry's trip to Japan is thus of record, and likewise it is not difficult to trace out the several steps by which his mission got under way. Some years before his voyage there had been an expedition of three American ships to Siam, where an American envoy accompanying the vessels, Edmund Roberts, on March 20, 1833 signed a treaty of commerce and amity, the first American treaty with a Far Eastern nation. Roberts on return to the orient in 1835 was commissioned to conclude a treaty with Japan, but died before reaching the island kingdom. After this effort, and after Cushing's successful conclusion of a treaty with China in 1844, another attempt to obtain the friendship and trade of Japan for the United States was undertaken by Alexander H. Everett, who was the first American commissioner to China under the Cushing Treaty. Everett because of illness was unable to reach Japan, and Commodore James Biddle, to whom the commissioner delegated his duties, arrived there in July 1846, but achieved nothing. After the Mexican War, and some further unofficial contacts by Americans with the Japanese, President Millard Fillmore in March 1852 appointed Perry commander in chief of the East India Squadron and special envoy to Japan.

Perry, in accord with the spirit of his times, had a large vision of his mission. In addition to opening Japan he believed it desirable for the United States to acquire territory in the Far East, and recommended taking the Ryukyu Islands. "Now it strikes me," the commodore wrote from Madeira en route to Japan, "that the occupation of the principal ports of those islands for the accommodation of our ships of war, and for the safe resort of merchant vessels of whatever other nation, would be a measure not only justified by the strictest rules of moral law, but, what is also to be considered, by the laws of stern necessity; and the argument may be further strengthened by the certain consequences of the ameliorization of the conditions of the natives, although the vices attendant upon civilization may be entailed upon them." Happily, Perry's recommendation of the Ryukyus was passed over. For the United States, the Ryukyu Islands would have proved another charge on American funds and patience similar to the Philippines. In American possession they would have served during the twentieth century as another hostage to Japan for American good behavior and pliability in the event of Japanese aggression. Yet strange are the ways of history, for the time would come when military necessity required the capture of the principal island of the Ryukyu group, Okinawa, at a cost of 45,029 American casualties—11,260 killed, 33,769 wounded—and at least several hundred millions of dollars.

Perry, reaching Japan in 1853, had some difficulty in treating with the Japanese before he eventually met with success. Until he could confer with officials of suitable rank and dignity, the commodore refused to discuss his mission with anyone. The Japanese in turn were not altogether happy to see Perry and would have been glad if he had sailed away. At last a Japanese potentate put his head into an eight-inch gun and lifted a sixty-four-pound iron cannon ball, and it was arranged that suitable individuals would receive Perry on shore and take from him, for delivery to the emperor, the letter encased in a gold box which the president or emperor of the United States had commissioned him to present. When Perry returned the following year he found the Japanese willing to conclude a treaty. The ruler of Japan at this time, the emperor's powerful viceroy the Tokugawa shogun, may have realized that it was futile for Japan to continue the isolationist policies of the past. The world had so shrunk, in terms of communication and trade, that an isolated Japan was an anachronism. The feudal society which had flourished for centuries in Japan was breaking down. A distinct merchant class had developed, possessing all the novel ideas of men of enterprise. This group was eager for foreign contacts, and the shogun in opening Japan followed the desires of these native merchants. As Finley Peter Dunne put it, in the words of Mr. Dooley, "Whin we rapped on the dure, we didn't go in, they come out."

Actually, Perry's treaty of 1854 was little more than a shipwreck convention, and was in no sense a broad commercial treaty such as

Cushing had secured at Wanghia in 1844. It remained for the first American diplomatic envoy to Japan, Townsend Harris, to negotiate a full-blown treaty of commerce and amity. The Harris Convention of 1858 set the pattern of American relations with Japan until the end of the century. It stipulated an exchange of diplomatic representatives, the opening of six ports for purposes of trade, provisions of extraterritoriality, and a schedule of tariff duties. Other nations concluded treaties on the pattern of the Harris Treaty, and they lasted until, from 1871 to 1911, Japan negotiated to end the extraterritorial concessions and other servitudes on Japanese sovereignty.

After conclusion of the Harris Convention the United States had the honor of being not merely the country which opened Japan to Western trade but the nation which received the first Japanese embassy. Japan sent a mission to America in 1860, and during its stay of three months it was feted, wined, dined, and received with enthusiasm and interest, despite the fact that the American nation stood on the brink of the Civil War. When the Japanese arrived in the national capital they visited Congress and found the Senate's proceedings of much interest. This was the first time that a Japanese mission had witnessed a national legislature at work. Second Ambassador Muragaki and some of his confreres remarked afterward that it looked like the fish market at Nihon-bashi in Yedo.

Perhaps more important than Japanese visits to Congress were the visits of the mission to the Washington navy yard, and acquisition of a wide selection of American ordnance which was sent back to Japan on the *Niagara* along with army and navy men to teach its use. The services of these men were declined by the shogunate, which was reluctant to reveal the state of Japan's defenses. The Japanese, one should add, already had learned how to use the Western-style guns.

2. The Open-Door Notes

By the end of the nineteenth century the westernization of the orient, despite some initial resistance, had proceeded rather far. The Japanese took over Western culture wholesale, in many cases jettisoning the heritage of centuries in favor of the latest Western nick-nack. One westernized Japanese destroyed a precious collection of Japanese prints to fill his house with cheap Western art. As for the Chinese, they at first proved more resistant to Western ways, but by the end of the century there was scarcely a locality in China, hinter-land or coast, where the influence of the Western world had not reached.

It was perhaps coincidental that the disruptive effect of westerniza-tion in China was accompanied by a decline in vigor of the Manchu dynasty. The Manchus had begun their reign with considerable pres-tige and power in the mid-seventeenth century, but after two hun-dred years the Taiping rebellion, together with disorders by the so-called Nien Fei bandits who ravaged large parts of the country, had shaken the Dragon Throne to its foundations. The authority of Peking was tenuous in the extreme by the end of the nineteenth cen-tury and it was obvious to all intelligent observers that the Manchu empire was breaking up, that a chaotic situation was arising not unlike that of India at the beginning of the eighteenth century. As in India, an opportunity presented itself to Western powers. But whereas in India only British power was able to take large advantage of the weak-ness of the native dynasty, in China in the 1890's all the major powers of Europe sought to take part in the spoils.

The first move was by the Russians, and their greed was quickly matched by that of the other nations. After the Japanese had defeated the Chinese in a war in 1894–1895, demonstrating to the world the weakness of the Manchu regime, the tsarist government concluded in June 1896 the Li-Lobanov Treaty providing the right to construct a railway across Manchuria—the Chinese Eastern Railway—as a short-cut for the Trans-Siberian route to Vladivostok. Moves by the other powers followed at once. When two German missionaries were murdered by Chinese bandits in the Shantung peninsula in November 1897, the Germans in early March 1898 extracted a convention giving them a 99-year lease on Kiaochow Bay and its port of Tsingtao, to-gether with economic rights in Shantung. Three weeks later the Rus-sians undertook to procure a 25-year lease of the southern part of the Liaotung peninsula including Talien-wan (Dairen) and Port Arthur, with the right to construct a railroad from Harbin in the north to the newly leased ports (this railroad, at first a feeder of the Chinese Eastern, became known after the Japanese acquired it in 1905 as the South Manchuria Railway). The British in a strategic counter took a 99-year lease of Kowloon opposite Hongkong and a lease on Wei-hai-wei on the Shantung peninsula "for so long a period as Port Arthur shall remain in the occupation of Russia." Meanwhile they had obtained other privileges from China, along with a pledge not to alienate to a foreign power any of the Yangtze Valley. The French obtained Kwangchow Bay in South China. Japan obtained rights in Fukien province opposite Formosa. Only the Italians, seeking in 1899 a naval station in Chekiang province, were successfully rebuffed.

The United States was at first oblivious to the impending chaos in China, and the probability that the Western nations would cut up the decrepit Manchu empire, although the turn of events in China coincided with the Spanish-American War and the somewhat fortuitous acquisition of the Philippine Islands by which the United States became a Far Eastern power. The British government in March 1898 had suggested a joint Anglo-American approach to the other Western powers interested in China, calculated to avoid a partition of the Chinese empire and a parceling-out of its trade among the partitioners. Because of the imminent war with Spain, President McKinley failed to heed the British request. Again, in January 1899, the British ambassador in Washington made an inquiry of the State Department, suggesting co-operation of London and Washington in the Far East. Once more the American government evinced no interest.

At this point came a personal intervention which always has intrigued students of American diplomacy. The Far Eastern adviser of Secretary of State Hay was William W. Rockhill, an "old China hand" and Sinologue intensely devoted to the welfare of the Chinese people. He feared that a partition of the Manchu empire would only mean further exploitation for the already downtrodden Chinese population. Rockhill was visited in the summer of 1899 by a friend from China, another old China hand, a Britisher named Alfred E. Hippisley. The latter suggested that in view of the concession-hunting in China the time was ripe for an American diplomatic move in favor of China, an attempt to obtain adherence by the powers of Europe to a commercial policy of the "open door" in China. The extraordinary nature of Hippisley's proposal becomes manifest when one realizes that Great Britain already had attempted twice to obtain the co-operation of the United States in promoting the open-door policy in China. Could it be that the British foreign office, wise in the ways of diplomacy, had undertaken to influence American policy through an intermediary?

Actually there appears to have been nothing untoward or devious about the connection of this policy with the Britisher, Hippisley, for the latter was a genuine friend of the Chinese people, as was his American confidant Rockhill. Hippisley had long been an official of the Imperial Chinese Maritime Customs Service, a British-administered organization but one distinct in interests, responsibility, and outlook from the Foreign Office. Hippisley by 1899 was second in charge of the Customs Service, was doubtless concerned over the Service's control of tariffs in the new spheres of interest of the Western powers, and for this reason alone had justification for seeking through Rockhill an American move to protect the open door and generally China's control over trade throughout the empire. Moreover, both he and Rockhill were students of Chinese history and culture, and they for this reason too were interested in a pro-Chinese diplomatic move by the United States. Hippisley had long been a Sinologue, and Rockhill was one of the world's authorities on Tibet. There was thus an easy explanation of why Hippisley proposed the open door to Rockhill and why the latter responded by forwarding Hippisley's proposition to Secretary of State Hay. The two men naturally would talk in terms of the threatened closing of the China market, which would attract the American people, rather than presenting an argument purely in terms of China's welfare or of China's control over her customs.

Hippisley, as is well known, drew up a memorandum on the open door. His friend Rockhill revised this analysis for presentation to President McKinley, and afterward put the substance of the revised memorandum in the form of diplomatic notes which, with minor changes, were adopted by Secretary Hay and sent out to Berlin, St. Petersburg, London, Paris, Rome, and Tokyo on September 6 and November 17, 1899. This was the first open-door note, containing the following three points:

"*First.* The recognition that no power will in any way interfere with any treaty port or any vested interest within any leased territory or within any so-called 'sphere of interest' it may have in China.

"*Second.* That the Chinese treaty tariff of the time being shall apply to all merchandise landed or shipped to all such ports as are within said 'sphere of interest' (unless they be 'free ports'), no matter to what nationality it may belong, and that duties so leviable shall be collected by the Chinese Government.

"*Third.* That it [each power] will levy no higher harbor dues on vessels of another nationality frequenting any port in such 'sphere' than shall be levied on vessels of its own nationality, and no higher railroad charges over lines built, controlled, or operated within its 'sphere' on merchandise belonging to citizens or subjects of other nationalities transported through such 'sphere' than shall be levied on similar merchandise belonging to its own nationals transported over equal distances."

The note could by no stretch of the imagination be described as epoch-making. The traditional American commercial policy toward China during the nineteenth century had been a policy of free competition among the powers for her trade—in other words, a policy of the open door in regard to China. There had not hitherto, it is true, been an effort to line up the other powers to favor this policy. The open door, as traditionally interpreted, had been a unilateral policy of the United States, contained only in treaties with China. But sooner or later it would have been elaborated in diplomatic intercourse with the nations interested in Chinese trade. To make multilateral this doctrine of fair trade in China was perhaps no more than a logical development of a traditional American policy. The first open-door note contemplated free commercial intercourse under the Chinese treaty tariff of five per cent—within the spheres of interest of the various powers. It did not contemplate abolition of the spheres of interest, although Hay's adviser Rockhill, to be sure, thought that by providing for collection of duties by the Chinese he had taken a stand in favor of protecting Chinese sovereignty within the spheres.

It was in the year 1900 that Hay made a second open-door effort, one far more important than the initiative of the previous year, and much different. An outbreak of antiforeign agitation in China, the Boxer rebellion, had required an expedition by an international force of 19,000 troops—including an American contingent—to rescue the besieged legations in Peking. On July 3, 1900, when it was uncertain whether the besieged legations in Peking would be saved, and when it seemed likely that after taking Peking the troops of the powers would engage in a grand division of Chinese territory, Hay made the bold and—in view of the conditions under which he made it—imaginative move of sending a circular note to the powers favoring the territorial integrity of China. This second open-door note, unlike its predecessor, was a novel statement of American policy. In the note of 1900 the secretary of state advanced to ground quite different from that covered by his note of the year before. In some ways the two open-door notes should not be coupled, for the second note in its stipulations regarding Chinese territorial integrity contradicted the note of September–November 1899. The first note had stipulated commercial freedom for all nations within any of the spheres of interest. In his second open-door note Hay announced that American policy sought to "preserve Chinese territorial and administrative entity," that is, that the United States was taking a stand against the further partitioning of China.

The second note, like the first, expressed the views of Hay's adviser Rockhill (and of his adviser, Hippisley), but neither Hippisley nor Rockhill nor Hay dreamed that the open-door policy would be more than a temporary buttress to Far Eastern peace. They did not envision that their diplomacy of the moment, "a kind of *modus vivendi*" as Rockhill described the first open-door notes, would become a cardinal doctrine of twentieth-century American policy in the orient. As the twentieth century advanced and Japan became ever more powerful in the Far East, threatening the integrity of China in numerous ways and on various occasions, American diplomacy tended to distort the sense of the second Hay open-door note. The idea of preserving Chinese territorial and administrative entity, in itself a somewhat ambitious policy, gave way almost unconsciously to the idea of downright guarantee of Chinese territory. There had never been a contractual guarantee of Chinese territory by the United States. But by 1941 the American public was virtually convinced that this was traditional American policy.

3. Rooseveltian Diplomacy, 1900–1909

The year 1900 was certainly a signal year in modern Chinese history, what with the suppression of the Boxer rebellion by the troops of the powers, and their forceful occupation of Peking. The nations imposed upon China a large claim for damages in the form of an indemnity of $738,820,707, distributed among Britain, France, Germany, Italy, Austria-Hungary, the United States, and Japan. The United States after accepting $4,000,000 to satisfy private claims, eventually remitted the remaining payments for the purpose of training Chinese students in America. The other nations kept the indemnities due them. In such wise the new century opened, but in 1900, it seems safe to say, the shape of the future was still uncertain. Settlement of the Boxer rebellion seemed to quiet affairs in the orient —for good, so many Americans and Europeans hoped.

In the year 1900 it was Russia, not Japan, which appeared to be the problem of the orient. Although Japan had defeated China in 1894–1895 in an exhibition of military prowess that boded ill for the future, when the powers had reached Peking and there was looting by some of the troops of the European nations the Japanese soldiers were well-behaved. In 1900 the Russians, far more than the Japanese, seemed the nation to watch. Russia had participated in a triple intervention along with Germany and France to thwart Japan in 1895, after the Japanese had won the war against China. At that time the tsarist government had insisted that Japan not take the southernmost part of Manchuria, the Liaotung peninsula, including a port on its tip which controlled the approaches to Peking. Faced with the intervention of three European powers, the Japanese in 1895 diplomatically withdrew their claims to Liaotung. The next year the Russians began moving into northern Manchuria under an agreement with the Chinese. By the time of the Boxer rebellion Russia was ready to occupy Manchuria, including all of the Liaotung peninsula, the territory denied to Japan in 1895. Russia also was showing considerable interest in Korea.

Russia was the power to watch—so the observers were writing at the turn of the century. Because of the clear record of Russian imperialism in the Far East, the powers, including the United States, were highly suspicious of the tsar's government. Theodore Roosevelt, upon succeeding the assassinated McKinley in the presidency, was thoroughly distrustful of the activities of tsarist Russia in the orient. After the Boxer rebellion, when trouble began to increase between Russia and Japan and war loomed, TR was happy to say that in case of a Russo-Japanese war he hoped Japan would win. The Russians were attempting to close Manchuria to foreign trade, on the theory that Manchuria was no longer a part of China. This was contrary to the idea of the open door, and other Americans than Roosevelt hoped that if Russia and Japan went to war, Japan would win and open Manchuria to trade. Japan would serve as houseboy for the open door.

The war between Japan and Russia began and ended with Russian naval defeats. After pressing the Russians to agree over a partition of Korea, and discouraged at the delay and evasion and the continuing expansion of Russian power in the Far East, Japan had severed diplomatic relations with Russia on February 6, 1904, and two days later suddenly attacked the tsarist fleet at Port Arthur, declaring war two days after hostilities began. Japanese troops invested Russian positions in Manchuria, giving no heed to the neutrality of Chinese soil, and in a matter of a few months, albeit with expenditure of over 100,000 Japanese lives, the island empire had worsted one of the most ancient of European nations. The last hope of the Russians was the thirty-two ships of the Baltic fleet, sent on a long voyage through the Mediterranean and the Indian Ocean to the Far East, only to be annihilated by Japan's Admiral Togo in Tsushima Strait.

What happened during the Russo-Japanese War of 1904–1905 was one of the surprises of the twentieth century—the abject defeat of Russia, the emergence of Japan as one of the first-class military powers of the world. Although they had disliked the Russians, the Americans had not bargained for this development. Japan, by defeating Russia, unsettled the entire Far East in a way that no event had done before, and the vulnerability of the Philippines began to appear as a major security problem for the United States. The Americans, perhaps, had only themselves to blame for this turn of affairs. They had for decades been doing their best to avoid any breakup of Japan similar to that of China, and in pursuing this purpose had done much to bolster Japan's military capabilities. American military assistance had begun with Perry's gift of one cannon from the *Saratoga*. The commodore had recommended to the Navy Department that two more be sent, for such gifts, he said, would on some future occasion be "returned a hundred-fold." The Japanese mission to the United States in 1860 had received a hundred muskets, four howitzers, shells and shell-filling machines. The United States sold three naval war vessels to Japan in 1863, and delivered them in 1865. Annapolis was opened to Japanese students in 1868. By contributing a number of political advisers to the Japanese government in the latter nineteenth century the United States further helped to make Japan a strong naval power. Mahan himself said that his writings had been more fully translated into Japanese than into any other language. But in the war of 1904–1905 the Japanese had suddenly exhibited the results of this American tuition in a new and startling and not altogether pleasant manner.

After initial requests from the belligerents, President Roosevelt undertook to mediate the war in the summer of 1905, and this task he performed with his usual aplomb, bringing his work of peace to a suitable end in the Treaty of Portsmouth, signed by Japan and Russia at Portsmouth, New Hampshire, on September 5, 1905. By this treaty Japan acquired the South Manchuria Railroad, the Liaotung peninsula under guise of a leasehold, and the southern half of Sakhalin Island. Russia acknowledged Japan's paramount interest in Korea.

The Portsmouth Treaty, narrowly considered, was a diplomatic accomplishment of the first order, and the American president eventually received the Nobel Peace Prize for his work in 1905. Unfortunately, in its long-term effects on American policy the treaty was hardly a triumph—indeed it was a disaster—for in reality it inaugurated the American-Japanese political antagonism that would plague American relations with the Far East during the first half of the twentieth century. Policy could no longer placidly continue in the nineteenth-century pattern of trade-Christianity-civilization. The Portsmouth Treaty, it is true, was probably the best treaty that either Russia or Japan could have obtained in the summer of 1905. The Russians were exhausted and the tsarist regime faced the first stirrings of the revolution that would engulf it in 1917. The Japanese were in equally bad straits, for their credit abroad was such as to dictate a speedy end to the war. Japanese finances had long been precarious, and the burden of further war in 1905 was almost too much to endure. The Japanese representatives at Portsmouth should have been satisfied with the peace treaty, and they were pleased, but they failed to get an indemnity from Russia, and obtained only half of Sakhalin. The government in Tokyo diplomatically allowed popular disappointment to focus on the American president who mediated the peace, rather than the Japanese envoys who signed it. Anti-American riots broke out in Tokyo, mobs burned four American churches, the United States embassy was placed under guard, and in subsequent years—as the Japanese spread further into Manchuria, taking advantage of Western weakness or preoccupation elsewhere—the rift in American-Japanese relations widened into a chasm.

There followed after the Portsmouth Treaty, during these uneasy years, three special agreements by which Japan and the United States sought to allay the suspicions of Portsmouth and somehow re-create the friendly atmosphere that had prevailed in an earlier era: the Taft-

Katsura Agreement (1905), the Root-Takahira Agreement (1908), and the Lansing-Ishii Agreement (1917). Unfortunately each agreement produced disagreement, and became a milestone in the antagonism developing between the United States and Japan. Each was accompanied by other untoward happenings and occurrences: the so-called Gentlemen's Agreement concerning immigration, the Knox neutralization scheme, the China consortium, the Twenty-One Demands.

The Taft-Katsura Agreement, a secret arrangement beween Secretary of War William Howard Taft and the Japanese premier, Taro Katsura, marked the effort of President Roosevelt to reach a harmonious arrangement with the Japanese government at the end of the Russo-Japanese War. It was obvious to Roosevelt that Japan was the coming power in the orient, and since the United States had acquired the Philippines, islands which lay at Japan's doorstep, it was prudent to placate the owners of the house. Placation meant giving away, in effect, an old edifice which lay close to the house, the kingdom of Korea. According to the Taft-Katsura "agreed memorandum," which supposedly bound only the administration then in power at Washington (though it is difficult to imagine how such an agreement could bind merely a single administration), the United States recognized Japan's dominant position in Korea, in return for which the Japanese disavowed "any aggressive designs whatever" on the Philippines.

No sooner was this memorandum drawn and the Portsmouth Treaty signed than trouble appeared with Japan, in an unexpected quarter—the segregating of Japanese school children together with Chinese and Koreans in the San Francisco schools. We have seen how the immigration of the Chinese to California in the years after the discovery of gold and during construction of the transcontinental railroad became in time an exceedingly sore point in California, and eventually forced an exclusion act through Congress in 1882. It was easy to exclude the Chinese, for the Chinese government was unable to do much more than protest such an act by the Americans. In the case of the Japanese, in the years after the Russo-Japanese War when the Japanese government was feeling its power and able to protest with vigor and effect, to take discriminating measures was far more dangerous. Yet in 1906, just a year after signature of the Portsmouth Treaty, the issue of Japanese immigration to California arose in this singularly ugly form. It is true that some adult Japanese had been attending grade schools—not a desirable situation, although these Japanese grownups were only trying to learn the English language. The action of the San Francisco school board was in any event precipitous and undiplomatic in the extreme and raised a storm in Japan. The whole issue of Japanese immigration to California suddenly came into the open, and the utmost diplomacy had to be exercised with the Californians, and with the Japanese, before the matter was settled by the Gentlemen's Agreement in 1907–1908. According to this agreement, a series of diplomatic notes, Japan would not allow laborers to obtain visas to the mainland of the United States, and thus halted the immigration which was causing so much trouble in California. The San Francisco school board, under its president— an erstwhile bassoon player under indictment for fraud—rescinded its rule.

Trouble again arose in California in 1913 when the legislature took under consideration a bill making it impossible for Japanese to own or lease land for agricultural purposes. President Woodrow Wilson was reduced to sending Secretary of State William Jennings Bryan to California in April 1913 to plead with the governor and the legislature. The discriminatory legislation as finally passed was so ingeniously worded as to sound less offensive than it was. Without directly affronting Japan or violating the letter of America's treaty obligations it barred Japanese from owning agricultural land. The Californians later in 1920 passed an act refusing to Japanese the right to lease agricultural land. Over a dozen states during the early 1920's followed California's example.

What with the increase of Japanese power in the orient signalized by the Russo-Japanese War, and the necessity of concluding an agreement for protection of the Philippines, the Roosevelt administration's original friendliness for Japan had dissipated. Relations between the two nations had not been improved by the San Francisco school controversy. Roosevelt in 1907 conceived the idea of sending the American battleship fleet around the world, stopping at oriental ports en route, in the hope that a display of American power would impress the Japanese. This was a typical Rooseveltian move, in its feeling for display and show of force, and TR later boasted in his *Autobiography* that it was "the most important service that I rendered to peace." This boast may have been true. Probably the battleship fleet did impress the Japanese people, as it also impressed the powers of

Europe, with the growing strength of America.

Meanwhile the Root-Takahira Agreement had been concluded on November 30, 1908, an agreement over which there has always been a controversy, for no one has ever established the precise meaning of this accord concluded by Secretary of State Elihu Root and the Japanese ambassador in Washington, Kogoro Takahira. In the exchange of notes between the two statesmen it was declared that the two governments wished to maintain the status quo in the region of the Pacific Ocean, together with the open door in China and that each would respect the territories of the other and support "by all pacific means at their disposal the independence and integrity of China and the principle of equal opportunity." This seemed to indicate that the United States would not challenge Japan's newly created position in Manchuria; the peaceful promises by Japan in turn pointed to another guarantee of the Philippines, together with Hawaii and Alaska. The Japanese doubtless considered the Root-Takahira Agreement a complement to their new position evidenced in the Anglo-Japanese Alliance of 1902, the Portsmouth Treaty, and agreements of 1907 with France and Russia. Secretary Root hoped and later affirmed that the agreement would ensure the open door in Manchuria rather than any special Japanese-fashion "status quo." There was no meeting of minds in the curious Root-Takahira Agreement, stemming as it did from the multiplying uncertainties and frictions of American-Japanese relations. It was one more attempt to find some formula that might make for better feeling between Washington and Tokyo.

4. *The Far East and the First World War*

The Far East, as we have seen, was in ferment in the years after the turn of the century, the decline of Manchu strength in China coinciding with the rising power of Japan. And these disturbing factors— Japanese power, the decline of China—were joined by a third complication, the embroilments of Russia in the Far East. The Russo-Japanese War had been an illustration of the novel difficulties in Asia.

The entire Far Eastern situation was enormously complicated by the developing antagonisms of Europe. Russia's diplomacy in the East, to name but one example, was closely linked to the deepening international crisis on the Continent. The alignments of the first World War were forming. The Triple Alliance of Germany, Austria-Hungary, and Italy soon would face the Triple Entente of Great Britain, France, and Russia. Far Eastern politics became the backyard of European politics. The German kaiser had striven for some time to interest his cousin, the tsar, in Far Eastern territory, to turn the attention of Nicholas II from Europe. William II and Nicholas II— "Willy" and "Nicky," as they signed their personal correspondence —had encouraged each other with the titles of Admiral of the Atlantic (Willy) and Admiral of the Pacific (Nicky). Insofar as Nicky took Willy seriously, and there is some evidence that he did, the ultimate result of these imperial pleasantries was the defeat of Russia by Japan and a weakening of the Franco-Russian alliance in Europe. It was, one should add, a somewhat mixed victory, for it meant too the weakening of the monarchical principle in Russia, which in due time had repercussions for European monarchs, as the kaiser would learn.

The quest of Great Britain for alliances and friendships in the years before the first World War—conclusion of the Anglo-Japanese Alliance of 1902, and after it the *rapprochement* with France signalized by the entente with Britain of 1904 and the Anglo-Russian Entente of 1907—also had its effects in the Far East. The Anglo-Japanese Alliance enlisted Japanese support of British interests in Asia and gave Britain a freer hand in Europe. The alliance was directed also, and this was Japan's *quid pro quo*, against Russia, for it promised that should Japan engage in a war with another power (that is, Russia) and that power be joined by a third power (that is, France, in accord with the Franco-Russian Alliance of 1894), then Britain would enter the war on the side of Japan. In effect this arrangement gave Japan assurance that in a war with Russia there would be no intervention by France.

This is not the place to set down in detail the Far Eastern ramifications of European politics; what mattered for American diplomacy was that after the Treaty of Portsmouth a new international arrangement took effect in the Far East, in large part a result of European political developments: Russia in 1907 concluded the entente with Britain, France had done so in 1904, and because of the already existing Franco-Russian and Anglo-Japanese alliances Japan therefore came to an agreement with Russia (Japan, Russia, France, and Britain would side against Germany in 1914). The Russo-Japanese *rapprochement* that took place during the years 1907–1910 was, of course, at the expense of China. Russia and Japan formally divided Manchuria into two spheres of interest, its southern part to Japan, its northern to Russia.

In view of this new alliance structure, any intervention by the United States in Far Eastern politics was likely to affect directly the European balance of power. Here was a new problem for American diplomacy in the Far East. But one must doubt whether the individuals who directed American policy after the era of Theodore Roosevelt really appreciated it. They knew that there had been a traditional American policy in the Far East, and that the rise of Japanese power had made that policy difficult. They saw the troubles in China, the crumbling of the Manchu empire which in 1911–1912 brought disintegration of the dynasty and proclamation of a republic. They had no sense of the connection of Far Eastern and European diplomacy. In the years between 1900 and 1914, and especially in the era 1905–1914, any sort of American diplomacy in the orient without knowledge of the factors and forces governing European international relations would have been foolish, or dangerous, or both.

Theodore Roosevelt had sensed the problems of American policy and he sought to placate Japan in the agreements of 1905 and 1908, but his successor President Taft unfortunately forgot the power equation in the Far East. Taft was a constitutional lawyer, and together with his secretary of state, Philander C. Knox, also a lawyer, he endeavored to promote American trade with China through legalistic maneuvering of a sort which would not have brought results in the nineteenth century, to say nothing of the twentieth. The two blunders of the Taft administration, and they were blunders, were the attempted neutralization of the existing Manchurian railways, sponsored by Secretary Knox, and the effort of the administration to promote a China consortium for developing Manchuria.

The Knox neutralization scheme was one of the most foolish proposals ever made by an American diplomat. The secretary of state was secure in his ignorance of Manchurian realities, that is, of the new friendship of Japan and Russia in Manchuria. He attempted through Britain, France, Germany, Japan, and Russia to obtain for China an international loan of sufficient size to enable that government to buy up all the foreign railways in China, including Manchuria, and thereby "neutralize" the roads by retiring foreign capital. As an alternative he suggested construction under neutral administration of a north-south railway through Manchuria from Aigun to Chinchow.

He overlooked the fact that the railroads of China, particularly Manchuria, had always been a prime means of foreign intervention, and that Russia's Chinese Eastern Railway in northern Manchuria and Japan's South Manchuria Railway were the thread on which these two nations had strung their interests in Manchuria. To ask those countries to neutralize their railway concessions was to ask retirement from an area over which wars had been fought in 1894–1895 and 1904–1905. The American secretary of state had made a preposterous suggestion. The European powers accepted the Knox proposal in principle, but would do nothing more. Japan argued in reply to Knox that his suggestion was at variance with the Peace of Portsmouth and arrangements for concessions in Manchuria made with China at the end of that conflict. The Russians, after perfunctorily expressing enthusiasm for the open door and equal opportunity in Manchuria— as the Japanese had also done—contended that Knox's proposal was against their interests and refused to accept it. As a result of the neutralization scheme, Japan and Russia concluded a new agreement in July 1910 strengthening their agreement of 1907.

Undaunted, Knox set out to force American capital into a new international consortium which was organizing to finance currency reform and industrial development in Manchuria. The United States went to the length of sending a special message from President Taft to the prince regent of China, begging the latter to look with favor upon American entrance into the consortium. The matter dragged on, and China was plunged into the revolution of 1911–1912, precipitated by foreign demands for concessions. The Americans finally were admitted to the consortium, but Wall Street financiers were reluctant to take part and demanded explicit government support. When Wilson became president in March 1913 he refused to support the consortium and allowed American bankers to leave what they had never wished to enter in the first place.

By the time of the Wilson administration, the American diplomatic position in the Far East had deteriorated to a grievous state, and with outbreak of the World War in 1914 the American government was beset with problems of neutrality. Little energy remained for Far Eastern matters. Neither the United States nor the European nations could do anything against the shameless demands made by Japan upon China in 1915. The Twenty-One Demands, as they were called, contained several conditions which if accepted by the Chinese would have brought that hapless nation directly under the control of Tokyo. The United States protested on May 11, 1915 that it would not recognize any situation forced upon China by Japan. Luckily the crisis passed when the Japanese decided not to force their most rigorous demands upon the Chinese.

But in 1917, when the United States entered the war, there came another opportunity for the Japanese, this time to obtain a concession directly from the Americans. France and Britain were sending missions to the United States in the spring of 1917, to arrange the policy and details of American participation in the European conflict, and the Japanese sent a special envoy, Viscount Kikujiro Ishii, but not on the same sort of mission the European governments were undertaking. Ishii was instructed to secure from the American government a recognition of Japan's position in Asia. Unblushingly performing his embassy, he threatened that Japan might go over to the side of Germany and abandon the Allies. Three times he told Lansing that Germany had sought to persuade Japan to forsake the Allied cause, and the hint was altogether obvious. The Lansing-Ishii Agreement was concluded on November 2, 1917 in this difficult atmosphere.

The agreement between Secretary of State Robert Lansing and the special Japanese ambassador was if anything more ambiguous than the Root-Takahira Agreement of nine years before. "The governments of the United States and Japan," it stipulated, "recognize that territorial propinquity creates special relations between countries, and, consequently the government of the United States recognizes that Japan has special interests in China, particularly in the part to which her possessions are contiguous. The territorial sovereignty of China, nevertheless, remains unimpaired . . ." Lansing always maintained that he had only recognized the "special interests" of Japan in China, interests of an economic nature created by geographical propinquity and contiguity. The Japanese translated the phrase "special interests" as "paramount interests," and refused to consider them as limited to economic concerns. Later Ishii wrote in his *Diplomatic Commentaries* that he and Secretary Lansing were only "performing the role of photographers, as it were, of a condition," namely, Japan's paramount situation in the Far East. "Even though Americans may destroy the print because it is not to their liking," Ishii added, "the negative will remain. And even if the negative also be destroyed, does not the substance of the picture remain?"

What could one conclude about all these perplexities of American-Japanese relations? Certainly there could be no doubt about Japanese intentions in Eastern Asia when in the year 1919 the peace conference for the first World War met in Paris. The Japanese by this time, not content with a sphere of interest in Manchuria and virtual hegemony over China, had made an effort to separate Siberia from Russia. Japan had sent over seventy thousand troops into Siberia, nominally to assist in the protection of Allied war materials stored at Vladivostok. The supposed purpose of sending these Japanese troops, together with contingents from other nations including the United States (the United States contingent in Siberia never numbered more than nine thousand), Britain, Serbia, Italy, and Rumania, had been to hold these stores against the Bolsheviks, who had taken over the Russian government in November 1917 and soon thereafter made a separate peace with the Germans. There was also, one should add, another purpose of the Allied troops in Siberia, namely to facilitate the exit from Russia of thousands of Czechs, former enemy prisoners freed by withdrawal of Russia from the war, who wished to pass over the Trans-Siberian Railway and take ship from Vladivostok to Europe, there to fight on the Allied side against Austria-Hungary to achieve an independent Czechoslovakia. A third purpose for Allied intervention in Siberia, set forth by the United States, was to assist the Russians with self-government or self-defense. But it was the hope of the Japanese to intrigue with Russian factional leaders and assist to power a pro-Japanese regime which some day might place Siberia under Japanese sovereignty. The Japanese war ministry defied the foreign office, and forced Japan's diplomats at home or abroad to defend the actions of the military. Eventually the Japanese government went back under civil control. Meanwhile the United States and the other allies withdrew their troops. Japanese troops left Siberia in October 1922.

At the Paris Peace Conference of 1919 there was, in addition to such difficulties with the Japanese, the problem of Shantung, the formerly German sphere of interest in China. If the Allied leaders at Paris had not recognized Japan's right to economic and other concessions in Shantung, the Japanese delegation would have retired from Paris. "They are not bluffers," Wilson told one of his assistants in 1919, "and they will go home unless we give them what they should not have." When a recognition of Japanese interests in Shantung was written into the Versailles Treaty the president accepted it, realizing sadly that it "was the best that could be had out of a dirty past."

Other advantages accrued to Japan at the Paris Peace Conference, for in addition to Shantung the Japanese were confirmed in their control over the former German Pacific islands north of the equator. Japan had taken the islands at the outset of the war, under a secret arrangement with Great Britain whereby the British took the German islands south of the equator. By the peace settlement of 1919 the islands went to Japan as a mandate, a special colonial trust, of the new League of Nations. The Japanese were supposed to administer these former German possessions for the benefit of the inhabitants thereof, but in fact the islands became Japan's private property and were fortified contrary to League rules for mandated territories.

The peace conference of 1919 marked generally a triumph for Japan. The island empire was included as one of the five great powers represented on the Council of Ten (to which each of the powers sent two delegates). This marked a large addition to Japanese prestige, for the council was designed to serve as a sort of executive body for the peace conference. Later, when the council gave way to the Big Four—private meetings of the leaders of Britain, France, the United States, and Italy—and the Big Three (Italy withdrawing), the Japanese received a careful explanation from President Wilson's adviser, Colonel Edward M. House, who assured one of the chief delegates from Tokyo, Baron Makino, "that the work of the Four will be submitted to him before its final adoption and that then the Big Four will be expanded into the Big Five."

Japan, it is true, did lose face at the conference when Makino in the last session of the League of Nations Commission, the committee for drafting the League Covenant, raised the issue of racial equality and asked for a statement in the preamble of the Covenant, then in final draft, of "the principle of equality of nations and the just treatment of their nationals . . . as a fundamental basis of future international relations in the new world organization." Under unbearable pressure from Prime Minister William M. Hughes of Australia, the British delegate at the commission meeting, Lord Robert Cecil, refused to admit the principle of racial equality. In the voting that followed the British and American delegations abstained, which was equivalent to voting against the Japanese proposal. This was an unpleasant pill for the Japanese representatives at Paris, but the gains to Japan at the con-

ference were otherwise so impressive and gratifying that the Japanese
in 1919 could well feel that, racially equal or not, they had achieved
a large and important place in the world family of nations, including
perhaps an unassailable position in the affairs of the Far East.

This latter notion was not the view of the great powers of the West,
in particular Britain and the United States, who at length reorganized
the affairs of the orient according to their desires, for a time, at the
Washington Naval Conference of 1921–1922—which subject must
be dealt with in another chapter.

Suffice to close this present chapter by remarking the transfer at
the end of the first World War of the bulk of the American fleet
from Atlantic to Pacific. There it remained as a counterpoise to the
Japanese navy during the increasingly critical relations between the
United States and Japan in the 1920's and 1930's. This transfer
symbolized the end of an era in American relations with Europe,
the period during which Americans feared Europe more than Asia,
and the beginning of a new outlook on world affairs in which the
security of the United States vis-à-vis Japan began to occupy the calculations of American strategists, military and diplomatic.

During the nineteenth century, as we have seen, three broad interests came to dominate American relations with the Far East.
American Far Eastern diplomacy in the nineteenth century resulted
in several treaties envisioning an open door for American commercial
enterprise. The open-door notes of 1899 and 1900 were further and,
at least in the case of the note of 1899, logical elaborations of this
policy.

At the beginning of the twentieth century new political complications appeared—the crumbling of the Manchu empire, the rise of
Japan to the position of a great power, the close connection of Asian
diplomacy with the diplomacy of Europe. These novel factors began
to plague the State Department, and produced several agreements
with Japan, together with such policy efforts as Secretary Knox's
neutralization scheme and his equally ill-advised support of the China
consortium. All such measures looked directly or indirectly to the
soothing of Japan and the adjustment of American interests to the
new and much more dangerous turn of Far Eastern affairs. American
relations with Japan nonetheless deteriorated, and by 1921 the specter
of war was fully visible, twenty years before the event.

ADDITIONAL READING

American relations with the Far East during the nineteenth century, in part because of their frequently exotic details, have interested many writers. A general account is Tyler Dennett, *Americans in Eastern Asia* (New York, 1922). Among the many books of merit on China are Kenneth Scott Latourette, *The History of Early Relations between the United States and China: 1784–1844* (New Haven, 1917); Ssu-yu Teng, *Chang Hsi and the Treaty of Nanking, 1842* (Chicago, 1944); J. K. Fairbank, *Trade and Diplomacy on the China Coast: The Opening of the Treaty Ports, 1842–1854* (Cambridge, Mass., 1953); Paul A. Varg, *Missionaries, Chinese, and Diplomats: The American Protestant Missionaries in China, 1890–1952* (Princeton, 1958); and, partly on China, C. M. Fuess, *The Life of Caleb Cushing* (2 vols., New York, 1923). See also Maurice Collis, *Foreign Mud* (New York, 1947). A general account is F. R. Dulles, *China and America: The Story of Their Relations since 1784* (Princeton, 1946). For Japan there is Arthur Walworth, *Black Ships Off Japan* (New York, 1946), concerning the Perry expedition; William L. Neumann, "Religion, Morality, and Freedom: The Ideological Background of the Perry Expedition," *Pacific Historical Review*, vol. 23 (1954), 247–257; Carl Crow, *He Opened the Door of Japan* (New York, 1939), on Townsend Harris; and Chitoshi Yanaga, "The First Japanese Embassy to the United States," *Pacific Historical Review*, vol. 9 (1940), 113–138. A biography of Horace Allen, the American missionary doctor and diplomat to Korea, is by Fred H. Harrington, *God, Mammon and the Japanese* (Madison, Wis., 1944).

A. Whitney Griswold's brilliant *The Far Eastern Policy of the United States* (New York, 1938) is best for American relations from the turn of the century until the mid-1930's. More detailed studies are Alfred L. P. Dennis, *Adventures in American Diplomacy: 1896–1906* (New York, 1928) and Charles Vevier, *The United States and China: 1906–1913* (New Brunswick, N.J., 1955). Among the many special works are Tyler Dennett, "The Open Door," in Joseph Barnes, ed., *Empire in the East* (Garden City, N.Y., 1934), a thoughtful, reflective account; Charles S. Campbell, Jr., *Special Business Interests and the Open Door Policy* (New Haven, 1951); C. S. Campbell, Jr., *Anglo-American Understanding: 1898–1903* (Baltimore, 1957); Thomas A. Bailey's *Roosevelt and the Russo-Japanese War* (New York, 1925), *Theodore Roosevelt and the Japanese-American Crises* (Stanford, 1934), and "The Root-Takahira Agreement of 1908," *Pacific Historical Review*, vol. 9 (1940), 19–35; and Betty Miller Unterberger, *America's Siberian Expedition: 1918–1920* (Durham, N.C., 1956), the latest scholarship. See also W. R. Langdon, trans., Kikujiro Ishii, *Diplomatic Commentaries* (Baltimore, 1936).

Standard biographies and diplomatic biographies are Howard K. Beale, *Theodore Roosevelt and the Rise of America to World Power* (Baltimore, 1956), an authoritative account of its subject, exhaustively researched; Tyler Dennett's *John Hay* (New York, 1933); Paul A. Varg, *Open Door Diplomat: The Life of W. W. Rockhill* (Urbana, Ill., 1952), a fascinating account of the high-strung, strange, yet likable scholar-diplomat; Henry F. Pringle, *The Life and Times of William Howard Taft* (2 vols., New York, 1939); Tien-yi Li, *Woodrow Wilson's China Policy: 1913–1917* (New York, 1952); Roy W. Curry, *Woodrow Wilson and Far Eastern Policy: 1913–1921* (New York, 1957); Russell H. Fifield, *Woodrow Wilson and the Far East: The Diplomacy of the Shantung Question* (New York, 1952).

CHAPTER
☆ 10 ☆

Latin America in the Twentieth Century

The relations of the United States with Latin America compare in one respect to relations with the Far East, namely that—as in Asia—there have been two major periods of policy. The first of these, which might well be described as the era of intervention, ran roughly from the time of the Spanish-American War down to the 1930's; American troops then retired after long occupations from Nicaragua and Haiti, and the United States cut supervisory ties with Cuba and the Dominican Republic. The second period in the relations of the Colossus of the North with her southern neighbors began at the end of the 1920's with enunciation of the good-neighbor policy and has continued to the present time—and will so continue, one must hope. In the first period, the era of intervention, the United States wrested Cuba from Spain, then in 1903 allowed the Panamanians to revolt from Colombia and cede a canal zone to the United States. After this came the series of interventions in the Caribbean area—the Dominican Republic, Nicaragua, Haiti—and in Mexico in 1913–1917. But when victory in the first World War removed the need for protection of the canal approaches in the Caribbean, and after the decade of the 1920's passed mostly in inaction, the United States in the 1930's recognized the need for a new policy toward the Latin republics, the policy of the good neighbor and the liquidation of protective imperialism.

This is not to say that prior to the end of the nineteenth century there were no relations worth noting between the United States and Latin America, for there were—such affairs as the 1826 Congress of Panama to which the United States sent delegates, the French intervention in Mexico in 1861–1867, the assembly of the first Pan-American Conference by Secretary of State James G. Blaine in Washington in 1889, the *Baltimore* episode in Chile in 1891–1892. Throughout the nineteenth century the Monroe Doctrine exercised a benevolent effect, translated into phrases that anyone could understand by Secretary of State Olney during the Venezuelan crisis in 1895–1896. If this were the first major invocation of the Monroe Doctrine since its enunciation in 1823, the existence of the presidential pronouncement and the increasing strength of the United States in the latter nineteenth century made it a theory of importance well before 1895. Even so, the diplomats of the United States when they had problems or concerns during the decades before the Spanish-American War were accustomed, on almost all occasions, to look to Europe. The first serious action by the United States government in the Western Hemisphere came at the time of the war with Spain.

1. *The Era of Intervention*

The deplorable situation in Cuba led in the early spring of 1898 to American intervention in that island, and Congress in the Teller Amendment stipulated prior to the declaration of war that the American nation would not acquire Cuba as a territorial possession. This self-denial did not mean that Cuba could not become a protectorate, which is what happened, and the terms of the protectorate over Cuba were laid down in the Platt Amendment to the army appropriations bill passed by Congress in 1901. According to its terms Cuba could not enter into any treaty impairing Cuban independence; the Cuban government was forbidden to contract any public debt in excess of ordinary revenues; the United States was authorized to intervene to preserve Cuban independence and maintain law and order; Cuba agreed to allow the United States navy to develop coaling stations (such as Guantanamo Bay, still held). The Platt Amendment was written into the Cuban constitution of 1901, after which American troops withdrew from the island. To be sure of preserving Cuba as a protectorate, the United States incorporated the amendment in a treaty with the newly constituted authorities in Havana, signed on May 22, 1903, which was not abrogated until thirty-one years later on May 29, 1934.

In general, it might be said, the Platt Amendment was not an uncalled-for infringement of Cuban sovereignty, for the islanders badly needed tutelage and preparation for self-government. It certainly was not a heavy burden on Cuban life, even if Latin patriots sought to describe it as such. American rights under the treaty of 1903 were not often exercised. Sometimes the Cubans, curiously enough, became heated at the government in Washington and at the American people, not because they intervened in Cuban affairs but because they refused to intervene—for example, during the Machado era of the early 1930's when the Cuban dictator Gerardo Machado ruled by terror. By 1958, with the Platt Amendment long dead and Fidel Castro leading a rebellion against the terrorist rule of Fulgencio Batista, one of the men who overthrew Machado, many Cubans again wished for some sort of American intervention. The Castro victory in January 1959 left some still wishing.

The Cuban experience, the first for the United States in the Caribbean, was mainly an effort to train a new government. A far different sort of intervention was the affair at Panama in 1903. President Theodore Roosevelt tired of the slowness of the Colombian senate in consenting to a canal zone for the United States in the Colombian province of Panama and protected a revolution which broke out in Panama by recognizing within three days the new Panamanian regime, with which TR soon signed a treaty giving rights to the United States for constructing a canal. This was a totally unnecessary affair, because Roosevelt could either have paid the price desired by the Colombians or he could have obtained instead a canal site across Central America through Nicaragua. TR was in too much of a hurry to build a canal. He was too much moved by the obvious need of the United States after 1898 for a canal—the increasing demand for cheap ocean transportation between the United States's east and west coasts, the hurried voyage of the *Oregon* around Cape Horn in 1898 to join the fleet off Santiago de Cuba, the existence after the Spanish-American War of the new Pacific possessions of the United States. One might charitably say that Roosevelt moved before he thought things out, although more probably he never thought things out but simply moved. Whatever the confusions, the intervention at Panama certainly constitutes the greatest blunder made by the American government among its Latin neighbors from the beginning of relations down to the present day.

The setting of the stage for the Panama drama began with some moves of American diplomacy prior to the coup of November 1903. Initially the United States had to arrange with Great Britain for abrogation of the Clayton-Bulwer Treaty of 1850, which had debarred either nation from exclusive rights in any canal built across the isthmus of Panama, and required neutralization of such a canal under international auspices. Abrogation was duly secured in the so-called second Hay-Pauncefote Treaty, concluded on November 18, 1901 by Secretary of State John Hay and the British ambassador in Washington, Sir Julian Pauncefote. The first Hay-Pauncefote Treaty, signed on February 5, 1900, had come to grief because it did not provide for American fortification of the proposed canal; the second treaty, by saying nothing about fortification, provided for it implicitly.

There then was the question of routes: Nicaragua or Panama. There had been much sentiment for cutting the canal through Nicaragua, instead of Panama, but in 1902 the Panama route became practically certain. For one thing, a number of important individuals in Washington, including President Roosevelt, became convinced that the Panama route was the easiest and best. For another, the Panama route became available. The New Panama Canal Company, a French company which owned the rights to the Panama route, reduced its price for selling out to the United States to a reasonable figure. This company was the successor of the concern which under direction of the builder of the Suez canal, Ferdinand de Lesseps, had gone bankrupt in 1891 after squandering $260,000,000 in a Panama canal, which the old company left only about two-fifths finished. The New Panama Canal Company had been asking $109,141,500 for its rights, until an American commission estimated that the Panama route was only about $40,000,000 cheaper to construct than the Nicaragua route, whereupon the New Company came down in its asking price to exactly $40,000,000. After this Congress passed the Spooner Act on June 28, 1902 stipulating that the canal should be constructed in Panama, the New Company receive its $40,000,000, provided an agreement could be made with Colombia, but if such an agreement could not be made the United States should come to an arrangement with Nicaragua and construct the canal there. President Roosevelt thereupon had Secretary of State Hay conclude a treaty with the Colombian minister in Washington, Dr. Tomás Herrán, and the Hay-Herrán Treaty of January 22, 1903 provided for payment of $10,-000,000 to Colombia and $250,000 annually as rental, the rental to begin in nine years. The United States was to receive a 99-year lease of the canal zone, subject to renewal.

At this point the Colombian senate, because of the indefinite nature of the lease and a stipulation for mixed American-Colombian courts in the canal zone, refused to ratify the treaty. The senators also knew that the franchise of the New Panama Canal Company would run out in the year 1904 and that the United States had promised in the Spooner Act to pay this company $40,000,000. They reasoned that Colombia might as well have this money and needed only to delay a year in order to get it. President Roosevelt was incensed. "Make it as strong as you can to Beaupré [A. M. Beaupré, the American minister to Colombia]," TR wrote Secretary Hay. "Those contemptible little creatures in Bogota ought to understand how much they are jeopardizing things and imperiling their own future." On August 17, 1903, he said that "we may have to give a lesson to those jack rabbits." On September 15 he referred to the Colombians as "foolish and homicidal corruptionists." On October 5 he said that it might be well "to warn these cat-rabbits that great though our patience has been, it can be exhausted." The president was deeply angered, and ready to welcome any turn of events in Panama that would take matters out of the hands of the Colombians. Since the New Panama Canal Company was as interested as the president in this matter, albeit for different reasons (the $40,000,000), it is readily understandable how word of the president's humor reached the ears of officers of the canal company, and the latter gentlemen wasted no time in seizing their opportunity. They were seconded in their enthusiasm, quite understandably, by the inhabitants of Panama who feared that the delay of the Colombian senate might lead the United States to choose the alternate waterway in Nicaragua and destroy the prospect, which otherwise would be excellent, for a boom in the Panamanian economy.

The company's initiative was prosecuted by two important agents. One was a French soldier of fortune who had formerly been de Lesseps' chief engineer, Philippe Bunau-Varilla. The other was the lawyer for the New Panama Canal Company, Nelson W. Cromwell of the New York firm of Sullivan and Cromwell. Working independently but complementarily to each other, they managed to engineer a revolution in Panama and to ease the way in Washington, if such easing were needed, for American recognition of the revolutionaries. Bunau-Varilla operated from Room 1162 in the Waldorf-Astoria in New York, which place he later wrote "deserves to be considered as the cradle of the Panama Republic." There he put together the constitution of the state and readied a declaration of independence; his wife stitched the new national flag. The flag looked very much like that of the United States, but with yellow instead of white for the background and two suns instead of stars. Preparatory to events, he also readied for himself a commission as Panama's first minister to the United States. Meanwhile the lawyer Cromwell was busy in Washington instructing members of the Senate about the plight of the suffering Panamanians. When the revolution came off in Panama on November 3, 1903 it was hardly unexpected, and everything occurred with complete success, thanks in part to arrival of the U.S.S. *Nashville* at Colón on the day before the revolution. The *Nashville* did not prevent the Colombians from landing troops to suppress the uprising—railroad officials in Colón failed to make transportation available to the Colombian troops. The railroad was owned by the New Panama Canal Company. But the presence of the American vessel lent substance to the hopes of the revolutionists for American support. At the other end of the new country, at Panama City, Bunau-Varilla's henchman Dr. Manuel Amador Guerrero, the new president of the republic, paid off the soldiers in the town at a rate allegedly of $80,000 for the local general, $10,000 each for the junior officers, and $50 apiece for the men. Amador made a speech and complimented his countrymen: "The world is astounded at our heroism! Yesterday we were but the slaves of Colombia; today we are free. . . . President Roosevelt has made good. . . . Free sons of Panama, I salute you! Long live the Republic of Panama! Long live President Roosevelt! Long live the American Government!"

Three days later the United States recognized the new regime, an interval between revolution and recognition which was considered appallingly short. Fifteen days after the revolution, on November 18, 1903, Secretary Hay and Minister Bunau-Varilla made a treaty granting to the United States in perpetuity the use and control of a canal zone ten miles wide across the isthmus of Panama. The American government agreed to pay $10,000,000 and an annual fee of $250,000, the same arrangement offered in the Hay-Herrán Treaty with Colombia, beginning nine years after exchange of ratifications which occurred in 1904. "The United States," according to the first article of this treaty, "guarantees and will maintain the independence of the Republic of Panama." This article made Panama a protectorate of the United States. The protectorate ended with a treaty between Panama and the United States signed March 2, 1936, ratified in 1939.

A question never answered about the Panama affair is, "Who received the $40,000,000?" The United States paid it to J. P. Morgan and Company for disbursement to the officers and stockholders of the New Panama Canal Company. No one knows to this day how this money was distributed.

American policy, as was said at the outset of this discussion, blundered in the business at Panama in 1903, in several respects. For one, the United States could easily have constructed a canal through Nicaragua, where the canal would have been much closer to the United States and saved time and trouble on coast-to-coast shipping. Probably, too, if President Roosevelt had been firm with the cat-rabbits of Colombia they would have accepted his offer of $10,000,-000. It would even have been better if the president had simply paid whatever price was desired in Colombia, for who received the money there was no business of his. Instead came this black mark on the record of the United States in Latin America, this obvious farce of a revolution in Panama, and Roosevelt in 1911 in a speech at the University of California compounded the Panamanian imbroglio by asserting that "I took the canal zone and let Congress debate." This was all Colombia needed, and Bogota turned in a bill for indemnity which the Democratic Wilson administration in 1914, the year the canal opened, came close to paying—so close that Roosevelt had to enlist his friend Cabot Lodge to block the appropriation in the Senate. After TR's death, and apparently inspired partly by prospects of American oil concessions in Colombia, the United States in 1921 paid $25,000,000 in what might be described as hush money.

Several other interferences by the United States occurred in the Caribbean area in the years after the Panama intervention: in the Dominican Republic in 1905, in Nicaragua in 1911, and in Haiti in 1915. None was as important as the Panama intervention, nor led to a permanent occupation as did the latter, but together these various interventions brought the United States into bad repute among the nations of Latin America and for a long time made extremely difficult any effective cordiality and friendship. The interventions in the Caribbean resulted largely from two concerns on the part of the United States: first, a missionary-like interest in the peace and well-being of the Caribbean countries; second, the United States' fear that disturbances in this area might invite foreign intervention from Europe. These understandable concerns did not mollify the Latins, who wanted no missionaries and felt thoroughly safe from Europe. They accused the United States of imperialism and, after President William Howard Taft in an effort to make American policy more palatable south of the border described it as "substituting dollars for bullets," the Latins had a new slogan against the United States—"dollar diplomacy."

The interference of the American government in the affairs of the Dominican Republic came hard after the treaty establishing a Panama canal zone, and the object was to prevent a European intervention in the Caribbean close to the canal. The problem arose in an oblique way. The first Hague Peace Conference of 1899, which met in the Dutch capital to consider ways to world peace and included twenty-six nations, among them the United States, had established a Hague tribunal for arbitration. Shortly thereafter, in 1902, a heated argument arose between Britain, Germany, and Italy, on the one hand, and Venezuela on the other, over some debts owed the European nations by Venezuela. The powers made a naval demonstration off Venezuelan shores. During this fracas the minister of foreign relations of Argentina, Luis M. Drago, announced what became known as the Drago Doctrine, that "the public debt can not occasion armed intervention nor even the actual occupation of the territory of American nations by a European power." The United States, uncertain of the validity of Drago's notion, sought a peaceful solution of the Venezuelan affair, urging resort by the powers to the Hague tribunal. The tribunal, trying to strike a balance between the intransigence of the Latin states and the need for nations to pay debts, decided that Venezuela should pay her debtors and that (this was the rub of the tribunal's judgment) payment should be first to the nations which had engaged in the naval demonstration. This decision put a premium on efforts to collect debts in the Western Hemisphere by force. When the Dominican Republic

in 1904 slipped into a condition of insolvency and the United States
faced the prospect of another European naval demonstration in the
Caribbean, President Roosevelt this time took upon himself the responsibility of obtaining justice for the European debtors.

"San Domingo is drifting into chaos," TR wrote his eldest son, "for
after a hundred years of freedom it shows itself utterly incompetent for
governmental work. Most reluctantly I have been obliged to take the
initial step of interference there. I hope it will be a good while before
I will have to go further. But sooner or later it seems to me inevitable
that the United States should assume an attitude of protection and
regulation in regard to all these little states in the neighborhood of
the Caribbean. I hope it will be deferred as long as possible but I
think it is inevitable." Roosevelt made an arrangement in 1905 that
the Dominican customs would be collected under receivership of an
agent appointed by the president of the United States, the agent to
pay out 45 per cent of customs proceeds to the creditors pro rata
after satisfying expenses of the receivership, and turn the remaining
funds over to the Dominican government. The arrangement was carried on by executive agreement until 1907, when the United States
Senate approved a treaty along these lines. The Dominican Republic
during most of its supervision by the United States until 1940 was
unoccupied by American troops, though for a period from 1916 until
1924 the marines were there. Under American control many measures
of value and advantage to the Dominicans were set on foot. "The
result," Samuel Flagg Bemis has written, "was a novel prosperity for
the republic accompanied by a frustration of revolutionary habits
hitherto confirmed."

It was at the beginning of this Dominican affair that Roosevelt
sought to make a corollary to the Monroe Doctrine, to the effect
that if Europe were to stay out of Latin America then the United
States ipso facto had a right to intervene. In his annual message to
Congress in December 1904 the president announced that "Chronic
wrongdoing, or an impotence which results in a general loosening
of the ties of civilized society, may in America, as elsewhere, ultimately require intervention by some civilized nation, and in the
Western Hemisphere the adherence of the United States to the
Monroe Doctrine may force the United States, however reluctantly,
in flagrant cases of such wrongdoing or impotence, to the exercise of
an international police power." Roosevelt explained himself further

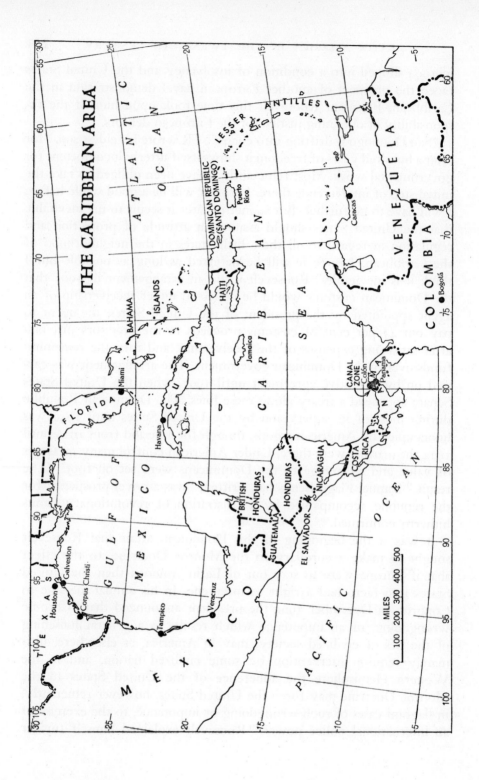

THE CARIBBEAN AREA

in a message to the Senate on February 15, 1905: "The United States
. . . under the Monroe doctrine . . . can not see any European
power seize and permanently occupy the territory of one of these
republics; and yet such seizure of territory, disguised or undisguised,
may eventually offer the only way in which the power in question
can collect any debts, unless there is interference on the part of the
United States." This was the famous Roosevelt Corollary.

The president must have hoped that his contribution to the Monroe
Doctrine would settle things in Latin America. It did settle them, for
a few years, until trouble appeared in Nicaragua where the dictator-
president, General José Santos Zelaya, tried to cancel the United
States-Nicaragua Concession, a mining property owned by a Pitts-
burgh corporation, the principal American property in Nicaragua,
so that he could sell it again for better terms. There were reports
that Zelaya had planned to make secret advances to Japan for a canal
treaty. The dictator was also trying to pull apart a treaty settlement
which Presidents Porfirio Díaz of Mexico and Theodore Roosevelt
of the United States had persuaded the republics of Central America
to conclude among themselves at Washington in 1907, according to
which they promised to submit all their disputes to arbitration and,
generally, not go to war with each other or foment revolutions in
each other's territories. Understandably, the United States had little
love for the Nicaraguan dictator. When a revolution against him
broke out in 1909 Zelaya executed two American citizens for laying
mines in the San Juan River in support of the revolutionists (the
Americans held commissions in the revolutionary army and considered
themselves prisoners of war). President Taft broke diplomatic relations with the Zelaya regime, and the dictator was overthrown. The
individual who had been secretary of the American concession in
Nicaragua, Adolfo Díaz, rose to power and his administration on
June 6, 1911 signed a treaty with Secretary of State Knox, the Knox-
Castrillo Convention, which was similar to the treaty of 1907 with the
Dominican Republic. It was identical with another treaty signed by
the United States in 1911 with Honduras. Knox would have liked to
deal the same way with Guatemala. The Senate rejected the Nicaraguan and Honduran treaties, but in Nicaragua the New York bankers
whom Secretary Knox had enlisted to set aright the finances of that
country went ahead anyway and with the help of the State Department set up a financial regulation. A revolution in Nicaragua against

President Díaz in 1912 brought at Díaz's request a "legation guard" of 2,700 marines, and except for a brief trial withdrawal in 1925, which did not work, the marines stayed until 1933. The country for a while in the mid-1920's was torn by civil war, but in 1927 the United States, represented by Henry L. Stimson, arranged for Nicaraguan elections; when the last marines retired in 1933 everything was for the moment peaceful and orderly. A financial supervision continued until 1944.

The Nicaraguan intervention was perhaps, as we can see it now, a mismanaged affair, not because it did too much in Nicaragua but because it did not do enough. The United States interfered barely enough to keep the elected government in power and the finances in order, but not enough to regenerate Nicaragua, as an effective protectorate had done in Cuba. The Nicaraguan intervention only aroused the animosity of other Latin American countries, and perhaps at that point the United States might well have become more drastic with its measures and done a thorough job.

The third American intervention in the Caribbean region in the years after the canal events—following upon the Dominican affair and the occupation of Nicaragua—was in Haiti in 1915. A revolution had raised Guillaume Sam to power as president in March 1915, and the new president faced a foreign debt of about $24,000,000, part of which was owed to American financial interests and much of the remainder to Europeans. The French and German governments in March 1914 had proposed a joint customs receivership with the United States, but this scheme had met with American disapproval and the coming of the World War occupied the attention of the two European governments. A revolution against President Sam broke out in the summer of 1915 and, after the president slaughtered 167 hostages, the populace of Port-au-Prince rose on July 28, seized President Sam, and quite literally cut him into small pieces and paraded these trophies around the capital city. At this juncture President Wilson instructed the marines to land, which they did, imposing a military occupation. President Dartiguenave, elected in August 1915, signed a treaty on September 16 under which the Haitian Republic became for all intents and purposes a protectorate of the United States. The treaty contained articles similar to those of the Platt Amendment for Cuba, and it was not terminated until 1934, when the marines left. Customs control continued in modified form until 1941. Haiti in 1918, one might add, had received a new constitution, written by President Wilson's assistant secretary of the navy, Franklin D. Roosevelt. FDR in the election of 1920 described it as "a pretty good constitution, too." Perhaps the constitution, along with the marines, helped make Haiti a more orderly place than it had been in the past.

An event of minor importance just before American participation in the first World War, 1917–1918, was purchase by the United States of the Danish West Indies, by a treaty of August 4, 1916. The Virgin Islands cost the government $25,000,000 and probably were worth it in view of their strategic location near the Panama canal.

In the 1920's and 1930's, after the first World War, many charges and countercharges were made about the conduct of the United States in the Caribbean region—the occupation or control of Cuba (1898), the Dominican Republic (1905), Nicaragua (1911), and Haiti (1915). Only Guatemala (controlled, some people said, by the United Fruit Company, an American concern), Costa Rica, Honduras, and El Salvador were left without benefit of direct American guidance, and so it was claimed that American actions in the Caribbean were in reality imperialism, similar to the nineteenth-century imperialism of France, Britain, and Germany in Africa and Asia. This argument overlooked the strategic reason for American action, the need to protect the canal. It ignored the humanitarian reasons for intervention. But because the humanitarian urges of the earlier part of the century had failed in some cases to bring all the blessings that reformers expected, and because after the first World War the genuine accomplishments of the era of intervention were brought under such severe attack and censure as imperialism, and because also the need for protective measures in the Caribbean had lost urgency with the Allied victory in 1918, the United States after a period of inaction began at the end of the 1920's to abandon its enterprises among the small Latin nations. The American government abandoned its controls and liquidated its imperialism, if such it was, of the years before its entrance into the first World War. A new era began, that of the good neighbor.

But before turning to discussion of this new policy one should mention the greatest of the interventions by the United States in Latin America, save only the Panama affair in 1903: the effort of President Wilson in 1913–1917 to intervene in Mexico to preserve

American lives and property in that area close to the American border.

2. *The Mexican Intervention*

The ruler of Mexico until 1911 was General Porfirio Díaz, under whose governance since 1877 the state had settled down and become prosperous, with many of its economic resources being exploited by foreign companies, particularly American. Díaz grew old, his control over the government slipped, and an increasing Mexican nationalism led at last to his retirement to Europe, where he died a poor man— he had not governed Mexico for his personal gain but for the good, as he saw it, of his country. The government after his departure passed into the hands of Francisco Madero, who was no match for the animosities and intrigues which swirled down on the City of Mexico after the old regime collapsed. Madero has been usually described as a dreamer, and so he was. Perhaps also he was crazy, for at one meeting with the American ambassador, Henry Lane Wilson, the president of Mexico placed a third chair in the circle and announced to the ambassador that a friend was sitting there. The friend was invisible, Madero explained, but there nonetheless. It was not unexpected that this visionary would run into trouble, and General Victoriano Huerta, after evicting Madero from the presidential palace early in February 1913, took over the government. Huerta then murdered Madero, together with Vice President Suarez, on the trivial claim that they had been shot while trying to escape. In actual fact this was a favorite Latin American way of execution.

The crisis in Mexico City occurred on February 9–18, 1913, the "tragic ten days" of Mexican history, and it caught the government of the United States in an uneasy position, for the Democrats and Woodrow Wilson were coming into Washington, Taft and the Republicans leaving the government. There was no American policy toward the events in Mexico until Wilson took office on March 4.

The new president had pronounced views on the Mexican situation. "I will not," he said privately, "recognize a government of butchers." He recalled Henry Lane Wilson and refused to appoint a successor. He laid down a policy on March 11, 1913 in regard to recognition of regimes in Latin America, declaring that recognition was "possible only when supported at every turn by the orderly processes of just government based upon law, not upon arbitrary or irregular force. We hold, as I am sure all thoughtful leaders of republican government everywhere hold, that just government rests always upon the consent of the governed, and that there can be no freedom without order based upon law and upon the public conscience and approval. We shall look to make these principles the basis of mutual intercourse, respect, and helpfulness between our sister republics and ourselves."

This new Wilsonian pronouncement on recognition, one should explain, stood in opposition to the recognition policy of the United States since the time when Thomas Jefferson was secretary of state. Jefferson had established the practice that any government in control of its territory and people—a government *de facto*—was a government *de jure* so far as the United States was concerned, to be recognized as soon as decently possible. Wilson now was undertaking to pass upon the legality of governments in Latin America, and presumably an illegal government would be for him, and his successors in office he doubtless hoped, an immoral government which it would be impossible to recognize. The Wilsonian theory for Latin America lasted until Secretary of State Henry L. Stimson revoked it on September 17, 1930 and went back to the practice of Jefferson. An exception to this rule of recognition was the Central American republics, which in the peace settlement of 1907 had sought, among other measures, to invoke a special recognition policy among themselves. These states, ridden by revolts and interventions across their several borders, had written out a code of proper revolutionary behavior, which even went to the length of stipulating what officials in a given government could and could not, by revolution, take office in a new regime. The treaty of 1907 was redrawn in 1923, and the United States, although not a signatory of the treaty of 1923, adhered to its specified recognition policy and followed the dictates of the treaty during revolts in Guatemala in 1930 and El Salvador in 1931. The Central American states themselves abandoned their agreement in 1934, at which time the United States reverted, for this area of the Western Hemisphere, to its general recognition policy in Latin America as laid down in 1930—which, as was mentioned, superseded Wilson's policy of 1913, returning American practice to that of Jefferson's time.

The president in 1913 thus refused to recognize Huerta the murderer, and he made his policy toward Mexico into a general policy toward all of Latin America, nonrecognition of any government which subverted the liberties of its people. This policy, he hoped, would freeze out the new dictator in Mexico City. It certainly would have done so in any of the smaller Central American states, but Mexico, as events turned out, was too large a state to handle in this way.

Huerta on October 10, 1913 threw 110 members of the Mexican chamber of deputies into prison and inaugurated a full-fledged military dictatorship. At this point President Wilson was still unwilling to interfere with open force in Mexico, though he was willing to use all diplomatic pressures. In a famous speech at Mobile, Alabama on October 27, 1913 he declared that the United States "will never again seek one additional foot of territory by conquest." Having set out his position he employed diplomacy for the next months to oust the Mexican general from power. He obtained the support of the British in this venture, promising to Sir William Tyrrell, the representative of the British foreign secretary Sir Edward Grey, that he would "teach the South American republics to elect good men" and that the United States would work to establish a government in Mexico under which foreign contracts and concessions would be safe. The British had been somewhat friendly to Huerta because they thought he would protect foreign investment, rather than undertake a series of social reforms as Madero was threatening to do. But the British, when Wilson duly approached them, withdrew recognition from Huerta.

Then came the Tampico incident, on April 9, 1914, when a boatload of American sailors landed at the port of Tampico from an American ship and by error entered a restricted area without permission from the local authorities. The sailors were arrested and publicly paraded through the streets of the town, after which the local commander, a Huertista, upon learning of the incident released the Americans and sent off an apology to Admiral Henry T. Mayo, commanding the American squadron off Veracruz. The affair might have ended there, but perhaps in memory of the *Baltimore* incident of over twenty years before, the admiral demanded a 21-gun salute to the American flag. President Wilson upon learning of the affair, and willing to make trouble for Huerta, backed him up. Wilson on April 18, 1914 issued an ultimatum to Huerta to salute the American flag or take the consequences; then, when the American government learned that a German steamer was scheduled to arrive at Veracruz with a load of ammunition for Huerta, Admiral Mayo was ordered to occupy the port forcibly. The occupation was accomplished on April 21 at the cost of 19 American dead and 71 wounded, the Mexicans losing 126 killed and 195 wounded. A difficult situation had arisen, because Wilson had not prepared the American public for this eventuality, and indeed the entire decline of American-Mexican relations had not been understood by the American people. To make matters worse, the followers of Huerta's enemy and rival in Mexico, the revolutionary commander Venustiano Carranza who was in the field against Huerta, condemned the occupation of Veracruz as wholeheartedly as did the Huertistas who controlled the town. Happily the ABC powers—Argentina, Brazil, and Chile—offered to mediate, and the affair blew over and the Americans eventually left. The adjournment of the incident was obscured by the fall from power of Huerta and the occupation of Mexico City by Carranza in August 1914, and by the beginning of the World War in Europe that same month.

The new government in Mexico City, headed by Carranza, who had disapproved of the Veracruz occupation, soon showed that it had no special love for the American government; having been helped into power by the United States, which had weakened the regime of Huerta, it virtually cut itself loose from all American influence. Wilson had received nothing for his trouble in 1913–1914. Unfortunately too, a split now occurred in the forces of President Carranza—the succession, one recalls, had been Díaz, Madero, Huerta, Carranza—and there appeared the formidable figure of Doroteo Arango, or "Pancho Villa," a wild and woolly character who could submit to control by no one and set out to pull down the government of his former friend Carranza. In the year 1915 fighting between the troops of Carranza and Villa swayed back and forth inconclusively, while the United States was busy worrying about conditions on the high seas because of the European war. The *Lusitania* was torpedoed in May 1915 and the crisis with Germany over its sinking lasted throughout much of the summer. But in 1916 American attention came back to Mexico, and for a while it appeared that the major problem of American foreign policy was not the fighting in Europe but the troubles south of the border.

Villa, to arouse an American intervention in Mexico and (so he hoped) to discredit Carranza, met a Mexican Northwestern train at Santa Ysabel on January 11, 1916 carrying 17 young American college graduates who had just come into Mexico from California under a safe conduct from Carranza to open a mine. Villa killed 16 of them on the spot. When this gesture failed to bring results he made a desperate raid into American territory at Columbus, New Mexico, on March 9, 1916, burning the town and killing 17 Americans. The United States government rose in wrath and President Wilson sent Brigadier General John J. Pershing across the border six days later, with several thousand troops. The expedition penetrated more than 300 miles into Mexico in search of the errant Villa. On June 18, 1916 when the situation had worsened—that is, when Villa was nowhere to be found—Wilson called out for protection of the border virtually the entire National Guard, some 150,000 men.

For the remainder of the year tension was considerable, although the meeting of a commission of Mexicans and Americans managed to neutralize the affair during the touchy period preceding Wilson's re-election in the autumn of 1916. Then the imminence of American involvement in the European war made advisable a withdrawal of the punitive expedition. The withdrawal was completed on February 5, 1917 and a chapter of American-Mexican relations was finished. The United States extended *de jure* recognition by sending Ambassador Henry P. Fletcher to Mexico City on March 3, a month before the declaration of war against Germany.

It was probably unwise of Wilson to interfere in Mexico, even to the extent of withdrawing the American ambassador as he did in March 1913. In the case of smaller Latin republics such policy held some hope of success, and perhaps in the nineteenth century it was not so difficult to coerce larger nations such as Mexico. But by the early twentieth century the time had passed for such action, for the nationalism of peoples everywhere in Latin America had risen to a point where the United States could not undertake drastic measures without raising local hatred and ill-feeling to a point where they not merely made the immediate measures useless but continued for years thereafter. It took nearly a generation after the Wilson intervention in Mexico before American relations with Mexico were placed on a solid foundation. Although Ambassador Dwight W. Morrow in the last years of the Coolidge administration spread much good will among the Mexicans, his conciliation and the policy of the good neighbor which followed it were not sufficient to prevent the Mexicans in the 1930's from nationalizing about $260,000,000 worth of American oil properties, for which the American companies received $42,000,000. Fortunately relations with Mexico continued calm through this nationalization—the United States simply allowed the Mexicans to take the American property—and by the time of the second World War it was possible for the two republics to co-operate congenially against the enemy in Europe.

3. *The Good-Neighbor Policy*

The phrase "good neighbor" was not original with President Franklin D. Roosevelt when in his inaugural address of March 4, 1933 he declared that "In the field of world policy, I would dedicate this nation to the policy of the good neighbor . . ." It was a phrase which in Latin American relations went back at least to the early nineteenth century, and was assuredly one of the most familiar clichés in the language of international intercourse. Roosevelt, indeed, used it in regard to the entire world in his address of 1933. President Herbert Hoover, his predecessor, in 1928–1929 used the phrase on several occasions during a preinaugural tour of Latin America. But it was Roosevelt who in the early 1930's presided over a marked change in American policy toward Latin America and the phrase has become associated, perhaps unjustly, with his name.

The relations of the United States with Latin America in an organized, international sense, a sense of Pan-Americanism, which was really the good-neighbor policy, began as early as 1826 when the Congress of Panama was called by the liberator Simon Bolívar as a convention of the states newly independent of Spain. The United States sent two representatives who failed to arrive in time for the meeting. Decades later, in 1881, Secretary of State James G. Blaine advocated closer commercial ties of the United States with Latin America, and hoped also to increase the prestige of his nation among the Latin countries, and so he invited the nations to a conference at Washington scheduled for November 1882. With the death of President Garfield, Blaine left office and his successor as secretary of state, Frederick T. Frelinghuysen, canceled the invitations. Grover Cleveland's secretary of state, Thomas A. Bayard, renewed them for a conference in 1888. Eventually Blaine, again becoming secretary of state in the following year in the administration of Benjamin Harrison, had the pleasure of presiding over the first Pan-American Conference which met from October 1889 until April 1890. Seventeen Latin American states attended, all except the Dominican Republic. Although the major goal of the United States, a customs union, was defeated, and although no machinery was set up for arbitration of disputes, which was another of Blaine's purposes, the International Bureau of American Republics was established. Later it became known as the Union of American Republics (with its secretariat, the Pan-American Union), and since 1951 as the Organization of American States (so phrased that it might include Canada; the Pan-American Union is now known as the Secretariat).

There followed three Pan-American Conferences in the early twentieth century—Mexico City in 1901–1902, Rio de Janeiro in 1906, and Buenos Aires in 1910—but little came from them. The fifth Pan-American Conference met at Santiago de Chile in 1923, again with few notable results. The sixth conference, at Havana in 1928, was notable not for the results of the meeting but because of the way in which the affair turned into a virtual rebellion of the Latin American nations against the power and influence of the United States. It was at this meeting that the envoy of El Salvador introduced a resolution against intervention, "that no state has a right to intervene in the internal affairs of another," a proposal directed, of course, against the interventions by the United States. President Calvin Coolidge's special representative at the meeting in Havana, Charles Evans Hughes—Coolidge himself had opened the conference by a visit and speech in the Cuban capital—finally could contain himself no longer, and stood up in the assemblage and spoke impromptu about what he denominated the "interposition" of the United States in the affairs of its neighbors. Hughes' speech, the last defense by American representatives of the policy of intervention, was terse and to the point. The distinguished former secretary of state asked the representative of El Salvador what the United States was to do "when government breaks down and American citizens are in danger of their lives? Are we to stand by and see them butchered in the jungle . . . ?" After this reply the Salvadorean withdrew his motion and the conference turned to other matters, less politically sensitive.

Hughes had made the final defense of the old policy, and even in the year he made it the United States realized that the old method of intervention was neither effective nor necessary. Both the appearance of Coolidge at Havana and the appointment of Hughes to head the

American delegation showed a new policy toward the Latins. The president's old college friend, Dwight Morrow, had gone to Mexico the year before, in 1927, and Morrow's appointment too showed the fear of the Coolidge administration that something needed to be done with Latin American relations. President-elect Hoover undertook his tour of Latin America in November 1928, and although some individuals claimed that he did this to get away from office seekers in the United States one must guess that there were less strenuous ways of escaping them than making 25 speeches and traveling for ten weeks in ten Latin countries. His tour, like the moves of Coolidge that same year, showed a change of policy.

Hoover in 1930 established through Secretary Stimson the new recognition policy. He tried also, without too much success, to settle a boundary controversy in the Chaco between Paraguay and Bolivia and the Leticia affair between Peru and Colombia (Peru had taken Leticia from Colombia). He also arranged for publication of a long memorandum drawn up in 1928 by Undersecretary of State J. Reuben Clark, which after an exhaustive exegesis of 236 pages showed that the Roosevelt Corollary of 1904 had no reason to be attached to the Monroe Doctrine. In a seventeen-page covering letter to Secretary of State Frank B. Kellogg, Clark explained, in authentic Department of State passive-voice style, that "it is not believed that this corollary is justified by the terms of the Monroe Doctrine, however much it may be justified by the application of the doctrine of self-preservation." Clark thus did not deny that the United States possessed the right in Latin American affairs of "interposition of a temporary character" (so Hughes liked to describe American intervention policy), but he denied that the Monroe Doctrine justified intervention. This notable memorandum, one of the most important statements of United States policy toward Latin America in the twentieth century, received reinforcement by statements from Stimson and Undersecretary of State William R. Castle. Stimson declared that the Monroe Doctrine was "a declaration of the United States versus Europe—not of the United States versus Latin America." Castle explained that the Monroe Doctrine "confers no superior position on the United States." The era of tutelage and instruction by force was plainly over.

The good-neighbor policy was, really, a nonintervention policy, and this policy, announced by both Hoover and Franklin D. Roosevelt, was formalized in resolutions of the several Pan-American Conferences that have met since 1933: Montevideo in 1933 (the seventh regular conference), Buenos Aires in 1936 (a special meeting), Lima in 1938 (eighth conference), Mexico City in February-March 1945 (special meeting), and, since the second World War, Rio de Janeiro in 1947 (special meeting), Bogota in 1948 (ninth), and Caracas in 1954 (tenth).

The conferences of 1933 and 1936 were probably crucial in obtaining from the United States specific expressions of intention not to interfere any more in Latin America. At Montevideo in 1933 the Latins, having seen the signs of change of policy, rose to the occasion with speech after speech. The distinguished historian of Cuba, Dr. Herminio Portell-Vilá, told the conferees: "Delegates, perhaps no other country has as important and special reason as Cuba for presenting a point of view on the very important problem of intervention or nonintervention. . . . Intervention is not only the 'curse of America,' but as a Cuban internationalist has said, it is the 'curse of curses' of any country, the cause of all evils of the Cuban Republic. Cuba was born with the congenital vice of intervention. . . . I wish to say . . . that the Platt Amendment and the Permanent Treaty have the evil of compulsion, for the people of Cuba did not accept either one freely, due to the fact that the country was full of North American bayonets."

The foreign minister of Argentina, Dr. Carlos Saavedra Lamas (who in the mid-1930's received the Nobel Peace Prize for a grand project for peace which many of the Latin nations signed and which virtually duplicated several treaties already concluded for Latin America and the Kellogg-Briand Pact for world peace sponsored in 1928 by the United States) said that any intervention, regardless of the reasons, was bad.

The Haitian delegate (the Americans were still unwelcome guests in his country) said that American marines and the American government had brought to his nation "indescribable anguish."

To such arguments, based not entirely on history, the United States representatives at Montevideo made no effort to reply, but instead accepted, to the surprise of the other delegates, the crucial part of the Convention on Rights and Duties of States: "No state has the right to intervene in the internal or external affairs of another." The chief of the American delegation, Secretary of State Cordell Hull, added a reservation mentioning "the law of nations as generally recognized and accepted," a broad enough hole to crawl through if the occasion demanded. This move, Hull announced, marked "the beginning of a new era." The Mexican delegate, perhaps unsatisfied with this sober appraisal, said that he wished "to submit my profound conviction that there is in the White House an admirable, noble, and good man—a courageous man who knows the errors of the past but who feels that the errors really belong to the past."

To effect its resolution for a new course, the United States evacuated Nicaragua in 1933 and the marines left Haiti in 1934. The Platt Amendment for Cuba was abrogated by a treaty between the United States and Cuba in 1934, and a similar treaty abandoned the American protectorate of the Dominican Republic in 1940.

At the special Buenos Aires Conference of 1936, called by the United States, the American government made a strenuous effort to better its friendships in Latin America. President Roosevelt journeyed to the Argentine capital on a battleship to open the conference in person, and the United States agreed to an undertaking of nonintervention more inclusive than that of Montevideo: "The High . . . Parties declare inadmissible the intervention of any one of them, directly or indirectly, and for whatever reason, in the internal or external affairs of any of the Parties." The text did not define intervention, thus leaving a useful loophole for the United States. Seeking to close this gap, the Latin states invited the Roosevelt administration to sign at Buenos Aires a Declaration of Principles of Inter-American Solidarity and Co-operation, in which the signatories "proclaim their absolute juridical sovereignty, their unqualified respect for their respective sovereignties and the existence of a common democracy throughout America." But this was put in the form of a declaration, rather than a convention which after ratifications by the several states would have been binding. Undersecretary of State Sumner Welles, referring to the nonbinding declaration, said diplomatically that it was a Magna Carta of American freedom and collective security.

The last two words of Welles' pronouncement, which appeared in international verbiage about this time, indicated that the purposes of the United States in the Western Hemisphere were changing. The good-neighbor policy had begun at the end of the 1920's as a reaction from the policy of intervention, a policy which was no longer necessary to protect the canal—matters in Europe seemed peaceful enough in 1928—and which had raised much ill will in Latin America and which needed to be replaced by a policy more in line with Latin American nationalism and *amour propre*. By the year 1936, Nazi Germany was moving actively in Europe to effect revision of the Treaty of Versailles, with the plan as it soon emerged of tearing up the treaty entirely and creating a new order in Europe and perhaps the world. Because of this novel exigency, the United States at the Buenos Aires Conference began to speak in terms of collective security, which for nearly a decade thereafter became the theme of Pan-American meetings. When war came in Europe the Declaration of Panama of 1939, a result of a meeting of foreign ministers of the American republics, established a security zone around the Americas south of Canada, which by 1941 was patrolled in vital areas by warships of the United States. The Declaration of Havana in 1940, made by another meeting of the foreign ministers, transformed into a Pan-American task what had long been a part of United States foreign policy, the No-Transfer Principle, that territory held in the Western Hemisphere by a non-American power could not be transferred to another non-American power. The Declaration of 1940 was designed to prevent Dutch and French territories in the New World from passing, after the fall of those nations in the Nazi spring offensive of 1940, under German control.

In the war of 1941–1945 against Germany and Japan the United States found that the Latin American republics all came to its support in one form or another. Eventually all of them declared war, and two of the republics, Brazil and Mexico, sent military contingents abroad —Brazil sent a division to Italy and Mexico an air squadron to the Far East. The Cuban navy co-operated against German submarines in the Gulf of Mexico. The American government obtained military bases on the soil of Brazil, Cuba, Ecuador, and Panama. In exchange for this assistance the United States gave all the republics except Argentina and Panama (Argentina did not declare war until March 24, 1945) $491,456,432.64 in lend-lease supplies.

Argentina proved difficult until almost the end of the war—a "bad neighbor," Secretary Hull later called her in his memoirs—and the United States used practically every means except severe economic sanctions and war to bring the Argentines into line. Most of the other Latin American nations gave lip service to the efforts by the United States to coerce Argentina. They were afraid of her, and also did not wish a principle of coercion introduced into their relations when with so much trouble they had just rid themselves, they hoped, of American intervention. The Argentines, declaring war on Germany in March 1945, were able to take part at the United Nations Conference in San Francisco when it met in April 1945.

But after the war as during the war, the Argentines refused their co-operation to the United States, and in the postwar era the fascist government of President Juan D. Perón in Argentina probably caused more concern in the United States than did any other development in Latin America. In its policy toward Argentina during Perón's rise and rule the United States government seems to have been thoroughly unsuccessful. In 1943–1945 it exerted heavy pressure to prevent Perón's rise to power, and in 1946 at the time of Perón's candidacy for president of Argentina the Department of State published a Blue Book virtually denouncing as a Hitler satellite the government of a country with which the United States maintained diplomatic relations. Perón enlisted the indignation of his countrymen at this interference and was handily elected president. Later the United States made an uneasy peace with his regime in return for measures against former Nazis and communists. By 1955 it was beginning to give the dictator financial support. Thereupon his countrymen rose up and threw him out. After his fall and exile, Perón was seen to have been a naive, childish individual who had succeeded in almost ruining Argentina's economy and bankrupting its government.

American diplomacy toward the Latin republics other than Argentina has not been nearly so eventful since 1945 as in the years before the war. President Harry S. Truman in April 1945, upon assuming the presidency, said that he would continue the good-neighbor policy. But there were no large gestures of the sort made by his predecessor at Montevideo and at Buenos Aires. Since the end of the second World War the problems of the United States in Latin America have seemed small, if compared with those in other areas of the world. For this reason, perhaps, and because in essentials the good-neighbor policy had been accomplished by 1945, there has been a lapse of diplomacy in the region.

The only international act in Latin American relations after the war which has had any considerable importance is the Rio Defense Treaty of 1947, concluded at the special conference held expressly for the purpose in Rio de Janeiro that year. This treaty, under Article 51 of the UN Charter which allows regional agreements for collective security, set forth that it was the duty of every American state to help meet an armed attack upon another American state or its territory until the UN Security Council should take effective measures to repel the aggression. The nature of the action to be taken by the American states was to be determined by a two-thirds vote in a meeting of foreign ministers of the Western Hemisphere, parties to the dispute not voting. No state could be required to use armed force without its consent—hence the United States by vote of the foreign ministers might have to cut diplomatic relations with another state, or cut trade, but it did not have to use (without its consent) armed force. The treaty went into effect after ratification by two-thirds of the signatories in December 1948 (it became effective, of course, only among the signatories). This was the principal international diplomatic act of the postwar era.

Whether there will be trouble in the future with Latin America is difficult to say at present, although it may well be that the spectacular growth of population in the Caribbean area and South America may bring a time when population will outrun resources and governments of these regions will be tempted to follow adventuresome foreign policies. That moment has not yet arrived. Population pressure has not reached such a degree as to raise fears in the minds of American makers of foreign policy, although in two of the small countries, El Salvador and Haiti, and in America's possession of Puerto Rico, population is already making much difficulty.

Problems may also arise out of the extremely unequal distribution of wealth and position in Latin America. The United States as a true democracy has become a sort of showcase to all Latin America, and many of the Latins with the increased advantages of education are going to ask questions about the medieval social structures in some of their nations. Getting these structures adjusted to modern twentieth-century realities may bring considerable political trouble, perhaps international trouble.

At the moment it appears to be wise policy for the United States to keep its fences in order in the Western Hemisphere, watching for possible crises, while it deals with the more exigent problems of Europe and Asia.

ADDITIONAL READING

The best general account of American policy toward Latin America is Samuel F. Bemis, *The Latin American Policy of the United States* (New York, 1943), which may be supplemented in detail by the volumes on the Monroe Doctrine by Dexter Perkins listed at the end of chapter 3. For twentieth-century Latin American policy see chapters in J. W. Pratt, *America's Colonial Experiment* (New York, 1950), together with the following volumes in the Harvard series on foreign policy: Dexter Perkins, *The United States and the Caribbean* (Cambridge, Mass., 1947); Arthur P. Whitaker, *The United States and South America: The Northern Republics* (Cambridge, 1948) and *The United States and Argentina* (Cambridge, 1954); H. F. Cline, *The United States and Mexico* (Cambridge, 1953).

Nineteenth-century diplomacy appears in J. B. Lockey, *Pan-Americanism: Its Beginnings* (New York, 1920); Alice Felt Tyler, *The Foreign Policy of James G. Blaine* (Minneapolis, 1927); Russell H. Bastert, "Diplomatic Reversal: Frelinghuysen's Opposition to Blaine's Pan-American Policy in 1882," *Mississippi Valley Historical Review*, vol. 42 (1955–1956), 653–671. Bastert is working on a book on Blaine and Pan-Americanism.

For the diplomacy of the Panama canal, see Wilfrid Hardy Callcott, *The Caribbean Policy of the United States: 1890–1920* (Baltimore, 1942); A. L. P. Dennis, *Adventures in American Diplomacy: 1896–1906* (New York, 1928); C. S. Campbell, Jr., *Anglo-American Understanding: 1898–1903* (Baltimore, 1957); H. K. Beale, *Theodore Roosevelt and the Rise of America to World Power* (Baltimore, 1956); E. T. Parks, *Colombia and the United States: 1765–1934* (Durham, N.C., 1935); together with the special studies by D. C. Miner, *The Fight for the Panama Route* (New York, 1940) and Gerstle Mack, *The Land Divided* (New York, 1944). For the statesmen involved there is Henry F. Pringle, *Theodore Roosevelt* (New York, 1931; available in paperback); Tyler Dennett, *John Hay* (New York, 1933); J. A. Garraty, *Henry Cabot Lodge* (New York, 1953). A curiosity, by the curious Frenchman who was one of the prime movers behind the Panama revolution, is Philippe Bunau-Varilla's *Panama: The Creation, Destruction, and Resurrection* (New York, 1914).

Charles C. Tansill, *The Purchase of the Danish West Indies* (Baltimore, 1932) is an exhaustive treatment.

On Mexican matters one should consult C. C. Cumberland, *Mexican Revolution: Genesis under Madero* (Austin, Texas, 1952), together with the excellent accounts in Arthur S. Link's *Woodrow Wilson and the Progressive Era: 1910–1917* (New York, 1954) and Link's *Wilson: The New Freedom* (Princeton, 1956).

President Herbert Hoover instructed the Department of State to publish the Clark Memorandum under the title, *Memorandum on the Monroe Doctrine* (Washington, 1930). Alexander De Conde, *Herbert Hoover's Latin American Policy* (Stanford, 1951) is a well-done general treatment. *Roosevelt's Good Neighbor Policy* (Albuquerque, N.M., 1950), by E. O. Guerrant, is a sprightly analysis. There are chapters on Latin America in *The Memoirs of Cordell Hull* (2 vols., New York, 1948).

For recent diplomacy see O. E. Smith, Jr., *Yankee Diplomacy: U. S. Intervention in Argentina* (Dallas, Texas, 1953) and A. Curtis Wilgus, *The Caribbean: Contemporary Trends* (Gainesville, Fla., 1953).

CHAPTER

☆ 11 ☆

Neutrality, 1914-1917

Although people in Europe and America had been talking about a war for years, few individuals had really expected it when it came at last in the first days of August 1914. Almost abruptly, the Dual Alliance of Germany and Austria-Hungary was at war with the Triple Entente of Britain, France, and Russia. The precipitating event of this struggle was the assassination of the heir to the Austro-Hungarian throne, the Archduke Francis Ferdinand, shot down in cold blood together with his wife at Sarajevo, the capital city of Bosnia, by a fanatical Bosnian revolutionary named Gavrilo Princip. The assassination took place on June 28, 1914. A month later the Austro-Hungarian government, suspecting with good reason the complicity of the Serbian government, declared war on the latter. This declaration brought into play the alliance system of Europe, and when Serbia's ally Russia entered the fray the other nations quickly followed, each fearful that an adversary might obtain an advantage in mobilization of its armies.

Signs of trouble had appeared in Europe toward the end of the nineteenth century. Ever since the early 1890's, when France in 1894 secured an alliance with Russia, the people and government of the United States had watched the development of a dangerous competitive system of alliances in Europe—for the Franco-Russian Alliance was designed to counterbalance the alliance concluded in 1879 between Germany and Austria-Hungary. Ten years after their alliance with Russia, the French obtained an entente with the British, and the lines were drawn for the war of 1914–1918.

Although the nations thereafter armed themselves to the teeth, few individuals in Europe or America really expected war. Americans and Europeans alike thought that a general European war, though often predicted, could not come, for they felt civilization had advanced too far to permit a war on the order of the Napoleonic wars of a century before. New designs in ordnance, naval and land, and other inventions in weaponry seemed to point to such a horrible toll in any new war that such a conflict was humanely unthinkable.

A series of untoward diplomatic events shook the peace of Europe in the first years of the twentieth century. Germany and France vied for influence over Morocco in 1905, and again in 1911. In the latter year Italy declared war on Turkey, to despoil the latter of the African territory of Tripoli. In 1912 there occurred a Balkan War of Turkey versus Bulgaria, Montenegro, Serbia, and Greece. When this conflict ended in 1913 it was followed almost without pause by another: Bulgaria against Serbia, Greece, Montenegro, and Rumania. But Western Europe seemed secure from war, until the shots rang out in Bosnia and the peace among the major powers of the Continent, preserved since 1871, came to a flaming end.

1. *The Problem of American Neutrality*

The eruption of a great European war in the first four days of August 1914 caught the government of the United States almost completely unprepared. The State Department in Washington had no inkling of the imminence of hostilities, having heard nothing from American diplomatic representatives abroad. The latter, although they were on the ground—residing in the dozen or so capitals of the European nations—failed to sense the coming of the catastrophe. The very existence of Sarajevo was unknown to the American minister to Belgium, Brand Whitlock, who during the crisis was at his country place outside Brussels writing a novel about rural life in Ohio. "I had never heard of Sarajevo," he later wrote. "I had not the least idea where it was in this world, if it was in this world." The American vice consul in Budapest, Frank E. Mallett, did send a warning of probable war to Washington, in a report dated July 13, more than two weeks after the assassination of the archduke on June 28. Mallett, being only a vice consul, hesitated to dispatch his report by the expensive cables, so he sent it by mail and it arrived in Washington on

July 27.

After the shock of the first days of August 1914, the American government through President Wilson proclaimed on August 6 its neutrality toward the European conflict. The vast majority of the American people expected to remain neutral during the fighting that followed. The war seemed another of those ordinary foreign combinations and collisions against which Washington had warned in 1796. Wilson on August 19 urged Americans to be "neutral in thought as well as in action." For the president the war was, to use the phrase of Ambassador Walter Hines Page in London, "this huge quarrel." At the outset Wilson could find no idealistic purpose in the war. He would have agreed with the British leader David Lloyd George, who later remarked that in 1914 Europe slithered into war. "America," Wilson said on July 4, 1919, "did not at first see the full meaning of the war. It looked like a natural raking out of the pent-up jealousies and rivalries of the complicated politics of Europe." As late as 1916 the president could say sincerely that with the objects and causes of the war "we are not concerned. The obscure foundations from which its stupendous flood has burst forth we are not interested to search for or explore." When in December 1916 he sought to mediate between the angry belligerents, he said that the objectives for which the Allies and the Central Powers claimed they were fighting were "virtually the same." A fond hope for neutrality characterized the entire American diplomatic stand in the years from 1914 to 1917.

The United States viewed the war in terms of international law and protection of neutral rights. The neutral rights of Americans, as laid down by the congressional plans for commercial treaties of 1776 and 1784, had stipulated a wide latitude for American trade during European wars: neutral ships would ensure the neutrality of goods carried, except for contraband ("free ships make free goods"); a narrow definition of contraband; neutrals had the right to trade between ports of a belligerent, that is, to take over a belligerent's carrying trade; blockades had to be conducted close to ports, with no paper blockades, so that any neutral carrier attempting to enter a blockaded port would be subject to "imminent danger." These principles had been codified in the Declaration of Paris of 1856, following the Crimean War of 1854–1856, and generally accepted by the major powers of Europe. A Declaration of London in 1909 further defined neutral rights, and although in the years between 1909 and 1914 the declaration was never ratified by enough nations to carry it into effect, Americans at the outset of the war believed that the belligerents would accept it. For everyone, Americans and Europeans alike, thought in 1914 that the new war would be along the lines of the Franco-Prussian War of 1870–1871, with fighting lasting little more than a few weeks or months. It seemed entirely feasible that in such a war the American view of neutral rights could prevail.

This hope, as events turned out, was vain. After the German rush through Belgium and down toward Paris ground to a bloody halt at the Marne in the autumn of 1914, the war turned into a trench conflict that lasted for four years, until November 11, 1918. The war on the high seas thereupon acquired the old familiar meaning. Both the Allies and the Central Powers found themselves short of almost all the materials requisite for a prolonged war. The Allies turned to the United States as a source of supply; they had no intention of permitting similar succor to reach the Germans. The Central Powers accepted the Declaration of London of 1909, for any definition of neutral rights was likely to assist a weak naval power. The British before the war had rejected the declaration, and the United States therefore had held up final ratification. After the war began the British continued to hesitate over the declaration, and then accepted it with reservations which amounted to rejection. The American government made some attempts to persuade the British to reconsider, and then settled down to seeking recognition by the belligerents of as many neutral rights as possible.

Two complicating factors, in addition to a rapidly developing British tendency to violate all inconvenient rules of neutrality, forced their way into American calculations at this point. These factors, both innovations in sea war, were Britain's employment of mines in quantity and Germany's use of the submarine.

Extensive use of mines first engaged the lawyers of the State Department when the British government on November 3, 1914 announced that the "whole of the North Sea must be considered a military area," and that henceforth all neutral ships should enter that sea by way of the Straits of Dover and stop at a British port for sailing directions though the mine fields. Extensive possibilities of cutting neutral trade with Germany arose when the British mined the North Sea, which according to international law was not territorial waters. The law of nations notwithstanding, the British in their North Sea proclamation took over as their own a huge part of the high seas. Thereafter the British checked on all North Sea traffic at the Straits of Dover. They delayed for weeks or months on some flimsy pretext any vessel carrying goods which although admittedly noncontraband was in some way useful to the Central Powers. The British meanwhile began to extend the contraband lists to include anything of remote value to their enemies. From the moment that the European war after the Marne changed from a war of movement to a war of position, the admiralty commenced the infringement of neutral rights, all the while attempting to enlarge neutral duties to a degree that would stop all trade with Germany. Mining the North Sea was the first major step in the elaboration of this policy.

Extensive employment of mines had not been part of nineteenth-century warfare. Nor had nineteenth-century war anticipated extensive use of the submarine. The submarine raised many difficult military, moral, and legal issues. The trouble began when the British mined the North Sea and the Germans retaliated by announcing in February 1915 that the waters surrounding Great Britain were henceforth to be considered a war zone in which vessels, presumably neutrals included, would be sunk by submarines without warning. There was no legal precedent for this German action other than the rule of international law permitting retaliation. The rule limited retaliation to actions in kind—but it was possible to argue that a British blockade by large mine fields sown far out on the high seas justified a loose German counterblockade by submarines. Even so, to render ineffective this German retaliation the British demanded that undersea vessels should act in accord with the accepted rules of warfare applicable to cruisers, then the only rules of international law applicable to the submarine. The Germans disputed this British contention: the submarine could not behave like a surface cruiser; it is one of the axioms of war that the nature of a weapon determines its tactics, and the submarine, then a weak and fragile vessel, could not afford to fire its torpedoes from the surface if there were any chance either of enemy gunfire or ramming, both of which defenses could be used by any ordinary merchant vessel.

Here lay the difficulty: the submarine, by nature an instrument of ambush, could not effectively follow the rules of cruiser warfare; a submarine had to act like a submarine. This necessity involved sinking merchant ships without warning. But the British, to give point to their contention that the submarine must act like a cruiser, armed their merchantmen early in 1915 and on February 10, 1915 secretly instructed them to ram submarines wherever possible. What could the Germans do? An armed merchantman firing on a submarine, or a merchantman attempting to ram a submarine, becomes *ipso facto* a vessel of war and is automatically subject to attack by the submarine, the latter using any means within its power to sink the merchantman. Yet the submarine captain, observing the rules of cruiser warfare, could legally go over to unrestricted warfare only after a merchant vessel had acted in a belligerent manner, and by that time it might well be too late for the submarine captain and his crew. Nor could the submarine, a cramped vessel, take on board the passengers and crew of a victim. To expect the submarine to behave militarily, morally, and legally like a cruiser was to demand the impossible. This is what the British government did demand, for understandable military reasons—the British wanted to prevent Germany from using submarines in an effective way.

When the Germans on February 4, 1915 announced unrestricted submarine warfare to begin two weeks from that date, February 18, the United States likewise protested Germany's submarine tactics, but from reasons moral and legal rather than military. The United States, in opposing Germany's use of the submarine in the first World War, argued largely from the sense of humanity and neutral rights. The inhumane aspects of submarine warfare were patent to everyone. The Germans themselves were uneasy about the inhumanity of submarine warfare, and felt able to justify it only as a necessary measure of war. As for neutral rights, American foreign policy had sought for almost a century and a half to make them prevail. Neutral rights had been codified in the nineteenth and early twentieth centuries after a persistent American effort. The United States, now a great power and recognized as such by the nations of the world, was not going to stand by meekly while the rules of neutrality, so painfully written into international law, were flouted. When the Germans in retaliation against Britain's mining of the North Sea declared unlimited submarine war, the president clearly made known the American position. Wilson edited the note which Secretary of State William Jennings Bryan dispatched to Berlin on February 10, 1915 and which set down in explicit terms that Germany would be held to a "strict accountability" for any American lives or property injured because of such a deviation from the accepted rules of warfare on the high seas.

Wilson in addition held out for the right of American citizens to travel, if they chose, on passenger ships of the belligerent powers, in practical effect those of Britain and France. This latter was a fateful request. It was something that Americans had not previously insisted upon—though in former wars the right to travel on belligerent ships had never been much of an issue, few Americans having business in Europe in those days. Travel on belligerent ships was to lead to so much difficulty during the first World War that some later writers on international law have argued that the United States should have forgone the right—which, so these writers have contended, was not a right in law anyway, but only a privilege. They have even argued that Wilson chose to interpret neutral rights in this way because he was partial to the British cause, wittingly or unwittingly, and demanded the utmost in neutral rights from the Germans. But even later, when the Gore-McLemore resolutions were presented to Congress in 1916 to the effect that no American could travel on a belligerent vessel headed for the danger zone in Europe, Wilson in acting to prevent passage of the resolutions certainly showed not the slightest favoritism for the British cause. He refused to surrender his position in this matter, and simply chose to construe neutral rights liberally to include the right of Americans to travel on belligerent ships.

The preceding pages have sketched in briefest terms the first belligerent actions against neutral rights, and the American response: (1) British mining of the North Sea in November 1914; (2) the German response of February 1915, unrestricted submarine warfare around the British Isles; (3) the American warning to Germany in February 1915 of strict accountability. These three initial steps in the breakdown of American neutrality were followed by (4) the sinking of the *Lusitania* in May 1915 and a consequent German promise to spare liners; (5) a new German campaign of unrestricted submarine warfare beginning March 1, 1916, under the claim that all armed merchantmen were warships; (6) an American note to Berlin, following the torpedoing of the unarmed French Channel packet *Sussex* (March 24, 1916), announcing that further attacks on unarmed ships would result in a breaking of diplomatic relations; (7) the final German announcement, after a temporary backdown over the *Sussex* "ultimatum," that effective February 1, 1917 all ships around the British Isles would be sunk without warning. This last German act brought a break in diplomatic relations between Washington and Berlin and was followed two months later by war.

It is interesting to notice that at the beginning of each year—1915, 1916, 1917—the Germans made an attempt to initiate unrestricted submarine warfare. Twice they gave in to American demands—after the sinking of the *Lusitania* in May 1915 and of the *Sussex* in March 1916. On the third occasion they did not give in and the United States went to war.

Germany's use of submarines, which eventually led to the entry of the United States into the first World War, had not been planned in advance of the war. The prewar head of the German navy, Admiral Tirpitz, did not believe in submarines, and 1914 found Germany with fewer submarines than England or France. Germany had 27, England 55, France 77. About half the German submarines were seaworthy. Two years were required to build a U-boat. By the beginning of 1915, when Germany first sought to carry on unrestricted submarine warfare, she had only twenty usable vessels. At any one time a third of these were in drydock, another third sailing to or from an assignment, and only a third—that is, seven—could be in striking position. It was actually with four submarines that Germany in February 1915 declared submarine warfare. When this move was re-enacted in 1916 the number of seaworthy U-boats had risen to a bare fifty, of which some were needed in the Mediterranean. At any given time in 1916 the Germans could only send eleven or twelve submarines into the Atlantic sea lanes. In the spring of 1917 Germany could send between twenty-five and thirty U-boats into western waters. It is curious how much havoc, diplomatically and militarily, a few submarines produced during the first World War.

2. *The American Case against Germany*

In retrospect there is no doubt that Germany's submarine measures, above anything else, brought the United States into the first World War in 1917. If the German government had used some other means of warfare against the Allies it seems certain that the United States would not have entered the war. This is not to say that the submarine issue alone antagonized the Americans, that there were no other issues on which the American people took issue with the Germans, but that the submarine issue was crucial in the American decision for war.

At the beginning of the war in 1914 the German government had blundered badly, so far as American opinion was concerned, by invading Belgium contrary to a solemn treaty of guarantee which Germany had signed. Americans were incensed by this act. Emotional and moralistic, they saw this attack by Germany on a weak neighbor, contrary to treaty, as a moral atrocity. The treaty of guarantee was admittedly old, almost a dead letter, negotiated in 1839, but it was a treaty and not a "scrap of paper" as the German chancellor, Theobald von Bethmann-Hollweg, described it to the British ambassador when the latter asked for his passports. Germany violated the treaty over the protests of the Belgians, whose King Albert is credited with an epigram when asked if the German troops could march through his country: "Belgium is a nation, not a thoroughfare." The Germans had marched, Belgium had futilely declared war, and the Belgian army after a stout defense had fallen back into northern France.

A German occupation followed in Belgium, and during its four years the Germans used the harshest measures to keep the restive Belgian population in order. When the British government on May 12, 1915 published the Bryce Report giving details of German atrocities in Belgium, the American public was revolted. Here, as in the invasion of Belgium in 1914, was a second black mark against Germany. It is true that in the light of postwar investigation the veracity of some of the deeds instanced in the Bryce Report has come into question. There are no proofs of many of the wanton cruelties set down in it. But Bryce had long been a student of the United States, had made a wide reputation in America by publishing in 1888 a two-volume study entitled *The American Commonwealth*, and had been British ambassador to Washington during the Taft administration. His name, in American eyes, lent support to the official British report on German atrocities. Bryce, as we now see, should have made some effort to investigate the volume with which he associated his name, but he did not. Yet despite the falsity of many of the British charges in regard to Belgium, there was a considerable case against German occupation policy there. The Germans in their conduct toward Belgium did not behave well. They executed some 5,000 Belgian civilians, some in large groups, chosen indiscriminately as hostages for Belgian good behavior. Whenever some German soldier was shot down by

Belgian patriots the Germans retaliated by shooting hostages. If the more lurid atrocity stories of violated women and bayoneted babies contained little truth, there remained this execution of hostages which, although perhaps militarily justifiable, was humanely outrageous. To the sensitive public opinion in America, an opinion highly idealistic, German occupation policy in Belgium was unspeakably reprehensible.

Publication of the Bryce Report had come at a time to heighten its effect. A few days earlier, May 7, 1915, was the date of the most shocking episode of the entire period 1914–1917, the sinking by a German submarine of the *Lusitania*, pride of the British merchant marine, largest and swiftest vessel on the transatlantic run. The Germans early in 1915 had announced their war zone around the British Isles, and this entailed sinking not merely warships and cargo ships but also liners. The Allies refused to believe that German submarines would attack the largest liners. There was a technical basis for such reasoning: until the *Lusitania* went down, the Germans had not been able to sink any vessel traveling faster than fourteen knots; because the liners were swift vessels it was deemed improbable that they could be attacked. And they possessed watertight bulkheads which presumably would minimize loss of life if they were attacked. Unfortunately, and contrary to such reasoning, Captain Turner of the *Lusitania* disobeyed his instructions as his ship came within sight of the Irish coast (he slowed down his vessel and refrained from zigzagging). Thus Commander Schwieger of the *U-20* managed (the following is from his ship's log) to get a sight on "four funnels and two masts of a steamer . . . Ship is made out to be large passenger steamer. . . . Clean bow shot at a distance of 700 meters . . . Torpedo hits starboard side right behind the bridge. An unusually heavy explosion takes place with a very strong explosion cloud (cloud reaches far beyond front funnel). The explosion of the torpedo must have been followed by a second one (boiler or coal or powder?). . . . The ship stops immediately and heels over to starboard very quickly, immersing simultaneously at the bow . . . the name *Lusitania* becomes visible in golden letters." With this act of inhumanity—1,198 people drowned, including 128 Americans—Germany committed one of the cardinal errors of the war.

No one remembered that the German authorities, in newspaper advertisements, had warned prospective passengers that the *Lusitania* was deemed subject to attack. No matter that the German emperor on June 6, after the *Lusitania* sinking, issued secret orders to his submarine commanders not to attack liners without warning, and that after an accidental attack on the British liner *Arabic* the German ambassador in the United States, although without authorization, made the imperial orders public. The American people were horrified at the sinking of the largest Atlantic liner. "Damnable! Damnable! Absolutely hellish!" cried the evangelist Billy Sunday.

More than any other single factor, Commander Schwieger's chance torpedo shot (he had, incidentally, almost finished his cruise; it was his last torpedo) hurt the German cause in America. The American people were incensed at Germany and with almost one voice supported the Wilson administration's diplomatic protests. When Secretary Bryan refused to sign a stiff note to Berlin and resigned his office on June 7, his devotion to his conception of moral law received little public sympathy. "I must act according to my conscience," the idealist remarked sadly at a luncheon after his last cabinet meeting. "I go out into the dark. The President has the prestige and the power on his side . . ." This final sacrifice of Bryan's political career was to no avail, for anti-German feeling was far too widespread. There was never, to be sure, any serious possibility of America going to war over the *Lusitania* outrage. The country was unready for such action, but it was ready for the strongest diplomatic protests.

The German case thus suffered in the United States because of the Belgian invasion and occupation and the sinking of the *Lusitania*. These acts were monumental instances of the German policy of *Schrecklichkeit* (frightfulness). There were other irritations, such as the crude attempts to sabotage American war industry which in December 1915 resulted in expulsion from the country of the German military and naval attaches, Captains Franz von Papen and Karl Boy-Ed. The Austrian ambassador in the United States, who bore the unfortunate name of Dumba, was also expelled after the British secret service intercepted and published some compromising correspondence, showing that he had been privy to schemes for fomenting strikes in munitions factories. Then there were the continuing incidents over German submarine warfare. After sinking of the *Lusitania* there was a lull as the Germans abandoned for the moment their unrestricted submarine tactics, but early in 1916 they again undertook all-out submarine warfare and a new crisis arose when a submarine sank the *Sussex* on March 24, 1916. President Wilson gave the German government a virtual ultimatum in the matter of unrestricted submarine warfare—that if the Germans used it again, a third time, the United States would break diplomatic relations. The German government for the moment backed down, and relations between Washington and Berlin became relatively placid for the rest of the year 1916, until the crisis of January 1917.

Meanwhile relations with Britain reached what was probably an all-time low during the entire war period. The British, having observed how successfully they had impressed the American people as compared with the clumsiness of the Germans, may have overplayed their hand and become too confident that no matter what they did their cause in America was safe. The British blacklist of American firms suspected of trading with the Central Powers raised particular difficulty in 1916. The British government had compiled a list of all firms, American or those of other neutral nations, suspected of trading with Germany or Germany's allies, and goods consigned to such firms were declared subject to capture and confiscation by the Royal Navy. Although the blacklist was generally accurate, it did mark a gross violation of neutral rights as historically interpreted by the United States. "This blacklist business is the last straw," Wilson wrote to his chief adviser on foreign affairs, Colonel Edward M. House. An order in council about this time had set aside all that remained in British maritime practice of the Declaration of London. The British army in 1916 ruthlessly suppressed an Irish rebellion, stirring up the hatred of Irish sympathizers in America. American relations with Britain in 1916 became almost as taut as those with Germany.

It was in this situation, facing a serious crisis with both the British and the Germans, that President Wilson undertook a mediation of the war, an effort to bring to an end in Europe what had become a terrible slaughter, and to end it with, as Wilson described his purposes, a peace without victory.

The initial proposal of mediation, which proved unsuccessful, was the House-Grey Memorandum. The president's trusted adviser, Colonel House, had been in Europe in the spring of 1915 and again a year later, in the spring of 1916. On the latter occasion the colonel had become definite in discussions with the British foreign secretary, Sir Edward Grey, and the two men together had sketched out a way to end the war: "on hearing from France and England that the moment was opportune," the United States would invite the belligerents to a peace conference; should Allied acceptance be followed by German refusal, the United States would probably enter the war against Germany; or if the conference met and failed to secure peace, "the United States would [probably] leave the Conference as a belligerent on the side of the Allies, if Germany was unreasonable." The cautious Wilson had inserted the second "probably" (bracketed above) when the House-Grey Memorandum came to him for approval.

Nothing resulted from this pacific effort. Sir Edward, like Wilson, became cautious and told House that the time to put the plan into effect would perhaps arrive with autumn. In the summer of 1916 the British expected to mount a great offensive on the Western front. The French, moreover, were fighting a gigantic battle at Verdun, and for them the time for mediation was later, not at the moment. But after the French held the Germans at Verdun they were less interested in mediation than before. As for the British, when they were defeated on the Somme they wished to wait until the military situation was more favorable. The Lloyd George ministry, replacing that of Herbert Asquith in December 1916, favored a policy toward Germany of a knock-out blow, and was more firmly against Wilson's "interference" than was the cabinet of Asquith. By this time the American president was highly irritated, for he and House had placed their hopes on the proposed plan of peace. The nonpursuit of the House-Grey Memorandum seemed to be one more of the difficulties which Great Britain was making in the latter months of 1916.

After the presidential elections in the United States, Wilson made a final mediation effort. The president at the outset was placed in a position of seeming to follow a German initiative, for the Germans on December 12, 1916 called for peace negotiations, hoping to gain the initiative by anticipating Wilson's move and catching him and the Allies off balance. He went ahead and on December 18 requested both parties to the war to state their war aims. The Allies obliged by asking for a settlement that the German government would not accept: "restoration of Belgium, of Serbia, and of Montenegro [the latter two nations, like Belgium, had been occupied] and the indemnities which are due them." After much prodding the Germans confidentially communicated terms to Wilson, but these were as impossible as those of the Allies: hegemony over Belgium, and a slice of France; only a small part of Serbia would be returned; much of Rumania was probably to pass to Bulgaria; there would have to be indemnities for Germany, and colonies. At the same time that they revealed their peace terms, the German government on January 31, 1917, sent word through Ambassador Johann von Bernstorff of a new unrestricted submarine campaign.

The German admiralty had concluded that there was an excellent chance of knocking Britain out of the war by a blockade of the British Isles, the blockade including not merely munitions but everything, particularly food coming to Britain from the United States, India, and Argentina (especially the latter two countries, for harvests in the United States had been poor in 1916). The admiralty and the leaders of the German general staff knew that unrestricted submarine warfare would bring the United States into the conflict on the side of the Allies, but they were prepared to take this chance. They knew that American armaments were almost entirely naval. Great Britain controlled the seas anyway, and if the American fleet were added to the British it would make little difference in the outcome of the war. The American peacetime army was of no military importance, and they calculated that before the United States could raise, equip, and train a great army, let alone transport it across the Atlantic, the war would be over. If the United States in 1917 had possessed a dozen ready army divisions the German government might well have hesitated. The United States did not have the ready army divisions, and Admiral Eduard von Capelle, Tirpitz's successor as minister of marine, declared in the Reichstag that the military significance of American intervention would be "zero, zero, zero!" The unrestricted submarine campaign began on February 1, and on February 3 Wilson severed diplomatic relations.

Between the breaking of relations and the declaration of war there was a lapse of two months during which Wilson and the country determined on a course of action. War was not inevitable even after Bernstorff received his passport, for the nation could have followed a course of armed neutrality. Wilson seems to have wavered during this crucial period, waiting until Germany had given unmistakable indication of how seriously she would take the protests of the United States over her violations of neutral rights and, generally, her conduct of the war.

Wilson conceivably had armed neutrality in view when during February he asked Congress for authority to arm American merchant ships. He was not given it; in the Senate a "little group of willful men" by filibuster kept the bill from coming to a vote before the Sixty-fourth Congress ended on March 4 under the then law.

Meantime, the course for the American government became clear. A German submarine on February 25 sank the Cunard liner *Laconia;* it was the *Lusitania* all over again. This news came to the White House almost simultaneously with intelligence of the Zimmermann Note, in which the German foreign secretary, Alfred Zimmermann, sought to entice the Mexican government into war, not yet declared, with the United States, promising that Mexico might "reconquer the lost territory in New Mexico, Texas, and Arizona." This incredible missive incensed President Wilson because it had been transmitted to Mexico from Berlin via the American embassy in Berlin and the State Department in Washington. Because of British control of the cables Wilson had allowed the Germans to use American channels; the Germans had used them to transmit a hostile message. American newspapers published the Zimmermann Note on March 1.

Wilson called Congress into special session. The Senate arranged to limit debate, but now it was asked to declare war rather than mere armed neutrality. President Wilson delivered his war message to Congress in person on April 2; the joint resolution declaring war was passed on April 6, with overwhelming majorities.

3. *The Decision for War*

To report these events does not altogether explain the official and popular decision for war. The reasons which took the United States to war in 1917 have been and will continue to be examined, questioned, and debated.

There had been the major issue of neutral rights between the United States and Germany, and this had brought the break in relations in February 1917. The issue had been presented to Americans in a startlingly graphic and poignant manner in the *Lusitania* disaster, and it is safe to say that nearly two years later, in early 1917, the sinking of the great liner was still in most American minds a large mark against the German cause. The Germans had refused to state publicly their war aims, and had followed their refusal by a third declaration of unrestricted submarine warfare.

There was the German invasion of Belgium and the severe and oppressive occupation policy of the Germans in that country.

There was the Zimmermann Note.

Also, while the decision was making, the issue of good versus bad was somewhat clarified by the first Russian revolution of March 12, 1917. The tsarist power was overthrown and a republic set up (this lasted until November 1917, when the Bolsheviks overthrew it). The Russian republic of March was substituted in the Allied coalition for an embarrassingly autocratic member and the change strengthened the feeling of Americans that the Allies were fighting the despotisms of Central Europe.

There were historical traditions and attitudes. It was easy for the people of the United States to recognize at this crucial time the tie of common language and kinship between America and Great Britain, to remember the somewhat neglected revolutionary bond between the United States and France.

There was also the trade in munitions and foodstuffs, the economic ties between the United States and the Allies. Despite the increased stringency of Allied measures and German countermeasures in 1914–1917, American foreign trade had by no means been eliminated. Trade with the Allies increased dramatically and took on the characteristics of a boom. Prosperity came to American industry, which had been in the doldrums at the beginning of the war. The American merchant made his profits, and likewise the American farmer received a share of the new commerce, since Britain stood in need of foodstuffs as well as of war material. The American economy by 1916 thus had become attuned to the requirements of the Allies. This is not to say, however, that economic bonds had a large part in bringing the United States into the first World War. As a result of the investigation of the American munitions industry by a Senate committee under the chairmanship of Gerald P. Nye of North Dakota in the mid-1930's, many Americans came to believe that in 1914–1917 it had been the bankers and the munitions makers—the "merchants of death"—who had driven the United States to war. This belief was partly responsible for the series of neutrality acts which Congress passed in the middle and later 1930's. But in actual fact there was not much truth to the merchants-of-death argument. One cannot doubt that many individuals, bankers and armament manufacturers, made fortunes from the wartime munitions trade. The United States Steel Corporation, to mention one example, flourished during the period and sweated out much of the

"water" with which it had been capitalized at the turn of the century
—the virtually paper issues of stocks and bonds, unsupported by physical assets of the corporation. Likewise such great banking houses as
J. P. Morgan and Company floated the Allied bond issues in the United
States and took handsome profits from such transactions. The Morgan
firm acted as Allied agent in this country in 1914–1917, and the
Morgan partners put some considerable pressure on the Wilson administration to permit floating of bonds and loans under the neutrality
proclamation of 1914. This pressure, the Morgan profits and those of
other financiers, and the profits of the munitions firms were uncov-
ered, so to speak, in the Nye investigation of the 1930's, and many
people at that time, anticipating uneasily another World War, were
quick to conclude that profiteers had taken the United States into the
war of 1914–1918. Still, there seems clearly to have been little if any
skulduggery involved in the financing and munitions-trading of the
first World War, and one should conclude that forces other than
these moved the country to belligerency in 1917.

There were persuasive and successful efforts to get United States
support for the Allies. These efforts supported another argument
much bruited about in the 1930's, again in anticipation of a second
World War, to the effect that crafty British propaganda in the years
of American neutrality in 1914–1917 had hoodwinked the American
people and finally brought them into the conflict on the side of the
British. The British government, according to the "disclosures" of
the 1920's and 1930's, had carefully set on foot a propaganda campaign to convert the United States to their side, and this campaign
had met with success. What should one conclude about this? Again,
there seems to have been an overstatement of a case. There is no question that the British government set up a special propaganda effort,
cleverly kept secret and unofficial, to enlist American sympathies with
the Allied cause. British books were sent over to the United States,
and speakers came to talk about the general similarity of English culture to that of Americans. Influential Britishers wrote letters to their
American friends, asking for sympathy with the cause in Europe. All
in all, a large effort went into bringing the United States into the first
World War. Since the United States entered the war, perhaps one
should say that the effort was successful—though this reasoning really
begs the question. There were many reasons, other than British propaganda, that brought the United States to declare war on Germany.

And one might say, in conclusion, that there is nothing wrong with one country representing its cause to another country—that the United States does this publicly and openly today, in its official information services, all over the world. The accusations about British propaganda current in the interwar years stemmed partly from fear of more propaganda and a second World War, and partly from sheer unacquaintance with the arts of peaceful persuasion. "Public relations" was a new industry in the United States as elsewhere in the 1920's and for some time thereafter, and there was fear of what might happen should the supposed wizards of press agentry set to work on national populations and deal in questions of foreign policy rather than tooth paste and cigarettes. This fear, as we now see, was unfounded, though the effects of propaganda of various sorts and sources upon life at mid-century have admittedly been of importance.

There was a consideration of national self-interest, however much it weighed. Some writers, notably Walter Lippmann, contemporaneously and later have sought to show that in 1917 the United States really entered the war to redress the balance of power in Europe, that is, to secure its national interests. Lippmann would argue that despite the many other factors mentioned above which moved the American government toward war, the final decision was taken in the highest circles in Washington on the basis of the world balance of power—the need to offset the military power of Germany, which was threatening to engulf the Continent, with the power of the colossus of the New World. According to the Lippmann contention, here was another time when the New World redressed the balance of the Old. This argument comes to rest uncertainly on the intuition and far-sightedness of the president and his advisers. The president is deemed to have acted implicitly on a balance-of-power basis, and also at the behest of some of his advisers, especially Bryan's able successor, Secretary of State Robert Lansing, who held the national interest up before Wilson. Yet, while it is not difficult to show that Lansing had a strongly developed sense of *raison d'état*—reason of state, or national interest—it is much more difficult to show such reasoning on the part of Wilson. It was certainly in the national interest to go to war and it might be comforting to believe that, since logic demanded entrance, logic was the source of action. From available evidence there is no proof that the American president in 1917 acted out of considerations different from those which moved his fellow citizens, and there is no evidence that his fellow citizens were moved by considerations of national interest.

Perhaps one should conclude that the reasoning which moved Wilson and the American people from the feelings at August 1914 to the remarkable singleness of purpose at April 6, 1917 (the Congress vote in favor of war was overwhelming, 82-6 in the Senate, 373-50 in the House) was a view of balance of power, but not the traditional view. The decision in 1917 was emotional, grounded in the belief, indeed conviction, that right, in the person of the Allies, was battling wrong, personified by the Central Powers. There was abroad, so Wilson and his fellow Americans believed, a concerted, highly organized, brutal, savage campaign against decency and morality, and in the early spring of 1917 evil was weighing heavily in the balance against good. The American people, having enjoyed throughout their history an abundant life in a material sense, having from their own successes come to believe that their principles were correct principles, lacking bitterness and cynicism about the motives and behavior of foreign peoples, were willing to take a stand against what most students even today would grant was a ruthless German military ambition. The American people, to the entire disbelief of contemporary foreign observers and to the disbelief of their own children of the next generation, were willing to take a stand in the world for principle. Americans in the long months of neutrality, from 1914 to 1917, had come to feel that their principles were being challenged. "The world," Wilson said in his war message, "must be made safe for democracy."

ADDITIONAL READING

See the titles listed at end of chapter 12.

CHAPTER

☆ *12* ☆

War and Peace

1. *Wartime Diplomacy, 1917–1918*

When the United States entered the first World War many questions at last were resolved or adjourned, and it was with considerable relief that the leaders of the American government could clear the decks, so to speak, and face the major problem that confronted them: defeating the Central Powers. Diplomacy during the war became of necessity a concern secondary to the military effort. Still, there was a place for diplomacy and a large one, in any war such as the conflict in 1917–1918, fought by a coalition. President Wilson—as would be true of President Franklin D. Roosevelt a generation later, in 1941–1945—found himself deeply involved in what might be described as "coalition diplomacy," the holding together and in some important instances the direction of the Allied war effort. The diplomacy of interallied co-ordination was a major concern in 1917–1918 and the president performed it brilliantly. There were, in addition, two other diplomatic tasks which Wilson undertook. One was in regard to Austria-Hungary—bringing pressure upon the Dual Monarchy to get out of the war. The other consisted of a calculated and eventually successful effort to persuade the German people to give up fighting and make peace with the Allies.

The principal diplomatic effort of the war years came over the business of interallied co-ordination. In the same month that the United States entered the war the British government sent a mission to America headed by the foreign secretary, Arthur Balfour, to discuss Allied requirements and seek to discover how the United States as a belligerent might best contribute to an Allied victory. Not to be outdone, the French simultaneously sent a mission consisting of René Viviani, a former premier, and also, to discuss military matters, Marshal Joseph Joffre. The Italians and Belgians likewise sent missions and, as we have seen in a previous chapter, the Japanese sent Viscount Ishii to the United States to obtain some concessions for the island empire which were not connected with the Allied war effort. Little came of any of these initial missions, including the mission of Ishii, but they did serve to emphasize at the outset of American belligerency the need for Allied co-operation in the common effort against the Central Powers.

One result of Balfour's visit was the setting up of a special system of contact between the British foreign secretary, once he had returned to London, and the American government. In a private arrangement that completely bypassed the State Department, Balfour set up a special British government code by which he could communicate directly with the chief of British military intelligence in the United States, Sir William Wiseman. Wiseman maintained a suite in a New York hotel which was directly above a suite occupied by Colonel House, Wilson's closest confidant. House, in turn, had a direct and private wire from his suite to the White House in Washington. It was a most effective arrangement. If exasperating to Secretary of State Lansing, who thus was left completely in the dark as to many Anglo-American arrangements on the highest level, it was probably for the best in many ways, for in this manner the British government could deal intimately with the American president instead of going through the rigmarole of sending formal notes between the respective foreign offices.

But this arrangement was efficacious only between the two English-speaking allies, and it was an arrangement of channels rather than a solution to the many problems of concern that confronted Britain, the United States, France, Russia and the other powers aligned against the Central Powers. After the United States entered the war the special Franco-British purchasing arrangements through J. P. Morgan and Company were dropped, as the Morgan Company rightly believed that it could not continue to carry on what was now a proper function of the government of the United States. This change required a new American organization, and the Morgan procedures were, unfortunately, not at once assumed by the government in Washington. There was muddle in this regard until an arrangement was made in late August 1917 for a purchasing commission in Washington. A protocol to this effect was signed by the United States, Britain, France, and Russia.

Such a purchasing commission could not co-ordinate the requirements of the Allies with those of the Americans themselves, which were increasing as an American army of enormous size and power began to come into being, and so pressure appeared for more co-ordination, perhaps an American mission to Europe. Colonel House's name was mentioned as a possible head for such a mission, and without hesitation President Wilson nominated House, who with a full complement of advisers arrived in London on November 7, 1917. The House mission performed yeoman service, conferring with the British until November 21, after which it went on to Paris and joined an Interallied Conference at which eighteen nations were represented, from Belgium to Siam.

The Interallied Conference of November 1917 was one of the most fruitful diplomatic events of the war, when one considers the many decisions that resulted, directly and indirectly. The first plenary session opened with a speech of welcome by the new French premier, Georges Clemenceau, who had just formed his ministry dedicated to victory, and who had promised that he would make a brief talk. He spoke five sentences, concluding: "The order of the day is work. Let us get to work." The conference thereupon adjourned for executive sessions of committees of technical experts. From this discussion at Paris came many important decisions. One was a plan that the Americans would place in France by the end of 1918 at least thirty divisions of troops, approximately a million men, available for the campaign envisioned for early 1919. As events turned out, the Americans had their million in France by June, 1918, and doubled the number by October. It was these fresh American troops which broke the back of the German army on the western front and enabled the Allies to win the war. There were other agreements at the Interallied Conference, such as the decision to send a battleship division to reinforce the British Grand Fleet. British naval authorities were extremely nervous over the accuracy of German naval gunfire as exhibited at the Battle of Jutland in 1916, the huge sea confrontation of the British and German fleets which with heavy British losses ended in a draw with re-

tirement of the German fleet. Appearance of American warships in
Europe, ensuring a preponderance of Allied naval power against a
possible second German challenge, greatly reassured the British naval
command. Another agreement at the conference in November 1917
in Paris was that the British and Americans together would close
the North Sea to German submarines by construction of a mine bar-
rage, which incidentally marked a reversal of the American stand
against mining of the high seas. There was also agreement at the conference on blockade policy, and on methods of rationing trade with
neutrals on the European continent so as to ensure that the neutrals
would not transship goods to Germany or Germany's allies.

The Interallied Conference set up a number of standing committees
which met in London and Paris. There was the interallied council on
war purchases and finance, the maritime transport council, the interallied naval council, the food council, the interallied petroleum conference, the interallied munitions council. The Europeans must have
been aghast at the organizational mania of the Americans, but because they needed American goods they complied with the desires
of the New World republic. As one Frenchman, André Tardieu,
put it (Tardieu was France's chief of a permanent commission of
co-ordination in the United States): "When Americans fall in love
with an idea, even if their enthusiasm does not last, it is always intense.
In 1917 and 1918, they had a passion for the organization of interallied war machinery, the weight of which was not always borne
gladly by Europe." Eventually, he concluded, the Europeans did
come to see that only through united efforts, rather than independent
measures, could the war be won.

The European Allies themselves on November 7, 1917, urged on
by military disaster on the Italian front, took a step in the direction
of unifying their efforts. The Italian army had cracked at Caporetto
on October 27, 1917, and in a short time three quarters of a million
Italian troops were killed, wounded, or made prisoner. This debacle
brought the British, French, and Italians to a meeting at Rapallo early
in November where they created an interallied Supreme War Council. The council was to act "as an agency for the adoption and maintenance of a general policy for the Allies in the prosecution of the
war, consistent with the total resources available and the most effective distribution of those resources among the various theaters of
operations." It was not a supreme command for the Allied forces—

that would not come until later, in the spring of 1918, when the almost successful German general offensive in the west forced the Allies to designate Marshal Ferdinand Foch as supreme allied commander. But if it were not a supreme command the Supreme War Council was a political organization of considerable importance. General Tasker H. Bliss, a former chief of staff of the American army, sat as one of the military advisers from the first meeting of the council. Colonel House represented the United States at the meeting in December 1917, and as Wilson's personal representative sat with the prime ministers of the other powers. After House's return to the United States the president appointed no one in his place, although permitting the councilor of the Paris embassy, Arthur Frazier, to attend as a "listener." Wilson wished to emphasize that the United States, having not signed the formal instrument of alliance between the Allied powers and having thereby assumed only the role of "associate" in the war, was not taking part in the Allies' political discussions. This, to be sure, was a false position and when in late 1918 the question of an armistice with Germany arose in the Supreme War Council, Colonel House entered its sessions and discussed the matter in fullest participation with representatives of the other nations.

One might conclude this discussion of the vitally important work of interallied co-ordination by again citing an opinion of André Tardieu. "Nations remember only the high spots of wars," he wrote in the 1920's. "What did they grasp of the tragic period of 1917–1918? The Rumanian disaster, Caporetto, the British Fourth Army, the Chemin des Dames. Were those the decisive events of the great struggle? No! The essential things were the problems of transportation, rotation of shipping and submarine sinkings, the financial problem, the problems of co-operation. Any shortcoming in the adjustment of effort, any breakdown in the machinery of supply, might have left our soldiers weaponless."

The United States, it can justly be said, was responsible for much of this work of interallied co-ordination.

Another of President Wilson's diplomatic tasks of the war period was bringing pressure upon the Central Powers with the hope of persuading them to give up fighting. This, like the diplomacy of co-ordination, was an informal sort of negotiation. It was much different from the usual note-sending and note-receiving that marks the normal peacetime dealing of nation with nation. There were no

American diplomatic representatives in Berlin nor—after the American declaration of war in December 1917—in Vienna, and American moves had to be made through special emissaries and through diplomatic posts in neutral countries.

The policy of the United States was generally well adapted to the situation of 1917–1918, for it focused its attention on Austria-Hungary. The German government had become extremely bellicose after the appointment in autumn 1916 of General Erich Ludendorff as quartermaster general of the imperial army, and there could be little hope for a peace offensive directed at Berlin. Austria-Hungary, however, had incautiously gone to war in 1914, and almost from the start was anxious to get out. The Austrian declaration of war on Serbia had set off the European alliance system, almost like a string of firecrackers, and the war had hardly begun before the old Emperor Francis Joseph was wishing for peace: if Austria-Hungary could get out with a black eye and no bones broken, the emperor said, he would be happy. Upon the death of Francis Joseph in late 1916, the young Emperor Charles came to the throne and was equally anxious for peace. Charles knew even better than his great uncle that the empire was torn by the dissension among its national minorities, which already had brought a high rate of desertion from the imperial army. If the monarchy did not soon have peace it would fall apart. To this inviting situation the United States directed a considerable diplomatic effort.

President Wilson and the American government nourished the hope of getting Austria-Hungary out of the war and, at the same time, maintaining the territorial integrity of the empire—avoiding its breakup into several small national states. There were unofficial and inconclusive conversations in Switzerland between emissaries of the Emperor Charles and an American resident in that neutral country, George D. Herron. There was a short exchange between Wilson and Charles, through the king of Spain. But Austria had become almost a captive state of the Hohenzollern empire. Strong bodies of German troops had deployed close to Vienna, and while the young emperor pursued his somewhat naive negotiations the Germans by indirect pressure kept him from going too far.

Meanwhile the nationalities subject to the Habsburg throne planned to capitalize the opportunity in a revolutionary sense, and by early summer of 1918 the situation was beyond repair. The nationalities, no longer satisfied with autonomy, demanded freedom. The American government acquiesced in this change in the situation, assuming that the Austro-Hungarian empire could not survive the war. In the summer of 1918 the United States recognized the Czechoslovak National Council in Paris and also the national aspirations of the empire's Serbs, Croats, and Slovenes. The Emperor Charles in October 1918 tried vainly to federalize his empire but the time had passed when such a move was possible. With jubilation the refugee Czechoslovak statesman, Thomas Masaryk, then in America, observed the collapse of his people's ancient Austrian enemy. This new political situation in Central Europe was, one should emphasize, created by the pressures of the war rather than any initiative on Wilson's part. The American president rather reluctantly used Central European nationalism to hasten the last stages of the war. He thereby obtained Austria-Hungary's capitulation seven days before that of Germany, in early November 1918.

Wartime diplomacy toward Germany had to move along different lines. The Second Reich, the empire of Bismarck, made by blood and iron in 1871 from the union of north and south Germany, offered no opportunity in 1917–1918—given the ardent Germanism which in the latter nineteenth century superseded German provincial feeling—to split the empire into its pre-1871 divisions. American tactics therefore were to separate the Berlin government from its people, under the somewhat meretricious but nonetheless useful argument that the government did not represent the people. With the German people, Wilson said in his war message, "we have no feeling . . . but one of sympathy and friendship." Similar statements appeared throughout his speeches in the period of American belligerency, 1917–1918.

The principal move by the American government to drive a wedge between government and people in Germany was the announcement, on January 8, 1918, of the Fourteen Points: (1) open covenants of peace, openly arrived at; (2) freedom of the seas; (3) removal, "so far as possible," of trade barriers; (4) reduction of armaments "to the lowest point consistent with domestic safety"; (5) equitable adjustment of colonial claims; (6) evacuation of Russia; (7) evacuation and restoration of Belgium; (8) assignment of Alsace-Lorraine to France; (9) readjustment of Italian frontiers "along clearly recognizable lines of nationality"; (10) "autonomous development" for the peoples of Austria-Hungary; (11) evacuation of Rumania, Serbia, and Montenegro, with access to the sea for Serbia; (12) reduction of Turkey to territory containing only peoples of Turkish descent; (13) independence of Poland, with access of Poland to the sea; (14) establishment of a league of nations. The chief motive of the Fourteen Points, one should explain, was to keep Russia in the war (the Bolsheviks had come to power on November 6–7, 1917) by a statement of more liberal war aims than Colonel House had been able to secure at the Interallied Conference at Paris in November 1917. There was also the need to reassure the Allied peoples that there was idealism in the Allied war aims. These were the immediate reasons, the impulse, behind Wilson's announcement of the Fourteen Points, but he directed his speech to the German people, hoping to persuade them to get out of the war. The Fourteen Points were a master stroke in what a later generation would describe as psychological warfare. The German people, learning of the Fourteen Points, could see that the Allies had a reasonable peace program, and they could ask themselves why they were continuing to fight in what had become a catastrophic world conflict.

Proof of the effectiveness of the Fourteen Points and other of Wilson's speeches explaining his peace program came when, prior to the armistice of November 11, 1918, the American president managed to obtain from both the Germans and Allies an express recognition—which in the case of the Allies became known as the "prearmistice agreement"—of the Fourteen Points as a basis of peace. This was one of Wilson's major triumphs as a diplomat. The prearmistice agreement became the foundation for the entire peace settlement at Paris in 1919. It was of the utmost historical importance, for without considering its pledges and exceptions no student can appreciate the Treaty of Versailles and the later German efforts to revise the treaty. The prearmistice agreement became possible when General Ludendorff, after a rupture of his lines in northern France, told the German civil government on September 29, 1918 that it must sue for peace and do so quickly. The government, which the German general staff had dominated for two years, displayed an unwonted initiative and at once asked for peace on the basis of the Fourteen Points, communicating directly with President Wilson and not the Allies. Wilson kept the negotiations in his own hands while he persuaded the Germans to democratize their government and drop the emperor. At the same time he persuaded the Allied statesmen—not without a broad hint from Colonel House, then sitting on the Supreme War Council in Paris, that the United States might make a separate peace—to accept the Fourteen Points. The British prime minister, Lloyd George, accepted the points with a reservation that there must be further discussion of Wilson's Point 2, freedom of the seas. The British also desired a large financial reparation from Germany, and so they drafted a reservation on this matter—it was written mainly by Sir William Wiseman—which was accepted by the French premier, Clemenceau, and the Italian premier, Vittorio Orlando. With these reservations, communicated to and accepted by the German government, together with explanation by Wilson to the Allies (but not to the Germans) that certain of the points such as Point 10 pertaining to Austria-Hungary had to be modified in view of recent events, the Germans on November 8 sent plenipotentiaries to Marshal Foch's railroad car, then in the forest of Compiègne in northern France, and there in the early morning of November 11, 1918 they signed the armistice.

2. The Paris Peace Conference

The war was over and the making of peace could begin. American diplomacy had enunciated the Fourteen Points as a basis of peace, and in the prearmistice agreement gained Allied approval of them. The Germans had consented to them. The diplomats of the New World would now have an opportunity to see how much of the American peace program could be secured at the peace conference.

Wilson decided to go in person to Paris, and this decision at the time and later was written down as a major diplomatic error. His presence assuredly put him into the hurly-burly of what was bound to be a difficult conference. The president had much to lose in personal reputation and little to gain by going to Europe to assist in making the peace. He went; and he obtained at Paris much of his program, notably the League of Nations, which an individual with less prestige might never have secured.

But did President Wilson at Paris lose some vital issues for the United States, apart from his victory on the League of Nations? There has persisted a popular belief in his "blunders" at Paris—a belief that a gullible American president, journeying to Europe to make peace in 1919, encountered issues which he did not understand, and that cunning European diplomats at Paris persuaded Wilson to give away everything that the United States won in the World War.

The simple process by which the Paris conference accomplished its tasks, in meetings of three or four of the leading statesmen, seemed to point to personal decision at the peace table. Three or four men, it was easy to believe, could make mistakes. Everyone watched with apprehension at the time, an apprehension which deepened into suspicion, as the conference followed a normal process of shrinking to a manageable size. Although it began with a large body of delegates, it was dominated at once by the Council of Ten (which was a reincarnation of the wartime Supreme War Council—foreign ministers and prime ministers or chief delegates of Japan, Italy, France, Britain, and the United States). It ended as a private meeting of the Big Four (the prime ministers of Italy, France, Britain; the president of the United States) and, frequently, the Big Three (Clemenceau, Lloyd George, and Wilson): Lloyd George, the politically agile prime minister of England, "a Welsh witch" as John Maynard Keynes described him; Clemenceau, conservative, uncharitable, realistic in the old-fashioned manner of diplomacy; Wilson, a great man in many ways, but edgy and irritable at Paris, and tired.

Even so, one must doubt that Wilson made many mistakes at Paris. Certainly on technical matters he was on almost all occasions hedged about by solid information from his advisers. There was much professional advice available in Paris, and the president was seldom in the predicament of having to make a subjective decision. Wilson needed this help. His declarations during the war months had been general in nature. The president, despite his background as a student of history, was not well grounded in European history. Colonel House as early as autumn of 1917 had therefore taken steps to marshal for the peace conference a corps of American specialists, and the resulting Inquiry, a group of experts drawn mainly from university faculties, devoted itself to minute examination of the problems of Europe, especially possible boundary changes in Eastern Europe. The Inquiry was a serious group, established for a serious purpose, and its information was in the main highly accurate. At the conference the experts of the Inquiry stood available to the president and other members of the American delegation. As events turned out, the Inquiry and a somewhat similar group in the British delegation, together with experts from the other Allied nations, wrote the major portions of the Versailles Treaty with Germany and the treaties with the other

Central Powers.

This is not to say that there were no large political questions at Paris subject to decision by the statesmen of the great powers, for there were such questions, running far beyond the technical into the political on a grand scale. One need only mention reparations—how much should Germany pay, and to whom? What should be done about Germany's border along the Rhine—should the border territory pass to France, or should there be provisions for demilitarization and occupation, with eventual retirement of Allied forces upon German good behavior? What should happen to the Saar, the rich coal-bearing valley—should it go to France permanently because of Germany's dynamiting of many of France's mines? There were the Polish questions, of borders and access to the sea; the difficulty of rearranging the peoples and borders of the Adriatic area, where, as in Poland, there was centuries-old confusion which had been adjourned so long as the Austro-Hungarian empire existed; the problem of the former Turkish territories in the Middle East, which had to go, apparently, to one or several of the victorious Allied powers; the need for parceling out former German colonies in the Pacific, including Germany's sphere of influence in the Shantung peninsula of China. In such political questions no experts could be of much help. Here the leading statesmen of the conference—Wilson, Lloyd George, Orlando, and Clemenceau—had to make decisions. But one should point out that even at these points, in the nontechnical areas, Wilson and the other leaders of the Allies could act only within definite limits, for each of them lacked the power of independent decision because he was curbed by the politics of democracy: Wilson was subject to advice and consent of the Senate; Lloyd George was heckled by the press in England, especially that of the sensational press magnate, Lord North-cliffe; Orlando had little power of decision because of the popular hysteria over Adriatic possessions, whipped up by patriots such as Gabriele d'Annunzio; Clemenceau was the prisoner of the French passion for revenge and security.

The idea is false that Wilson had a wide area of decision at Paris and blundered badly because of his personal foibles and incapacities, thereby losing the peace. Personal decisions—blunders—could hardly characterize the peace conference of 1919. The idea of a personal conference flourished in the overimaginative brains of newspaper correspondents, and in the disappointments and disillusions of nations which after 1919 did not have what they wanted. It was easy to point to three or four elderly men sitting in a book-lined study in Paris, and to say that "*There* was the trouble," whether it was there or not.

The results of the conference gradually became evident in the months from its beginning on January 18, 1919 until signature of the treaty with Germany on June 28, 1919—the fifth anniversary of the assassination of the Archduke Francis Ferdinand at Sarajevo. The majority of the 440 articles of the Treaty of Versailles were technical and noncontroversial. A few of them stood out in importance or in seeming importance. The first twenty-six comprised the Covenant of the League of Nations. The Covenant became, incidentally, the first twenty-six articles of all of the Paris peace treaties (St. Germain with Austria, Trianon with Hungary, Neuilly with Bulgaria).

In the German treaty, Article 231 was the famous war-guilt clause, which blamed Germany and her allies for beginning the war in 1914. Perhaps a special error of the German treaty, fraught with future difficulty, was the postponement of setting of the amount of reparations which Germany was to pay, and the fact that reparations were to include the cost of Allied pensions. The boundaries of Germany in the west underwent some changes. Alsace-Lorraine was given to France. Two small patches of land, Eupen and Malmédy, went to Belgium. The Saar valley was placed for fifteen years under a temporary League administration, with its future status to be decided at the end of that time; the mines of the Saar went to France, and if the territory was returned to Germany by plebiscite in the year 1935 the Germans were to purchase the mines. There were to be no German fortifications west of a line fifty kilometers east of the Rhine, and certain German territory west of the Rhine was to be occupied by Allied troops for periods of five, ten, and fifteen years. In the east, Germany's province of East Prussia was separated from the remainder of German territory by a Polish corridor—a severe settlement excusable on the basis of self-determination and Poland's need for access to the sea, inexcusable to Germans who for centuries had possessed the corridor lands. Danzig, the former German port now in the new corridor, was denominated a free city under control of the League of Nations. In Upper Silesia, in southeast Germany, there was a plebiscite to determine what lands would remain German and what would go to Poland. In the north of Germany two parts of

Schleswig were to decide their nationality, Danish or German, by plebiscite. Germany under the Treaty of Versailles lost nearly four million people in the east, a third of whom were of German nationality. Altogether she lost by the treaty over six million people, or one-tenth of her population. She lost one-eighth of her territory.

The problems of the Paris conference were extraordinarily numerous, but the treaty with Germany was not a vindictive instrument in view of the more than four years of bitter fighting which preceded it. It compared favorably indeed to Germany's Treaty of Brest-Litovsk with Bolshevik Russia, signed on March 3, 1918, by which Russia gave up all claims not merely to Poland, Finland, and the Baltic states, but to the Ukraine and the Caucasus. If Germany had won the war in the west she would have demanded annexation of the Briey-Longwy iron district from France, Liége from Belgium, and in addition a close economic control over Belgium. One can say therefore that Allied ambition was considerably less than the German during the first World War. And under the Treaty of Versailles and the other treaties with defeated nations there was always the hope of the League of Nations. President Wilson hoped that such imperfections as would appear in the peace settlement could be taken to the new international tribunal where there could be discussion, compromise, and peaceful change.

It is saddening to reflect upon the manner in which this peace settlement of 1919 was lost, of how the divisions among the Allies which became evident at the Paris Peace Conference lasted for twenty years thereafter, and enabled Germany, the defeated power at Paris, to begin another World War. It was tragic that at Paris the Italian delegates had to appease their own public at home and champion more territory for Italy than would have passed to her under the terms of the generous Treaty of London of 1915 (Fiume, seized after the war by Italian patriots led by d'Annunzio, had not been offered to Italy under the Treaty of London). The Japanese used the conference to enforce their claims on Shantung, the large Chinese province containing thirty million people, and in view of the small contribution of Japan to the defeat of Germany this was an excessive demand, embarrassing to the Allies and so humiliating to China that there was bound to be future trouble. The French representatives at the Paris conference were forced by their public opinion (if they did not already think this way themselves—certainly Clemenceau did) to be bitter and grasping; this course was mistaken, although entirely understandable for a nation which had lost 1,385,000 of its finest young men, with more than three million wounded. The British under the leadership of Lloyd George were not interested in territorial acquisition, even if the colonial premiers were determined to acquire control of the former German colonies. Despite the empire's grievous loss of 947,000 men killed, British leaders desired to promote Germany's economic welfare. But the British prime minister was opportunist in his approach to politics, whether national or international, and he lent uncertainty and something of cheapness to a meeting which needed dignity and a convincing atmosphere.

President Wilson, in poor health towards the close of the conference after a serious attack of influenza in April 1919, did his best to hold up American ideals to the peoples.and statesmen of Europe. In this effort he was in fair measure successful, but he became so preoccupied with the task that he failed to keep in touch with the changing political situation in the United States and eventually lost at home everything that he gained abroad. He persisted in believing that domestic politics would be adjourned not merely for the period of the war, but for the period of peacemaking as well. He failed, and it was a foolish error, to appoint to the American peace delegation domestic political leaders of standing. Neither General Bliss, nor Colonel House, nor Secretary Lansing, nor the former diplomat Henry White, could keep him in touch with political developments in the United States. Wilson lost contact with American public opinion, despite a trip home in February and early March of 1919 to sign necessary legislation and plead the cause of the League of Nations to members of the United States Congress. If the Congress seemed slightly inattentive, it might have been because the Republican Party had gained control in both the House and Senate as a result of the November 1918 election. After return to Paris the president worked incessantly, and when the moment came in June 1919 to sign the German treaty he was close to exhaustion.

Apart from the understandable errors of peacemaking forced upon the statesmen of the great powers by public opinion in their home countries, one might mention at this point a special factor, namely Russia, which while much talked about in the springtime and summer of 1919 was left undecided at the peace conference. If the Paris conferees made a cardinal error, above and beyond any other mistakes, it was their sidestepping of the Russian question. Russia, to be sure, had been much in the minds of the Allies ever since the tsarist government had disappeared with the first Russian revolution of March 12, 1917. After the first revolution people hoped that the new government would prove more efficient than the old and that the Russian front, from being something of a holding operation, would become a serious theater of operations against the Germans. Instead the weak republic gave way in November to the Bolsheviks, and at once the strange group of fanatics, so they seemed, led by Vladimir Lenin and Leon Trotsky, threw in the sponge and made peace with the Germans at Brest-Litovsk on March 3. This was a large blow to Allied fortunes, for it enabled the German army to transfer many of its divisions from the Russian front to France. Luckily for the Allies, the Germans were not thorough enough in transferring troops—they could have sent across Germany far more than they did—and the western front held again in 1918 despite a great German offensive.

But at the peace conference at Brest-Litovsk the Bolsheviks led by Trotsky had talked long and loud about the rights of workers in Europe and their oppression by the capitalists, and this doctrine, though poked fun at in Allied newspapers, began toward the end of the year 1918 to worry Allied leaders. When after the German surrender the reds set up a communist regime in Bavaria, and when early in 1919 the radical premier of Hungary, Michael Károlyi, surrendered his government to the communist revolutionary Béla Kun, and when the Russians entered the Ukraine after the Germans left it—with all these happenings people everywhere began to wonder about this movement known as communism. There was a "red scare" in the United States, and in other countries, in 1919. The statesmen at Paris worried about the durability of any peace they might conclude, finding themselves in the position of winning a war only to make the world safe for communism, hardly an attractive prospect.

What to do about the Bolsheviks in Europe was one of the major questions at the peace conference, but unhappily the problem was never resolved. Some individuals such as Winston Churchill and Marshal Foch were all for sending troops to Russia and putting the Bolsheviks down by force. Yet such an expedition ran counter to all the feelings among Allied peoples at the time—it was impossible to stir up enthusiasm for more fighting, after November 1918, and anyway it seemed that perhaps with the passage of some months the

Russian confusion would right itself. Britain and France sponsored various "white" leaders in Russia in 1919 and 1920, and the occupations of Siberia and Murmansk, originally for military purposes, tended at times to become political interventions. But the attitude of President Wilson, which was to let the Russians find a new course according to their own preferences, gradually prevailed. This did not mean that Wilson himself was willing to recognize the Bolshevik regime, for he was not, and he so instructed his last secretary of state, Bainbridge Colby, in the summer of 1920. Colby announced the non-recognition of communist Russia because the regime had subverted popular government, and this policy prevailed until another Democratic president changed it in 1933. Meanwhile the opportunity for intervention in Russia, if there had ever been one, had passed away as the regime of the Bolsheviks established itself during the 1920's and 1930's beyond any chance of destroying it.

The difficulty in regard to Bolshevik Russia, the reason why the problem was not solved, was in the main, as mentioned, the war weariness of all the Allied peoples. Public opinion had by 1919 turned to other concerns than the problems arising out of the World War. People were tired of war and wished to hear no more about it, not even about its settlement by the peace conference at Paris. By the autumn of 1919 when the Versailles Treaty was ready for approval by the nations of the world, the treaty encountered something close to indifference. "In this autumn of 1919," wrote John Maynard Keynes, then in process of composing a polemic which bitterly criticized the treaty, people were "at the dead season" of their fortunes. "The reaction from the exertions, the fears, and the sufferings of the past five years is at its height. Our power of feeling or caring beyond the immediate questions of our own material well-being is temporarily eclipsed. The greatest events outside our own direct experience and the most dreadful anticipations cannot move us. . . . We have been moved already beyond endurance, and need rest. Never in the lifetime of men now living has the universal element in the soul of man burnt so dimly."

Keynes's words were intended to describe popular feeling in England and France, but his description was true of the United States as well. In America the exertions of the war, while great, had not been beyond endurance. They had been endurable, and the nation in a war in Korea some thirty years later would lose more than half as many young men as in the first World War (Korea: 36,647 killed; first World War: 53,398 dead). The American exertion in 1917–1918, however, had been a great one in a spiritual sense. The American people had gone to war hoping for accomplishments not possible at the moment, such as making the world safe for democracy. To Europeans this latter phrase was a slogan but to Americans for a brief period it became a reality. When that reality faded and disappeared in the petty quarrels of the Paris Peace Conference there came immense weariness with internationalism, and it could be said of Americans as of Europeans that "Never in the lifetime of men now living has the universal element in the soul of man burnt so dimly." Americans were ready to retreat from participation in the peace settlement, and they were ready for the general retreat into isolation which characterized the next twenty years of their diplomatic history.

3. Lodge versus Wilson

The withdrawal of the United States from Europe after the first World War became obvious when the Senate in 1919–1920 refused three times to advise and consent to ratification of the Treaty of Versailles. Here was a public announcement to all the world that the American government would be strictly an onlooker while the nations of Europe attempted to repair the war's grave damage to their political, social, economic, and intellectual life. Yet an acute observer in the United States might have predicted this American withdrawal from "foreign entanglements" long before it became obvious in the Senate's refusal of the Treaty of Versailles. There had been premonitory rumbles from the retired sage at Oyster Bay, Theodore Roosevelt, who during the months of American participation in the war had been unable, despite initial resolves, to refrain from public jeers and sarcasm at what he described as Wilson's idealism. TR had thought that Wilson during the period of neutrality had been a pacifist, afraid to fight. Roosevelt in his private correspondence during the war vented his spleen without stint or limit (to borrow a Wilsonian phrase). "That skunk in the White House"—so he was heard to describe the president over the telephone to a friend. Roosevelt still had a hold of the affection of the American people, and his opposition boded ill for Wilson's program. When Wilson, upon the

advice of party leaders, broke the wartime domestic political truce
by asking for return of a Democratic Congress in the November 1918
elections, the lid was off, and the president's party was defeated at
the polls.

Wilson contributed in other ways to the undoing of his international
program. Upon American entrance into the war he made a serious
error in pitching his war speeches on too high an emotional level.
His oratorical gifts ran away with him, and he made the fight too
much of a struggle for justice and morality and right principle. These
had been the values to which American politicians since the beginning of the republic had appealed. These were such slogans as could
always stir the idealistic American electorate. But the American
people by 1917 sadly needed tuition in the facts of international life,
namely, that a great power must act affirmatively in the world, that
to protect its interests it could not enter the world balance of power
only when it felt like it but would have to keep military weight constantly in the balance, in time of peace as well as of world war. Wilson
talked, instead, about moral responsibility and legal rectitude. He was
so incautious as to announce on one famous occasion that the balance
of power was forever discredited. Likewise he stressed during the
war the importance of a parliament of man without inquiring carefully into mankind's willingness to depend on such an assemblage for
settlement of international disputes.

Still, the most important factor militating against the continued
participation of the United States in the work of world peace after
1918, a factor more important than any mistakes that Woodrow
Wilson made, was the traditionally isolationist outlook of the American people toward foreign affairs. The American people, as mentioned, lacked international political training. Although the intellectual upbringing of Americans had been intensely political, politics
always stopped at the water's edge. The generality of Americans did
not know about the sort of politics that went on between nations.
The century which separated Waterloo from the World War had
allowed Americans to engage in a Civil War and develop half a
continent without serious threat of foreign intervention. In 1919,
having "paid their debt to Lafayette," the American soldiers returned
home and divested themselves not merely of their uniforms but of all
friendly remembrance of the cause for which they had fought. The
World War to them became an unpleasant interlude, an interruption

to the normal processes of life in the United States. The traditional American public attitude of isolation could easily reassert itself in 1919. There had been no intellectual preparation for what the war-time president's critics soon were describing as Wilsonian inter-nationalism.

The role of Senator Henry Cabot Lodge in the Senate's rejection of the Versailles Treaty becomes intelligible when one realizes the forces which lay behind him and which he so well represented. To say that Lodge was the architect of America's post-Versailles isola-tion would be a gross misstatement. The senior senator from Massa-chusetts stood for traditional nineteenth-century ways of American international behavior. He represented the post-Waterloo belief that in foreign affairs America must have a free hand. Lodge loved England, and visited many friends there on his summer trips abroad. He was happy to see the United States enter the war on the side of England against Germany in 1917. After the danger of German power disappeared he wished to return the United States to the time-honored policy of the free hand. The leading element in Lodge's attitude to-ward the League and the Treaty of Versailles was traditionalism. The treaty's failure in the Senate was a result of this prevailing intellectual current. No single man or small group of men could change it. Po-litical leaders, if they wished to stay snugly in office, had to act within it, and this is what Henry Cabot Lodge did.

At the outset of the anti-League battle, Lodge found considerable support in the Senate for his stand against the treaty. The presi-dent's war leadership had taken away much of Congress's usual power, and the senators were aching to display their importance. Wilson had failed to consult congressional leaders while drawing up the Covenant in Paris. He had gravely offended the Senate by refusing to appoint a member of that body, preferably a Republican member, to the peace commission. Lodge found animosity toward Wilson among his colleagues, and just before midnight on March 3, 1919, the day before the session of Congress was to end, he read to the Senate in a clever maneuver a round-robin statement signed by thirty-seven Republican senators and senators-elect (two other Republican sena-tors added their names by telegraph the next day) which advised that "the constitution of the league of nations in the form now pro-posed . . . should not be accepted by the United States," and that the proposal for a league of nations should be taken up for discussion at Paris only after the conference had negotiated peace terms with Germany.

This was a clear ultimatum to Wilson from more than one-third of the Senate's membership. The president ignored it.

Meanwhile, and as a result of the November 1918 elections, the Republican Party organized Congress. By a majority of 49 to 47 (there would have been a tie if Henry Ford had won the close contest in Michigan) the Republicans organized the Senate in 1919, and Henry Cabot Lodge became chairman of the foreign relations committee. Of the committee's membership of seventeen, ten were Republicans, among them six irreconcilably anti-League senators. The irreconcilables would dominate the Republican majority and thus the committee itself. With Lodge as chairman the committee could determine the conditions under which the Senate received and considered the Covenant. Ex-President Taft and many others individuals accused Lodge of stacking the committee against the Covenant. To this accusation the senator neither at the time nor later made a reply. In his posthumous book, *The Senate and the League of Nations*, his comment was that "It will be seen at once that this was a strong committee and such as the existing conditions demanded."

By the spring of 1919, with the situation in the Senate ominous, two moderate Republican leaders, former President Taft and President A. Lawrence Lowell of Harvard, cabled Wilson in Paris that it was essential to soothe the Senate's feelings. This soothing, they believed, might be done by a few small changes in the Covenant, including a Monroe Doctrine reservation. Wilson managed, though with some difficulty, to insert such a reservation in the Covenant's Article 21. But needless to add, no small changes would accommodate Lodge, who wished for a complete return to traditionalism in American foreign policy.

The tactics of the senator were to prolong the preliminaries and to delay the Senate's advice and consent to the treaty until American opinion came around to his side. Lodge in the summer of 1919 studiously procrastinated when the treaty in the course of senatorial procedure came first before the committee on foreign relations. He consumed two weeks reading the document aloud. Most of his colleagues absented themselves from the committee chamber, and on at least one occasion the committee clerk left the room, leaving Lodge reading to himself. He then arranged public hearings, an unprecedented step in consideration of a treaty, which required six additional weeks. The senator obtained for the foreign relations committee an invitation to the White House for a conference with the president, and there on August 19, 1919 Wilson answered senatorial questions for three hours. Lodge's tactics finally drove Wilson into a rash act, a speaking tour for the treaty—and this in turn had a most unexpected result.

In September of 1919, in twenty-two days, the president delivered thirty-six speeches averaging about an hour in length, traveled more than eight thousand miles, and stood up in a swaying automobile during a dozen parades. Sixty-two years old, worn by illness and the rigors of negotiation at Paris (not to speak of the requirements of twenty months of war leadership), Wilson was unable to stand the strain and collapsed at Pueblo, Colorado on September 26, 1919. His assistants hurried him back to the White House, where he suffered a paralytic stroke.

Had Wilson died that glorious night in Pueblo, while cheer after cheer swept through the huge auditorium, he would have met a hero's end. Ex-Senator Beveridge, one of the president's most vicious critics, later remarked that if this had happened Wilson would have become a greater martyr than Lincoln. His beloved Covenant would have passed the Senate. Instead there came the collapse and the stroke, and for seven and one-half months the president lay almost helpless in the White House. The stroke thickened his speech, and withered the left side of his face and body. "My God, the President is paralyzed!" Dr. Grayson cried as he burst out of the sick man's room shortly after the attack. Mrs. Wilson later wrote that "for days life hung in the balance." For weeks and months, leaders of the administration could approach the ailing man only through his wife, who took it upon herself to decide what specific written communications she would pass in to her husband. The president did not meet the cabinet during this time, and in his sickness grew suspicious of everyone. He broke with Colonel House, and cavalierly dismissed Secretary Lansing. During his illness the Treaty of Versailles met defeat in the Senate.

4. *The Defeat of the Treaty*

The position on the treaty taken by the so-called irreconcilable senators, led by William E. Borah of Idaho, was of critical importance.

The irreconcilables had pledged themselves to do everything in their power to achieve the treaty's rejection. They became known as bitter-enders and the Battalion of Death; according to a recent critic they possessed a state of mind compounded of "varying amounts of traditionalism, ignorance, bigotry, fear of the untried, prejudice, personal pique, partisanship, political ambition, and a natural bent for destructiveness." Their chief Borah, had never been outside of the United States, but this had not prevented him from becoming a senatorial expert on foreign affairs. Indeed, the "lion of Idaho" succeeded to the chairmanship of the committee on foreign relations when Lodge died in 1924. Borah was enormously effective on a rostrum, and was considered one of the orators of his generation. His talents unfortunately seemed always on the side of obstruction and hypercriticism, and although an honest individual (he was the only irreconcilable for whom Wilson retained respect) he was much given to making debaters' points against whatever subject he was opposing. It was the Idahoan's propensity for contrariness which prompted Washington wits to comment, when they saw Borah taking his daily horseback ride in Rock Creek Park, that it was marvelous that horse and rider were both going in the same direction. In the fight over the Treaty of Versailles the Idaho senator was uncompromising. He declared that if he had his way the League of Nations would be "twenty thousand leagues under the sea." He wanted "this treacherous and treasonable scheme" "buried in hell," and insisted that he would not change his mind if Jesus Christ himself came to earth and pleaded for the Covenant. Borah's forensic gifts were ably seconded by the leather-lunged Senator Hiram Johnson of California, by the narrow legal erudition of Senator (formerly Secretary of State) Philander C. Knox of Pennsylvania, the wit of Senator George Moses of New Hampshire, and the active mentality of Senator Frank Brandegee of Connecticut. There was also the demagogy of Senator James A. ("Jim") Reed of Missouri, a Democrat. Only a dozen or so in number, the irreconcilables were formidable in ability.

Their strength provided Senator Lodge with an excuse, if he needed one, for organizing the defeat of the Treaty of Versailles. Lodge maintained at the beginning of his senatorial maneuvering against the treaty that he was in reality in favor of the treaty and the League of Nations if these two Siamese twins (the Covenant was part of the treaty) could be given suitable reservations during their passage through the Senate. Most of the Republican senators, except Porter

J. McCumber of North Dakota who sided with the Democrats, favored either mild or strong reservations. Lodge was ostensibly a strong reservationist. But as majority leader he had to keep all Republicans—mild, strong, and irreconcilable—under control, a difficult task because of the margin, two votes, by which the party had organized the Senate. The irreconcilables led by Borah were threatening to jump the party traces.

Borah had never been a reliable party man. The nightmare of 1912 when Theodore Roosevelt split the Republican Party and gave the election to Wilson was ever in Lodge's memory. Borah and the other irreconcilables in 1919 threatened the elderly majority leader with a secession from the party if they did not have their way in the Versailles Treaty. On one occasion Lodge complained that certain senators were browbeating him by addressing him in language which "no man of my age should be obliged to hear." According to Lodge's most recent biographer the Massachusetts senator came to an agreement with Borah. If Borah and his fellow irreconcilables would support the party during the preliminary voting on reservations they could vote against the treaty's final passage. If the treaty failed they would achieve their objective, and if it passed it would be less objectionable than the Wilsonian proposal of a treaty without reservations.

In retrospect the motives of the several Republican factions in the Senate appear rather clearly. The irreconcilables wished for the total defeat of the treaty, including of course the League of Nations. Theirs was the pure, unadulterated traditionalist stand in international affairs. As for those senators who were willing to vote for the treaty with reservations of varying severity—the strong reservationists and mild reservationists—they too were traditionalists, although the wartime Wilsonian infection had influenced their judgment. They feared for what they would have loosely described as American rights and wished distinct reservations of American sovereignty. Senator Warren G. Harding, a strong reservationist, was typical of this feeling when he asserted that "I could no more support mild reservations that I could support mild Americanism." The task of Lodge as Republican manager of the Senate was clear: it was to avoid at all costs a party split. Given Lodge's traditionalist views of American policy and a personal dislike he harbored for Wilson, it should have been obvious that he would almost welcome the chance to hold his party together at the expense of the Treaty of Versailles.

By the end of the summer the foreign relations committee under Lodge's leadership had therefore produced thirty-eight amendments and four reservations, later boiled down into fourteen reservations. The United States, according to these reservations, in case of its withdrawal from the League reserved to itself sole judgment as to whether it had fulfilled its obligations under the Covenant. The American government could not accept a territorial mandate under the League without vote of Congress. The Council and Assembly could not consider questions which pertained to the domestic jurisdiction of the United States. The Monroe Doctrine was "wholly outside the jurisdiction of the League of Nations" and entirely unaffected by any provision of the Treaty of Versailles. America withheld its assent to the Shantung settlement, and reserved complete liberty of action. Congress might enact, if it wished, a law in regard to appointment of American representatives to the League. The reparations commission of the League would have no right to interfere with trade between the United States and Germany, without the consent of Congress. American expenses in the League would be subject to an act of appropriation by Congress. The committee asked for the right to increase armaments of the United States, under any League plan of disarmament, in case the United States were threatened with invasion or engaged in war. Nationals of covenant-breaking states, residing in the United States, might continue their normal relations. The American government must have the right to regulate private debts, property, rights and interests of citizens of the United States. Assent was withheld to the section of the Versailles Treaty setting up an international labor organization, until Congress voted approval. The United States was to be protected against any unequal vote, in the League, of the British empire.

In particular Lodge's committee criticized Article 10 of the Covenant, which the committee considered a dangerous departure from the vital principles of American foreign policy. Lodge chose to see foreshadowed in Article 10 the end of a safe and wise tradition. The nation had never consented to commit itself in advance to international actions except in obvious cases such as intervention by foreign powers in the Western Hemisphere; but in Article 10, according to Lodge, the nation would bind itself to decisions by an alien body sitting in Europe. Yet the perils of Article 10 were largely imaginary.

A close reading of the Covenant revealed the article as less than dangerous. League members undertook to "respect and preserve" (but not specifically to guarantee) "as against external aggression" (*aggression* was a difficult word to define) each other's "territorial integrity and existing political independence" (what this meant was not altogether clear). Nonetheless Lodge's committee balked at Article 10. The senator's close friend, Elihu Root, pointed out that so far as concerned the phrase "respect and preserve" he was willing to agree to "respect," but that "to preserve" was tantamount to "guarantee." President Wilson, on the other hand, declared Article 10 the "heart of the Covenant" and insisted that any reservation of the article was utterly unacceptable.

On November 19, 1919 the Senate voted twice on the treaty. The first roll call was with the fourteen Lodge reservations. The vote was 39 for, 55 against (the irreconcilables voting with the Democrats). A second roll call on the treaty without reservations resulted in 38 for, 53 against. Both with and without reservations the treaty failed to obtain a simple majority. In a third and final vote on the treaty on March 19, 1920, after there had been added to the Lodge reservations a fifteenth reservation favoring the independence of Ireland, the treaty failed again—49 for, 35 against—lacking seven votes of the necessary two-thirds majority.

It was Woodrow Wilson's misfortune, unlike his counterparts in American history, Lincoln and Franklin D. Roosevelt, to live on into the final act of his era, and when he died in 1924 he had seen his handiwork discredited. One of his last moves as president was to insist that the election of 1920 be a "great and solemn referendum" on the League and the treaty. Two Ohio newspaper editors, Harding and James M. Cox, competed for the presidency in 1920, and the election was a travesty of Wilson's solemn referendum. Cox with courage came out in favor of the League, but Harding's managers played safe by taking the advice of the wily Senator Boies Penrose of Pennsylvania, who told them to "Keep Warren at home. Don't let him make any speeches. If he goes out on a tour, somebody's sure to ask him questions, and Warren's just the sort of damn fool that'll try to answer them." The amiable Harding confined himself to "bloviations" (as he liked to describe his campaign oratory and statement making) from his front porch in Marion, Ohio. It was said that during the campaign he took fourteen different positions on the

League. It was in one of his speeches that he accidentally made the
famous declaration that "America's present need is not heroics but
healing; not nostrums but normalcy; not revolution but restoration."
In vain did thirty-one prominent Republicans, among them Nicholas
Murray Butler, Henry L. Stimson, President Lowell, and ex-president
Taft, issue a manifesto near the end of the campaign advising that
Harding favor the League of Nations. The only result of this be-
lated effort to remind the candidate of the large pro-League faction
within the Republican Party seems to have been an inclusion of a
favorable reference to the League in the first draft of Harding's inaugural address; but, so the story goes, Mrs. Harding blue-penciled
the reference during one of her revisions of the text.

Such was the fate of the great crusade which had begun for
America in 1917. "We have torn up Wilsonism by the roots," Lodge
rejoiced after learning of Harding's unprecedented majority of seven
million votes. The hopes of humanitarians that the World War would
inaugurate what Lord Robert Cecil called a "great experiment" in
keeping the peace, that the war to end war would not have been
fought in vain, disappeared when the traditionally isolationist views
of the American people reasserted themselves after the war. The
League of Nations, President-elect Harding told his fellow citizens in
his victory speech, was deceased. "You just didn't want a surrender
of the United States of America; you wanted America to go under
American ideals. That's why you didn't care for the League, which
is now deceased." Senator Lodge announced, more bluntly, that the
League was dead. The United States under the Harding administration terminated the technical state of war with Germany by resolution
of Congress, July 2, 1921, and signed a Treaty of Berlin on August
25 confirming to the American government all rights stipulated in
the Treaty of Versailles. Similar treaties followed with Austria
(August 24) and Hungary (August 29), and a series of later pacts
established diplomatic relations with Turkey and with the seven new
states which had emerged from the war in Eastern Europe.

ADDITIONAL READING

The literature of American diplomatic history has certain marked
"bulges" in periods that at the time or later were controversial, and such

is the case for the first World War. Throughout the 1920's and 1930's and during the second World War there was interest in the failure of the Treaty of Versailles in the Senate and there was concern over the problem of world organization; both of these have reflected themselves in the literature. Likewise during the 1930's, as the second World War approached, much interest was taken in the period of American neutrality that preceded entrance into war in 1917. Woodrow Wilson, the man and statesman, has continued to excite controversy; Wilson's career, marked as it was by large successes and by final defeat, has stirred the interest of biographers. For reasons such as these the era of the first World War has produced an array of books and articles comparable to writing on the Civil War and American entrance into the second World War.

Books dealing with the outbreak of the first World War in Europe are innumerable. Heading the literature are the volumes by Sidney B. Fay, *Origins of the World War* (2 vols., New York, 1929) and Bernadotte Schmitt, *The Coming of the War* (2 vols., New York, 1930). Schmitt has brought his account up to date in "July 1914: Thirty Years After," *Journal of Modern History*, vol. 16 (1944), 169–204. A new study is Luigi Albertini, *The Origins of the War of 1914* (3 vols., London, 1952–1957). A popular account of the coming of the war is Ludwig Reiners, *The Lamps Went Out in Europe* (New York, 1955). Two fascinating biographies of prewar diplomats are Harold Nicolson, *Portrait of a Diplomatist* (New York, 1930), a study of Nicolson's father, Sir Arthur Nicolson; and Charles W. Porter, *The Career of Théophile Delcassé* (Philadelphia, 1936).

A general account of America's involvement in the war, unsympathetic to the Wilson administration, is Walter Millis, *Road to War: America, 1914–1917* (Boston, 1935), a most interesting and able work. C. C. Tansill, *America Goes to War* (Boston, 1938) is a more detailed anti-Wilson study. A general account of America's involvement appears in P. W. Slosson, *The Great Crusade and After: 1914–1928* (New York, 1931). The best work of American scholarship—and this is proved partly by the fact that its author's interpretation of the period has held up remarkably through the years—is the three volumes by Charles Seymour, the dean of writers in this field: *Woodrow Wilson and the World War* (New York, 1921); *American Diplomacy during the World War* (Baltimore, 1934), still the most balanced study available; and *American Neutrality: 1914–1917* (New Haven, 1935), stressing the importance of the submarine in the declaration of war against Germany. Arthur S. Link, *Woodrow Wilson and the Progressive Era: 1910–1917* (New York, 1954) is the latest view on its subject, in essential agreement with Seymour.

Richard W. Leopold, "The Problem of American Intervention, 1917: An Historical Retrospect," *World Politics*, vol. 2 (1950), 405–425 is the best introduction to books dealing with American policy in 1914–17. Merle E. Curti, "Bryan and World Peace," *Smith College Studies in History*, is sympathetic to that statesman. For Bryan's successor see *War*

Memoirs of Robert Lansing (Indianapolis, 1935); together with the sketches by Julius W. Pratt, "Robert Lansing," in Samuel F. Bemis, ed., *The American Secretaries of State and Their Diplomacy* (10 vols., New York, 1929), vol. 10, 47–175; and Daniel M. Smith, "Robert Lansing and the Formulation of American Neutrality Policies, 1914–1915," *Mississippi Valley Historical Review*, vol. 43 (1956–1957), 59–81. As for the involved question of neutral rights, an able account is R. G. Albion and J. B. Pope, *Sea Lanes in Wartime* (New York, 1942). The United States after entrance into the war reversed its practice on neutral rights and duties, if not its position; for this story see Thomas A. Bailey, *The Policy of the United States toward the Neutrals: 1917–1918* (Baltimore, 1942). W. E. Lingelbach, "England and Neutral Trade," *Military Historian and Economist*, vol. 2 (1917), 153–178 is an excellent account, unfortunately published in a defunct periodical. For the most spectacular event of the neutrality era see Thomas A. Bailey, "The Sinking of the *Lusitania*," *American Historical Review*, vol. 41 (1935–1936), 54–73, based on Commander Schwieger's diary and other materials; and more recently the popularization by A. A. and Mary Hoehling, *The Last Voyage of the Lusitania* (New York, 1956; available in paperback).

There was much concern in the United States during the 1920's and 1930's over whether or not the nation was talked into war in 1914–1917 via propaganda from the Allies. This concern, as we now see, overrated the effect of propaganda. Typical of the genre is James Duane Squires, *British Propaganda at Home and in the United States from 1914 to 1917* (Cambridge, Mass., 1935). More interesting and worthwhile are such studies as James M. Read, *Atrocity Propaganda: 1914–1919* (New Haven, 1941). For its special subject, see Armin Rappaport, *The British Press and Wilsonian Neutrality* (Stanford, 1951).

An excellent little volume which deserves close and careful reading is Samuel R. Spencer, Jr., *Decision for War: 1917* (Rindge, N.H., 1953). Spencer examines the importance of such events as the Zimmermann Note and Germany's sinking of the British liner *Laconia*. E. H. Buehrig's *Woodrow Wilson and the Balance of Power* (Bloomington, Ind., 1955) considers the possibility that Wilson came out for war because of Germany's threat to the balance of power in Europe and the world.

In the perspective of our own time American wartime relations with Russia have appeared far larger in importance than they did in 1917–1918, and here the student may consult the study presently in progress by George F. Kennan, entitled *Soviet-American Relations: 1917–1920*. The first volume, *Russia Leaves the War* (Princeton, 1956), won the Pulitzer prize in history; the second is *The Decision to Intervene* (Princeton, 1958). On this general subject of Russian-American relations see also Betty M. Unterberger, *America's Siberian Expedition: 1918–1920* (Durham, N.C., 1956).

The best introduction to Wilson books is Richard L. Watson, Jr., "Woodrow Wilson and His Interpreters," *Mississippi Valley Historical*

Review, vol. 44 (1957–1958), 207–236, an expert analysis. Robert H. Ferrell, "Woodrow Wilson: Man and Statesman," *Review of Politics*, vol. 18 (1956), 131–145 contains an appraisal of Wilson that is not elaborated in this text. Biographically the best studies of Wilson have been done by Arthur S. Link, *Wilson: The Road to the White House* (Princeton, 1947) and *Wilson: The New Freedom* (Princeton, 1956), the first two volumes in a masterful portrayal of Wilson and his times; and Arthur Walworth, *Woodrow Wilson* (2 vols., New York, 1957), the best finished biography. See also the short biography by J. A. Garraty, *Woodrow Wilson* (New York, 1956), a beautifully written essay. An early biography, still attractive, is William Allen White's *Woodrow Wilson* (Boston, 1924). See in addition H. C. F. Bell, *Woodrow Wilson and the People* (Garden City, N.Y., 1945).

The centennial of Wilson's birth in 1956 inspired several notable books about Wilson, among them John Wells Davidson, *A Crossroads of Freedom: The 1912 Campaign Speeches* (New Haven, 1956); Em Bowles Alsop, ed., *The Greatness of Woodrow Wilson* (New York, 1956), a series of essays by authorities; Edward H. Buehrig, ed., *Wilson's Foreign Policy in Perspective* (Bloomington, 1957), a splendid set of five essays; Arthur P. Dudden, ed., *Woodrow Wilson and the World of Today* (Philadelphia, 1957), essays by Link, Eric F. Goldman, and William L. Langer; Arthur S. Link, *Wilson the Diplomatist: A Look at His Major Foreign Policies* (Baltimore, 1957) by the leading student of Wilson and his times; and Alexander L. and Juliette L. George, *Woodrow Wilson and Colonel House: A Personality Study* (New York, 1956), a plausible psychological analysis.

Books on the peace conference and the Senate's defeat of the Treaty of Versailles could fill libraries, and one can only list a few of the obvious titles. First in the order of events would come Harry R. Rudin's excellent *Armistice: 1918* (New Haven, 1944). A summary of peace-conference literature appears in Paul Birdsall, *Versailles Twenty Years After* (New York, 1941), and because the literature has not changed greatly since its publication this book continues to be useful. Thomas A. Bailey's *Woodrow Wilson and the Lost Peace* (New York, 1944) and *Woodrow Wilson and the Great Betrayal* (New York, Macmillan, 1946), combined in one volume in 1947 under the title *Wilson and the Peacemakers*, is an able synthesis. Stephen Bonsal's *Unfinished Business* (Garden City, 1944) and *Suitors and Suppliants* (New York, 1946) set out Colonel Bonsal's experiences from his diary. Another diary, with comment, is Harold Nicolson, *Peacemaking* (Boston, 1933), an admirable account. John Maynard Keynes's *Economic Consequences of the Peace* (New York, 1920) has the famous characterizations of the Big Three and some acid comments on the peace. L. L. Gerson, *Woodrow Wilson and the Rebirth of Poland: 1914–1920* (New Haven, 1953) explores this complex subject. G. B. Noble, *Policies and Opinions at Paris: 1919* (New York, 1935) is an important work. Details appear in Hunter Miller, *The Drafting of the*

Covenant (2 vols., New York, 1928).

On the fate of the Treaty of Versailles in the United States, see Dexter Perkins, "Woodrow Wilson's Tour," in Daniel Aaron, ed., *America in Crisis* (New York, 1952); W. Stull Holt, *Treaties Defeated by the Senate* (Baltimore, 1933), chapter 10; Henry Cabot Lodge, *The Senate and the League of Nations* (New York, 1925), a long apology, buttressed by appendixes and extensive quotations, with personal comment on Wilson; Selig Adler, *The Isolationist Impulse* (New York, 1957); R. J. Bartlett, *The League to Enforce Peace* (Chapel Hill, N.C. 1944), concerning the principal private American organization for a league of nations; F. P. Walters, *A History of the League of Nations* (2 vols., London, 1952).

For statesmen and influential people of the time there are such volumes as J. M. Blum, *Joe Tumulty and the Wilson Era* (Boston, 1951), on Wilson's private secretary; André Tardieu, *France and America* (Boston, 1927); Allan Nevins, *Henry White* (New York, 1930); C. G. Bowers, *Beveridge and the Progressive Era* (New York, 1932); P. C. Jessup, *Elihu Root* (2 vols., New York, 1938); R. W. Leopold, *Elihu Root and the Conservative Tradition* (Boston, 1954); C. O. Johnson, *Borah of Idaho* (Toronto, 1936); J. A. Garraty, *Henry Cabot Lodge* (New York, 1953); H. F. Pringle, *Life and Times of William Howard Taft* (2 vols., New York, 1939); Charles Seymour, *Intimate Papers of Colonel House* (4 vols., Boston, 1926–28); John M. Blum, *The Republican Roosevelt* (Cambridge, Mass., 1954). The valedictory of the League fight appears in Samuel Hopkins Adams, *Incredible Era: The Life and Times of Warren Gamaliel Harding* (Boston, 1939).

CHAPTER

☆ 13 ☆

The Twenties

1. The United States and Geneva

Joseph C. Grew as ambassador to Japan in the 1930's became one of America's most trusted diplomats, but earlier in his life when he was not so well known and was American minister to Switzerland in the 1920's he had to be extremely careful not to be seen near, and of course not in, the League of Nations buildings at Geneva. Once a correspondent of the Chicago *Tribune* found Grew near the entrance to that den of internationalists, and the minister spent several uncomfortable days until arrival of the Paris papers showed that the meeting had passed unnoticed.

Charles Evans Hughes, President Harding's secretary of state, for a while allowed League of Nations communications to the American government to be received at the State Department without acknowledgment.

The United States during the 1920's, and this was true also of most of the 1930's, was in the world but not of it. American foreign policy was devoted to the principle of peace, and the republic did not belong to the chief world organization dedicated to that ideal. As years passed and the heat of battle over the Covenant of the League of Nations subsided, there was an increasing interest in the nonpolitical activities of the Geneva institution. The first American flirtation with the League was over restricting the world-wide opium traffic, and a delegation from the United States, arriving in Geneva in 1924, gradually learned to take part in this cause, although not before it on one occasion temporarily walked out of a committee meeting, "acting on motives of delicacy," that is, fear lest its presence imply American recognition of the League. There followed a careful participation in such other League activities as regulation of the international traffic in arms (1925), a communications and transit conference (1927), a general economic conference (1927), abolition of import and export restrictions (1927), economic statistics (1928), counterfeiting of currency (1929), codification of international law (1930), and buoyage and lighting of coasts (1930). These activities, of course, were nonpolitical, unconnected with the large problems of international affairs.

One of the more notable American activities at Geneva was membership in the preparatory commission for the Geneva Disarmament Conference, to the meetings of which the United States sent a delegation. The preparatory commission commenced its dreary life in 1926, incident to Germany's joining the League in that same year. The duty of the commission was to draw up a draft treaty on disarmament which the nations would debate in the future conference. The commission's meetings turned into technical controversies against some types of armament and in favor of other presumably less aggressive varieties. During five years of wrangling a subcommittee alone used 3,750,000 sheets of typescript, enough to permit the commission's Polish or Swedish delegations to walk home on a path made of committee paper. Finally in 1930 the preparatory commission produced a draft convention which upon the meeting of the General Disarmament Conference at Geneva in 1932 was promptly scrapped.

But in the annals of United States co-operation with the League, the most important issue was whether or not the United States should join the World Court. The League's World Court, more properly known as the Permanent Court of International Justice, has often been confused with the Permanent Court of Arbitration established in 1901 after the first Hague Peace Conference. The Hague court was not permanent, but comprised only a panel of international jurors from which disputing nations might draw for arbitration of controversies. The World Court consisted of a group of judges who sat during court sessions at The Hague and passed upon cases brought before them. Any state, whether a member of the League or not, could belong to the World Court by subscribing to its protocol. There was little danger to national sovereignty in joining because the jurisdiction of the court was always optional.

The idea of a world-wide international law presided over by a court has always found favor among legal-minded American diplomats, as well as among many private American citizens interested in world peace. President Harding made the first gesture toward American adherence to the World Court protocol when he commended it to the Senate in February 1923. Three years later, on January 27, 1926, the Senate approved, 76 to 17, but with five reservations of which the last was the most important: ". . . nor shall it [the Court], without the consent of the United States, entertain any request for an advisory opinion touching any dispute or question in which the United States has or claims an interest." This was a singularly foolish reservation, but it arose out of the Senate's concern about approaching the untouchable League of Nations. Why an American judge on the World Court could not have given a little advice to the League, once in a while, was difficult to understand. Of course a large political question might by some odd chance come before the court—and did, in fact, when the question of *Anschluss*, in the form of joining Austria to Germany in a customs union, was taken to the court in 1931. But if the United States had ventured an opinion in this matter, would it have made any difference in the broad course of European and world history?

The Senate in 1926 believed that for an American judge to give an advisory opinion would make a large difference. The court question continued wearily on. The elder statesman Elihu Root, who had taken part in 1920 in drawing up the World Court protocol, tried to draw up a compromise between the Senate and the forty-eight nations members of the court, and at the age of 84 he made a trip to Geneva in 1929 to revise the protocol. President Herbert Hoover in 1930—without much enthusiasm but, so one observer reported, to enable "old Elihu Root to die happy"—resubmitted the court proposal to the Senate with the Root compromise. There the matter languished until 1935, when Hoover was gone, Franklin Roosevelt was president, and the Senate was roused to action. But an eleventh-hour campaign of opposition led by William Randolph Hearst and the Detroit "radio priest," Father Charles E. Coughlin, deluged Washington with tens of thousands of protesting telegrams, and on January 29, 1935, the court failed to receive a two-thirds vote, 52 in favor, 36 opposed. A shift of seven votes would have saved the day.

The court issue had engendered a long debate during the fifteen years it was before the Senate, and in retrospect one must lament the energy expended on so minor a cause. Some individuals, such as Elihu Root, devoted almost all their time to the court; yet the issue was never as important as that. The American ideal of an international court could never in the 1920's and 1930's have been realized fully, given the weakness of international law. Perhaps the World Court approach to international order was logically right, and thus should have had more hearing than it received. There is much to say for so rational an approach to foreign relations, and it may be a mistake to write it off completely as a waste of time. Still, in terms of the customs and habits of nations in the 1920's the World Court was not a practical measure for bringing about world peace, and an effective court may well prove to be nothing but a noble dream in the power-dominated twentieth century. After establishment of the United Nations a second World Court appeared, this time known as the International Court of Justice instead of the Permanent Court of International Justice. All members of the United Nations are members of the new world court, which is entitled to give advisory opinions on legal questions to the General Assembly and Security Council. Little has been heard yet from the court or its activities.

One should not conclude this account of American co-operation with the League without mentioning the so-called war debts, a discordant factor in post-1918 United States relations with Europe. Though not directly connected with the League, the question served to raise a wall of antagonism between the United States and its debtor nations which were virtually all League members.

During the war the Allies had stretched to the utmost their private credit in the United States; when in 1917 the limit of this was in sight they turned to the American government, which freely lent money raised by the liberty- and victory-loan drives. Some seven billion dollars was advanced to the European powers in this way, and approximately three billion more was included in loans after the end of hostilities. After the war the debtors halted their interest payments on these public loans pending readjustment downward of the interest rate, originally five per cent. Congress in 1922 created the World War Foreign Debt Commission, which between 1923 and 1930 re-negotiated the debts to an average interest rate of 2.135 per cent, and made the obligations payable over sixty-two years. The principal plus interest over that period would have totaled more than twenty-two billion dollars. Terms extended to the debtors varied somewhat according to ability to pay; the British government in 1923 was allowed a reduction of interest to 3.3 per cent, whereas France (1926) received a new rate of 1.6 per cent and Italy (1925) 0.4 per cent.

It was comparatively easy to speak of debts and interest rates, and everything appeared to be settled by the mid-1920's, but the American government gradually discovered that signature of renegotiated notes by the debtor nations did not mean intention to pay. Part of the difficulty of payment consisted in problems of exchange. To obtain dollar exchange it was necessary for debtor countries to sell goods or services directly or indirectly to the United States, and the alternative was to send gold shipments. The latter interfered with the "cover" for domestic currencies. As for the former course, it was impossible to send large supplies of goods over the American tariff, raised in 1922 and again in 1930. Postwar subsidies to American steamship companies deprived the European nations of one of their traditional ways of obtaining dollars. The nations might have paid the debts somehow if they really had wished to do so. They did not, and as is frequently the case, they united against their creditor. The French set the tone of this rebellion by rechristening Uncle Sam "*l'Oncle Shylock*," and Parisian editors instructed their cartoonists to change the stars on Sam's hat to dollar signs. There followed a series of diplomatic maneuvers by the debtors. The first move, taken before American renegotiation of the debts, linked debt payment to the payment of German reparations under the Treaty of Versailles.

According to Article 231 of that treaty, Germany was responsible for beginning the war, and Article 232 specified that Germany would have to pay the costs arising out of war damages, including both physical damages and pensions to Allied veterans. The German government in 1919 had no choice but to accept the Allied view of reparations. But collection from Germany soon began to grow difficult, partly because of the drastic postwar currency inflation which reached its peak in 1923 when the mark sank to $\frac{1}{4,000,000,000,000}$ of a dollar. The Germans made no effort to stop the inflation. They did not wish to pay reparations, were almost eager to appear as bankrupts. The French government, itself in financial difficulties, nonetheless hopefully maintained that *le Boche payera tout*, the Germans would pay for everything, including French obligations to the United States. The British government accepted the French idea of linking debts and reparations, and Foreign Secretary Balfour in a note of August 1, 1922 announced this formally as Britain's policy. "In no circumstances," he said, "do we propose to ask more from our debtors than is necessary to pay our creditors . . ." He was stating a consensus not only of London and Paris but of all America's debtors. It was to no avail that American presidents from Wilson to Hoover refused to connect debts with reparations, for the linkage had already been accomplished by the statesmen of Europe.

During the 1920's the flimsy structure of international payments to debtors and creditors preserved an appearance of stability. As holes appeared they were filled—by the Dawes Plan of 1924, which put German reparations on a plan of payment, and by the Young Plan of 1929, which reduced the original estimate of reparations, set in 1921 at thirty-three billion dollars, to eight billions payable over $58\frac{1}{2}$ years at an interest rate of $5\frac{1}{2}$ per cent (the total reparations bill under the Young Plan, including principal and interest, would have been about twenty-six billions). Although the United States had no official part in these two plans, they bore the names of American financiers serving privately, Charles G. Dawes and Owen D. Young. It was curious that the number of annual installments for reparations under the Young Plan equaled exactly the then remaining number of European debt installments to the United States as determined by the renegotiations of the Foreign Debt Commission.

The whole arrangement for debts and reparations finally broke under the weight of the Great Depression in the years after 1929. The United States in June–July 1931, under the leadership of President Hoover, negotiated a moratorium on both reparations and war debts. The purpose was to save American private loans in Germany which would have become uncollectible had reparations payments continued. The American banking structure was so weakened by the depression that for the bankers to lose their German collateral would have invited wholesale bank closures. Hoover in his moratorium was forced to acknowledge tacitly the connection between reparations and war debts, because the European nations would not consider temporarily giving up reparations unless the United States postponed debt payments. Unfortunately, despite the moratorium of mid-1931, American credits in Germany were frozen solid by the end of the summer, and American investors lost the large amounts of money which they had pumped into Germany after 1924, several billions. This money had far more than enabled Germany to make her annual reparations payments (part of which, of course, went circuitously to the United States as war debt installments). It is true that had American money not gone to Germany it would have passed into the New York stock market and been lost there, but American funds in the 1920's in Germany financed the re-equipment of large segments of German heavy industry, which a decade later as armament industries were turned against their benefactors by Hitler. Much American blood and treasure had to be expended during the second World War on the destruction of these industrial complexes. In the post-1945 period the United States has helped rebuild them once more.

When the American government by 1931 had come around to the European interpretation of debts and reparations—that they were inseparable—Germany declared itself unable to continue reparations. The European Allies, as we have seen, refused to agree to a moratorium on reparations unless the United States agreed to postpone payment of the war debts. Shortly thereafter the Allies in effect canceled reparations at Lausanne in June 1932 when they lowered the reparations bill to $750,000,000. This arrangement depended upon a renegotiation of the war debts by the United States, but the damage had been done. The Germans would pay no more; neither would the Allies. When for the first time after expiration of the Hoover Moratorium the semiannual debt installments fell due on December 15, 1932, Britain paid, as did Italy, Czechoslovakia, Finland, Latvia, and Lithuania. The rest of the nations defaulted or made useless gestures such as depositing part payments in blocked accounts. Finland was the only European country after 1933 which attempted to continue paying its debt.

In anger, Congress in 1934 passed the Johnson Debt Default Act, prohibiting government loans to nations in default of their debts. The neutrality laws of 1935–1939—about which more later—reiterated this prohibition of government loans to debtors. The Lend-Lease Act of 1941, on the other hand, allowed the president in a latitudinarian way to "lend, lease, or otherwise dispose of" government properties, and the neutrality laws were amended in 1942 so as not to apply when the United States was at war.

In surveying the sad history of the war debts one must conclude that when a loan is likely to be considered a gift, statesmen should accept the inevitable and make a virtue of necessity. This was the course followed in the second World War, but during the first war there was no precedent for such largesse, and time-honored custom dictated that nations should pay and not repudiate their debts. Under this then prevailing practice the United States asked for payment, and no other single postwar international policy pursued by the State Department met with such cordial approbation from American tax-payers. President Coolidge allegedly remarked of the European debtors that "They hired the money, didn't they?" To his generation he seemed uncommonly sensible. His countrymen failed to compre-hend the manner in which the war debts estranged them from their friends in Europe, who were already distrustful because of the American attitude toward the League of Nations. Any advantages accruing from the minor nonpolitical co-operation of the United States with the League were wiped out by the bad feeling engendered over the war debt and reparations issues. The bond of sentiment be-tween the United States and the democratic nations of Western Europe, a bond which in 1917–1918 had been so strong, was stretched in the postwar years almost to the breaking point. With the coming of a second World War the strained friendship of Americans and Europeans would require extraordinarily careful at-tention.

2. *Alternatives to the League—Treaties of Peaceful Settlement*

The United States during the 1920's, outside the League of Nations, felt that it had to do something for world peace. The Department of State tried to discover alternatives to the League which would be acceptable to the American people, and from this search came two general lines of procedure in American diplomacy—treaties for avoidance of war, and treaties of disarmament. These alternatives to the League were compatible with the American tradition of isolation and neutrality in international affairs. Insofar as they were not an adequate international program in the 1920's, they indicated that the traditional principles, isolation and neutrality, were inadequate. But treaties for avoidance of war and treaties of disarmament were the American prescription for world peace in the 1920's. They were even announced as cure-alls, and in the early 1930's Secretary of State

Cordell Hull supplemented them with his ideas of economic disarmament by lowering tariff barriers through reciprocal trade agreements. Such alternatives to the League of Nations, it is not unfair to add, had slight effect in promoting world peace.

What kind of treaties for the avoidance of war concerned the United States government after the refusal in 1919–1920 to adhere to the League of Nations? During the 1920's there flourished interest in a program of bilateral arbitration and conciliation treaties, and Secretary of State Frank B. Kellogg made some considerable effort to satisfy the popular demand for these pacts. He discarded in 1927 the arbitration formula first employed successfully at the State Department twenty years earlier by Elihu Root—a formula excepting from arbitration questions affecting the United States's vital interests, independence, or national honor, or disputes involving third parties—in favor of a formula reserving from arbitration only cases involving domestic questions. This was a dubious improvement, for a reservation of domestic jurisdiction was large enough to permit evading almost any arbitration. Even so, the Kellogg arbitration treaties sounded, at least, as if they were broader than the Root treaties.

Kellogg in 1928 likewise undertook to extend the United States's network of conciliation treaties as established before the first World War by Secretary William Jennings Bryan. These treaties, concluded between the United States and twenty-one foreign countries, provided that in event of questions threatening peaceful relations the signatories would wait a year before resorting to war. They were known as "cooling-off" treaties. During the cooling-off period a panel of commissioners, selected in advance, was to determine the difficulties at issue and attempt conciliation. Bryan when he had concluded the treaties in 1913–1915 had appointed commissions, but with lapse of time the personnel in many cases died and nothing was done about new appointments. Kellogg filled out the commissions again.

This move, like the change in formula for the arbitration treaties, had little effect upon the course of American diplomacy. No nation has ever resorted to the provisions of the Bryan concilation treaties. Nor is there a single recorded instance of the employment in an international controversy of the Root or Kellogg arbitration treaties. Some Americans interested in the obvious merits of arbitration and conciliation have comforted themselves that the existence of the innumerable Bryan, Root, and Kellogg treaties has served somehow to allay international tensions.

Perhaps one may be permitted an extra remark or two on the treaties of arbitration with which the United States so concerned itself in the 1920's and for some years prior to the first World War. This sort of agreement between nations, like the World Courts, had long appealed to Americans, one of the first notable uses of arbitral commissions being in Jay's Treaty in 1794. Later there was the Geneva arbitration of 1871, and at least the form of an arbitration in the Alaska boundary dispute of 1903. Then in 1899 there had assembled at The Hague the grand conference of the powers of Europe, including the United States, which established an international panel of arbitrators, the Permanent Court of Arbitration. A similar Hague Conference met in 1907 and passed among other measures the Porter Resolution, championed by the American delegate Horace Porter, allowing intervention by nations to collect a debt from another country if the delinquent state refused arbitration or an arbitral award. Other projects for arbitration might be mentioned, including two unsuccessful efforts at treaties, the Olney-Pauncefote Treaty of 1897 with Great Britain and the Taft arbitration treaties of 1911 with Britain and France. The former failed to obtain the advice and consent of the Senate and the treaties of 1911, while they passed the Senate, were killed by unacceptable reservations.

But when all was said and done, arbitration never seemed more than of minor and episodic importance in the history of American diplomacy. The idea, so attractive to the international lawyer and to the theoretical student of foreign relations, proved in practice an awkward way of conducting affairs between nations. Statesmen were almost never willing to try it unless, as in the Geneva arbitration, everything was rigged to obtain an agreed conclusion, in which case arbitration was a sort of smokescreen behind which crucial diplomatic moves were made.

Arbitration has faded away in international affairs, and little is heard about it at the mid-twentieth century. It has no attraction to present-day statesmen, nor to popular opinion. At the turn of the century American public opinion regarded arbitration highly. Theodore Roosevelt could say of the Root treaties that he "went into them because the general feeling of the country demanded it." Perhaps people in our own time have come to realize that the nineteenth century was the most renowned legal century of modern history, a moment when it seemed as if world order might be brought into reality, when rules for peaceful intercourse among nations appeared not as dreams but possibilities. Perhaps Americans today know that after the turn of the twentieth century, with its great power conflicts, its two world wars and threat of a third, arbitration has receded into the realm of dreams, along with so many other noble projects such as binding international law and a truly powerful world court. Arbitration had passed out of the area of practicality at the turn of the century, some years before Elihu Root took it up. The idea was *passé* indeed by the time of the secretaryship of Frank B. Kellogg in the 1920's.

But it was not through bilateral treaties of arbitration or conciliation that the United States made its largest effort for pacific settlement of international disputes after the World War, for this effort came at Paris in 1928 when Secretary Kellogg, together with representatives of the great powers, signed a treaty for renunciation of all war and for settlement of all disputes by peaceful means. Nearly every nation in the world eventually signed the Kellogg-Briand Pact, except a few such holdouts as Argentina, Bolivia, El Salvador, and Uruguay, together with five uninvited little countries—Andorra, Monaco, Morocco, Liechtenstein, and San Marino.

A dull topic for discussion, the Kellogg Pact: so it might seem if superficially considered. Actually it marked some of the shrewdest diplomacy one can discover in international relations in the twentieth century. Its roots went back to the first World War and France's position as a result of that war, when after the armistice of 1918 the French had what might be described as acute feelings of insecurity. France had triumphed over Germany during the war only by alliance with Britain, Russia, and the United States, and Frenchmen not without reason were worried about the future of their country, with a small birth rate and a population of about forty million as opposed to Germany's sixty-odd million and rapidly increasing population. France after 1918 suffered from "pactomania," a desire to sign promises with anyone in or out of Europe to protect *la patrie* on some untoward day when Germany might seek revenge for the first World War. In the quest for security the French foreign minister of the later 1920's, Aristide Briand, one of the cleverest diplomats of the past half century, offered to Secretary of State Kellogg a pact between France and the United States pledging both countries never to go to war against each other.

This offer by Briand was intensely embarrassing to Secretary Kellogg, who at first sought to stall it. Briand made the proposal of an antiwar treaty in 1927 because he was attempting to drag the United States into his security system in Europe. The proposal of perpetual peace between the United States and France was in truth a negative military alliance. If America were to sign such a promise it meant that regardless of how hard the French pushed the United States in violation of neutral rights (as the British had done in 1914–1917), in any future war when France was, say, fighting Germany, the Americans could not side in reprisal against France, for the antiwar treaty would prevent it. Kellogg, of course, wanted nothing to do with such a proposition.

The American secretary of state was furious with Briand. And not the least part of Kellogg's ill humor came because he discovered that the foreign minister had marshaled in support of this antiwar proposition the many American private organizations for world peace which had sprung up before and especially after the war. Many important private American citizens, who knew how to put pressure on the government in Washington, began to demand of Kellogg that he sign with France. Women's organizations, led by such personalities as Miss Jane Addams and Mrs. Carrie Chapman Catt, made Kellogg's life miserable with their visitations and expostulations. The secretary, who was known privately to possess a Ph.D. in profanity and invectives, swore at the "—— —— pacifists," but to no avail. He made it known through intermediaries that he wanted the peace organizations to leave him in peace. Finally he discovered a way to outwit the French foreign minister, and the resulting treaty became the Kellogg-Briand Pact, America's greatest contribution to peace in the interwar years.

There is a well-known and justly admired axiom of diplomacy to the effect that the more signatories to an agreement the less binding it becomes, and Kellogg invoked this hoary truism against his antagonist in December 1927, proposing to Briand a multinational treaty renouncing war. There was enormous glee in the State Department. Kellogg's able assistant secretary of state, William R. Castle, who had been behind the widening of the original French proposal, wrote privately in his diary that the trick had been turned, that Briand was now out on a limb, that the foreign minister was caught with cold feet which were going to be positively frozen when the State Department drove him out into the open. As for Briand, the foreign minister after Kellogg's counterproposal made one maneuver after another to drop the whole business of an antiwar pact. Every time he suggested that a committee of jurists or a conference of foreign ministers examine Kellogg's counterproposal, the secretary of state refused to be taken in, and Briand became ever more embarrassed as his American opponent invited other states to adhere to the antiwar pact. It was getting, indeed, to be a public humiliation of the foreign minister of France. It was all that Briand could do to stand up against the perverse zeal of the Americans. Himself a possessor of the Nobel prize for peace, which he had won earlier in the 1920's for the Treaty of Locarno among France, Britain, Italy, and Germany, he could not resist indefinitely the public pressure, in Europe as well as America, that he take a position for peace.

Finally, Secretary Kellogg became enamored of the new multi-national proposal, originally conceived only to counter Briand, and began to believe that such a pledge against war by the nations of the world would help prevent future wars. After he placed within the proposed antiwar treaty enough reservations of self-defense and other matters to make the pact agreeable to prospective signatories, Kellogg was able to persuade the French foreign minister to bring the powers together in Paris for a ceremony of signature, which was done by the great powers—other nations acceding thereafter—on August 27, 1928.

The treaty contained two substantive articles: first, "The High Contracting Parties solemnly declare in the names of their respective peoples that they condemn recourse to war for the solution of international controversies, and renounce it as an instrument of national policy in their relations with one another"; second, "The High Contracting Parties agree that the settlement or solution of all disputes or conflicts of whatever nature or of whatever origin they may be, which may arise among them, shall never be sought except by pacific means."

Statesmen signed the Pact of Paris with tongue in cheek, and the only discernible influence of this grand treaty was to inaugurate a fashion whereby wars would be fought under justification of self-defense and without formal declaration of hostilities. An American senator, during debate over ratification of the treaty, said that it was an international kiss. Senator Carter Glass of Virginia announced to his colleagues that he intended to vote for the pact "but I am not willing that anybody in Virginia shall think that I am simple enough to suppose that it is worth a postage stamp in the direction of accomplishing permanent peace." But the pact had large popular support, and in the United States was politically irresistible. Many people believed that with it they had taken a large step in the direction of peaceful settlement of international disputes. Ever since the Senate and Woodrow Wilson had defeated the Treaty of Versailles, numerous Americans had felt badly that their country had abandoned the world after the crusade of 1917–1918. To them it seemed that the heart of the world was broken when the United States stayed out of the League. They were willing to believe that a private American measure such as the Kellogg-Briand Pact, if coupled with arbitration and conciliation treaties and co-operation with the League in humanitarian tasks and the World Court, could indirectly redress the loss to the Geneva organization of American abstention from membership. In the year 1928 there was rejoicing that the United States, once more, had put its weight in the scales for righteousness. Few Americans understood the politique that lay behind the Kellogg-Briand Pact. If they had they would have been sorely disappointed.

3. Another Alternative to the League—Disarmament

The Kellogg-Briand Pact and the bilateral arbitration and conciliation treaties were the American substitutes for the League. In addition the State Department relied on treaties of disarmament, or as the term came to mean, limitation of armament. The idea flourished after the first World War that large armaments had caused the war, and that if the nations of the world would limit their weapons, peace would follow. Disarmament gained support not merely from the American people but from their political leaders, most of whom after 1918 were sincerely anxious for the United States to set Europe an example of arms limitation. The United States's influence for disarmament lay chiefly, one should add, in naval arms, for the American postwar military establishment was weak in land armaments.

The immediate problem in naval disarmament at the end of the first World War was that of the three major naval powers, Great Britain, the United States, and Japan, the latter two were threatening a naval race. This postwar rivalry presented serious questions for all three powers, but especially for the Japanese. Japan, despite a strengthening of its economic position during the war, could not continue a naval competition over an indefinite period of time, for by 1921 one-third of the Japanese budget was going into naval construction and maintenance. Moreover, other factors did not favor Japan. To be sure, Japan during the World War had destroyed the balance of power in the Far East, but with the armistice of 1918 the balance in Europe had also been destroyed, to the disadvantage of Japan. France and Great Britain could redistribute their sea power to distant parts of the world and were better able to defend their territories and interests in the Far East than at any time since the rise of the German navy at the turn of the century. At the end of the war the main American battle fleet was transferred to the Pacific, the base at Pearl Harbor was developed, and there was talk of bases in the Philippines and Guam to match Britain's base at Singapore. Should Britain and America achieve between themselves an entente, a working relationship of their navies, there was danger of Japanese isolation. For Japan, a conference on limitation of naval arms had its attractions. It was shrewd diplomacy for Japan to begin a retreat before compulsion changed it into a rout.

For the Americans and British it was equally obvious that a naval conference might be convenient. Although there was a considerable rivalry between the high commands of the American and British navies—a feeling on each side that the other navy was too large—and although there was talk at the end of the World War of an Anglo-American naval race, still neither Congress nor Parliament would have voted appropriations for such a contest. The British government was hard-pressed for money after the World War and could never have survived an expensive arms race with the United States. As for the American navy, it had emerged from the war almost as large as the British, and the high command of the American navy was all set to resume the postponed building stipulated in the naval act of 1916, but Congress by 1921 was in a balky mood and let it be known that no money for such a purpose would be forthcoming. Co-operation, not antagonism, was the obvious course for the two English-speaking nations. It was common sense that the British and American navies undertake a mutual limitation in a diplomatic conference. And by co-operating in naval policies the two powers would be able to present a unified front to the Japanese.

In the United States, before the end of Wilson's second administration, Senator Borah was trumpeting for a conference. The Harding administration, wishing to head off the British who were about to propose a meeting, offered on July 11, 1921 to organize a conference in Washington. The intention was to deal with both sea and land armaments, but the conference after coming together devoted itself to naval arms.

Representatives of nine invited nations met in Washington on November 11, 1921 to observe formally the third anniversary of the armistice. The following day they held their first plenary session. In addition to delegations from the United States, Britain, and Japan there were representatives of the lesser naval powers, France and Italy, and because it was impossible to deal with Japanese armaments without considering problems of the Far East, China obtained an invitation to the meeting, as did also Portugal (because of Macao), the Netherlands (the East Indies), and Belgium (interests in Chinese railways, and a concession at Tientsin). President Harding gave a stirring address, and then came the surprise of the occasion: the permanent chairman of the conference, Secretary of State Hughes, in what seemed an ordinary speech of greeting, declared suddenly that "the way to disarm is to disarm." In regard to the possibility of an armaments race Hughes said that "There is only one adequate way out and that is to end it now." He thereupon offered some devastatingly concrete suggestions.

Consternation reigned in the hall. According to the journalist Mark Sullivan, when the secretary made his enumeration of British ships to be sunk Admiral Sir David Beatty "came forward in his chair with the manner of a bulldog, sleeping on a sunny doorstep, who has been poked in the stomach by the impudent foot of an itinerant soap-canvasser seriously lacking in any sense of the most ordinary proprieties or considerations of personal safety." All the official documents in the world, Sullivan later wrote, "can't convey as much essential fact to the distant and future reader as did the look on Lord Beatty's face to the historian who had the advantage of being in the room when Mr. Hughes, in that sensational opening speech of his, said that he would expect the British to scrap their four great *Hoods*, and made equally irreverent mention of the *King George the Fifth*."

During the following days some American naval officers went

about saying, half humorously, in a paraphrase of an old Latin *morituri salutamus*, "We who are about to be abolished, salute you."

Hughes's proposals for limitation of naval armaments, considered revolutionary at the time, were in actual fact rough approximations of then existing naval strengths, although (as he made so plain in his speech) it would be necessary for the powers to scuttle some craft to achieve his proposed figures. What he had proposed amounted in tonnage to what a newspaperman happily described as a scale of 5-5-3-1.67-1.67. After adjustment to be completed in the year 1942, Britain and the United States would have parity at 5 (a battleship tonnage of 525,000, aircraft carriers 135,000), Japan a ratio of 3 (battleships 272,000; carriers 81,000), and Italy and France 1.67 (175,000; 60,000). Although for the three largest naval powers these figures were based roughly on existing naval strength, ships built and building, for France and Italy the ratio was an arbitrary figure. Neither of the latter nations had embarked upon a postwar battleship program, but it was essential to assign them a ratio because Britain was insisting upon a two-power standard against Continental navies— the British fleet must equal the combined strength of the two largest Continental navies—and would have refused otherwise to accept a ratio with Japan and the United States.

After the initial confusion and protests the major conferees accepted these figures. French pique at a ratio equal only to Italy's made it impossible for Hughes to extend limitation beyond the categories of battleships and aircraft carriers (the latter were limited because the powers might otherwise have converted their excess battleships into carriers).

Limitation of armaments was the major but not the sole task of the Washington Conference, for in the work of persuading the Japanese to accept a battleship and carrier ratio inferior to Britain and the United States the conference made several political arrangements in the Far East. Japan consented to refrain from further fortification and construction of naval bases in some of her island groups—the Kuriles, Bonins, Ryukyus, Pescadores, also Formosa and Amami-Oshima—and in return Britain and America agreed not to construct additional fortifications or bases in their possessions east and north of Singapore and west of Hawaii. The result was to expose Hong Kong and the Philippines in event of future war. One must add, however, that Japan's possession of the Marianas, Marshalls, and Carolines, taken from

Germany during the World War, virtually precluded a successful defense of the Philippines, and Secretary Hughes at the Washington Conference was giving away only what had already been lost. Hong Kong, of course, was from the beginning indefensible. The agreement was binding until December 31, 1936, subject thereafter to termination upon two years' notice. It was believed that Japan, so long as she had an inferior naval ratio, could safely be allowed mastery of the far Pacific, and the peaceful behavior of Tokyo governments for the remainder of the 1920's seemed to confirm the wisdom of this decision. The Washington Conference in effect partitioned the world among the three naval powers: Japan dominated the Far Eastern seas, the United States the Western Hemisphere, and Britain from the North Sea eastward to Singapore.

The naval treaty as concluded on February 6, 1922 became known as the Five-Power Treaty. A Four-Power Treaty signed on December 13, 1921 had as its purpose the abrogation of the Anglo-Japanese Alliance of 1902, which had been periodically renewed until 1921.

In the renewal of 1911 the Japanese government had suggested that the treaty be inapplicable against any nation with which either ally had a general treaty of arbitration. When the Senate loaded down with reservations the Anglo-American arbitration treaty negotiated in the administration of President Taft, the British government had a private understanding with the Japanese that under no circumstances could the alliance be invoked against the United States. After the World War, and in view of the possibility of a Japanese-American naval race, the British in 1920 announced publicly that the Anglo-Japanese Alliance would not apply in event of hostilities, but Prime Minister Arthur Meighen of Canada became worried and at an imperial conference in the summer of 1921 demanded—against opposition of his colleagues from Australia and New Zealand who feared an ostracized, vengeful Japan—that the mother country abrogate the Japanese Alliance. The Four-Power Treaty proved the vehicle for this task.

Ostensibly the treaty extended responsibility for keeping peace in the Far East to the United States and France, in addition to Japan and Britain, but the pact contained only (1) a pledge to respect each other's "rights in relation to their insular possessions and insular dominions in the region of the Pacific Ocean"; (2) a promise that in any controversy (excluding matters of domestic jurisdiction) between the signatories pertaining to the Pacific Ocean, not settled by diplomacy, the disputants would invite the other members to a conference; (3) an agreement for consultation in event a nonsignatory should threaten the rights of the parties; (4) specific abrogation of the Anglo-Japanese Alliance. Shortly after the Washington Conference, Elihu Root stated the effect of the pact when he declared, "I doubt if any formal treaty ever accomplished so much by doing so little."

The United States during the conference was able to obtain a Nine-Power Treaty, a pledge by all the conferees at Washington to respect the principle of the open door in the Far East and to refrain from using the unsettled situation in China to advance their special interests at the expense of nationals of other countries. The former promise, reaffirming the open door, strengthened the individual pledges given to Secretary of State Hay in 1899. The promise to refrain from exploiting the unsettled situation in China restated the second open door note of 1900. This latter promise had been a secret protocol to the Lansing-Ishii Agreement of 1917, and its inclusion in the Nine-Power Treaty was followed a year later on April 14, 1923 by cancellation of the 1917 agreement.

There were three other Far Eastern arrangements at Washington. The attention which the Senate had given to Shantung during the debate over the Versailles Treaty indicated that this question would have to be solved before any treaty for naval limitation could be ratified, and the Japanese delegates at Washington in separate negotiation with representatives of China, with Secretary Hughes and Lord Balfour serving as impartial observers, agreed upon evacuation of troops from the Shantung peninsula and return of Chinese sovereignty and customs control, subject to retention by Japan of important economic concessions. The second arrangement by Japan at Washington had to do with the Pacific island of Yap, where cable rights were granted the United States. Thirdly the Japanese promised an early end to their occupancy of parts of Russian Siberia and the northern half of the island of Sakhalin. Siberia was evacuated in 1922, northern Sakhalin in 1925.

Japan thus was the principal loser at Washington. This humiliation, preceded by refusal of the Paris Conference to grant the principle of racial equality, followed in 1924 by the United States's complete barring of Japanese immigration, badly hurt Japanese pride, serving to create a situation where not too many years later Japan would use mercilessly a deteriorating political situation in Europe to expand her power in Asia.

To the American people the Washington Conference of 1921–1922 appeared only as a triumph for peace. The Senate approved the naval treaty with a single dissenting vote—President Harding had profited from one of Wilson's most egregious errors at the Paris Peace Conference and appointed to the American delegation to the Washington Conference two senators, including Henry Cabot Lodge. There had been fear before the conference that the United States by engaging in a naval race would be acting the role of a militarist nation, not unlike imperial Germany under the kaiser and Admiral von Tirpitz. Instead the American government reaffirmed one of the doctrines of Mahan, that Anglo-American co-operation was the foundation of world order, and that policies antagonistic to Britain were the height of folly. It is noteworthy that America was willing to limit its naval armaments without attempting to solve the many questions of neutral rights which had so recently embroiled relations between Washington and London. The decisions of the Washington Conference much impressed the peoples of Britain and the United States, creating the somewhat questionable faith that great powers could confer successfully over their vital interests—that the conference method was one of the best ways of diplomacy. Moreover, many Americans came to believe that their country could most effectively make its contribution toward world peace by actions taken outside the League. The Republican Party announced modestly in its platform of 1924 that the Washington Treaty was "the greatest peace document ever drawn." Probably the conference was a success when one considers that battleships had a reduced part in the second World War. A limit on their construction did not detract from the safety of the Allied nations.

The Washington Conference was not, of course, the end of naval rivalry among the great powers. A naval race developed after 1922 in the smaller categories of warships. From this cruiser race between Britain and Japan the United States abstained for several years, and early in 1927 President Coolidge called a new disarmament conference to discuss the competition. At a meeting which began in Geneva on June 20, 1927 and ended on August 4 there were representatives of Britain, the United States, and Japan. France and Italy did not attend, the French from pique because of the parity granted between them and Italy at the Washington Conference, the Italians because the French would not attend. The Geneva Conference of 1927 was a fiasco, for neither the British nor Japanese were willing at that time to halt their cruiser race. The efforts of the Coolidge administration were embarrassing, for diplomatic rumors were set on foot in European capitals that President Coolidge had made "insufficient preparation" for the conference, which was equal to saying that Coolidge was an ignoramus in international affairs. In retaliation Congress in early 1929 passed an appropriation for fifteen heavy cruisers (10,000 tons, 8-inch guns) and an aircraft carrier.

Here was the sort of language which nations understood, and after inauguration of President Herbert Hoover there were explorations by his ambassador to London, Charles G. Dawes, and the new British prime minister, Ramsay MacDonald. Hoover invited Mac-Donald to visit the United States, the visit in October 1929 proved a success, and the London Naval Conference assembled on January 21, 1930.

The London Conference addressed itself to limitation of naval categories not undertaken at the Washington Conference, and the result of a three-month deliberation was a limit on cruisers, submarines, and destroyers. There were no political questions on the agenda, such as had figured so prominently at Washington. The Japanese delegation nominally accepted a ratio of 3 in the lesser naval categories as compared with 5 for Britain and America, but Japan achieved parity for submarines and destroyers and virtual parity, through an involved provision, in heavy cruisers—at least until December 31, 1936, by which time the entire naval question was to be re-examined. The London Treaty was a three-power engagement, although France and Italy signed the document with the other powers on April 22, 1930. The two European nations pledged themselves to negotiate their differences, but after two years they gave up in disagreement.

With the London Conference the question of disarmament virtually ceased to have meaning for European and American diplomacy. Two further conferences were held—the League-sponsored General Disarmament Conference which met on February 2, 1932 at Geneva, and a second London Naval Conference which convened in 1935—but neither achieved any results. Although the conference at Geneva opened with several weeks of enthusiastic speeches, when the fifty-nine nations set to work there was no agreement. The conference enjoyed spurts of activity when various of the great-power delegations proposed limitation schemes. President Hoover on June 22, 1932 suggested an across-the-board reduction of one-third of all arms, but this idea died when seconded by Germany, the disarmed nation. German rearmament under Hitler ended the conference, which in 1934 adjourned "temporarily," never to meet again. As for the second London Conference, commencing in December 1935, it came to grief on the demands of the Japanese delegation for complete parity with Britain and the United States, but in the background was the increasing strength of the Germany navy which forced the British government to invoke the so-called "escalator clause" of the London Treaty of 1930 by which signatories were released from their commitments when a nonsignatory threatened their national safety. The grand campaign for peace through disarmament, begun in 1921 with much hope and some minor achievement, disappeared in another naval race which terminated in war in 1939–1941.

Disarmament, the principal American alternative to membership in the League of Nations, hence proved of little value. So also did the other alternatives—the Kellogg, Root, and Bryan treaties, and the Kellogg Pact. The United States did little for the broad problems of world peace by supporting the noncontroversial health and other humanitarian activities of the League.

On the other hand it is doubtful if American membership in the League of Nations could have halted the drift toward a second World War. Most of the European nations were themselves unwilling to enforce peace after the armistice of 1918. France and her friends, especially Czechoslovakia under the inspiration of the Czech statesman Eduard Beneš, would have made of Article 10 of the Covenant an ironclad guarantee against aggressors if they could have gained enough support for such a course, but this they were never able to do because of the stand against enforcement of peace taken by Great Britain and the Dominions and the former neutral nations during the war—the Baltic countries and others.

As for any American initiative and success in the direction of enforcing peace (if the United States had joined the League), such would have been hardly imaginable. By the first anniversary of the armistice the buoyant enthusiasm of the American people for making peace and justice prevail throughout the world, the enthusiasm which had carried the nation to victory in 1918, had begun to fasten itself to the almost hopeless ideas which dealt with world peace in terms of law rather than force, which offered the possibility of peace everywhere by signature rather than by continuing and ardent labor. Thereafter it was impossible to make Americans realize that a foreign policy had to be backed by military force rather than words. They wished to remain aloof from troubles outside the Western Hemisphere, and convinced themselves that they could do so by formulas.

The American people, one must conclude, had been improperly schooled for their sudden participation in the first World War. Having remained for nearly a century on the fringes of world international affairs—their last passing acquaintance being the overemphasized dangers of European intervention at the time of the Monroe Doctrine —they had forgotten the hard ways of international politics, and during the fighting of 1917–1918 had allowed their idealism such free reign that they were not mentally prepared for the rigors of peacemaking which followed. The disappointments of the Paris Peace Conference combined with the traditionally isolationist beliefs of the American people, and helped the defeat of the Covenant and peace treaty in the Senate. From then on American diplomats did their best to assist the cause of peace without exciting the isolationist sentiments of their fellow citizens. It was an impossible task. The greatest nation in the world could not remain apart from the main international current of the time. Its interests were too scattered geographically and too numerous not to become entangled in those of other nations. The international education of the American people, which had virtually ceased in the 1920's, was further neglected in the dangerous years after 1933, until it began once more with startling suddenness on December 7, 1941.

ADDITIONAL READING

The best short introduction to the period of the 1920's in American diplomacy is Allan Nevins's *The United States in a Chaotic World: 1918–1933* (New Haven, 1950); a volume in the series entitled *Chronicles of America*, this book neatly brings together the leading issues of the time. Selig Adler, *The Isolationist Impulse* (New York, 1957) sets out the presiding American philosophy toward international affairs. For "atmosphere" see Samuel Hopkins Adams, *Incredible Era: The Life and Times of Warren Gamaliel Harding* (Boston, 1939); and Frederick Lewis Allen, *Only Yesterday* (New York, 1931; available in paperback).

Two books by Denna F. Fleming, *The United States and the League of Nations: 1918–1920* (New York, 1932) and *The United States and World Organization: 1920–1933* (New York, 1938) describe the course of American diplomacy toward the League and its organs. The definitive history of the League, in its technical aspects, is F. P. Walters, *A History of the League of Nations* (2 vols., London, 1952). Elihu Root's efforts on behalf of the World Court may be followed in P. C. Jessup, *Elihu Root* (2 vols., New York, 1938); and R. W. Leopold, *Elihu Root and the Conservative Tradition* (Boston, 1954). For their special subjects see H. G. Moulton and Leo Pasvolsky, *War Debts and World Prosperity* (New York, 1932) and Herbert Feis, *The Diplomacy of the Dollar: First Era, 1919–1932* (Baltimore, 1950).

The diplomacy of the Kellogg Pact appears in Robert H. Ferrell, *Peace in Their Time* (New Haven, 1952), which may be supplemented with J. E. Stoner, *S. O. Levinson and the Pact of Paris* (New York, 1943), which deals with the efforts of a Chicago lawyer to rid the world of war; and J. C. Vinson, *William E. Borah and the Outlawry of War* (Athens, Ga., 1957), concerning the lion of Idaho. See also David Bryn-Jones, *Frank B. Kellogg* (New York, 1937).

Disarmament as an avenue of American foreign policy in the 1920's and early 1930's has inspired a fairly large literature. For the Washington Naval Conference the best introduction is Harold and Margaret Sprout, *Toward a New Order of Sea Power* (Princeton, 1940; 2d ed., 1943), together with George T. Davis, *A Navy Second to None* (New York, 1940), both excellent accounts of American naval power during and after the first World War. C. N. Spinks, "The Termination of the Anglo-Japanese Alliance," *Pacific Historical Review*, vol. 6 (1937), 321–340 is a first-rate article. The local color of the conference appears in Mark Sullivan, *The Great Adventure at Washington* (New York, 1922); Sullivan attended the meetings as a reporter. J. C. Vinson, *The Parchment Peace* (Athens, Ga., 1956) defines in a most informative way the Senate's part in the Washington Conference—its influence on the treaties drawn up by Secretary Hughes. The secretary's work appears in detail in Merlo J. Pusey, *Charles Evans Hughes* (2 vols., New York, 1951), a brilliant biography, winner of the Pulitzer prize; and briefly, in better perspective, in Dexter Perkins's *Charles Evans Hughes and American Democratic Statesmanship* (Boston, 1956). For the London Naval Conference of 1930 see the account in Henry L. Stimson and McGeorge Bundy, *On Active Service in Peace and War* (New York, 1948), together with the remarks in *The Memoirs of Herbert Hoover: The Cabinet and the Presidency, 1920–1933* (New York, 1952). There is an account of the conference in Robert H. Ferrell, *American Diplomacy in the Great Depression* (New Haven, 1957). A general survey of disarmament appears in Merze Tate, *The United States and Armaments* (Cambridge, Mass., 1948).

CHAPTER

☆ 14 ☆

The Great Depression

The United States after the first World War refused to join the League of Nations, and instead elaborated an American policy for international peace consisting of two principal courses of action— signature of treaties of disarmament and signature of treaties for peaceful settlement of international disputes. These, one might say, were the American plans, the American nostrums, for world peace. In the 1920's they did not appear as nostrums but as entirely adequate measures, and American statesmen were inclined at times to dispute with the statesmen of Europe as to whether the League or, in reality, the American measures such as the Washington Conference treaties of 1921–1922 and the Kellogg-Briand Pact of 1928 had provided the basis for European and world peace after the first World War. In any event there was no serious challenge to the structure of peace in the 1920's, probably because the world was economically prosperous during that time, and because also the labors and rigors of the war had been so many and large that people everywhere wanted to forget about the very word "war." And so down to the year 1929, and for some time beyond it, Americans felt that they had discovered a satisfactory route to peace.

Unfortunately for such feelings, in the Great Depression decade of the 1930's the people of the United States as well as other nations discovered that world peace was not as secure as they had assumed. Treaties of disarmament and of peaceful settlement, or the League of Nations as it existed in the 1920's without American support, could provide a sense of international community during a quiet period, but these measures could not stand up when the going became rough in the 1930's. The Great Depression had a dual effect in undermining peace. It turned the attention of peoples of democratic countries to their own domestic economic welfare and made them reluctant to look at the broader problems of international peace, problems that lay beyond their national borders. The depression also persuaded the peoples of some countries that the most drastic sort of national leadership was the only way their personal condition might be bettered. It gave impetus to the institution of dictatorship, for the dictators could easily claim that they had the key to national solvency, that they knew how to take their countries out of the Great Depression. As a result of the preoccupation of democratic governments with what was hopefully called recovery, and of the rise of totalitarianism in Europe and Asia, the peace of the world fell apart. A series of major international events in the latter 1930's dealt terrible blows to international peace. By the end of the decade the nations of Europe, soon to be followed by nations outside of the Continent including the United States, found themselves in the second World War.

A decade of American policy, and of work for peace by the League of Nations, proved ineffective when the shadow of totalitarian governments fell over large areas of Europe and Asia. Hitler became German chancellor in January 1933, and started at once to tear down the democratic Weimar Republic which during the 1920's had offered so much hope for the future of European politics. Sometime also in the worst years of the Great Depression, between 1929 and 1933, Mussolini adopted a policy of revision, by which he meant change, peaceful or otherwise, of the Treaty of Versailles. The Italian dictator ceased devoting himself to making the trains run on time, and turned to serious pursuits, looking for diplomatic victories which would deflect the thoughts of his people from poverty and the drabness of post-1918 Italy. By the mid-1930's this policy led him into the arms of Hitler. Likewise the worst sort of nationalism seized Japan in the Far East. The Japanese army got out of hand in 1931 and occupied all of Manchuria, and this venture was followed by a full-scale Sino-Japanese War beginning in 1937. Trouble in the Far East brought sheaves of diplomatic protests from Washington, for ever since 1899 and the first Hay open-door note the United States had been pursuing a policy dedicated to friendship with Japan and to preservation of Chinese sovereignty. But it gradually became evident to Americans that nothing short of military defeat could deter the Japanese from further aggressive acts. It was a disillusioning experience during the 1930's to see thirty years of Far Eastern policy dissolve in war.

The other concerns of this chapter—the London Economic Conference, the Hull-Roosevelt reciprocal trade agreements, recognition of Soviet Russia, and the neutrality acts of 1935–1939—these represented no new crises in American foreign policy. They were only a continuation or attempted continuation of policies long adhered to by the republic's diplomats. The neutrality laws were an extension of the attempt in the 1920's to legislate war out of existence. Americans had always put their faith in law, and when the grand international statute of the 1920's—the Kellogg-Briand Pact—proved worthless, the people of the United States passed their own antiwar laws to keep war away from the Western Hemisphere. As for recognition of Soviet Russia in 1933, this accorded with the traditional American policy of recognizing the government *de facto* as the government *de jure*, whether or not the form of government was pleasing to the United States. The Reciprocal Trade Agreements Act of 1934 embodied the idea of trade reciprocity which occasionally had been employed, although never long enough to prove its merits, in American tariff acts. The London Economic Conference was in harmony with a traditional American diplomatic theory, infrequently practiced, according to which trade barriers wherever possible were to be lowered.

1. *Trouble in Manchuria, 1929–1933*

President Herbert Hoover and Secretary of State Henry L. Stimson directed American diplomacy in the years from 1929 to 1933, the most difficult years of the Great Depression. The president and his secretary were men of ability, yet different in temperament. Hoover was a cautious, careful man who believed in peace and disarmament. Stimson, a Long Island squire and ex-secretary of war under President Taft, was given to quick and not always careful judgments on international affairs, and overestimated the martial ardor of the American electorate. One must say immediately, however, that Stimson, like his chief, Hoover, believed in the American postwar policies of disarmament and peaceful settlement, and despite occasional snap suggestions

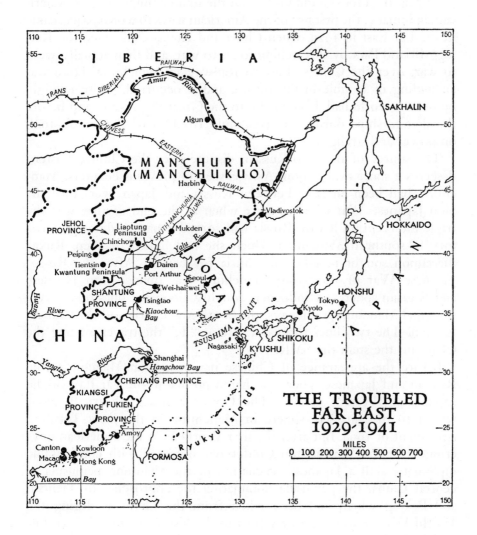

THE TROUBLED
FAR EAST
1929·1941

MILES
0 100 200 300 400 500 600 700

on foreign affairs he almost always ended with the same views as the president. Under such leadership well-meaning caution was the key to American policy, foreign and domestic.

During the Hoover administration the first entanglement of American diplomacy, the first test of the American ways to world peace, came in the Far East in 1929, when China and Russia challenged the Kellogg-Briand Pact by threatening to go to war, and then actually went to war, over the Chinese Eastern Railway in Manchuria. Here was an inkling of trouble in the future, and it occurred, oddly enough, before the world had descended into the Great Depression and before the dictatorships during the economic troubles of the 1930's took on power and strength.

The source of the Sino-Russian dispute over the Chinese Eastern deserves a short explanation. As was seen in previous chapters, Manchuria had been an issue between Russia and Japan ever since the Sino-Japanese War of 1894–1895 when at the end of that war the triple intervention led by Russia had forced Japan to disgorge territory in southern Manchuria which she had hoped to keep. Russia thereupon sought to take Manchuria for herself. After the Russo-Japanese War of 1904–1905 Manchuria was divided into Japanese and Russian spheres of influence, roughly along the lines of the two principal Manchurian railways, the South Manchuria and the Chinese Eastern. The two lines formed a sort of "T," the traverse being the CER and the stem the SMR.

Before the appearance of Chinese nationalism in Manchuria, the Russian and Japanese spheres bothered no one in the Far East or the capitals of Western nations. The United States halfheartedly consented to the Japanese sphere in Manchuria in the Root-Takahira agreement of 1908. But after the first World War the American government at the Washington Conference obtained with considerable diplomatic skill a Japanese evacuation of the Shantung peninsula in central China, the peninsula dominating the approaches to Tientsin and Peking which had been taken from the Germans during the World War. This gave a new turn to the history of Far Eastern imperialism. The Chinese nationalists under Sun Yat-sen and Chiang Kai-shek foolishly believed that the Western powers would look with approval and joy upon the abolition of spheres of interest and foreign possessions and extraterritoriality in all China, including Manchuria. Pursuing this reasoning, the Chinese sought in 1929 to oust the Russians from the Chinese Eastern Railway and regain for China the Russian sphere of influence in northern Manchuria. Chinese politicians in Nanking reasoned that they should assert themselves first against the Russians, who were communists and not respected by the powers of the West. General Chiang and his supporters also hoped to gain a victory in foreign affairs which would turn Chinese thoughts away from the difficult and still unsolved, and perhaps insoluble, Chinese domestic problems.

The details of the Sino-Russian imbroglio over the Chinese Eastern in Manchuria during the summer and autumn of 1929 need not detain us. The Chinese acted first by expelling the Russians from management of the railway, and after violent expostulation the Soviet government beginning in August 1929 sent troops against the foolhardy Chinese and forced the Nanking regime to sue for peace. Unfortunately, after the initial seizure of the Chinese Eastern Railway by the Chinese, Secretary Stimson in Washington became excited and raised the subject of the Kellogg-Briand Pact with both China and Russia. Although the Nanking and Moscow governments promised to settle their dispute by peaceful means, the Russians in the autumn nonetheless invoked the right of self-defense and began a military campaign against the Chinese. The Kellogg Pact, which to many Americans was the very foundation of pacific international relations, looked (to use the expression of an American diplomat) like thirty cents. Stimson made still another mistake near the end of the affair, actually after the Chinese had sued for peace, when in a circular note in late November 1929 he admonished the belligerents to cease fighting. The note was communicated to the Soviet Russian government, unrecognized by the United States since the Bolshevik revolution of 1917, by the French ambassador in Moscow. The result was an insulting unofficial communication via the public press from the Russian vice commissar of foreign affairs, Maxim Litvinoff, who told Stimson to mind his own business.

Litvinoff in 1929 thus had his small moment of triumph against the well-meaning but inexperienced Stimson. The latter soon turned to other international matters besides Manchuria, particularly disarmament, with which he would have to deal at the London Naval Conference of 1930 and the General Disarmament Conference in 1932. The secretary of state's first two years of office were in fact largely concerned with disarmament, being only momentarily interrupted by the diplomatic fiasco over Manchuria. Stimson, however, learned in 1929 that quick action in Far Eastern matters, even if confined to verbal admonitions, could lead to grave embarrassment. The Kellogg-Briand Pact after its initial invocation in 1929 never looked the same, and proved useless when a much more important conflict broke out between the Chinese and Japanese in Manchuria beginning with a Sino-Japanese clash at Mukden on September 18, 1931. This conflict the Japanese liked to call the Manchurian incident; Stimson preferred, and rightly, to call it the Far Eastern crisis.

The crisis found part of its origin in the actions of the Chinese against the Russians in 1929. In their inept effort to seize Russian property in Manchuria, the Chinese managed to convince the Japanese that the South Manchurian Railway and all of Japan's other possessions in Manchuria, territorial and otherwise, which depended upon that railway, were endangered by the growing nationalism of the Chinese government. A second factor persuading Japan to move against China in Manchuria was the Great Depression, which struck with especial harshness in the Japanese islands, bringing misery to peasants and city workers. Among other difficulties for Japan, the bottom fell out of the silk market in the United States, and this catastrophe, combined with Chinese nationalist boycotts of Japanese cotton goods, meant a crisis in Japan's foreign trade, almost half of which was in silk and cotton goods with China and the United States. Manchuria, so it seemed, might provide under Japanese rule a safe area for Japan's trade, an area unaffected by foreign tariffs.

Added to these factors was increasing unrest in the Japanese army, a rebellious spirit among many of the younger officers. Until the decade of the 1920's the Japanese officer corps was the preserve of the upper classes, who contributed the bulk of the higher-ranking officers. The army had always been a peasant army, and in the years after the first World War when democracy achieved a temporary popularity in Japan the peasants began to rise into the officer corps, bringing into the army a new type of officer who was in reality half-educated— overly professional, ultrapatriotic, suspicious of Western ideas and intentions. These young officers, many of them old enough to know better, began in the latter 1920's to agitate and conspire against their elders, with vague ideas of overthrowing the government in Tokyo and establishing a "Showa restoration," a moral regeneration of Japan. Showa was the reign name of the Emperor Hirohito. The Meiji restoration of 1867 had rejuvenated the nation politically, they believed, by returning to the emperor the political powers usurped by the shoguns, and a Showa restoration would reform the nation's morals which had been debauched by the politicians. This was, to be sure, inexact historical reasoning, for the emperors in Japan have never enjoyed much real power, either in the early centuries before their domination by the shoguns or after the Meiji restoration. Still, the typical young officer believed in this restoration theory, and he had the courage of his ignorance. There was, one should add, a strong admixture of socialist thinking in this program of the young army officers. But after the Manchurian incident beginning on September 18, 1931, the older army officers gradually infiltrated the restoration movement of their younger confrères and in 1936 purged it of its socialist tendencies, leaving only its patriotism. This was a virulent residue. The younger officers eventually came back into control as their conservative superiors retired; the result was the attack on Pearl Harbor and a suicidal effort to achieve *Hakko Ichiu*, The Eight Corners of the Universe Under One Roof.

But to return to the incident of September 18, 1931, which inaugurated the Far Eastern crisis.

After alleging an explosion along the main line of the South Manchuria Railway a few miles north of Mukden, and claiming that Chinese troops in the vicinity had sought to blow up the track of the South Manchuria Railway, the Japanese army in Manchuria, the so-called Kwantung Army, on the night of September 18 under leadership of its young officer elements began occupying Manchuria. In a few days the Japanese spread out along the line of the SMR, and during the winter of 1931–1932 they audaciously took the Russian sphere of interest in Manchuria, the northern part of Manchuria bordering the line of the Soviet-controlled Chinese Eastern Railway. Manchuria was set up as an "independent" puppet empire called Manchukuo with Kang Teh (the boy emperor of China deposed in 1912; also known by the names Hsuan T'ung and Henry Pu-yi) as "sovereign." In Russia the Soviet regime was so busy collectivizing the farms and forwarding the second five-year plan that it could only watch the Kwantung Army's movements in nervous fear, hoping that the Japanese would not invade Siberia (there was sentiment in Japan for such an excursion). By the spring of 1933 all Manchuria including the province of Jehol had fallen, and the government in Tokyo temporarily persuaded the army to follow a policy of relative moderation. For the next several years the Japanese government was an unsteady coalition of bureaucrats and army and navy officers. As time passed the bureaucrats of pacific inclination dropped out of the government, the navy grew more warlike as it observed the successes of totalitarianism in Europe during the years 1935–1939, and the army became supreme when in autumn 1941 the fire-eating General Hideki ("Razor Brain") Tojo, a sympathizer with the young officers, assumed the premiership.

The future did not stand revealed to American officials in Washington in September 1931, and President Hoover and Secretary Stimson spent the remainder of their time in office until March 1933, when the Manchurian affair came almost simultaneously to an end, attempting to halt Japan's aggression and if possible to persuade the Japanese to return the captured territory to China. The first policy adopted by Stimson and Hoover was one of inaction, for they remembered the fiasco over the Chinese Eastern in 1929. They hoped also that the League of Nations would take jurisdiction and persuade the Japanese to cease and desist. An American chargé d'affaires in Geneva in October 1931 sat at the League Council for a few days while Council members summoned up courage to invoke the Kellogg-Briand Pact. In November–December, Ambassador Dawes went over to Paris from his post in London and from the confines of a suite in the Ritz sought to inspire the League Council, then in session at the Quai d'Orsay. Not much came from Dawes's exhortations, except some additional feeling of American solidarity with the League during the Far Eastern crisis. This was more feeling than fact, for suspicion of the League dominated American relations with that organization throughout the interwar era. In Paris in 1931 Dawes had been careful to stay in his hotel, and never once did he cross the Seine to the Quai d'Orsay to meet with the League Council.

Shortly after this Paris meeting of the Council came further Japanese acts in Manchuria. The Japanese army occupied the South Manchurian town of Chinchow on January 2, 1932. This produced a statement of the American position toward aggression which became known as the Stimson Doctrine.

Secretary Stimson on January 7, 1932 announced that the United States could not "admit the legality of any situation de facto nor does it intend to recognize any treaty or agreement . . . which may impair the treaty rights of the United States or its citizens in China, including those which relate to the sovereignty, the independence, or the territorial and administrative integrity of the Republic of China, nor to the international policy relative to China, commonly known as the open door policy; and that it does not intend to recognize any situation, treaty, or agreement which may be brought about by means contrary to the covenants and obligations of the Pact of Paris of August 27, 1928, to which Treaty both China and Japan, as well as the United States, are parties."

The Stimson Doctrine, inspired in 1932 by Japan's conquest of Manchuria, was later applied by the United States to conquests by other nations in Europe. It has, however, obtained little support from other nations of the world and hence has failed to become a part of international law.

One might remark parenthetically, about the Stimson Doctrine, that authorship of the note of January 7, 1932 was afterward a subject of some controversy, or if not controversy then confusion, between Stimson and Hoover. Stimson had obtained the idea of such a declaration of nonrecognition of the fruits of aggression from President Hoover in a cabinet meeting in November 1931, but the phrasing of the announcement was Stimson's. Hoover in the presidential election of 1932 took credit for the doctrine, saying in his acceptance speech that "I have projected a new doctrine into international affairs." The idea of nonrecognition so attracted him that despite defeat in November 1932 he afterward asked some cabinet members to prepare testimonial letters on the subject, which they did in the interest, as Hoover later put it, of "accuracy of historic fact." Stimson himself never claimed sole authorship of the idea of nonrecognition, but the idea nonetheless has taken his name.

It has been argued that there were two doctrines in 1932—a Stimson Doctrine and a Hoover Doctrine, the former implying sanctions of military force and the latter relying only on the sanction of international public opinion. This does seem contrary to the case in 1932, where there was not any essential difference of opinion between the president and the secretary of state. Stimson for a while in the autumn of 1931 had talked privately of military sanctions, but they were never within the realm of possibility and Stimson gradually came to understand as much. Public opinion in the United States would never have stood for them. Hoover, of course, a profoundly peaceful man, did not favor military sanctions or even economic sanctions (such as an embargo on war material) against Japan in 1931–1933.

The Stimson Doctrine, announced early in January 1932, had no effect on Japanese aggression, for it was late that same month that Japanese naval forces began an attack on the Chinese port of Shanghai; and Stimson on February 23, 1932 had to make a second statement of policy reinforcing his doctrine. The attack on Shanghai had little relation to the Japanese army's activities in Manchuria, despite what might seem to be the logic of Japan's military position in China: logic would indicate that the Japanese in 1931–1933 planned to take over all of China, and that the first move in Manchuria was to be followed by an attack on Shanghai and if that were successful then attack elsewhere along the coast and eventually penetration into and occupation of the interior regions as well. In actual fact this was not the Japanese plan of conquest. There was no careful plan of conquest then or later. Japan's actions in China were an unco-ordinated series of movements, a crazy quilt of military campaigns. A Japanese admiral in Shanghai in early 1932 thought that because of some Chinese attacks on Japanese citizens residing in the port he was justified in occupying part of the city. He met unexpected resistance, and eventually after the Japanese had brought in well over 50,000 regular army troops the campaign was given up. But for a while in the spring of 1932 it looked to outside observers as if full-scale war was spreading over China. The Japanese air bombardment of a defenseless Chinese sector of Shanghai, the Chapei quarter, was an outrageous act that fired Western indignation. It persuaded Secretary Stimson that he should make another statement of the American diplomatic position relative to the Far East, and this he did in what has become known as the Borah Letter of February 23, 1932.

Conceived in the form of a public letter to the chairman of the Senate foreign relations committee (Stimson felt that if he sent a note to Japan he would receive a caustic reply), the Borah Letter restated eloquently the American stand against Japanese aggression. The secretary hinted that if Japan persisted in attacking China the United States might abrogate the Five-Power Naval Treaty of Washington. Stimson said that problems in the Far East "were all interrelated. The willingness of the American government to surrender its then [1921] commanding lead in battleship construction and to leave its positions at Guam and in the Philippines without further fortification, was predicated upon, among other things, the self-denying covenants contained in the Nine Power Treaty, which assured the nations of the world not only of equal opportunity for their Eastern trade but also against the military aggrandizement of any other power at the expense of China."

At the end of his letter to Borah, Stimson placed a noble statement of American purposes toward China which showed the essentially humanitarian instincts of American Far Eastern policy: "In the past our Government, as one of the leading powers on the Pacific Ocean, has rested its policy upon an abiding faith in the future of the people of China and upon the ultimate success in dealing with them of the principles of fair play, patience, and mutual goodwill. We appreciate the immensity of the task which lies before her statesmen in the development of her country and its government. The delays in her progress, the instability of her attempts to secure a responsible government, were foreseen by Messrs. Hay and Hughes and their contemporaries and were the very obstacles which the policy of the Open Door was designed to meet. We concur with these statesmen, representing all the nations in the Washington Conference who decided that China was entitled to the time necessary to accomplish her development. We are prepared to make that our policy for the future."

The Borah Letter Stimson afterward regarded as the most important state paper of his career, and it was an eloquent statement of Japan's wrongdoings and the American position toward them, but neither it nor the Stimson Doctrine deterred the Japanese. World public opinion, which Stimson hoped to stir, remained occupied by the increasingly acute economic problems of the Great Depression. Stimson proved himself a competent lawyer, and made a most careful summation to the jury, but the jury was not listening.

This was the public mood, in the United States and elsewhere, when the League of Nations on October 1, 1932 released a report on conditions in Manchuria. At the end of the Paris Council meeting in November–December 1931 the League had appointed a commission, and this body, headed by Lord Lytton of England and including Major General Frank R. McCoy as an unofficial American representative, had gone out to the Far East and interviewed government leaders and other individuals in China, Manchuria, and Japan. Laboring through the summer in Peking, the commission produced the famous review of Manchurian conditions known as the Lytton Report. It was written largely by two American assistants to the commission, George H. Blakeslee of Clark University and C. Walter Young of Johns Hopkins. The report sidestepped responsibility for the Mukden clash of September 18, 1931, but stated unequivocally that subsequent Japanese actions had gone far beyond any requirement of the original incident. The report found the Japanese claim of self-defense inadmissible. While fully recognizing Chinese delinquencies of administration in Manchuria prior to the Japanese attack, and granting the need of Japanese citizens in Manchuria for protection, the report put the blame for aggression on Japan. As for the Japanese puppet state, Manchukuo, the report said that it could not "be considered to have been called into existence by a genuine and spontaneous independence movement" as the Japanese claimed. The Japanese army, the commission discovered, was in full control.

The League of Nations adopted the Lytton Report with its recommendations, an autonomous Manchuria under Chinese sovereignty, on February 24, 1933, but it was too late by this time to do anything against Japan in Manchuria—and the League had never intended to, anyway. That same day, February 24, the first anniversary of publication of Stimson's letter to Senator Borah, the Japanese delegation at Geneva made a dramatic exit from the League. Japan announced permanent withdrawal from the League of Nations, taking as a souvenir the Pacific islands held under League mandate. The chief Japanese delegate at Geneva, Yosuke Matsuoka, told the League Assembly that as Christ had been crucified on the cross, so was Japan being crucified by the nations of the League. Privately Matsuoka explained that the powers had taught Japan the game of poker but after they had acquired most of the chips they pronounced the game immoral and took up contract bridge.

This was the sad diplomatic end of the Manchurian affair. Hostilities in Manchuria petered out and were ended formally by the Tangku Truce of May 31, 1933. Secretary Stimson in Washington took satisfaction that the League in adopting the Lytton Report in February 1933 had endorsed the Stimson Doctrine of nonrecognition of Manchukuo. He at that moment could not know that in the future cases of Ethiopia, Austria, and Czechoslovakia, League members would forget about nonrecognition of the spoils of aggression. He did not realize that Japan in walking out of the League of Nations had set an easy example for other nations which did not wish to honor their international pledges—Germany left the League in October 1933, Italy in 1937. The American secretary of state in January 1933 conversed for a few hours with President-elect Franklin D. Roosevelt, and hopefully sought to persuade FDR to continue the Hoover-Stimson policies in the Far East. With that the Hoover administration bowed out and the Roosevelt administration bowed in.

2. The Diplomacy of the New Deal

During the first and second administrations of President Franklin D. Roosevelt the American people continued largely to live apart from the realities of international relations. The diplomacy of the United States from 1933 to 1939 relied no longer on disarmament and treaties of peaceful settlement, for by the time the Hoover administration went out of office it was fairly clear that those American alternatives to the League of Nations had proved ineffective. Even so, the only new Rooseveltian device for world peace, reciprocal trade agreements, was no more effective than the policies of FDR's Republican predecessors. Roosevelt had no opportunity, of course, to return the country to the policies of his illustrious Democratic predecessor, Woodrow Wilson. At no time after the spring of 1920, least of all in 1933 and after, was it possible to have taken the United States into the League. The temper of American opinion would never have allowed it. The memory of the clever anti-League propaganda of Senator Lodge and the Battalion of Death in 1919–1920 had solidified many ancient American prejudices, and an international body such as the League seemed to the average American citizen an impossible organization for his country to join. When William Randolph Hearst in February 1932 confronted the Democratic candidate for the presidency with the League issue, FDR came out flatly against membership. In the election of 1932 repeal of the eighteenth amendment was a far greater issue than any international matter.

But overreaching any issue of the 1932 campaign and dominating the policies of the first two Roosevelt administrations was the Great Depression, which had settled down over the country like an enormous blight. The depression, which lasted until 1941 and American entry into the second World War, was the most calamitous domestic disaster in the history of the United States, excluding only the Civil War. Roosevelt came into office with a mandate to do something about the depression, and from the outset of the New Deal foreign affairs took a place subordinate to economic and social reform. No one who can remember the grim depression days will assert that Roosevelt had any choice about his program. He had to take care of the immediate problem, which was to get the economy off dead center, the condition he found it in on the morning of his inaugural when every bank in the country had closed. It does not help to say with the advantage of hindsight that for Roosevelt foreign affairs, the rapidly expanding power of totalitarian regimes throughout the world, should have been more important than domestic matters. Roosevelt had to do something about the depression.

The London Economic Conference (June 12–July 24, 1933), where the United States together with sixty-three other nations was represented, offered a typical example of the influence of the Great Depression on American foreign policy during the first two Roosevelt administrations. Here, when an international measure was suggested that might have undermined the president's domestic economic program, Roosevelt did not hesitate to withdraw all American support. This conference had been called for the summer of 1933 to increase world trade through such measures as reduction of tariffs, stabilization of currencies, perhaps some agreement on war debts owed to the United States. The purpose of the conference—to increase trade— was always plain, although many proposals of the nations looking toward achievement of the purpose were uncertain. Roosevelt's secretary of state, Cordell Hull, acting in the midst of this confusion, produced a plan to facilitate world trade through tariff reciprocity, and Hull went off to London hoping to achieve a general treaty for lowering of tariffs. He hoped that the treaty would both help world trade and ensure world peace through the bonds of an international exchange of goods and services. But President Roosevelt, fearful of tariff reduction during the depression, deeply involved in the spring and early summer of 1933 in pushing through Congress the first measures of the New Deal, vetoed the proposal while the secretary was en route to the conference.

There then arose the question of currency stabilization, allowing the free exchange of one currency for another. When the conference began its deliberations it appeared that many of the delegates at London wished currency stabilization via some sort of return to the gold standard by such leading financial nations as the United States and

Great Britain, especially the United States. The British government in
1931 had gone off the gold standard, which meant that the pound
sterling was no longer convertible easily into other currencies (a
paper currency convertible at any time into gold could always be
exchanged for other paper currencies). Many countries had followed
the British off gold, including the United States under the Roosevelt
administration in March and April 1933. World trade was thrown
into an uproar, for without a gold standard the value of national
currencies in world trade was tied to the value of national exports: if
country A did not need the goods of country B it was difficult to sell
to country B; country A would not want B's currency which was
good only within country B; if A wished to sell its own goods to B,
it had to find country C which wished B's goods; then A would take
some of C's goods—or else work another deal between C and D, or
on down the alphabet until A found some nation with goods which A
needed. The intricacies of trade without the gold standard become
readily understandable. The problem in the summer of 1933 was somehow to free the world's currencies, so that there would be no need
for each nation desiring foreign trade to go suitoring to other nations,
making detailed private arrangements for trade.

Currency stabilization, the nations believed, would have a tonic effect on world trade, but such a measure President Roosevelt would
not allow. When a proposal was sent to the president he vetoed it in
a sharp message to the American delegation at London on July 2,
1933. This message, one should add, exploded the sole remaining hope
of the London delegates, since the president had already forbidden a
general treaty for American tariff reciprocity. FDR torpedoed the
London Economic Conference, to use the figure of speech current at
the time. He did it for domestic economic reasons, not because he
did not wish to assist in the business of world peace. Roosevelt took
a stand against stabilization because he feared that to make the dollar
convertible upon demand, tying its value to the ups and downs of
world trade, would jeopardize his recovery program. With the coming of the Great Depression the dollar had risen in value—a dollar
would buy much more in 1933 than it had in 1929. This change placed
debtors in the unenviable position of repaying loans contracted in the
1920's when the dollar had less value. The president wished to de-
preciate the dollar, at least to its level in the 1920's, and depreciating it
would be difficult if the dollar's value were tied to world exchange

conditions and, hence, out of his control.

Many individuals in 1933 and later believed that the collapse of the London Economic Conference was a catastrophe for world peace, that Roosevelt's action destroyed the last great hope for peace by conference before the second World War. Certainly FDR's message of July 2, vetoing currency stabilization, not merely destroyed all hopes for the meeting but worsened world trade in addition, for it gave assurance that the United States would have nothing to do with the gold standard. Still, Roosevelt was taking the only possible course in 1933 when he put American economic recovery ahead of world recovery. "The world," he had remarked in his message, "will not long be lulled by the specious fallacy of achieving a temporary and probably an artificial stability in foreign exchange on the part of a few large countries only. The sound internal economic system of a nation is a greater factor in its well-being than the price of its currency in changing terms of the currencies of other nations." This declaration was hailed by FDR's countrymen in 1933 as an American financial declaration of independence. Few Americans in the depth of the depression would have supported international measures at the expense of the American economy.

The administration, however, soon showed something resembling contriteness for its behavior when in 1934 Secretary Hull announced a proposal to reduce tariff barriers all over the world. Hull's scheme was what he had hoped to offer at London the year before—tariff reciprocity.

Tariff history has always been an interesting aspect of American history, and much has been written about it. Perhaps the most important single fact about the American tariff is that the exports of the United States have seldom exceeded ten per cent of the total of American annual production, and therefore the effect of the tariff in the United States has been principally upon domestic prices. A tariff on rails, for example, kept out foreign rails that might have undersold domestic rails. After the first World War, as we have seen, the tariff served to prevent payment in goods and services of the World War debts, public and private, although on the other hand the debts probably could not have been collected anyway, even with a lower American tariff. Large international loans often become political issues and possibility of payment diminishes directly in proportion as the exigency disappears in which the loans were contracted. As for promoting international peace via an increase in international trade, a special argument which Hull in 1934 adduced to support his new trade-agreements program, one can only say that the tariffs of the world were lowest in the nineteenth century and that the nineteenth century marked the most warless period in modern history. It is difficult to know whether this was cause and effect (and which was which?), or coincidence, or the result of world dominance by British power in the form of the British navy; or perhaps the nineteenth century was a period of such phenomenal industrial growth, marking the spread through Western Europe and North America of the industrial revolution, that in such a time of physical development the nations of the world were too busy to fight each other often or for long.

Be that as it may, Secretary Hull was a firm believer in low tariffs. He was convinced that lower tariffs meant world peace. Roosevelt, with what appears to have been mild enthusiasm, sponsored reciprocity tariff legislation in accord with the wishes of his secretary of state, and the Hull-Roosevelt Reciprocal Trade Agreements Act passed Congress and received the presidential signature on June 12, 1934. It permitted executive lowering of the tariff to an extent of fifty per cent of any tariff schedule, providing that foreign nations would make similar adjustments in schedules in which the United States had an interest. Almost all concessions made would be extended automatically to other nations. The advantage of the Hull program was that tariffs could be adjusted without the express consent, on each schedule, of Congress, and hence adjustment could be made in the national interest and not that of some lobbyist.

As for the effects of the Hull-Roosevelt reciprocity program, they have been difficult to gauge, for the 1930's and 1940's and 1950's have proved extraordinarily disturbed years for foreign trade. The rearmament of Europe and coming of the second World War and the perplexities of the postwar years have obscured the results of American tariff reciprocity. Some individuals have ventured that American trade has increased greatly because of reciprocity. Cordell Hull in 1940 thought that the program was begun for "the express purpose of expanding our exports. . . . I submit that it has done so." Writing in the same year an economist, Grace Beckett, concluded (with perhaps undue caution) that reciprocity "seems to offer the only feasible program which will obtain some of the advantages of the international division of labor in a world filled with trade restrictions."

Another diplomatic act of the early New Deal period was recognition by the United States of the government of Soviet Russia. Because of the numerous outrages and horrors with which the Bolshevik Party had achieved and maintained power in Russia, and because the communist government represented expropriation and anticapitalism and had repudiated the debts of the tsarist regime and the short-lived provisional republic of 1917, the American government had refused recognition during the 1920's. The Bolsheviks did not increase their popularity by the constant emission of crude revolutionary propaganda which kept American officials stubborn. Nonetheless many businessmen in the United States and liberal leaders who considered communist Russia a social experiment rather than a dictatorship favored recognizing the Bolsheviks. This agitation grew in volume as the depression made businessmen sensitive to any, even remote, possibilities of foreign trade, and the result finally was diplomatic recognition.

How a nation such as Russia could have conducted any large-scale foreign trade with the United States should have been a mystery, for Americans needed nothing that Russia produced, and the Russians had no money (at this time they had not sent political prisoners in sufficent numbers into the Kolyma gold fields). Because of Bolshevik repudiation of the wartime debts, loans were out of the question. But in the lurid possibility of Russian trade the dream was more important than reality. Here was another instance like China, where the existence of a large population in a large territory seemed without further explanation to mean enormous trade. The Roosevelt administration gave in to the economic arguments for recognition.

There were some other and minor reasons for recognizing communist Russia. For one, the increasing danger of a Japanese move against Russia in the Far East helped bring together the Soviet and American governments. Moreover, the American people had sickened of all the argument over recognition, pro and con, and remembered only that the now discredited Republican administrations of the 1920's had opposed relations with the Russians. Recognition of Soviet Russia by 1933 was a stale problem, tiresome and boring, and negotiations between Maxim Litvinoff, who had become Soviet commissar for foreign affairs, and President Franklin D. Roosevelt were completed with hardly a hitch.

In a formal exchange of notes on the day of recognition, November 16, 1933, Litvinoff promised that his country would (1) abstain from propaganda in the United States, (2) extend religious freedom to American citizens in the Soviet Union and negotiate an agreement to guarantee fair trial to Americans accused of crime in Russia, and (3) reopen the question of outstanding claims of both governments.

There followed a serious effort by the United States to improve relations with Russia. The president appointed as ambassador to Moscow the wealthy William C. Bullitt, who in a burst of enthusiasm departed for Russia to demonstrate his friendliness and that of his countrymen for the struggling socialists of the former tsarist empire. Between 1934 and 1936, at which latter date he was transferred to Paris, Bullitt made heroic efforts for American-Soviet friendship, including equipping of some Russian citizens with baseballs, bats, and gloves. American businessmen likewise did their best to obtain Russian orders. American private citizens, some of them of the most impeccably patriotic antecedents, demonstrated with effusion their friendship for Russia. Apropos this latter phenomenon of the 1930's, Eric Goldman in a recent book has cited a news item in the Baltimore *Sun* for November 8, 1937: "Wearing a black ensemble with orchids at the shoulder, Mrs. William A. Becker, national president of the Daughters of the American Revolution, attended the reception at the Soviet Embassy last night to celebrate the twentieth anniversary of the Russian Revolution." Unfortunately, such camaraderie was to no avail. Moreover, American trade with Russia, so fondly anticipated, diminished after recognition instead of increasing. The Russians remained suspicious and difficult and forgot, if they had not from the beginning intended to ignore, their promises through Litvinoff in the prerecognition agreement. One can only conclude about this effort by the Roosevelt administration to improve relations with Soviet Russia that the Russians repulsed a sincere effort with as much hardness and disdain toward the well-intentioned American republic as they again would show after the second World War.

A word remains about the neutrality acts of 1935, 1936, 1937, and 1939, which together with Secretary Hull's tariff-reciprocity agreements represented almost the sole discernible new moves by the United States toward the nations of Europe in the decade before the second World War. A series of stark international events shook Europe to its foundations in the four years beginning with 1935. The first was the Italian conquest of Ethiopia, which began in 1935 and ended the next year. German reoccupation of the Rhineland came in 1936, which made Germany militarily defensible against the French army by securing the approaches to the Rhine, and separated the French from their Czechoslovak allies. Occupation of the Rhineland broke down France's post-1918 alliances with the nations of Eastern Europe—Czechoslovakia, Rumania, and Yugoslavia (the Little Entente). The year 1936 saw the beginning of the Spanish Civil War, a death struggle between liberals and conservatives in Spain. The liberals drew in the radicals, and the reactionaries joined the conservatives. Germany and Italy sent help to the Franco regime, Russia to the Republicans. When peace came in 1939 it was a peace of exhaustion. The accession of General Francisco Franco to power in Spain, one should add, marked a sad deterioration in Western democratic fortunes, for the Spanish caudillo was a reactionary, opportunistic gentleman of the eighteenth century rather than the twentieth, who brought an intellectual, economic, and political blight to Spain during the years after the end of the civil war; during the second World War the Allies had terribly difficult dealings with this Machiavel as he wavered between the German and Allied sides, waiting to see who would win the war. Meanwhile in March 1938, after rebuilding German military power, Hitler forced the *Anschluss* with Austria, and in September 1938 he took the Sudeten territory from Czechoslovakia after negotiation at Berchtesgaden, Godesberg, and Munich with the British prime minister, Neville Chamberlain, the French premier, Edouard Daladier, and the Italian dictator Mussolini. After having said in these conversations that the Sudetenland was his last demand, Hitler in March 1939 took most of the remainder of Czechoslovakia. Mussolini seized Albania in April. In midsummer the German Fuehrer precipitated the Danzig crisis with Poland, and on September 1, having waited until the crops had been harvested, he began the second World War.

During these catastrophic four years of European history the United States contented itself with enacting neutrality statutes. A special committee of the Senate headed by Gerald P. Nye of North Dakota had begun in 1934 to investigate profiteering in the United States during the first World War. The investigation lasted into 1936, and the Nye committee's voluminous testimony and exhibits helped condition the American people for staying neutral during Europe's new time of troubles. The Senate munitions investigating committee turned up little of a sensational nature, for it proved that many individuals had made sizable profits during the first World War, a conclusion which might have been evident without any investigation. Insofar as the committee showed that co-operation existed during the war between Wall Street banking firms (J. P. Morgan *et al.*), ammunition concerns (the "merchants of death"), and the Wilson administration, the American people in the mid-1930's became convinced that such co-operation was collusion, that sinister forces in 1917 had taken the nation into a war which it did not want. There would be no such nonsense again. In an act of Congress of August 31, 1935, which was hurried through both Houses after the Italian attack in Ethiopia, the Roosevelt administration renounced some of the traditional rights of neutrals which had caused difficulty during the first World War, in the hope that the maritime troubles of that war which had led to American entry in 1917 would not repeat themselves in the Italian crisis. Mussolini had been making balcony speeches about Italy's destiny, and gave the distinct impression that interference by anyone in the Ethiopian adventure would mean instant war. The Duce believed what he said. According to the Neutrality Act of 1935, an avowedly temporary affair, the president after proclaiming the existence of a state of war had to prohibit all arms shipments to belligerents and could forbid American citizens to travel on belligerent vessels except at their own risk. Roosevelt signed the neutrality act reluctantly, and remarked in irritation that it was calculated to "drag us into war instead of keeping us out." This was unlikely, but after passage of the act the president and the State Department could no longer bargain with Mussolini, and could make no effective protests against the Italian bully's attack on a small tribal African state, because in advance the United States had given up any possible trump cards such as sending supplies to the Ethiopians. The president managed to obtain from Congress a six-month limit on the arms embargo. He had hoped that Congress would permit him to use the embargo only against aggressor nations, but Congress refused.

In following years the United States revised and refined its neutrality laws. The act of February 29, 1936, forbade loans to belligerents. A joint resolution of Congress on January 6, 1937, embargoed shipments to the opposing forces in the Spanish Civil War (the act of 1935 had applied only to war between nations and not to civil wars).

A new act of May 1, 1937, brought together the provisions of previous legislation and added some new stipulations: travel on belligerent vessels was now forbidden, rather than allowed at the risk of the traveler; the president was authorized to list commodities other than munitions which belligerents might purchase in the United States and transport abroad in their own ships (this "cash and carry" provision of the act of May 1, limited to two years, expired by the time the European war began in September 1939). The May act of 1937 did give the president some discretion, for a tricky wording permitted FDR to move only when he could "find" a war. It stipulated that "Whenever the President shall find that there exists a state of war between, or among, two or more foreign states, the President shall proclaim such fact . . ." When in July 1937 another war broke out—this time in China between Japanese and Chinese troops near Peking, the beginning of the long conflict which closed in 1945—Roosevelt refused to invoke the neutrality legislation on the technical ground that he did not find a war. The Sino-Japanese War of 1937–1945, like the "Manchurian incident" of 1931–1933, was an undeclared war, such being the fashion of the 1930's to get around the inconvenient promises of the Kellogg-Briand Pact. On technical ground Roosevelt could claim to find no war in China, and this technicality served his purpose of making munitions available to the beleaguered Chinese.

Thus the neutrality acts by 1937 had begun to appear not always in the national interest of the United States. Their invocation in the new Far Eastern war would have assisted the aggressor, not the victim. After the second World War broke out in Europe, Congress in November 1939 revised the neutrality laws, repealing the embargo on arms and ammunition and authorizing "cash and carry" exports of war material to belligerent powers. Because this late revision of the neutrality regulations assisted the belligerents who controlled the high seas, that is, Britain and France, opponents of changing the laws argued that Congress was committing an unneutral act, unfavorable to Germany. Actually the act of November 4, 1939 reasserted the right of the United States to sell munitions of war to any nation which had the shipping to come and get them. Neutrality according to international law had never meant that a nation had to even up its trade with opposing belligerent nations. In any event the argument over the Neutrality Act of 1939 became academic when the United States in following months unmistakably demonstrated its sympathy for the

Allies with such moves as the Lend-Lease Act of 1941. By this time the neutrality acts had been proved futile. They played no part whatsoever in keeping the United States at peace. It was absurd to pass legislation preventing American munitions trade with the European belligerents, to attempt to legislate the country "out of the first World War," for the causes of American entry into the first war differed markedly from those of entry into the second.

In the history of American diplomacy the decade of the 1930's, like the preceding decade, is a cheerless subject for analysis. The initial years of the Great Depression, from 1929 to 1933, passed in uncertainty, in expostulation to Japan but nothing more. Secretary of State Stimson and President Hoover were men of peace who did their best during an extraordinarily difficult domestic economic crisis. They realized that their measures were not altogether adequate, but they hoped that time would work for peace. It was impossible to imagine the course of history in the following years. The structure of peace arranged at Paris in 1919 had been challenged in the Far East by 1933, but it still appeared fairly secure in Europe. Almost all Americans, who did not realize that peace was indivisible, believed that Japan could have her little aggression in Manchuria and that the Peace of Paris, buttressed by the Washington Conference treaties and the Kellogg-Briand Pact, would endure.

During the first two administrations of President Franklin D. Roosevelt, the people of the United States continued to think primarily in terms of the Great Depression, the effect of the depression on their own individual lives. Americans beginning in 1933 were preoccupied by the New Deal in domestic affairs, the grand effort to escape from the Great Depression, and they had little time or inclination to examine the course of international affairs. President Roosevelt in 1935 told Prime Minister Joseph A. Lyons of Australia that never again would the United States be drawn into a European war, regardless of circumstances. Representative Louis Ludlow of Indiana in 1935 first introduced his resolution in the House proposing a constitutional amendment that, except in the event of an invasion of the United States or its territorial possessions, the authority of Congress to declare war should not become effective until confirmed by a majority vote in a national referendum. Congress came close to passing the resolution in January 1938, and held back only because of a personal message from

President Roosevelt to the speaker of the House of Representatives. Pacifist feeling was much in vogue everywhere, in Europe as well as America, during these years. In England many young men were taking the Oxford Oath that they would never fight for king and country. Before the leading Western democracies—Britain, France, and the United States—understood what was going on outside their national borders it was almost too late. The dictatorships of the world instituted the series of calamitous events: Ethiopia, the Rhineland, Spain, China, Austria, Czechoslovakia, Albania, Danzig. The time arrived when American diplomacy, as we see in retrospect, might have joined Britain and France in the stand against aggression. The United States, engrossed in the effort to achieve domestic economic recovery, renounced diplomacy in favor of neutrality.

Down to the end, confusion and inaction characterized American policy. Many prominent Americans had only the slightest notion of the holocaust that was preparing in Europe. Senator Borah in July 1939 announced publicly that there would be no second World War, and offered as authority his own private sources of information. When Hitler and Stalin on August 23, 1939 signed the Nazi-Soviet Pact, which gave Hitler a free hand in the West and was in a real sense the crucial diplomatic arrangement prior to outbreak of the war, the chairman of the House committee on foreign affairs, Representative Sol Bloom, called at the State Department and told a department officer that the crisis was not serious and that he had "doped out" why Hitler had come to terms with Russia: to give himself an asylum when he should ultimately be thrown out by the Germans. No other country, Bloom said, would accept him. At the height of the crisis in August 1939 there was little that American diplomats could do except await its end. The brilliant State Department career officer, Jay Pierrepont Moffat, wrote in his diary on August 26–27, 1939 that "These last two days have given me the feeling of sitting in a house where somebody is dying upstairs. There is relatively little to do and yet the suspense continues unabated." Headlines and radio flashes at the beginning of the second World War on September 1, 1939—GERMAN PLANES ATTACK WARSAW, ENGLAND AND FRANCE MOBILIZE—found the country almost as bewildered as it had been a quarter of a century earlier, in August 1914.

ADDITIONAL READING

The Great Depression dominated American diplomacy for a decade after 1929, and so the proper introduction to the era is J. K. Galbraith, *The Great Crash: 1929* (Boston, 1955), a witty account. A general view of the period is Allan Nevins's *The New Deal and World Affairs: 1933–1945* (New Haven, 1950), a volume in the *Chronicles of America;* for the Hoover years see Nevins's *The United States in a Chaotic World* (New Haven, 1950). Robert H. Ferrell, *American Diplomacy in the Great Depression: Hoover-Stimson Foreign Policy, 1929–1933* (New Haven, 1957) undertakes a detailed analysis of the Hoover years. For the two presidents, Hoover and FDR, one should consult *The Memoirs of Herbert Hoover: The Cabinet and the Presidency, 1920–1933* (New York, 1952); Frank Freidel's brilliant multivolume study *Franklin D. Roosevelt* (Boston, 1952–   ), of which the first three volumes take its subject to the inaugural in 1933 (*I. Apprenticeship*, 1952; *II. Ordeal*, 1954; *III. Triumph*, 1956); John Gunther, *Roosevelt in Retrospect: A Profile in History* (New York, 1950); James M. Burns, *Roosevelt: The Lion and the Fox* (New York, 1956); together with Dexter Perkins's excellent *The New Age of Franklin Roosevelt* (Chicago, 1956). The secretaries of state, Stimson and Hull, have each left their explanations—Stimson in his memoir written with the assistance of McGeorge Bundy, *On Active Service* (New York, 1948), an intelligent and fascinating account; and Hull's own *The Memoirs of Cordell Hull* (2 vols., New York, 1948), written just like the secretary's speeches, but laden with information together with asides on such subjects as the secretary's favorite game, croquet. On Stimson see also the critical appraisal by Richard N. Current, *Secretary Stimson: A Study in Statecraft* (New Brunswick, N.J., 1954). Accounts by subordinate State Department officials are William Phillips, *Ventures in Diplomacy* (Boston, 1953); and Nancy Harvison Hooker, ed., *The Moffat Papers: Selections from the Diplomatic Journals of Jay Pierrepont Moffat* (Cambridge, Mass., 1956). The Moffat diary is a rare piece, deserving of a much more extensive publication; no student of the 1930's can afford to neglect this source.

For the Far Eastern crisis of 1931–1933 there is the personal account by Henry L. Stimson, *The Far Eastern Crisis* (New York, 1936), which should be supplemented by the smaller section in Stimson's memoirs. Sara R. Smith, *The Manchurian Crisis: 1931–1932* (New York, 1948) views the troubles of the era in terms of a challenge to the League of Nations. For the inside of Japanese politics, one of the motive forces of the trouble in the orient, see Delmer M. Brown, *Nationalism in Japan* (Berkeley, 1955); and especially the absorbingly interesting study by Richard Storry, *The Double Patriots* (Boston, 1958). Storry relates that as a double shot of whiskey has twice the strength of a single shot, so some Japanese citizens during the 1920's and 1930's and early 1940's sought to be double patriots.

On American recognition of Russia one should consult the prior troubles in the United States at the end of the first World War, the *Red Scare: A Study in National Hysteria, 1919–1920* (Minneapolis, 1955) by Robert K. Murray. William A. Williams, *American-Russian Relations: 1781–1947* (New York, 1952) covers the entire span of relations with attention to the early twentieth century, and R. P. Browder, *Origins of Soviet-American Diplomacy* (Princeton, 1953) surveys the years before and immediately after recognition. See also Thomas A. Bailey, *America Faces Russia* (Ithaca, 1950).

There is as yet no adequate account of the neutrality legislation during the latter 1930's. A balanced view of part of the neutrality period appears in the volume by William L. Langer and S. Everett Gleason, *The Challenge to Isolation: 1937–40* (New York, 1952), the first of a two-volume study of American entrance into the second World War, 1937–1941. See also Selig Adler's *The Isolationist Impulse* (New York, 1957). An example of the antiwar agitation of the mid-1930's, with due attention to all the war-scare bogeys of the day, is H. C. Engelbrecht and F. C. Hanighen, *Merchants of Death* (New York, 1934).

To Pearl Harbor, 1939-1941

One feels a sense of tragedy in watching a great nation enter a world war. The course of American diplomacy in the years before December 7, 1941 is a somber, melancholy spectacle. American arms had brought victory to the Allies in the first World War, but afterward the United States threw away the advantages of the victory and sought to retire into the safe and sane nineteenth century when foreign relations were one of the least concerns of the successive administrations in Washington. For a while during the post-Versailles decades it appeared that the new American withdrawal—it was never complete isolation, for the American substitutes for the League indicated concern for world peace—would prove as successful as had the policies, or lack of them, of the nineteenth century. Especially in the golden period of the later 1920's, the tide of world prosperity supported a hope of washing away everywhere the rancors and antagonisms of the first World War. Instead, the Great Depression washed away prosperity and with it the hopes of the 1920's. By the time the United States had recovered its poise and, no longer preoccupied with domestic concerns, could look about—by the later 1930's—the peace of the world was almost irreparably lost.

American policy toward Europe in the later 1930's had little effect upon the course of events. The only discernible diplomatic action of the American government against the advance of aggression everywhere in the world was a series of personal communications which the president dispatched to the dictators during several of the

371

European crises. President Franklin Roosevelt in a letter of September 27, 1938 counseled peace to the dictators at the time of the Munich crisis. On April 14, 1939, after the Nazi occupation of Prague, the president in an open letter asked the German and Italian leaders to avow friendly intentions toward a long list of thirty-one specified European and Middle Eastern nations. Hitler on both occasions denied warlike intentions and restated German grievances. On August 24, 1939, Roosevelt again appealed to the dictators, beseeching them to settle their problems by peaceful means rather than war. All this effort was to no avail.

When war broke out on September 1 the American government still had the Neutrality Act of 1937 on its statute books, making it impossible for friendly foreign nations to purchase arms and ammunition in the United States, even if they undertook to carry these war materials in their own ships. The Neutrality Act of 1937 was revised in an act of November 4, 1939 to accommodate the sorely pressed Allies who, unlike Hitler, had not prepared for war. This change in the neutrality laws of the United States, according to President Roosevelt's critics, was an unneutral act. One must doubt that it was unneutral. Its provisions were as permissible under international law as were those of the Neutrality Act of 1937. But there can be no doubt that as month succeeded month and the position of the Allies became more desperate, the policies of the American government underwent changes which were, in reality, unneutral. Finally in the autumn of 1941 a large-scale undeclared war broke out between Germany and the United States in the Atlantic: American naval vessels were convoying foreign ships and sinking German submarines on sight; the German U-boats were retaliating wherever possible by torpedoing American destroyers. Yet war, when it came, did not stem from American unneutrality in the Atlantic, but came suddenly despite the correct and careful policy of the United States in the Pacific. Detractors of the American president, claiming that Roosevelt purposely exposed the Pacific fleet to a Japanese attack, have since described the events of December 7, 1941 at Pearl Harbor as the back door to war.

1. The War in Europe, 1939–1940

When the war opened in September 1939 the Allies at once looked to American industry for assistance in building their supplies of war material, and in November the president signed the revised neutrality act which permitted assistance. Meanwhile, on September 5, two days after France and Britain declared war on Germany, Roosevelt had proclaimed American neutrality under the act of 1937. He announced on September 8 a limited national emergency, a rather unprecedented state of affairs which no American president had ever proclaimed before and which, presumably, FDR himself thought up in order to indicate American interest in the European conflict and yet at the same time avoid worrying Congress and the people by proclamation of an unqualified national emergency. Announcement of the latter might well have seemed like a prelude to American entry into the European war.

For the next few months little more of a concrete nature occurred to indicate the Roosevelt administration's essentially deep sympathy for the cause of the Allies in their fight against German aggression. In the early months of the war it appeared that a *Sitzkrieg*, a stalemate, had developed on the Western front, and during the months until the spring of 1940 this "phony war" made the armament situation of Britain and France seem far less precarious than it was, even in the presence of much placing of armament orders in American factories. In the winter of 1939–1940 President Roosevelt became ever more open in his castigation of the Nazi German government. Some of the utterances in his fireside chats were strong statements about the personalities in control of a government with which the United States was nominally at peace. But beyond verbal condemnation, and the general facilitating of Allied war material purchases, the United States did not go. It took the shattering events of the Nazi spring offensive of 1940 to bring the administration to an understanding of the power and danger of the German government and people under the demonic guidance of their Fuehrer.

The German offensive of 1940 had long been in preparation, and it came with the full fury of planning and purpose. First occurred the occupation of Denmark and the conquest of Norway. Then German troops pushed into the Netherlands, Belgium, and Luxembourg, down toward the French Channel ports. Meanwhile the main German drive laced through the allegedly impassable Ardennes forest and moved via Sedan to the Channel. Next followed the turning of France's Maginot line—the ponderous French fortifications were taken from the rear. The French and British infantry and light tanks, no match for the

German Panzer divisions, were brushed aside like so much chaff. Soon it was a race with time, to see whether the British and some remnants of the French forces could escape over the Channel from the encircled port of Dunkirk. By June 4, 1940, 338,226 troops, mostly British, had got across to England. They had lost all equipment excepting their side arms and their nerve. This latter quality proved far more important than anything else they could have taken with them. The new prime minister, Winston Spencer Churchill, considered by many the greatest statesman in British history, defiantly announced in Parliament that "we shall not flag or fail. We shall go on to the end . . . we shall fight in the seas and oceans, we shall fight with growing confidence and growing strength in the air, we shall defend our island, whatever the cost may be, we shall fight on the beaches, we shall fight on the landing-grounds, we shall fight in the fields and in the streets, we shall fight in the hills; we shall never surrender, and even if, which I do not for a moment believe, this island or a large part of it were subjugated and starving, then our Empire beyond the seas, armed and guarded by the British Fleet, would carry on the struggle, until, in God's good time, the New World, with all its power and might, steps forth to the rescue and the liberation of the Old."

No American statesman at such an hour could have failed to see the stakes in the world conflict, and Franklin D. Roosevelt set to work with vigor to assist the beleaguered British government and people. In his annual budget message of January 1940 the president had already requested $1,800,000,000 for national defense, an unprecedented expenditure in time of peace, and he had asked for additional appropriations of $1,182,000,000. He called for production of 50,000 combat planes a year. He requested $1,277,000,000 more on May 31 for military and naval requirements, and in response to an urgent appeal from Prime Minister Churchill the War Department on June 3 began releasing to Britain surplus or outdated stocks of arms, munitions, and aircraft. The War Department turned stocks back to manufacturers who sold them to the British. Over $43,000,000 worth went across the Atlantic in June 1940.

Other measures were quickly forthcoming. In a move not devoid of political overtones (Roosevelt was toying with the idea of a moratorium on domestic politics, much as Lincoln had sought a political truce in the early days of the Civil War) FDR appointed two prominent Republican leaders, Henry L. Stimson and Frank Knox, as secretaries of war and of the navy. It was possible also to interpret this move as an effort to silence Republican criticism of the administration's pro-Allied measures, although criticism of Roosevelt's actions was not always patterned on party lines. In any event, one must say that both appointees, Stimson and Knox, were strong and able men who served their country well in the emergency which began in June 1940 and continued for over five years. Knox died under the strain in 1944. Stimson, in an atmosphere of triumph and honor, returned to private life in 1945.

In addition to the bipartisan appointments of Stimson and Knox, the president undertook in other ways to prepare the country for the struggle which he felt was approaching. In early autumn of 1940 he discussed defense problems with Prime Minister W. L. Mackenzie King of Canada, and agreed to establish a permanent joint board of defense. On August 31, with the consent of Congress, the first units of the National Guard were inducted into federal service. On September 2 the president, in an executive agreement with the British government, traded fifty World War I destroyers in exchange for the right to 99-year leases on naval and air bases in Newfoundland, Bermuda, the Bahamas, Jamaica, St. Lucia, Trinidad, Antigua, and British Guiana. This he announced as "the most important action in the reinforcement of our national defense . . . since the Louisiana Purchase." Then on September 16, 1940 the Burke-Wadsworth Bill became law, providing for selective service, the first peacetime compulsory-military-training program in the United States.

With these measures behind him the president went before the country as a candidate for a third term in the White House, running against the liberal Republican, Wendell Willkie. This campaign, one may say in retrospect, might have been used by both candidates—Willkie, like FDR, favored aid to the Allies—to educate the American people to the realities of international affairs. Unfortunately it was not. The presidential campaign of 1940 was a lost opportunity. Both candidates marred the campaign by a conscious trimming of foreign-policy issues. Willkie and FDR almost outdid each other in promising peace to the American electorate. It is true that the American people naively asked for, and were reassured by, such empty promises. It is also true that Willkie honestly, and despite the feverish injunctions of many of his political supporters, came out in favor of the Roosevelt administration's pro-Allied activities. Yet the rigors of electioneering finally drove Willkie into saying that "If you elect me president I will never send an American boy to fight in any European war." Not to be outdone, the president himself, at Boston on October 30, 1940, told American mothers that "I have said this before, but I shall say it again and again and again: Your boys are not going to be sent into any foreign wars." At Buffalo on November 2 he said: "Your President says this country is not going to war." It was only a few months after the campaign that American troops were en route to Greenland and Iceland; a little more than a year later the president had to take his promise back, completely.

With the assurance of another four years of office, Roosevelt moved ahead in his plans for aid to Britain against Germany. In a fireside chat on December 29, 1940 he told the nation that it should become "the great arsenal of democracy." In his annual message to Congress on January 6, 1941 he enunciated the Four Freedoms—freedom of speech and expression, freedom of worship, freedom from want, freedom from fear. Then, having done all these things, having laid the moral and material basis of aid to Britain against the German tyranny, he turned to two new and pressing problems. British credit in the United States was running out, and the Johnson Act of 1934 prevented the floating of public loans. The requirements of British defense were so large that no private loans could possibly cover them. The president in his annual message of January 6, 1941 produced a new formula, "lend-lease." Then there was a second problem: a sudden increase in the effectiveness and rigor of German submarine warfare in the Atlantic made necessary some sort of naval protection for British ships transporting the American-made goods to England.

2. *Lend-Lease and Its Aftermath*

Lend-lease was the first major policy of assistance toward Great Britain adopted by the Roosevelt administration. It was a massive contribution to the defeat of Nazi Germany. Previous measures, such as the Neutrality Act of 1939 and the destroyers-bases deal of 1940, had looked in the direction of an Allied victory, but lend-lease was a move of substance that reduced these other acts to insignificance.

Its inspiration lay in Britain's dire need, but more intimately it was a result of the increasing personal cordiality between the two leaders of Britain and the United States. Roosevelt had been corresponding with Winston Churchill since the beginning of the European war, and the delighted Churchill—who at the outbreak of the war was first lord of the admiralty—had replied over the mysterious signature of "Naval Person." Upon becoming prime minister in May 1940 he changed his signature to "Former Naval Person." Through the medium of this correspondence the two statesmen of the English-speaking peoples kept in contact, and the president was in a position to know quickly the difficulties of his British opposite. It was in response to Britain's needs, so persuasively and personally represented by Churchill, that Roosevelt in January 1941 proposed to Congress the Lend-Lease Act: "H.R. 1776"—so some unknown person had numbered the epoch-making bill when it came before the House of Representatives. According to its terms the president could "lend, lease, or otherwise dispose of," to any country whose defense was vital to the United States, arms and other equipment and supplies to an extent of an initial appropriation of $7,000,000,000. Fiscally the Lend-Lease Act made history for the size of its original appropriation, which was more than ninety times the amount of the national debt which Secretary of the Treasury Alexander Hamilton had refunded in 1790. By the end of the war the United States had appropriated for lend-lease more than $50 billion, a gigantic sum which would have been incomprehensible to the nation's founding fathers. H.R. 1776 did not, to be sure, go through Congress without objection. There was a vociferous debate during the first three months of 1941 which for bitterness and passion has rarely been equaled in American history.

The reasons for the bitterness of the debate over lend-lease were not difficult to perceive. For one, it was clear that with the proposed Lend-Lease Act the Roosevelt administration was irreparably committing the United States to the Allied cause; from this act onward there could be no turning back. For another, the administration's opponents in Congress had been resisting the president's measures of help to Britain with the increasing conviction that such opposition was hopeless—and their despair translated itself easily into passionate outbursts on the floor of the Senate and House. For a third, there was much concern, part of it political but part of it utterly sincere, that the president, so recently re-elected to an unprecedented third term of office, was pushing his views too far in Congress and throughout the country, that he had an obedient congressional majority and was hoodwinking the people and moving steadily in the direction of a dictatorship. All this misgiving may seem nonsensical by hindsight, but many individuals in 1941 were agitated. Debate over lend-lease brought their feelings to the surface.

Probably the most outspoken accusation came from Senator Nye, long an opponent of President Roosevelt, who in a remark which alluded to the Agricultural Adjustment Act of 1933 announced that "The lend-lease-give program is the New Deal's triple A foreign policy; it will plow under every fourth American boy." Roosevelt was outraged. He angrily denounced "those who talk about plowing under every fourth American child." He told his press conference that he regarded Senator Nye's remark as "the most untruthful, as the most dastardly, unpatriotic thing that has ever been said. Quote me on that. That really is the rottenest thing that has been said in public life in my generation."

Nye's crude metaphor was beyond question misplaced and inappropriate, and the president had reason to lose his temper. Nonetheless the administration did approach lend-lease, a momentous piece of legislation, in a not entirely candid way. Roosevelt, it has sometimes been said, was at his worst when moving indirectly, and in the case of lend-lease he came to the proposal's defense in a way which at the least might be described as inaccurate. He must have known that the measure would probably lead to war, and certainly that if it led to peace this end could come only after the United States for a long time had exposed itself to the danger of German retaliation while giving aid to the British. An administration official, Jesse Jones, said during the lend-lease debate that "We're in the war; at least we are nearly in it; we're preparing for it." This utterance FDR turned with the comment that lend-lease would be administered not as a war measure but, on the contrary, as a peace measure. Roosevelt denied that lend-lease contradicted the spirit, if not the terms, of the Neutrality Act of 1939.

The administration's supporters maintained vehemently that lend-lease would not lead to war. Senator J. W. Bailey of North Carolina remarked that "It is said that the passage of the bill will lead to war. I do not know whether it will or not. I think those who predict that it will lead to war are in a pretty safe position, because there is a great deal of probability that war is coming, either course we take, and, when it comes, those who say it will come on account of this pro-

posed act will say, 'Now it has come on account of the act.' Those
who take the affirmative have to take the responsibility for events.
The man who takes the opposition side is always in a fortunate
position; he is not responsible for anything; he can always say, 'I did
not advocate it.' I question whether the passage of the pending bill
will lead to war, and I say its object is to head off war."

Representative E. V. Izak of California said in the House that "I
lost all patience with my people when they came to me during the
last campaign and said: 'Please don't get us into war.' I said, 'Don't
look at me. I am not getting you into war, but there is one man who
has the power to do that, and that is Mr. Hitler. Look at him.' "

And so debate went on. As we have seen, the president under the
proposed act could make any arrangements with other nations which
he deemed satisfactory, which implied much congressional trust in
the president's discretion. Roosevelt did not have to report to Congress
in any way on anything he did under the law. Because authorship of
H.R. 1776 was unknown, many individuals believed (and they were
right) that the proposed act had emanated from the White House;
the anonymity and surmise lent an air of conspiracy to the debate in
Congress. As Representative Karl E. Mundt of South Dakota remarked, "We find this piece of legislation—surreptitiously conceived,
individually disclaimed, of unknown parentage—placed before us,
like a baby in a basket on our doorstep, and we are asked to adopt
it." Perhaps Representative Dewey Short of Missouri summed up this
belief in lend-lease as a conspiracy when he said that "You can dress
this measure up all you please, you can sprinkle it with perfume and
pour powder on it, masquerade it in any form you please . . . , but
it is still foul and it stinks to high heaven. It does not need a doctor,
it needs an undertaker."

All this was to no avail. "An Act to Promote the Defense of the
United States" became law on March 11, 1941. As a direct result of
the act, with its enormous supplying of aid to Britain against Nazi
Germany, a virtual state of war broke out in the autumn of 1941 along
the Atlantic seaways.

The approach of President Roosevelt to this undeclared war was,
like his approach to lend-lease, indirect, and it is fair to say that the
president's incapacity for indirect action lent to his words during the
spring and summer and autumn of 1941 some color of untruthfulness.
Congress, not altogether certain of presidential intentions with lend-

lease, had written into the act a statement as follows: "Nothing in this Act shall be construed to authorize or to permit the authorization of convoying by naval vessels of the United States. Nothing in this Act shall be construed to authorize or to permit the authorization of the entry of any American vessel into a combat area in violation of section 3 of the Neutrality Act of 1939." The president denied for several months in 1941 that he had any intention of instituting convoys. Meanwhile he set on foot measures which in result if not in avowed purpose were equivalent to convoying.

After passage of the Lend-Lease Act the president began almost at once to feel out public opinion on convoys, through statements by himself and by friends and members of the administration. FDR on March 15 began a move toward convoying by a radio address in which he said he would maintain a bridge of ships to Britain. On March 16 Senator Carter Glass of Virginia said he favored convoys if the president intended to imply that in the radio address. Next day the Committee to Defend America by Aiding the Allies, a group of important private individuals with easy access to the White House, came out for convoys. In a press conference on March 18 Roosevelt parried questions on convoys. Secretary of the Navy Knox said on March 20 that the Navy Department had no plans for convoys. On March 27 Senator Glass again said he was in favor of convoys. Then on March 31 Senator Charles W. Tobey of New Hampshire and Representative Harry Sauthoff of Wisconsin introduced in the Senate and House a joint resolution against convoys.

Tobey made a speech in which he explored the convoy question. He found himself opposed by Senator Alben W. Barkley of Kentucky, the Senate majority leader, who argued that Germany already had the right to declare war on the United States because of America's violation of neutrality by aiding Great Britain with lend-lease. Barkley could not see any further danger from convoys. Tobey asked his opponent if he was defending convoys.

Barkley: "Oh, no; the Senator knows that I am not."

Tobey: "I am asking the Senator in good faith."

Barkley: "And I am answering the Senator in good faith; if we have violated international law in such a way as could result in a declaration of war against us by Germany, we have already done that, and the convoying of ships would be only an incident."

A little later Tobey observed that "there is always a straw that breaks the camel's back, and that straw in my judgment, will be when, as, and if we send convoys to transport goods to belligerent nations."

Barkley: "That will depend upon events that we cannot now foresee."

Tobey: "Does not the Senator feel so, too?"

Barkley: "I will express my views upon that subject when the occasion has arisen."

Tobey: "In the words of the advertisement, 'If eventually, why not now?'"

Barkley: "I do not think it is possible for anybody today, even including the wise Senator from New Hampshire, to foresee conditions that may exist."

The colloquy drifted off into irrelevancies, led by Barkley.

Such was the interesting exchange on the Senate floor between the president's spokesman and an opposition senator, and if no light emerged it did serve to further interest in the proposition of convoys. Tobey, aroused over the matter, apparently gave information to the New York *Daily News*, published on April 17, 1941, to the effect that American naval vessels were giving assistance to the British far out into the Atlantic, doing patrols and reconnaissance, even sailing between opposing enemies on the high seas and daring one side to shoot. In reply the president's press secretary, Stephen Early, declared that American naval vessels were operating far out in the Atlantic "on neutrality patrol," flashing news of alien ships in uncoded messages that anyone could listen to. American ships were carrying out their original instructions, he said, "to observe and report," and they were "keeping war from our front doors." Early said that the president, after reading a morning paper, thought its account had woven the long-time and historic policy of the United States into a story which was a deliberate lie.

Shortly after this, on April 25, FDR made an explanation of the difference between a convoy and a patrol. There was the same difference between the two operations, he said, as between a cow and a horse ("if one looks at a cow and calls it a horse that is all right with the president, but that does not make a cow a horse"). Roosevelt recalled that in pioneer days the wagon trains going westward had armed guards, and also scouts. The rule was, he explained, to keep the trains more than two miles from where the Indians were. He elaborated this pioneer example by saying that it was not safe to wait until the Indians got two miles away, but advisable to ascertain whether the Indians were 200 miles away.

Meanwhile on April 9 the president had signed an agreement with the Danish minister in Washington which included Greenland in "our sphere of co-operative hemispheric defense." Hitler launched his rash attack on the USSR in June. On July 7 there was an agreement with Iceland similar to that with Denmark. Under these arrangements United States military forces received convenient new bases for their "patrols" to protect their "security zone" and "patrol areas."

Two months passed after occupation of Iceland before there began to occur a perhaps not unexpected series of untoward incidents. The first, probably the most important, was the attack by a German submarine on the United States destroyer *Greer*, off Iceland, on September 4. The president took a strong view of this engagement. Roosevelt made a broadcast about the *Greer* on September 11 in which he said the vessel "was carrying American mail to Iceland. . . . She was then and there attacked by a submarine. . . . I tell you the blunt fact that the German submarine fired first upon this American destroyer without warning, and with deliberate design to sink her." He announced that he had given sink-on-sight orders to the navy, a decision which, he said, was the "result of months and months of constant thought and anxiety and prayer."

Without doubting the care that went into the president's decision, one should perhaps explain that the circumstances of the *Greer* attack were not altogether as the president described them. In his radio address he had, indeed, engaged in the time-honored diplomatic practice of *suppressio veri, suggestio falsi*. The *Greer* while en route to Iceland had been informed by a British plane of the presence of a submarine about ten miles directly ahead. The *Greer* gave chase, trailing the submarine and broadcasting its position for three hours and twenty-eight minutes, during which the British plane dropped four depth charges, when the submarine fired a torpedo which crossed the *Greer* about 100 yards astern. The destroyer answered with a pattern of eight depth charges; the submarine replied with another torpedo that missed the *Greer*. The chase went on for a while, with more depth charges, and the American ship finally gave up and proceeded to Iceland.

The sink-on-sight order came on September 11. The navy on

September 16 announced convoying in the Atlantic as far as Iceland.

There followed a month later, on October 17, the torpedoing with severe damage of the destroyer *Kearny* by a German submarine west of Iceland, with loss of eleven American lives. FDR on October 27 delivered a long and vehement address, in the course of which he said that "America has been attacked. The U.S.S. *Kearny* is not just a Navy ship. She belongs to every man, woman, and child in this Nation." The *Kearny* had also been attacking German submarines when she was torpedoed.

The tanker *Salinas* sank on October 30, 1941.

The destroyer *Reuben James* was torpedoed on the night of October 30, with loss of 96 officers and men.

The issue was clearly drawn between the United States and Germany—of that there could be no doubt. A series of unneutral acts had demonstrated the sympathies of the Roosevelt administration: lend-lease and convoying had put the case clearly enough. The leader of the German Reich knew in the autumn of 1941 that the government of the United States was his enemy.

There remained, in the course of events in the Atlantic, a touch of high principle, produced by President Roosevelt and Prime Minister Churchill during their dramatic meeting in Argentia Bay off Newfoundland in mid-August 1941. It was during this meeting that they drew up the Atlantic Charter.

The Charter of August 14, 1941 was not a signed document, only a press release, a statement of principles agreed to by the participants at the Argentia meeting, but its informal nature did not lessen its importance. A document analogous to the Fourteen Points, it set out what were to be American and to some extent British aims for the remainder of the war years. It later was written into the United Nations Declaration of January 1, 1942 and adopted by all the Allies against Nazi Germany. In this joint declaration Roosevelt and Churchill pledged that their countries sought no aggrandizement, territorial or other; second, "they desire to see no territorial changes that do not accord with the freely expressed wishes of the peoples concerned"; third, they announced the right of all peoples to choose their own form of government; fourth, "access, on equal terms, to the trade and to the raw materials of the world"; fifth, economic collaboration among nations; sixth, freedom from fear and want; seventh, all men had the right "to traverse the high seas and oceans without hindrance"; eighth, disarmament of aggressors and limitation of the arms of peace-loving peoples. The Charter admittedly was not as explicit as the Fourteen Points—it was in fact downright vague in a number of its pronouncements—but it did declare in rounded terms the war aims of the American and British peoples. Churchill, as the war progressed, came to see that some of the Charter's provisions were visionary, and during a dinner at Yalta in 1945 he pointedly told Roosevelt that the Charter was not "a law, but a star." The American president, however, took the Charter seriously, and Churchill and the other Allies were therefore persuaded to take it into account.

Thus the United States had come in the Atlantic, through principle and practice, to virtually a state of belligerency against Germany, although in spite of these unneutral actions there was still no declared war in the Atlantic between the two nations. For the moment it suited the German dictator's purposes that there be no declaration of war. Hitler apparently believed that with the attack upon Russia in June 1941, an attack which at its outset came within a hair's breadth of victory, he could ensure his domination of the continent of Europe—afterward, he would settle scores with both England and the United States.

What would have happened had Russia collapsed in 1941 is an interesting subject for speculation. It is difficult to see how British and American power alone could have defeated a triumphant Germany, unless the war would have gone on for years and perhaps decades. Roosevelt took a grave chance in coming to the defense of Britain when he did. Russia fortunately did not collapse in 1941, and history saved the reputation of an American president.

In retrospect it is easy to see where the German dictator made his mistakes. He could have nicely confused the American people in 1940–1941 by a magnanimous peace with France. He could have offered an olive branch to England, and used every stratagem to convince the somewhat gullible Americans that he alone was holding back the Bolsheviks along the marches of Eastern Europe. Then, had he placated the Russian people in the captured areas of their country, instead of victimizing and enslaving and decimating them, he might have swept forward all the way across the steppes of Siberia in the guise of an anticommunist crusader. Doubtless the leaders of the American and British governments knew too much already about the bestial nature of the Nazi regime, but a careful propaganda effort might have caused trouble among the divided and confused American people. Luckily for the United States this historical nightmare never became real.

Thus far we have sketched the measures of the American government at the outbreak of the war in Europe, and analyzed in some detail the mobilization of American resources which began after the successful German spring campaign against France in 1940. By the final month of the year 1941 the American navy was engaged in open although undeclared warfare with the German submarine fleets in the western Atlantic. Still, the event which plunged the United States into war derived from an entirely different development, the deterioration of American-Japanese relations in the summer and autumn of 1941.

3. Pearl Harbor

Ever since the Mukden incident of September 18, 1931, relations between Washington and Tokyo had been strained. For that matter, ever since the victory of Japan over Russia in 1904–1905 and the subsequent refusal of the Japanese to be houseboys for the open door, distrust had existed between the two Pacific nations, a distrust which on several occasions before 1931 had overcome the normal reticences of international discourse. At such moments as the segregation of Japanese school children in San Francisco schools in 1906, the Twenty-One Demands of 1915, and the exclusion of Japanese immigrants from the United States in the immigration act of 1924, Japanese anger at the American government rose to fever pitch. Long before the occupation of Manchuria, official relations between the two countries had become far from congenial.

The Manchurian affair initiated a precipitous decline in Japanese-American cordiality, and when in 1937 the Japanese army, having virtually taken over the civil government in Tokyo, went into China in a large way and began to seize China's main coastal cities and as much of the hinterland as could be easily held, relations between Japan and the United States sank lower and lower. The military operations of the so-called China incident were conducted on a ferocious scale. The Manchurian incident was marked by almost no atrocities by Japanese soldiers, but the China fighting in 1937 and thereafter was appallingly inhumane, perhaps as many as 100,000 Chinese soldiers and civilians being murdered in the sack of Nanking alone. In marked contrast to the doubted information about increasing Nazi brutalities in Europe, the American people quickly learned of this bloodletting in China, where the American missionary effort both Protestant and Catholic had for decades been large; the missionaries wrote home terrified letters about what was happening before their very eyes. President Roosevelt apparently believed at this time that public opinion was ready for some sort of positive policy. He proposed in a speech in Chicago on October 5, 1937 that there be an international quarantine of aggressors as the only means to preserve peace. He did not, it is true, pursue this policy at the Brussels Conference, held on November 3–24, 1937 by all the signatories (save Japan) of the Nine-Power Treaty. At Brussels the United States, along with the other nations, took a weak position and the conference broke up in despair. Still, the president was beginning to think of action. When on December 12, 1937 some firebrands in the Japanese army willfully sank the United States river gunboat *Panay*, with loss of two American lives, the administration felt strong enough to demand from the Japanese government an immediate apology, reparations, and guarantee against further incidents. The Tokyo regime, hardened though it was, gave in at once to the blunt note of Secretary Hull.

Relations continued to deteriorate after 1937. When the second World War commenced in Europe in 1939, the Japanese awaited events until after the fall of France in the early summer of 1940; then the Tokyo government on September 27, 1940 signed a Tripartite Pact with Germany and Italy. High government officials in Washington at once began to worry lest the three fascist powers were now concerting their policies, and that while Japan alone of the three aggressor nations had not yet entered the lists against the Western democracies, she would enter in due time, presumably the worst possible time for Britain and America.

What, in truth, was the purpose of the Tripartite Pact of 1940? Did it as good as tell the world that Japan intended a new move of expansion in the Far East at the expense of American interests, and therefore was enlisting Germany to assist her in event of a head-on collision with the United States? If Japan expanded further in the Far East, if she moved into territory other than China, it would be either (1) Siberia or else (2) the much more attractive lands of the Dutch East Indies, French Indochina, British Malaya and Burma, perhaps

Australia and New Zealand. It was axiomatic that the United States, while attempting to bolster England in the fight in Europe, could not allow Japan to knock down the British empire in Asia. An advance not into Siberia but into Southeast Asia, Australia, and New Zealand might well bring an American declaration of war. Even so, it was an error to construe the Tripartite Pact as aimed against the United States. Actually Germany in 1940 was seeking to enlist Japan in the forthcoming campaign against Soviet Russia, planned for the spring of 1941. The *Realpolitiker* in Berlin hoped that Japan would enter Siberia at the same time that the German army crossed the Russian borders in the West.

It was true, of course, that the Japanese had made up their minds by 1940 to turn southward—but Allied diplomats in so reading the Tripartite Pact obtained the right conclusion from the wrong evidence.

The southward advance seemed necessary to the Japanese as the only solution of a crucial problem of military logistics. Japan's oil reserves were so small that they could not support a major and prolonged war. Japan depended upon imports from the United States for eighty per cent of her oil. As the military planners in Tokyo saw it, they must take the oil of the Dutch East Indies. The strategists of the Japanese army and navy were resigned to the fact that the southward advance meant a war with the United States. Hence they planned to destroy at the outset the principal American military force in the Pacific, the American fleet based on Pearl Harbor in Hawaii. From such a blow, they hoped, the American navy would require months and perhaps years to recuperate. During that period, Japan could so expand her power through the Far East that she would become impregnable to American counterattack. Then, the United States having become involved in the war in Europe, American political leaders would negotiate a peace with Tokyo, and allow Japan to keep her new "co-prosperity sphere."

Such a scheme of conquest may today seem foolhardy and irresponsible in the extreme, and perhaps it was. One might ask how the Japanese military, who were not complete fools, could have sponsored it. The minds of men, one can only conclude, are always capable of self-delusion. As for the leaders of the Japanese army and navy, they were mostly men of narrow background and intensely professional experience, incapable of making the large appraisals and informed guesses which are the rudiments of statesmanship. Japan's military planning was never the careful plotting and analysis which was later attributed to it. The Japanese military leaders really did not know where they were going. Japanese aggression was a jerry-built structure which moved uncertainly forward, one event leading crazily to another. It is easy to see now that the plan of the young officer enthusiasts led by General Tojo was an immense gamble. It would have been better for Japan in 1940–1941 to have obtained an agreement with the United States. The Japanese military, unfortunately, were unable to see a middle way out of their predicament. They could not see that honorable peace was an acceptable alternative to capitulation or war. Typical of Japanese reasoning was the contention of an admiral at an imperial conference—that because of the vulnerability of the Japanese military machine to a cutting off of foreign oil imports Japan was like a patient who was certain to die if you did nothing, but might be saved by a dangerous operation.

The southward advance was chosen, instead of Siberia. The German government learned with surprise in the early spring of 1941 that Japan was negotiating a nonaggression pact with Russia. Foreign Minister Yosuke Matsuoka signed the pact in Moscow on April 13 with Foreign Minister Vyacheslav M. Molotov. The Russians already were anticipating the German attack which came on their western border in June, and they were happy to secure their eastern flank in Manchuria against the Japanese. Japan likewise secured her northern flank, and her armies could pursue the cherished southward advance.

The first move came quickly. The Japanese announced on July 25, 1941 that together with the Vichy French government of Marshal Henri-Philippe Pétain (the Vichy government controlled that part of France unoccupied by the Germans) they were undertaking a joint protectorate of Indochina. There was no reason why Japan should protect Indochina, except that Japanese troops could thereby menace the Philippines. Access to the airport at Saigon, acquired several months before, had already brought the British bastion of Singapore within easy range of Japanese bombing planes.

Not to be outdone, President Roosevelt on July 26, 1941 issued an executive order freezing Japanese assets in the United States. This ended all trade, forcing even those Japanese ships in American ports to depart in ballast. Among other things the president's executive order cut off all exports of oil.

Back in the summer of 1940 the United States had begun to embargo strategic materials to Japan—scrap iron, steel, and certain types of oil products—and in following months additional embargoes were placed until on January 27, 1941 Ambassador Joseph C. Grew in Tokyo warned that "There is a lot of talk around town to the effect that the Japanese, in case of a break with the United States, are planning to go all out in a surprise mass attack at Pearl Harbor." Actually this was the very time that Admiral Isoruku Yamamoto began planning the Pearl Harbor attack. When Grew's premonitions reached the United States they were mulled over by the Office of Naval Intelligence, but ONI placed no credence in them. Between January and July 1941 much war material continued to go out from America to Japan. Only high-octane gasoline and aviation lubricating oil were openly forbidden in trade, and other types of petroleum products flowed in a stream across the Pacific to the Japanese army and navy. But on July 26 this trade came to a sudden end.

Both the United States and Japan began preparing for war. President Roosevelt in the summer of 1941 nationalized the Philippine forces, and appointed the Philippine field marshal and former United States army chief of staff, Douglas MacArthur, as commanding general of army forces in the Far East. Meanwhile Japanese army planners drafted plans for major strikes against the Malay peninsula, the Philippines, and Pearl Harbor. Yet both nations needed time. The Japanese militarists needed a few months to train their carrier air groups to destroy the United States Pacific fleet, and America needed time for new naval construction and to reinforce the army in the Philippines.

There followed several months of last-minute diplomatic negotiations—which, let it be added, were sincere on both sides. On the American side President Roosevelt and Secretary of State Hull were anxious for peace if they could obtain it with honor. On the Japanese side the diplomats of the Tokyo government did not know what their military were up to. The Japanese ambassador in Washington, Admiral Kichisaburo Nomura, was an honorable man, a typical Japanese conservative, who knew that his poverty-stricken country should not attempt to play the role of the frog which wanted to become a bull. Nomura with good reason was *persona grata* at the State Department. He knew nothing of the plans of the militarists in his homeland.

Nomura's superior, Premier Prince Fumimaro Konoye, was a well-meaning individual but of weak tendencies, a person known in Japan as a liberal, yet as premier in 1937 he had said that China should be "beaten to her knees." Konoye in 1941 was window dressing for the militarists, and in early September they impatiently gave him six weeks to reach a settlement with the United States. The terms: America would have to turn China over to Japan. With this impossible proposal as his only program, Konoye sought a Pacific conference with Roosevelt. But the latter, well advised by Secretary Hull, who suggested that the Japanese be invited to detail their program in advance of any meeting, refused to meet the Japanese premier. The six-week deadline came and passed. Konoye, forced to resign, gave way to a new premier, General Tojo, the Razor Brain, in whose keeping events now lay.

The crisis moved rapidly toward a showdown. Ambassador Grew in Tokyo did not know exactly what was going on in the councils of the militarists, but in a cable of November 3 he warned Secretary Hull that Japan might resort to war measures with "dramatic and dangerous suddenness." Perhaps he recalled that all of Japan's modern wars, in 1894, 1904, and 1914, had begun without formal declaration of hostilities. Nomura in Washington on November 5 received instructions that it was "absolutely necessary" to come to an agreement with the United States by November 25. A special ambassador, Saburo Kurusu, another man of good will, made a hurried flight from Japan to assist Nomura in these negotiations. On November 20 the two Japanese ambassadors made what they regarded as their "absolutely final proposal," a rather immodest request for resumption of oil exports and noninterference by the United States in Japan's China incident. Secretary Hull realized that granting these was impossible, given the rising American popular temper. Americans might permit trimming on European matters, but they would allow their government no compromises with the Asiatic Axis partner, Japan. The American people did not realize how close their country was to war, but it is doubtful if in 1941 they would have permitted a "Munich" in the Far East, even had they known the seriousness of affairs.

For a short time Washington officials did consider some sort of *modus vivendi*. Military preparations were in a perilous state—an army contingent was at sea near Guam, the marines were just pulling out of Shanghai where for years they had been protecting American commercial interests, and 21,000 troops were scheduled to sail from the United States for the Philippines on December 8. Secretary Hull prepared a three-month *modus vivendi*, which included some concessions on oil, and submitted it to representatives of China, Great Britain, Australia, and the Netherlands in Washington. The Chinese government violently opposed the idea. Winston Churchill described it as "thin diet for Chiang Kai-shek." And, in any event, a *modus vivendi* would have been unacceptable to the Japanese. Premier Tojo in Japan already had rejected any compromise along the lines of Hull's draft, and so when the State Department dropped the matter nothing was lost.

Hull then presented the Japanese with a long document dated November 26, which among other requests asked the Japanese to get out of China. At the Tokyo war crimes trial after the end of the war, General Tojo admitted that the note of November 26 was little more than a restatement of the Nine-Power Treaty of Washington, to which Japan had been a party, but twenty years after the Washington Conference the Nine-Power Treaty was unacceptable to Japan's rulers. On December 1 a cabinet council met in the Imperial presence in Tokyo and ratified General Tojo's decision to make war on America, Great Britain, and the Netherlands. The Pearl Harbor striking force, which had already sailed, was notified that X-day was December 7. Nomura and Kurusu, unaware that the die had been cast, were instructed to present the Japanese reply to the November 26 proposal at 1:00 P.M. Washington time, December 7, which was twenty minutes before the striking hour at Pearl Harbor.

The intensely interesting details of the Pearl Harbor attack have been carefully described from both the Japanese and American sides in a number of books and essays easily available to serious readers. Briefly, the Japanese attack force of six carriers, escorted by two battleships and a full complement of cruisers, destroyers, and submarines, sailed undetected through high seas and fog. When the fleet changed course toward Hawaii, on the final lap of the voyage, one of the carriers hoisted to its masthead the identical flag which the revered Admiral Togo had displayed on his flagship before the battle of Tsushima Strait in 1905. It was a great moment in Japanese history when on Sunday morning, "the day that will live in infamy" (as President Roosevelt would describe it in his war message), the attacking Japanese planes roared over Pearl Harbor and found the battleship fleet exactly where it was expected, tied up to the mooring quays along the southeast shore of Ford Island.

The valor and heroism of the surprised and trapped seamen will long live in the annals of American naval warfare. More than 2,300 lives were lost that terrible Sunday morning. Eight battleships capsized or were otherwise put out of action. Fortunately for the United States, Admiral William F. Halsey was away with a carrier striking force on a special mission, and his precious ships escaped the disaster in the harbor. Fortunately too, the Japanese in their attack virtually ignored the installations and fuel tanks at Pearl Harbor, destruction of which would have presented grave logistic problems and perhaps forced a removal of the fleet's remaining ships to the American west coast. Still, the Japanese attack on Pearl Harbor, despite such miscalculations, was appallingly successful. American entry into the second World War occurred after an unprecedented naval disaster.

4. *The Theory of the Back Door*

Was Pearl Harbor the back door to war?

This question was to trouble many Americans for years to come. Debate over the circumstances of American entry into the second World War had to await the end of the war itself, but in 1945 it rose to the surface of public discussion and raged for the next four or five years—until the loss of China to the communists in 1949 and its sequel in 1950, the Korean War, turned attention to what seemed an even more serious kind of skulduggery than Pearl Harbor.

While it lasted the controversy over Pearl Harbor was an acrimonious affair. John T. Flynn, the well-known journalist, blew the lid off the Pearl Harbor controversy in 1945 when immediately after V-J Day he published his pamphlet *The Final Secret of Pearl Harbor*. He showed that the American government in the months before entry into the war had cracked the highest Japanese secret code, the so-called purple cipher, and had been reading Japan's innermost diplomatic and military secrets long before the attack of December 7, 1941. Pressure for a congressional investigation became overwhelming, and Congress authorized a special joint committee which sat from November 15, 1945 to May 31, 1946. Its record of hearings encompassed approximately 10,000,000 words, and this mountain of evidence was published in October in 39 volumes. But the joint committee came to no agreement as to the meaning of its evidence, and publicly registered its uncertainty in a report containing dissenting majority and minority views.

Argument continued, with the key question being why the Pearl Harbor disaster had occurred if the government was so well-informed on Japanese intentions. Some individuals chose to believe that there had been an intelligence lapse before the fleet disaster—that plenty of warnings had come from the decoded intercepts but they were not properly evaluated. The intercepts (according to this view) came in bits and pieces to the desks of leading administration officials, military and civil, and these busy people did not have time enough to evaluate them. Another interpretation of the Pearl Harbor disaster, however, was that the intercepts and other important pieces of information were ignored, purposely left unassembled, because President Roosevelt had "planned it that way." He had determined to expose the fleet to the Japanese so as to force the reluctant American nation into the second World War. This latter belief produced a veritable school of "revisionist" historians led by the historian and sociologist Harry Elmer Barnes. As Barnes pointed out in a book entitled *Perpetual War for Perpetual Peace*, Pearl Harbor was a dastardly plot. "The net result of revisionist scholarship applied to Pearl Harbor," he wrote, "boils down essentially to this: In order to promote Roosevelt's political ambitions and his mendacious foreign policy some three thousand American boys were quite needlessly butchered. Of course, they were only a drop in the bucket compared to those who were ultimately slain in the war that resulted, which was as needless, in terms of vital American interests, as the surprise attack on Pearl Harbor."

What can one make out of this sort of accusation? Have the revisionists ever succeeded in proving their case about Pearl Harbor? In actual fact they have not, for an enormous amount of scholarship, revisionist and antirevisionist, has been expended on the subject of Pearl Harbor, and no one has emerged with clear proof, even a trace of proof, that the American president in 1941 purposely exposed the Pacific fleet to achieve his goals in foreign policy. For the revisionists, apparently, a wish has been father to the thought. Many of them wanted to believe that President Roosevelt was a villain, and by a quick leap or two of the imagination they managed to turn wishes into conviction.

Admittedly a circumstantial case can be constructed in support of revisionist history. It is true that the authorities in Washington prior to December 7, 1941 badly bungled some warning messages to the various Pacific commands, messages based on information derived from the Japanese intercepts. These messages employed customary military circumlocution in an effort to seem mindful of all occasions and eventualities; the Pearl Harbor commanders interpreted the messages as a warning against sabotage—and among other precautions they bunched their planes on the runways where they made convenient targets for Japanese attack. Likewise it is true that Roosevelt at the very moment of Pearl Harbor was contemplating a message to Congress recommending American entry into the war, and the Japanese attack saved him the trouble of arguing with skeptical congressmen.

The back-door theorists have borrowed support from the treatment of the army and navy commanders at the unfortunate Hawaii base, Admiral Husband E. Kimmel and Lieutenant General Walter C. Short. They were hastily—and, the present writer believes, most unfairly— cashiered after the Japanese attack; their treatment by the Washington administration was so ungenerous as to suggest that they were needed as scapegoats to remove suspicion from higher authorities. General Short died in 1949, but Admiral Kimmel lived to publish a book in 1955 hinting broadly that Short and he were scapegoats for the president of the United States. One of Kimmel's friends, Rear Admiral Robert A. Theobald, who was in command of fleet destroyers at the time of the Japanese attack, wrote a book with the same title as the pamphlet by Flynn, *The Final Secret of Pearl Harbor*, and openly accused the late president of exposing the fleet and thereafter sacking the military commanders at Hawaii.

But no one has really proved any skulduggery at Pearl Harbor, and the burden of proof must rest with Roosevelt's detractors. Nearly all the records of the United States government have been opened to public or congressional scrutiny, and no proof of a presidential plot has yet appeared. Even the personal correspondence between Churchill and Roosevelt—a series of some 1,700 missives, most of which have been published although they might have been expected to remain for some time inviolate to the scrutiny of historians—has provided no incriminating evidence.

It ought to be possible therefore to settle the argument for revisionism by an argument drawn from what might be termed common sense. What man, one might ask, having risen to the presidency and enjoyed two successful terms in office, would jeopardize his life's reputation, not to speak of the fate of his country, to engage in a plot so crude that it sounds as if it came out of the sixteenth century, the era of Niccolo Machiavelli? Common sense refuses to believe in the possibility of such a course. Moreover, in so large and unwieldy an establishment as the government of the United States it is enormously difficult to set a conspiracy on foot without someone revealing it. Many people must be privy even to the highest secrets of state, and it is inconceivable that conspiracy could advance in such a situation. Even if he were thwarted by the German government's refusal to declare war against the United States because of American aid to Britain, in supplies and convoying, it defies common sense to believe that President Franklin D. Roosevelt would have constructed in diabolical cleverness a Pacific back door to war.

Personalities and recriminations aside, the fact is that the Japanese attack in 1941 on the Pearl Harbor battleship fleet united the American nation as no other single event could have done, and at last took the country into the second World War at the side of Britain and Russia. Once again, as Churchill had hoped a year and a half before, "in God's good time, the New World, with all its power and might," came to "the rescue and the liberation of the Old." The American people finally realized that a generation of diplomatic error had to be redeemed in war. They and their leaders had been well intentioned. The mistakes of the post-Versailles years had been partly their own fault, partly that of others, partly a conjunction of unfortunate circumstances. But the error of the times, wherever the responsibility, had to be redeemed. When the signal towers at Pearl Harbor on Sunday morning, December 7, 1941, messaged the United States the stupefying news,

AIR RAID PEARL HARBOR THIS IS NO DRILL

there began the first of what proved to be 1,351 days of war.

ADDITIONAL READING

For the years 1939 to 1941 there are available the excellent volumes by William L. Langer and S. Everett Gleason, *The Challenge to Isolation: 1937–40* (New York, 1952) and *The Undeclared War: 1940–1941* (New

York, 1953). This account of American entrance into the second World War, published by the Council on Foreign Relations, was based on exhaustive study of available manuscript and printed sources. The eminence of its authors and sponsorship has ensured an account that will stand for some time to come. A shorter study dealing with the same period is Donald F. Drummond, *The Passing of American Neutrality: 1937–1941* (Ann Arbor, Mich., 1955). Two bibliographical surveys are Louis Morton, "Pearl Harbor in Perspective," *United States Naval Institute Proceedings*, vol. 81 (1955), 460–468; and Wayne S. Cole, "American Entry into World War II: A Historiographical Appraisal," *Mississippi Valley Historical Review*, vol. 43 (1956–1957), 595–617.

Events during 1939–1941 can be traced in many memoirs and special works. The plight of Europe appears poignantly in Winston S. Churchill, *The Gathering Storm* (Boston, 1948), *Their Finest Hour* (1949), and *The Grand Alliance* (1950), the first three volumes of *The Second World War* (6 vols., Boston, 1948–1953). For the fall of France, one of the most dramatic and saddening events of the early part of the war, see the brilliant memoir by Edward Spears, *Assignment to Catastrophe* (2 vols., New York, 1954–1955), by a key British official and confidant of Churchill. See also Harold Butler's *The Lost Peace: A Personal Impression* (London, 1941). H. L. Trefousse, *Germany and American Neutrality: 1939–1941* (New York, 1951) is a competent monograph. The activities of American diplomats in Paris and London have been examined critically by William W. Kaufmann, "Two American Ambassadors: Bullitt and Kennedy," in Gordon Craig and Felix Gilbert, eds., *The Diplomats* (Princeton, 1953). Among the many other studies and memoirs see Walter Johnson, *The Battle Against Isolation* (Chicago, 1944), an account of the Committee to Defend America by Aiding the Allies; Wayne S. Cole, *America First* (Madison, Wis., 1953), the history of the America First Committee; Henry L. Stimson and McGeorge Bundy, *On Active Service* (New York, 1948); R. N. Current, *Secretary Stimson* (New Brunswick, N.J., 1954); *The Memoirs of Cordell Hull* (2 vols., New York, 1948); and Robert E. Sherwood's *Roosevelt and Hopkins* (New York, 1948; available in paperback), a wonderfully lucid history written from the Hopkins papers by the well-known playwright.

For American-Japanese relations prior to the Pearl Harbor crisis consult Joseph C. Grew, *Ten Years in Japan* (New York, 1944). Grew's later memoir, *Turbulent Era: A Diplomatic Record of Forty Years, 1904–1945* (2 vols., Boston, 1952) does not include the diary extracts printed in *Ten Years*. A well-done survey is F. C. Jones, *Japan's New Order in East Asia: Its Rise and Fall, 1937–45* (New York, 1954). New light on Roosevelt's quarantine speech in 1937 appears in Dorothy Borg, "Notes on Roosevelt's 'Quarantine' Speech," *Political Science Quarterly*, vol. 72 (1957), 405–433. Paul W. Schroeder in an American Historical Association prize volume has examined *The Axis Alliance and Japanese-*

American Relations: 1941 (Ithaca, 1958). See also Frank W. Iklé, *German-Japanese Relations: 1936–1940* (New York, 1957).

Pearl Harbor has inspired a large literature, much of it based on the voluminous *Pearl Harbor Attack: Hearings before the Joint Committee on the Investigation of the Pearl Harbor Attack* (39 vols., Washington, 1946); together with the summary *Report on the Investigation of the Pearl Harbor Attack* (Washington, 1946). The best summary of this material, beautifully written, is Walter Millis, *This Is Pearl!* (New York, 1947). When Secretary Knox first heard news of the Japanese attack he said to Admiral Stark that it must be an attack on the Philippines. "No sir," replied Stark, "this is Pearl!" The naval side of the surprise appears in Samuel Eliot Morison's *The Rising Sun in the Pacific: 1931–April 1942* (Boston, 1948), a volume in Morison's *History of United States Naval Operations in World War II* (14 vols., 1947——). Walter Lord, *Day of Infamy* (New York, 1957; available in paperback) is a "the day when . . ." approach, of a type presently in vogue. Herbert Feis, *The Road to Pearl Harbor* (Princeton, 1950) is a carefully researched study, probably the most authoritative yet published.

The "back door to war" books are numerous, but most of the nuances of this interpretation appear in Harry Elmer Barnes, ed., *Perpetual War for Perpetual Peace* (Caldwell, Idaho, 1953). See also the first of the genre, John T. Flynn, *The Final Secret of Pearl Harbor* (New York, 1945); together with Charles A. Beard, *American Foreign Policy in the Making: 1932–1940* (New Haven, 1946) and *President Roosevelt and the Coming of the War, 1941: A Study in Appearances and Realities* (New Haven, 1948); George Morgenstern, *Pearl Harbor: The Story of the Secret War* (New York, 1947); Charles C. Tansill, *Back Door to War* (Chicago, 1952); Rear Admiral Robert A. Theobald, USN (ret.), *The Final Secret of Pearl Harbor: The Washington Contribution to the Japanese Attack* (New York, 1954); Husband E. Kimmel, *Admiral Kimmel's Story* (Chicago, 1955). Antidotes to the above are the review of Morgenstern's book by Samuel Flagg Bemis, "First Gun of a Revisionist Historiography for the Second World War," *Journal of Modern History*, vol. 19 (1947), 55–59; and the review of Beard's second volume by Samuel Eliot Morison, *By Land and By Sea* (New York, 1953), chapter 15, "History through a Beard," pp. 328–345. Richard N. Current, "How Stimson Meant to 'Maneuver' the Japanese," *Mississippi Valley Historical Review*, vol. 40 (1953–1954), 67–74, ably explains a difficult quotation from Stimson's diary. On November 25, 1941 the secretary of war dictated to his diary the remark that "The question was how we should maneuver them [the Japanese] into the position of firing the first shot . . ." Interpreted by Roosevelt's detractors as proof that the administration was planning to sink the Pacific fleet, this quotation indicated nothing of the sort. Everyone, Current contends, expected the Japanese to be smart enough not to attack American territory, and Stimson hoped that FDR, perhaps through a message to Congress, could convince the American people that a Japanese move against Siam or the Netherlands Indies or Malaya—even though it was not directly against American territory—was proper cause for a declaration of war. The Japanese move, when made (and if the ground had been properly prepared for it in America), could be announced as "firing the first shot."

☆ **16** ☆

The Second World War

The two world wars of the twentieth century have been fought by coalitions, in 1914–1918 by the Triple Entente and Dual Alliance, during 1939–1945 by the Axis powers and the Allies, and in gathering and holding the several parts of the coalition the diplomat was in both periods a truly important individual. In the second World War, maintenance of the Allied coalition of the United States, Great Britain, and Russia required exacting exercise of the art of diplomacy. There was no serious trouble in fusing the war efforts of America and Britain. After December 7, 1941 the hard-pressed British were eager to work with their new ally, the United States. Not that there never was dissension between the two English-speaking allies, for there was plenty, but in every large question no doubt ever existed that a compromise sooner or later could be made. Maintenance of the coalition with Russia was far more difficult. Sometimes relations trembled in the balance over arrangement of the smallest matter. Mutual trust was a perennial problem between the English-speaking nations and the Russians. Even in the period of extreme military hazard, the years 1941–1942, the communist regime was sometimes difficult and unco-operative. Fortunately diplomacy managed to hold the coalition together to the end of the war.

The implementing of the coalition—it is almost impossible to treat the second World War without lapsing into its jargon—became the special business of conferences between the allies. There were meetings between the British and the Americans, and between the British and the Russians. There were conferences of the Big Three: Teheran (November–December 1943); Yalta (February 1945); Potsdam (July–August 1945). These last conferences occupied an especially prominent place in operation of the Allied coalition. How much did the spectacular meetings of the Big Three accomplish? Was it not true that lower-level diplomacy, coupled with the exigencies of the war, took the coalition through to victory? Meetings of the leaders during the second World War, it seems fair to say, if they accomplished little else must have produced some bonhomie which helped carry forward the war effort. There doubtless were, moreover, a number of decisions of a delicate, highly political nature which were far easier to take during a face-to-face conference than through the toils of the lower-level conferences. Administratively there were problems difficult for subordinates to solve, and when issues became pointed and were of importance, a personal conference of leaders was an expeditious way of reaching decisions.

1. *The Time of Emergency*

The period of emergency in the conduct of the war was beyond doubt the years 1941–1942. In the summer of 1941 Germany had attacked Russia, and it was on December 4, 1941 that a German task force reached the gates of Moscow and momentarily breached the city's outer defenses. The exhausted German soldiers of the army group of Field Marshal von Kluge gazed off into the distance, for a day or two, and saw the towers of the Kremlin. At this moment of crisis the Japanese government rushed precipitately into the war with a successful attack on the American fleet at Pearl Harbor.

During ensuing weeks and months it often seemed that the Allies could not survive. To Americans, reading the wordy optimism of their newspapers, the full crisis was never quite evident, but to military planners in Washington there came during the winter and spring of 1942 a cold feeling of the imminence of defeat. The official historian of the American army, Kent Roberts Greenfield, has written that the winter and spring of 1942 was a period of "terrific stress and anxiety." American experts gave the Russians little chance of survival. Nor did it seem that the Japanese were going to be stopped easily in the Pacific. Twenty years of Pacific diplomacy collapsed in the weeks after Pearl Harbor when the Japanese army and navy spread out to the island possessions of the United States, the Netherlands, and Great Britain, reaching southward toward an almost defenseless New Zealand and Australia.

Small wonder that when the American government arranged for a ceremony in Washington on January 1, 1942, at which representatives of the twenty-six Allied warring countries signed the United Nations Declaration, there was no quibbling by the Russian ambassador about any of the principles of the Atlantic Charter, which document had been included *in toto* in the Declaration. Nor did the American government question what measure of acceptance the Russians were offering. The military picture of the moment dominated all diplomatic considerations.

Throughout the year 1942 military necessity kept inter-Allied dissension to a minimum, and if there was ever a time when coalition diplomacy proved easy, this was it. The United States welcomed the Russians as allies, as had the British the previous summer. There was little skepticism in America's welcome to Russia. There was no undertone of opportunism such as characterized Churchill's private remark that "If Hitler invaded Hell, I would make at least a favorable reference to the Devil in the House of Commons." The hope in the United States, a hope which the circumstances of the moment would seem to have supported, was that under wartime pressure Russian patriotism had supplanted communism as the motive force of the government of the USSR. It seemed entirely possible that Russia would drop her communist theories and return to her traditional friendships in the West. The Soviets, for example, in 1943 announced dissolution of the Comintern, the international propaganda arm of the Communist Party which had caused so much strife in the 1920's and 1930's. This at the time seemed an act of signal importance—although unfortunately the Comintern would reappear in 1947 under the name of Cominform.

America's first year in the war, the time of peril, saw little Allied dissension, but it did mark some considerable American embarrassment vis-a-vis the Russians over the question of a second front in France. The Soviets wished to draw German divisions from the Russian front, and pressed the issue of a second front in every possible way. It worried American planners, who knew that even if the United Nations cause could survive the trials of the first year of the coalition, at least another year would have to pass before the United States could marshal its resources and build its military power to a level where a large-scale second front in France—anything larger than a small bridgehead—was a possibility. Opinion swayed to and fro in the spring and early summer of 1942. It was embarrassing that the troops of the United States and Great Britain were not engaged in fighting the Germans at this crucial time, except for some British activity against General Erwin Rommel's mixed force of Italians and Germans in North Africa. This Anglo-American inactivity was an embarrassing fact. Almost the full weight of German power was falling on Soviet Russia. American military planners wished ardently to make a move in 1942, to open a small bridgehead in France with Operation Sledgehammer, and follow it the next year with the big drive, Operation Roundup. In late 1942 President Roosevelt, during a conversation with the Russian foreign minister Molotov, promised a second front within the year. Prime Minister Churchill in conferences with Roosevelt at Hyde Park and Washington (June 18–27) argued against a cross-Channel attack that year, and in July the British flatly refused to support it. Roosevelt persisted in believing that an attack should be made somewhere, and out of the confusion, and the embarrassment of not providing the Russians with support, came the proposal of an invasion of North Africa.

The political situation in North Africa was such as to welcome an Allied invasion, so the British and Americans believed. Parts of North Africa were French protectorates and one portion, Algeria, was an actual department of France. When the French had met defeat at the hands of the Germans in June 1940 they had reconstituted a feeble government at the southern French city of Vichy, and the Vichy regime had retained allegiance of the North African provinces of Tunis and Morocco and the department of Algeria. The Vichy government was headed by the aged Pétain, assisted by Admiral Jean François Darlan and Pierre Laval. It was in many ways a defeatist regime and seemed on occasion much too pro-German. Its political vulnerability provided the Western Allies, Britain and the United States, with an opportunity to occupy French North Africa. The Allies believed that the army and civil officers in this area would welcome British and American troops, and from North Africa the invasion of Europe might eventually be launched. In the event, this turned out to be a fond hope. The Allied landings in North Africa actually almost miscarried. In the invasion of November 1942 cooperation was obtained from the French only because Admiral Darlan happened by chance to be in North Africa and was able to persuade the local French army commanders to welcome the Allies. One should add that co-operation with Darlan, an individual of mixed character, later led to much soul-searching by some Allied publicists and writers, and after the war there was a heated argument over whether such co-operation was justified on grounds of military necessity; the present writer believes it was justified—though many of his readers will disagree.

But to return to the subject of the North African invasion. This invasion, it should be remarked, was essentially a compromise move. Secretary of War Stimson argued vigorously with the president against the operation. Stimson believed that the North African invasion, decided upon in July 1942, delayed the eventual cross-Channel attack for an entire year. Still, what could the Americans do in 1942 without co-operation from their British ally? The British had been fighting Hitler for three years, and urged their superior wisdom in matters of strategy. Indeed the then chief of the imperial general staff, Sir Alan Brooke, in a book of memoirs published a dozen years after the war, has argued that the Americans were strategic morons, and that only through British and especially his own superior wisdom was disaster averted in 1942. Sir Alan in that year comforted the Americans by telling them they could still have Operation Roundup in 1943, and that the North African affair would be preliminary. The chief of staff of the American army, General George C. Marshall, and his naval opposite, Admiral Ernest J. King, predicted that North Africa's Operation Torch would kill Roundup, which it did. Sir Alan in his memoirs has confessed that he intended it to do so. The North African affair was in truth a political decision, rather than a matter of strategy. Perhaps it had to be. President Roosevelt was convinced that American troops had to become engaged somewhere, and the only feasible move—lacking support from the British for Sledgehammer—was Torch. General Marshall years after the war told the distinguished naval historian Samuel Eliot Morison that "the great lesson he learned in 1942 was this: in wartime the politicians have to do *something* important every year. They could not simply use 1942 to build up for 1943 or 1944; they could not face the obloquy of fighting another 'phony war.' The 'something' . . . was Operation Torch . . ."

The difficulty over supporting the Russians in 1942 and the decision to go into North Africa raised in peculiarly sharp form a fundamental conflict in strategy between the British and Americans which was not adjourned for two years thereafter, namely, whether it was better to make a frontal invasion of the Continent via France, or to move northward into Europe from the Mediterranean via Italy and Yugoslavia. This issue had come to American attention for the first time during the conference between Roosevelt and Churchill at Argentia Bay in 1941, when American military planners accompanying the president were appalled at the gingerly nature of British strategy. By the year 1944, when American troops came to constitute a preponderance of the strength of the Western Allies, it was possible to insist on American strategy, and the Allies thereupon went into France. But the strategic argument of France v. the Balkans persisted throughout the war, and some postwar literary strategists have flayed the American frontal strategy in much the same manner as has Sir Alan Brooke in his memoirs. So perhaps this controversy is worth examination at this point.

The British view of proper Anglo-American strategy for the second World War is not difficult to state. Churchill and the British government had devoutly desired the invasion of North Africa in 1942, albeit for reasoning different from that of the American president. Churchill had always in mind such military butcheries as Passchendaele and the Somme during the first World War, when hundreds of thousands of British soldiers died in a series of dreadful and futile offensives. Apropos of British reluctance to fight again on the Continent, Morison in a published lecture has recalled the simple inscription on a tablet erected by the British government in Nôtre Dame de Paris: "To the glory of God and to the memory of one million men of the British Empire who fell in the Great War, 1914–1918, and of whom the greater part rest in France." When General Marshall, in England for staff conversations, was arguing vehemently for a cross-Channel invasion of Europe, the late Lord Cherwell said to him, "It's no use—you are arguing against the casualties on the Somme." Churchill was not going to risk more such massacres simply because the Russians were crying for help and the Americans eager to assist them.

There were two further reasons which may have prompted the British to oppose a cross-Channel invasion. For one, British strategists and especially Churchill bore in mind the political purpose of the war—to defeat Hitler Germany without bringing down the structure of Western civilization on the Continent. For this reason it appeared desirable to adopt toward Europe a strategy resembling that employed against Napoleon in the war of a century earlier, a strategy of beleaguerment, of probing at the periphery of the Continent, of feeling one's way cautiously, and perhaps moving through the Balkans and Central Europe to the Ruhr and Rhineland, North Germany and Berlin. Churchill may also have had in mind a campaign to open a route of supply to Russia through the Dardanelles and Bosporus, which if successful would have vindicated the ill-fated effort that he had sponsored during the first World War, an unsuccessful campaign that for years had clouded his political career. The British for such reasons as this elaborated their policy of cautious containment, a first step of which could be the taking of North African bases.

What can one conclude about this Anglo-American argument? Perhaps it is correct to say that Torch, the compromise of 1942, was a wise preliminary for the cross-Channel invasion in 1944—that establishing a bridgehead in France in 1942 and a full-scale second front in 1943, as hoped for by General Marshall and Admiral King and President Roosevelt and Secretary Stimson and many other American leaders, would have been too dangerous, given the strength of German forces in France in those years, given Allied, especially American, inexperience in warfare, given the need for time to beat down the German submarine fleets in the Atlantic and time also to produce landing ships and tanks and the innumerable other requirements of land warfare on a vast scale. Some of the Mediterranean operations which followed the Torch landings, especially the Italian campaigning of the last year or so of the war, were strategically questionable, but the initial North African occupation did have justification pending the build-up of Allied strength to a point where the cherished cross-Channel invasion was likely to succeed. It would have been a terrible blow to the Western Allies if in 1942 they had attempted Operation Sledgehammer, the proposed bridgehead operation, and been hurled off the Continent in a repetition of the British debacle at Dunkirk in 1940.

But is it not true that the cross-Channel strategy which eventually prevailed in 1944 proved an unwise move from a political point of view, just as Churchill in 1942 had been sensing it would be? Did not the Allies lose Central Europe and the Balkans to the Russians because they chose the cross-Channel attack in 1944, rather than an invasion up through Italy and the historic Ljubljana Gap into Europe's (to use Churchill's phrase) "soft underbelly"? Actually there is little to be said for this argument, so frequently presented in the years after the second World War. The compromise of 1942, the Torch operation, made sense at the moment, but by 1944 British strategy had become outmoded. Once the Allies had the requisite strength there were far more advantages in an attack across France than up through Yugoslavia. It was fortunate that the Allies did not pursue the British peripheral strategy after 1943. Had they done so it is possible that the American and British forces could have obtained control of Belgrade, Bucharest, Budapest, Prague, and Vienna, instead of those capitals passing to the Russians. On the other hand it is also possible, even probable, that an American-British advance through the Balkans and Central Europe might have bogged down in the difficult terrain of that region, with the consequence that the Russian armies, rolling across the North German plain, would have reached the Ruhr and Rhineland and passed on into the Low Countries and France—with results for the postwar political organization of the Continent which can readily be calculated. Even in its strictly political possibilities, not to speak of its military difficulty, British strategy was less effective than the opposing American strategy. It was far better to give Russia the Balkans and Central Europe rather than the Continent's vastly more valuable northern and western areas.

So Churchill's losing out on his peripheral strategy, after an initial success in 1942, was all for the best. He fought to the bitter end. At one point in 1943 he put up a terrific argument for a landing on the island of Rhodes, and was still arguing after Roosevelt and Stalin at the Teheran Conference in December 1943 tried to dissuade him. At Algiers in January 1944, during an informal meeting with the Americans he announced with full Churchillian rhetoric, holding onto the lapels of his coat as if making a speech in the House of Commons: "His Majesty's government cannot accept the consequences if we fail to make this operation against Rhodes!" General Marshall, present at the meeting, told the prime minister that "No American is going to land on that goddam island!"

2. From Casablanca to Quebec

With the year 1943 the tide of war turned in favor of the Allied coalition, and there could no longer be any serious cause for worry, after the victories of that year and the triumphs of the year that followed. The only question concerned the time necessary to defeat an enemy who was imaginative, brave, tenacious, even fanatical. By the beginning of 1943 the German and Italian troops in North Africa, numbering about 250,000, were falling into a hopeless position and would be forced to surrender on May 13, 1943. Meanwhile the beginning of a new phase of the war in Russia came with the German surrender at Stalingrad, February 2, 1943. This victory, in which twenty-two German divisions, including a galaxy of German generals, were made prisoners, was followed in the summer of 1943 by the complete failure on the Russian front of a German general offensive.

Although the crucial points in a conflict seldom become visible until after the fighting has ceased, it began to be evident in 1943 that a change for the better had come in the Pacific war as well. In the Pacific the United States first had suffered the disaster at Pearl Harbor; not too long after that had come the inevitable surrender in the Philippines, on May 6, 1942. But then in the summer of 1942 came the first good news from the Pacific: the Japanese were driven back from Midway on June 3–6, in a victory of naval aviation that forbade further Japanese advances. A year later, by mid-1943, United States forces in the Pacific were on the offensive everywhere.

When victory thus came into sight—and it was visible at the beginning of 1943—there appeared a need for a statement of Allied policy toward the enemy, some statement that would hold the coalition together until the end of the war. The squabbling over spoils that had broken so many coalitions must not occur. The embarrassment of not being able to provide a second front in France either in 1942 or 1943 must be relieved; there was the bare possibility that the Russians in disgust might make an arrangement with the Germans, as they had done under other circumstances in August 1939. With these purposes in mind Roosevelt and Churchill meeting in a conference at Casablanca, January 14–24, 1943, announced the doctrine of unconditional surrender.

The doctrine was carefully premeditated, and was no off-the-cuff pronouncement as Roosevelt later liked to make out. The president, as Robert Sherwood has remarked, "often liked to picture himself as a rather frivolous fellow who did not give sufficient attention to the consequences of chance remarks," and so he made light of the calculation that went into his new doctrine, unconditional surrender. He talked carefully from notes, that day at Casablanca. He had just managed to get two bickering French generals—Henri H. Giraud and Charles de Gaulle—to shake hands, and this, according to FDR's fanciful recollection, brought to mind a chain of ideas: "We had so much trouble getting those two French generals together that I thought to myself that this was as difficult as arranging the meeting of Grant and Lee—and then suddenly the press conference was on, and Winston and I had had no time to prepare for it, and the thought popped into my mind that they had called Grant 'Old Unconditional Surrender' and the next thing I knew, I had said it."

Whatever the incidental errors that attached to it, the new doctrine of unconditional surrender was singularly important for Allied diplomacy during the second World War. This policy, along with that of the Balkan *v.* cross-Channel strategy, has stirred much debate among postwar analysts and writers. Was unconditional surrender a wise policy? Is not every surrender, by definition, a surrender on conditions? The diary of the Nazi propaganda minister, Josef Goebbels, reveals the joy with which that functionary presented to the German people the choice between fighting or groveling before the Allies. The Allied declaration of unconditional surrender appeared to him as a godsend, for it would, he thought, spark the German people to fight for an honorable peace. It proved what he had always told them, that surrender to the Allies could only be dishonorable. The military analyst of the *New York Times,* Hanson W. Baldwin, has written that unconditional surrender was one of the blunders of American diplomacy during the war. It prolonged the war, Baldwin believes, and encouraged the Germans to fight to the last man, leaving for the Allies in 1945 a country which was the most complete shambles ever seen by conquering soldiers.

On the other hand Elmer Davis, who conducted the Office of War Information and to whom in 1941–1945 fell much of the burden of explaining to the American people the nation's wartime policy, has defended this policy of unconditional surrender. Davis argues that the policy served notice on our allies, in particular the Russians, that there would be no premature peace with Germany. Moreover, so Davis contends, "the unquestionably good effect of unconditional surrender—an effect which was its primary purpose," was upon the Germans themselves. It prevented them from telling again the story they told after 1918, that they had not been defeated militarily in the field but had been stabbed in the back by civilian revolutionists in

Berlin. To the argument that the policy of unconditional surrender left no responsible government in Germany with which the Allies could negotiate, Davis answers that there never was any chance for a government to arise with which the Allies could have negotiated. The Germans could not, certainly did not, unseat the Hitler regime. Their random wartime conspiracies against Hitler were heroic but naive affairs, easily put down by the Gestapo. Even the conspiracy to assassinate Hitler which miscarried on July 20, 1944, with such tragically terrible results for thousands of the conspirators and their relatives and friends, was an amateurish plot with little chance of success. To crush the regime required an absolute military defeat.

Certainly it was impossible to negotiate with the Hitler regime, which was the most bestial government known since the statistically clouded times of the medieval Huns and the fabled slaughters of the ancient oriental satrapies. No negotiated peace was possible with the regime that had slaughtered literally millions of people, men and women and children, by machine guns and starvation camps and efficient gas ovens, giving to the world's languages a new word, *genocide*.

But whatever the virtues—or defects—of unconditional surrender, it does seem true that the doctrine, for perhaps twenty months after its enunciation in January 1943, held off the making of wartime commitments that would have prejudiced the postwar settlement. The principle of "no predetermination," a rather jawbreaking idea, was finally abandoned, and with questionable results, in a conference at Moscow on October 9–18, 1944 when Churchill and Stalin agreed to divide the Balkans into spheres of interest. According to one version—there has been no official confirmation of these figures—Russia was assigned a 75/25 or 80/20 preponderance in Bulgaria, Rumania, and Hungary, while in Yugoslavia Russia and Britain would share influence 50/50. It was agreed also that the Curzon Line, a roughly ethnographic line in Eastern Poland proposed as a boundary in 1919, would be the new postwar Polish boundary, and that Poland, having thereby lost territory to Russia in the east, would be given a western boundary along the Oder, obtaining compensation at the expense of Germany. The American government, not a party to these arrangements, let it be known that it would not be bound by them. It was American policy to refrain from division of spoils until the peace conference at the end of the war. Divisions of territory, so the United States maintained, were one of the prime methods of disrupting a coalition prior to the end of a war. The British government agreed with such reasoning in the period of emergency, the year 1942, but underwent a change of mind, if not of heart, when as victory approached it became evident that the Russians could make their own pleasure prevail in Eastern Europe, with or without agreement with the English-speaking Allies. Britain felt that an agreement might at least confirm British interests in Yugoslavia and in Greece (where according to Churchill's memoirs the ratio of British-Russian influence was to be 90/10, in favor of Britain). Perhaps Churchill thought it was better to formalize the inevitable in Eastern Europe, with the hope of getting something in the process.

Having set forth the doctrine of unconditional surrender at Casablanca in January 1943, the leaders of the United States and Britain communicated it to the Russians, who for the moment accepted it. For the rest of the year the attention of the two English-speaking governments was occupied with the North African campaign, the seizure of Sicily (July 10–August 17), and the invasion of Italy (September 3). Forcing the retirement of Mussolini—who afterward escaped to North Italy and founded another Italian government under German sponsorship—the Allies began the slow movement up the boot of Italy toward Rome. They also prepared for the cross-Channel invasion.

Throughout the year 1943 arguments over strategy raged between the British and American governments. The question again was whether to enter the Continent through the Balkans and Central Europe or by crossing the Channel. This time the British, despite the tireless importunities of Churchill, lost to the Americans, who possessed more troops and equipment and were in a position to dictate strategy. By the end of the year there was no longer doubt as to the cross-Channel operation. Planning it, however, required, in Western eyes, some co-ordination with the Russian front, and there followed the Teheran Conference, November 28–December 1, 1943.

Held at the capital of Iran, the conference was attended by Roosevelt, Churchill, and Stalin. It was the first three-power conference on the highest level. Actually, other than a promise by the Russians to co-ordinate their campaigns with the projected invasion of France, little resulted from the meeting. It did produce a plan for an international organization to keep the peace, an idea of the Americans which was accepted with some enthusiasm by the British and with less interest by the more skeptical Russians. Stalin at Teheran reiterated a promise made at the Moscow Conference of foreign ministers (October 19–30, 1943) to enter the war against Japan after hostilities ended in Europe.

Before going to Teheran, Roosevelt and Churchill had a meeting at Cairo with Generalissimo and Mrs. Chiang Kai-shek. The meeting was apart from the Teheran proceedings because the Russians had not yet entered the Far Eastern war and did not desire to antagonize the Japanese. At the Cairo Conference (November 22–26, 1943) the United States, Britain, and China promised to prosecute the war against Japan until the Japanese surrendered unconditionally. Japan was to be deprived of all Pacific islands acquired since 1914. Manchuria, Formosa, and other territories taken from China by Japan were to be restored to China. The three powers were "determined that in due course Korea shall become free and independent." At a second Cairo conference (December 4–6, 1943) the president and prime minister met the president of Turkey, Ismet Inönü, and received and gave pledges of support in the war against Germany— albeit without Turkish hostilities, not declared until February 23, 1945.

In concluding this account of the era when the coalition, having passed through the emergency, stood in sight of victory, there remains the year 1944, a year of campaigning and heavy fighting. Diplomacy languished during 1944. Churchill and Roosevelt did meet again in the late summer at Quebec (September 11–16, 1944), where the two leaders heard Secretary of the Treasury Henry Morgenthau offer a plan for postwar Germany. On September 15, 1944 the president and the prime minister initialed an abbreviated version of the Morgenthau Plan, under which Russia and other devastated countries could "remove the machinery they require" from Germany, the heavy industry of the Ruhr and Saar to be "put out of action and closed down" and these two German provinces placed under indefinite international control. The plan initialed at Quebec, phrased in Churchill's own words, included a much-quoted statement that the measures for the Ruhr and Saar "looked forward to" conversion of Germany into a country "primarily agricultural and pastoral in character."

This was, beyond question, a silly proposition. Morgenthau's scheme ignored the fact that the German people could not live without the industrial complex erected in their country, the center of eco-

nomic life on the Continent. The Morgenthau Plan, whatever the intentions of its author, was a starvation plan. President Roosevelt rejected the proposal later that year, and Churchill eventually admitted
that initialing it was an error. Churchill seems to have been willing
to accept the Morgenthau Plan tentatively because at the time he
needed a large postwar American loan and the chief exponent of the
plan was secretary of the treasury. When news of the scheme leaked
out it had an unfortunate effect in Germany, playing into the hands
of Propaganda Minister Goebbels. Hitler in a New Year's message
to the German people drew attention to what he described as a plot
of the British, Americans, Bolsheviks, and "international Jews," which
he said would result in the "complete ripping apart of the German
Reich, the uprooting of 15 or 20 million Germans and transport
abroad, the enslavement of the rest of our people, the ruination of
our German youth, but, above all, the starvation of our masses." In
the years after the war much was made in the United States of the
fact that the Morgenthau Plan as originally drawn gave virtual control
of Germany to Soviet Russia (the Russians along with other nations
of the Continent were to control Germany), and that the plan had
been worked out by Morgenthau's chief assistant at the treasury,
Harry Dexter White, who after his death in the early postwar years
was accused of Communist Party affiliations. No one, let it be added,
has proved that the Morgenthau Plan was Soviet in origin. Perhaps
one should simply remark, in conclusion, that the proposal and its
temporary and partial adoption at Quebec in September 1944 was an
unfortunate but small chapter in American diplomatic history. The
scheme of the secretary of the treasury was an amateur proposal,
typical of many that have occurred in American diplomacy.

3. Yalta

The Yalta Conference (February 4–11, 1945) properly began the
third and final period in the history of the wartime coalition, the
period of disintegration, of dissolution and disillusion. By the time
the conference met, the wartime coalition had outlived its military
usefulness. Germany was a doomed country by 1945, with many
of its cities in rubble from Allied bombing, with its eastern and western areas ravaged by the encroaching Allied armies—the Russians
coming from the East, the British and Americans from the West.

Americans at the beginning of 1945 were preparing to cross the Rhine. Hordes of Russian soldiers had approached to within a hundred miles of Berlin. Soviet armies had concluded a victorious peace with Finland, occupied Rumania, Bulgaria, most of Poland, and driven deeply into Hungary, Yugoslavia, and Czechoslovakia. Understandably, when the war's end was near, there was no longer serious need for the Allied coalition, which was beginning, although ever so imperceptibly, to dissolve. A conference meeting under such circumstances was bound to encounter trouble.

The Yalta Conference, held at what had been the Crimean resort of the last tsar of Russia—the Livadia Palace built by Nicholas II in 1911 some two miles from the town of Yalta—did not at the time seem to be a meeting of despair and cynicism, a conference during which the hopes of the world disappeared in an orgy of secret agreement and bickering, with the evil genius of Moscow receiving benefits and giving none. The American nation did not at the time receive the impression of Yalta which has tempted many later writers to believe that the fruits of the war were lost in an eight-day meeting. Churchill buoyantly sent a message to Roosevelt on January 1, 1945, in advance of a preliminary Anglo-American meeting at Malta (held January 30–February 2, 1945): "No more let us falter! From Malta to Yalta! Let nobody alter!" A few days later in a telegram of January 8 the prime minister was becoming gloomy: "This may well be a fateful Conference, coming at a moment when the Great Allies are so divided and the shadow of the war lengthens out before us. At the present time I think the end of this war may well prove to be more disappointing than was the last." Still, this was a momentary reaction, and it never infected the spirits of the Americans at Yalta. Roosevelt and his advisers concluded their labors in the Crimea in a spirit close to exaltation. They felt that the postwar world was going to be safe —that the world had been saved for freedom and peace in a way which would have gladdened the heart of Woodrow Wilson. There was to be, verily, a new world. It would have been unbelievable to leaders of the American government in early 1945 had they been told that their hopes were not merely to be dashed, but the meeting in which they had seen their vision of a New Jerusalem would soon be described by many of their countrymen as a conference of blunder and surrender.

What is the truth about Yalta? The Yalta Conference was by all odds the most important of the wartime diplomatic meetings, and in the light of later controversy it deserves a close and sharp look. It dealt with essentially four issues: (1) voting arrangements in the new United Nations; (2) general policy toward the liberated governments of Eastern Europe, and specific policy toward the postwar government of Poland; (3) the immediate postwar governance of Germany; (4) Russia's joining the war against Japan.

Of these issues at Yalta, arrangements pertaining to the UN were probably of minor importance. Steps toward formation of the United Nations had already been taken before Yalta, notably at the Moscow Conference of foreign ministers in October 1943, when a joint declaration by Great Britain, the United States, the USSR, and China projected "a general international organization, based on the principle of sovereign equality of all peace-loving states, and open to membership by all such states, large and small, for the maintenance of international peace and security." It was after return from this conference that Secretary Hull declared extravagantly that if the provisions of the Moscow Declaration were carried out there would be no need for "spheres of influence, for alliances, for balance of power or any other of the special arrangements through which, in the unhappy past, the nations strove to safeguard their security or to promote their interests." At Yalta the date was set—Wednesday, April 25, 1945—for opening of the San Francisco Conference to work out the constitutional details of the UN. The three great powers at Yalta were in perfect agreement on their need for a right of veto in the UN. Stalin favored a veto even on discussion of matters at the UN, but Churchill and Roosevelt prevailed on him to allow the right of free speech in the new Parliament of the World. With this issue resolved, the Soviet dictator lost interest in the proposed world organization and turned to other matters.

In the meantime he had asked for and received Assembly seats for Byelorussia and the Ukraine, a concession by the Western statesmen which later brought much criticism of the Yalta Conference. The Russian argument was that the British empire was well represented in the Assembly, and that to confine a great power like Russia to one seat was unfair. The Russians at first asked for sixteen seats, one for each of the Soviet republics. The Russian ambassador to the United States, Andrei Gromyko, argued that any of the Soviet republics was more important than Guatemala or Liberia. To the query as to whether the Russian republics had been given control of their foreign relations Gromyko had answered that they soon would have such control. Finally the Russians compromised on three seats, and it was agreed that the United States also might request three seats. The American government has never asked for this bonus representation. The multiple-seat concession to Russia at Yalta has provoked a good deal of criticism from American public opinion—although it is difficult to see what advantage the Russians gained by their increased Assembly representation.

In the matter of Eastern Europe the Yalta Conference has also been criticized. Here attack frequently has been directed to the Yalta Declaration on Liberated Europe, drafted by the State Department and accepted almost *in toto* by the conferees, which specified free elections and constitutional safeguards of freedom in the liberated nations. It was employed as a propaganda device by the Soviets, who never seriously considered putting it into effect. In retrospect the pledges of the Soviets in the declaration appear almost grotesque: "By this declaration," the United States, Britain, and Russia announced, "we reaffirm our faith in the principles of the Atlantic Charter, our pledge in the Declaration by the United Nations, and our determination to build in co-operation with other peace-loving nations world order under law, dedicated to peace, security, freedom and general well-being of all mankind." The Yalta Declaration on Liberated Europe had the immediate result of lending to the activities of the Soviet occupation authorities in Eastern Europe a certain sanctity and authority conferred by the democratic allies. Conspicuous posting of the text of the declaration throughout the liberated areas made the task of occupation easier. What followed is now well-known. The Soviets pursued their own brand of democracy in the liberated countries, first by means of coalition governments. The communist members of the coalition, supported by the Red Army, then infiltrated every position of responsibility in the government. Even so, the Yalta Declaration did some good, for without it the Russians might have omitted the coalition stage of their takeover of Eastern Europe in favor of a brutal takeover without attempt at legality. In this respect the Yalta Declaration may have given the East European peoples two or three years in which they had some freedom. Moreover, the declaration is the one Russian promise for this area of the Continent with which the United States and Britain have been able to reproach the Russians. It is a contractual arrangement which Russia violated.

But then one comes to the case of Poland as decided at Yalta, another matter about which the West has felt uneasy. Germany's attack on Poland had brought on the war in 1939. The British and Americans both felt during the war that an independent Polish government was essential in any acceptable postwar organization of Europe. Great Britain had guaranteed Polish national existence in 1939, and in the United States six million Americans of Polish descent laid constant and heavy political pressure upon President Roosevelt. The Western Allies at Yalta did the best they could for Poland, and spent more time at the conference discussing Poland's postwar frontiers and government than any other subject. Churchill described the Polish question as "the most important question" before the conference. Still, Poland by February 1945 had been almost completely occupied by the Red Army, and any arrangements made at Yalta in regard to Poland had to be made out of hope rather than with certainty that they would be put into effect.

The Polish boundary question was straddled at Yalta—after much discussion—with tentative agreement on the Curzon Line as the eastern boundary, but disagreement over the western boundary. Roosevelt and Churchill were not averse to a line along the Oder River, but as for continuing it southward along the Western Neisse—that was something else, and the decision was that "the final delimitation of the Western frontier of Poland should thereafter await the Peace Conference." This decision was reaffirmed at the Potsdam Conference of July–August 1945. The peace conference for Poland never met, and the Russians made their own bilateral arrangement with Poland of the Curzon Line in the east and the Oder-Western Neisse in the west.

The Western Allies reserved their consent to Poland's boundaries, but in the matter of Poland's postwar government the Americans and British at Yalta made what with hindsight appears to have been an ill-advised concession. The Russians received clearance to expand the so-called Lublin Committee, a Soviet-sponsored group of Polish-Russian communists, by including in it representatives of the Polish government-in-exile then domiciled in London. The government-in-exile in London had far more right to claim the postwar government of Poland than did the cardboard Lublin Committee, propped as the latter was by the Russian army and Russian funds. The Soviets knew that their Polish organization was a fraud, and they were willing to "broaden" it and dress it in legitimacy by inclusion of members from the London Polish government. Not long afterward, all the noncommunists were squeezed out of the newly organized Warsaw government. The Western powers sensed the danger of trying to combine oil and water, Lublin and London, but they felt that they could do little more than accept Russian promises. At Yalta there was still hope that the Russians had changed their spots, that it would be possible to live amicably with the communist regime, and in that hope and possibility the agreement on postwar Poland was consummated. In retrospect it appears that it would have been far better to have championed the London Poles, even at the risk of the government of Poland going to the Lublin Committee. It went to the committee anyway.

But perhaps this was the best that could be done. Roosevelt's adviser, Admiral William D. Leahy, said to the president at the time that the Polish agreement was so elastic that the Russians could "stretch it all the way from Yalta to Washington without ever technically breaking it." Roosevelt agreed: "I know, Bill—I know it. But it's the best I can do for Poland at this time."

There thus was a certain inevitability at Yalta in regard to the postwar government and boundaries of Poland. The provisions at Yalta for extra Russian seats at the UN Assembly, while not inevitable, were unimportant. Division of Germany into zones of occupation was an easier part of the Yalta proceedings, and was done with success because the war map of the moment, while giving Russia Eastern Germany, gave the Western Allies the rich industrial complex of West Germany. This was no even division, but the Russians had to accept it because of the war map.

Planning for the division of Germany had preceded the Yalta Conference by a number of months, and when the Western Allies met Stalin in the Crimea they were fairly certain of what they desired in the way of occupation zones. A European Advisory Commission met in London in 1944 and recommended that Russia receive the eastern third of Germany, and that the southeastern zone go to the United States and the northwestern zone to Britain. There was to be joint control of Berlin, and an Allied Control Commission for Germany. These proposals came before Churchill and Roosevelt at the Quebec

OCCUPATION ZONES IN GERMANY AND AUSTRIA

SWEDEN

DENMARK

RUSSIAN CONTROL

EAST PRUSSIA

Danzig

POLISH CONTROL

AMERICAN CONTROL

Hamburg

Stettin

FOUR-POWER OCCUPATION

Berlin

Bremen

Elbe R.

Oder R.

BRITISH ZONE

NETH.

RUSSIAN ZONE

POLAND

Warsaw

Vistula R.

Neisse R.

Leipzig

Dresden

Cologne

BELG.

Rhine R.

Frankfurt

Prague

AMERICAN ZONE

FRENCH ZONE

LUX.

Nuremberg

CZECHOSLOVAKIA

FRANCE

Munich

FOUR-POWER OCCUPATION

RUSSIAN ZONE

Vienna

Salzburg

Danube R.

Budapest

HUNGARY

Innsbruck

FRENCH ZONE

BRITISH ZONE

SWITZERLAND

MILES

0   100   200   300

YUGOSLAVIA

Based on a map in Winston Churchill, TRIUMPH AND TRAGEDY (*Houghton Mifflin Company*)

Conference in September 1944, and the two statesmen agreed, Roosevelt reserving control by the United States over Bremen and Bremerhaven as enclaves within the British zone for purposes of supplying American troops in Bavaria. At Yalta this was essentially the arrangement for German occupation, with Roosevelt and Churchill persuading Stalin to allow to liberated France an occupation zone "within the British and American zones." The Russian leader was at the outset against the idea of a French role in the occupation of Germany. Overlooking his own delinquency in the Nazi-Soviet Pact of August 1939, he said that France had "opened the gate to the enemy" in 1940 and "contributed little to this war." Churchill cagily remarked that "every nation had had their difficulties in the beginning of the war and had made mistakes." Stalin gave in, and France obtained not merely an occupation zone but a place on the Allied Control Commission.

In the matter of German reparations, agreed upon at Yalta in a hedged and general way, it was decided that a reparations commission should be set up, with instructions that "the Soviet Union and the United States believed that the Reparations Commission should take as a basis of discussion the figure of reparations as twenty billion dollars and fifty per cent of these should go to the Soviet Union." The British opposed naming any reparations figure, and managed also to write into the instructions a statement of purpose, "to destroy the German war potential," rather than the more broadly phrased Russian statement, "for the purpose of military and economic disarmament of Germany." All in all—so a recent student of this complicated subject, John L. Snell, has concluded—"the reparations decisions at Yalta constituted a thinly disguised defeat for the Russians and a clear-cut rejection of the Morgenthau plan and the Quebec agreement of September, 1944."

But it was not chiefly its provisions for Germany nor its stipulations for Eastern Europe or the UN that later gave the Yalta Conference notoriety. Rather it was the provisions for Russia to enter the Far Eastern war. Here one comes to the nub of the Yalta controversy. Agitation over the Far Eastern provisions of Yalta has become a political matter in the United States, with the Democratic Party, in power in 1945, generally defending Yalta's Far Eastern terms, and the Republicans characterizing them as a "betrayal of a sacred trust of the American people." Entrance of Russia into the war against Japan was unnecessary—so runs the accusation—and it was not merely obtained at Yalta, it was bought, at an outrageous price.

The reason for the Yalta concessions to obtain entrance of Russia into the Far Eastern war was, simply, that President Roosevelt's military advisers told him they needed Russian help. The military situation appeared downright difficult for the United States. American military leaders estimated that the war in Europe would last until July 1, at least, and that the Pacific war would require (and this with Russian help) another year and a half, that is, until December 1946. How long the war would take without Russian help, no one knew. Japanese troop strength at the time of Yalta was impressive, in terms of men (but ignoring armaments, which it later turned out that they did not have). The Japanese had 2,000,000 to 2,500,000 troops in Japan, 1,000,000 in China, and 1,000,000 in Manchuria and Korea. The United States by the end of the war had sent only about 1,459,000 army troops and 187,500 marines into the Pacific, and scattered them from Australia to Alaska. Casualties were high in operations against the Japanese. Shortly after the Yalta Conference came the costly attack on Iwo Jima, an island two and one-half miles wide by four and two-thirds miles long, on which the marine corps lost nearly 7,000 dead and 20,000 wounded. Okinawa, invested soon afterward, cost 11,260 dead and 33,769 wounded. At Okinawa the Japanese sank 36 ships and damaged 368 others. It is understandable that Roosevelt and his advisers at Yalta desired Russian entrance into the Far Eastern war. American military leaders estimated that an invasion of Japan would cost at least half a million American casualties, even if Japanese forces in China, Manchuria, and Korea stayed on the mainland. Douglas MacArthur, who later described as "fantastic" the Yalta concessions for Russian entrance into the Pacific war, told a Washington staff officer in early 1945 that Russian support was essential for the invasion of Japan. According to a memorandum of a conversation of February 25, 1945 sent by Brigadier General George A. Lincoln to General Marshall, "General MacArthur spoke of the strength of the opposition to be expected in invading the Japanese home islands. He declared that planning should start at once, that heavy firepower would be needed to cover the beachheads, and that as many Japanese divisions as possible should first be pinned down on the mainland, principally by Soviet forces." When Russia on August 8, 1945, invaded Manchuria, MacArthur declared flatly, "I am delighted at the Russian declaration of war against Japan. This will make possible a great pincers movement that cannot fail to end in the destruction of the enemy." Such was the feeling of Roosevelt's advisers at the time of Yalta, and it explains a number of the Yalta concessions to Russia.

As everyone now knows, the military estimate of Japan's strength was inaccurate. Actually Japan was on her last legs at the time of Yalta. In the summer of 1944 the marines had captured Saipan, and this defeat spelled the beginning of the end of Japan's will to fight. The cabinet of General Tojo resigned on July 18, 1944 in shame and disgrace, and from that moment onward it was a matter not of *if* but of *when* Japan would surrender. Russian assistance was not needed, when by the early summer of 1945 (after the Yalta Conference, and before the Russians entered the Far Eastern war) United States submarines sank ferry boats passing between the islands of Japan, and when the American fleet engaged with impunity in offshore bombardments. The taking of bases other than Saipan—Okinawa, Iwo Jima, and others—secured air strips within easy bombing range of every part of Japan. The huge B-29 bombers in their fire raids wreaked havoc upon the island empire. Even before the dropping of the atomic bombs at Hiroshima (August 6, 1945) and Nagasaki (August 9), the dreadful daily bombing raids had proved comparable in deadliness to the atomic explosions. At Hiroshima 135,000 people were killed or wounded, but in the conventional raids on Japan the total of deaths ran to 241,000. It was an apocalyptic end for the Japanese. No intervention by Russia in Manchuria was necessary to bring down the bamboo edifice that had once been the center of the Japanese empire.

At Yalta the Russians agreed to join the war against Japan in "two or three months" after defeat of Germany, and when Germany fell on V-E Day, May 8, 1945, it was presumed that the Russians would join the Far Eastern war sometime in August. In return for this dubious service (which at the time seemed necessary) the Russians received the territory and privileges in China and the Pacific region that they had enjoyed prior to the Russo-Japanese War of 1904–1905: Southern Sakhalin and the Kurile Islands, railroad concessions throughout Manchuria (disguised as a joint Sino-Russian venture in railroading), and Port Arthur and Dairen (the latter was internationalized, meaning that it was free for Russian use).

It was embarrassing, but necessary, to obtain Chiang Kai-shek's acquiescence to these territorial infringements on Chinese sovereignty, and this necessity has since agitated some of the critics of Yalta. Even so, anyone conversant with the wartime military situation in China must grant that Chiang had done virtually nothing to expel the Japanese from his country. In 1945 he was still in his miserable and remote capital at Chungking. His troops had no control of any sort in Manchuria, not to speak of the seacoast which had passed to the Japanese in 1937–1938. For Chiang to give Russia rights in territory which he did not possess was no concession. True, the Western Allies at the Cairo Conference in 1943 had promised complete restoration of Chinese sovereignty. Yet there had been no real Chinese control over Manchuria since the end of the nineteenth century when Russia received her first large concessions, and a restoration of Chinese sovereignty did not preclude restoration of Russian privileges. It is technically possible for a nation to exercise sovereignty at the time that its territory is to some extent encumbered by servitudes. Extraterritoriality had been a commonplace in the orient in the nineteenth century, and the United States had not relinquished its extraterritorial privileges in China until 1943. Admittedly this is a bit of a technical argument in favor of the Yalta agreement on Russian privileges in China. There is something to be said for the broad, more equitable interpretation of international arrangements. The difficulty in 1945 was the seeming necessity of getting Russia into the Far Eastern war. This meant obtaining an ally for Chiang Kai-shek, which the latter statesman, in view of his own minuscule contribution to the war, should have welcomed. Chiang signed a treaty with the Russians in August 1945. The unfortunate aspect of the matter was that he was not consulted in the Yalta arrangement—but again, had he been consulted there almost certainly would have been a leak to the Japanese of the imminence of Russian intervention. As Roosevelt said at Yalta to Stalin and Churchill, anything told the Chinese "was known to the whole world in twenty-four hours."

Yalta was beyond dispute the climax of coalition diplomacy. It was the moment when the issues of the war, in all their complexity, came to focus. Most of these issues were not decided at Yalta, for they already had been decided in one way or another. Stalin had twice promised, informally at the Moscow foreign ministers' meeting of October 1943, formally at Teheran, to enter the war against Japan.

Arrangements for the postwar Polish government over which so much bitterness later would appear had been anticipated during the October 1944 meeting in Moscow of Stalin and Churchill. Eventual settlement of the problem of Eastern Europe, despite the promises at Yalta, was also set forth at the Moscow Conference of 1944. Other illustrations could be cited to show how the Yalta Conference usually focused issues, and then formalized them, rather than "settled" them.

The conference was memorable, too, because it was the second and last meeting of the wartime Big Three. Something seemed strange about Stalin sitting later for formal Big Three pictures with Clement Attlee and Harry S. Truman. By the time of the Potsdam Conference the war in Europe was over and the war against Japan almost won, and the new faces at the Potsdam conference table symbolized the end of an era. During the war there had been high emotion and drama of a sort that would have pleased a Shakespeare. A coalition mastered the world and the triumvirs of that coalition, Stalin, Churchill, Roosevelt, lent grandeur to what in every sense was a crucial point in history—the second World War.

The uncertainties of the following decade have in many instances tended to rub the grandeur off the effort of 1939–1945. The recriminations over Yalta have made Americans, as well as the peoples of other nations, forget the generous emotions of the war years, and ridicule what in many ways was the grandest crusade ever undertaken by the American nation. After a decade and a half of disillusion it is now possible to see the beginning of a deeper understanding of the recent war, to see a more sensible view emerging. Americans are looking away from the lurid brilliance of Yalta, and fastening their attention on the essential tragedy of a nation such as Germany going down to ruin behind a psychopathic dictator, and the tragedy of a nation with all the virtues of the Russian people denied postwar freedom and peace by an oriental despotism.

But this is more properly a subject for the chapters that follow. Here let us review in a few sentences the nature of the diplomacy of the victorious Allied coalition. There were three stages in the coalition—the period of emergency (1942), the period when victory came into sight (1943–1944), the period of disintegration (1945). The Yalta Conference coincided with the coalition's decline. In the years of disillusion which followed Yalta it was easy to fasten blame for the world's woes upon a spectacular meeting of three elderly men at a Crimean summer resort. In attributing such blame history was repeating itself, for at Paris a quarter of a century earlier other old men had sat in a book-lined library and drawn down upon themselves the maledictions of a succeeding generation.

ADDITIONAL READING

The second World War, like the war of 1914–1918, has produced a spate of memoirs and scholarly studies, and in sketching out this literature it is difficult to know where to start and stop. Herbert Feis, *Churchill, Roosevelt, Stalin* (Princeton, 1957), analyzes the interallied diplomacy of the war and is an excellent piece of scholarship, a likely first reference for the inquiring student. See also William L. Neumann, *Making the Peace: 1941–1945* (Washington, 1950); and Chester Wilmot, *The Struggle for Europe* (New York, 1952). A critical account of political-military strategy appears in Hanson W. Baldwin, *Great Mistakes of the War* New York, 1950). Samuel Eliot Morison, *Strategy and Compromise* (Boston, 1958), is a brilliant analysis, countering the assertions in Arthur Bryant, *The Turn of the Tide* (New York, 1957), the diaries of Lord Alanbrooke. Paul Kecskemeti, *Strategic Surrender: The Politics of Victory and Defeat* (Stanford, Calif., 1958) considers among other topics the unconditional-surrender formula of the Casablanca Conference.

No one can study the war of 1939–1945 without appreciating the influence of Winston Churchill, the great British prime minister. Churchill's importance historically has not lessened—and probably has greatly increased—with publication of his memoirs, the last three volumes of which consider the war from 1942 to 1945: *The Hinge of Fate* (Boston, 1950); *Closing the Ring* (1951); and *Triumph and Tragedy* (1953). An investigation of Churchill's strategic views is Trumbull Higgins, *Winston Churchill and the Second Front 1940–1943* (New York, 1957). The best biography is Alan Moorehead's *Winston Churchill: In Trial and Triumph* (Boston, 1955), a model of brevity, judgment, and literary skill.

For titles about Roosevelt, see books listed at the end of chapter 14. The vast literature on FDR ranges from volumes about "that man in the White House"—such as John T. Flynn, *The Roosevelt Myth* (New York, 1948)—to such defenses as Arthur M. Schlesinger, Jr., "Roosevelt and His Detractors," in E. N. Saveth, ed., *Understanding the American Past* (Boston, 1954).

The memoir output for the second World War has been prodigious, and the following are leading accounts: *Memoirs of Cordell Hull* (2 vols., New York, 1948); R. N. Current, *Secretary Stimson* (New Brunswick, N.J., 1948); H. L. Stimson and McGeorge Bundy, *On Active Service* (New York, 1948); E. R. Stettinius, Jr., *Lend-Lease: Weapon for Victory*

(New York, 1944) and *Roosevelt and the Russians* (Garden City, N.Y., 1949); Ernest J. King and Walter M. Whitehill, *Fleet Admiral King* (New York, 1952), an excellent volume; William D. Leahy, *I Was There* (New York, 1950), by an individual who as FDR's military aide saw as much high-level diplomacy as any official of the American government save only the president; Walter Millis and E. S. Duffield, eds., *The Forrestal Diaries* (New York, 1951), diary jottings, letters, and memoranda; Sumner Welles, *The Time for Decision* (New York, 1944), *Where Are We Heading?* (New York, 1946), and *Seven Decisions that Shaped History* (New York, 1951); Robert E. Sherwood, *Roosevelt and Hopkins* (New York, 1948; available in paperback); Dwight D. Eisenhower, *Crusade in Europe* (Garden City, N.Y., 1948); Harry C. Butcher, *My Three Years with Eisenhower* (New York, 1946), by the general's naval aide.

For American diplomacy toward specific countries, two notable books deal with Germany: Henry Morgenthau, *Germany Is Our Problem* (New York, 1945), by the author of the Morgenthau Plan; and A. W. Dulles, *Germany's Underground* (New York, 1947), an account of the tragic uprising on July 20, 1944 by the German opposition to Hitler. Dulles was the representative in Switzerland of the Office of Strategic Services, the American wartime intelligence organization. Relations with Vichy France appear in William L. Langer, *Our Vichy Gamble* (New York, 1947), a defense of the Department of State's policy; and Paul Farmer, *Vichy—Political Dilemma* (New York, 1955). Russian relations are set down by the American wartime ambassador, William H. Standley, *Admiral Ambassador to Russia* (Chicago, 1955); and the military head of lend-lease, Major General John H. Deane, *The Strange Alliance* (New York, 1947). Spain's dealings with the United States, the wartime maneuverings of Generalissimo Francisco Franco between the Axis and the Allies, are considered by the American ambassador, the well-known historian Carlton J. H. Hayes, *Wartime Mission to Spain* (New York, 1945); and the economic adviser to the Department of State, Herbert Feis, *The Spanish Story* (New York, 1948).

Turning to the Far Eastern theater of warfare where the United States bore the brunt of defeating Japan, there are several excellent paperback books on the military operations of the war: Saburo Sakai with Martin Caidin and Fred Saito, *Samurai;* Yasuo Kuwahara and Gordon T. Allred, *Kamikaze;* Mitsuo Fuchida and Masatake Okumiya, *Midway: The Battle that Doomed Japan;* Masatake Okumiya and Jiro Horikoshi with Martin Caidin, *Zero;* C. Vann Woodward, *The Battle for Leyte Gulf.* Masuo Kato's *The Lost War* (New York, 1946) is a poignant account by a Japanese newspaperman interned in the United States after Pearl Harbor who later went back to Japan and watched his country go down to defeat. Toshikazu Kase, *Journey to the Missouri* (New Haven, 1950) is by a distinguished Japanese diplomat. Robert J. C. Butow, *Japan's Decision to Surrender* (Stanford, 1954) is the best book on its subject. See also J. C. Grew, *Turbulent Era* (2 vols., Boston, 1952) and F. C. Jones, *Japan's*

New Order in East Asia (New York, 1954). Books on American wartime relations with China are listed at the end of chapter 18.

The question of Yalta—whether or not Yalta was a "sell-out"—has agitated publicists and the American public ever since the Yalta apportionment of territory and influence between the Western Allies and Soviet Russia. A special congressional request to the State Department resulted in the United States Government's publication in 1955 of the Yalta conference papers in a special volume in the series *Foreign Relations of the United States*. That volume has been carefully digested and compared with other memoir and documentary publications in the excellent book edited by John L. Snell, *The Meaning of Yalta* (Baton Rouge, La., 1956). General MacArthur's allegations on the subject of Yalta led the Department of Defense to take the extraordinary step of releasing from its records 105 pages of documents entitled *The Entry of the Soviet Union into the War Against Japan: Military Plans, 1941–1945* (Washington, 1955); this report shows that MacArthur approved of the Yalta arrangements for Soviet assistance against Japan. Helpful articles on Yalta are Rudolph A. Winnacker, "Yalta—Another Munich?" in *Virginia Quarterly Review*, vol. 24 (1948), 521–537; Ellis M. Zacharias, "The Inside Story of Yalta," *United Nations World*, vol. 3 (1949), 12–16, arguing that erroneous intelligence estimates brought the Yalta effort to enlist Russia against Japan; Louis Morton, "The Military Background of the Yalta Agreements," *The Reporter*, April 7, 1955; and Raymond J. Sontag, "Reflections on the Yalta Papers," *Foreign Affairs*, vol. 33 (1954–1955), 615–623, defending the Yalta agreements as the only agreements that could have been made, given the temper of the times. Sontag believes that in the light of what happened in the following decade it was entirely proper that the United States made a sincere effort to get along with the Soviet Union, for otherwise we would have uneasy consciences today.

Europe, 1945-1950

After every one of the major wars in American history—the revolution, the Civil War, the first and second World Wars—there has been a letdown, a time when people relaxed from wartime trials and enjoyed peace with unaccustomed vigor and abandon. The greater the war the greater the letdown, and the first few years after 1945 were a relaxed, loose, and frivolous time; the nation enjoyed itself as never before in its history. The end of gas rationing came in 1945, and soon afterward the end of other rationing; "the boys" came home; the cars moved out on the roads; the night clubs expanded their seating capacities. The United States in 1945 and 1946 in no sense experienced what occurred in postwar Britain—continued rationing, and a general tightening of belts. Neither did it experience the troubles of Continental nations—dropping production, rising unemployment, and lack of food and fuel by large segments of the population. Americans enjoyed themselves in a burst of postwar spending and self-indulgence, which when compared to the austerity of other nations, victor and defeated alike, seems in retrospect almost callous.

This letdown, the wonderful feeling of relaxation after the war, accounts largely for the aimlessness of American diplomacy in the two or three years after V-E and V-J days. The purposes of American diplomacy understandably became lost in the general hubbub. After all, who wanted to think about diplomacy when the nation had just won the largest war in human history? Peace was to be enjoyed —meanwhile, let the diplomats play their private games; so Americans thought.

There were other, if less important, reasons for the course of American diplomacy after 1945. For one, the leadership of the republic's diplomacy was not all that it might have been. When Vice President Harry S. Truman on April 12, 1945 was elevated to the presidency by the death of President Roosevelt, he had little knowledge of foreign affairs. He had been vice president for a few weeks, and had had almost no briefing on the conduct of American foreign relations. Nor could he receive assistance from James F. ("Jimmy") Byrnes, his inexperienced appointee as secretary of state (Byrnes replaced Edward R. Stettinius, Jr., in July 1945; Stettinius had replaced Hull in December 1944). Jimmy Byrnes was an able politician who during the war had made himself almost indispensable to President Roosevelt as a troubleshooter, ferreting out problems and their solutions with admirable efficiency, but when translated into the State Department he discovered himself in a milieu different from American domestic politics. For some months, perhaps for most of the time that he held the secretaryship (until January 1947), he moved slowly, attempting to take the measure of his responsibilities.

The nation's diplomacy, thus in trouble, was further crippled by the precipitous demobilization of the American armed forces. During the war the enormous military power of the United States had given a strength to the country's diplomacy that it had not possessed since the time of the first World War when for a fleeting moment there was another large army in being. If only some of American wartime military power could have been retained, if the draft could have continued to feed into the army and navy and air force just a part of its wartime levies of young men, the series of defeats that befell American diplomacy in the postwar years might not have occurred. Hindsight makes this easy to see. At the time no one worried. There was a compelling pressure for demobilization, and the Washington government had little choice except to let the magnificent war machine of May 1945 disintegrate within half a dozen months under a ruinous point system that released first the armed forces' most experienced members.

But the overwhelming desire for letdown, for return to normal ways of behavior and thought, was the chief cause of our woes after the second World War. Desire for relaxation carried everything before it. Few individuals looked for trouble in foreign affairs, and almost everyone chose to enjoy the postwar domestic prosperity to the limit. The United Nations, President Roosevelt had believed, would care for future international rivalries. There would be few problems from Soviet Russia. The Russians, almost all Americans thought in 1945, would be peaceful and easy to get along with. General Dwight D. Eisenhower concluded after a trip to Moscow that "nothing guides Russian policy so much as a desire for friendship with the United States," and this was the prevailing view. When in 1946 and 1947 Soviet intentions became all too clear, written in actions and verbiage that everyone could understand, it was nearly too late to do anything. Americans found that they were without the means to make their will prevail, short of a preventive atomic war which was humanely unthinkable. There was no conventional military machine to back the nation's diplomacy, and two or three years were necessary to rebuild the military forces. Besides, the country was repelled by the idea of turning again to military pressure in foreign relations. It sought for a while with considerable success to institute a program of economic aid to Europe and the Middle East and Asia. Part of that program, the Marshall Plan, resuscitated the faltering economies and wrought startling improvements in the material well-being of the Continent. Even so, the threatened subversion of pro-Western regimes in Greece and Turkey, the need to buttress them militarily as was recognized in the Truman Doctrine of 1947, and the continuing use of strong-arm methods by the Russians in such cases as the Berlin blockade of 1948–1949, all gave indication of trouble ahead. Something more than economic measures was necessary to stop communism. The nation in 1950 woke with a start when the communist invasion of South Korea demonstrated the importance of a military as well as an economic policy. For five years the United States had sought, with growing distraction, to pursue its own national prosperity, and in 1950, on June 25 to be exact, the postwar letdown came to an end.

1. *The United Nations*

In the brave new months after victory, probably nothing characterized the times more hopefully for Americans than did creation in 1945 of the United Nations. The UN would provide, its American supporters believed, a solvent for national rivalries. It would be the

Parliament of the World of which poets long had sung. An American president in 1919 had revealed a vision of world government which failed to obtain popular support. Woodrow Wilson, so his supporters were saying while the second World War was still being fought, had been "ahead of his time." By 1945 time had caught up with the prophecy, many Americans were approaching the new world organization with a childlike faith that within a few years was humbling to recall. The UN was to be the government of the brave new world, the mistakes of 1919 would not be repeated. Because of the United Nations, so carefully established before the war had ended, there would be no muddle and descent into international anarchy such as marked the two decades after the armistice of 1918.

The intention of the United States to establish and participate in a new world organization had become obvious well before the end of the second World War. In the year 1943 both houses of Congress passed resolutions—the Fulbright Resolution in the House (September 21, 1943), the Connally Resolution in the Senate (November 5, 1943)—stipulating for, as Representative J. William Fulbright put it, "creation of appropriate international machinery with power adequate to establish and to maintain a just and lasting peace, among the nations of the world." The Senate, with due attention to its traditions, added in the Connally Resolution that the "general international organization" should be "based on the principle of the sovereign equality of all peace-loving states." A year later, in 1944, the United States invited Britain, Russia, and China to meet in Washington to plan for the new organization, a meeting held from August 21 to October 7, at a mansion known as Dumbarton Oaks—the meeting thereby becoming known as the Dumbarton Oaks Conference. Its draft proposals became the basis of the UN Charter when the latter was drawn up at the San Francisco Conference of the following year.

Delegates of fifty nations attended the grand conference at San Francisco which opened on April 25, 1945. President Truman gave the speech of welcome. The resultant UN Charter was signed on June 26, and established a General Assembly of all member nations to meet periodically, each nation with a single vote, together with a Security Council of eleven members in continuous session. There were to be such other organs as an Economic and Social Council, an International Court of Justice (sitting at The Hague, replacing the old and similarly titled League organization, the Court of International Justice), a Trusteeship Council, and a Secretariat. The Senate of the United States advised and consented to the UN Charter on July 28, 1945 by a vote of 89 to 2. Other nations quickly added their assents, and the Charter went into effect on October 24, 1945. The first meeting of the General Assembly was held in London on January 10, 1946; the Security Council convened the same month. The headquarters of the new organization was not to be in the location of the discredited League—Geneva, Switzerland—but in the metropolis of the Western Hemisphere, New York City, in a new skyscraper along the Manhattan range. This splendid slim tower of steel and glass, sumptuously appointed, has since been visited by (to use the skeptical description of Reinhold Niebuhr) multitudes of Americans prompted by piety or school principals or women's clubs. These Americans seemed to regard the UN as a kind of super-government that could guarantee peace if only devotion to it were absolute. Viewing the UN's headquarters in their own country, Americans apparently believed that this time the world organization, the UN, would work.

Had they examined the UN Charter with greater care they might have found in it reason for skepticism, or at least for reservation, because in some ways the new organization was a less imposing institution than the old League of Nations. The preamble to the Charter was impressive enough, though rather bitter-sweet when read in the light of the world's history after 1945. "We the peoples of the United Nations," it began in a vein reminiscent of the constitution of the United States, "determined to save succeeding generations from the scourge of war, which twice in our life-time has brought untold sorrow to mankind, and to reaffirm faith in fundamental human rights, in the dignity and worth of the human person, in the equal rights of men and women and nations large and small, and to establish conditions under which justice and respect for the obligations arising from treaties and other sources of international law can be maintained, and to promote social progress and better standards of life in larger freedom, and for these ends to practice tolerance and live together in peace with one another as good neighbors, and to unite our strength to maintain international peace and security, and to ensure, by the acceptance of principles and the institution of methods, that armed force shall not be used, save in the common interest, and to employ international machinery for the promotion of the economic and social advancement of all peoples, have resolved to combine our efforts to accomplish these aims." Such was the auspicious beginning. But as one read further in the Charter, into the substantive articles, he discovered some qualifications in its detailed constitutional arrangements. The very length of the Charter—the Covenant of the League of Nations had 26 articles; the UN Charter required 111—gave it an air of uncertainty, recalling the manner in which state constitutions in the United States frequently have been drawn to great length so that the governments inaugurated under them would not merely be precisely informed of their duties but limited in their powers. Perhaps, however, the length of the Charter was a scheme to hide the inevitable reservations of national sovereignty —the "loopholes," as the two express reservations of the Covenant of the League had been known. There were two similar loopholes in the Charter, just as all-encompassing as those in the Covenant. Part 7 of the UN Charter's Article 2 reserved to member nations "matters which are essentially within the domestic jurisdiction of any state." Article 51 thoughtfully set forth that "Nothing in the present Charter shall impair the inherent right of individual or collective self-defense . . ." Taken together, the provisions for domestic jurisdiction and self-defense would allow any scheming nation to wiggle out of its UN commitments, if it so desired. An additional loophole was the veto power over any UN actions held by the five permanent members of the Security Council, the United States, Great Britain, the USSR, France, and China. Every possible contingency thus was fenced in, in advance.

If one analyzed the Charter carefully he found that it bound its membership to little more than good behavior. It certainly was no stronger than the League of Nations. And it was positively weaker when one considered that the Charter showed a startling lack of the procedures and regulations for members in event of international trouble that had marked the Covenant of the League of Nations. The Covenant specified procedures in case of war or threat of war. The Charter did little except declare "breaches of the peace" (the word "war" does not appear in the articles of the Charter, except twice in the phrase "second World War") as the proper business of the membership, without stating what should thereafter be done. A skeptic or a cynic might have asked what was gained by the 111 new articles, other than the admission to membership of Soviet Russia.

The Russians, having been expelled from the League in 1939 during the war with Finland, would have nothing to do with the old world organization and insisted upon a completely new one. Now there was the new one, weaker organizationally than the old.

Quite apart from its constitutional inadequacies, the UN developed a special functional weakness in the years after 1945, a weakness which deserves some mention. This was the unanticipated rise of the General Assembly to a position of importance within the UN organization, accompanied by the decline in prestige of the Security Council. The increased role of the Assembly was not, as said, anticipated by the UN's founders. The San Francisco Conference had established the Security Council in a belief that in this select body of eleven members, dominated by five great powers possessing permanent seats and the right to veto any action deemed detrimental to their interests, the work of watching over the world could easily be accomplished. In the springtime of 1945 there was little anticipation, at least on the American side, that American-Russian relations would soon deteriorate to a point where the Council could hardly function at all. The Americans in drawing up their list of powers for permanent membership in the Council also did not anticipate how drained of energy the British were in 1945, how Great Britain's stature in a year or two or three would decline to that of a virtually second-class power. France also had appeared to the United States as a far more important nation than postwar events proved. Likewise it was, apparently, a mistake to have included China among the permanent members of the Council, for neither was China a great power in 1945 nor could Nationalist China fairly represent the Chinese people after 1949, when the Kuomintang was driven from the mainland to Formosa. The Security Council, as constituted in 1945, was crippled from the start. This most important policy-determining arm of the UN did not in any major respect represent the true distribution of strength, military and diplomatic, throughout the world.

The idea behind organization of the Security Council as a body dominated by the great powers was essentially a good one, for this meant, if the idea worked as planned, that nations holding dominant power in the UN were also the nations truly responsible for maintenance of peace throughout the world. The UN structure, as conceived in this way, contained the prime requisite for any well-planned political organization—a linking of power and responsibility. But the idea went awry in the unforeseen diminution of power of Britain, France, and China, and the new antagonism between the United States and the Soviet Union. This development soon led to confusion within the UN; then the United States confounded the confusion by adopting a policy of taking major political questions, many of them with profound implications for the controversy between the two superpower groups, to the General Assembly. The Assembly, the planners of the UN had assumed, was to be a talking place, a kind of town meeting with extremely limited powers, a forum where the smaller nations of the world could have representation without power. The United States for its own reasons decided that it would be good to have "decisions," resolutions of support, from the General Assembly, and went to the Assembly for such notable decisions as that to resist the North Korean invasion of South Korea in June 1950.

By soliciting support from the Assembly, the United States placed itself in a delicate position. It would not always be convenient for the American government to solicit Assembly support. But the Assembly, having been solicited by the United States, began to take its support seriously, as something to be given or withheld as the case might require. The Assembly was a large and unwieldy organization, including the numerous new nations of Southeast Asia and the Middle East. Hence whenever the Assembly gave or withheld support in the form of a resolution many nations voted—nations other than Latin America and Western Europe and the British empire—and it was difficult to be sure of the votes. The Asian-Arab bloc, if the United States were not constantly on guard, could team up with the Latin-American nations and secure an Assembly majority. This majority would not have the faintest correspondence to world power. But for better or worse, a modicum of power passed to the Assembly, after the abdication of the Security Council, and how the United States would handle this new development was a matter for time to tell. Some thoughtful people, observing the irresponsibility of the Assembly and the impossibility of reaching decisions in the Security Council, were beginning to believe that the UN was finished so far as constructive work was concerned. It was, they believed, a place of passion, of unreason, frequently of utter confusion, with little regard for the problems of the great powers of the world.

An especially confused polarization developed in the UN, often discussed as a division between "East" and "West." These two terms have probably become inextricably imbedded in the language, but they need comment, even if in a digression. They are inaccurate if only in that the "West" division includes such eastern nations as the Philippines and Japan, and would also like fervently to enroll India and many other Asiatic countries. It is unfortunate that the language of discussion in western countries thus tends to concede all eastern countries to the communist bloc.

In the first years after the war the confusions of the UN's organization, structural and functional, were only in part apparent. The UN in its first days was a forum of deadlock, with the *nyet* of Russian representatives echoing through the meetings of the Security Council, with the two superpowers at odds over all kinds of international proposals. It was, perhaps, unfortunate that the new world organization should have been asked to help solve at this time one of the most difficult problems ever presented to any government, national or international—the problems of limitation and reduction of atomic arms.

It was on January 24, 1946, two weeks after its opening meeting, that the UN Assembly created a commission to study the control of atomic energy. The American elder statesman, Bernard M. Baruch, on June 14, 1946 proposed an international atomic development authority to which the United States would turn over its atomic bomb secrets, provided that there was an international control and inspection of bomb production not subject to big-power veto, and that further manufacture of bombs would cease and existing stocks be destroyed. "We are here," Baruch told the UN's Atomic Energy Commission, "to make a choice between the quick and the dead. That is our business. Behind the black portent of the new atomic age lies a hope which, seized upon with faith, can work our salvation. If we fail, then we have damned every man to be the slave of Fear. Let us not deceive ourselves: We must elect World Peace or World Destruction." The Soviet Union, unfortunately, was not willing to accept the Baruch proposals, balking in particular at the American elder statesman's demand for international control and inspection. The Russian representative in the Security Council, Andrei A. Gromyko, in a speech on March 5, 1947 remarked that "Logic tells us that any thought may be reduced to an absurdity. This applies even to good thoughts and ideas. The transformation of atomic-energy control into an unlimited control," Gromyko said, "would mean to reduce to an absurdity the very idea of control of atomic energy in order to prevent its use for military purposes. Unlimited control would mean an unlimited interference of the control and controlling organ—or organs—in the economic life of the countries on whose territories this control would be carried out, and interference in their internal affairs. . . . the authors of the so-called Baruch plan completely ignore national interests of other countries and proceed from . . . the interests actually of one country; that is, the United States of America."

The issue of atomic limitation and control by the UN thereupon deadlocked. Testimony to this saddening fact was the McMahon Act of 1946, reorganizing the American domestic atomic program under a new civilian five-man Atomic Energy Commission. There were two atomic tests at Bikini in July 1946. The UN had proved incapable of halting the atomic armaments race.

2. *The Nadir of American Diplomacy*

In the early postwar period of 1945–1947, faith in the UN was coupled, as we have seen, with a dominant American mood of letdown, relaxation—which insofar as it expressed itself in policy was marked by a desire to "get out of" Europe and "get out of" Asia. Troops and military forces in those distant places should come home. The world should return to its prewar habits, nations "standing on their own feet" without American aid and sustenance. The nations should "get off the U.S. taxpayer's back." If this were done, so Americans thought, everything would be just fine. In the merry chase at home, the effort to get caught up in cars and refrigerators and deep-freezers and all the other items that had gone out of production during the war, there was enough to do without thinking of foreign countries.

Despite the popular mood, diplomacy could not come to a stop. International relations continued, whether Americans saw any value in them or not. In the initial postwar period, accommodation with Russia was the purpose and goal of American diplomats. This turned out to be largely a negative rather than positive effort, to preserve a wartime alliance that the Russians found no longer useful. The wartime alliance had begun to break, even before the end of the war in Europe, and the stresses and strains were visible at the Yalta Conference, but for some time thereafter the West sought futilely to arrange some kind of friendly settlement with the East. Everyone in 1945 hoped for one world, a family of nations. The UN "*has* to work," people said. One world or none. The atomic bomb would unify or destroy the world. Such ideas as co-existence, containment, and cold war, utterly foreign to American wartime hopes, were not talked of by the people and statesmen of the United States until 1947 and thereafter.

There were rumblings of trouble as early as the spring of 1945, but they were unknown to the American public. President Roosevelt a short time before his death had admitted to Senator Arthur Vandenberg that "Just between us, Arthur, I am coming to know the Russians better . . ." President Truman had discovered shortly after entering the White House that American dealings with Russia had been a "one-way street," and the new president talked turkey to the Russian foreign minister, Molotov, when the latter visited Washington a few days before the opening of the San Francisco Conference. "I have never been talked to like that in my life," Molotov said. "Carry out your agreements," Truman answered, "and you won't get talked to like that."

Uneasiness over Russian relations continued. On May 12, four days after V-E Day, Prime Minister Churchill sent a memorable telegram to President Truman: "What is to happen about Russia?" he asked. "What will be the position in a year or two, when the British and American Armies have melted and the French has not yet been formed on any major scale, when we may have a handful of divisions, mostly French, and when Russia may choose to keep two or three hundred on active service? An iron curtain is drawn down upon their front. We do not know what is going on behind. There seems little doubt that the whole of the regions east of the line Lübeck-Trieste-Corfu will soon be completely in their hands. To this must be added the further enormous area conquered by the American armies between Eisenach and the Elbe, which will, I suppose, in a few weeks be occupied, when the Americans retreat, by the Russian power. . . . Thus a broad band of many hundreds of miles of Russian-occupied territory will isolate us from Poland. . . . Surely it is vital now to come to an understanding with Russia, or see where we are with her, before we weaken our armies mortally . . ."

This magnificent advice went unheeded. It came too soon to be followed. The American government prepared hopefully for the Potsdam Conference, held on July 17–August 2, 1945. As an earnest of good will toward Russia, President Truman ordered American troops to begin withdrawal from the advanced positions they held in central Germany. In the final rush of the war the Western Allied troops had penetrated beyond their Yalta-allotted zones of occupation on a front 400 miles in length and at one point 120 miles in depth. Despite Churchill's plea, the United States gave up this territory, beginning the withdrawal on June 21. Americans hoped that at Potsdam no force or threats of force would be necessary, that the good work begun so auspiciously at Yalta, the work of establishing the hopes of peoples everywhere for a lasting peace, would be carried forward decisively to a settlement of European problems and, perhaps, a preliminary settlement of Far Eastern affairs. (Japan was a secret subject for discussion at Potsdam, as at Yalta, for the Soviet Union had not yet entered the Far Eastern war.) And it was one of the ironies of history that the British statesman who so recently had given the American government such a good piece of advice was forced to attend Potsdam while the results of an election in his home country were still in doubt. Churchill brought to Potsdam the leader of the British Labour Party, Clement Attlee, and when it became known during the meetings of the conference that Attlee had won the election he replaced Churchill at the closing sessions.

The diplomacy of accommodation with the Russians was pursued at the Potsdam Conference amid the gardens and brownstone splendor of the Cecilienhof, once the country estate of the last Crown Prince William of Hohenzollern. Surrounded by history, the conference had every inspiration for success, but what had gone before—the eagerness to please the Soviets, the withdrawal by the Western Allies into their zones of occupation, the disavowal of Churchill's leadership by the British people, the uncertainties of American leadership—these were the decisive factors at Potsdam, together, of course, with Russia's vast army in possession of all Eastern Europe: East Germany, Czechoslovakia, Poland, Yugoslavia, Bulgaria, Rumania, Albania. The decisions of Potsdam, like those of the wartime conferences, were foreordained. The Russians admitted that they had made a private deal with the Polish Provisional Government of National Unity (dominated by the Lublin Committee) whereby Poland received a slice of Germany, the line of the Oder and Western Neisse rivers, in compensation for Poland's loss to Russia of the territory east of the Curzon Line. The Western Allies at Potsdam could do nothing about this accomplished fact, the new Polish border drawn within Russia's zone of East Germany, except to vow in the conference's protocol that "the final delimitation of the western frontier of Poland should await the peace settlement."

There were two other, and minor, developments at Potsdam. President Truman proposed that the principal waterways of the world—Panama, the Bosporus, Kiel, Suez, the Rhine-Danube waterway from the North Sea to the Black Sea—be opened to trade and passengers of all the world. This scheme was perfectly agreeable to the British, Churchill declaring it "remarkable and important," but it meant in effect, through opening the Rhine-Danube waterway, an opening up of the iron curtain, and this the Russians would not allow. The proposal slipped into oblivion. The other development of some importance at Potsdam was the so-called Potsdam Declaration, a statement by Britain and the United States that the Japanese should give up the fighting in the Far East. "We call upon the government of Japan," Truman and Churchill announced on July 26, 1945, "to proclaim now the unconditional surrender of all Japanese armed forces, and to provide proper and adequate assurances of their good faith in such action. The alternative for Japan is prompt and utter destruction." Had the Japanese known that the words of the declaration were barbed by the explosion of the first atomic bomb on July 16 at Alamogordo, New Mexico, they might have heeded the warning from Potsdam, but they did not know of the successes of Allied science. When they surrendered a few days after the Potsdam meeting it was, in an immediate sense, because of the sudden Russian military intervention in the war, perhaps also because of the atomic bomb, and only to a minor extent, if any, because of the Potsdam Declaration.

After the Potsdam Conference came the interminable meetings in Europe and America of the Council of Foreign Ministers, in which nothing seemed to be accomplished. There were four meetings of the foreign ministers during the first year of peace, and the meetings went on and on. The ministers talked and argued but could come to no agreement. The apogee of disagreement was reached at the Moscow meeting in the spring of 1947, when there were forty-four sessions devoted to proposed treaties of peace for Germany and Austria.

The regular meetings of the Council of Foreign Ministers, as had been the case with the Potsdam Conference, were disappointing in their results. Nor was the Paris Peace Conference of 1946, a series of special meetings of the foreign ministers of Great Britain, France, the Soviet Union, and the United States, held between the dates of April 25 and October 15, a triumph for American diplomacy. It gave a short-lived independence to Hungary, Rumania, and Bulgaria, which the Russians soon snatched away. It provided for Finnish independence, which Finland somehow maintained, perhaps because as an independent country Finland was able to pay more reparations to Russia than would have been the case if the Finns had not received their independence. As for the conference's deliberations on Italy, that nation was a province of the two Western allies, Britain and the United States, and they could have controlled Italian destinies with or without a Paris Peace Conference. The Paris meetings ratified the Western decision to give Italy independence. The conference had the effect, although the democratic allies at the outset had fervently hoped that this would not be, of confirming the military settlement made in Europe at the end of the war in 1945. Indeed, after one combined the results of the Paris Peace Conference with the results of the various regular meetings of the foreign ministers during 1945–1946, together with the accomplishments of the Potsdam Conference, he discovered that the settlements might have been predicted by any neophyte: where the Red Armies stood, there the Russians organized and manipulated governments to their own taste; wherever the West had stationed its forces, it retained local political control.

Despite what in retrospect appears to have been an obvious situation, the loss of Eastern Europe to the communists was at the time an unnerving experience for the Western powers. At the end of the war there had been high hope that the Russians in their preserve of Eastern Europe—Hungary, Rumania, and Bulgaria, together with the already nominally free Yugoslavia, Poland, and Czechoslovakia—would maintain political freedom in the occupied nations, in accord with the Yalta Declaration on Liberated Europe. There would be, so Americans hoped, free elections in Eastern Europe, after which the reconstituted governments would continue to allow political freedom. It was one of the most disillusioning experiences of the postwar era to see the Russians ignore the Yalta Declaration and subvert to communism the East European governments. At the Potsdam Conference in 1945 Stalin had made the Soviet position clear when he said that "any freely elected government would be anti-Soviet and that we cannot permit." Even so, Western statesmen did not think the Soviet dictator would follow such a course of open domination as he did in Eastern Europe, for it seemed impossible that he would stoop to such outrageous behavior.

As mentioned briefly in the preceding chapter, conversion of the small countries of Eastern Europe into Soviet satellites was in each case, including even that of Czechoslovakia (February 25, 1948), a legal affair, accomplished by infiltrating the postwar coalition governments. In these war-devastated nations it had proved extremely difficult at the war's end to establish any kind of democratic government. Before the war, when conditions had been far more favorable, most of these countries had succumbed, in one form or another, to totalitarian regimes. In 1945 it was necessary to begin anew. Still, these nations were making the effort to fulfill the promises of the Yalta Declaration on Liberated Europe, and it appeared quite probable that the humiliations and trials of the war years had invigorated a spirit of democracy that had always been latent. Old and new political parties began to appear and there was some sign of life politically, but at that moment the communist parties in Eastern Europe through a devious process of force, intimidation, and assimilation took over the other political parties. The favorite communist gambit was to form a coalition government, a practical necessity in the first postwar months, and then to obtain for their own party the key cabinet portfolio, the ministry of the interior, which in most European countries controls the police. From this vantage point a communist minister could institute measures of a sort that members of other parties, seeking political freedom, discovered stifling to party effort and initiative. From the ministry of the interior the communists in the former Axis satellite nations reached out to the government bureaucracies, and before the usually somewhat naive democratic leaders realized what was happening, the jig was up. Once a communist premier and cabinet took over, dissident politicians found themselves silenced and, in many instances, with one-way tickets to Siberia.

The communization of Hungary was a typical case of Russian postwar behavior behind the iron curtain. As is related by Stephen D. Kertesz in his fascinating volume *Diplomacy in a Whirlpool*, after the end of hostilities in Hungary there appeared a National Independence Front, a coalition established during the German occupation by underground leaders of the Smallholder, Social Democrat, and Communist parties. Later three other parties were admitted to the Front. The Hungarian Communist Party was careful at first to disguise its intentions, and announced to the weary Hungarian people that democracy was the best policy, and even went so far as to pose as protectors of religion, affirming that the Christian churches were worthy of support. As for the Russians, so the Hungarian communists said, they were interested only in annihilating fascism and had no intention of interfering with Hungarian domestic politics.

There followed the organization of a Hungarian government by the Independence Front with co-operation of the communists. Members of the provisional government were chosen with care, to give the populace confidence. The new prime minister and two other cabinet members were generals of the old prewar regime of the conservative Admiral Nicholas Horthy. But the new minister of the interior was a crypto-communist, and he at once set about organizing the police all over the country.

Then, in March 1946, came an attack against the largest noncommunist party, the Smallholders, by a left-wing bloc under communist leadership. The bloc gave ultimatums to the Smallholders in the name of the progressive Hungarian people, asking for expulsion from the national assembly of "reactionary" deputies. The Smallholders under pressure expelled twenty-one deputies, but after this step toward self-liquidation the party still held a parliamentary majority. Soon after, however, the Hungarian police discovered a plot and arrested the secretary-general of the Smallholder Party, Béla Kovacs, whose "confessions" before he died—in Russian captivity—implicated other members of the party including the prime minister, Ferenc Nagy. Nagy was in Switzerland on vacation when the crisis culminated at the end of May, and he could resign in personal safety. The Smallholder speaker of the national assembly, Monsignor Béla Varga, fled Hungary to avoid arrest, and eventually came, as did Nagy, to the United States. The collapse of the Smallholders was followed by annihilation of the other parties and establishment of a "people's republic" on the approved Moscow model.

Observing this process of communization, American diplomatic representatives in Eastern Europe, in Budapest and Bucharest and Sofia and Belgrade and Warsaw and Prague, protested without end, but to no avail. It was humiliating and frustrating to watch the subversion to communism of so large and important an area, without being able to do a thing about it. The diplomacy of the United States in 1945 and 1946 reached a nadir. Never in the twentieth century had American prestige in Europe fallen so low. And this within two years of the tremendous victory of 1945.

Some at the time and later would believe that Soviet actions in 1945–1946 were shrewdly calculated, and that the undoubtedly low estate of American diplomacy by the end of the year 1946 was a masterly piece of work, achieved by the genius of the Soviet dictator. Here, so it might have seemed, was diplomacy worthy of Bismarck, Talleyrand, or Vergennes. Stalin had accomplished everything he wished, and without war.

One must take exception to this view that Russian postwar actions were, as examples of the diplomatic art, masterpieces of calculation and achievement. Soviet diplomacy was beyond doubt shrewd, but it was a cheap kind of shrewdness, a petty, narrow shrewdness that gained short-term advantages while losing long-term advantages of far greater value. First of all, one must say that many of the Soviet actions in the early postwar years were unnecessarily aggravating to the West. The Russians could have accomplished the subversion of the East European governments with much greater finesse. Indeed, subversion of those governments, from the Russian point of view, should not have been necessary. An independent government can be subservient without enslavement, and subservience might have sufficed for Russia's purpose of economic exploitation. Few military advantages were to be gained from control of the satellites. Militarily the positions of the Red Army in the satellite countries were of doubtful value in 1945 and subsequent years, and with achievement of parity in atomic bombs between Russia and the United States the value of those positions declined further. The satellite armies, so carefully trained, have proved politically unreliable. The only gain that the Soviets could have realized from the satellites was economic. Their physical occupation and political subversion was unnecessary. And every movement of this sort in East Central Europe antagonized the Western nations.

There were other Soviet blunders in the years immediately following the war. At Yalta and Potsdam the Russians had sponsored a demarcation of occupation zones in Germany that gave the West the most valuable part of the country, the industrial portion that later became the heart of the West German state. The setting up of the German Democratic Republic made this a permanent division of territory. Western Germany in terms of wealth is second only to France on the continent of Europe today. Moreover, when in Great Britain the Churchill government lost the election in 1945 and gave way to the Labor Party, an avowedly socialist party, there was opportunity for the Soviets to flatter this new Labor government, and perhaps try to separate it from its ally, the United States. Instead the Russians rebuffed the British Laborites. They chose to treat the British Labor Party with the same contempt that they had shown the Churchill regime. There was similarly shabby treatment of the French government. Already, during the war, the Russians had refused to consider the French a great power, and it was with difficulty that Britain and the United States persuaded Stalin to permit the French to supervise a zone in Germany and a section of the Anglo-American area in Berlin. In such manner the new Fourth Republic of France found itself insulted by the Eastern colossus at a time when honeyed treatment might have drawn France into the communist camp. In somewhat similar fashion the Russians frightened the smaller nations of Western Europe into association with the Western allies. By these tactics—shrewd in the short term, erroneous over the long run—the USSR by its own ineptitude unified the West instead of dividing it, creating by its actions that which it most feared. Soviet tactics by 1947 produced the Western policy of containment. The following year the Soviets, by forcibly taking over Czechoslovakia in the so-called Czech coup, made possible the passage of the Marshall Plan through Congress.

A famous article, "The Sources of Soviet Conduct," appeared in the American journal *Foreign Affairs* in 1947. Written by a "Mr. X," later identified as George F. Kennan of the State Department, the article made a classic plea for a new Western policy toward Russia. Russian wartime and postwar expansion, Kennan argued, was only another example of the migrations westward of barbaric peoples from the recesses of the Asiatic heartland, a migration similar to that of the Mongol conqueror of the thirteenth century, Genghis Khan. The best diplomacy for the United States, the persuasive Kennan said, was containment, a policy less than war itself, but a policy of opposing force with force, of drawing a line, a defense perimeter (as the military men liked to describe it), and warning the Russians "Thus far shall you go, and no farther." It was clear, Kennan wrote, "that the main element of any United States policy toward the Soviet Union must be that of a long-term, patient but firm and vigilant containment of Russian expansive tendencies. . . . such a policy has nothing to do with outward histrionics: with threats or blustering or superfluous gestures of outward 'toughness.' . . . demands on Russian policy should be put forward in such a manner as to leave the way open for a compliance not too detrimental to Russian prestige." Kennan's article ended with an apostrophe to manifest destiny: ". . . the thoughtful observer of Russian-American relations will find no cause for complaint in the Kremlin's challenge to American society. He will rather experience a certain gratitude to a Providence which, by providing the American people with this implacable challenge, has made their entire security as a nation dependent on their pulling themselves together and accepting the responsibilities of moral and political leadership that history plainly intended them to bear."

Shades of 1898! And in the enormously troubled era of fifty years later!

3. *The Truman Doctrine*

It was in the early spring of 1947, with Western Europe in economic and military peril, with the nations of Eastern Europe falling like ninepins under complete communist control, that the United States turned to a policy of containment. Early in the year the government of Great Britain had found itself unable to guarantee further support to the pro-Western governments of Greece and Turkey. The British on February 21 communicated this intelligence privately to Washington, with the advice that if after April 1 the United States could not pay the bill, economically and militarily, for these two nations, then Greece and Turkey would have to shift for themselves, presumably falling to communism. It was a difficult situation. President Truman took the only acceptable course in the face of this threatened disaster and prevented it by a program of economic and military aid to Greece and Turkey and other nations willing to resist aggression, a program that in its sweeping general justification of aid took the appellation of the Truman Doctrine.

Senator Arthur Vandenberg, the Republican Party's leading expert on foreign affairs, urged that Truman make his proposal of aid in a speech before Congress, and in accord with this advice the president went before a joint session on March 12 and asked for $400 million for military and economic aid to the Greek and Turkish governments. In a message notable for its frank and forthright approach he estimated that the United States had contributed $341 billion toward winning the second World War. He pointed out that the assistance he was recommending to Greece and Turkey amount to little more than ⅒ per cent of the wartime investment. "I believe," the president said, "that it must be the policy of the United States to support free peoples who are resisting attempted subjugation by armed minorities or by outside pressures." Great responsibilities, the president remarked, had been placed upon the United States by the swift movement of events, and he was confident that Congress would face these responsibilities squarely.

Congress proved decisively in favor, and the aid bill passed by a vote in the Senate of 67–23 (April 23) and in the House of 287–107 (May 9). This first appropriation under the Truman Doctrine, signed by the president on May 15, was a relatively small program, in view of the outlays that followed under the Marshall Plan and the North Atlantic Treaty Organization, but it was a beginning, and as such marked an upward turn in American diplomatic fortunes. If Greece and Turkey had succumbed to the increasing pressure—Greece was almost surrounded by Albania, Yugoslavia, and Bulgaria, all communist states; Turkey had a long border with the USSR—Western Europe might have followed in the wake of such a disaster. The two East Mediterranean nations had never before been associated with the American national interest, and it was a novel procedure for President Truman to convince the national legislature and the American people that two such foreign localities had now, perforce, come within the American defense perimeter.

Opposition to the Truman Doctrine nonetheless was voluble and sharp. One of the arguments against the program was that the Greek government was undemocratic, corrupt, and reactionary, that Turkey was not a democracy and had been neutral during most of the war. Why (so ran the argument) attempt to defend the free world by aiding such questionable governments? Or, why not let Greece and Turkey pass into the communist orbit, since those two nations merely would be exchanging one form of undemocratic government for another? The Truman administration could only argue that in matters of foreign policy it was not always possible to choose between white and black. Then too, the government of Greece might evolve toward more democratic ways if it could be economically buttressed. The government of Turkey was already moving from its era of tutelage under Mustafa Kemal toward an era of fuller democratic government. Future governments in Ankara and Athens might turn out to be different from the governments of the moment. Under noncommunist regimes the future was at least hopeful, whereas under communist regimes it would become disastrous.

Some opponents of the Truman Doctrine in Congress and in the public press during the spring of 1947 raised the argument that the doctrine bypassed the United Nations. The UN, they claimed, was the place to develop plans for economic assistance on such scales as were required in Greece and Turkey. This argument appeared frequently in the speeches and pronouncements of members of Congress and others whose friendship for the UN had never been warm, and whose sudden stand in favor of handing over the fate of Greece and Turkey to the UN sounded suspiciously like buck passing.

During the debate over the Truman Doctrine, Representative Walter H. Judd, a former medical missionary to China, drew a comparison between American aid to Greece and Turkey and American aid to China which was momentarily embarrassing to the Washington administration. Judd wanted to know why the United States in 1947 was urging the communists in one country—China—to co-operate with China's accredited regime, and opposing communists in other countries with arms and economic aid. Here was a sincere argument, using an analogy not easy to refute. Undersecretary of State Dean Acheson hedged in his answer to Judd, saying that the situation was different. China was a place unlike Turkey and Greece. The point, of course, was that despite the global implications of the Truman Doctrine it was impossible to aid such a large country as China. Later, in 1954, it turned out that it was too late to assist even such a small Asian country as Indochina. The Truman Doctrine in its practical effect was limited to Western and Mediterranean Europe.

It was a noble gesture, the Truman Doctrine, but it came too late to suffice by itself for containing Russian expansion. Immediately after the appropriation for Greece and Turkey passed Congress, indeed while it was in passage, it became evident that more than just aid to Greece and Turkey was necessary to stem the rise of communism. In the spring of 1947 Americans began to realize that all Europe was sick, and that something had to be done quickly, some measure of relief to Europe undertaken on a grand scale, else the Continent would fall irresistibly under the sway of Moscow. Hanson W. Baldwin in the *New York Times* of March 2, 1947 reviewed the "plague and pestilence, suffering and disaster, famine and hardship, the complete economic and political dislocation of the world." He remarked that the United States was "the key to the destiny of tomorrow; we alone may be able to avert the decline of Western civilization, and a reversion to nihilism and the Dark Ages." The economic situation in all Europe in the spring of 1947 was desperate. With support from the temporary relief organization, the United Nations Relief and Rehabilitation Administration (UNRRA), due to end (UNRRA was launched late in 1943 and came to an end on March 31, 1947), Poland, Hungary, Greece, Italy, Austria, and Yugoslavia found themselves in a bad way. It was at this time that Winston Churchill described Europe as "a rubble heap, a charnel house, a breeding ground of pestilence and hate." Everywhere in Europe people lacked sufficient food, clothing, and shelter. Drought had killed most of the 1946 wheat crop, and the severe winter of 1946–1947 cut the prospects for the crop of 1947. In France between three and four million acres of wheat planted in the autumn were destroyed in January and February 1947. In England at this time a coal shortage became so serious that London found its electric power shut off for hours every day. What would the United States do about a Europe on the verge of economic breakdown? Would it pursue a do-nothing policy, and let the pro-Western governments in Britain, France, and elsewhere pass out of office, to be succeeded by less friendly and, in some instances, by communist cabinets?

Having already taken a step in the direction of economic aid to Greece and Turkey, the Truman administration found the way clear to a more general and ambitious program of aid to all Western Europe. President Truman on January 21, 1947 had replaced Secretary of State Byrnes by General George C. Marshall. The new secretary in a commencement address at Harvard in June 1947 announced the program that was to bear his name, the Marshall Plan.

4. *The Marshall Plan*

In conceiving the Marshall Plan the American secretary of state brought together various ideas and opinions of his subordinates in the State Department, linked them to the eagerness of President Truman to arrest the progress of world communism, and contributed his own decisive and forthright approach. The resultant plan as the secretary elaborated it tentatively before the Harvard assemblage on June 5, 1947, was pre-eminently the result of staff work in the Department of State. It was the kind of work that the department had not done for a long time, since fifteen years before when Henry L. Stimson was secretary of state. When Marshall had taken over the State Department he had told his undersecretary, Acheson, to straighten out the lines of command, and to set the unwieldy organization on the kind of footing that would enable it to function and would prevent the suffocation of every idea that sought to make its way from desk officers through the hierarchy to the office of the secretary. When the Truman Doctrine injected a new note of decision into American diplomacy, the already reorganized department sprang to life, and produced a ferment of ideas that set the secretary to thinking about a general plan of European economic assistance. Charles Bohlen, a department career officer who later became ambassador to Russia, drafted Marshall's Harvard speech, using memoranda prepared by the head of the department's new policy-planning staff, George Kennan, and by the department's expert assistant secretary for economic affairs, William L. Clayton. It was teamwork in the best sense.

In his speech Marshall called upon the European governments to help themselves by drafting a program of mutual economic aid, to which the United States would make a substantial contribution. He told the European nations that instead of bringing their various shopping lists to the United States, as had been the case with lend-lease and UNRRA, the nations should get together and decide among themselves the best allocation of resources. Only after such decision would the United States contribute. "It is already evident," he said, "that before the United States Government can proceed much further . . . there must be some agreement among the countries of Europe as to the requirements of the situation and the part those countries themselves will take. . . . The initiative, I think, must come from

Europe. . . . The Program should be a joint one, agreed to by a number, if not all, of the European nations."

There was, incidentally, no stipulation in Marshall's original proposal that it should include only the nations of Western Europe. The secretary defined his offer of aid to Europe as "everything up to the Urals." The Marshall Plan encompassed Russia and her satellites in Eastern Europe, and the Soviets could participate if they wished.

In this provision for an all-European program there might have been the death of the Marshall Plan, even before it passed beyond the stage of proposal. If the Russians had participated in the plan they could have wrecked it, either through their devious activities or else by their mere entrance. For it was almost inconceivable that Congress would have voted the appropriations necessary to put the Marshall Plan in business if the Russians had chosen to join in Secretary Marshall's proposed program. Fortunately the Russians did not join, although there was momentary wavering.

It is to this day uncertain whether they were ready to join, or merely making a show of interest and then backing out at the first opportunity. Secretary Marshall did not believe that the Russians would join, but there seems to have been a closer call than anticipated. Foreign Minister Molotov in June 1947 arrived in Paris for a meeting of the foreign ministers of France and Britain to discuss the Marshall proposal, and brought along a delegation of some three-score Russian experts and economists. What happened thereafter is obscure, except that he withdrew from the conference. One theory is that the Soviet minister of foreign trade, Anastas Mikoyan, was in disagreement with Molotov over the Marshall Plan, Mikoyan wishing the USSR to join and Molotov opposing. Another hypothesis is that the Soviets thought there would be another lend-lease, and that all they had to do was ask for goods and get them. Another theory is that they balked when they discovered the Marshall proposal would mean a good deal of supervision of their own Soviet economy. Another, that the restiveness of the Soviet satellites drove the Russians to make an appearance in Paris. Another: that recovery involved, so far as Britain and France were concerned, rejuvenation of the German economy, and Molotov was unwilling to support this. For whatever reason, he left the Paris conference. The satellites, some of them with reluctance, were forced to forswear the Marshall Plan, and Russia petulantly announced her own bogus program of economic aid to Eastern Europe, known as the Molotov Plan.

The way was open for action by the American Congress, and action was forthcoming. Debate on Marshall's proposal of June 1947 had begun during the autumn and early winter, and in January 1948 the time of decision arrived. By this date it was apparent that Congress would not balk. Senator Robert A. Taft believed that there was not much good that could come out of helping foreigners for it would only spread bankruptcy from Europe to America, but he said he would vote for the European Co-operation Act. Anguished left-wingers such as Henry A. Wallace, the former secretary of agriculture and of commerce, denounced the proposed aid program as a wanton attack on the Soviet Union, a "Martial Plan." But Wallace had little support in Congress. The initial Marshall Plan appropriation of $5 billion passed easily and was signed by President Truman on April 3. There was an accompanying appropriation of $400 million for military and economic aid to China, to quiet the "China first" members of Congress.

Seventeen European nations together with the Free State of Trieste gathered in Paris in April 1948, and formed the Organization of European Economic Co-operation, or OEEC, an international coordinating body that would represent all European partners in the plan. To these eighteen states the United States, via the Marshall Plan, gave through the Economic Co-operation Administration, or ECA, between April 3, 1948 and January 1, 1952, the sum of $12,285,200,-000. Three nations took over half this amount. England obtained $2,800,000,000, France $2,600,000,000, Germany $1,300,000,000. Italy received over a billion, the Netherlands nearly that much. Iceland took the smallest amount, $27,000,000. Such was the Marshall Plan in operation.

It was a noble effort by the United States, and in its effect upon the European economy it showed itself vastly worthwhile, for European production in 1950 was 45 per cent higher than in 1947, 25 per cent higher than in 1938, the last prewar year; in 1952 production was 200 per cent over 1938. By the end of the Marshall Plan in 1952 there was an economic base in Europe, a solid foundation on which the United States could build an alliance against the USSR. An effective military alliance would have been impossible in 1947.

All this for the reasonable expenditure of about $12 billion, a negligible sum compared to the near $1 trillion income of the American economy during that same period. These $12 billion were only a fraction of America's liquor bill over the same period. Unconvincing were the claims of some political leaders in 1947 and thereafter that European aid was bankrupting the nation, that the billions sent to Europe would force the United States Treasury into fiscal chaos, ending the American way of life. The country in 1947–1950 enjoyed an unprecedented prosperity, and hardly felt the expenditures of the Marshall Plan.

When the plan ended in 1952 after the beginning of the Korean War, with production in Europe still rising in a manner most encouraging to the people and government of the United States, there were perhaps two problems that Marshall aid had undertaken to solve without complete success. If the plan had hoped to make Europe more efficient in production and marketing techniques and if it had sought to capture the sympathy of European workers so as to wean them away from communism, it had been something of a failure, for those two goals were not altogether achieved. Europe by 1952 was still inefficient economically. Much of its trade was throttled by cartels, if not by trade barriers at national borders. As for the workers of Europe, in Italy and France (although not in England, Scandinavia, Germany, Austria, Luxembourg, the Netherlands, and Belgium) they had failed in the early years of the Marshall Plan to receive much benefit from the new production that the plan achieved. The poor in Italy and France had not become poorer, but the rich grew richer. Italian and French workers were dissatisfied with their lot, and not unwilling to express their feelings by voting communist in national elections. Even so, despite such difficulties the Marshall Plan provided a healthy economic base in Europe, from which reforms, economic and democratic, might be made in the future. This was no ordinary accomplishment.

The Korean War eventually brought an end to the Marshall Plan, an end to exclusively economic aid to the countries of Western Europe. There had been a stipulation that not a cent of Marshall Plan aid should go into military supplies. Early in 1951 the United States informed Europeans that further American assistance would have to be allotted for defense purposes. (This, incidentally, was not as large a blow as it appeared, for Europe and chiefly Germany benefited hugely from the "Korean boom" in the world market.) By 1952 the

United States was giving eighty per cent of its aid to Europe in military weapons and the other twenty in defense support. By 1952 the plan, the European Co-operation Administration or ECA, merged with its competitor, the Military Defense Aid Program or MDAP, in the Mutual Security Agency, MSA (in 1953 rechristened the Foreign Operations Administration or FOA; in 1955 rechristened the International Co-operation Administration or ICA).

5. *The Berlin Blockade*

A crisis of more than momentary importance in the first half-decade after the war was the Berlin blockade of 1948–1949, which for a time appeared to be a prelude to a third World War. Prior to the Korean War no crisis looked so dangerous as this Russian attempt in 1948 to seal off Berlin from Western access by rail or road, and to force the Western Allies thereby into a change of their German policy. The blockade took its origin in the efforts of the Western Allies to unify their zones in Germany, once the honeymoon period with the Russians was over. The Western Allies, Britain and France, led by the United States, felt that they had to do something in the years 1946 and 1947 and early 1948 to bring the collapsed German economy to its feet again. This effort involved a series of moves toward a West German government which the Russians construed as a challenge to their own occupation policy in Eastern Germany. In an effort to force a settlement of the German issue in their favor, that is, to establish a communist government for all of Germany, the Soviets in 1948 undertook their blockade of the Western zones of Berlin.

Prior to the reforms instituted by Allied authorities in Germany—reforms led by the imaginative American military commander, General Lucius D. Clay—the West Germans had lived on the "cigarette economy," in which the American cigarette had replaced the inflated Reichsmark as a standard of value. Food rations in the Allied zones were set at 1,500 calories daily, well below the normal requirement. Steel production in Germany in the year 1946 was down to 2.6 million tons. There was little incentive to work, Communist Party memberships began to increase, the American army was spending $1,000,-000,000 a year in relief funds to feed the hungry Germans, and there was a compelling pressure from the United States to get the Germans off the American taxpayer's back. There was, in truth, every reason for the Allies to attempt to get their zones organized economically.

These moves antagonized the Russians and led to the showdown over Berlin. General Clay at first had persuaded the British to fuse their zone in Western Germany with the American zone, and the result was "Bizonia," which with addition of the French zone became "Trizonia." In the spring of 1948 a conference of the Western powers in London invited the Germans to elect delegates to a constitutional convention which would create a new government for West Germany. In June 1948 the Allies instituted a drastic currency reform in Western Germany, repudiating 90 per cent of the Reichsmarks then circulating and substituting a new and soundly controlled money. Almost at once the sparks of economic life began to flare up throughout the cities and countryside of Allied-occupied Germany. There commenced such a renaissance of economic life as has hardly been seen during the course of modern history. The Russians, doubly disturbed by this economic-political revival under Western capitalist auspices, moved to stop it with the Berlin blockade beginning April 1, which became total on June 24, 1948.

That there could have been such a thing as a Russian blockade of Berlin and an Allied airlift would have seemed incredible to Americans in 1945. The United States had been uninterested in Berlin in 1945. In the closing days of the war General Eisenhower's victorious Western armies had moved far into Germany, and could without much trouble have arrived in Berlin at the same time as the Russians, and perhaps before. But despite Prime Minister Churchill's urgent pleas the Americans refused to take Berlin with or ahead of the Russians. As Eisenhower informed Washington, "May I point out that Berlin is no longer a particularly important objective." The chiefs of staff in Washington agreed, and President Truman concurred, and Berlin was conquered by the Russians, who allowed the Allies to occupy specified zones within the city. Access to those zones was through Russian-held territory. But few individuals worried in 1945 over the security of the Western Allies' position in Berlin, over the fact that the Soviets could blockade at will the Western sectors of the city.

The only thing that saved West Berlin in 1948–1949 was the Allied right to an air corridor to the city across the Soviet zone of East Germany. Fortunately the Western powers had an agreement to this effect with the Russians, and the Soviets—so the Allies hoped—would not interfere with this route. The only alternative means of supplying West Berlin with food and fuel was to push through armed road convoys. An airlift seemed at the outset impossible in 1948, but the Allies were determined to stay in Berlin. The odds appeared impossible for democracy, but General Clay had cabled the Pentagon on April 10, 1948 that "WHEN BERLIN FALLS, WESTERN GERMANY WILL BE NEXT. IF WE MEAN . . . TO HOLD EUROPE AGAINST COMMUNISM, WE MUST NOT BUDGE . . . IF WE WITHDRAW, OUR POSITION IN EUROPE IS THREATENED. IF AMERICA DOES NOT UNDERSTAND THIS NOW, DOES NOT KNOW THE ISSUE IS CAST, THEN IT NEVER WILL AND COMMUNISM WILL RUN RAMPANT. I BELIEVE THE FUTURE OF DEMOCRACY REQUIRES US TO STAY." The challenge, therefore, was taken up. The Allied air forces by dint of quick work and improvisation brought together enough planes from all over the world to accomplish what by any standard was a gigantic task. General Clay had estimated that by the winter of 1948–1949 it would be necessary for the Allies to bring in 4,500 tons of food and fuel a day. By October 1948 the average daily airlift haul was approaching 5,000 tons. One day in April 1949, 1,398 Allied planes landed a record 12,941 tons. The planes came in every 61.8 seconds. Altogether, Allied planes ferried 2,325,500 tons of supplies to the city, an average of more than a ton for each of the 2,100,000 inhabitants of West Berlin.

Not merely, of course, did the Western powers supply the people of their zones in Berlin. The airlift produced in Berlin and throughout Europe a tremendous wave of pro-Allied enthusiasm. Sight of the hundreds of giant transports circling down over Tempelhof airdrome was an indication of Western power that thrilled Berliners, and the morale of the inhabitants of that embattled city rose to such heights that the Russians in disgust called off their blockade on May 12, 1949. The way was clear for a West German government. The way was clear in all Europe for the Marshall Plan. And with the Marshall Plan, Americans hoped, would come sufficient economic power that the Europeans in a not too distant future might be able to participate in defense of their countries against a possible Russian invasion.

In this present chapter nothing has been said about the origin and development of the North Atlantic Treaty Organization which occurred in 1949 and subsequent years. NATO was a logical accompaniment of the Marshall Plan: the plan prepared the economic base from which a European military plan could be constructed. NATO, however, remained subordinate to the Marshall Plan until 1950 and the Korean War, and so it is perhaps better to put off discussion of it until a subsequent chapter dealing with Europe from 1950 onward.

As for President Truman's program of Point 4, the fourth of a series of suggestions that the president elaborated in his inaugural address of January 1949, this in a sense was a world counterpart to the Marshall Plan. It promised technical assistance—American agricultural, mechanical, medical, and administrative knowledge—to the so-called underdeveloped countries (incidentally, those countries heartily disliked the word "underdeveloped" with its unintended meaning of American superiority). In financial outlay it has never come near equaling the expense of the Marshall Plan, and generally one can say that Point 4 has been much more promise than fulfillment. Only here and there have efforts at amelioration been made, at places where either a small amount of money could do a large amount of good, or where "pilot projects," demonstrations of effectiveness of aid, could hope to bring in further assistance from other quarters. Appropriations for Point 4 in its first year amounted to $35,000,000, and outlays since then have not been large. Perhaps the chief difficulty with the program was that the United States, despite its vast wealth, could not underwrite the economies of all the poorer nations of the world. And it was difficult to obtain public support in the United States for Point 4; Americans in the war and postwar years already had paid out a great deal for foreign assistance and were disinclined to finance economic development indefinitely for no more precise purpose than developing underdeveloped countries. Many were ready to hear ridicule; the head of the International Co-operation Administration, in charge of Point 4 work, was accused of various absurdities and delinquencies: providing striped pants for Greek undertakers and bathtubs for Egyptian camel drivers; supplying wild grass seed for sowing along Lebanese highways; flying Arabs to Mecca; building roads for the royal Cadillacs in Saudi Arabia; and—that ancient political accusation!—iceboxes for Eskimos (there was "absolutely no trace of iceboxes for Eskimos," the harassed administrator protested, "nor are we in the business of furnishing aid to the Eskimos").

The first five years of peace in Europe after the second World War, one might conclude, marked a period of numerous trials and troubles, and by 1950 when recovery was at last in sight the Far East erupted in the Korean War, spelling new trouble. The course of power and politics on the Continent had proved far different from what Americans had expected in the rosy haze of V-E Day, 1945. Europeans and Americans by 1950 had nonetheless come together against the menace of Russian communism. Matters were not yet out of danger, but the worst, so Americans hoped, was over.

ADDITIONAL READING

The years between 1945 and 1950 were an era of disillusion when the wartime gospel preached by Wendell Willkie, *One World* (New York, 1943) dissolved into a highly dangerous Russian-American rivalry. Such a volume as that edited by Raymond Dennett and J. E. Johnson, *Negotiating with the Russians* (Boston, 1951) would have seemed impossible to Americans in 1941–1945. The motif of the period became that expressed in the title of Walter Lippmann's *The Cold War* (New York, 1947).

General books on the era, dealing in part with American diplomacy, are such volumes as Eric F. Goldman's *The Crucial Decade: America, 1945–1955* (New York, 1956), a lucid, witty, intelligent sketch after the fashion set by Frederick Lewis Allen's social history of the 1920's, *Only Yesterday* (New York, 1931); and Herbert Agar, *The Price of Power: America since 1945* (Chicago, 1957). See also Chester Wilmot, *The Struggle for Europe;* and W. S. Churchill, *Triumph and Tragedy* (Boston, 1953). For American statesmen there are Harry S. Truman, *Memoirs* (2 vols., Garden City, N.Y., 1955–1956); William Hillman, ed., *Mr. President* (New York, 1952), a volume compiled with Mr. Truman's active assistance; James F. Byrnes, *Speaking Frankly* (New York, 1947), in which Truman's second secretary of state looked carefully over his career; James F. Byrnes, *All in One Lifetime* (New York, 1958), by the same author with a different time-perspective; Robert Payne, *The Marshall Story* (New York, 1951); and *The Pattern of Responsibility: Edited by McGeorge Bundy from the Records of Secretary of State Dean Acheson* (Boston, 1952), a compilation of speeches and papers.

The important subject of Germany appears in Hajo Holborn, *American Military Government* (Washington, 1947); Marshall Knappen, *And Call It Peace* (Chicago, 1947), a first-hand account of the early years of occupation; Eugene Davidson, *The Death and Life of Germany* (in press), a brilliant analysis of the occupation down to West German independence in 1955; Lucius D. Clay, *Decision in Germany* (Garden City, N.Y., 1950), and *Germany and the Fight for Freedom* (Cambridge, Mass., 1951), the former the memoirs of the American military commander, and the latter volume a brief essay; W. Phillips Davison, *The Berlin Blockade: A Study in Cold War Politics* (Princeton, 1958).

For its special subject see Stephen Kertesz, ed., *The Fate of East Central Europe* (Notre Dame, Ind., 1956), essays by a dozen or so experts; together with Kertesz's own excellent volume, *Diplomacy in a Whirlpool* (Notre Dame, 1953).

The turning point in American policy toward Europe is set out philosophically in George F. Kennan, "The Sources of Soviet Conduct," *Foreign Affairs*, vol. 25 (1946–1947), 566–582; and historically by Joseph M. Jones, *The Fifteen Weeks (February 21–June 5, 1957)* (New York, 1955). A special study is Harry B. Price, *The Marshall Plan and Its Meaning* (Ithaca, N.Y., 1955).

The actions of leading American officials—diplomats, military men, administration figures—appear in D. D. Eisenhower, *Crusade in Europe* (Garden City, N.Y., 1948); A. B. Lane, *I Saw Poland Betrayed* (Indianapolis, 1948), by the American ambassador to Poland; W. B. Smith, *My Three Years in Moscow* (Philadelphia, 1950), by the American ambassador; W. D. Leahy, *I Was There* (New York, 1950), by FDR's military confidant who stayed on under Truman; A. H. Vandenberg, Jr., ed., *The Private Papers of Senator Vandenberg* (Boston, 1952); Walter Millis and E. S. Duffield, eds., *The Forrestal Diaries* (New York, 1951); John P. Armstrong, "The Enigma of Senator Taft and American Foreign Policy," *Review of Politics*, vol. 17 (1954–1955), 206–231, a trenchant analysis of the isolationist senator's meandering views on foreign policy; William S. White, *The Taft Story* (New York, 1954), a careful biography.

The Far East, 1945-1959
(Part I)

Americans in the years since the end of the second World War have
heard more about Far Eastern affairs than ever before in their history.
In magazines and newspapers, from public rostrums and private platforms, information and misinformation about the Far East have poured
forth in flood proportions, and there is no indication that the flood
is in any way receding. The years since 1945 have been an era of
intense interest in the orient. John Hay could announce a policy of
the open door at the beginning of the twentieth century and hear
polite applause from certain interested segments of the American
people, but even a minor pronouncement from Dean Acheson or
John Foster Dulles on Far Eastern policy at once touched off long,
sharp, and acrid debate.

One easily understandable reason for public interest in the Far East
has been the vast extent of American involvement in the area during
and after the war of 1941–1945. After fighting and winning the war
against Japan, the United States was forced to occupy the Japanese
Islands, half of Korea, parts of the Chinese mainland, and island
groups off the Asian coast: Ryukyus, Bonins, Volcanoes, Marshalls,
Carolines, Marianas. Then came two events in the orient of large importance for American diplomacy, the communization of China and
the Korean War. In the confused debate about these events, punctu-

ated by President Truman's dismissal of the popular General Mac-Arthur as American commander in the area, there ensued more controversy than Americans had heard since President Franklin D. Roosevelt led the country to adopt measures assisting the European Allies against Germany in the crucial years 1939–1941. And the problems that followed the Korean cease-fire, such matters as Japan's resumption of a place in world affairs, disposal of the Matsu, Quemoy, and Tachen island groups, the place of Formosa in world affairs, the crisis of Indochina, likewise have engaged Americans of both political parties in argument and debate.

There has been in recent years a new intellectual attraction of Americans toward the Far East, which has accompanied the diplomatic-military events and further increased American interest in the orient. During the Hay era at the turn of the century people in the United States considered the East a strange place, quaint and backward. There was from earliest times little inclination to welcome orientals into the Western Hemisphere; it was all right to take Western civilization to them but it was not right if Chinese, Japanese, Indians, or Southeast Asians wished to leave their own area of the world. In the years after 1945 American views changed drastically. There was a new conviction that the East was an undeniable fact of life, that it was a part of the world whether the West cared to admit it or not, and that in the interests of world peace it would be a good idea to be friendly to Eastern states and statesmen. Among many Americans there was belief that the nations of Europe had bungled Far Eastern problems and allowed a conflict to develop there in 1931–1933 that spread some years later to Europe and the entire world. Had the Europeans taken more pains with the orientals, so ran popular feeling in the United States, the train of calamities that came after the Manchurian incident might have been stopped at the outset. It was now necessary, many Americans thought, to have some kind of meeting intellectually of East and West; there had to be intellectual rapport between the two major divisions of the human race, else confusion of purposes might be followed by incidents that would lead to another world war. When shortly after the end of the second World War the American philosopher F. S. C. Northrop published a book entitled *The Meeting of East and West*, carrying the good tidings that the cultures and civilizations of East and West could meet in the undifferentiated esthetic continuum, Americans bought thousands of copies of the book. Perhaps they did not read beyond the first chapters but they were expressing their hope that somehow, in some way, the hundreds of millions of human beings in the orient might come into some kind of spiritual communion, and perhaps thereby international co-operation, with the peoples of the Western world.

As for the idea long held by American businessmen that the East contained illimitable markets for the products of the nation's industry, that notion had died in the experience of the past forty or so years, and it had little to do with American concern over the Far East after 1945. After the second World War one heard little about four hundred million customers or the other old-time cries for commercial expansion. At the turn of the century the markets of Asia had seemed enormously attractive because *fin de siècle* businessmen were expecting a depression, some kind of permanent blight on the national economy, if they could not dispose of their goods to such buyers as the people of Asia. The American businessman eventually discovered to his sorrow that the Asians had no capacity to pay. And during the second World War had come realization that the American domestic market was capable of far greater consumption than anyone had suspected, that if the American worker were paid a high wage he would turn his wage into purchases. One of the principal impulses to American relations with the Far East in the nineteenth century and in the heyday of imperialism at the end of the century, the attraction of trade, was largely absent in the years after the second World War.

American interest in Asia after 1945 was, in sum, a compound of military involvement and intellectual attraction. The United States had sent its troops into the area during the war, but in the postwar years and quite apart from the presence there of military forces there developed this belief that the two parts of the world must meet on some sort of intellectual plane to further the good life of everyone concerned.

As for the subsequent vicissitudes of American Far Eastern policy, one cannot contend that they originated entirely or in large part from this curious composite of military commitment and unabashed good will. Admittedly good will is a property not always appreciated in international affairs and sometimes an invitation to troublemakers, but to say that the American view of East Asia or policy toward East Asia was the moving force behind the disturbances and trials of Asian politics after 1945 is gross oversimplification. The course of affairs in the Far East would have been much the same regardless of United States policy toward that area.

1. *Nationalist China Prior to 1945*

Probably the communization of China was the single event that, more than any other happening in the orient, bothered Americans in the years since the end of the second World War, and it is as good a place as any to begin discussion of American Far Eastern policy in recent times. Why did China go communist in the first four years of the postwar era? How could China after a century of friendship for the United States, since the Cushing Treaty of 1844, turn on its good friend and benefactor at a moment when Americans faced in Soviet Russia the most implacable and dangerous foe they had ever had?

This in truth is not an easy question to answer. The victory of the Chinese communists was no simple proposition, and to understand what happened to China in the years after the war one must look back to the events of Chinese history in the 1920's and 1930's and early 1940's.

China, as mentioned in previous chapters, had undergone a time of troubles near the beginning of the twentieth century because of the breakdown of the Manchu dynasty's control over large areas of the Chinese subcontinent. The Manchus had been governing China ever since the mid-seventeenth century and their power, as had held true of the dynasties before, was in a decline following an initial era of some vigor. In the mid-nineteenth century serious trouble came with the Taiping rebellion and the Nien Fei uprisings, and by the turn of the century there was no question but that a new regime was due. The Western powers and Japan sought momentarily to partition the empire themselves, but because of the imminence of war in Europe— not, incidentally, because of the American open door policy—the powers abandoned this effort and matters rocked along uncomfortably until almost without effort the Chinese themselves overthrew the Manchu dynasty in 1911–1912.

The next dozen years was a swirling period when government after government assumed power in a nominal way in Peking, and when in the provinces there was competition for place and power by a large number of local warlords. This competition was not greatly different from what had been practiced during the last years of the Manchus, but it became more apparent once the traditional central authority disappeared. For a while one of the leading functionaries of the Manchu court, Yuan Shih-kai, ruled from Peking, and he would have liked to have changed his rule, which was described to the European nations as republican, into another empire with himself as the first monarch of the new dynasty. His efforts came to naught and Yuan died in 1916, according to a Chinese phrase, "from eating bitterness." Confusion continued, the warlords ruled in their satrapies throughout China, and whatever warlord was the most powerful and closest geographically to Peking took over the Chinese government and acted as if he were the government. This confusion was all very frustrating to Chinese diplomatic representatives abroad but they tried as best they could to maintain the fiction that their government was united and powerful, and frequently they managed to put a rather respectable face upon what was in truth a chaotic situation at home.

As events gradually revealed the course of the future, a revolutionary movement in the south of China proved the most important intellectual and military movement in China for the 1920's and 1930's and the first years of the 1940's, for it was from Canton that the Kuomintang or Nationalist Party took its origin and in time moved northward to assume the rule of China in the name of the Chinese people. The Kuomintang was the creation of the old-time revolutionary, Dr. Sun Yat-sen, who in 1924 elaborated his Three Principles of the People: People's Nationhood (nationalism); People's Power (democracy); People's Livelihood (variously translated as livelihood, socialism, or communism). Dr. Sun had long been a revolutionary, and it was his custom to foment revolution from the French concession of Shanghai where he lived in a house on the Rue Molière, a convenient location, for when revolutions were unsuccessful he scurried to the safety of French extraterritoriality and escaped the revenge of his enemies. Later he would proclaim that foreign concessions were one of the chief causes of China's difficulties, but for a while he was glad to use their facilities. At any rate Dr. Sun was not too successful as a revolutionist until some Russian communist agents came into China and, beginning in 1923, assisted him in organizing both his party and his army. The autocratic nature of the Kuomintang Party owes much to the inspiration of Dr. Sun's Russian communist advisers in the early 1920's, who taught the doctor—Sun was a medical doctor, not a doctor of philosophy—how to establish a party with unswerving obedience to its leader. The Nationalist army likewise was modeled most profitably on the advice of Sun's communist assistants, and some of his officers (including the young Chiang Kai-shek) even had been to Moscow and studied the organization of the Red Army so as to understand communist military theories at first hand. By the mid-1920's everything was ready in South China for the march north, and Dr. Sun set out with his party and his army to take over the Chinese government.

The takeover was successful, although two events of importance occurred during the move of the Nationalists northward which changed the character of the revolution. First Dr. Sun, who had suffered from cancer, died in Peking in 1925, the leadership of the Kuomintang Party passing to his chief general, Chiang Kai-shek. Second, General Chiang discovered that the communists in his entourage were not as amenable to his advice as he may originally have hoped. In 1927 Chiang put them down, and thereby established his authority over the party as leader and interpreter of the revolution. The move of the Nationalists northward, having met with these events, concluded in triumph in 1927 when Chiang occupied Nanking and in 1928 when he took Peking. The seat of the National government was kept at Nanking rather than at the traditional location, Peking, because the latter city was too close to Manchuria and thus subject both to attack by the Manchurian warlord and also to dominance by the Manchurian powers, Japan and Russia.

The years between 1927 and 1937, from the Kuomintang taking of Nanking to the Japanese attack on China in which Japan occupied Nanking and began forcing the Nationalist regime into the Chinese hinterland, were the era when Chiang Kai-shek tried as best he could to secure his control over China and present a united front toward the foreign powers and, generally, to convert the Chinese peasantry to the Three Principles of the People as laid down by his mentor Dr. Sun Yat-sen. There was hope among the Western nations that Chiang would be able to introduce into the Nanking regime not merely nationalism but some considerable elements of democracy, the second of Dr. Sun's principles. There was hope that the Chinese, if given Western support, would be able for the first time since the heyday of the Manchu dynasty in the eighteenth century to put their nation's house in order. For a time, it must be admitted, success seemed to be coming to the Nationalists. The control of the regime stretched out from Nanking, taxes began to flow toward the Nationalist treasury, and in 1928 the warlord of Manchuria, General Chang Hsueh-liang, announced his allegiance to the Kuomintang; everything looked as if with luck China would convert itself into a unified national state on the model of Western nations. There was talk early in this era of relinquishment of extraterritoriality by the Westerners and Japan. Then the Chinese went too far—first with the Russians in the Chinese Eastern Railway affair of 1929, next when in a fit of idiocy they began to tinker with Japanese prerogatives in the South Manchuria Railway, precipitating in 1931 the Manchuria incident by which Japan seized, within two years, all of Manchuria. Pressure thereafter mounted against the Nationalist regime, and Chiang's government tottered on several occasions. In 1937 the Japanese, observing the preoccupation of the Western nations with the series of untoward events in Africa and Europe, decided that the time had come, as Premier Konoye put it, to beat the Chinese to their knees. The Japanese attack on China's coastal cities in 1937 began a new and miserable era for the Nationalist regime.

The Sino-Japanese War of 1937 and thereafter began with a series of horrible massacres of Chinese civilians and soldiers by the Japanese troops, at Nanking and other places, and the character of the war, thus established in ferocity, never changed during the years that followed. The Japanese were angered that the regime of Chiang Kai-shek retreated to Chungking and there received American support. Their anger and frustration resulted finally in an alliance with Germany and the attack on Pearl Harbor. But American aid to the Chinese only increased after this catastrophic event, and by the years 1943 and 1944 the American government was virtually propping up the Nationalist regime in Chungking—the regime might well have fallen otherwise—by shipping over the hump of the Himalayas supplies and instructors for the Chinese army and by maintaining in Chinese territory Major General Claire L. Chennault's Fourteenth Air Force. General Joseph W. Stilwell established himself in Chungking not merely as American commander of the China-Burma-India theater, the CBI, but also as military adviser and chief of staff to Chiang Kai-shek. Stilwell thereupon sought to galvanize the Chinese armies to resistance against the Japanese, and part of his endeavors consisted of trying to obtain the military co-operation, perhaps with American supplies, of the Chinese communist armies.

What was the strength of Chinese communism by the time of the second World War? The communists in China by the war years were a strong group but not the dominant group, and as late as 1945 (when Stalin on August 14 made a treaty with the Nationalist regime, apparently in the belief that the Nationalists would remain the dominant group in China) it did not seem possible that mainland China within a relatively short period could pass entirely under communist control. Communism in China had been a faltering affair, and whatever strength the communists possessed by 1945 had come only after years of careful labor and some serious setbacks. Russian communists had attempted in the early 1920's to spread the revolution to China, but they had sought to do it by revolutionizing the views of city workers, an effort that failed miserably. Communism, according to the accepted party line, was to make its first conquests intellectually in the cities of China, the workingmen were then to be made communists and their efforts, according to Russian theory imported into China, would promote and eventually realize the revolution. The city communists in the mid-1920's attached themselves to the Nationalist movement of Dr. Sun Yat-sen and his successor Chiang Kai-shek, and perhaps their leaders hoped that with time they could control that movement. But Chiang surprised them and put them out in 1927. Communism in China languished after its defeat by the Nationalists, and until a deviationist named Mao Tse-tung undertook to revolutionize the peasantry rather than the city workers, achieving the revolution by a means other than that prescribed by the doctrinaires of Moscow, there was no success at all. When attacked by the Nationalists the country communists resisted heroically, and in 1934 they set out on the long roundabout trek from Kiangsi province to remote Shensi in China's northwest, where they sought to establish themselves for a revolution which they foresaw distantly in the unknown future. The coming of the war between the Japanese and the Nationalists in 1937 was a heaven-sent boon to the Chinese communists, who because of united front tactics were enabled for a while to pose as patriots against the Japanese and in the meantime were relieved of Nationalist military pressure. Gradually they improved their position in their capital city of Yenan and established areas of control behind Japanese lines throughout China, but their power by the end of the second World War was by no means strong.

During the war, naturally, they feared to enter any coalition with

Chiang Kai-shek, remembering the draconian measures he had taken against them nearly twenty years before in 1927 at Hankow, and the many years required before communism again gained any strength in China. When Stilwell tried to get the communists and Nationalists together he doubtless misguessed the situation.

The unsuccessful wartime effort of General Stilwell to bolster Chinese resistance by reforming the Chinese armies, if not through uniting the communist and Nationalist forces then through reorganizing and invigorating the troops of Chiang Kai-shek, was decidedly a heroic proposition. It might even have succeeded if it had not been for several factors, chief among which was a personal incompatibility between the American commander and Chiang Kai-shek. Stilwell also was undercut both by General Chennault, who believed that airpower alone would save China and had many private channels through which he sent these views to Washington, and by many wellwishers of China in the United States who thought that whatever General Chiang desired it should be given to him and not with advice as to how to use it. But the largest difficulty that developed was the dislike of Stilwell for Chiang and vice versa. The two men could not get along. Chiang did not like to be told the truth with bluntness, and "Vinegar Joe" Stilwell could tell the truth only in such a way. One of the semihumorous aspects of the war in the Far East—and it would have been a downright hilarious business if so much had not been at stake—was Stilwell's private-diary treatment of Chiang Kai-shek. The American commander referred to the generalissimo of China as "Peanut" and "a crazy little bastard." And at one point in their relations, when Stilwell had presented to Chiang what appeared virtually as an ultimatum from President Roosevelt that he reform his armies, Vinegar Joe repaired to his quarters and wrote out a bit of doggerel, the "Peanut Poem," which must go down as a wartime classic:

> I've waited long for vengeance—
> At last I've had my chance.
> I've looked the Peanut in the eye
> And kicked him in the pants.
>
> The old harpoon was ready
> With aim and timing true,
> I sank it to the handle,
> And stung him through and through.

The little bastard shivered,
And lost the power of speech.
His face turned green and quivered
As he struggled not to screech.

For all my weary battles,
For all my hours of woe,
At least I've had my innings
And laid the Peanut low.

I know I've still to suffer,
And run a weary race,
But oh! the blessed pleasure!
I've wrecked the Peanut's face.

This masterpiece was very probably read by General Chiang, whose agents constantly were about Stilwell's quarters in Chungking and made every effort to read his correspondence and dispatches.

But very probably Stilwell did not care, for he had observed the miserable morale of Chinese troops in the field, the corruption that ran rampant through the entire Nationalist government and down through the Nationalist army command to the junior officers, and he saw that if the endless manpower of China were ever to be marshalled effectively in a military way there would have to be the most serious sort of reform of the Chinese armies and probably the Chinese government. General Chiang's face, if saved at the moment, would only be lost later.

Stilwell had the faithful backing of his military superiors in Washington, General Marshall and Secretary of War Stimson. Even so, the dissatisfaction of various of General Chiang Kai-shek's supporters once their monetary and other interests promised to be affected by Stilwell's proposed reforms turned into a veritable campaign against the doughty American commander, and this, linked to the insubordination of Chennault and the opinions of various important Americans who made flying visits to China, resulted in President Roosevelt's ordering Stilwell relieved in 1944.

Stilwell's successor, Lieutenant General Albert C. Wedemeyer, did not take a strong stand against the military and other delinquencies of the Nationalist government. The efforts of the American government became more diplomatic.

Wedemeyer was assisted by Major General Patrick J. Hurley, who in November 1944 was appointed American ambassador to Chungking and sought to help Nationalist China through the war. Just what the effect of Hurley's mission was, beyond a general pouring of oil on troubled waters, is difficult to measure, though the general, whom no one could ever accuse of the slightest communistic leanings, tried as had Stilwell to bring the Nationalists and communists together in a coalition government. His work in this regard must have amused or amazed the Chinese, for Hurley (who had been born in Choctaw Indian country) liked to demonstrate a blood-curdling Comanche yell. He chose to loose this salutation to the Chinese communists at Yenan—Mao Tse-tung, Chu Teh, Chou En-lai, and others—when he first met them on an official ambassadorial visit at the airport of their city. Hurley did his best in China; his was not an easy mission, and he found himself undercut at times by his nominal subordinates in the foreign service accredited as observers at Yenan and elsewhere. These included John Stewart Service, John Paton Davies, and several other foreign-service officers whom Hurley came to believe were pro-communist. At any rate Hurley's disgust mounted to a point where, after recall to the United States in the autumn of 1945, he resigned in a huff in November of that year. He charged publicly that his work had been sabotaged and he engaged thereafter in a crusade against disloyal Americans that eventually found much sympathy among his fellow countrymen.

Such was the condition of American diplomacy toward China in 1945 when—through few efforts either by the Nationalists or the communists, though admittedly more by the Nationalists—the Pacific War on August 14 came to a sudden end after the explosions at Hiroshima and Nagasaki and the declaration of war by Russia on Japan.

2. The Communization of China

In the years that followed, down through 1949, the communists achieved control of China. This diplomatic defeat, if not the greatest suffered by the United States in the postwar era, was certainly one of the most dramatic and disheartening turns of events. For a century the United States had acted *in loco parentis* to the Chinese, and in four short years the work of a century disappeared with little left to show for it except a small enclave of Free China on Formosa and, on the continent, a heated outpouring of diatribe and accusation of American imperialism tinged with sarcastic description of the United States as a paper tiger. When the Chinese treated their good friends the Americans in this way it was difficult to take, and when such treatment occurred at the moment when throughout the world the American government was being attacked by the Soviet communists it was almost too much to bear.

What was the course of American diplomacy in the crucial years for China following V-J Day? By autumn of 1945 Ambassador Hurley was recalled, and he was replaced in 1946 by a long-time Presbyterian missionary in China, the distinguished president of Yenching University in Peking, Dr. John Leighton Stuart, who remained ambassador to China until his resignation in 1952. Ambassador Stuart presided at the American embassy in Nanking during the downfall of the Nationalist regime, and his brilliant and touching memoir, *Fifty Years in China*, is one of the best accounts available on why China went communist.

The ambassador watched a succession of American special missions to China, and saw them fail, one after the other. The Chinese problem was too much for them. The essential difficulty, as he wrote in his memoirs, was "a gigantic struggle between two political ideologies with the overtones of democratic idealism perverted by bureaucratic incompetence on the one side, succumbing to a dynamic socialized reform vitiated by Communist dogma, intolerance and ruthlessness on the other. And the great mass of suffering inarticulate victims cared for neither but were powerless to do anything about it." "The party members on both sides were a mere fraction of the huge, disorganized, inarticulate, amorphous population." The Chinese people "were neither Kuomintang nor Communist but merely Chinese, desiring to be allowed to live their own lives with a minimum of government interference or oppression." Given this difficulty, given the struggle between the two political factions in China, the fight to the end for leadership of the Chinese nation, there was little that the United States was able to do unless by a considerable intervention in Chinese affairs, and this neither the American nor the Chinese people desired.

At the end of the war the Americans did do a large favor for the Nationalist Chinese by ferrying, both by boat and plane, thousands upon thousands of Nationalist troops into the Japanese-occupied areas so that they could take over those localities ahead of the Chinese communists. Likewise the Nationalists received huge amounts of American surplus military equipment. By such heroic efforts the Nationalist regime was saved at least temporarily, and this move offset the advantage accruing to the communists when the latter at the close of the war either captured from the Japanese or received from Russian troops in Manchuria stocks of Japanese arms and equipment.

The first and major diplomatic attempt by the United States to assist Nationalist China in the postwar years was the mission of General George C. Marshall, who went out to the Far East as special ambassador in December 1945, following Ambassador Hurley's resignation, to attempt to bring together the communists and Nationalists in the tradition of Stilwell and Hurley. After a year Marshall gave up the job as lost and returned to the United States to become secretary of state, replacing James F. Byrnes on January 7, 1947. The hope of the Marshall mission was first to obtain a truce in fighting between the communists and Nationalists and second to persuade the two sides to join in a coalition government. They were then to disband their armies except for a relatively small number of troops of both sides which were to be brought into a single Chinese army and trained by American advisers. The Joint United States Military Advisory Group, JUSMAG, some 1,000 officers and men, was brought to Nanking in the hope that it could advise on organization of the coalition force of the coalition government, neither of which, unfortunately, ever came into being. A truce between the Nationalists and the communists did, however, continue spasmodically through much of the year 1946.

The hopes of the Marshall mission were bright at first; Ambassador Stuart later believed that the two sides came close to agreement. In retrospect, given what apparently was the detached view of Stalin at this time—the Russian dictator seems to have advised the Chinese communists to make peace with the Nationalists, believing that the Nationalists were the winning side in China—there may have been some possibility of bringing the two sides into a rough and tentative agreement. Still, most of the leaders of both sides, Nationalist and communist, were the same individuals who had taken part in the arguments of the 1920's and 1930's and there was a personal feud between the two groups, quite apart from their intellectual and other differences. Animosities long ago had gotten out of control on both sides.

Chiang, for instance, had said publicly that "the Japanese are only lice on the body of China, but Communism is a disease of the heart." The communists in like vein criticized the Nationalists. Moreover, the communists quickly realized the weakness of the Nationalists when the latter came back to the coastal regions after the war. Many of the Nationalist leaders in the coastal cities behaved in the most shameful fashion, and grafting in connection with the Chinese version of UNRRA, CINNRA, reached heights unknown even in China. Thus the only hope for the Nationalist government, namely keeping the political support and sympathy of city businessmen and the students and intellectuals, was dashed by this conquistador spirit of the Nationalists' return. The communists knew this.

General Marshall later said, apropos his efforts to form a coalition government, that the communists favored the idea because they "felt the Kuomintang was just an icing on the top and all its foundations of public support had become almost nonexistent or at least hostile, so if they could ever get the thing in the political arena they would win . . . it would not have been hard but a rather easy thing for the Communists to dominate the government." The general also understood the reluctance of the Nationalists to let in the communists: "I read yesterday [these remarks were made privately in October 1949 at a special meeting of Far Eastern experts in the State Department] of the death of Hannegan, the former Chairman of the Democratic National Committee. He came out to China and I asked him: 'Did you ever know anybody in political life that gave up something unless he just had to?' He said, no, offhand he couldn't think of anyone. Well, here was a whole party being asked to give up the position they were in and admit a two-party procedure of government. Now, when I say 'give-up' you see, it differs from the ordinary two-party situation in this country, because the man held sort of a double office. He might be a General in the army but he is also, well, he is also the National Committee which really determines laws, and he was enjoying the preferment of pay and everything of that sort."

After the smoke began to clear in China, so to speak, following the Japanese surrender, the weakness of the Nationalist regime became altogether apparent. When both sides violated the Marshall truce, and when the Nationalists in 1947 began a full-scale military campaign against the communists in Manchuria, the fate of the Chiang Kai-shek government was quickly sealed.

Ambassador Stuart told General Marshall when the latter left early in January 1947 that there were three courses for American policy in China: (1) sufficient aid to the Nationalist government together with advice and controls so that it could defeat the communists; (2) a half-hearted course; and (3) complete withdrawal of the United States from efforts to bolster any regime in China. Stuart preferred the first course to the other two, and the third course to the second. The United States followed the second. Perhaps, however, it was the only possible course for the American government, considering the post-war letdown among the American people and the increasing difficul-ties with the Russians in the years 1946 and 1947 culminating in the Truman Doctrine and the Marshall Plan of the latter year. The United States throughout the early postwar era was busily looking at Europe, and it is worth noting that the Berlin blockade began in 1948 at the crucial time of the Chinese revolution, and ended in 1949 when the communists had almost taken over mainland China. Stepping in full-scale in China might have involved committing several divisions of American troops, perhaps as many as twenty or thirty, which was an impossible policy at the time short of a general mobilization which neither Congress nor the American people would ever have supported.

If one were to assess the relative contribution to the fall of Nation-alist China on the mainland, the chief portion would lie with the Chiang regime, the second with the communists, the third with the Russians who supported the Chinese communists at least spiritually (there is little or no proof of any Russian material support to the Chinese revolution), and the least portion with the United States.

General Chiang himself contributed to the debacle because, despite his willingness to pursue any course that was for the good of China, he had become accustomed through long years of power and com-mand to construing the welfare of China in terms of his own welfare. Not that the general was a grafter, for he was not; but he was in-clined to believe that only he could rule China properly, and his ad-visers were often corrupt and incompetent or both. The result was a bureaucratic mess, from the top down, that could hardly have been worse.

The support of the Chiang regime through the years had come to rest essentially upon the landlord class in China. But land reform—one aspect of the People's Livelihood set forth by Sun Yat-sen as the third of his principles—was one of the most pressing demands of the peasant Chinese, a demand to which Chiang could not afford to listen and which played straight into the hands of the communists, who posed as agrarian reformers. While Chiang was reorganizing his regime in the cities after the war, the communists revolutionized the countryside. The Nationalist government, as we have seen, was also extraordinarily inept in the manner of its return to the coastal cities of China. This was no way to win friends and influence people. Thus Chiang tidied up the job of self-destruction by alienating his possible new supporters, the businessmen and students.

The United States sought to shore up the Nationalist regime, but with no good results; in fact many American measures became propaganda for the communists. The Marshall mission and even more the useless military mission in Nanking, JUSMAG, gave the communists their rallying cry that the Americans were pitting Chinese against Chinese, supporting the Nationalists in their war against the communists. General Wedemeyer suddenly reappeared in China in 1947 with a staff of investigators and without much finesse drew together a brutally frank report on the Chinese government, only in part published two years later, which criticized the Chinese and further alienated support, both American and Chinese, from the Chiang Kai-shek regime. In the same year, 1947, such private Americans as William C. Bullitt and Congressman Walter H. Judd came out on junketing tours of China and after a quick reconnaissance made speeches or allowed statements to be published in China and in their homeland which told Americans what was wrong with the Chinese and vice versa, again to the embarrassment of people in the field such as Ambassador Stuart who were trying as best they could to help the Chinese people. Meanwhile the Nationalist campaign in Manchuria drew off the best of Chiang's troops, and thereafter it was a matter of time until his defeat.

Government affairs by early 1949 were in utter confusion. Chiang Kai-shek had quit the Nanking regime and was in nominal retirement at his native village in Chekiang, although he was apparently giving orders to his troops by long-distance telephone. The highest officers of the government, including the acting president, Li Tsung-jen, were in Nanking; the administrative and other officials were in Canton. Everyone was looking obliquely at Formosa, considering the possibility of retreat to that haven of safety. The Nanking troops were unpaid (or paid in so-called gold yuan, Nationalist paper, which was equivalent to being unpaid). Their pay was set at four Chinese dollars silver a month, worth two American dollars, and this pay in silver would have made them willing to fight. Ambassador Stuart, seeking to devise ways to use unspent ECA funds to pay the troops, learned that for several months the top ranking Nationalist generals had been holding 30,000,000 silver dollars. They continued to hold them. Nanking fell, and the government moved to Canton, which fell, and Chungking, which fell, and then to Formosa. On December 9, 1949 the Kuomintang cabinet began to function in Taipei, the capital of Formosa.

Until the last, incompetence was the order of the day. The Nationalists sought to stop the wild inflation of their final months by instituting on August 19, 1948 a new currency, the gold yuan already mentioned, equal to four United States dollars, which was handled not by their own treasury officials but by a private and respected group of Shanghai citizens who were to publish statements each month of the issues and backing of the currency. By the end of September 1948 the gold yuan, despite brutal measures taken by Chiang Kai-shek's eldest son, Chiang Ching-kuo, against speculators in Shanghai, had lost 98 per cent of its value. The generally increasing scarcity of goods could not help but prove inflationary, and the fall of Tsinan in Shantung province at this time—the communists were advancing on Nanking—helped the yuan along toward worthlessness. Ambassador Stuart discovered after this gold yuan fiasco that the Nationalists had nearly $300,000,000 in bullion. He estimated that $10 million would have bought up all the gold yuan in circulation, then worth $75 billion at face value.

All the money that the United States had put into China between 1937, the beginning of the Sino-Japanese War, and the departure of the Nationalists from the mainland in 1949 had gone down the drain, so far as concerned shoring up the Nationalist regime. The $275 million in Marshall Plan funds appropriated in the spring of 1948 had proved of doubtful value, for such aid was too little and too late; economic projects could not save the Nationalist government in 1948. The $125 million simultaneously voted by Congress as a special China fund for the Chinese government to use in any way it wished had no effect affirmatively on the situation. Because of the slowness in filling Chinese orders for weapons the United States was more criticized for its assistance than praised. And what weapons arrived in China were mostly wasted by troops unable to use them, or else fell into the hands of the communists through desertions by individual soldiers or sell-outs by their generals. Communist forces taking over Tientsin in January 1949 were completely supplied with American equipment. The communists entered Peking during the same month with a long retinue of American tanks.

Grants and credits in the twelve-year period 1937–1949 had come to the large total of $3,523 million. About 40 per cent had been authorized before V-J Day and the remainder thereafter. This did not include so-called sales, virtually gifts, to the Chinese government of American military- and civilian-type surplus property made since V-J Day, material with a procurement cost of over $1,078 million. Nor did such totals include large quantities of ammunition left by American forces in China and transferred by the United States to the Chinese government at the end of the war, nor the cost of special missions to China, nor of relief contributions through such agencies as the World Health Organization.

It is a strange commentary on United States policy toward China that in the postwar years 1945–1949 the American government con-tributed about $2 billion in grants and credits to the Chinese, while at the same time the Russians before their retirement from Manchuria took $2 billion worth of machine tools and other booty, stripping many factories bare, hauling off to Siberia everything that was port-able, and that the net result of this subtraction and addition by the two powers was the almost universal impression among the Chinese people that the Russians were their benefactors and the Americans their oppressors.

Perhaps the dislike arose from the United States having too sud-denly exerted its power in the Far East, from the old criticism which had focused on the British and the French as imperialists and colonial exploiters becoming unfairly but all too easily attached to the United States. General Marshall, in describing our difficulties in the Far East after the war, not particularly in China, has remarked that on one occasion "One of our Generals said 'good morning' to somebody and that was reflected in all the papers as a hideous example of our duplicity."

On October 1, 1949 the Central People's Government of the People's Republic of China was formally inaugurated at Peking and began to seek recognition from foreign governments. The Soviet

Union recognized it the next day, October 2. The Nationalist government severed relations with the USSR on October 3, and the following day the United States announced that it would continue to recognize the Chiang Kai-shek government. The Chinese communist regime upon taking office quickly stabilized the currency and set about stopping corruption among the officialdom. The revolution was over—or perhaps it had just begun.

3. *Free China and Communist China*

At the outset of the period 1949–1959 and immediately after the communization of the mainland there came the Korean War, and this in the United States gave inspiration to a debate of impressive proportions about American Far Eastern policy and general military strategy, which will be treated in the next chapter.

The war and the debate led to some changes of American policy toward Formosa—toward Free China—which are worth setting down at this point. When the Korean War broke out, President Truman ordered the Seventh Fleet to protect Chiang Kai-shek against any aggression from the mainland, and this order was coupled with a directive forbidding Chiang's armies from crossing the Formosa Strait to mainland China. But during the presidential election of 1952 there was much criticism of the order restraining Chiang: the president of Nationalist China had been leashed, so the cry went, and if he were unleashed he might reconquer China. Leading members of the Republican Party in the United States were determined to free Chiang for the mainland invasion, and so President Dwight D. Eisenhower gave Chiang the go-ahead in his first state-of-the-union address on February 2, 1953. The new policy lasted for about a year and a half, during which Chiang did not move an inch from the position he had been in while on leash. Finally, in a treaty between the United States and Free China concluded on December 2, 1954 both countries guaranteed each other's security, pledged alliance, and promised that either country before taking action toward communist China would concert its measures with those of the other country. This latter provision effectively re-leashed President Chiang, for he thereafter could not move without permission from the United States.

In the autumn of 1954, and again in 1958, trouble occurred in connection with Nationalist-occupied islands—the Tachen, Quemoy, and Matsu island groups—off the coast between Formosa and the mainland. The two Quemoy islands lie about five miles off the Chinese mainland, about 105 miles west of Formosa. On September 3, 1954 the communist Chinese—who from their moment of triumph in 1949 onward had been proclaiming their intention of liberating Formosa from the Nationalists, and made an explicit announcement to that effect in the summer of 1954—began shelling with coastal batteries some of the Tachen Islands. The Nationalists replied with their own artillery and with announcements of a fight to the finish. The *New York Times* published grim pictures of Nationalist soldiers huddled in scooped-out holes and caves with their rifles at the ready. With the fall of the island of Yikiangshan in January 1955 the situation looked dangerous, and President Eisenhower obtained from Congress an extraordinary resolution giving him authority "to employ the armed forces of the United States as he deems necessary for the specific purpose of securing and protecting Formosa and the Pescadores [these latter islands were occupied by the Nationalists] against armed attack, this authority to include the security and protection of such related positions and territories of that area now in friendly hands and the taking of such other measures as he judges to be required or appropriate in assuring the defense of Formosa and the Pescadores." The fall of Yikiangshan made evacuation of the Tachen group a military necessity, but the two other island groups involved in the controversy, Matsu and Quemoy, which commanded the approaches to important harbors in the Fukien province of mainland China and were possible staging points for a Nationalist invasion of communist China, were retained by the Nationalists. Whether the United States would support Chiang Kai-shek in defending these islands was never made clear at the time or thereafter by the American government, on the theory (not admired by America's European allies) that it was good policy to keep the communist regime in China guessing.

This island fracas might have been a small affair except for the possibility of irresponsible action by the Nationalists, who were all the while looking in the direction of assistance from the United States Seventh Fleet. Further, because the affair occurred immediately after the tragic French disaster at Dienbienphu in Indochina, and in the midst of the domestic political hullabaloo in the United States over release by the State Department of the Yalta papers, there was

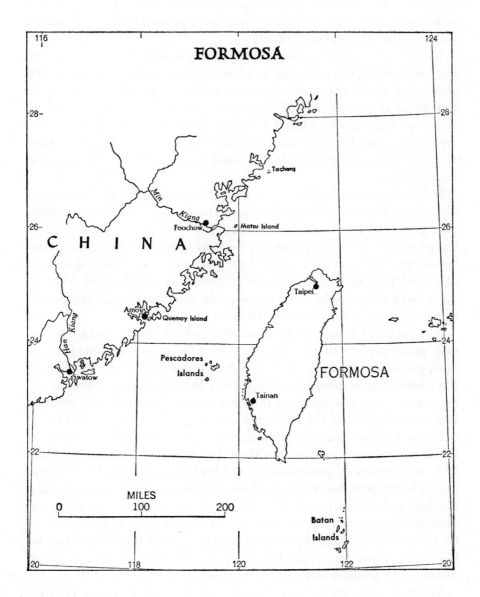

FORMOSA

CHINA

Min
Kiang
Foochow
Tachens
Matsu Island

Han
Kiang
Amoy
Quemoy Island
Swatow

Pescadores
Islands

Taipei

FORMOSA

Tainan

MILES
0   100   200

Batan
Islands

much sentiment for stern action against the communists, perhaps using American planes to bomb Fukien on the mainland and any possible marshalling places for ships for the supposed Formosa invasion. Happily the affair quieted down.

In 1958, when the communists again bombarded the Quemoys, they seemed to be trying primarily to embarrass the United States. At one point they were firing only on even-numbered dates; supplies could thus reach the semibeleagured garrison on alternate days. When Secretary of State Dulles visited Formosa in October 1958 the shelling resumed during his stay, stopped after he left. No military decision was reached, and the ticklish offshore-islands question lingered on in uncertainty.

What, however, had been happening in the meantime in communist China, the home of all but a small fraction of the Chinese people, now governed by the regime of Mao Tse-tung in Peking? China, in the words of Mao (who, actually, used the expression for all of Asia), "stood up" beginning in 1949. The power of communist China, as exhibited first in the Chinese intervention in the Korean War in 1950–1953 and more lately in propaganda and diplomacy, became one of the large question marks of the world.

The face of China could not be changed overnight, and undoubtedly many aspects of the old, corrupt, inept China remained in the new, yet there was from the first a sharp break with the old China in the administrative practices of the new. In ways totally unknown to former Chinese governments the new communist state was efficient bureaucratically, and the efficiency was applied in a terroristic regime over the Chinese people which likewise was something new among Chinese governments. Not that there had been no massacres and terrible vengeances of governments and leaders on the hapless Chinese people in the past, but these had been inefficient uses of terror, mostly illogical and of short duration. The new use of terror was unprecedented. Executions of opponents of the regime may well have numbered into the millions. Against the background of these novel uses of bureaucracy and terror, the Chinese communists put forth a claim to great-power status among the powers of the world.

What was the precise strength and weakness of this new regime? It was easy to speak in general, rather than particular, about China. Just precisely what was going on in the new Red China was not easy to discover, though enough became known through escapees and through unconscious disclosures in communist publications to enable makers of policy in the West gradually to perceive certain stresses and strains of the regime. During an initial period of honeymoon everything had seemed to be going well, and many Chinese everywhere, not merely in mainland China, were proud that their country at last was unified under what gave every evidence of being a strong government. The intervention in Korea gave more support to the belief that China had really stood up. But in the years since the Korean truce there have been signs that all is not so well in China, though this is not to say that revolution against the regime is around the corner or will occur in the foreseeable future. Some such signs have been perceived in the incessant propaganda campaigns among the Chinese people by the government, a technique necessary for communicating with an illiterate peasantry. The Chinese have been sloganed to death, so it might seem, with such campaigns as the three-anti movement—anti-corruption, anti-waste, anti-bureaucratism. There was also the five-anti movement (anti-bribery, anti-tax-evasion, anti-fraud, anti-stealing state property, and anti-theft of state economic secrets). A momentary relief was the Rectification Campaign announced by Mao Tse-tung in February 1957 in terms of a Chinese classic, "Let the hundred flowers bloom." The government invited criticism, and obtained a large amount of it, whereupon it clamped the lid down and began a new campaign known as "weeding the garden."

Underlying all the self-criticism and the sloganeering was the sometimes silent but always pressing problem of population. In China today there is a veritable population explosion. An announcement of the communists, given out as a triumph but undoubtedly made with many secret misgivings, was that there were 600 million Chinese. One suspected that the statistics for this count were perhaps more reliable than old-time Chinese statistics where one just chose a number, any number; maybe there were not yet 600 million Chinese, but if not then there soon would be. It was quite possible that the Chinese population was increasing as the available statistics said, at a rate of 2.2 per cent a year, and thus might reach the enormous total of 800,000,000 by 1967, in which case the mere increase in Chinese population would equal by that time the entire population of the United States, and perhaps exceed it. What this meant in terms of China's economy was utterly clear, for despite the most strenuous program of industrialization the population would be growing more rapidly than the capacity to care for it. The gloomy predictions of the early nineteenth-century philosopher of population, Thomas Malthus, may have come true in China.

By imitation of Russian methods, the Chinese sought to escape this vicious population spiral, but probably to no avail. There were two five-year plans, the first beginning in 1953 and the second in 1958. Results of these were impossible for outsiders to measure, but in no case could they have been startling because China was terribly poor in the major requirements for industrialization, coal and steel and oil. A necessary concomitant to the five-year plans, again taking a page from the experience and doctrine of Stalin, was collectivization of agriculture—because of the need to place the Chinese peasantry under close supervision so that the state could extract the last ounce in agricultural production to obtain capital to build industry, since capital obviously was not going to come in large amounts from outside China. Spectacular results numerically were announced for Chinese collectivization, and by the end of the year 1955 and out of a peasant population that (accepting the official Chinese statistics) numbered about 480,000,000, supposedly 60 per cent were turned into agricultural producer co-operatives. In June 1956 the total, precise enough to be suspicious, was 91.7 per cent. Rumor and some verification coming from communist China was to the effect that this collectivization functioned according to the Russian experience: that is, was ineffective. Agriculture is an occupation that requires numerous careful and personal tasks, and close supervision is impractical if attempted contrary to the will of the agriculturist. Whereas about 8 million workers on American farms turn out more food than the United States can use or export, some 50 million on the Soviet collective farms do not raise enough food for a scant seventh more people (200 million compared to 175 million). The Chinese peasant discovered that the produce of collectivized farms went to the state at starvation prices. Collectivization appeared to have lowered agricultural output, rather than raised it, and probably took innumerable Chinese peasants to the edge of existence or beyond.

The meaning of all this domestic turmoil and supposed reform in communist China was fairly clear for American diplomacy, namely, that China was not the great power in terms of long-run economic strength and inherent capability that Americans had come to think she was. Mao was strong, but China was weak. The communist government of China was distinctly a second-class dragon as compared to the first-class dragon to the north. Communist claims to the contrary, there were still flies in China. And from this some students concluded: (1) that the best course for American policy toward China was to continue its original tactics of no-aid, no-trade, no-recognition and thus push the Chinese further into the arms of the Russians; (2) that the Chinese were indeed a liability to the Russians, for the Chinese possessed a prime problem, agriculture, which the Russians under much more favorable circumstances failed to solve; and (3) that American policy therefore would be pushing the Chinese into the Russians' arms at the very time that the Russians discovered that they had to give rather than take in Eastern Europe. In addition to placing a millstone around the neck of Soviet Russia, such a policy might bring Mao and his fellow revolutionaries to the view that their primary concern had to be the welfare of the Chinese people, the advancement of Chinese nationalism instead of Russian communism. At such a point, so ran this theory, the United States could make some deal with the Chinese government, engage safely in negotiations, and extricate itself from what was an unsettled and embarrassing impasse, America's refusal to treat with the Chinese communist regime in Peking. If we waited long enough, and meanwhile built up economically and militarily the other Asian countries, we might eventually be able to reduce the intransigence of the new Peking government and bring the communists to their senses.

This was an interesting theory, and it would be comforting to think that it was correct. Unfortunately there was no way to prove its correctness short of trying it, in which case, if it should fail, the results—driving the Chinese communists inseparably into the arms of the Russians—might be decidedly against the national interests of the United States. The proponents of the above view claimed that the Red Chinese were already in the arms of the Russians and there was nothing to lose.

They contended that Formosa, the present domicile of Chiang Kai-shek, could be made into another West Berlin, or West Germany. Formosa could become a showcase at the front door of communist China, proof that the democratic way, reliance on the dignity of man and his own resourcefulness if left to go his way without inhuman pressures, was the best course for Asia as well as for Western Europe.

In this respect one should state that Formosa, since the establishment there of Chiang Kai-shek, had beyond question proved an island of some intellectual freedom for the million or more of mainland Chinese who went there with Chiang. While there was not complete freedom of speech in Formosa, and while some individuals feared that if the government of that island passed under control of Chiang Ching-kuo a tight dictatorship would ensue, still there was a large freedom of behavior in Formosa if contrasted to the mental confinement of mainland China. And economically Formosa had progressed under Chiang's rule. The standard of living there was not high, but it was high for an Asian economy. Much money had been poured into Formosa by the United States, there had been a large-scale land reform, and the general economic picture was fairly bright.

So one could conclude that the scene of two Chinas, recognized and unrecognized, had some contrasts favorable to the West. True, matters were unsettled, and perhaps with eventual relinquishment of the Formosa government by Chiang Kai-shek they would worsen, but the view was not too discouraging, ten years after the debacle of 1949.

The record of American relations with China by the year 1959, one might conclude, had been one of co-operation and friendship for a hundred years until in 1949 it fell to pieces, and a decade later it had not been put together again. Perhaps it never would be, although any honest observer of the American scene in 1959 would at once have remarked the hearty good will present among people of the United States toward the people of China, the fervent hope of Americans that somehow the Chinese people, with all their virtues and the tragedies of their history, might come at last into national and individual happiness. The regime in Peking, if it accepted in friendship the good will of Americans and the willingness to help that it surely implied, had opportunity to become the greatest government in all Chinese history, instead of pursuing the old Manchu oppressive tradition albeit with a twentieth-century bureaucracy, terror, and ideology.

ADDITIONAL READING

An excellent introduction to the present chapter is John K. Fairbank, *The United States and China* (Cambridge, Mass., 1948) by the professor of Chinese history at Harvard. Books on Asia dealing in part with China, by acknowledged scholars, are Paul H. Clyde's first-rate volume, *The Far East: A History of the Impact of the West on Eastern Asia* (3d ed., New York, 1958); Claude A. Buss, *The Far East* (New York, 1955); Fred Greene, *The Far East* (New York, 1957); George E. Taylor and Franz H. Michael, *The Far East in the Modern World* (New York, 1956); Kenneth S. Latourette, *A Short History of the Far East* (New York, 1957) and *The American Record in the Far East: 1945–1951* (New York, 1952); and Harold M. Vinacke, *Far Eastern Politics in the Postwar Period* (New York, 1956). A potpourri of essays and occasional pieces, some dealing with Asia, is G. F. Hudson, *Questions of East and West: Studies in Current History* (London, 1953). Worth any student's attention for its readability and shrewd generalization is Guy Wint, *Spotlight on Asia* (London, 1955; paperback).

Dorothy Borg's *American Foreign Policy and the Chinese Revolution, 1925–1928* (New York, 1947) is valuable for background and for the period named in its title.

For wartime American relations with China there is Herbert Feis, *The China Tangle: The American Effort in China from Pearl Harbor to the Marshall Mission* (Princeton, 1953), a scholarly account based on all available printed and manuscript materials. A fine piece of journalism reflecting the authors' disgust with Kuomintang China is Theodore H. White and Annalee Jacoby, *Thunder Out of China* (New York, 1946). See also Theodore H. White, ed., *The Stilwell Papers* (New York, 1948), published after the general's untimely death, with an introduction by Mrs. Stilwell, containing Vinegar Joe's plain thoughts on some highly political subjects. The diary is a mixture of letters, diary jottings, and commentary by the editor.

The years of China's fall to communism, 1945–1949, appear in colorful detail in Pierre Stephen Robert Payne, *The Marshall Story* (New York, 1951); Don Lohbeck, *Patrick J. Hurley* (Chicago, 1956); and more authoritatively, with equal attention to color, in John Leighton Stuart's excellent *Fifty Years in China* (New York, 1954). Leighton Stuart was alarmed and worried by the fact that he was brought home from China just prior to publication by the Department of State in August 1949 of its voluminous *United States Relations with China: With Special Reference to the Period 1944–1949* (Washington, 1949), the so-called China White Paper. This book of 1054 pages consists of two approximately equal parts, a detailed chronology and documentary annex. That it was compiled *ex parte* the United States against Nationalist China admits of no doubt. Stuart felt that it was a serious matter for the government to publish confidential conversations of its diplomats within a very few years of the event, and has contended that because of the possibility of such publication diplomats in the future will become guarded in their reports to Washington. This seems an admissible criticism, although in recent years there has been hurried declassification of all manner of materials, and publication of the White Paper follows what for better or worse is now an American pattern. Stuart believes that some of the documents compromised Chinese and other individuals who believed they were speaking to him in private, and this delicate problem may well have been neglected in publication of the White Paper. At any rate, whatever one thinks of the White Paper, it has been a boon to historians and will continue so to be, until the annual documentary publication, *Foreign Relations of the United States*, comes to the year 1949, which may be—given its usual 15-year lag—the year 1964 or thereabouts.

Anyone reading the White Paper would be interested in the Department of State's mimeographed "Conference on Problems of United States Policy in China," the stenographic report of the proceedings of a conference of Far Eastern experts held at the department on October 6, 7, and 8, 1949. This has been declassified and contains statements by General Marshall and other participants.

For Free China there are two books which need revision, Joseph W. Ballantine, *Formosa: A Problem for United States Foreign Policy* (Washington, 1952); and Fred W. Riggs, *Formosa under Chinese Nationalist Rule* (New York, 1952).

On communist China one should consult the colorful account by Derk Bodde, *Peking Diary: A Year of Revolution* (New York, 1950), which sets out the communist occupation of Peking. See also the travel books by Frank Moraes (editor of *The Times of India*), *Report on Mao's China* (New York, 1953); and Robert Guillain, *600 Million Chinese* (New York, 1957). Richard L. Walker, "Guided Tourism in China," *Problems of Communism*, vol. 6 (Sept.–Oct. 1957), 31–36, gives the standard tourist's itinerary. At one point, Walker writes, the tourist visits Mao Tsetung's birthplace and talks to an uncle of his; and it has been discovered that the "uncles" work in shifts.

Studies of communist China include W. W. Rostow, *The Prospects for Communist China* (New York, 1954); and Richard L. Walker, *China under Communism: The First Five Years* (New Haven, 1955), a lively and interesting book. For Sino-Russian relations see David Dallin, *Soviet Russia and the Far East* (New Haven, 1948); Robert C. North, *Moscow and Chinese Communists* (Stanford, 1953); and Howard Boorman *et al.*, *Moscow-Peking Axis: Strengths and Strains* (New York, 1957), a study by four experts for the Council on Foreign Relations which sees no prospect in the foreseeable future that the ties between Russia and communist China will weaken because of any possible American action, either by continuing or by changing our present China policy.

An exciting intellectual excursion into the problems of Asia is Edwin O. Reischauer's *Wanted: An Asian Policy* (New York, 1955).

The Far East, 1945-1959
(Part II)

The relations of the United States toward China have beyond doubt been the most exigent American concern in the Far East in the years after 1945, and for this reason they have been dealt with in detail in the preceding chapter. They were not, however, the only question in the orient to occupy the attention of the American public, for there were many questions of diplomacy in regard to Japan and the new nations of Southeast Asia, not to mention the two succession states of British India—India and Pakistan. Likewise there was the Korean War, and the "great debate" in the United States on Far Eastern affairs that occurred during the presidential election campaign of 1952. These matters are the business of the present chapter.

1. The Occupation and Democratization of Japan

Of the many unexpected events and strange occurrences in the Far East in the past decade or two, none was more spectacular than the occupation of Japan by the United States armed forces and the democratization of that country under the rule of General Douglas MacArthur. At the end of the war MacArthur set himself up in Tokyo and began to order the course of Japanese affairs. The American general became a latter-day shogun, something of an emperor, a dictator. Who in 1941 could have foretold such a turn of affairs?

MacArthur proved a happy choice for the job in Japan. His critics would always describe him as a little larger than life, as an ambitious man who had done everything in his career with a success more complete than he deserved, but no matter how one felt about the general there could be no doubt that in his first years in Tokyo he lent a prestige and authority to the occupation that no other American could have given it. When MacArthur's limousine drove up to his office, a respectful crowd of Americans and Japanese was always on hand. When the general left Tokyo on his homeward trip in 1951, recalled in the atmosphere of censure by President Truman, Japanese lined the route to the airport. MacArthur in Japan became a strange kind of democratic autocrat who ordered the new Japanese constitution to be composed by his underlings, apparently writing in a few phrases himself, and then presented the constitution to the Japanese people with such commanding presence that of their own free will they ratified it and were thankful. When he finished his work at Tokyo the Japanese were largely governing themselves, the economy of the nation was booming, the Japanese government was on the high road to independence and foreign recognition.

Even so, the occupation left many marks on Japanese life. American occupation authorities promoted a revived Japanese labor movement, land reform, freedom of the press, woman suffrage, educational reform, and efforts to give the average Japanese some protection against what had been an oppressive and brutal police. These measures acquainted all classes of Japanese society with ideas of freedom and liberty. When the Japanese received their national independence in the Japanese Peace Treaty Conference held at San Francisco on September 4–8, 1951, and when the occupation soon afterward came to an end, it proved impossible to turn the clock back, impossible to repudiate all the occupation reforms.

Admittedly, some American measures during the occupation were not altogether successful. The Americans sought to "humanize" the emperor, and in a New Year's rescript of January 1, 1946, Emperor Hirohito repudiated "the false conception that the Emperor is divine." How much change this announcement could make in Japanese attitudes was difficult to say. Probably there was little change. Likewise, American efforts failed to break up the concentration of business enterprise in Japan. Ever since the industrialization of Japan in the later nineteenth century, business enterprise had been concentrated in the hands of a small number of wealthy families, the *zaibatsu* such as the Mitsui and Mitsubishi, and it was the hope of American occupation authorities that decartelization might create economic democracy. Despite an active program of decartelization it proved an extraordinarily difficult task to change the pattern of an economy. To play safe, to avoid risking a collapse of the Japanese economy through perhaps economically dangerous methods of cartel control, it was finally decided to keep the cartels, to follow a policy of "putting the cartel before the hearse."

What has been the shape of Japan since September 8, 1951? Will the reformation of the postwar years continue into the future? These are difficult questions to answer, for perhaps there has not been enough time since 1951 to judge Japan's reorientation carefully and intelligently. Some matters are fairly clear. For example, it appears certain that the spirit of militarism in Japan has for the moment almost disappeared. Too many Japanese were killed in the war: the battle losses among soldiers, sailors, and airmen, the casualties from the American air force's fire bombings in Tokyo and elsewhere, and the holocausts at Hiroshima and Nagasaki were terribly costly. All in all the tragedy of the second World War was by 1945 so omnipresent in Japan that militarism could no longer have its old attraction. The so-called MacArthur constitution contained a clause renouncing war that was reminiscent of the Kellogg-Briand Pact of 1928, and sounded for this reason altogether American in expression, but the Japanese apparently accepted this remarkable clause in good faith, glad to be excused from further fighting. According to the constitution the Japanese people "forever" renounced "war as a sovereign right of the nation and the threat or use of force as a means of settling international disputes." To carry out that hope, the constitution continued, "land, sea, and air forces, as well as other war potential, will never be maintained." When these provisions of American military government first appeared they evoked little or no criticism. Later, during and after the Korean War when it seemed necessary that Japan establish defense forces of strength and size, the general public antipathy in Japan toward military men and measures had hardly lessened.

One may fairly conclude that the new Japan has thus far proved worthy of American confidence. Under MacArthur the Japanese nation was not remade in six years. "The Japanese people since the war," MacArthur told Congress in 1951, "have undergone the greatest reformation recorded in modern history." There could be some doubt about this. Still, the new Japan is a nation far different from the one that upset the peace of Asia in the years before and immediately after Pearl Harbor.

2. Korea and the Korean War

American occupation of Korea, unlike that of Japan, encountered grave troubles of an unexpected sort, which led not to peace but to further war. The difficulties in Korea were caused in general by the post-1945 antagonism between the United States and the Soviet Union. In particular they stemmed from the division of Korea in 1945 into two zones of occupation, Soviet and American, separated by the thirty-eighth parallel.

Choice of the thirty-eighth parallel was a military decision, of the peculiarly military-diplomatic variety that occurred in several areas in Europe and Asia at the end of the war. The thirty-eighth parallel was a fair dividing line, for it left more territory and less population above the line, and the reverse below. A division had to take place because at the time of V-J Day the American commander in the area was unable to move his troops into Korea until September 8. Japan surrendered rather suddenly, and it took some time to bring up troops for occupation duty. Had there been no such arrangement as the thirty-eighth parallel the Russians easily could have moved down from Manchuria and occupied the entire peninsula. Later critics of American policy might have remembered that. No one at the time, certainly not the military commanders on the spot, anticipated a division of the world between communists and noncommunists, and the consequently unfortunate results for Korea.

After this division of Korea in 1945 the events that led to the Korean War are not difficult to trace. In September 1947, when East-West tensions were in evidence, the United States informed the USSR that it was referring the question of Korean reunion and independence to the United Nations. In January of the next year the Russians announced that the UN commission scheduled to visit Korea would not be permitted to enter North Korea. Elections were held in South Korea in May 1948. The government of the American-sponsored leader in South Korea, Syngman Rhee, in December 1948 signed an agreement with the United States for economic and military assistance. A People's Republic meanwhile had been set up in North Korea in September.

At this juncture there came some unfortunate pronouncements by American government and military leaders. In a speech in January 1950 Secretary of State Dean Acheson declared that South Korea would be expected to defend itself, and other statements by Acheson and by General MacArthur indicated that the American government did not consider South Korea, or for that matter Formosa, among the territories in the Far East that it would defend against attack. South Korea, the strategists said, was not within the American defense perimeter. General MacArthur at this time stated that only a lunatic would fight on the mainland of Asia. These announcements of military lack of interest in Korea later became the subject of wide criticism, and during the campaign that preceded the presidential election of 1952 it was said that Secretary Acheson in January 1950 had virtually announced to the communists that Korea could be taken without American interference.

Actually, the communists could have read American intentions from the condition of the American army, for unless the army made a strenuous effort it was too weak to engage in any war in Korea. It was altogether unprepared for war. The secretary of defense in 1949–1950 was Louis Johnson, an able appointee but dedicated to the proposition that the defense budget of about $14,000,000,000 was large enough to defend American interests abroad. The atomic bomb, he believed, would make up for the weakness of the United States army's total ground forces of approximately ten under-strength and ill-equipped divisions. American military unpreparedness, rather than any such factor as public statements by the secretary of state or General MacArthur, probably accounts for the willingness of the USSR to permit the North Koreans to invade South Korea in 1950. The American people and their leaders allowed the military forces of the United States to disintegrate after the second World War and there was almost nothing to stop the North Koreans when the invasion started. Lack of military preparation was incidentally no party matter in the United States. It was a national policy. If the Democratic Party which was then in power failed to provide for the army, there was little pressure from the Republican opposition to increase appropriations. Indeed there was the reverse. So the cause of the

Korean War has appeared in retrospect.

At the outset of the Korean War the United States was therefore at a considerable disadvantage. When the North Koreans attacked on June 24, 1950 and caught the defending forces of the South Koreans off guard, American forces based in Japan could give little support; there was only the weak occupation garrison, and it was well understood that the American strategic plan in the Far East contemplated defense of Japan and Okinawa and the Philippines but not of Korea. As everyone knows, Korea and also Formosa were quickly brought within the American line of defense. President Truman on June 27 instructed the Seventh Fleet to patrol Formosa Strait and authorized use of the navy and air force in Korea; on June 29 he gave General MacArthur permission to use army combat and service troops "to insure the retention of a port and air base in the general area of Pusan." MacArthur had said that only a lunatic would fight on the mainland of Asia, but within months of this remark the general found himself directing a major military operation there.

Several reasons were involved in the decision to send troops into Korea, although the purpose of preserving American prestige in Asia and throughout the world was obviously paramount. In some authoritative quarters it was suggested that by allowing the North Koreans to attack, the Russians were feeling out a soft spot in American defenses. There was another theory, somewhat corollary, that the Russians were seeking to give the world a demonstration of Soviet strength and American weakness. A third hypothesis was that the USSR was testing our resolution. This hypothesis urged that the North Korean invasion was analogous to Hitler's reoccupation of the Rhineland in 1936, and that if the United States in 1950 did not stand up to Russia there would only occur—as after 1936—further aggressions and ultimately a major war. A fourth view, advanced by John Foster Dulles, then in charge of preparations for the Japanese peace treaty, was that the Korean aggression was an attempt by Russia to block American efforts to make Japan a full member of the free world. The attack would halt the American attempt to create in South Korea an Asian republic, a "hopeful, attractive Asiatic experiment in democracy."

Militarily the commitment of American troops to the Korean peninsula was certainly undesirable. Although Korea was a minor threat to Japan, and in the high noon of the age of imperialism when Japan coveted Korea it had often been said that the Korean peninsula was a

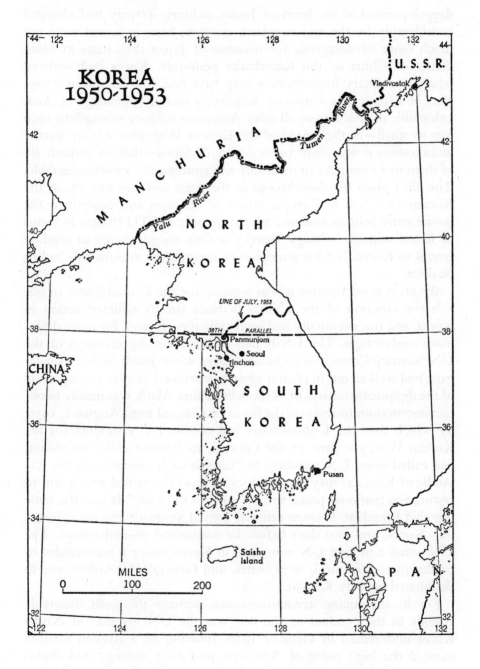

KOREA
1950·1953

U. S. S. R.

Vladivostok

MANCHURIA

Tumen River

Yalu River

NORTH

KOREA

LINE OF JULY, 1953

38TH PARALLEL

Panmunjom

Seoul

Inchon

CHINA

SOUTH

KOREA

Pusan

Saishu
Island

MILES
0   100   200

JAPAN

dagger pointed at the heart of Japan, military strategy had changed considerably by the mid-twentieth century; bases in Korea were not much more advantageous for invasion of Japan than bases in Manchuria or China or the Kamchatka peninsula. Korea had outlived whatever military importance it may have had. For American strategists in 1950 it was a military liability, a useless appendage of Asia, vulnerable to attack from all sides. American military strength in 1950 was so small—at the height of the Korean War after a hasty partial mobilization it was only twenty-four divisions—that to commit six of them to a minor Asian peninsula was strategically most undesirable. The ideal place for those troops in the tense and taut months of the Korean War was in Europe, where in numbers and equipment the Soviet army held an immense advantage over NATO troops. In terms of broad military strategy there was thus no advantage in sending troops to Korea, but for a number of nonmilitary reasons this had to be done.

By great good fortune it was possible for the United States to obtain the sanction of the United Nations for its military action in Korea, and this eventually had some military—though far more diplomatic—advantage. The USSR had been boycotting meetings of the UN Security Council since January 1950 when Jacob Malik, its delegate, had walked out in protest against continued Western recognition of the diplomatic envoys of Nationalist China. Malik was unable to obtain instructions to re-enter the Security Council until August 1, 1950, by which time the United States had obtained UN support for the Korean War. On June 27 the Council, its Russian colleague absent, had called upon UN members to "furnish such assistance to the Republic of Korea as may be necessary to repel the armed attack and to restore international peace and security in the area." It was the same day that President Truman ordered United States air and naval forces into Korea, and two days before he authorized ground troops. The UN voted a unified UN command in Korea under a commander to be designated by the United States, and General MacArthur was so designated on July 8, 1950.

For its diplomatic accompaniments, perhaps the most debatable episode in the conduct of the war was the UN invasion of North Korea undertaken in October 1950. Invasion of a Russian satellite marked the high point of American post-1945 strategy and diplomacy. And the invasion of North Korea, following General Mac-

Arthur's brilliantly conceived Inchon landings in September, brought Chinese intervention on a massive scale. Although he had taken few precautions, MacArthur was certain that the invasion of North Korea would prove successful. Leaders in Washington, diplomatic as well as military, approved the thrust because they felt it would be a hopeless task to put Korea on its feet if either Chinese or North Korean communists remained in control of the dams and power stations along the Yalu River, North Korea's northern boundary with Manchuria. In invading North Korea, a communist country, MacArthur appears to have counted on the same boldness that had stood him in such good stead in Japan. He apparently hoped that a determined move to the North Korea-Manchuria border would work out well and would not bring Chinese intervention. He failed to reckon the difference between the demoralized people of a defeated Japan and the high-spirited Chinese communists who had just won a long civil war.

The Chinese intervention brought a second American retreat down the peninsula toward Pusan (this time during the cold Korean winter). Then, after recouping their strength, the Americans began another push upward, a sort of slow-but-sure "meat grinder" advance known in army parlance as Operation Killer. Confronted with this new American tactic, the communists through the Russian delegate of the Security Council, Jacob Malik, raised the subject of a truce. The truce was reached on July 27, 1953, after a frustrating two years of talk between American and North Korean representatives meeting most of the time in an improvised "truce tent" at a place called Panmunjom.

3. The Great Debate

Meanwhile had come a great debate in the United States over the conduct of American diplomacy in the Far East—one of the most vociferous arguments in recent years. It concerned notable and specific events: the loss of China to the communists in 1949; the beginning of the Korean War in 1950; President Truman's seemingly abrupt dismissal of General MacArthur in 1951; and it was at its climax in the presidential election of 1952. These events led many people in the United States to survey recent American policy in the orient and draw conclusions of a startling sort.

The loss of China to the communists had, first of all, been a most difficult event for Americans to endure. China had been the focus of American interest in the orient since 1784. China had been the hope of American traders and businessmen. It had been the center of American missionary activity since the days when young students went out to the East to work for "the evangelization of the world in this generation." Partly as a result of China's expenditure of the Boxer indemnity for educational purposes, more Chinese students had come to America than had the nationals of any other Far Eastern country. The Kuomintang government had consisted in large part of American-educated Chinese. When in so severe a period of international tension as the years after 1945 China went over to the camp of America's enemy, it was a signal for more soul-searching by makers of United States policy and by the general public than had occurred in generations. Someone, so it seemed, had lost China.

The Korean War of 1950, like the failure of American policy in China, bothered many American citizens. Korea seemed the wrong place for the United States to fight, after failing to fight communism in China. The Korean War, unlike other American wars, did not proceed toward any discernible conclusion; it seesawed indecisively up and down the Korean peninsula, moving strangely from one almost unpronounceable place name to another. The war seemed a thoroughly unsatisfactory affair, and many Americans were beginning by 1951 to air their perplexities. Was there not something wrong with the administration in Washington? There had been revelations of spy activities in the United States, a conspicuous instance having involved Alger Hiss, a former State Department official and New Deal appointee. The Department of State was vulnerable to partisan attack because Secretary of State Acheson had been friendly with Hiss. Democratic administrations had been in power in Washington since 1933, and it was not difficult to argue that any disasters of foreign policy since that time, including Korea, had been the result of their errors, unpremeditated or intentional, inspired by "leftist" views or perhaps allegiance to communism. As Senator Joseph R. McCarthy of Wisconsin was reported to have said, "How can we account for our present situation, unless we believe that men high in this government are concerting to deliver us to disaster? This must be the product of a great conspiracy on a scale so immense as to dwarf any previous venture in the history of man."

In the presence of such dissatisfaction came the dismissal of General

MacArthur. President Truman removed the general from command because he had flagrantly disobeyed a presidential order against pronouncements on foreign policy by government officials without prior clearance from the State Department. MacArthur had disagreed with some of the strategic and diplomatic views of the Truman administration, and with little regard for the consequences and in fact perhaps as a direct challenge to the president, the general talked openly to reporters and sent communications to friends at home, one of them a letter to the Republican speaker of the House of Representatives, Joseph W. Martin, which was an open invitation to President Truman to dismiss him or acquiesce in the general's judgment. Truman, with the unanimous support of the joint chiefs of staff in Washington, dismissed MacArthur from all Far Eastern commands. The American people, irritated over Korea and China, used the occasion of MacArthur's relief to give the discharged general a welcome the like of which had not been seen in the United States since the Lindbergh enthusiasm of 1927 and Admiral Dewey's reception in 1899.

MacArthur came home in triumph. San Francisco, New York, and innumerable other localities went wild for the general. After MacArthur Day in New York City the department of sanitation reported that the MacArthur litter weighed 16,600,000 pounds; the previous record had been 3,600,000. It was the general's first visit to his country since a short trip from the Philippines in 1937, and the homecoming may have been warmer for this reason, perhaps also because he and the nation were to each other such unknown quantities. But whatever the ingredients of his welcome, it could have been construed only as a demonstration against the Truman administration. The president did not greet the general on the steps of the White House, but MacArthur achieved the next best recognition in being invited to address a joint session of Congress, with his speech broadcast over the national radio and television networks.

The dismissal of MacArthur and the general's reception in the United States faded from public memory, and American diplomacy and politics continued in their accustomed courses. President Truman, who sat out the storm, guessed correctly that MacArthur's star would come down almost as quickly as it went up. The MacArthur hysteria provided an occasion, however, for a careful public statement by the Truman administration of the basic principles and purposes of American diplomacy during the Korean War, and this statement deserves some attention. When the general's greeting had run its course, two senatorial committees in May and June of 1951 held "an inquiry into the military situation in the Far East and the facts surrounding the relief of General of the Army Douglas MacArthur from his assignments in that area."

The MacArthur hearing, for those American citizens who followed its stenographic reports closely, was extremely enlightening. After the Chinese had intervened in North Korea in late November 1950, MacArthur had spoken out in favor of attacks on the Chinese mainland. The general had been giving the impression that the slow pace of the war, the moving up and down the Korean peninsula, had derived entirely from strategic blunders by politicians and political generals in Washington. Such allegations were major political attacks in the pre-presidential campaign atmosphere of the capital in 1951–1952, and the Truman administration's answer to its deposed proconsul may have taken some inspiration in the political need for a defense. Certainly much of the great debate of 1951–1952, defense and offense, carried implications for the presidential campaign. Even so, the administration's response had a ring of sincerity. General Omar Bradley, chairman of the joint chiefs of staff, put the administration's reasoning succinctly. "Taking on Red China," Bradley said at the hearings, would have led only "to a larger deadlock at greater expense." "So long," Bradley said, "as we regarded the Soviet Union as the main antagonist and Western Europe as the main prize," the strategy advanced by MacArthur "would involve us in the wrong war at the wrong place at the wrong time and with the wrong enemy."

Nothing could have been clearer than Bradley's statement of the American position. It was a position that derived not from blunders by politicians and political generals, but from careful consideration of all the factors in the United States's politico-military policy. MacArthur had failed to understand the many responsibilities of his government, and had advocated a policy in the Far East that was sheer military in nature. He had been so ill-advised as to push his views in the public press and in letters to congressmen, rather than keep his opinions in the proper military channels. After the controversy over his dismissal had cooled, the Bradley-Truman view of strategy and diplomacy seemed sensible.

There remained the presidential campaign, toward which much of the great debate over foreign policy, as mentioned, had been directed. The Korean War became perhaps the prime issue of the campaign, although it was accompanied on the Republican Party's side by two others, corruption in the government and communism in the government. The Republican platform argued that Allied morale in Asia was crumbling because Russia's "Asia first" policy contrasted so markedly with the American policy of "Asia last." General Eisenhower, the Republican nominee for president, eventually was moved to declare that if elected he would "go to Korea" and straighten things out. Eisenhower, for this reason among others, was elected. Soon after his inauguration, and perhaps because of his trip to Korea, the Korean War came to an end with the armistice of July 1953. The great debate ended with it.

The Truman administration's views on Korean strategy had prevailed. Eisenhower in his short period of office during the war did not change the Korean strategy of limited war—of war for a limited purpose, the containment of Soviet-inspired aggression in Korea—and achievement of this purpose, one can fairly say, marked the basic achievement of the Korean War. This was a large success of American policy, this turning into victory of what on all sides in June 1950 and again in November–December of that year had looked like imminent defeat.

Other events of diplomatic importance followed from the Korean conflict. The war encouraged the United States to a far larger rearmament than it had already begun in 1948 and 1949. The United States roused its allies in Europe and made an heroic effort to put teeth into NATO, engineering the appointment of General Eisenhower as supreme commander of NATO forces. Likewise there were some marked economic effects of the Korean War. It seems fairly certain that although the Korean War did not pull the United States out of an economic recession—the downward economic trend that had begun in 1949 had reversed itself well prior to the North Korean invasion—it did give an impetus to the American economy that sent it spinning ahead to what over the next half-dozen years proved to be ever higher levels of production, wages, and employment. Two months after the Korean War began, employment crossed the 62,000,000 mark, two million beyond the fondest dreams of New Dealers at V-J Day. And there was even a sort of mental fillip that came with the Korean War.

Many of the post-1945 worries of depression, memories of the Great Depression that had only been temporarily stilled in the United States by the prosperous years of the second World War, were laid to rest, at least for a while, during the Korean boom. With release from this fear, the economy for several years thereafter moved ahead with unheard-of confidence.

The facts set out above do not make a triumph of the tragedy of Korea. No one in the United States is soon going to forget the casualties during that conflict: 33,647 young men killed in action. And the cost of the war was many billions of dollars. Perhaps this price in men and treasure was not too great for the major benefit of Korea, the limit that the war placed, at least temporarily, upon Soviet aggression throughout the world.

4. *Southeast Asia, India, and Pakistan*

For the five years from the end of the Korean War, the history of American diplomacy in the Far East was relatively uneventful. The ebb and flow of daily diplomatic communication with the capital cities and the statesmen of the various Asian countries continued without let-up, but by the end of the war in Korea, so Americans hoped, the basic settlement of territories and peoples in the orient had been made. There remains for the present chapter some account of American diplomacy toward Far Eastern nations other than Korea, Japan, and China—namely, Southeast Asia, India, and Pakistan.

In Southeast Asia the United States played a part during the post-World War II years in the attainment of Indonesian independence. The agreement between the Netherlands government and the Republic of Indonesia, by which both parties concluded a truce and the Netherlands agreed to Indonesian independence, was concluded by a UN team, including the American representative Frank P. Graham, aboard the USS *Renville* on January 17, 1948. After this agreement the Dutch in November 1949 transferred sovereignty over the Netherlands East Indies (except Dutch New Guinea) to the Republic of the United States of Indonesia.

In regard to the Philippine Islands, so long a charge upon American patience and funds, Congress fulfilled its promise under the Tydings-McDuffie Act of 1934 by granting the islands independence on July 4, 1946, despite the interruption and chaos of the Japanese occupation from 1941 to 1945. The results of independence were at first unfortunate. General MacArthur had advanced the candidacy of Manuel Roxas as president of the Philippines; Roxas, who died in April 1948, was succeeded by Elpidio Quirino. Under the administrations of these two statesmen affairs in the islands reached a state of crisis. By 1950, when the American government found itself embroiled in Korea, government in the Philippines had deteriorated to such a degree that there was grave doubt as to whether the commonwealth could survive as an independent state. An economic commission sent out to Manila in that year, headed by a former undersecretary of the Treasury, Daniel Bell, found that much of the $1,500 million given the Filipinos between the years 1945 and 1950 as economic aid and payments of various kinds had found its way into the hands of grafters, profiteers, and high officials of the government. Meanwhile the insurrectionary activity of the communist-led Hukbalahaps (Huks) was attracting many of the poverty-stricken country people, who had received no relief from their own government and saw some possible relief in communism. It was a serious situation, which fortunately was retrieved in the nick of time by election in 1953 of the reforming Philippine leader Ramón Magsaysay, under whose enlightened administration order was restored throughout the islands, especially in the ranks of the Philippine army and in the government bureaucracy. After some momentary discouragement American pride was restored in the Philippine Islands as a "show case of democracy" in Asia. It had been a close call.

Another and far more serious American diplomatic difficulty in the Far East occurred over Indochina in 1954. By that year French forces in Indochina were finding themselves in a hazardous position against the communist-led Vietminh forces. The familiar communist guerilla warfare was proving a nightmare to the young French army conscripts and volunteers of the Foreign Legion. Native troops were difficult to officer and not always trustworthy. The government in Paris had taken a stand against the independence movement in Indochina, driving many of the native nationalists into the communist fold. There seemed little hope that anything could be done to retrieve the situation. American military aid had been sent via France to Indochina by the hundreds of millions of dollars, with little result. In the spring of 1954 a force of French and Indochinese troops were bottled up at a place named Dienbienphu, and this name, so strange-sounding to Western ears, began to take on emotional meaning as word of the defenders' desperate plight spread through the newspapers of the Western world.

Fresh from the experience of Korea and determined to pursue a policy of no appeasement of aggression in Eastern Asia, the Eisenhower administration found itself hard pressed. There seems to have been some serious debate as to whether American troops, or even the atomic bomb, should be used to free the trapped garrison at Dienbienphu. According to one pieced-together account by an enterprising American reporter, the United States came close to intervention on two different occasions in April 1954. Eventually the decision was reached that intervention was too risky, that the result might be the general war that everyone feared could grow out of such local wars as those in Korea and Indochina, and that the course of wisdom was to let the garrison fall and to hope that no such military humiliation would again mark the hostilities in Indochina. It was a saddening decision. Dienbienphu with its 12,000-man garrison fell on May 7, 1954.

With Dienbienphu the people of the United States may have realized for the first time in their nation's career that there was a physical limit to American power. Throughout the nineteenth century the United States seemed always to be a giant that continued to grow —and so also it had seemed in the first half of the twentieth century. At Dienbienphu in distant Indochina the United States at last contemplated a situation where American power meant little. The same situation, of course, had obtained in post-1945 China, but high officials in Washington had never reached the point of debating the advisability of military intervention in China, immediate and massive. This point was reached sharply and suddenly in the crisis of 1954 over Indochina. Dienbienphu was a chastening experience in American history.

Secretary of State Dulles sought unconvincingly to cover the national weakness by attending an international conference on Far Eastern matters at Geneva. The conference opened on April 26, 1954, and after more than two months of discussion the French and Vietminh leaders agreed to divide Indochina at the seventeenth parallel, with the communists to the north. The truce was signed on July 20, 1954. Most observers at the time felt that within only a few years the communists by peaceful penetration might well take over the remainder or Vietnam portion of the former French colony. Instead the American-sponsored president of Vietnam, Ngo Dinh Diem, proved himself a doughty political leader, and the new country within months of its birth showed a surprising vitality.

After the Geneva Conference, Secretary Dulles made another diplomatic effort to cover the partition of Indochina when on September 6, 1954 representatives of the United States, Great Britain, France, Australia, and New Zealand, meeting in conference at Manila with three Asiatic nations—the Philippines, Thailand, and Pakistan— signed a pact providing for a Southeast Asia Treaty Organization (SEATO), on the pattern of NATO, stipulating that an attack upon one of the signatories would be recognized as dangerous to the peace and safety of the others. What would happen after such recognition was a matter for determination by each individual nation signatory of SEATO. One could doubt if this treaty changed to any degree the balance of power and diplomacy in the Far East, although it gave the appearance of a new bulwark against communism.

A word remains about American relations with India and Pakistan, those two new and important powers that replaced British India in 1947. Was the transfer of government from Britain to two independent nations of any consequence for the foreign relations of the United States? Actually, there were some consequences, though none was drastic. In the case of India the United States was soon to discover a leader of neutralist sentiment in the United Nations. The independent government of India, led by Jawaharlal Nehru as both prime minister and foreign minister, took the stubborn point of view that security came from peace rather than peace from security, that creation of military blocs against the Soviet Union and its satellites could result only in creation of counterblocs, that—in other words—the way to end the cold war was not through aligning nation against nation but, instead, through finding areas of agreement between the United States and its friends and the Soviet Union and its friends. The Indians thought that Americans were obsessed by communism; the government of India was friendly to communist China; Nehru took a cautious line toward Russia's suppression of the Hungarian uprising in 1956 at the very time when he was castigating Britain (the former colonial power) for military intervention in Egypt; the Indians flirted with the communists in other ways that bothered the Americans. The Americans felt, on the other hand, that Indian neutralism was a result of India's sheer inexperience with Russian communism, that the Indians had been too busy with securing their national independence from the British before and after 1947 to understand how the Soviets during the same period had abandoned pledges and turned world peace upside down. American diplomats told the Indians these facts and views; they were answered by more neutralist arguments and, in 1951, with requests for large loans to import wheat. The combination was all that some Americans could stand, and a little more.

If these difficulties of Indian-American relations were not enough, there was American policy toward Pakistan and (as Indians believed) toward Kashmir. The Indians watched with intense misgivings the signing of a military agreement in 1954 between the United States and Pakistan, by which Karachi received economic credits and military supplies. Pakistan joined SEATO and the Baghdad Pact (for this latter, see the next chapter). These moves had a double effect upon India: they showed India's Moslem rival following an independent line in foreign policy, vying for leadership perhaps with India herself; and they seemed to foreshadow an arms race between the two successionist states. They had been at active and bitter issue over Kashmir, the large province to the north of the Indian subcontinent which, under a Hindu maharaja, requested accession to India in October 1947. But Pakistan claimed Kashmir, and the Indian case was weakened by the fact that three-fourths of the province's population of four million was Moslem. Civil war broke out in Kashmir. There followed several futile UN efforts to arrange a plebiscite. And then, in 1954, came the arms agreement between the United States and Pakistan. This the Indians interpreted as American support for Pakistan in Kashmir.

The thorny problems of American relations with India and Pakistan will not probably meet with solution for some years to come, though one should hasten to add that in general there are far more points of agreement than of disagreement between the United States and India and that this fact has been realized by Indian leaders on unemotional occasions. Whatever difficulties have existed in American relations with India and Pakistan, one might conclude, have been underlain by a large amount of mutual good will. Certainly between the peoples of India and the United States, or Pakistan and the United States, there is no enmity—if only because most Americans know little about either. And as the United States in the nineteenth century had gone through an era of national bumptiousness, so might India in the twentieth.

America's sermonizings to the world had often occurred at moments when the federal union was beset by large social and economic problems; so might India's. India, and Pakistan too, would have a long road to travel before the pressure of population upon extremely thin economic resources would lessen. Their main tasks lay in domestic reconstruction, each nation solving its own problems and, internationally, learning first to get along with each other. This was the logic of the situation. But no Indian, of course, could be expected to foreclose his sovereign right to a large foreign policy. And given the US-USSR frictions of the 1950's, it was perhaps useful to hear an independent voice in world affairs.

American policy in Asia thus was having some successes and some failures by the mid-twentieth century, but no wise man would venture predictions of its course for even so short a time as five or ten years. The United States faced many problems in the orient. It was obvious that what was happening in the Far East was a drastic, rapid awakening of the native peoples to currents of thought that had been common in the Western world for a century and more. Nationalism was the chief of these ideas to emerge after the second World War. There had been Indian nationalism and Chinese nationalism and Japanese nationalism for many years before the era 1939–1945, and nationalism had been nascent in other of the countries of Asia, but during the war the last of the colonial ties were snapped and peoples in Asia saw that the future was increasingly a matter for their own making. The peculiar brand of Asian nationalism championed by the Japanese was short-lived in its effect upon Japanese-occupied countries, but it encouraged a genuine native nationalism that appeared with force and vigor as soon as the Japanese left and the former occupying powers sought to return. The French and Dutch learned this truth far later than the British, with the result that in the Netherlands East Indies and in Indochina there were vicious civil wars before the occupying powers relinquished control. None of these developments had been foreseen by American diplomacy in 1945.

The Harvard historian Edwin O. Reischauer pointed out in a brilliant book, *Wanted: An Asian Policy*, published in 1955, that the United States and other Western nations had three resources of policy toward Asia: military, economic, and ideological. Reischauer appreciated the occasional need to apply military power, the necessity for the West to maintain in the orient as in the occident a respectable military capacity, but he believed that Americans and Europeans had erred by pursuing in the main a military policy. Ten years of experience with military policy—incidentally the most costly choice of policy—had proved it largely futile, for coercion had failed in the Netherlands East Indies and in Indochina and it had succeeded only under special conditions in Korea. The policy of economic support and maneuver, which the Western powers had engaged in desultorily, was so slow and uncertain in action that it could not hope to have much immediate influence upon day-to-day, pressing needs of Western diplomacy. The industrialization that was attempted in the East could not increase productivity to keep up with the increase of native populations. The average Indian or Indochinese or Japanese was likely to find himself no better off despite new industrial techniques and experiments.

The level on which the West could reach the East, Reischauer believed, was the intellectual or ideological. By urging approach at this level he was not advocating the popular but vague American view of the late 1940's, a "meeting of East and West," but a concrete, serious effort by Americans and other Westerners to present democracy to Asians as an active, serious, immensely practical way of life. The ideological was the cheapest line of approach, he argued, far cheaper than military or economic assistance. Democracy, so presented, would be attractive to Asians, who found its ideas vastly enticing and its theories intensely interesting. In this regard, he counseled, we should not be disturbed if ideological debates in Asia veered from one extreme to another. We should not worry if our ideas were accepted only to be juxtaposed with utterly impractical ideas—more likely than not, communist ideas. Economic debates especially, he pointed out, were far more theoretical in the East than in the United States, because the crude economies of most of the new Asian countries had given them so little experience against which to measure theory.

In the course of time and with good fortune democracy might win out in the East. It was up against grave difficulties, when even the more democratic Eastern nations had only a relative handful of people competent to staff, lead, and control the governments, an elite leadership exercising some kind of tutelage and experiencing little enlightened restraint from the bulk of the citizenry. In any economic program of large proportions it was possible that in the East the totalitarian methods of communism might prove momentarily more effective than the vacillations of a primitive and precarious democracy. Communism had an undeniable ideological appeal in Asia, and halfway through the twentieth century the diplomats of the United States found themselves hard put to defend their system of government against the spurious claims of the Bolshevik Revolution. The State Department, confronting the post-1945 difficulties and disasters in the Far East, could only hope that time would work in favor of democracy, the cause of the United States.

ADDITIONAL READING

For general books on the Far East, see titles at the end of the previous chapter. An able introduction to Japan is Edwin O. Reischauer, *The United States and Japan* (Cambridge, Mass., 1957), which may be supplemented by John K. King, *Southeast Asia in Perspective* (New York, 1956). For their special subjects two interesting books are J. B. Bingham, *Shirt-Sleeve Diplomacy: Point 4 in Action* (New York, 1954) and Eugene Staley, *The Future of Underdeveloped Countries* (New York, 1954).

Harry E. Wildes's *Typhoon in Tokyo* (New York, 1954) criticizes the "occupationnaires," although it is written by one of them. Another book on the occupation is E. J. Lewe Van Aduard, *Japan: From Surrender to Peace* (New York, 1954). Elizabeth G. Vining, *Windows for the Crown Prince* (Philadelphia, 1952), by a well-known writer of children's books who became private tutor to Crown Prince Akihito, tells a touching story of its author's efforts—successful, we must hope—to instruct "Jimmy" (the crown prince) in democratic ways. Consult also such MacArthur biographies as John Gunther, *The Riddle of MacArthur* (New York, 1951); Charles A. Willoughby and John Chamberlain, *MacArthur: 1941–1951* (New York, 1954), by the general's intelligence chief, and Louis Morton, "Willoughby on MacArthur: Myth and Reality," *The Reporter*, Nov. 4, 1954, a rebuttal; Courtney Whitney, *MacArthur: His Rendezvous with History* (New York, 1956), a fulsome account; Frazier Hunt, *The Untold Story of Douglas MacArthur* (New York, 1954), sheer hero worship; and Richard H. Rovere and Arthur M. Schlesinger, Jr., *The General and the President and the Future of American Foreign Policy* (New York, 1951), the "meat axe" approach to MacArthur's reputation, by a writer for the *New Yorker* magazine and a professor of history at Harvard.

For the Korean War the best account is probably S. L. A. Marshall, *The River and the Gauntlet* (New York, 1953), by the distinguished military commentator. See also Guy Wint, *What Happened in Korea* (London, 1954; available in paperback); and the book by one of the

American military commanders, Mark W. Clark, *From the Danube to the Yalu* (New York, 1954). After the war in Europe, Clark had served for a time in the Allied occupation of Austria. An intelligent set of essays is Melvin B. Voorhees, *Korean Tales* (New York, 1952). The Council on Foreign Relations has published L. M. Goodrich, *Korea: A Study of United States Policy in the United Nations* (New York, 1956). Consult Alexander L. George, "American Policy-making and the North Korean Aggression," *World Politics*, vol. 7 (1954–55), 209–232; and Carl Berger, *The Korea Knot* (Philadelphia, 1957). Donald Portway's *Korea: Land of the Morning Calm* (London, 1953) is a view of the country and its people.

The great debate of 1951–1952 appears in the "MacArthur hearings," the *Military Situation in the Far East: Hearings before the Committee on Armed Services and the Committee on Foreign Relations* (5 vols., Washington, 1951). Only in a democracy could such an outpouring of information and allegation be published so soon after events, for all the world to read and ponder. A notable book by a member of the United States Senate is Joseph R. McCarthy, *America's Retreat from Victory: The Story of George Catlett Marshall* (New York, 1951). See also John Lord O'Brian, *National Security and Individual Freedom* (Cambridge, Mass., 1955) and Norman A. Graebner, *The New Isolationism: A Study in Politics and Foreign Policy since 1950* (New York, 1956).

American diplomacy toward India has been set down in Chester Bowles, *Ambassador's Report* (New York, 1954). Excellent pieces of reporting are Robert Trumbull, *As I See India* (New York, 1956); and Carl T. Rowan, *The Pitiful and the Proud* (New York, 1956), about a tour through India by an American Negro journalist. Edwin F. Stanton's *Brief Authority* (New York, 1956) is an admirable account of a career diplomat's service in—among other places—postwar Thailand. Francis B. Sayre, *Glad Adventure* (New York, 1957), a most interesting autobiography, contains observations on Thailand by an American long familiar with the country. George McT. Kahin, *Nationalism and Revolution in Indonesia* (Ithaca, N.Y., 1952) discusses a nation about which many Americans are ill informed. E. J. Hammer, *The Struggle for Indochina* (Stanford, 1954) was a timely book, for the country was partitioned in the year of the volume's publication. C. M. Roberts, "The Day We Didn't Go to War," *The Reporter*, Sept. 14, 1954 seems to be an inside account of the Indochina crisis of 1954; Roberts relates how Washington officials considered sending military assistance to the trapped French garrison at Dienbienphu, but eventually decided that intervention in so faraway a conflict was too risky. Robert A. Smith, *Philippine Freedom: 1946–1958* (New York, 1958) discusses a complex subject. A useful book is John W. Coulter, *Pacific Dependencies of the United States* (New York, 1957). See also the excellent book by Earl S. Pomeroy, *Pacific Outpost* (Stanford, 1951).

CHAPTER

☆ 20 ☆

Europe and the Middle East, 1950-1959

Since the end of the second World War the forward movement of Russian communism, politically and militarily, has been distressingly rational in its large outlines, and the organization of the later chapters of the present book, ones hopes, displays this fact. The first Soviet move was toward the nations of Western Europe, where the troubles of the war had brought military, social, and economic ills of a seemingly insoluble sort and where, according to communist dogma, the contradictions of the capitalist system were about to deliver these nations into the hands of the revolutionary workers of the world. This first move was stopped largely by American policy activities related to the Truman Doctrine, the Marshall Plan, and the North Atlantic Treaty Organization (NATO).

Blocked at this point, the USSR allowed the North Koreans to start a war in the Far East, which if successful might have spread communism throughout Asia and made Russian satellites of the weak governments in that part of the world. Again the United States responded, this time with military force, and if the UN-US successes in Korea of 1950–1953 did not prevent the partition of Indochina in 1954, they at least brought proof that there would be no easy conquest of Asia by the USSR if the United States could help it.

At this moment the Russian government looked back to Europe

and observed the strengthening of Western defenses by NATO and the dangers of moving against those defenses either directly or by fomenting internal disorders in the Western European countries. Europe likewise was giving the Soviets some trouble, for the Russians to their embarrassment had to deal with riots in Eastern Germany in 1953 and then, in 1956, with great rebellions in Poland and Hungary. The rebellion of the Poles proved in large part successful; the Hungarian uprising was put down but only with an open use of force. By the end of the year 1956 the Russian position in Europe was not an enviable one.

Thereupon the Russians found in the Middle East a fine area for intrigue and a convenient occasion which could not fail to embarrass the West. Two of the important Western Allies, Britain and France, together with Israel, were entangled in the Suez crisis with Egypt. The Suez events aroused against the British and French an Arab nationalism which was already extremely strong, and as a result Anglo-French prestige in the Middle East fell to zero. When the United States at the height of the crisis opposed this action of its allies, the world was treated to the spectacle of the United States and Russia together opposing two of the NATO powers. And two years later—when the Americans sent marines to prop the shaky pro-Western regime in Lebanon and the British sent paratroops into Jordan—the further firing of the temper of Arab nationalism delighted the Soviets. A troubled West faced a rampant pan-Arabism that was not averse to allying itself with Russia and threatened to sweep Western democratic influence entirely out of the Middle East.

1. *The Strengthening of NATO in the Early 1950's*

The North Atlantic Treaty was signed in Washington on April 4, 1949, by representatives of the United States and eleven European powers. NATO's original members were, in addition to the United States, the nations of Benelux (Belgium, the Netherlands, and Luxemburg), France, Britain, Canada, Italy, Portugal, Denmark, Norway, and Iceland. Greece and Turkey joined NATO in February 1952, and West Germany joined in 1955, making a total of fifteen countries. By Article 5 of the treaty the signatories agreed that an attack upon one would be an attack upon all, to be followed by individual or collective resistance under the stipulations of Article 51, the "collective self-defense" article of the UN Charter. For the United States, membership in NATO was an epoch-making proposition, for not since the Treaty of Mortefontaine of the year 1800, when the United States disengaged itself from its French alliance, had the American government been bound in peacetime by a treaty of alliance. Signature of the North Atlantic Treaty in 1949 indicated clearly that the era of American isolation had ended.

Three Russian moves of strength against the West had led first to the creation and thereafter to the build-up of NATO—the communist coup in Czechoslovakia in February 1948, the Berlin blockade of 1948–1949, and the Korean War of 1950–1953. The communist seizure of power in Czechoslovakia aroused the West and led to talk of military action to counter such Russian moves. During the turmoil in Prague the Czech foreign minister Jan Masaryk, a son of the founder of the republic and well known in the West, died in an apparent suicide under circumstances suggesting that the communists had pushed him out of a window. Soon afterward came the Berlin blockade, which made the West wonder how far the Russians were willing to go in violating the war's territorial settlement—to move the iron curtain westward perhaps to the Atlantic Ocean? NATO was organized while the blockade was in progress.

If there were any uncertainties as to Russian intentions, these were resolved by outbreak of the Korean War in 1950. Thereafter the Allies set out in earnest to construct a strong military force in Western Europe, for it seemed that only by opposing force with force could the position of the West against Russia be made tenable. General Dwight D. Eisenhower, the American military commander of the second World War, went to Europe in 1951 to establish the Supreme Headquarters, Allied Powers in Europe, known as SHAPE, and his command received the available standing forces in Western Europe which at the time consisted of 15 army divisions together with a handful of planes.

Eisenhower's presence in Europe galvanized the NATO powers, and large plans were drawn for a NATO force that on the ground would almost be able to defend Western Europe against the Red Army divisions in Eastern Germany and the satellite nations. There was talk of building by 1954 a force totaling 96 divisions including reserve units. These goals were reconsidered at the NATO Council meeting in Lisbon in February 1952, from which issued a plan to raise a force of 50 divisions and 4,000 aircraft by the end of that year. At the defined time this plan was largely met: 25 divisions were to be ready for combat and all were on hand by December 1952; 25 more divisions in reserve were to be available in thirty days, and all but three or so were ready. The aircraft goal fell short by between 200 and 300 planes.

This achievement came at a time when the Korean War was drawing to an end, and in the year 1953 the European powers, surveying the better prospects for peace in the Far East, began to reconsider their NATO goals and to think about slowing their ambitious plans. The goal for 1953 had been 75 divisions and 6,500 aircraft; this was revised downward to fifty-six divisions and 5,500 aircraft. For the following year, 1954, the provisional goal had been 100 divisions, excluding the armies of Greece and Turkey; this goal was reset at 62 divisions. In May 1955 the force consisted of only 46 ready divisions with a roughly equivalent number of reserve divisions, together with 6,000 planes. In 1957 the tally of ready forces stood at about the same figure.

In such ways did the military components of NATO rise toward a force of considerable strength, but it is easy to see that the original hopes of the United States and the other nations never came to maturity. In Western Germany the United States contributed five battle-ready divisions and the British government contributed four divisions; and this army was the heart of NATO as it appeared in the later 1950's. The West German government, after admission into NATO in 1955, promised twelve divisions, but by 1958 only three were organized and they were much under strength. The French contingent to NATO dwindled rapidly from 1954, when units were sent to fight rebellions in Tunisia and then in Algeria. French troops to the number of 650,000 were in Algeria by 1957, and France's NATO troops were down to two under-strength divisions. The ready strength of NATO had to be reckoned in terms of the Anglo-American troops, the strong Turkish army of twelve divisions, eight Italian divisions, the six divisions of Greece, together with four and a half divisions from the Benelux nations.

The purpose of setting out this military picture in some detail is to point out how Western military strength in Europe leveled off after the Korean War, and to indicate the essential weakness of NATO troops vis-a-vis Russian forces in the later 1950's despite the effort of

the United States to bolster this NATO force. Soviet divisions opposing NATO were estimated at 85 in 1957. In addition there were
70 satellite divisions. Although the reliability of at least some of the
satellite troops was dubious, there could be no question that if a
ground war of the conventional type fought during the second World
War were again to occur in Western Europe, the victory would
quickly go to the Russians. NATO commanders said so, openly.
General Alfred M. Gruenther said in 1956 that NATO was not strong
enough to defend Western Europe. He and his successor, General
Lauris Norstad, counted on holding back the Soviet hordes with
atomic weapons. The NATO troops were a burglar alarm, a trip
wire—that is, if NATO troops should become heavily engaged with
the Russians the pressure would be a signal for the use of tactical
atomic weapons against the Soviet forces. The NATO commanders
spoke in terms of confining such an atomic war to the battlefields,
but many commentators, as will be pointed out in the following
chapter on atomic weapons and diplomacy, believed it impossible to
define such a so-called tactical use of atomic weapons. This disagreement led some individuals to query the usefulness of the NATO
forces, which—so they contended—being unable to do much more
than function as an alarm, might well be dispensed with. There was
a good argument in the notion that either NATO had to be strong
enough to fight without tactical atomic weapons or else had little use.

In connection with the buildup of NATO the new state of West
Germany was able to increase its bargaining power with the Western
Allies by obtaining a grant of full sovereignty on May 5, 1955, ex-
changing as a *quid pro quo* a contribution of German troops to NATO.
The West German government found itself in the enviable position
where both the *quid* and the *quo* were to its advantage, although the
Western powers, especially the United States, felt rewarded by the
German troop contribution. Ten years after the defeat of 1945 a
German government thus received full sovereignty in Europe, a
remarkable event which few individuals would have predicted on
V-E Day. In view of the French preoccupation in the mid-1950's
with a rebellion in Algiers, relatively small German measures of
rearmament were enough to bring to being on the Continent a German army larger than the French.

The issue of Germany's troop contribution to NATO was complicated and is worth some comment, although with passage of time

it has begun to take on the appearance of a detail within the larger scene of diplomacy in Europe and the world. The United States at the beginning of the Korean War was mightily anxious to include a German contingent within NATO, and without much finesse impressed this sentiment upon its NATO Allies. The French were disturbed by this notion of German rearmament within so short a time after the recent troubles, and not unnaturally approached reluctantly and cautiously the business of Germany's inclusion in NATO. In October 1950 the French premier of the moment, René Pleven, pulled a special rabbit out of his hat, the Pleven Plan, which as it had developed by 1952 was called the European Defense Community (EDC). This scheme was readily understandable as a linked expression of French dislike of German rearmament and concession to the obvious need for German troops in NATO. EDC was a compromise by which German contingents would be included within NATO but in a military organization no larger than the divisional level: the divisions of various members of EDC would be mixed together at the corps and army level. This was the chief point of EDC, and there were subsidiary provisions for a joint military budget for the multinational European defense force, the budget to be raised by assessing each member country a share relative to the size of its national income.

EDC commended itself to American diplomats if only because of the need that they felt in 1952 for haste in bringing together a European force to oppose the Red Army. The Americans virtually thrust it upon Pleven's successors until—partly for a reason unconnected with German rearmament, to be mentioned in the next chapter—the French, who had repudiated Pleven, scuttled EDC by a rousing vote in the national assembly in August 1954. This, despite Secretary of State Dulles's famous pronouncement of December 1953 that if EDC did not pass the assembly the United States might have to make an agonized reappraisal of its European commitments.

The Germans soon afterward were admitted to NATO by another stratagem, more involved if really less soothing to French fears of a new German army than had been the case with EDC. The new solution was to refurbish a treaty that had been concluded between Britain, France, and the Benelux countries in 1948: the Brussels Pact alliance known also as Western Union. In its revised form, christened Western European Union or WEU, its original signatories offered membership to West Germany and Italy, which promptly accepted.

WEU was not an organic union like EDC, but an alliance, and it allowed Germany to keep more control over her armed forces than would have been the case under EDC. After joining WEU, West Germany was invited to become a a member of NATO, and all armed forces of WEU were to be subject to the NATO supreme commander, who now was referred to as the Supreme Allied Commander, Europe, or SACEUR. The French assembly approved WEU on December 30, 1954.

One should point out in any discussion of West Germany's entry into NATO that this move had an economic as well as military basis which was well understood by the European powers, especially Great Britain. The trouble was that the Western Germans, with their defense problems taken care of by their erstwhile enemies, had been able prior to 1955 to have a special advantage in competition for foreign markets—the West Germans had no production facilities tied up in military work and could produce goods for export at an advantage over their Western European competitors. The British in particular felt the competition of West Germany during the Korean War boom and after, and when nine per cent of Britain's total national product and fifteen per cent of her metal and two-thirds of her scientific brain power was being consumed in the armament race, this business of German competition was no laughing matter.

Even after the Germans were persuaded to take up the burden of their own defense, Britishers were inclined to point out how the Germans were still the leading war profiteers of Europe. The American army in the latter 1950's was spending so many dollars annually in West Germany that this expenditure helped the West Germans keep ahead nicely in dollar exchange. One British statesman was moved to say plaintively to an American colleague that it might be advisable for Scotland to threaten an attack on England so the English could have a rich American army stationed in their midst.

In the present discussion of Britain and NATO to which we have come in roundabout fashion after discussing the rearmament of Germany, there should be some account of the effect upon NATO, not yet entirely realized, of the British White Paper on Defense which appeared on April 4, 1957. According to newspaper accounts, NATO commanders were staggered by the announcement in the White Paper of drastic cuts in British defense expenditures.

The White Paper, published by the British government during a parliamentary debate over the national budget, proclaimed the defenselessness of the British Isles because of the new atomic weapons and their missile carriers and said that Britain planned to abandon most of her conventional military forces and rely, on the one hand, upon what amounted to little more than local police forces of a conventional sort, and on the other, on atomic and hydrogen bombs. The paper did not envisage an immediate withdrawal of British troops from the Continent, but it was clear from its general tone and some specific recommendations that British troop strength in Europe would be cut sooner or later. The British government in the White Paper announced a reduction of its four-division NATO contingent from 77,000 to 64,000 men, with further reductions to follow. General Norstad, the NATO commander, had been stressing that what strength NATO then possessed was an irreducible minimum if his forces were to provide a defense shield for Western Europe, but the British government, afflicted as a result of the Suez crisis with an alarmingly weak financial condition, decided upon reduction and there was little that General Norstad could do about it.

Some observers felt that Britain, by refusing in the White Paper to consider her NATO contribution as irreducible, was moving toward neutralism in the military competition between the United States and the USSR. The British move, they thought, would encourage similar moves by other NATO governments, most of which were beginning to feel after the Korean War that there was a relaxation of Russian pressure in Europe and that anyway the NATO forces were not of large value. As has been mentioned previously, those forces were too weak to prevent a Russian invasion unless they should use atomic weapons; given the impossibility of tactical use of atomic weapons, the peace of Europe rested upon the balance of terror; NATO forces were therefore a military waste.

The desire of America's allies by the late 1950's to get disentangled from NATO got some support in a notable series of lectures over the BBC in London in the autumn of 1957 by the American historian and former diplomat George Kennan. The adroit Kennan proposed something close to destruction of NATO and made a deep impression upon his British and European listeners. He suggested that the Western powers and Russia conclude a peace treaty over Germany in which the Germans would be allowed to unite their country under treaty guarantee that they would not rearm. This plan would effectively take Germany out of NATO, but the price, Kennan argued, would be worth it. He pointed out that the then American position toward German unification was based on what at first seemed to be the unexceptionable right of Germans to determine their allegiance between East and West and to ally with either side. In actual fact, opportunity to exercise this right meant that a reunified Germany would almost certainly be an ally of the West, for the Germans held no love for the Russians. Since the Russians could never agree to German reunification in the face of such a likelihood, the best way to obtain reunification was to neutralize the country. This program would not merely make the Germans happy and liberate the oppressed East Germans, but it would also remove the entire German problem from world politics including the extremely dangerous and touchy area of Berlin, where Russians and Westerners stood daily at loggerheads. Moreover, it would raise the possibility of a Russian withdrawal militarily from the East European satellites—Premier Wladyslaw Gomulka of Poland had already announced that the moment Russian troops left East Germany he would negotiate for their retirement from Poland. Kennan believed that such a retirement from Poland and even the other more securely controlled satellites might become possible, that the pressures of European opinion would become overwhelming and the Kremlin would have to give in.

The fact that this proposition, whether sound or not, found much approval in Britain and elsewhere was important for American diplomacy. Such a proposal for a neutral Germany, if carried into effect, would abandon the hope that a West German contingent of twelve divisions could be added to NATO. Perhaps it would obviate much of the reason for NATO's existence. Secretary of State Dulles dismissed Kennan with a wisecrack and former Secretary Acheson offered some sharp statements against his erstwhile subordinate. Kennan nonetheless was popular in Britain and other of the NATO countries.

2. *Russian Embarrassments in the 1950's*

One of the most momentous developments for American foreign policy in recent years, an event for which the United States was decidedly not responsible, was the death on March 5, 1953, of Joseph Stalin. The headlines came suddenly. On March 4 they announced:

STALIN GRAVELY ILL AFTER STROKE. On March 5: STALIN SINKING: LEECHES APPLIED. Then on March 6: STALIN DEAD. A grand state funeral took the tyrant to his public tomb—at least for a while his public tomb—alongside the body of the great Lenin, and there were muffled reports that Stalin had been quietly eliminated by his associates in the Kremlin. The world turned to the more important speculation of how the leader's decease would affect Russian foreign policy. That it would, no one doubted.

The first trouble for the successors came when they loosened some of the rigorous controls over the Russian and satellite peoples that had marked the last years of the old dictator. Even a small measure of freedom was dangerous, and this small measure led to an uprising in East Berlin in June 1953 that spread throughout Eastern Germany. In the Stalin Allee, the grand avenue of East Berlin that was to be the showplace of the workers' paradise, some German construction workers quit their jobs in protest over an increase of their work requirements, their so-called norms, and paraded down the street, calling upon other workers to join them. The parade turned into a riot and then a demonstration of almost the entire populace of East Berlin against the Russians. Tanks belonging to the Russian army in Berlin were attacked by workers with stones and paving bricks. The officials of the East German government, in a state of mind close to terror, pleaded with their fellow countrymen to go back to work. The revolt spread to other cities in East Germany; there were mass meetings throughout West Berlin and the cities of West Germany; and the riots did not subside until Soviet troops broke up the demonstration and until it was certain that there would be no armed assistance from the Western-occupied part of Germany. Clearly, these events showed that Russian rule of the East Germans after eight long years had been unsuccessful; that the young men and women of the East zone of Germany who had been painstakingly indoctrinated with communism were the first to throw it over; that probably the East-zone military units being organized and trained by the Russians would be extremely unreliable adjuncts of any Soviet army invading the West.

The East German revolt of 1953, if unsuccessful for the Germans, at least gave Western observers reason to feel heartened. There was no question but that the cause of the West was looking up in the hitherto supposedly lost areas behind the Iron Curtain.

If the German revolt stemmed from relaxation of Stalinist bonds, from encouraged hopes that were not gratified quickly enough by the East German and Soviet authorities, then the new leaders of the USSR faced some large problems within their domain and would have to reimpose Stalinist severity if they were to have any chance of keeping the lid down on their restive subjects. But three years later on February 24–25, 1956, the Russian leader Nikita S. Khrushchev (for reasons as yet not altogether divined in the West) denounced his former master Stalin to a secret gathering of the Twentieth Congress of the Soviet Communist Party in Moscow. This speech, soon leaked and since famous, gave new hope and led to new revolts of the East European peoples. Some eight months later Moscow's two satellites, Poland and Hungary, were in open revolt, and the Poles by a combination of good fortune and discretion managed to obtain from the Russians a large measure of freedom. The Hungarians went too far with their revolution and brought about a communist terror and reimposition of the communist puppet government by force of Russian arms. The Khrushchev speech, coupled with some relaxation of secret-police measures in the satellites, appears to have had this remarkable effect.

The speech of Khrushchev in early 1956 constituted one of the most important documents of the twentieth century. It was leaked to the West apparently by officials of the Polish government, and the Department of State in Washington became Khrushchev's publisher when it released the text in April 1956. The speech well rewarded close reading and was published in book form by the Columbia University Press. In this impassioned address, punctuated by frequent and tumultuous applause and other sounds of approval or astonishment throughout the great hall in Moscow, Khrushchev set down many, though presumably not all, of his former chief's delinquencies. It turned out that Stalin was enormously vain, given to faking his own biography both by claiming authorship of books he did not write and by interpolating whole sections favorable to himself and his genius. He was enormously suspicious, and even came to believe that one of his oldest associates, Klementi Voroshilov, was an English agent—he had microphones planted in Voroshilov's house. Stalin was enormously jealous of his military achievements and during the war was accustomed to sit in his office tracing the front lines on a globe. He lost his composure when the Germans pressed close to

Moscow in 1941 and for days was unable to take hold of his government duties. But more important than these delinquencies were his hatreds and deceits; he personally sent thousands of innocent people to their deaths in the latter 1930's and by his example led to purging and liquidation of hundreds of thousands and perhaps millions of Russians. As late as 1951 Stalin arranged the execution of a member of the politburo, Nikolai Voznesensky. Khrushchev disclosed that the politburo had little power of decision itself and in fact had operated in the late Stalin years mostly in fragmented committees—quartets, quintets, septets, etc.

The cult of the individual, the impassioned Khrushchev declaimed, had to be destroyed, and if he did not tell all the evils of Stalinism, he told enough. His sincerity was obvious enough to give his speech the ring of truth. His revelations shook the communist parties in all the nations of the world and led to personal reassessments of the sort that had occurred in 1939 when Stalin had taken Russia temporarily, via the Nazi-Soviet Pact, into the camp of the Germans.

Beyond question this speech was important and appears to have led traceably to the outbreaks in Hungary and Poland in October 1956, two of the largest troubles encountered by the USSR in recent years.

A history of American diplomacy is no place to set down these internal developments of Soviet government and politics in their full details, but because the two revolts of 1956 did have meaning for Russian strength—or weakness—in Eastern Europe and because this obvious weakness in satellite territories subtracted markedly from Russian military strength and political prestige, it deserves recounting in its general outline.

The Polish revolt was the more interesting because it was successful and presented a model for other satellites seeking independence. The Poles, it should be noted, had managed to preserve some independence during their years under communism. Poland had never been completely in the hands of the Stalinists and even the Polish Stalinist leader Boleslaw Bierut appears to have advised subordinates against too draconian measures in his country. When after Stalin's death the word came down from Moscow that destalinization was the order of the day, the Poles could argue that their quiet opposition had been politically correct. Then in the summer of 1956 came riots in Poznan by workers who had tired of their exploitation for the Soviet Union. These riots had been observed by Westerners who were in Poznan visiting an international fair and hence were fit subject for advice from Moscow, but the rioters were in fact treated gingerly by the Polish Communist Party and were let off without much chastisement after surprisingly fair trials. The Poznan riots and their careful settlement, as events turned out, were a straw in the wind giving indication of larger developments, in the course of which Wladyslaw Gomulka moved from the status of a disgraced and imprisoned former functionary to become chief of the Communist Party in Poland.

Gomulka appears to have been a shrewd operator. Having recently experienced the rigors of a Polish communist prison, he was guided by caution and a sense of what might happen to him and his collaborators in event their plans failed. He managed to marshal behind his leadership the support of the Polish people and with this he set out to follow his own course. On October 19 when he was suddenly confronted in Warsaw with an august Moscow delegation consisting of Khrushchev, Molotov, Mikoyan, and the politburo member Lazar Kaganovich, he threatened an armed uprising against any Soviet-inspired military coup. Khrushchev at this point backed down, realizing that it was better to have a national communist in charge of Poland than start a civil war between Russian and Polish communists, to the ruin of Soviet prestige throughout the world. Gomulka on his own side was careful to prevent excesses by Polish patriots anxious to abandon not merely the Russian tie but communism as well. He seems to have realized that the hope of his leadership, the opportunity for achieving Poland's national independence, lay in the foundation of a Titoist regime, a government modeled on that of Marshal Tito of Yugoslavia, who had managed through control of his army and party apparatus to maintain independence against Moscow. Tito had come to power in Yugoslavia with communist help during the second World War. Although himself a Moscow-trained communist, he was too spirited a person to be a Moscow puppet, and gathering about him the patriotism of the Yugoslav people he had cut loose from Russian direction in 1948. By adroit maneuvering—obtaining economic assistance from both West and East, but especially from the West—Tito had managed to create and maintain an independent communist government. The example of Yugoslavia lay at hand, and Gomulka seized it. He moved carefully but surely. He was willing to break up premature strikes by Polish students, and dispersed a student demonstration on October 22, 1956. In this uneasy position, halfway between two worlds, the Polish leader managed to gain control over his country.

Whether the compromise in Poland could last was a problem for the future, and probably no one, not excepting Gomulka the liberator (?), could look far into it. The Poles may have learned after the disheartening fortunes of their national existence since 1918 that only through care and caution in their present position could they make their national way. Poland's military situation had always been difficult, for the nation lay exposed on the north European plain between Russia and Germany. It possessed no natural defenses. Its population was too small to oppose either of its larger neighbors. Moreover, when Gomulka took charge of the country and defied the Russian leaders, although in a fairly tactful way, the Polish economy was in difficult straits. He would have to solve economic and political problems at the same time, hoping for continued co-operation from his countrymen, which in the twentieth century few Polish leaders had ever obtained.

The outburst in October in Budapest was a different affair from its beginning, for the Hungarians found no resting-place between satellite and independent status. The communist leader Imre Nagy sought, as had Gomulka, to hold his countrymen from excess, but students and army officers leading the revolt found themselves on an irresistible popular wave; communists were turned out of power, many were pursued and killed; Cardinal Joseph Mindszenty, Roman Catholic primate of Hungary, entered Budapest in triumph to the ringing of all the city's church bells broadcast for the world to hear. This was too much for the Russians, already humiliated by the triumph of national communism in Poland, and after some initial confusions it became clear that the revolt in Hungary would be snuffed out. It was. The Soviet army feigned a withdrawal from Budapest on October 30 but on November 4 reappeared and, city block by city block, reconquered the city from its own people.

The deaths of the rebels could not obliterate the meaning of their country's revolt—that in Hungary as in Poland communism had been rejected, however firmly imposed; that despite a decade or more of indoctrination the youth of satellite nations was unwilling to forgo nationalism for communism.

3. *The Suez Crisis*

The Suez crisis occurred at the same time as these Russian troubles in Eastern Europe, a moment which could not have been better so far as the Soviets were concerned. The Suez fiasco in the Middle East showed the disunity of the Western Allies in a most glaring way and drew the world's attention from Russia's defeat in Poland and Russia's grisly triumph over the revolution in Hungary.

This 1956 crisis over the Suez had been long in preparation and it might be well to look back into its origins, for only in its historical context can it be understood.

Here one could write in long detail of the background of British and French policy in the Middle East and such detail would be entirely relevant although too extensive for inclusion in the present account. French interest in the Middle East went back to the nineteenth century, when the French government acted as protector of the Christians in Lebanon against the Turks. British interests likewise reached back into the nineteenth century: Benjamin Disraeli in 1875 had managed the purchase of the khedive of Egypt's 44 per cent share in the Suez Canal Company; the British had bombarded and subdued Alexandria in 1882 and had maintained a temporary occupation of Egypt for forty years, until 1922. In that year Britain unilaterally terminated the protectorate, leaving details for future negotiation, which were finally settled in an Anglo-Egyptian treaty of 1936. Meanwhile the British and French during the first World War had managed by military action against the Turks to become heirs to the Middle Eastern fragments of the former Turkish empire. The two European powers secured their new hegemony by mandates from the League of Nations and during the 1920's and 1930's it was the word from London or Paris that came down to the Middle Eastern capitals and made or unmade prime ministers and chiefs of staff. During the second World War large bodies of Allied troops maintained peace in the area and only in 1945 and thereafter did a new basis of government become possible.

The new regimes, as they set themselves up with their grants of freedom from Britain and France after the second World War, were in many ways shadow governments, tribal arrangements that had little relation to the geographical realities of the Middle East, and it has often been pointed out that such cartographical monstrosities as Iraq, Jordan, or Syria could not have expected to continue indefinitely in their original shapes. In the early years after 1945, everyone hoped against hope that the Middle East would remain quiet or semi-quiet while the greater problems of Europe and Asia were attended to. The appearance of the State of Israel in 1948, when the British abandoned the Palestine mandate, did not represent any large calculation by Western statesmen; the hasty recognition of the new state by the United States within eleven minutes was a reflection of domestic American politics more than anything else. Few Americans or citizens of Britain and France had time to give much thought to the Middle East in that hectic year 1948, the year of the Marshall Plan's first operations, of the Berlin blockade, and of communist successes in China. That area of the world rattled along, so to speak, and the new nations of the Middle East went their new ways with apparent stability and little attention. In the year 1950 Britain, France, and the United States concluded a Tripartite Declaration under which they promised, among other things, to prevent any border changes by the Arab states or Israel: "The three Governments, should they find that any of these States was preparing to violate frontiers or armistice lines, would, consistent with their obligations as members of the United Nations, immediately take action, both within and outside the United Nations, to prevent such violation." Although this part of the declaration proved later to be a dead letter, another part provided for a virtual arms embargo, a careful measuring of requests for arms by the Arab nations or Israel, so that there would be no arms competition by these small nations. In such fashion everything continued in fairly good order until February 1955, when Israeli troops, in retaliation for border incidents by the Egyptians, made a large raid against Egyptian army forces in the so-called Gaza Strip area adjoining Israel. Thereupon, the Egyptian government under its new nationalist leader Gamal Abdel Nasser announced negotiation in September 1955 of an arms deal with Russia and Czechoslovakia. This was the thin entering wedge for serious trouble.

There had been troubles even before 1955. The prime minister of Iran, Dr. Mohammed Mossadegh, had precipitously nationalized the Anglo-Iranian Oil Company in 1951 and raised a large row with Great Britain. But eventually things came back under control in Iran, the shah abdicating in August 1953, then returning and appointing

THE MIDDLE EAST

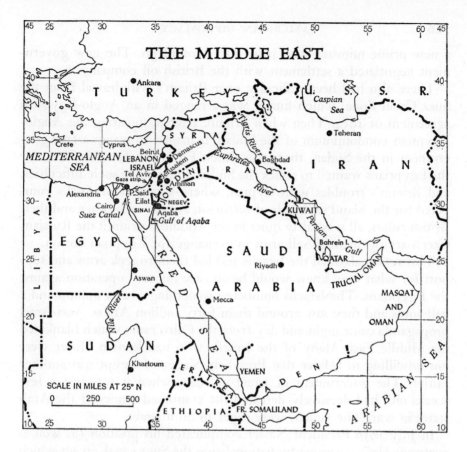

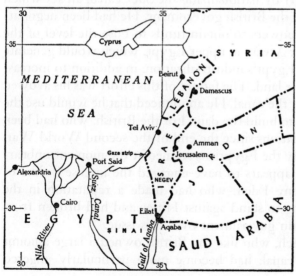

a new prime minister who jailed Dr. Mossadegh. The new government negotiated a settlement with the British oil company.

There also had been difficulty over Britain's withdrawal from the Suez Canal Zone, which finally was arranged in an Anglo-Egyptian agreement of 1954. Then when Britain, after terminating the Anglo-Egyptian condominium of the Sudan, managed to set up a free government in the Sudan, there was much Egyptian dissatisfaction, for the Egyptians wanted to annex the Sudan. Other than such difficulties, and Britain's troubles with Cyprus, where Greeks and Turks competed for the island with acts of terrorism against each other and their British rulers, all was fairly quiet in the Middle East until the Russian-Czech arrangement to sell arms in exchange for Egyptian cotton.

This action alarmed the Israelis and led them to seek arms and support for what they knew would be an easy military operation against the Egyptians. The Israelis numbered something over a million and a half souls and they saw around them forty million Arabs. Anti-Israel propaganda came night and day from the Cairo radio which blanketed the Middle East. Many of the Israelis who had known Hitler were not unwilling to believe that President Nasser of Egypt was another Hitler. The government of Israel in 1948, when it was just a few weeks old, had decisively defeated the combined armies of the Arab states in war. The Israelis were eager to do it again.

In July 1956 President Nasser complicated his position (as well as everyone else's position) by nationalizing the Suez canal, an act which won him the enmity of the British government. He had been negotiating with the Western powers to obtain funds to raise the level of the Nile by a higher dam at Aswan in upper Egypt, which would generate electricity to promote Egypt's industrialization, in addition to increasing the area of cultivable land. The failure of this effort was his avowed reason for nationalizing the canal. He announced that he would use the income from the canal to build the dam. For the British, who had been treated to many humiliations since the end of the second World War, to be thus humiliated by the Egyptians seemed at the moment unbearable. President Nasser appears to have engaged the intense dislike of Prime Minister Anthony Eden, who had made a reputation in the 1930's for being willing to stand against Hitler and had broken from the Neville Chamberlain government over this issue.

Meanwhile the French, who like the British owned a large amount of stock in the Suez canal, had become more particularly angered at Egypt because of the Egyptians' support for the rebels in Algeria.

The makings of trouble were thus at hand and there followed in the summer of 1956 something that may only be described as an intrigue, apparently first between the Israelis who wished to have a whack at Nasser, and the French who were angry because of smuggling of arms to Algiers, and lastly the British.

In retrospect one can see that the military operations of early November could have been handled by the forces of Israel alone, which in a brilliant little campaign of a few days, between October 29 and November 2, 1956, finished off all Egyptian troops in the Sinai peninsula and could easily have cut straight to Cairo and taken all Egypt if they had not been stopped by the intervention—possibly without Israeli knowledge—of Britain and France. The two Western powers gave both the Israelis and Egyptians an ultimatum on October 30 that they refrain from military operations within ten miles of the canal, which allowed the Israelis to occupy a hundred miles of Egyptian territory. When the Egyptians ignored the ultimatum, the British and French brought their forces into the canal area, shelled and occupied Port Said. The Egyptians blocked the canal with wrecks. There followed a diplomatic, military, and economic impasse at Suez until the United Nations at the instance of Canada created a UN Emergency Force, UNEF, which beginning in mid-November arrived in the Middle East and by Christmas 1956 had replaced the British and French, with the Israelis retreating to their home base.

In the course and sequels of this complex crisis the United States joined with Russia in opposing Britain and France, the Russians threatened to shoot missiles into the Western capitals and to send "volunteers"—that is, troops—to the Middle East; the United States said that volunteers meant war, the Egyptians in effect held the blocked canal as a hostage, there was sabotage of the Iraq oil pipeline through Syria, the British pound sterling came within an ace of devaluation, two British cabinet ministers resigned, there was indication that India and Pakistan might withdraw from the Commonwealth and join forces with a new international African-Arab-Asian bloc; the United States and especially Secretary of State Dulles received an exceedingly bad press in Britain and France, the Israelis were angry because they lost their chance to destroy Nasser; Nasser rose in stature to be the most powerful and attractive of all the Arab leaders,

Prime Minister Eden lost the Nobel Peace Prize for which before the Suez operation he had been a candidate, went to Jamaica for three weeks to recuperate from what could not have been a more maladroit piece of diplomacy, and not long afterward relinquished the seals of his office to Sir Harold Macmillan.

The lesson of Suez was plain for everyone to read: use of armed force by the Western powers could no longer secure their interests in the Middle East. As Guy Wint and Peter Calvocoressi have written in their excellent little book, *Middle East Crisis:* "The fundamental British error has been to persist too long in a policy that has been overtaken by events. . . . The alternative to staying is going away. In 1947 the British left India lock, stock, and barrel. . . . Withdrawal may be repugnant and is certainly risky, but once the facts dictate it, it needs to be made sharply. Failure to realize this in the Middle East led to . . . an achievement for which it would be hard to find a parallel in the history of British diplomacy."

British and French prestige had vanished from the Middle East. Arab resentment was for a moment deflected from the United States because of the undeniably firm American stand against the Suez venture of its Allies. But the Americans were susceptible to the same illusions as the British and French, and two years later, in a not exactly analogous situation, they also made a show of armed force in the Middle East and focused upon themselves the hostility of the Arab world.

4. *The Lebanon and Iraq Crisis of 1958*

The crisis of 1958, like that of two years before, represented a move by the West—this time the United States—to stop by force the power of Arab nationalism. In 1957 after the Suez fiasco, the two Arab states of Egypt and Syria formed a union, turning themselves into a United Arab Republic under the presidency of Gamal Abdel Nasser. The small sheikdom of Yemen allied itself with this new combine. Nasser set out to unite the entire Middle East by feeding the fires of Arab nationalism. He could thus inspire internal revolts in Arab countries, promote their union with the United Arab Republic, and nationalize the oil-producing properties. If successful, he would have not merely a more powerful position from which to confront the Western Allies and also Soviet Russia, but he could help solve the internal problems of Egypt and some of the other poorer Arab states by obtaining control over the oil revenues of the region. By nationalizing the canal in 1956 he had taken control of the most important means of transport, and this move had not yet been offset by Western construction of large oil tankers which could profitably make the run around South Africa. This all made sense from a Middle Eastern point of view, and the only courses open to the West were either to retire from the area or come to an accommodation with the United Arab Republic, or, and this was a poor alternative, to seek alliance with the few anti-Nasser leaders in the Middle East who still had some control over their governments. This latter course, which was the one taken by the West, meant Western military support to the regimes in Jordan and Iraq and Lebanon.

The government of Premier Nuri es-Said in Iraq, with its seat in Baghdad, had long been as pro-Western as Nuri could make it and at the same time retain power, and so Iraq became the foundation of this Western policy. Iraq in February 1955 had made an alliance with Turkey, the Baghdad Pact, and the two nations had then been joined by Pakistan and Iran and Great Britain. The purpose of this alliance was to form a group with NATO in Europe, SEATO in the Far East, and the Rio Pact allies in the Western Hemisphere. On paper these various regional alliances against communism looked impressive; unfortunately, the Baghdad Pact was a fragile creation because it pivoted on the government of Nuri es-Said in Iraq. This government was doing its best after Suez to contain what the West was beginning to call Nasserism in the Middle East, but this undertaking was difficult when the enthusiasm for Arab unity was running so high, fanned day after day as the Cairo radio talked of a united Arab people. Abruptly, on July 14, 1958, a revolt erupted in Baghdad, led by the Iraqi army. Troops occupied the capital in the early morning and King Feisal, of Iraq, his uncle, the crown prince Abdel Illah, and Premier Nuri es-Said were all murdered. The new army "republican" government was at once recognized by President Nasser's United Arab Republic, the Baghdad Pact seemed to cave in and the position of the West in the Middle East looked insecure in the extreme.

The Eisenhower administration at once moved to ensure the independence of Lebanon, threatened also with Nasserism. Before the nationalist coup in Iraq there had been a civil war in Lebanon, a confused struggle of political factions embittered by a Christian-Arab antagonism, the pro-Nasser and anti-Nasser feeling of the Lebanese, and a general division of the tiny country between its westernized city dwellers in Beirut and the inhabitants of the small towns and the hill areas. After the murders in Baghdad the pro-Western president of Lebanon, Camille Chamoun, a Maronite Christian, asked for immediate military support from the United States. President Eisenhower sent American marines into Lebanon. The forces of protection, welcomed enthusiastically by President Chamoun, soon numbered 14,000, almost equivalent to an army division. They landed under protection of the United States Sixth Fleet, much in evidence in the Mediterranean at this time, whose publicity officers announced that it was ready for all eventualities.

Simultaneously British troops, crossing Israeli territory en route, were flown from Cyprus to Amman, the capital of Jordan, where the anti-Nasser leader King Hussein was in dire straits with a near-bankrupt treasury, an unreliable army, the example of Iraq, and a noisy pro-Nasser sentiment among his citizenry. These troops, to the number of 3,000, were received by Hussein, who had asked for them, and were stationed at the airport at Amman, presumably to protect the Jordanian capital in event of revolution.

Here, then, was a new move by force into the Middle East, with American and British troops instead of British and French. It was a dangerous move, considering the force of Arab nationalism and the willingness of the Soviet Union to pose as the friend of the Arabs. Newspapers in the United States proclaimed a time of crisis and peril. In the days after the Iraq revolution and the British and American military moves, there was a heated verbal exchange between the West and Soviet Russia, with Khrushchev indulging hints of open warfare, branding the Americans as fascist aggressors and enemies of the Arab people. President Nasser spoke out strongly against the United States. President Eisenhower in a statement after the marines entered Lebanon said that they were going there to protect the little country against communism and the terroristic tactics of the president of the United Arab Republic. During the remainder of July and through August, the controversy wore on, with proposals by Khrushchev of another summit meeting and counterproposals by Eisenhower and Prime Minister Macmillan and talk of what the UN could do or should do. By the end of the summer a new regime took office in Lebanon under the Lebanese army commander Fuad Chehab. The fate of Jordan was unclear, although the United States and Britain engaged in a frantic operation to bring in oil and other supplies to bolster its economy and secure Hussein against Nasser.

It was no easy matter for the Americans to decide what to do about the Middle East, after the measures of the summer of 1958. Americans had the distinct feeling that short of Russian invasion of the area, with all that could mean for the extension of communism into Africa and Asia, there was no national interest of the United States in the Middle East that was worth a war.

The United States, as became clear during the Lebanon and Iraq crisis, had two hostages to fortune in the Middle East: oil and the State of Israel. For the moment the problem of Israel was not pressing and hence was largely a theoretical matter. Israel at the moment was strong enough militarily to resist all the Arabs in combination. But if Arab nationalism were to invigorate the armies of the Arab states and make them a little more efficient, Israel would be in serious trouble and what would the American government do?

The problem of oil was more pressing (even with the United States still by far the world's largest producer), for Europe vitally needed the oil of the Middle East, without which its economy would collapse. And the United States vitally needed Europe. Only if the United States were willing drastically to cut down its own domestic oil requirements, probably moving the majority of Americans' cars off the highways, could enough oil come from the Western Hemisphere to care for Europe and make the Western Allies secure against Middle Eastern oil blackmail.

It appeared that the best course for American diplomacy in the Middle East was to re-examine carefully the extent of American interests in the area, and to design a policy to fit those interests. This course would require examination of the oil contracts by American and other Western companies with the Middle Eastern governments. It would probably also involve an honest bargaining over the contracts between the West and the Arab nationalists, with willingness to do business even under nationalization so long as the terms were fair, but with determination to pull out and to refuse to buy Middle Eastern oil if the terms were unfair. In pursuit of this course, the United States would necessarily take an interest in spreading oil revenues from the "have" nations such as Iraq and Saudi Arabia and the little tribal sheikdom of Kuwait (170,000 people; one-seventh of the world's known oil reserves) to the "have-not" nations of Egypt, Syria, Jordan, and Lebanon. This course would also mean an open discussion diplomatically of the problem of Israel, which since the Arab military defeats of 1948 had appeared in Arab eyes as the second largest problem in the Middle East, next only to the "colonial" schemes of the United States, Britain, and France. In this regard it would be essential somehow for Western statesmen to convince both the Israelis and the Arabs that the two peoples could live together, to their mutual benefit, and "living together" would mean some arrangement by the Israelis to settle the status of the Arabs who during establishment of Israel had left the country. These Arabs, from 500,000 to 600,000 in number, were one of the reservoirs of hatred and fanaticism in the Middle East, and the United Nations Relief and Works Agency was spending $30,000,000 annually to feed them and the 450,000 Arabs in the part of Palestine annexed by Jordan at the time of the 1948 armistice. An accommodation on such matters as the above would have to be arrived at. An imaginative American diplomacy could accomplish it.

President Eisenhower in 1957 obtained congressional approval of a resolution which became known as the Eisenhower Doctrine, expressing the determination of the United States to use its armed forces in behalf of any Middle Eastern state which requested "aid against overt armed aggression from any nation controlled by international communism." Accompanying this new doctrine was a crash program of economic assistance totaling $200,000,000. Inspired by the Lebanon and Iraq crisis, the president in August 1958 spoke before the UN and offered a plan for economic development in the area. Whether these measures were well thought out, whether they reached to the root of Middle Eastern troubles, was difficult to say. At least they were efforts, and the latter two—the economic plans—seemed to be moving in the right direction.

Toward the end of the 1950's, events had come a long way since the beginning of the decade when the United States was largely ignoring the Middle East and bolstering NATO in anticipation of a Soviet attack in Western Europe. It was easy in the fall of 1958 to believe that American-Russian relations had come no closer to solution. But if one looked at the state of the world at that later time he saw that there was a fairly stable situation in Europe and likewise in Asia, and that if in the Middle East there was trouble and the United States was embarrassing itself *à la* Suez in Lebanon and Jordan, still the Middle East troubles were far more susceptible to settlement than had been those of the Far East and Europe. If successes had occurred in these latter places, an intelligent diplomacy might achieve peace in the Middle East.

ADDITIONAL READING

General views of American life and national and international policy in the years since 1945 are Eric F. Goldman, *The Crucial Decade* (New York, 1956) and Herbert Agar, *The Price of Power* (Chicago, 1957). See also David M. Potter, *People of Plenty* (Chicago, 1954), which puts its finger on one of the prime factors in American life today. George Kennan has given his interpretation of foreign policy in a small volume, *Realities of American Foreign Policy* (Princeton, 1954). Kennan's *American Diplomacy* (Chicago, 1951; available in paperback) is a short and most interesting view of American policy since 1900. More controversial were his Reith lectures of 1957, *Russia, the Atom, and the West* (New York, 1958). Robert E. Osgood's *Ideals and Self-Interest in America's Foreign Relations: The Great Transformation of the Twentieth Century* (Chicago, 1953); and Alexander DeConde, ed., *Isolation and Collective Security* (Durham, N.C., 1957) seek to explain the forces behind American foreign policy today. Especially worth attention is the short essay by Dexter Perkins, "American Foreign Policy and its Critics," in Alfred H. Kelly, ed., *American Foreign Policy and American Democracy* (Detroit, 1954), pp. 65–88; although Perkins deals here with the sometimes hypercritical commentaries of Kennan and also Hans Morgenthau of the University of Chicago, his remarks have their own sharply intelligent point of view. See also Perkins's *The American Approach to Foreign Policy* (Cambridge, Mass., 1952).

For year-to-year detail of American foreign relations in recent times an excellent source is the annual *United States in World Affairs*, compiled by the staff of the Council on Foreign Relations.

For biographical accounts of President Eisenhower and Secretary Dulles, see Robert J. Donovan, *Eisenhower: The Inside Story* (New York, 1956); Merlo J. Pusey, *Eisenhower, the President* (New York, 1956); and John Robinson Beal, *John Foster Dulles* (New York, 1957). The latter book created a furor because it purported to record conversations in which the secretary of state acknowledged having gone to the brink of war in pursuing America's diplomatic aims.

Turning to the general subject of Europe, Theodore White in *Fire in the Ashes: Europe in Mid-Century* (New York, 1953), shows with the brilliant writing one expects of this reporter that there is the spark of life in Europe and that the prophets of gloom and doom who surveyed Europe at the end of the second World War were mistaken. Blair Bolles, *The Big Change in Europe* (New York, 1958) brings the subject of White's volume up to date. A reliable and readable survey of Europe and the world at mid-century is Hans W. Gatzke, *Present in Perspective* (Chicago, 1957; paperback).

As for American diplomacy toward Europe, the first-magnitude subject of NATO is dealt with by Lawrence S. Kaplan, "NATO and Its Commentators: The First Five Years," *International Organization*, vol. 8 (1954), 447–467, an excellent bibliographical survey; Massimo Salvadori, *NATO* (Princeton, 1957); together with the recent and authoritative volume by Ben T. Moore, *NATO and the Future of Europe* (New York, 1958). For Britain, an instructive article is Alastair Buchan, "Mr. Macmillan Charts a Course," *The Reporter*, Feb. 21, 1957, pp. 26–28. A recent and controversial account of France is Herbert Luethy, *France Against Herself* (New York, 1955; available in paperback), an effort to analyze what is wrong politically with Frenchmen. Herbert L. Matthews, *The Yoke and the Arrows: A Report on Spain* (New York, 1957) is hostile to the Franco regime, and should be read by anyone concerned for the fate of about $1,000,000,000 that the United States by 1958 had spent or would soon spend for air bases and other projects in Spain. Henry Wallich surveys the *Mainsprings of the German Revival* (New Haven, 1955), offering an economist's explanation for what happened during the years after Hitler. See also Eugene Davidson's excellent *The Death and Life of Germany* (in press).

For the United States and Russia there is Harrison E. Salisbury, *American in Russia* (New York, 1955); Henry L. Roberts, *Russia and America: Dangers and Prospects* (New York, 1956; available in paperback); and C. L. Sulzberger, *The Big Thaw* (New York, 1956). Interesting documents appear in *The Anti-Stalin Campaign and International Communism* (New York, 1957), Khrushchev's speech and the responses of communist leaders and organs in other nations; Paul E. Zinner, ed., *National Communism and Popular Revolt in Eastern Europe: A Selection of Documents on Events in Poland and Hungary, February–November 1956* (New York, 1957); and *Report of the Special Committee on the Problem of Hungary* (New York, 1957), the official, factual report on the Hungarian revolution submitted to the United Nations General Assembly.

Turning to the Middle East, there is M. A. Fitzsimons, "The Suez Crisis and the Containment Policy," *Review of Politics*, vol. 19 (1957), 419–445; and Guy Wint and Peter Calvocoressi, *Middle East Crisis* (London, 1957, paperback). For American policy see John C. Campbell, *Defense of the Middle East* (New York, 1957). For local color, camels and all, consult Carleton S. Coon, *Caravan: The Story of the Middle East* (New York, 1951); T. Cuyler Young, ed., *Near Eastern Culture and Society* (Princeton, 1951); Khalil Totah, *Dynamite in the Middle East* (New York, 1955); D. Van der Meulen, *The Wells of Ibn Saud* (New York, 1957); James Morris, *Sultan in Oman* (New York, 1957), and *Islam Inflamed* (New York, 1957); and Sir John Bagot Glubb, *A Soldier with the Arabs* (New York, 1958).

CHAPTER

☆ 21 ☆

The Diplomatic Revolution: The New Weapons and Diplomacy

Until recent years the art of diplomacy, it is fair to say, has rested on the possibility of war. From time out of mind, diplomats have proceeded on the assumption that should their missions fail, should the nations to which they are accredited prove contentious rather than peaceful, there was always the recourse of war. Often this possibility, intimated in a veiled and delicate diplomatic hint, was sufficient to bring intransigent nations around to the point of sweet reasonableness. There have been many historic occasions when hints of war, backed by undoubted willingness and ability to wage war if necessary, have settled international disputes. The historian can say with confidence that if the possibility of war had suddenly been removed from the diplomatic arena, the result would have been virtually a revolution in the conduct of diplomacy.

This possibility has in truth been removed in the years since 1945, for invention of the atomic bomb has made war so unbearably destructive that none of the possessors of atomic weapons has been willing to open hostilities on a large scale.

International hatreds today are as implacable as any since the beginning of the modern era, since the renaissance and reformation at the end of the middle ages. Yet there is no war. The intense reluctance of the powers to engage in war, their continuing refusal to submit their rivalries to what our nineteenth-century ancestors were wont to describe as the arbitrament of the sword, is the fundamental diplomatic fact of our time. Nuclear war has become, in the words of former Secretary of State Dean Acheson, "the brooding omnipresence, under the shadow of which the nation-states impinge on one another." The technical feasibility of nuclear war, the insufferable human consequences of a nuclear Armageddon, has shifted the foundations of diplomacy and caused a diplomatic revolution.

In the years after 1945 the great powers have tried to adapt their thinking and talking to the new picture of power and politics in the world. During the years of American atomic monopoly, from 1945 to 1949, Soviet Russian diplomats felt keenly their country's lack of atomic weapons and apparently chose to adopt as a kind of defense mechanism a provocative verbiage, a ferocity of language previously unknown in diplomatic intercourse. Russian diplomatic talk continued its sharpness for a few years after 1949 when there was atomic inferiority. It is true that from the time of the Russian revolution of 1917 negotiation with the Soviets had usually lacked the amenities and *politesse* traditional to diplomacy, but in the post-1945 years there was a new virulence in the language of Russian negotiators caused in part by embarrassments of the atomic arms race.

As for American diplomats in the post-1945 era, they talked in the accustomed politeness of diplomacy, but sometimes gave a tone to their negotiation that carried reminder of the existence, in American possession, of a weapon of unprecedented strength. Diplomats of the United States, realizing that for several years after the end of the war their country possessed little military strength from which to negotiate, other than the bomb, were forced to remind their opponents on occasion of the existence of this special ace in the hole.

As for the allies of the United States (among whom only Great Britain had the bomb and she not until 1952) they betrayed what might for lack of a better phrase be described as psychological insecurity. America's allies, especially Britain, felt that they were too close to the seat of Russian power, too exposed to quick Russian retaliation, to play as forthright a role in diplomacy as the Americans, and they resented the veiled remarks by diplomats of the United States that the USA possessed a powerful bomb which it would if necessary use. This reluctance by weak allies to follow the American diplomatic lead became apparent in the years after 1949 when the

Russians were building bombs. "No annihilation without representation" was the plea of the British and French.

Such has been the behavior of diplomacy in the shadow of the atomic bomb. The new weapons have brought a diplomatic revolution. Today there is considerable reluctance to engage in full-scale warfare. On the Russian side there seems to be understanding that in an atomic war the gains of a quarter-century of slow, painful, immensely costly five-year plans could disappear in radioactive dust. On the American side there now is understanding that to send the planes of the Strategic Air Command (SAC) to Russia would mean Soviet retaliation on cities and industrial centers in the United States, assuming that the Soviet air force were not destroyed by our strike. And there is fear that Russian attack on the United States might be more effective than American attack on Russia. The United States has 168 metropolitan areas with more than 50,000 inhabitants, and their location is well known. Russia has considerably fewer such areas of concentration of industry and people. The Americans for many years have published detailed maps of their country, freely available to all comers at the corner gas station. The Russians have never been so obliging. Target selection in Russia would be much more difficult than in the United States. Of course, if SAC simply went after industrial targets and cities (in air-force language, "bombing by the telephone book," that is, by sheer population), the task of selection would not be too difficult.

This armament situation brings up another aspect of the diplomatic revolution: a strong admixture of military knowledge has become essential to the work of every high-level American diplomat. The diplomat is virtually a soldier. Gone are the days when American diplomats could remain ignorant of the military capabilities of their country, when they could make diplomatic statements without the slightest military calculation, secure in the knowledge that three thousand miles of Atlantic and five thousand miles of Pacific would shield their country during the months or years necessary to build an adequate war machine. American diplomacy since 1945 should have operated as never before from close knowledge of American military capacity. Any diplomacy that neglected military considerations lived in unreality. Diplomats in the mid-twentieth century had to become military strategists. And are the requirements of this role too much for diplomacy? Has not the diplomat become a sort of latter-day dinosaur, stranded by the rush of historical events, unable because of the enormous complexity of military affairs to make his way in the new situation?

Existence of the new weapons, and the weakness of defense, had a profound effect upon the course of American diplomacy in the years after the second World War. It was in this era of the diplomatic revolution that the United States had to confront the problem of Soviet power, a power which represented, to use the phrase of George F. Kennan, "the greatest test of statesmanship that our country ever faced." American-Russian tensions had to be dealt with in the tricky and treacherous era of atomic power. In happier times, when requirements upon diplomats were far less heavy, the Russian problem would have been difficult enough, but its solution in a climate of thought surcharged with the possibility of annihilative warfare was almost more than statesmanship could bear.

American diplomats found their work indisputably easier in the days when the nation's atomic power was stronger than that of Russia. As we have seen in previous chapters, James F. Byrnes, George C. Marshall, and Dean Acheson all had to wrestle with extremely difficult questions and crises, and they met with success and with failure. But until about 1953, the United States had kept the lead in atomic power, first by monopoly and then by superiority. If this did not prevent such bold Russian actions as the Berlin blockade, the latter undertaken the year before the Russians exploded their first atomic bomb, it gave a security, however tenuous, to the conduct of American policy.

As practical equality in atomic bombs developed about 1953, and as hydrogen-bomb tests by both superpowers were imminent, diplomacy became truly difficult. The most exacting problems of diplomacy thus appeared during the secretaryship of John Foster Dulles, appointed by President Eisenhower in 1953. Some observers criticized American diplomacy under Dulles as a diplomacy of public relations, of sloganeering rather than substance, of series of statements often contradictory which left the student bewildered but gave the man in the street an illusion of activity and brisk purposefulness at the State Department. While this criticism had some validity, it was less perceptive than at first seemed. The statement-making of the Dulles era reflected the uncertainty of American policy in the face of virtual atomic equality with Russia. There were other reasons, in addition to the weapons race, for Dulles's troubles. He took over the State Department during the last crotchety days of the old dictator Stalin, and he experienced diplomatically the uncertainties and initial confusions of the dictator's successors. Dulles also was handicapped because the Eisenhower administration allowed itself to get behind in some aspects of the armaments race with Russia—notably the competition for missiles, intermediate-range and intercontinental. But if for no other reason than the general evening-up of the arms race during the Eisenhower era, Secretary Dulles found himself in more straitened diplomatic circumstances than did his predecessors.

The Eisenhower-Dulles team hopefully announced in its opening years several new policies, or new courses announced as new policies. There was talk of liberation of the captive nations of Eastern Europe, of an agonizing reappraisal of America's relations with its allies, of a new look in American military defenses. Each of these policies was born under the exigencies of the diplomatic revolution and took its course under the compulsions which attached to that revolution in 1953 and thereafter, the virtual equality of Russian and American atomic power.

It is unnecessary in the present pages to repeat some of the comments about these policies made in previous chapters, except to point out how in each case diplomatic choices narrowed markedly because of existence of the new weapons. Consider the policy of liberation, so boldly announced during the presidential campaign of 1952. Almost the sole activity in line with this policy was to send balloons over Eastern Europe bearing cheery messages of good will from the United States to the peoples of the satellite nations. The American government did nothing when the workers of East Berlin and other East German cities revolted in June 1953, nor during the Hungarian and Polish revolts of 1956. At these critical moments the Eisenhower-Dulles policy of liberation became indistinguishable from the Truman-Acheson policy of containment. The United States in truth could not risk driving the USSR into atomic war to liberate the captive peoples of the satellite nations between Western Europe and Russia. It is worthy of note that the Western spokesmen of the captive peoples, leaders of the East European emigration to the West after 1945, did not favor forcible liberation, and for the same reason that deterred the American government—the terrible vengeance that Russia might wreak on all Europe in event of an attempted Western military liberation of Eastern Europe.

As was set forth in a previous chapter, the projected reappraisal of 1953, second on the list of Eisenhower-Dulles diplomatic pronouncements, was an attempt to bluff France into co-operating with NATO when the United States was doing its best to incorporate West Germany in the military alliance against Russia. The bluff had no effect other than to antagonize the French, who voted down the proposed European Defense Community that would have brought German divisions into NATO. Part of the reason why EDC failed of adoption was the diplomatic revolution. The French government had little stomach for war in an atomic age with the nation's beautiful cities exposed to Russian atomic bombs. Frenchmen gave every indication that they would not be pushed into close co-operation with NATO and the nominal issue of inclusion of German units in that organization did not go far beneath the surface of French reasoning. Many Frenchmen preferred neutralism to provoking a Russian attack. It was to no avail that the American government threatened withdrawal of its military forces from Europe—an agonizing reappraisal of its European commitments—because the French knew that the Americans could not afford for their own good reasons to withdraw divisions from Western Europe and abandon NATO even if NATO became little more than an Anglo-American army.

The new look, another Eisenhower-Dulles principle, was an attempted return to an atomic strategy rather than continuance of the combined atomic-conventional strategy which the nation had adopted after the opening of the Korean War in 1950. Secretary of Defense Charles E. Wilson first announced this new policy in 1953. Secretary Dulles defined it in January 1954 as a basic decision "to depend primarily on a great capacity to retaliate by means and at places of our own choosing." With this, he later said, "you do not need to have local defense all round the 20,000-mile perimeter of the orbit of the Soviet World." In March 1954 Vice President Richard M. Nixon stated what the new look meant: "We have adopted a new principle. Rather than let the Communists nibble us to death all over the world in little wars, we will rely in future on massive mobile retaliatory powers." This new strategy was defined visibly when in March 1954 the United States exploded its large H-bomb in the Pacific. But actually the new look, this post-Korea effort to go back to an atomic strategy, was naught but an attempt to reduce military expenditures with little reasoning behind the effort other than a wish for sheer reduction. The Eisenhower administration desired to reduce arms costs from the average post-Korea figure of about $40,000,000,000 toward—but of course not anywhere close to—the 1945–1950 average of around $14,000,-000,000. From this wish for savings in the cost of armaments came the slogan "more bang for the buck," and the attraction of wish and slogan and political hope was compelling until the administration realized that reductions in conventional military power would have an automatic effect on the conduct of American diplomacy. "Diplomacy without armaments," Frederick the Great once said, "is like music without instruments." If this aphorism needed qualification in the mid-twentieth century, it still carried truth. A wide range of armaments was especially necessary in the day of limited war (for limited war was the only feasible kind of armed conflict after invention of the new weapons; total war had become almost too repulsive for practical consideration). The years 1953–1954 were no time to reduce the military establishment and rely primarily on atomic weapons when the type of war to be anticipated was limited war, totally unsuited to atomic strategy.

Eventually the budgetary inspiration of the new look yielded to a more long-range view of American armaments and most of the proposed cuts in conventional military power were abandoned. The new look, however, had an important effect on American strategy which at the time passed almost unappreciated. In 1954, the year of most of the official pronouncements about the new look, a most important strategic decision was reached by the American joint chiefs of staff: United States military forces in Europe in December 1954 received delivery of a number of 280-millimeter atomic cannon— "Atomic Annie," as the new gun was affectionately named. Shortly thereafter, the American army in West Germany announced acquisition of field artillery battalions equipped with Corporal and Honest John missiles. It became known that atomic bombs were stockpiled in Germany. In public speeches the leaders of the American armed forces announced that their cannon and missiles would see use in any future war with Russian forces in Europe. The impression they gave was that atomic cannon and missiles were just a little more powerful than ordinary artillery and represented only one more and rather minor miracle of American science. Magazines in the United States published army press releases with pictures extolling the virtues of the huge new cannon, and the cannon looked like a cannon, which was reassuring.

What most people failed to understand were the consequences if armies in the field used such small atomic weapons for tactical purposes. An atomic explosion was an atomic explosion whether propelled out of cannon or by rockets or dropped from planes, and equipment of American armies in Europe with these small atomic weapons meant conversion of the armed forces to atomic strategy. And in any future war, tactical use of atomic cannon and rockets would be a signal, so many informed commentators in the United States and Europe believed, for all-out use of atomic weapons. The tactical use of atomic weapons was impossible. Who could tell when tactical employment shaded into strategic employment? No military writer or practitioner has ever been able to draw a clear line between tactics and strategy. Choice of atomic weapons for America's NATO forces was a fateful and perhaps fatal step. Viscount Sir Bernard Montgomery put the case frankly: "The reason for this action is that we cannot match the strength that could be brought against us unless we use nuclear weapons." He said that with this decision "we have reached the point of no return as regards the use of atomic and thermonuclear weapons in a hot war." Bluntly, the use of tactical weapons in the field meant hydrogen bombs on the homeland.

In the eyes of many military experts this new reliance of America's armed forces in Europe on an atomic strategy was most unwise. It was bad enough, they contended, that such a new policy gave support to the pleas for reduction in arms costs which had been heard increasingly since the end of the Korean War. To some experts the new look seemed to be a pandering by the administration to uninformed public opinion. But by far the worst aspect of the new look, they believed, was that reliance on atomic strategy would unsettle American diplomacy throughout the world. The United States would have no forces to meet the inevitable limited wars which the Russians would start in the Middle and Far East. Such was the contention of General Matthew B. Ridgway, whose clash of views with the Eisenhower administration over reduction of the army led to his retirement after a single term as army chief of staff. Whether he and the numerous military experts who agreed with him were wrong about America's military requirements, time would tell.

Perhaps the diplomatic revolution had not altogether impressed itself upon the American government and people by the late 1950's. Perhaps there lingered a feeling that the old type of diplomacy, the old familiar diplomacy that depended ultimately on force, still had its place. About all that one could conclude was that the Eisenhower administration, in an era of virtual atomic equality with Russia, did find that some of its policies, such as liberation and the agonized reappraisal, were difficult to pursue.

What, then, were the diplomatic possibilities for the United States in the new and strange age after 1945? How could American diplomacy so estimate the possibilities of each moment in the era of the diplomatic revolution that it could maintain the national interest in a world at peace?

The word most commonly used by strategists of the West to describe the purpose of Western policies was deterrence. The West hoped to deter the Soviet Union—to maintain sufficient military strength and diplomatic agility to persuade the USSR to refrain from either limited or atomic war, to keep roughly the post-1945 balance of territory and peoples throughout the world, to avoid the unknown but obviously dangerous possibilities of full-scale war. This was Western policy: to avoid war, to keep peace with honor, until in some distant and wonderful future the suspicions of Russian leaders would cool and the world could turn with full attention to the problems of peaceful living.

The uneasiness of East-West relations would have to be kept under control through a period of years. Deterrence perhaps would give the world time to cool down. In the enormous armaments race, so obvious to all readers of daily newspapers at the mid-century, the two sides would have to remain roughly equal, the chief runners abreast of each other and neither tempted to take advantage by some large lead. The peace would be in danger should some situation occur in armaments where, for example, one side's manned bomber would be neutralized before its ICBM became mechanically operable, in effect canceling its capacity for nuclear war and tempting a great power possessing nuclear strength to move while its adversary's retaliatory power had been rendered ineffective.

Diplomats calculated their national advantages with more unsureness at the mid-twentieth century than ever before. There had been an almost miraculous, or diabolic, invention of new weapons in the years since Hitler in 1939, an almost forgotten date, had invaded

Poland and begun the second World War. The diplomats' task required almost more information than intelligence could comprehend. One could hope that they would not turn to guessing instead of rational investigation, that they would not proceed on a day-to-day basis hoping that today's decision would ensure the possibility of another decision tomorrow, that by no chance in some large enemy country would the process of decision-making pass into the hands of such an irrational individual as another Hitler or Stalin who might in his warped intelligence find justification for nuclear war and plunge the world over the brink.

The nearest American diplomatic analogy to the problems of the 1950's was offered by the problems of the early years of independence, when the nation's diplomats learned to counter the tricks and dissimulations of Europe's professional diplomats. The analogy was none too close when one realized that diplomacy in the later eighteenth century, despite its deceits, was still a profession of gentility and mutual respect. The worst a diplomat could expect in those days, an unwanted war, could in no way be as destructive as war in the 1950's. Secretary of State Dulles was called upon to do much better than the best of America's diplomats in the era of national foundation. Benjamin Franklin, that wisest of eighteenth-century Americans, had an easy task at Paris compared to Dulles's daily surveys of the prospects for peace and existence. Dulles had no Vergennes, no Richard Oswald, to deal with, men of common background and some trustworthiness. Franklin never had to negotiate with a shifting coalition of statesmen who lived to a totally different ethic.

A mass of problems confronted American diplomats at the mid-century. There was the problem of their country's allies, whether the United States could count on their assistance in crisis. Our allies could be frightened away by our own diplomatic ineptitude. As a close student of our atomic diplomacy, William W. Kaufmann, has put it, the United States had to be extremely careful of its allies, displaying "a willingness to act as the leader of a coalition rather than as the principal of a kindergarten." (But perhaps, so some devotees of one-solution atomic strategy were beginning to believe, allies were not necessary when the ICBM might remove the need for overseas bases for the American strategic air force and even the necessity for that air force itself.)

There was the problem of keeping the American government free of military domination when so much diplomacy was of a military nature and subject to the requirements, real or imaginary, of secrecy in the name of national security.

There was the problem of keeping a large military establishment ready for eventualities and of justifying this military establishment to the American people. Many Americans were concerned that their friends and relatives were confined unwillingly within the air force or army or navy. The secretary of state would have to convince the nation of the unpalatable truth that the military establishment was his only hope for conducting foreign policy and that without armaments of all kinds, conventional as well as atomic, the diplomacy of the United States might become ineffective.

There was the cost of atomic weaponry, piled onto that of the regular military establishment, a large problem for Americans to reckon with. Military costs were so high that they encouraged searches on the part of both the government and its citizenry for cheaper solutions, hopeful efforts to find easy formulas for solving difficult problems. There would always be the question as to whether the American taxpayer might fail to understand why each year his income tax was so high. The bulk of the tax went for national defense, and the cost of that defense was astonishingly high, about—as we have seen—$40,000,000,000. Of this sum the Atomic Energy Commission each year was spending over $2,000,000,000, or the same amount of money spent during the entire war period on atomic weapons. A five-inch shell in the second World War cost about $100, but a single navy Terrier guided missile, the modern substitute for a five-inch antiaircraft shell, in 1958 cost about $60,000 without its launcher. During the war of 1941–1945 submarines cost between $5,000,000 and $7,000,000; nuclear-powered submarines cost between $45,000,000 and $60,000,000. A fighter aircraft in the second World War cost about $125,000; jet fighters cost about $1,250,000. A B-52 heavy bomber with spare parts cost over $7,000,000. Technological breakthroughs in production of the H-bomb or the new rockets and missiles could make expensive plant investment useless or nearly useless overnight. It was necessary frequently to initiate weapons projects in several ways, employing different theoretical approaches until experiment could show the correct course. (On February 25, 1958 the "last of the Navahos," the last of the unsuccessful and obsolete

Navaho missiles, was fired at the missile proving ground on Cape Canaveral, closing a program that had cost about $700,000,000 but was canceled in the summer of 1957. It was necessary, defense officials argued, to have expensive "booboos" of this sort.) But if the demands of an economy-minded public should override informed strategic thinking, the result might well be a cutting down of experiment and preventing of quick results. Would the people support this long-term armament program to an extent necessary to keep up with the program supported by the controlled economy of Russia?

There was, lastly, the problem of education. The people would have to learn the requirements of their country's contemporary diplomacy and this learning was difficult without careful study of the nation's diplomatic history. But to what use? Education had been the vain hope of eighteenth-century philosophers and nineteenth-century liberal reformers, and in the twentieth century the best-educated country in Europe, Germany, had adopted a foreign policy full of error and mistake, precipitating the world into its present difficult position.

One thing was certain, that foreign relations by the middle of the century had become the central problem of the great republic of the New World.

ADDITIONAL READING

For what has become a strange new subject since 1945, that of atomic weapons and diplomacy, there is a large literature, and although some of it is trivial and some of it has become dated there are books of lasting value and importance to which the student interested in this most important subject can turn. There is no single book that deals generally with what might be described as atomic diplomacy, but several volumes provide together an excellent introduction. One might begin by reading the brilliant work by Walter Millis, *Arms and Men* (New York, 1956; available in paperback), which sets out in historical perspective the military history of the United States and its connection with high policy from 1775 to date. Millis's last chapters, "The Hypertrophy of War" and "The Future of War," are among the best essays he has ever published. Reading of this work might be followed with three small books which explain in lay language the problem of atomic weapons: David Bradley's *No Place to Hide* (Boston, 1948; available in paperback) by a naval doctor present at the Bikini explosions in 1946; and two books by

Ralph E. Lapp, *Atoms and People* (New York, 1956) and *The Voyage of the Lucky Dragon* (New York, 1958). One should then read the essays, especially those by the editor, in William W. Kaufmann, ed., *Military Policy and National Security* (Princeton, 1956).

A recent and much-heralded volume, somewhat at variance with the Kaufmann book because it foresees the possibility of limited atomic wars, is Henry A. Kissinger, *Nuclear Weapons and Foreign Policy* (New York, 1957; abridged edition available in paperback). This book was the result of discussions by a group of leading American experts on foreign policy held at the Council on Foreign Relations in New York. William W. Kaufmann's review of this book, "The Crisis in Military Affairs," *World Politics*, vol. 10 (1957–1958), 579–603, is an able analysis: Kaufmann believes that Kissinger is sloppy in his thinking; that his sources are open to question; that he is not complex enough, or subtle enough, in his analysis; and that, in sum, the book is essentially polemical rather than thoughtful.

Two personal accounts of work with the atom are Arthur H. Compton, *Atomic Quest* (New York, 1956), by the Nobel prize laureate in physics; and Gordon Dean, *Report on the Atom* (New York, 1954), by the late former chairman of the Atomic Energy Commission. The British physicist and Nobel prize-winner, P. M. S. Blackett, has used his scientific knowledge in exploring *Atomic Weapons and East-West Relations* (Cambridge, Eng., 1956). A commentary on the world of atomic physics, with oblique views into the personal rivalries among physicists and into the debates of the Atomic Energy Commission on such large questions as whether to build the H-bomb, is the fascinating publication of the AEC, *In the Matter of J. Robert Oppenheimer: Transcript of Hearing before Personnel Security Board* (Washington, 1954).

Turning to military problems and atomic weaponry, there are the works by the British air marshal and strategist, Sir John Slessor, *Strategy for the West* (New York, 1954) and *The Great Deterrent* (London, 1957). Slessor's American opposite, the former secretary of the air force Thomas K. Finletter, has written of *Power and Policy* (New York, 1954), together with *Foreign Policy: The Next Phase* (New York, 1958). A new work is James M. Gavin, *War and Peace in the Space Age* (New York, 1958). When General Matthew B. Ridgway retired from the army he published an able memoir, *Soldier* (New York, 1956), criticizing the Eisenhower administration's reliance on air-atomic power at the cost of the army's ability to defend the nation in nonatomic wars. In this regard see Robert E. Osgood, *Limited War: The Challenge to American Strategy* (Chicago, 1957). See also F. O. Miksche, *Atomic Weapons and Armies* (New York, 1955); and Hanson W. Baldwin, *The Great Arms Race* (New York, 1958). No study of the effect of weapons in the modern world can ignore the highly suggestive essays by Bernard Brodie, in such magazines and journals as *Harper's*, *The Reporter*, *World Politics*, and *Foreign Affairs*.

Special studies are Elis Biörklund, *International Atomic Policy during a Decade: 1945–55* (Princeton, 1956); and Klaus Knorr, *The War Potential of Nations* (Princeton, 1956).

Well worth attention is the *Bulletin of the Atomic Scientists,* a journal published in Chicago and dedicated to the social aspects of their work by the atomic scientists of the United States.

Appendix

John Jay (*1745–1829*)—1784–1790—The Continental Congress

Thomas Jefferson (*1743–1826*)—1790–1793—*President* George Washington

Edmund Randolph (*1753–1813*)—1794–1795—*President* George Washington

Timothy Pickering (*1745–1829*)—1795–1800—*Presidents* George Washington *and* John Adams

John Marshall (*1755–1835*)—1800–1801—*President* John Adams

James Madison (*1751–1836*)—1801–1809—*President* Thomas Jefferson

Robert Smith (*1757–1842*)—1809–1811—*President* James Madison

James Monroe (*1758–1831*)—1811–1817—*President* James Madison

John Quincy Adams (*1767–1848*)—1817–1825—*President* James Monroe

Henry Clay (*1777–1852*)—1825–1829—*President* John Quincy Adams

Martin Van Buren (*1782–1862*)—1829–1831—*President* Andrew Jackson

Edward Livingston (*1764–1836*)—1831–1833—*President* Andrew Jackson

Louis McLane (*1786–1857*)—1833–1834—*President* Andrew Jackson

John Forsyth (*1780–1841*)—1834–1841—*Presidents* Andrew Jackson *and* Martin Van Buren

Daniel Webster (*1782–1852*)—1841–1843 *and* 1850–1852—*Presidents* William Henry Harrison, John Tyler, *and* Millard Fillmore

Abel Parker Upshur (*1791–1844*)—1843–1844—*President* John Tyler

John Caldwell Calhoun (*1782–1850*)—1844–1845—*President* John Tyler

James Buchanan (*1791–1868*)—1845–1849—*President* James K. Polk

John Middleton Clayton (*1796–1856*)—1849–1850—*President* Zachary Taylor

Daniel Webster (second service)

Edward Everett (*1794–1865*)—1852–1853—*President* Millard Fillmore

William Learned Marcy (*1786–1857*)—1853–1857—*President* Franklin Pierce

Lewis Cass (*1782–1866*)—1857–1860—*President* James Buchanan

Jeremiah Sullivan Black (*1810–1883*)—1860–1861—*President* James Buchanan

William Henry Seward (*1801–1872*)—1861–1869—*Presidents* Abraham Lincoln *and* Andrew Johnson

Elihu Benjamin Washburne (*1816–1887*)—1869—*President* Ulysses S. Grant

Hamilton Fish (*1808–1893*)—1869–1877—*President* Ulysses S. Grant

William Maxwell Evarts (*1818–1901*)—1877–1881—*President* Rutherford B. Hayes

James Gillespie Blaine (*1830–1893*)—1881 and 1889–1892—*Presidents* James A. Garfield, Chester A. Arthur, *and* Benjamin Harrison

Frederick Theodore Frelinghuysen (*1817–1885*)—1881–1885—*President* Chester A. Arthur

Thomas Francis Bayard (*1828–1898*)—1885–1889—*President* Grover Cleveland

James Gillespie Blaine (second service)

John Watson Foster (*1836–1917*)—1892–1893—*President* Benjamin Harrison

Walter Quintin Gresham (*1832–1895*)—1893–1895—*President* Grover Cleveland

Richard Olney (*1835–1917*)—1895–1897—*President* Grover Cleveland

John Sherman (*1823–1900*)—1897–1898—*President* William McKinley

William Rufus Day (*1849–1923*)—1898—*President* William McKinley

John Hay (*1838–1905*)—1898–1905—*Presidents* William McKinley *and* Theodore Roosevelt

Elihu Root (*1845–1937*)—1905–1909—*President* Theodore Roosevelt

Robert Bacon (*1860–1919*)—1909—*President* Theodore Roosevelt

Philander Chase Knox (*1853–1921*)—1909–1913—*President* William H. Taft

William Jennings Bryan (*1860–1925*)—1913–1915—*President* Woodrow Wilson

Robert Lansing (*1864–1928*)—1915–1920—*President* Woodrow Wilson

Bainbridge Colby (*1869–1950*)—1920–1921—*President* Woodrow Wilson

Charles Evans Hughes (*1862–1948*)—1921–1925—*Presidents* Warren G. Harding *and* Calvin Coolidge

Frank Billings Kellogg (*1856–1937*)—1925–1929—*President* Calvin Coolidge

Henry Lewis Stimson (*1867–1950*)—1929–1933—*President* Herbert C. Hoover

Cordell Hull (*1871–1955*)—1933–1944—*President* Franklin D. Roosevelt

Edward Reilly Stettinius, Jr. (*1900–1949*)—1944–1945—*Presidents* Franklin D. Roosevelt *and* Harry S. Truman

James Francis Byrnes (*1879–　*)—1945–1947—*President* Harry S. Truman

George Catlett Marshall (*1880*–)—1947–1949—*President* Harry S. Truman

Dean Gooderham Acheson (*1893*–)—1949–1953—*President* Harry S. Truman

John Foster Dulles (*1888*–)—Commissioned 1953—*President* Dwight D. Eisenhower

Index